How to Produce

CREATIVE

PUBLICATIONS

•• •• ••

Traditional Techniques & Computer Applications

Thomas Bivins •• William E. Ryan
University of Oregon   University of Oregon

Printed on recyclable paper

NTC Business Books
a division of *NTC Publishing Group* • Lincolnwood, Illinois USA

Book Design by Thomas Bivins and William E. Ryan

Library of Congress Cataloging-in-Publication Data

Bivins, Thomas.

How to produce creative publications : traditional techniques and computer applications / Thomas A. Bivins and William E. Ryan.

p.   cm.

Includes index.

ISBN 0-8442-3493-1 (hard cover); 0-8442-3495-8 (soft cover)

1. Printing. Practical—Layout. 2. Printing. Practical—Layout—Data processing. 3. Associations. institutions. etc.—Publishing. 4. Corporations—Publishing. 5. Desktop publishing. I. Ryan William E. II. Title.

Z246.B58 1990

686.2'2544—dc20   90-60193

1995 Printing

Published by NTC Business Books, a division of NTC Publishing Group.
©1991 by NTC Publishing Group, 4255 West Touhy Avenue,
Lincolnwood (Chicago), Illinois 60646-1975 U.S.A.

Contents

Foreword

Desktop publishing, as a concept, is quite young. As a reality, it is even younger. I first coined the term "desktop pubishing" in October of 1984 to describe what people could do with PageMaker. The combining of text and graphics on a page using a microcomputer is no longer a revolutionary concept. Today, both the term "desktop publishing" and the reality of desktop publishing have become commonplace.

As we move into a new decade, computers are rapidly becoming an indispensable tool of both business and education. The fact that we live in an information age makes the acquisition of computer literacy a vital component of our everyday lives. The benefits of computers are now being enjoyed by nearly every element of our society. We are no longer faced with a lack of technology. What we are now faced with is the question of how people are going to use the technology they already have.

I am constantly reminding people that a computer is only a tool. Even the best-designed software program will not compensate for a lack of basic skills. We in the industry are already moving to become a more active player in education, and it is gratifying to see that others are taking seriously the task of educating users. Books such as this provide the necessary link between the availability of desktop publishing and the skills needed to make the concept a working reality. The journey that leads from the mind to the page is often fraught with pitfalls, not the least of which is mastery of not only the technology but also the basic skills so necessary for successful results. Within these pages are contained the necessary roadmaps to make that journey a fruitful one. This is the kind of guide we all need to see more of.

Paul Brainerd
CEO, The Aldus Corporation

Introduction

Every day in the United States, and around the world for that matter, hundreds of thousands of publications are created for and by organizations. These publications are aimed at a variety of audiences: employees, shareholders, members, volunteers, communities and countless others, and come in dozens of shapes and sizes—newsletters, brochures, magazines, annual reports, pamphlets, booklets, posters, flyers and direct mail pieces are just a few.

Anyone assuming the responsibilities of putting together a publication for an organization for the first time has quite a lot to learn. But that person also has quite a lot of information to draw from. Most beginners don't realize that the vast number of publications they see (and would like to emulate) are based on a few basic designs. All adhere to basic writing and editing principles. And all either try to inform or persuade. In fact, the differences are far fewer than most people might think.

For our purposes, we'll concentrate on what we consider to be the **basic publications**—those most common to most organizations, whether they are profit or non-profit, whether their aim is to inform or to persuade. These are newsletters, magazines, annual reports and brochures. Once you have mastered the techniques of writing, editing and designing these basic forms, they are easily applied to other publications (with, perhaps, the exception of traditional newspapers). For example, if you have been assigned to produce a booklet on employee benefits but the information is too long and complex to be included in a simple brochure, you simply adapt the material to a magazine-style layout. A working knowledge of the fundamentals of the basic publication formats will allow you to experiment with more complex formats later on.

Why the Computer Has Made Such a Difference

Probably the single most revolutionary invention of the last century has been the computer. Scarcely fifty years ago, a computer able to do the simplest calculations took up an entire room. Today, even the most complex work can be done at your desk. When the microcomputer became commonplace only a very few years ago, it seems that life changed for millions of people. For the publishing industry, however, the most significant change followed invention of the hardware itself. The microcomputer changed the way we do nearly everything; page-layout *software* programs changed the way we think about and execute publications in particular.

One of the earliest, some say the first, page-layout programs was *PageMaker*, invented by Paul Brainerd and a handful of friends. Its original target audience was newspaper publishers. When that audience proved to be basically unreceptive, Brainerd turned to business. As it turned out, page-layout software revolutionized the way organizations thought about in-house publication. What once had to go through the traditional writing, editing, typesetting, pasteup and printing process could now be done in a few, simple steps.

What Is Desktop Publishing?

Although it took several long years for "desktop publishing" to catch on, it is now sweeping the country. The term **desktop publishing** is a bit of a misnomer because "publishing" involves much more than just the writing and laying out of a publication—which is all the software claims to do. True publishing entails *all* the printing and production stages, testing the product in its respective markets, creating a marketing and distribution plan, and the myriad other details that make publishing a complex and often risky business.

What this software, and the increasingly sophisticated hardware, allow is the involvement of fewer intermediaries in the publication process. To some, this is a blessing; to others, a curse. What has happened is that everyone with a computer and the necessary software is producing a publication—with or without the background necessary to do so.

As Paul Brainerd (now president of Aldus Corporation) once quipped, "A desktop publishing program won't make you a designer." What the revolution in computer publishing has done is provide the writer, editor, and designer with another tool to better accomplish their respective jobs. *Without the knowledge and experience gained through a study of the basics of writing, editing and design, however, even the best computer hardware and software won't help you.*

The computer has made a tremendous difference. Word processing programs, once cumbersome and nearly impossible to work with, allow us to write, delete, move whole copy blocks, copy between files, index, outline and do other tasks that once took hours and days to accomplish on a typewriter. The computer has allowed writers and editors to facilitate their work through the on-line interchange of information (or exchange of disks). Editors can now edit on screen, and the writer can watch—if she or he has the nerve. And, the designer and artist can see their work come to life on the screen and have it instantly delivered into their hands as fast as a laser printer can print. Working together, writers, editors, designers and artists have made the most of this revolutionary tool, but they haven't done so without countless hours of training in the basics of their professions. Providing training in the basics is a major part of what this book is all about.

How to Use This Book

This book was written with the beginner in mind. It details the basics of publication. It deals only with the primary publication forms. You will not find a computer manual here. What you will find is a textbook covering the traditional approaches to writing, editing and designing, and a discussion of the basic concepts of applying computer technology to these traditional tasks.

We expect that you will read your hardware and software manuals. If you don't, you'll certainly suffer for it in the end. What we will help you with are the elements your software manuals don't tell you about—and the kinds of things your software won't do for you. We'll help you to become a better writer and a better designer and, we hope, show you the possibilities inherent in the application of computer technology to your work.

We have organized this book so that you can learn some of the traditional approaches to writing, editing and designing basic publications. Most of us assume that we can learn by doing, and, to a certain extent, we can. However, on-the-job training often leaves out much of the "why" of tasks and focuses only on the "how." We have tried to compensate for that in a number of ways. This book is organized around a framework composed of "hows" held firmly together by a mortar of "whys."

Remember, attempting to create publications without knowing the basics of writing and design is like falling into the water without knowing how to swim. Your chances of staying alive in the medium are slim at best.

Briefly, then, here is how the book is organized.

- To begin with, the book is comprehensive in its approach. It should be read in its entirety, sequentially. Each chapter builds upon preceding chapters; and although you can certainly skip around, you will be constantly referred to other chapters containing the information necessary for a complete understanding of any given subject.

- The book is divided into two parts: **Part I** outlines the elements of publication (all its parts), and contains specific, computer-related information. **Part II** deals only with the four basic publication formats. If you have obtained this book to read only the last four chapters, be forewarned that they are basically meaningless without the first seven.

- **Chapters 1–2** deal with the key elements of basic publication—writing and design. In each, you will find *detailed* information on these subjects. Consider these two chapters as a primer for what follows. Without them, subsequent chapters will seem incomplete.

- **Chapters 3–7** deal with the individual and specific elements of publication ranging from graphics to layout. Each of these chapters is divided into two sections: the first deals with the traditional approach to the topic and the second outlines the benefits of using computers to accomplish the same tasks.

We are acutely aware of the short "lives" of computer hardware and software. What was brand new two years ago is now obsolete; however, at least two-thirds of the information in this book has been around for decades or longer. The basics of good writing and good design will outlast each software and hardware upgrade. In fact, every upgrade in technology seems to affirm the need for these basics on the part of the the human operator. Without this knowledge, all the sophisticated hardware and software in the world won't help.

We have attempted to keep the computer-oriented information contained herein at a generic level. We simply want to show you how the technology has enhanced and expedited the process of publication. In most instances, we have referenced the most advanced hardware and software available. In fact, we have used it to develop this book (see the colophon at the end of the book for a detailed look at how it was put together). What we have learned, we have tried to pass on to you in the hope that you will see the possibilities inherent in the new technology. Just don't rely too heavily on it. The human element is the one we can't mention enough, and it's the one without which none of the other is important.

Acknowledgments

It is often awkward for co-authors to thank the various individuals who helped them as a generic unit since so many of those individuals worked either with one or the other of the authors, and not necessarily with both. So following are our individual acknowledgments.

For their generosity and beautiful work, this author extend his thanks to all the artists, illustrators, photographers, designers, creative directors and art directors who made the artwork and featured pages that appear here. They helped make this book a reality.

In particular, I would like to thank Tom Russell and Kathy Getsey of Whittle Communications; D. J. Stout, *Texas Monthly*; Kathy Carlisle and Ron Dumas of NIKE Inc.; Kit Henrichs and Allyson Merkley, Pentagram—San Francisco; Lee Eide, Aster Publishing Corp.; Kay Hanafin, John Hornall and Jack Anderson of Hornall Anderson Design Works; Steve Liska, Liska Associates; Kathy Keene and Jim Prendergast of Hill and Knowlton; Matt Bertolone-Smith, Media Index Publishing, Inc.; Michael Gunselman, Gunselman & Polite; Pat and Greg Samata of Samata Associates; Tracy Wong, Goodby, Berlin & Silverstein; Kirk Kahrs, Maritz Communications; Thomas Kitts and Robert Bailey, Bailey/Warner Group; Joan Kurfin, Leo Burnett USA; Thomas Ryan, Thomas Ryan Design; Gary Sluzewski, *Cleveland Magazine*; Jeff Hackett, Florence Crittenton Home; and Kathleen Shay and Andrea McHone, Miller-Freeman, Inc. For all my students, old and new—particularly Saxon Woon, Andrea McHone, Jarrett Jester, Greg Brown, Jan Hawkins, Katie Miller, Suzanne Sunada, Chris Keleher, Laura Staroski, Brian Alvstad, Janet Kimball, Chris Staub, Debbie James and Becky Owston—thanks for all you have taught me. I would also like to thank Mario Garcia, Ken Metzler, Don Monroe, Daryl R. Moen, Raymond Roseliep, Robert Bohle, Peggie Stark and Roy Paul Nelson for past and present insights and advice.

Finally, I thank my wife, Jan Ryan, for her help, patience, encouragement and love.

—William E. Ryan

We would also like to thank the Dean of the University of Oregon School of Journalism, Arnold Ismach, for his generosity in allowing us to use the many support services of the school throughout this project. I am especially grateful for the provision of the high-end computer system on which this book was written, designed and laid out. Without it, the job would have been near impossible to complete. In the same light, we would be remiss if we did not thank Paul Brainerd, President of Aldus Corporation for his kind and flattering foreword to this book. It was Paul who supplied the software with which the book was laid out, as well as the gift that allowed for the computerization of all the faculty offices at the School of Journalism. He has been a generous friend and supporter of his *alma mater*.

We would also like to thank the people at NTC Business Books who cajoled, prodded, inspired, and always supported us; especially Anne Knudsen who had this project dumped into her lap when it was already halfway done and who not only came quickly up to speed, but who ended up being a guiding force behind its completion.

Finally, I would like to thank my wife, Lonnie, who never once complained that I spent more time in front of my computer than I did with her over the past two years. Perhaps it was a relief.

—Thomas H. Bivins

We would both like to dedicate this book to our families for their patience and understanding.

Part One

The Elements of Publication

Writing

Design

Typography

Photography

Illustration

Layout

Printing

All forms of writing for basic publications have one thing in common—they are supposed to be written well. Beyond that, they are different in many ways. These differences are related primarily to intent, style, format and medium. Writing for corporate magazines and newsletters, for example, employs standard magazine writing style (which is to say, a standard magazine style of journalism). Newsletter writing, on the other hand, is leaner, shorter, and frequently uses a straight news reporting style. Folders (commonly referred to as brochures) are, by nature, short and to the point. Copy for posters and flyers is shorter still, while pamphlets and booklets vary in style and length according to purpose.

There are basically only two reasons for an organizational communication piece to be produced: information or persuasion. The approach to writing these pieces depends, to a great extent, on the purpose to which they are to be put. Before you ever put pen to paper (or text to screen), you have to begin the whole process from an organizational perspective. This means planning.

Almost all writing goes through, or should go through, several stages before it reaches publication. Before you start writing, a plan by which your message will reach its intended audience and accomplish its intended purpose has to be developed. One of the most useful techniques for planning written communication is **management by objectives** (MBO). MBO allows you to set objectives in advance for your written communication, and provides you with the criteria you need to measure the message's effectiveness all along the way. By adapting an MBO approach to writing, you can derive at least three stages, or processes, you must go through to achieve success in your written communications—planning, writing and evaluation.

The **Planning Process** includes:
- Setting objectives and criteria for evaluation
- Analyzing the target audience(s)

- Picking the most appropriate medium or media
- Researching the topic

The **Writing Process** includes:
- Setting message strategy
- Researching and developing the appropriate style
- Organizing the message
- Writing the message

The **Evaluation Process** includes:
- Testing your message in advance of distribution
- Evaluating the message during and following the program

The Planning Process

Setting Objectives

Objectives relate to your publication's purpose and should be realistic and measurable. For basic publications, there are three types of objectives: informational, attitudinal and behavioral. Informational objectives are used most often to present balanced information on a topic of interest to your target audience. Attitudinal and behavioral objectives relate more to persuasive messages.

For instance, if you are simply attempting to let your employees know that your organization has developed a new health care package, your objective might read something like this:

> To inform all employees of the newest options available in their health care benefits package by the end of the October open enrollment period.

Notice that the objective begins with an infinitive phrase. Objectives should always be written this way. Notice, too, that the number of employees is addressed ("all"), and a specific time period for the completion of the objective is also included. In a complete communications plan, this objective would be followed by the proposed tactic for its realization and a method by which its success could be measured. For example:

> To inform all employees of the newest options available in their health care benefits package by the end of the October open enrollment period by placing informational brochures in each employee's paycheck over the next two months. Personnel will keep a record of all employees requesting information on the new health care plan during the open enrollment period.

If, on the other hand, your objective is attitudinal or behavioral, your message is probably persuasive. There are three ways you can attempt to influence attitude and behavior:

- You can create an attitude or behavior where none exists. (This is the easiest of these three because, if none exists, there is usually no predisposition on the part of your target audience.)

- You can reinforce an attitude or behavior. (This is also relatively easy to do because your target audience already believes or behaves in the way you desire.)

- You can attempt to change or alter an attitude. (This last is the most difficult to accomplish and, realistically, shouldn't be attempted unless you are willing to expend a lot of time and energy on an, at best, dubious outcome.) See the following material on audience types.

An example of an attitudinal objective might be:

> To create a favorable attitude among employees concerning the changeover from a monthly pay disbursement to a twice-monthly pay disbursement.

Methods for measuring this type of objective range from informal employee feedback to surveying attitudes some time after the changeover has gone into effect.

An example of a behavioral objective might be:

> To increase the number of employees in attendance at the annual company picnic by 25 percent by mailing out weekly reminders to the homes of employees four weeks prior to the picnic.

Obviously, measuring the effectiveness of this objective is easier; however, if you don't see an increase in attendance, you will have to do some serious research into the reasons why. And, be aware that these reasons might not involve your message or its presentation at all. You might have simply picked the Sunday of the big state fair to hold your picnic. The lesson here is, don't ever conclude that your message is automatically the problem without exploring all variables affecting its desired results.

Analyzing the Target Audience

Imagine holding a complex conversation with someone you don't know at all. If you are trying to persuade that person of your point of view, you will have a better chance if you know his or her predispositions in advance. The same holds true for written communication. In order to write for an audience, you have to know that audience intimately. What you need to know about your target audience depends to a great extent on what your objectives are.

As discussed previously, basic publications are typically used for either information or persuasion. A lot depends on which of these two uses your particular piece will be put to. Think, for instance, of the racks of brochures you find at a travel agency or the thousands of publications you see at a typical convention attended by hundreds of suppliers of products or services who are vying for your attention. Their chief aim is persuasion, and their attempts begin with the look of the piece itself. We are all attracted to certain colors and graphic styles. Persuasive publications have to rely on the "look" as the element that first hooks the prospective reader.

On the other hand, think of all those publications you've seen at government agencies or received through the mail as a result of having requested information. They frequently are less glitzy, more straightforward, and simpler in style. They don't have to be designed to attract your attention (or persuade you to pick them up). They are designed to inform you, and they assume that you have already chosen to read them.

Developing a reader profile

Knowing for whom you're writing is probably the most important factor in setting message strategy. The success of a publication will be determined, to a great extent, on how well you've "aimed" your message. The best way to write is to write for an imagined reader, an individual to whom you are speaking directly. In order to understand this individual, you need to know him or her personally. To do this, you will have to develop a profile of this "typical" reader.

There are a number of methods for collecting information on your target audiences ranging from fairly expensive formal research to secondary research gathered from such sources as the library or your own organization to simply asking the person who gave you the assignment who the audience is. Many writers are put off by the notion of having to gather hard-core information about their readers; unfortunately, many a publication has totally missed its audience by not doing so.

If you can't afford the luxury of a formal survey, try gathering demographic information from other departments within your own organization. For example, if your organization has a marketing department and your publication is external, you might be able to extract some solid audience demographics from existing marketing research. And don't discount the value of a visit to the library. Government documents such as the *American Statistics Index* (*ASI*) can be invaluable sources. *ASI* is actually a compendium of statistical material including the U.S. Census and hundreds of periodicals that can be obtained directly from the sponsoring agencies or from the library itself. *ASI* also publishes an alphabetical index arranged by subject, name, category and title.[1]

Other sources of market information include the Simmons Market Research Bureau's annual *Study of Media and Markets*. This publication includes information on audiences for over a hundred magazines with readership delineated by demographic, psychographic and behavioral characteristics. When using secondary research such as this, be aware that you will find much information that is not directly applicable to your target audience. You not only have to know where to look, but you also have to know how to decipher what you read and apply it to your situation.

There is also one other important factor to consider at this point: how your target audience feels about your subject. In most persuasive endeavors, there are three types of audiences: *those already on your side, those opposed to your point of view,* and *those who are undecided.* Most persuasive appeals are, or should be, aimed at the last.

As most experienced persuaders know, convincing the hard-core opposition is not a reasonable objective. Persuading those already on your side is like preaching to the converted—a waste of time (unless you want to stir them to some action). Thus, most persuasion is aimed at the undecided. Remember, however, that even the undecided have opinions. Those opinions may not be fully crystallized, and this leaves them open to the persuasive appeal. One final question must be answered if you expect to be successful: Why are they going to be reading your publication?

Anticipating readers' expectations

If you don't know why your audience is reading your publication in the first place, you certainly can't know what they expect to get from it. Whatever their reasons, you had better know them. Ask yourself some questions.

- What do they know about your topic already? Never assume they know anything; however, don't talk down to them. How do you reach a compromise? Find out what they do know. Remember, people like to learn something from communication. It is best, however, to limit the amount of new information somewhat so as not to overwhelm your readers.

- What is their attitude toward you? Remember the three basic audiences for any persuasive piece? You'll need to determine whether your audience is on your side, against you, or unconvinced. This is a primary concern. To the extent possible, it is also a good idea to try to determine what their image of you or your organization is. Determining audience attitude is often an expensive proposition because it usually requires formal research; however, if the best you can do is make an educated guess based on a small focus group or even intuition—it's better than nothing at all. It is much easier to persuade when you know that you have credibility with your reader.

- Is your publication to be used in a larger context? In other words, is your publication part of a press kit, for instance, or a direct-mail package, or one of many handouts at a trade show? This knowledge will determine your readers' level of attention and their receptiveness. Always consider the surroundings in which your piece will be used if you want it to have the maximum impact.

Choosing the Appropriate Medium

It's strange to note that most nonwriters who are seeking some sort of publicity automatically assume that a brochure is the route to take, or, if the message is meant for employees, a newsletter. Of course, these may both turn out to be sound suggestions. The problem is that any *assumptions* you make concerning the most appropriate medium for your message could be disastrous. As in all stages of the planning process, selecting the right medium or media is a decision that should be based on sound knowledge of a number of factors. Doug Newsom and Alan Scott have designed a series of important considerations to be used in choosing the right medium for your message.[2]

- **What audience are you trying to reach and what do you know about its media usage patterns and the credibility ratings for each medium?** Many target audiences, for instance, simply do not watch television or listen to the radio. Others don't read newspapers regularly or subscribe to magazines. You need to know, first off, whether your intended audience will even see your message if it is presented in a medium they don't regularly use. Research tells us, for example, that businesspeople read the newspaper more than do some other groups, and rely on it for basic news and information. Other groups may rely on television almost exclusively for their news and information. For each of these groups, the credibility of the medium in question is vital. Again, businesspeople cite newspapers as a more credible source for news and information than television; however, for many people, television is far more credible.

- **When do you need to reach this audience in order for your message to be effective?** If time is of the essence, you'd best not leave your message for the next issue of the corporate magazine.

- **How much do you need to spend to reach your intended audience and how much can you actually afford?** It may be that the only way to achieve the result you're looking for is to go to some extra expense such as a brochure with more glitz or a full-color newsletter. Although every job has budget constraints, it's best to know from the start exactly what it will take to accomplish your objectives .

After these tough questions have been answered, you will still need to ask four others.

- **Which medium (of those you've listed above) reaches the broadest segment of your target audience at the lowest cost?** The answer to this question will give you a "bottom-line" choice of sorts because cost is the controlling factor in answering it. It might be that you can reach all of an employee audience with an expensive corporate magazine, but two-thirds of it with a less expensive newsletter.

- **Which one has the highest credibility and what does it cost?** Here, the correct answer will give you the additional factor of credibility which is key if your audience is discriminating at all. There are always those for whom the least credible of sources is still credible (otherwise, gossip tabloids would go out of business). But, for the honest communicator, credibility is important to the success of any messages.

- **Which medium will deliver your message within the time constraints necessary for it to be effective?** Again, a critical letter distributed companywide may be a lot more timely than a well-written article in next month's corporate magazine.

- **Should a single medium be used or a combination of complementary media (media mix)?** Remember, each element in an overall communications program may require a specialized medium in order for that portion of the message to be most effective.

Obviously, the more you know about your audience, the better you will be at selecting just the right medium for your message; however, you must also understand that certain media criteria often dictate message and message format. For instance, brochures "demand" brevity, as do flyers and posters; corporate magazines allow for fuller development of messages; newsletters offer more space than brochures but less than magazines; pamphlets offer space for message expansion and place fewer demands on style; and annual reports require strict adherence to SEC guidelines.

You must also consider cost, lead time for writing, editing, layout, typesetting, pasteup, printing and distribution. In short, selecting the most appropriate medium for your message is a complex endeavor. Be forewarned, therefore. No assumptions should be made about the acceptability of any particular medium. Until you have considered, at the least, the questions posed earlier, you will probably only be guessing on your choice of an ideal medium.

Researching Your Topic

Obviously, as is the case in all forms of writing, you must know your topic. Research techniques can run the gamut from formal research, such as surveys and questionnaires, to simply checking the library.

Most writers who work for in-house publications have access to the organization's research material for their informational or persuasive pieces. Much of the research can be accomplished in house. You can check with various departments for information on your topic and obtain previously published material from in-house and other sources. After you have been at this type of work for a while, you will undoubtedly have a well-stocked "swipe file" in which you have collected everything you (or anyone else) has ever written about your subject area. In essence, you become a standard journalist gathering background information for a story. You should never start writing until you have sufficient background on your subject to do so.

For many articles, human interest is important. This is where interviews come in. Firsthand information is always best when you can get it. Interview those intimately involved with your topic and use their information when you write. Interviewing is a special skill and it takes a lot of practice. Who you interview will have a great deal to do with how informative or interesting your interview will be. Although you can't control who you interview, you can prepare so that you can make the most out of your meeting. Following are some tips to help you through a successful interview.

- Prepare your interviewees in advance of the interviews. Contact them well in advance, set a convenient time for the interview (convenient for them, not you), and make sure they know exactly what you are going to cover and why. That way, they can also prepare for the interview by gathering pertinent information—or, at the very least—their thoughts. Ask if you can *talk* with them, not *interview* them. A talk puts people at ease—an interview often makes people tense and formal.

- Do your homework. Collect background information on the people you're going to interview, as well as the topics. Don't be embarrassed by your own ignorance of the topics. If you really know the subject, you can save a lot of time by asking for confirmation or denial of specifics rather than in-depth explanations.

- Write down a list of questions that you want answered. Work from the general to the specific, but be prepared to let the interview range according to the interviewee's responses. Often, an answer will open new areas of inquiry or suggest an angle you hadn't thought of before. Be ready to explore these new avenues as they come up. Ken Metzler, journalist, educator and author of *Creative Interviewing,* claims that the best interviewers should not only expect surprises, but should also provoke them by their willingness to explore new areas rather than follow a strict set of questions.[3]

- Break the ice. Open your interview with small talk. Try a comfortable topic, such as the weather, or, if you know something about your interviewee, a familiar topic that is nonthreatening. Almost any topic will do; most of the time, something will suggest itself naturally.

- Make sure all key questions are answered. As your interview progresses, don't be afraid to range freely, but return occasionally to your preset questions. Although the information you gather exploring other avenues may add greatly to your collection of relevant facts, remember to cover all the ground necessary for your article.

- If you are going to use a tape recorder, check to make sure that your interviewee is comfortable with being taped, and that you have fresh batteries or that an electrical outlet is available. And, even though you are taping, always take notes. This physical activity usually puts the interviewee at ease by showing that you are listening, and it serves as a good backup if your recorder stops functioning or your tape runs out. Your recorder should not occupy the space between you and your subject. Move it a little to the side, but make sure the microphone component isn't obstructed. The space between you and your subject should be free of any object that may be a source of distraction. (You should also keep your note pad in your lap, if possible, or simply hold it.)

- If you are ever unsure of a quote or think you might have misunderstood it, ask your subject to repeat it. Even if you are taping the interview, accuracy on paper and in your own mind is worth the slight pause.

- Be prepared to have to remember some key conversation *after* your interview is officially over. Most of us are aware of the phenomenon that Ken Metzler calls the "afterglow effect," when dinner guests, for example, stand at the door with their coats on ready to go, and talk for another thirty minutes. The same thing usually happens in an interview. You've turned your recorder off and put your pad away, and on your way out the door, you'll have another ten minutes of conversation. In this relaxed atmosphere, important comments are often made. Remember them. As soon as you leave, take out your pad and write the comments down or turn on your recorder and repeat the information into it. However, always make sure that your interviewee is aware that you are going to use this information as well. Don't violate any assumed "off the record" confidences.

Remember, get as much as you can the first time out. Most interviews range from thirty minutes to two hours. A follow-up interview, providing you can get one, will never be as fruitful or relaxed as the first one.

The Writing Process

Setting Message Strategy

Message strategy has to do with your approach to developing a message, or messages, that will reach your targeted audiences with the desired result. Following the MBO method of organization, your message strategies should logically follow your goals and objectives and contribute either directly or indirectly to them. You will need to develop individual message strategies for each of your target publics as well based on what you have learned about them through your research. Remember, the strategy or strategies you employ will be determined, to a great extent, by your audience's makeup, predispositions and perceived needs.

Sandra E. Moriarty has described five basic message strategies (which she calls **stratagems**) that can be used as summary statements describing the general orientation of an overall creative strategy.[4]

- **Information.** An information strategy is usually a straightforward statement of fact best used on audiences interested enough to seek out the information you can provide. This strategy is frequently employed for such messages as new product announcements, consumer awareness campaigns, public information programs and as supplemental messages (such as position statements) to persuasive campaigns.

- **Argument.** This message strategy assumes that there are at least two sides to the issue you are addressing. Messages employing the argument strategy are usually persuasive in nature and require an audience that is already interested in the issue and able to process information fairly well. Argument strategy makes frequent use of reasoning and logic and is best structured to reach either those already convinced or neutral and open to logical reasoning.

- **Image.** Image strategy is used to develop or maintain a strong, memorable identity for a person, idea, product or organization. It attempts to "bundle" perceptions into a single concept or symbol representing the subject of the message. The best-used imagery often results in a perception that the image itself *is* the subject, not just a symbolic representation of the subject. This technique is frequently associated with political candidates and parity products that depend on a connotative association in order to differentiate among them.

- **Emotional strategies.** Emotional messages are generally intended to persuade. They are best utilized in dealing with those already on your side or neutral. Emotional messages will rarely convince the hard-core opposition. Traditionally, these depend on the use of emotionally laden words, images or style elements, such as the structure of a speech or the use of certain "hot buttons" in a message. Most of us think of emotional strategies as useful only in the context of emotionally charged issues; however, everything from political candidates to soft drinks can be sold through emotional appeal or association of the "product" with an emotion, such as patriotism or romance. Moriarty also cites humor as an emotional strategy because typically it makes us feel good about the message.

- **Entertainment.** Moriarty includes this strategy specifically for advertising purposes because it is usually presented in "highly competitive and cluttered environments." Remember, however, that, like humor, entertainment can be an excellent strategy for "selling" your ideas, philosophies or whatever regardless of the medium or format. The entertainment value of a message helps it gain and maintain attention. Like image, entertainment as a strategy is often used to sell parity products.

As a rule of thumb, persuasive pieces are usually heavy on the positive attributes of your service, philosophy or product. They need to be written in lay terms and frequently benefit from words with emotional impact. Information pieces can get away with far fewer emotionally packed words and are frequently longer. After all, their aim is to inform; the assumption is that your audience is already convinced of the point being addressed, or at least interested.

The informative piece should be balanced and complete. Its purpose is to let your readers in on something they may not know or may have an incomplete picture of. Many times, however, even the strictly informative piece contains a bias. After all, you are informing based on your point of view. The intent is often to publicize something like a new product or service, to set the record straight on a vital issue affecting your organization, or simply to let your readers know what's up with your organization. Whatever the intent, the informational publication has to stick to just that—information. If your point of view is so strong as to evoke opposition, you'd better be writing a piece to persuade.

Developing the Appropriate Style

Most of us have a problem. The problem is that not many of us learned to write the way we do in school—instead, we learned on the job, picking up bad habits and having those habits further ingrained by people who couldn't write it down much better than we could. Writing well means writing logically. Accepted elements of style are simply the most logical ways to write so that we make the most of our words.

If you understand some of the accepted methods of "good" style, you can begin to apply them to your personal writing. You obviously don't want to change an already good writing style. But, you should always think about your approach, changing those things that you would like to change while leaving what is good intact.

Good Word Usage
Slang and jargon

All industries have their jargon. Banks call certificates of deposit "CDs," journalists call paragraphs "graphs," police call a record of arrests a "rap sheet," and highly technical industries develop entire dictionaries of shorthand notations. As a writer, observe certain guidelines in your use of jargon. Use jargon in external information pieces only if they are going to be read by experts in the field; for the lay readers, use jargon if you can explain it in lay terms, or if the terms have fallen into general usage. The use of jargon in internal pieces is also acceptable.

When jargon becomes cumbersome, ambiguity results. For example, what are commonly referred to as "legalese" and "bureaucratese" are really the overuse of jargon. Benjamin Franklin knew as well as anyone that language can sometimes get in the way of understanding. During the early days of the republic, a great debate raged over the right of average citizens to vote. Many thought that only property owners should have that right, thus restricting a vital component of the democratic process to the wealthy. Franklin was opposed to this point of view, and his supporters, known as Franklinites, explained it this way:

> It cannot be adhered to with any reasonable degree of intellectual or moral certainty that the inalienable right man possesses to exercise his political preferences by employing his vote in referenda is rooted in anything other than man's own nature, and is, therefore, properly called a natural right. To hold, for instance, that this natural right can be limited externally by making its exercise dependent on a prior condition of ownership of property, is to wrongly suppose that man's natural right to vote is somehow more inherent in and more dependent on the property of man than it is on the nature of man. It is obvious that such belief is unreasonable, for it reverses the order of rights intended by nature.

Now, Franklin agreed with this, but he also knew that most people wouldn't understand the level of language. He explained it like this:

> To require property of voters leads us to this dilemma: I own a jackass; I can vote. The jackass dies; I cannot vote. Therefore, the vote represents not me but the jackass.

Other words, such as *impact* and *input,* have now become jargon in many industries. They sound "trendy" to many people and give them a false sense of belonging to a select group of "experts."

Jargon: I have asked Ms. Pomeroy to *input* the latest cost figures so that we may have the results by 4:00 this afternoon. [*a noun misused as a verb*]

General: I have asked Ms. Pomeroy to *enter* the latest cost figures so that we may have the results by 4:00 this afternoon. [*a verb used correctly*]

Jargon: The severe downturn in the economy has negatively *impacted* our industry. [*a noun misused as a verb*]

General: The severe downturn in the economy has negatively *affected* our industry. [*a verb used correctly*]

In your efforts to write clearly and concisely, remember that the object of written communication is to communicate. In other words—don't "fuzzify."

Exactness

Exactness is an art. Most of us tend to "write up" when we assume a formal style. Perhaps our fifth-grade teachers thought we sounded more mature when we wrote that way and we assumed that was the way we were supposed to write. Not so. When we "write up," we lose precision. What we should strive for is clarity, and clarity can be achieved most easily from the exact use of words. Much of our writing is read by people who know something about us and what we do, but that is not always the case

One way to avoid confusion is always to use words whose denotative meanings are most closely matched by those of your audience. The denotative meaning of a word is its "dictionary" meaning.

Connotation is the meaning suggested by a word or words other than their dictionary meaning. Connotative meanings are a matter of association. Some words may have a negative connotation for one group and a positive one for another.

> John had finally returned to the town in which his mother had given birth to him and in which he had grown up. [*The denotative meaning of this sentence is clear, but there is little connotative meaning.*]
>
> John had finally returned to his hometown. [*Not only is the denotative meaning clear, but now we have a word which has a definite connotative meaning—usually a positive one.*]

Think of the different connotative meanings for words such as *liberal, conservative, freedom, democracy, communism,* and *patriotism.* Words with multiple connotations may not be the best words to select if you are striving for exactness.

Exactness requires that you be specific. We all know people who deal in generalities. Writing in generalities is even worse. When we read a piece that has been written in general, nonspecific terms, we can't help but feel that something is being left out—perhaps on purpose.

Specific words are precise and limited in definition. General words are less precise and cover many possible meanings, both denotatively and connotatively.

General	Specific
car	Honda, Accord LX
people	New Brunswickians (New Brunswickites?)
animal	cat
precipitation	rain

Abstract words, on the other hand, deal with concepts or ideas that are intangible such as *freedom* or *love*. It is not wrong to use such words, but there is a chance that they will be misinterpreted.

Remember to be precise when you write (and when you talk). Ambiguity will net you only frustration when you realize that others can't respond in specifics to your generalities.

> *General:* Marisa, please take this report to word processing and tell them it's a rush job. [*Show me something that isn't a rush job!*]
>
> *Specific:* Marisa, please take this report to word processing, and tell them we need it by 3:00 this afternoon. [*Now word processing has a specific deadline*]

Keep it fresh

A long, long time ago, all expressions were original. Today, we're frequently stuck with trite or overworked expressions or chichés. These should be avoided like an IRS audit. The problem with using clichés or worn out words is that they may be entirely overlooked by your reader who has probably seen them a thousand times.

> *Trite:* Nine out of ten times Harcourt is wrong in his instant analysis of a problem.
>
> *Better:* Most of the time Harcourt is wrong in his instant analysis of a problem.

Many forms of writing, including journalism, have developed certain chichéd expressions. Some of these expressions are acceptable shortcuts that aid understanding; others are trite and detract from meaning. It is usually unnecessary, for instance, to speak of someone as:

> John Smith, who was born and raised in Chicago...

It is much easier to say:

> John Smith, a native of Chicago [or Chicago native]...

The key is to recognize cliches and understand when they can be useful and when they can hurt your message. Remember, good writers avoid worn out words and opt instead for a fresh approach.

Keep it active

For most basic publication writing, you will want to use the active voice instead of the passive voice. This means, give the action to the subject of the sentence, not the object. For example:

Passive Voice:	The decision was made by the corporate CEO to discontinue all employee benefits until employees, in his words, "show a little respect for my office."
Active Voice:	The CEO made the decision to discontinue all employee benefits until employees, in his words, "show a little respect for my office."

The main reason for using the active voice is that it brings immediacy to your writing and places the action where it belongs—with the subject of each sentence. Passive voice is reserved, for the most part, for academic or scholarly writing where, for some unknown reason, it is not only acceptable, but often required. (Perhaps no one wants to take credit for the action.)

Good Sentence Usage

Wordiness

Wordiness is a habit that most of us fall into at one time or another. Perhaps, as was mentioned earlier, we once thought it meant we were writing in a formal style. Actually, the opposite is true. Formal English should be no more wordy than informal English. In fact, it should be even more precise because it is formal. As a writer, you will find that the best way to eliminate wordiness is through editing. You probably already have more editors than you need, but you are still your own best editor.

When you edit, strike out the needless phrases and words that add no additional information to your work, and clarify with precise words.

First Draft:	I would appreciate it if you could set up a meeting for sometime in the late afternoon, midweek, for our next, important get-together.
Revised Draft:	I would appreciate it if you could set up a time sometime late Wednesday afternoon for our next meeting.
Final Draft:	Please set up a 3:00 meeting for next Wednesday.

Naturally, you don't want to be brief to the point of abruptness, but you can see what the editing process can do to clarify your message. The key is to make sure that all important information is covered in enough detail to be useful to the reader.

When you edit for exactness, avoid those words or phrases that are meaningless.

First Draft:	We would like to attempt to schedule our very next company picnic to be held in or around the city of Wilmington in order to facilitate transportation by employees to the site.

Revised Draft: We want to schedule our company picnic in Wilmington to make it easier for employees to attend.

Plain, but to the point. Unfortunately, we often overclarify in an attempt to make our messages understood; however, much of what we write is simply redundant or not needed for clarification.

The in-basket is completely full. [*How can it be incompletely full?*]

The meeting date has been set for March 31, the last day of the month. [*The 31st has always been the last day of March on my calendars.*]

Sentence length

Short sentences are easier to read. This also applies to word length. On the other hand, too much of anything can lead to monotony. The key to good style is to vary the sentence length. Don't string together short, choppy sentences if they can be joined to form more interesting, compound sentences.

Monotonous: Harvey walked into the office. He sat down. He began to type on his 1923 Underwood. It was the typewriter with the black, metal carriage. Harvey hated typing this early in the morning. He was never fully awake until at least 10 o'clock.

Varied: Harvey walked into the office, sat down and began to type on his 1923 Underwood with the black, metal carriage. He hated typing this early in the morning, since he was never fully awake until at least 10 o'clock.

Notice that related ideas are linked as compound sentences. Linking unrelated ideas is an easy mistake to make, and the resulting sentences often sound silly.

Harvey walked into the office, sat down and began to type on his 1923 Underwood. It was the typewriter with the black, metal carriage, and he hated typing this early in the morning.

Another way to prevent monotony is to alter sentence order. One of the best ways to alter this order is to use a subordinate clause first.

Because of his dislike for early-morning typing, Harvey never showed up at work prior to 10 o'clock.

Before you start on that report, come into my office for a little chat.

And don't forget—beginning a sentence with a conjunction is perfectly acceptable. Remember, though, that even conjunctions have meanings and usually infer that a thought is being carried over from a previous sentence.

Not only was Harvey later than usual, he was downright tardy. And I wasn't the only one to notice. *(Implies that the information is being added to the previous thought)*

Not only was Harvey later than usual, he was downright tardy. But I was probably the only one who noticed. *(Implies a contrast with the previous thought)*

Good Paragraph Usage

The paragraph represents a series of related sentences. Although there is no set number of sentences you should include in a paragraph, it is instructive to note that paragraph length is shorter today than it has been in the past. Short paragraphs invite readership while longer paragraphs often put the readers off.

The key is coherence, which means that ideas must be unified. You can give unity to your paragraphs in several ways.

Make each sentence contribute to the central thought. The first sentence should generally express the theme of the paragraph. Although the thematic statement may actually appear anywhere in the paragraph, the strongest positions are at the beginning or the end; however, the end is usually reserved for a transitional lead into the following paragraph.

> Our annual operating budget is somewhat above what we expected due to the increase in state allocations to higher education this fiscal year. The result will probably be an increase in departmental allowances with the bulk of the increase showing up in the applied sciences. Although Arts and Sciences have been "holding up" well, we don't expect that they will be able to maintain this independence for long. As a result, their departmental budgets will also reflect this positive financial shift. Next year's outlook is a different story.

The lead sentence sets the theme for the entire paragraph, this year's budget. The final sentence indicates that the next paragraph will probably deal with next year's budget. What you want to avoid are unrelated sentences. If they are truly unrelated, then they deserve a paragraph of their own. If they are slightly related, then the relationship needs to be pointed out.

Arrange sentences in a logical order. The best way to achieve unity is to arrange your sentences in a logical order and provide smooth transition between them indicating their relationship. There are several ways to group sentences to show ranking including chronological order, space order, and order of climax.

Chronological order

Time order and chronological order are sometimes synonymous, although chronological often implies a direct mention of time or dates.

> The growth of communication in the northernmost regions of America was rapid and coincided roughly with the development of the land itself. In 1867, shortly following the Civil War, the first telegraph line was strung between Dawson Creek and Whitehorse. By the turn of the century, the lines had been extended through to Seattle, on the Southeastern coast, and Anchorage, along Prince William Sound. The First World War saw a flurry of development as military involvement increased in the region. And with this involvement, came a windfall of communication development which lasted until 1959.

Time order is most appropriate when explaining the steps involved in an action.

> Changing a typewriter ribbon is a relatively easy task. First, pull the ribbon-release lever, and remove the old ribbon. Throw it away. Remove the new ribbon from its box, insert it onto the spindles provided for it and snap it down. Next comes the hard part. Pull out enough ribbon to place around the ribbon guides against the platen and thread it through the "slots" in the guides. Return the ribbon-release lever to its original position. You are now ready to type.

Space order

Space order implies movement from one location to another: right to left, up to down, east to west, high to low, and so on.

> It rained all day yesterday. The weatherman had shown in glaring detail how the jet stream would carry the warm, moist low front from the snow-filled Cascades of the Northwest, over the Rockies, onto the plains, and finally into my backyard on the Atlantic coast. Apparently, it hadn't lost anything in the transition.

Order of climax

Order of climax means that the arrangement of sentences moves from the least important element to the most important element in the paragraph, or in ascending order of importance. The climax is usually the concluding sentence.

When arranging sentences in order of climax, consider moving from the general to the specific or vice versa. Sometimes, moving from the familiar to the unfamiliar will soften the blow of dealing with a new idea.

> When we view each member of our office staff as an individual, we sometimes develop tunnel vision. We have to understand the larger picture in order to alleviate this problem. They are all a part of a much larger organism. Together they form departments. Departments form divisions. The larger company is composed of these divisions and the company is part of a much larger conglomerate. To take the analogy further, the conglomerate is only one of the hundreds of such groupings which help make our system of economics one of the most successful in the world.

Make logical transitions between sentences. Related ideas are given further unity by the use of logical transitions between sentences. A good transition usually refers to the sentences preceding it. Remember that a transitional word or phrase also has a meaning. Make sure the meaning adds to the understanding of the sentences around it.

> The floor plan was completely haphazard; *furthermore,* it appeared to crowd an already crowded office area. (*Furthermore* indicates an addition to the thought begun in the first clause.)

> Don Johnson was the first to try the new water fountain. *On the other hand,* he was the last to try the potato salad at the last company picnic. (The phrase indicates contrast.)

> Fourteen employees were found to be in violation of company policies forbidding alcohol on the premises. *Consequently,* inspection of employee lockers will probably become commonplace. (The indication here is that the second sentence is a result of actions in the first.)

> The rate of consumption has tripled over the past eighteen months. *In short,* we have a severe problem. (This indicates a summary or explanation.)

> Jeremy covered the news desk. *Meanwhile,* Judy was busy copying the report before Wally returned and discovered it was missing. (This is an indication of time placement.)

One of the major problems associated with the use of transitional words and phrases is the reliance on a very few common groupings. Many people tend to use words such as *however* to bridge every transitional creek. After a while, its use becomes monotonous. The answer? Vary transitional phrases. There's always another word you can use. Think about it.

The same applies to transitions between paragraphs. Use words and phrases that tie the thoughts together and form a smooth bridge between subject changes. After all, even dissimilar ideas need to be linked. If they are so dissimilar that you can't link them logically, they don't belong in the same paper.

Paragraph Development

There are a number of ways to develop your paragraphs to show unity and coherence. The following paragraph is an example of developing a definition to add unity to a paragraph.

> There are a number of ways of viewing the office water cooler; however, to a social scientist, it is a communal gathering place at which ideas and information are freely disseminated. It is an informal location, usually outside the territorial boundaries of any one employee and therefore accessible to all on an equal footing. It is the traditional "oasis," shared by any who are in need of water and at which all are free to share. To imply that this communal ground is the "property" of any one individual or department is to negate its real value. At it, we not only quench our thirsts for liquid, but for information outside the formal boundaries of protocol.

Frequently, classification will serve to relate like ideas in the same paragraph.

> There are three categories of clerical aid within the company. At the lowest rung of the pay scale is the clerk. A clerk's job includes light typing, no shorthand, much filing, and a tremendous amount of running around. Next up on the scale is the secretary. More typing is involved (at a much faster speed and with more accuracy), much filing, some shorthand, and a great deal of running around. At the top is the executive secretary. Typing is a must (at great speeds and with great accuracy), good shorthand, much filing, and more running around than the Stanford University track team.

The main idea can be made more coherent by comparing or contrasting it with a like idea.

> *Comparison:*
>
> A committee meeting is like a football game. The chair is the quarterback, and so is the directing force; however, the members are the players without whom no goal can be obtained. The key to the game plan, then, is to coordinate the players into a single unit with a single goal. The players must be made aware that a unified, or team, effort is integral to the accomplishment of that goal and that the quarterback is the director—not the coach. He recommends; he does not command.

> *Contrast:*
>
> The typical office environment is orderly. Without order, little can be accomplished. Remember the recess periods of your school days? You were able to act freely, without consideration of the restrictive environment of the classroom. You were free to explore your voice, your agility, and your mastery of fast-paced games not suited to the indoors. Once inside, however, you were required to conform to the

needs of the classroom—quiet and order. Within these confines, work can be accomplished with a minimum of disturbance; and the accomplishment of that work is as important in an office environment as in a classroom.

One of the best ways to develop a paragraph and its central idea is to show cause and effect. Most things in life are a result of something else. For most of us, though, it takes some thought to trace cause and effect.

The so-called open office environment popular in newer buildings today has its roots in several trends. Since the mid-1970s, energy conservation has been a major concern in the United States. The open office requires less heat in the winter and less cooling in the summer, due mainly to the lack of walls. In the place of these walls, we now have "dividers" which, although they serve to mask sound, allow for the free circulation of air throughout an entire floor. In addition to conservation, open offices serve to homogenize workers by removing the traditional boundaries of high walls and closed doors. Employees now have access to each other through a network of openings, yet maintain the margin of privacy needed for individual productivity.

Obviously, a paragraph need not be restricted to any single method of development but can benefit from a combination of approaches. The key, of course, is to be clear. Any method which promotes clarity is a good one.

Straight News Style

A great many writers are unfamiliar with what journalists call "straight news." More than anything else, this phrase refers to a style of writing, common to newspapers, known as the *inverted pyramid*. Technically, this means putting all the pertinent information needed for a cursory understanding of the story theme in the opening paragraph, then working in a descending order of importance through to the end of the story. There are several reasons for the growth of this fairly peculiar style of writing. First, it allows busy editors to cut a story from the bottom up without having to worry about eliminating any critical information. Because newspaper stories are measured in column inches, every inch counts. An editor in a hurry, and with only six inches of space to fill, can safely cut a story written in inverted pyramid from the bottom up until it fits. The other reason most cited is the penchant of newspaper readers to read *only* the first couple of paragraphs of any given story. If you are able to pack most of the pertinent information into the first few paragraphs, then readers are able to scan stories (which most do anyway).

Whatever the reason, the inverted pyramid makes sense for shorter, straight news stories. *Straight news* also implies that the story is free of embellishment and bias and comes straight to the point. It doesn't require a fancy lead in or an elaborate close. Consider the following straight news story that appeared in a student newsletter.

Counselors' Association 'hires' PRSSA

The American Mental Health Counselors Association (AMHCA), a representative association for community counselors, has hired PRSSA to develop and implement a series of communication projects.

The projects began last spring when a committee of five PRSSA members developed a PR plan for AMHCA. The comprehensive plan is targeted at present and potential members. The two main objectives of the plan are to strengthen AMHCA as a membership organization and to create awareness of AMHCA among its target audiences.

After receiving approval for the plan from AMHCA board members, PRSSA was asked to develop more specific projects. This fall, a committee of eight PRSSA members worked on two projects. The first was to develop a logo and slogan for AMHCA to be used on all informational materials. The logo, now finished, symbolically represents the safety and shelter of a hearth, utilizing a stylized Hebrew symbol for home and well being. The second project involved redesigning an existing AMHCA brochure. The committee developed a whole new layout and cover design.

The committee will also continue to develop projects winter and spring terms. The main project will be a series of brochures for AMHCA. The brochures will range from information on membership to information on mental health counseling. Other upcoming projects include writing a series of public service announcements to be broadcast nationally for Mental Health Week in March.

"Overall, the project has been a great experience for all of us involved," said committee chairperson, Wendy Wintrode.

Notice that the story opens with what journalists refer to as a lead. The most common type of lead found in a straight news story is known as a *summary lead;* it answers several important questions about the story: who, what, when, where, why and how. Most journalists know that it is almost impossible, and unnecessary, to try to include all of these elements; however, the most germane points should be covered. Remember, that although a lead is typically the first paragraph of a story, it sometimes continues into the second paragraph as well. Look again at the lead (first two paragraphs) in the preceding story.

Who?   The American Mental Health Counselors Association.

What?   Has hired PRSSA to develop and implement a series of communication projects.

When?   The projects began last spring.

Where?   Unless there is a specific need to pinpoint the place, this element isn't needed.

Why?   This is usually the most difficult to explain and least often appears in the lead, but is expanded upon as the story progresses. In this case, however, the answer is the final sentence in the second paragraph.

How?   The answer to this one, like the answer to "why," is usually found later in the story. In this case, it is developed throughout the remainder of the piece.

Be advised that although the most common straight news lead is the summary lead, other types are also used—the delayed lead for example. In this type of lead, the point of the story is delayed slightly while an interesting angle is developed or a character is set up through a quote, or a scene is set through description. For example:

School children all over the country will soon be learning the three *R*'s on a *C* thanks to a $1 million grant from Associated Products

Corporation (APC). APC has recently donated the money to set up a fund for the purchase of educational computers that, when combined with APC's newest software, will teach reading, 'riting and 'rithmetic in a whole new way—on computers.

If this reads less like straight news than the preceding story's lead, then you've discovered why straight news rarely uses a delayed lead. Delayed leads most often appear in feature-type stories because they are excellent ways to set a scene, introduce a character or simply attract and hold attention.

Feature style

The feature story produces what the name implies—a feature. Its style is more relaxed, takes a point of view, discusses issues, people and places. It creates ambience by using "color"; that is, it uses words creatively to describe what is happening. In a straight news story, the focus is on an unbiased presentation of facts; in a feature story, the emphasis is on description. Consider the following feature story based on the straight news story above. Only the first few paragraphs and the closing are included here.

Clearing up the confusion over mental health

What's the difference between a therapist, psychologist, psychotherapist, psychiatrist, and a counselor? If you don't know, you're among the millions of people who are confused about the multi-tiered mental health counseling field.

In an effort to clear up some of the confusion, the American Mental Health Counselors Association (AMHCA) has "hired" a university student group to produce a public information campaign for them.

The Public Relations Student Society of America (PRSSA) at the University of Oregon has been retained by the Association to develop a program of information that will better define the various roles contained under the umbrella term "mental health counselor." Jane Weiskoff, regional director of AMHCA says that the confusion seems to stem from a misconception over what constitutes a "counselor." "In the mental health profession, there is a perceived hierarchy," she says. "Psychiatrists are seen as being at the apex of the field with psychologists, therapists, and other counselors falling into place under them. We'd like to clarify and possibly alter that perception."

Part of the plan, which has already been produced and approved, is to establish and maintain contact with current AMHCA members through a series of brochures and an updated and redesigned association newsletter. These informational pieces will carry the message that mental health counselors come in a variety of forms with a variety of educational and training backgrounds, and that each of these levels is suited to certain types of counseling. The goal is to establish credibility for certain of the counseling functions not fully recognized at this time by the general public and the mental health profession....

... If committee chairperson Wendy Wintrode has her way, the term "mental health counseling" will soon have a completely different, and definitely more expanded, definition. "We want everyone to know that professionalism doesn't begin and end with a small clique at the top—it is the guiding force behind the entire field of mental health counseling."

As you can see, this story is considerably different from the straight news version. The facts are still here, but the focus is on creative information presentation. The lead is a question (a typical delayed lead strategy). Answering that question becomes part of the story itself. Quotes are used liberally. They not only validate and lend credibility to the subject being discussed, they add *human interest*. Human interest is rather loosely referred to as anything that highlights the human element in a story. We too often associate it with syrupy stories about children or animals; however, human interest ranges from simple inclusion of the human "voice" in a story to an entire profile featuring a single person. In fact, the term *profile* usually refers to a feature story done on one person or on one aspect or issue relating to one person, although companies or products can be profiled as well. The following lead is from a profile on a corporate legal department and its head. Notice how the scene is set before the subject is introduced.

> Sitting behind a cluttered desk, boxes scattered around the office—some still unopened—is the new head of Associated Products Corporation's Law Department, Ed Bennett. Ed is a neat man, both in appearance and in speech. As he speaks about the "new" Law Department, he grins occasionally as though to say, "Why take the time to interview someone as unimportant as a lawyer?" That grin is deceiving because, to Ed and the other attorneys who work for Associated Products Corporation, law is serious business.

To add human interest is merely to add the human element to a story. Information without this element is only information. With it, information becomes more interesting, more personal, more attuned to readers' experiences. Consider the following broadcast news lead.

> A little girl stood for the first time today to receive a new teddy bear and a check for $75,000 from the Society for Needy Children. Eight-year-old Mary Patterson accepted the check on behalf of the children at the St. Mary Martha's Children's Hospital. The money represents the culmination of a year-long fundraising drive by the Society.

If you're trying to reach people with your message—I mean really reach them—injecting human interest is often the best way to do it.

Organizing the Message

A sentence is a syntactically related group of words that usually expresses a single idea. A paragraph contains a number of sentences structured around a single theme. So too, a complete piece of writing, whether it's a press release or an article for the company newsletter, contains a series of paragraphs on a single theme and unified by logical transitions.

For many of us, the writing is the easy part—planning is the snag. And the toughest part of planning is deciding exactly what to say and what to leave out. Most of us tend to overwrite; we err on the side of too much information when less is usually better. In the words of one observer: "Writing is like summer clothing—it should be long enough to cover the subject, but brief enough to be interesting."

The first job of writing, then, is to choose your subject and be selective about the information needed to cover it. There are several ways to accomplish this task. One of the easiest ways is to work from a very general topic to a more specific one.

banking -> withdrawing and making deposits -> avoiding lines ->
using automatic tellers -> using automatic tellers in the lobby

This may seem insanely simple, but the act of putting your ideas on paper does help focus your thoughts and crystallize those ideas.

Naturally, your theme is intimately tied to your purpose. If, for instance, you wish to encourage bank patrons to use the automatic tellers in the bank lobby, it may be necessary to come directly to the point in your pitch, using one of the traditional writing approaches. Among the most common approaches are:

Exposition—used to inform or explain
Argumentation—used to convince or persuade
Narration—used mostly for its entertainment value
Description—used to explain through verbal "pictures"

In most publications, narration is the least frequently used form of writing except in feature-type stories; however, the other methods are often used in combination to present information to readers. A lot depends on whether you are trying to be persuasive or simply present information.

The outline
There are three rules to good writing:

1. Organize.
2. See rule one.
3. See rule two.

One of the best ways to organize is with an outline. It is intended as a guideline for constructing the finished product; it should include only the body of the piece to be written and the order of the points you wish to make. (The introduction and conclusions are not main points but separate points and should be so noted in the outline.)

Selecting points
Selecting what points to cover in your publication depends on space and topic. The trick is to have each point bear directly on the thesis of the message—what you are trying to communicate.

A general rule of thumb is to *have at least two, but not more than five, main points in your message.* If you try to stick to this number, you are less likely to run out of space or fail to cover your points in the kind of depth necessary. In order to limit the number of points you will cover, you need to follow some guidelines.

- **Select mutually exclusive points**. Don't present the same information more than once. Each point should cover new ground and follow from preceding points rather than reiterate them.

- **Arrange points according to relationship**. Points of equal weight are called **coordinate** points; points which support other points are called **subordinate** points. In an outline, this usually means that major headings (for instance, those beginning with Roman numerals) are coordinate points in a global sense. Points that follow (lettered "A, B, C," etc.), are subordinate to these global points. However, any point that elaborates on another point is subordinate to that point. The trick in constructing an outline is to make all points that are preceded by Roman numerals parallel in importance. Likewise, all points that are preceded by a capital letter ("A, B, C," etc.) should be parallel, and so on.

The central idea

Once you have decided on your purpose, try to write down your central idea in a single sentence or thesis statement. Suppose, for example, that your goal is to inform the general populace about the nature of telephone fraud—clearly an information-based communication. (However, if you also want your audience to act to prevent or report phone fraud, your message, in part, will be persuasive.) What is your thesis statement? It might be something like this:

> If you are an aware consumer, you are less likely to become a victim of telephone fraud.

In a single sentence, you have set down the controlling idea of your message, which can now be elaborated upon. The next step is to develop a working plan or rough outline.

Before you begin an actual outline, however, you might want to list some ideas that are appropriate to the topic. These ideas can be in the form of a simple list. Let's say, for instance, that by using the above thesis statement as a reference point you have decided to follow the approach of an "imagined Q & A."

> What is phone fraud?
>   —FTC definition
>   —What are fraudulent callers selling?
>   —Examples of types of callers
>
> What do callers say?
>   —Examples of "pitches"
>
> How to protect yourself
>   —List of actions when being solicited over the phone
>
> How to take action
>   —Provide information on who to call

Now you have a beginning. In the case of an imagined Q & A, you will probably want to address the points one by one, leading the reader through the following sequence: definition of problem, examples of problem, protective measures and call for action.

The topic outline

The most common type of outline is the topic outline. It is the easiest to jot down and the quickest way to organize scattered thoughts.

> Central Idea: If you are an aware consumer, you are less likely to become a victim of telephone fraud.
>
> I. Federal Trade Commission definition
>
> II. What are they selling?

A. A number of things:

   1. film club membership
   2. vacations
   3. donations to c rities
   4. church-sponsored events

III. What do they want?

   B. Money sent directly to them

   C. Your credit card number

Arranging points

The order in which you arrange your main points will affect your readers psychologically. Most messages have a tendency to arrange themselves; that is, the subject matter often lends itself to an easily recognizable order. When in doubt, however, rely on the traditional ordering methods: chronological, space order, cause–effect, problem–solution. Chronological and space order were covered earlier in this chapter, so let's look at the other two.

• **Cause-effect:** Cause-effect and problem-solution are probably the approaches most frequently used. Cause-effect simply requires that you relate information in such a way that you spell out a clear causal relationship (usually working from the cause to the effect) between two items. For instance, you could be trying to point out that lack of sufficient knowledge about telephone fraud is costing your state millions of dollars a year. You will need to draw clear and logical connections between telephone fraud (the stated cause) and loss of consumer buying power (effect).

• **Problem-solution:** This is similar to cause-effect in that you work from one to the other in a logical progression. If you are trying to get your readers to try something for the first time or to accept a certain approach as being the answer to a problem facing them, then this is the way to go.

   There are two ways to set up problem-solution. One approach is to jump right in with the solution by describing it and what it does while also describing the problem it solves. The more effective approach (and often the most dramatic) is to set up the problem first, relate it to your readers' personal interests, and then give the solution. In the following example, teachers are the targeted audience.

> It's not an easy time to be a teacher. Community expectations of teachers are high, and students are perhaps more demanding than ever before. Today's children, brought up on TV, know more at an earlier age and frequently challenge their teachers just to keep up.

> Some long-time educators say that children of the TV generation are more passive than their predecessors and have shorter attention spans. As a result, today's teachers have to concentrate as much on performing—developing teaching methods that catch and hold students' interest—as on teaching a subject.

> Many children also seem to need more individual attention and encouragement from their teachers to perform well. Unfortunately, in today's crowded public school classrooms, sometimes there's just not enough teacher to go around. Slow learners don't get the individual help they need, and better students, capable of

learning at a faster rate, become bored and lose interest in school.

What's the answer?

We've known for years that computers can help children learn. What we've ignored is the fact that computers can also help teachers teach. Consider these findings...

The introduction

The introduction is usually written after the rest of your outline is completed. It is probably the most important aspect of your message and deserves appropriate attention when it is written. Your introduction, like a lead in a feature or news story, is used to "hook" your readers. Naturally, there are some guidelines that will help you develop your introduction.

- **Open with an attention-getter**. There are many ways to open a persuasive message: with humor, analogy, anecdote, drama or by posing a question. When you write an introduction, try out several approaches before deciding on which best fits your tone. Of course, keep your intent in mind. For example, a good writer won't alienate his or her audience by using too flip a tone if the subject is serious. At the same time, don't ever be afraid to use a little humor if the tone can be lightened without harming the message or the image of the organization or client. For instance:

    Analogy: Your students are hungry for knowledge. They're not satisfied with the traditional meat-and-potatoes approach to education.

    Question: Can you name the most underpaid professional job in the United States today? If you guessed teacher, you're right.

- **Establish a relationship with your readers**. Once you get your readers' attention, you have to keep their interest. This means that you have to establish a relationship with them. First, however, you need to know what your present relationship is (if you've done your audience analysis properly, you'll know). Then, you have to determine what relationship you need to develop to get your message across. One of the best, and subtlest, ways to establish a relationship is to use personal pronouns such as "we" and "us." Although this sometimes sounds phoney, most of the time it is not noticed at all and will probably make your readers feel that you're one of them.

    Remember, however, that most people like to think that you know more than they do. Why else should they bother to read your information? But, they don't like to think that you're a whole lot smarter.

- **Establish credibility with your readers**. Help them to believe you by showing that you know what you are talking about. This often means "introducing" yourself and your qualifications before presenting an opinion concerning the issue at hand. Sometimes, of course, you can establish credibility through what you say.

    We at the National Education Association know what it's like to be a teacher. We should, we've been in the business of representing American teachers for over 50 years.

- **Establish common ground**. By explaining similar interests, experiences or goals, you show your readers that you are like them. Speak their language. If you can show commonality and establish your credentials at the same time, do it.

- **Motivate your readers**. Let your readers know how important it is that they read your information. Show them, right off the bat, what's in it for them.

  > How would you like to have a teaching assistant who not only involves each student on an individual basis, but also can do this for all of them simultaneously? Sound like a dream come true?

Conclusions

Readers seek psychological closure. They need to have things wrapped up for them. Shakespeare was famous for wrapping up his plots neatly at the end of his plays. You can often accomplish closure by referring back to the beginning of your piece. This gives the readers a sense that they have witnessed a complete process. There are several ways to attain the closure necessary to end your message effectively.

- **Summarize the main points**. It is always a good idea to reiterate your main points at or near the end of your message. Reiteration is especially important if you have covered the allowable points in some detail. By summarizing, you are reminding the reader of what you've said.

  > Are computers worth it? In a nutshell—yes. They involve students on an individual basis with modern, interesting techniques. They help the slow as well as the fast learners equally without interfering with either's pace. They can teach all the traditional subjects in a modern, involving way. And, they can take some of the burden off the teacher, allowing for more personal interaction.

- **Remind the reader of the importance of the topic**. Remember when you told your readers what was in it for them? Tell them again. Or, if you haven't told them yet, now is the time to do it. Often, it is appropriate to reiterate your introduction in a slightly altered form.

  > Is anything more important than a child's education? Not that we know of. And there's no better way to "free up" some time for you to work with students individually than through a computer-based curriculum.

- **Make an appeal**. This is usually reserved for the persuasive message when a call to action is often appropriate.

  > If you think this is the kind of classroom environment you'd like to work in, let us know. Just fill in the attached mail-back card and we'll have a representative contact you. Try us out. We think you'll be hooked on computer education.

Writing the Persuasive Message

Writing a message that persuades is not easy. First, you have to have a crystal-clear understanding of what it is you want your readers to do in response to your persuasive effort. This means that you have to be able not only to convey your message in the clearest possible terms, but also be responsive to opposing points of view.

It is important to note here that the persuasive message is normally audience centered. Your persuasive strategy will be based on who your audience is and how they feel about your topic.

The strategy of the persuasive piece ideally is to inform, and while informing, persuade. The approach you use probably will be based on how receptive your audience is to either emotional or rational appeal. Historically, audiences react best to a combination of both. There are times, however, when a purely emotional or purely rational appeal will work best. The key is good audience analysis.

Remember, a hostile audience usually won't be convinced. A sympathetic audience doesn't need to be convinced. And, an undecided audience is as likely to be convinced by your opposition as by you. The difference in strategies employed for each of these audiences can be great. For instance, if you are writing for a friendly audience, an emotional appeal may work very well. For an undecided audience, a rational appeal supported by solid evidence may work best. If your neutral audience is uninterested, you'll have to stress attention-getting devices. If they are uninformed, you'll have to inform them. And if they are simply undecided, you'll have to convince them.

Developing an approach

You might want to consider approaching development by referencing the psychological state of your readers. This is known as the audience-centered approach and includes three basic techniques: the motivated sequence, the imagined Q & A, and attitude change.

The motivated sequence

The motivated sequence is a common tactic used by persuaders. It is organized in five steps.

1. **Attention.** You must first get their attention. This means that you have to open with a bang.

2. **Need**. Next, you have to establish why the topic is of importance to the readers. Set up the problem statement.

3. **Satisfaction.** Present the solution. It has to be a legitimate solution to the problem.

4. **Support.** You have to support fully your solution and point out the pitfalls of any alternatives. Otherwise, your readers may not be able to comprehend completely the advantages of your solution over others.

5. **Action.** Finally, call for action. Ask your readers to do something, and make it as easy as possible to take action.

The imagined Q & A

In the imagined Q & A, you structure your message by imagining questions or attitudes that your readers might have if they could express them instead of sitting silently reading your publication. For instance, you might imagine, based on some audience analysis, that your audience is fairly lethargic. In that case, your first step is to wake them up—get their attention. Next, ask yourself the questions they might be asking you, albeit silently.

- Why even talk about this subject? Tell them the importance of your topic to them. Tie your topic to their concerns.

- For example? Don't just leave them with your point of view. Give them examples. Support your proposal.

- So what? Let them know what all of this means to them, and tell them what you want them to do.

Covering all sides

Most novice writers assume that all you are obligated to do in a persuasive piece is present your side. This is an especially dangerous assumption if the opposing side has sound arguments of its own. Ideally, you have excellent reasons for preferring your arguments to theirs. If your arguments really are sound, they will stand up to comparison. To that end, you will often find it advisable to present opposing viewpoints for the purpose of showing yours as the better alternative.

You may assume that your audience is at least familiar with opposing arguments. Thus, you will need to admit to these arguments and begin to refute them. In most cases, it is advisable to address counter arguments only after you have presented your own side. Try using the following guidelines:

1. State the opposing view fairly. Make your audience believe that you are fair-minded enough to understand that there *is* another side and that you're intelligent enough to understand it.

2. State your position on the opposing view. Now that you've shown that you understand the other side, state why you don't think it's right—or, better yet, not totally right. This indicates that *you* find at least some merit in what others have to say—even the opposition.

3. Support your own position. Give the details of your side of the argument. Use logic to build your position, not emotion. The trick is to strike a balance between logic and emotion while leaning toward logic and emotional control.

4. Compare the two positions and show how yours is the most viable. If you've done your work well up until this point, then your audience will already see the clear differences between the two sides. Strengthen their understanding by reiterating the differences and finishing with a strong statement in support of your side.

The Evaluation Process

Now is the time to test your message. You'll need to test it on several levels in order for your assessment to be accurate. Go back and look at the steps listed at the beginning of this chapter for planning your communication. You'll have to test your final message at each of the four levels if you are to succeed in meeting your objectives.

First, do your messages reflect your original objectives? Is it clear to you that these messages are directly related to your objectives? You should ask yourself why each message has been developed. If the answer relates to accomplishing one of your objectives, then the message has succeeded at that level.

The next three steps (target audience, message strategy and choice of medium) all have something in common for testing purposes: they can all be tested at one time. The best approach is to test them on actual members of your target audience. Focus group testing has become a fairly common practice for those in advertising, marketing and public relations. This technique requires that you assemble a small group (eight or so) of your target audience, present them with the message, and ask for their reactions. The best way to set up a focus group is to hire a moderator who is experienced with asking these types of questions and interpreting the responses properly. Don't assume that because you are the writer, and the closest to the project, that you can interpret audience feedback clearly. In most cases, you are *not* the one best suited to perform the focus group moderation. In either event, your approach can be fairly formal (a written questionnaire to be filled out following the presentation), or informal (open-ended questions asked in an open discussion among the participants). The key is to design your questions in advance and to cover all the areas you need to analyze.

For example, be sure to cover the appropriateness of the language to your audience. Is it difficult to follow or have too much jargon or technical terms? Do they understand the message? Does it speak to them, or do they feel it is meant for someone else? Is the medium appropriate? Would they take time to read it if it came to them in the mail? As an insert in their paychecks? In the corporate magazine? Answers to these questions should give you a fair idea of how your larger audience will react to your message.

One other method of testing appropriateness of message is through readability formulas. Readability formulas analyze everything from the level of education needed to understand your message, to the number of personal pronouns used (which analyzes the level of friendliness of tone). Two of the most common readability formulas are described here.

The Gunning Fog Index

1. Select a sample of 100 words from the middle of your message.
2. Count the number of sentences and divide that number into 100 to find an average sentence length (ASL).
3. Count the number of words consisting of three syllables or more in the 100 words. Do not include proper nouns, compound words like *typesetting*, or words that end in *ed* or *es*.
4. Add the totals from steps 2 and 3 and multiply by 0.4.

Figure 1.1 _____

The Gunning Fog Index. *The resulting score approximates the number of years of schooling required to read the piece. College graduates usually can read at about a score of 16 while most best sellers are written at 7-8. Obviously, if your piece is intended for vertical distribution, such as a company magazine, you will need to reach an "average" audience. Newspapers, for instance, write at about the sixth-grade level.*

The Flesch Formula

1. Select a sample of 100 words from the middle of your piece.
2. Count the number of sentences; divide that *into* 100 to find the average sentence length (ASL).
3. Count the number of syllables in sample and divide this figure *by* 100 for the average word length (AWL).
4. Plug the resulting figures from steps 2 and 3 into the following formula:

Readability = 206.835 − (84.6 x AWL) − (1.015 x ASL)

5. Interpret the scores based on the following scale:

70–80 = very easy (romance novels)
60–65 = standard (newspapers, *Readers Digest*)
50–55 = "intellectual" magazines (*Harpers, The Atlantic*)
30– below = scholarly journals, technical papers

Figure 1.2 _____

Flesch Formula. This formula is based on ease of reading determined, to a large extent, by the length of words. This assumes that polysyllabic words slow down and often confuse the reader. Other formulas guage the degree of familiarity by noting personal pronouns, for instance.

This sort of evaluation is known as *preparation evaluation*. Obviously, it can only tell you if the message and the way it's packaged and presented are acceptable to your target audience. What it won't tell you is whether or not your audience will respond to your message. For that, you'll have to wait.

There are a number of methods for judging the effectiveness of your communication once it is distributed, ranging from expensive to relatively inexpensive, and from complex to simple. Let's take the simplest first: readership surveys.

Readership surveys are simple questionnaires usually included with your publication (as in a corporate magazine or newsletter) that seek to find out whether anyone is really out there. A few, plainly put questions—about what interests your readers the most, the least, what they would change if they could, what they would include or leave out—will tell you a lot. Most commercial publications run the occasional readership survey just to make sure they're operating on the same wavelength.

On the more expensive level are formal, statistical surveys measuring everything from whether your readers are actually receiving your message, to whether or not they're changing their attitudes or behaviors because of it. These surveys are best left to highly qualified specialists who will probably charge you a great deal to ask the right questions and properly interpret the answers; however, the results can be invaluable if persuasion is your aim. Remember, behavioral change can often be easily measured in increased sales of your new widget, attendance at the company picnic (remember to factor in the free beer as a contributing variable), more votes for your candidate, or a decrease in the number of complaint letters you receive on an issue. Attitude change, on the other hand, is more difficult to measure but, nonetheless, equally as important.

Modern survey techniques, contrary to what critics say, *can* accurately define attitudes and measure shifts in them. Because of the complexity of the operation, however (and the need to perform both a pre- and a post-survey in order to have something to compare), you will have to pay the price. Good research isn't cheap. For most of us involved in publication production, research usually means counting the mail and weighing the negative against the positive (understanding that most people will write you with a complaint before they write to congratulate you on the marvelous job you're doing). But, don't pooh-pooh the idea of formal research if you're dealing with a complex issue or if your organization's image is on the line. In the communication business, you simply can't afford to be wrong—which means, you can't afford to guess.

NOTES

[1] For an excellent work on gathering information, see Lauren Kessler and Duncan McDonald, *Uncovering the News* (Belmont: Wadsworth Publishing Company, 1987).

[2] Doug Newsom and Alan Scott, *This Is PR* (Belmont: Wadsworth Publishing Company, 1985), p. 213.

[3] Ken Metzler, *Creative Interviewing* (Englewood Cliffs: Prentice-Hall, 1989).

[4] Sandra E. Moriarty, *Creative Advertising* (Englewood Cliffs: Prentice-Hall, 1986), pp. 62–65.

If desktop publishing was a revolution, word processing was its harbinger. For years, secretaries, clerks and writers of all kinds struggled with traditional word processing tools. From the simple pen or pencil to the clumsy but memory-capable *mag-card* typewriter, the tools of the writer have become increasingly sophisticated. The problem, of course, was that many writers balked at the new technology. Mark Twain was one of the first American writers to buy and use the typewriter, but he rejected it in favor of the pen, finding the machine too clumsy for his tastes.

In the same way, modern writers were slow to adopt the computer as a method of composing and setting down their words. And no wonder. The earliest computers were linked to huge mainframes and weren't designed for anything as mundane as text typing. Then came the revolution. Now, we'd be hard put to find an office *without* a computer. Secretaries can't find jobs without computer knowledge these days, and it is the unwise college student who doesn't gain this vital skill prior to graduation.

Since word processing burst upon the scene, software programs have abounded. The earliest programs were cumbersome and quirky. Now they run the gamut from highly sophisticated to simple. With so many options, how do *we* choose a word processing program? Most of us just use the one that came with our computer. In fact, we tend to become almost religiously devoted to the first program we learned. The reason is that it is time-consuming and often frustrating to have to learn a new program; and old habits, formed when we learned to use our first program, are hard to break. At the rate software is being updated, it's enough just to keep up with the changes in the program we are using.

How to Choose a Word Processing Program

Even if you learned on a particular software program, there comes a time when it might not do everything you need. At $200 to $500 a whack, "trying out a program" could be a costly practice. Here are a few tips for deciding on just the right word processing program for you.

Pick a program that meets *all* of your needs, not just some of them. First, decide if ease of use is more important than certain special features. The more features incorporated into the program the more difficult it will be to learn and use. For example, do you need a program that indexes to write copy for a newsletter? Maybe you can find a program that will serve both purposes and still be easy to use.

If you are switching to a Macintosh-compatible word processing program from a PC-based program, or vice versa, be prepared for some changes in your software. Although many people can handle both systems with ease, most prefer one over the other.

Pick a program that will not limit document size. Although you will probably be working with smaller documents, it pays to use a program that will allow long documents without tying up primary memory on your computer. For instance, some word processing programs use primary memory to store the file you are working on. Once you fill that primary memory, you're done—whether you like it or not. You are forced to save very small files to disk each time. Eventually, you're going to want to work on longer documents.

Pick a word processing program that is compatible with your page layout program. This is a key feature of any word processing program for a desktop publisher, especially if you are going to be using your word processing program to produce the text for desktop publishing. Software incompatibility can cause some real problems, and the fact that there are levels of incompatibility makes it even more difficult to match up your programs. For example, some word processing files can't be transferred at all to your page layout program. Others will transfer, but only as "text" files. That means your original formatting is lost. Some display other quirks when transferred such as losing everything bold or italicized. Read the documentation that came with your page layout program. It will tell you not only which word processing programs work with it, but also which versions.

Software manufacturers update their programs frequently, both to add new features in order to keep up with the competition and to eliminate bugs in earlier versions. These manufacturers don't ask each other's permission before updating. The result is often that the newest version of a word processing program won't match the parameters of your existing page layout program. You usually have to use your old version of the word processing program until the page layout program is updated.

Compatibility problems also occur among other types of programs for many of the same reasons. One solution is to use software manufactured by the same company for everything. That's nice in theory, but most of us find that any given software company excels in one or two areas and not all of them. For instance, Aldus was the first into the market with a page layout program, *PageMaker*. In fact, it became the industry standard for Apple computer systems. However, if you work on PCs, you're going to find other programs more responsive, such as *Ventura Publisher* from Xerox, or Quark *Xpress*. And although you might find some auxiliary programming from the same company for use with your page layout program (Aldus also makes *FreeHand* for instance), it's not realistic to expect that you'll find them all.

Some computer hardware comes with bundled software—packages containing "everything you'll need" for your new computer. Don't be fooled. There is no *one* company with a corner on the market for any given type of software.

Pick a program that is compatible with the programs of the other people who will be working with you. Nothing is more frustrating than knocking off a 3,000-word article only to discover your layout artist uses a page layout program that won't accept your word processing program's format. Many word processing programs have built-in converters or translators allowing files written in one program format to be transferred to another format. However, formats don't usually convert *in toto* and leave many problems, such as no paragraph indents or missing type style commands in the newly converted version of the file.

Compatibility across hardware system types is also a problem, especially if you are working on a mixed system with some people using IBMs and others Macintoshes. If you are all linked through a local area network (LAN), sharing a system should cut down on transfer problems. Most networks support convert programs that allow you to use Macintosh-generated files on PCs and vice versa. In addition, there are hardware converters available that can transfer data among disparate system types or even disk sizes and formats, and the newest Macintosh comes with a built-in convert program allowing it to read directly from PC disk formats.

Read software reviews for straightforward information on the strengths and weaknesses of potential software purchases. A number of reputable magazines provide monthly reviews of both software and hardware, including *PC World, BYTE, MacUser, Macworld, Publish* and many others. But don't just take the word of reviewers and friends. Obtain a test version and try it out. Many software companies will gladly send you a sample of their program to test out before you purchase. They are fairly complete as to the various functions they'll perform, but normally don't allow you to save your work. In other words, they give you just enough to whet your appetite.

Remember, selecting the right word processing program is one of the most important decisions you'll make as a desktop publisher. It pays to take your time. If you try to project your needs as far ahead as possible now, you will save yourself a lot of heartburn later on.

Chapter 2

Design is central to the success of any communication. In fact, most designers—this one included—would go so far as to suggest that design is just as important an element of a publication as writing. Don't get me wrong. If your writing stinks, graphic cartwheels and high design acrobatics won't cover up the smell. Writing works without a net. Nothing can save it, save thoughtful rewrites. However, the point must be made that good design attracts and holds readership, while bad design repels and discourages it. If you don't get them in the tent, they won't see the show.

Like it or not, we read externally first and internally second. Which is to say that we judge publications not only by their covers, but by their overall visual appearance. Design provides an outward structure upon which we further communicate our messages, sell our soap, project our images, inform our publics and otherwise hang our corporate hats. Companies think nothing of spending incredible sums of money for trademarks, company seals, logos and other symbols to suggest their quality, integrity, dependability and consistency or to draw visual attention to themselves. They appreciate outward image when it's rolling down a street painted on the sides of their trucks, being stacked on shelves or signing off a magazine advertisement. Too often, however, the same companies lose sight of design's importance when it comes to their publications.

But make no mistake. Whether the publication is internal—a newsletter, benefits folder or employee recruitment kit—or external—a brochure, annual report or company magazine—its design requires careful planning. Without structure, visual thought and order, your publication will not get the attention it deserves. No matter how well written and carefully edited your message may be, readers will pass over poorly designed print materials. It's as simple as that.

For these reasons, then, it is necessary for us first to understand and be able to use basic design principles. Second, it is important to develop a vocabulary, so that we might communicate clearly with designers, printers and other publication professionals. Third, we should know how the eye moves through a page (so we can direct and redirect visual traffic) as well as understand how to attract and hold readers. Finally, we must comprehend the "parts of sight" as clearly as we know the parts of speech.

Design: What It Is and Why It Might Be Greek to You

Before venturing further, we need to define what we mean by design.

Essentially, design is the act of bringing order to whatever surrounds us. It is planning and organizing physical materials and shaping and reshaping our environment to accommodate specific needs. It is not magic, accomplished with mirrors, black cat bones and sleight of hand. And there's nothing particularly mysterious about it.

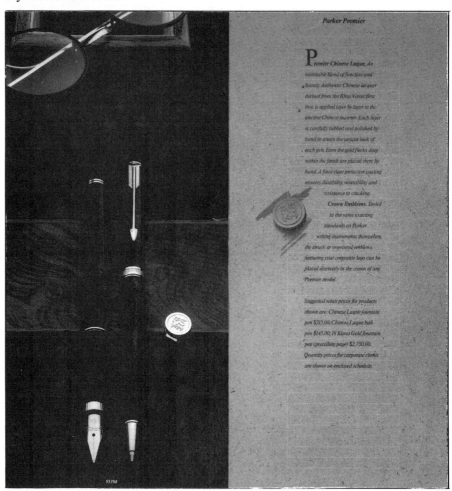

Figure 2.1 _____

The copy for these pages begins, "An inimitable blend of function and beauty." Although directed to the Parker Premier pen set, it sums up the simplicity, function and high aesthetics of this design. Samata Associates used a very narrow format—5-1/2" x 11-1/2"—to contribute to the stylish and slender qualities of the product. The copy block closely approximates the size and shape of the pens in the photography, and the pens intersect the birdseye maple box. (Our eyes are always drawn to intersection points.) Textures from the hand-crafted, laquered pen contrast slightly with those from the wood, giving Terry Heffernan's photography a warm, inviting feel. Paul Thompson did the photo illustration on the right page. The Parker brochure was designed by Pat and Greg Samata; Dan Fredericks wrote the copy. Reprinted with the permission of Parker and Samata Associates.

Figure 2.2

Texas Monthly *"set out to document the relationship between people and their painted images," and in so doing, art director D. J. Stout designed the entire feature using engraved plaques for the article's title and for all IDs. A fitting solution. Stout has also blocked all the type—the subhead, copy area and Danny Turner's photography credits—at the same width as the title plaque and generously framed it, as if it might be a painting. Reprinted with permission of* Texas Monthly.

There are logical reasons why design probably seems foreign and troublesome to us, though. For one thing, few of us have had much visual education. That looms especially ironic when you consider how much our learning and survival depend upon sight. Think about it: with few exceptions, our verbal literacy is learned, broadened and specialized through vision—i.e., through reading and writing skills. We study letters, words, spelling, vocabulary, grammar, syntax, style, writing and literature. Grammar is apt to be central to our language studies from third grade through our first year of college. Writing begins before we start our formal educations, first by learning to recognize a set of abstract symbols, and then to form them; and writing runs fully through all the years of our educations. Visual studies, however, tend to end somewhere between the second and third grades when crayons are either thrown or taken away.

Another reason why we underestimate the impact of design is the effortless nature of sight itself. Our eyes receive and process line, shape, texture, color, intricate spatial relationships and other complex visual information almost instantly—so long as we keep our eyes open, we don't run red lights, fall down stairs, try to open the wrong end of a beer can or trample people. That sight works so easily is both good and bad. Good in that our visual sense operates automatically, is well greased and complete beyond our wildest dreams. Bad in that we take it for granted and often assume that to have sight is to have visual literacy. Of course this is no more the case than to assume that to be able to speak a language is the same as to also read and write that language.

It should come as no surprise, then, that design seems foreign to us. It enjoys its own vocabulary, grammar, syntax, composition and meaning. Additionally, it possesses a unique literature, history and heritage; one that, in fact, precedes written language. But happily, acquiring this new visual "language" is considerably less painful than the average root canal procedure.

This chapter cannot provide sixteen years of visual education, an art history review and a full discussion of aesthetic theory at a single sitting. However, with an earnest read and review it can provide

- a crash course in design principles

- a basic visual and design vocabulary

- a primer of sorts for visual literacy, discussing the parts of sight, and showing how to direct vision and steer the viewer through publication designs.

Finally, the design chapters of this text will alert you to the idiosyncrasies and special design concerns of specific collateral print materials and provide design insights and solutions unique to each of those publications.

But Is There a Difference?

The next question, then: Do collateral materials require different design approaches, principles and strategies? Or, more simply stated, do you design differently for collateral materials?

Yes and no. Or, as Winnie the Pooh might suggest, it all depends.

There is a set of design principles that applies to whatever we create, regardless of intent, style, medium or format. In each instance, we plot a visual course that becomes the blueprint for our publication's architecture. And although publication formats vary, just as buildings differ, they possess similar structural principles, just as skyscrapers, shopping malls, museums and homes have some characteristics in common. Publications, like buildings, employ a structural plan that mixes serious pragmatic and aesthetic concerns while providing a sound framework and foundation.

Every publication deserves a good design that takes into account its format, medium and intent. For example, the exaggerated vertical configuration of a brochure presents a set of spatial concerns much different from those of a poster. The brochure's long, relatively small and narrow area is arranged in a series of panels—of equal or unequal size—that can be folded two, three or more times, vertically or horizontally. These properties make the brochure's continuity and sequence especially important.

The medium also brings its own eccentricities and needs to the design. While an annual report may bear a strong resemblance to a magazine—and the best ones seem to—it requires special care to design a report that communicates with its many audiences while conforming to exacting SEC requirements that prescribe everything from logistics to point size. Designing a poster that will be read from across a room by a moving audience—or that may itself be moving—presents a different challenge. Or the poster itself may be moving. With apologies to Marshall McLuhan, the medium is the message. The point is that the medium brings its own unique eccentricities and needs to the design. Where or when possible, the good designer extends constraining boundaries, borrows from other media and steals or recreates from the present or the past.

Intent also figures squarely into the design formula. Let's assume that a company has had a financially disastrous year. While it can easily afford a full-blown, four-color report with portraits of smiling CEOs in three-piece, charcoal gray suits, perceptive company planners might decide that a more austere approach is warranted. For that fiscal year, anyway. Or, perhaps due to a corporate takeover or a major image overhaul, a company decides to completely reposition itself and court a changed or new audience. To do so, it redesigns everything from newsletter to logotype. Simply put, your purposes affect the look and structure of what you publish.

Your designs should also reflect your audience and their needs. Here's a quick example. When our students of advertising design and magazine design get caught up in their formal design concerns, they sometimes forget their audiences, without really meaning to overlook them. When this happens they need to be refocused. In one instance, we asked them to design a full-page advertisement for a national candy company that the ad will appear in *Boy's Life*, a monthly magazine for the Boy Scouts of America. The advertisement should target six-to-ten-year-old boys. After they've completed the assignment and each has provided rationales and presented their work, we bring a Cub Scout into the classroom to react to their work and, more importantly, to explain what each of the ads means to him. It's a good exercise, and a lesson well learned. Professionals should do more of the same.

Here's another example. A few years ago, Interlake, Inc. had a problem with their corporate image. Once a highly respected and competitive steel company, they'd foreseen trouble from foreign competitors and had completely reshaped the company through divestiture and by moving into ferroalloys, packaging, material handling and conveyance systems, strategic metals and die-casting. But they continued to be perceived as an iron/steel conglomerate. Kirk Kahrs, then creative director of HGSO in Chicago, was asked to write and design an annual report and launch an advertising campaign to turn the image around.

Figure 2.3 _____

On the opposite side of this folded piece, a connect-the-dots cow has a bright color block adjacent to it which says: "If developing software was as simple as dot-to-dot...we'd be out to pasture." This Sakai Nishi-McMullen brochure for Computer Language *magazine was designed to be read folded out. Designers Burt Sakai and Stacy Nishi-McMullen angled the contents page to catch attention and add to the brochure's informality. The call-outs are executed by hand and gain notice while remaining very personal. Nice touch. Design by Sakai Nishi-McMullen. Type by Sakai Nishi-McMullen and Andrea McHone. Reprinted with permission from* Computer Language, *a publication of Miller-Freeman, Inc.*

Figure 2.4

This Interlake annual report is nearly a direct replica of Time. What better way to be informative, change perspective and deliver the news than with a news magazine format, especially with one so perfectly copied? (Also see **Figure 2.5**.*) This Financial World award winner is as functional as it is unique. For example, instead of editors and staff its masthead consists of corporation officers, directors and operating executives—that along with information on the annual meeting, dividend reinvestment plans, 10-K forms and other particulars mandated by the SEC. Kirk Kahrs, then creative director at HGSO, said, "We didn't miss anything. Even the copy is as terse and snotty as Time's. We stole the type, photography styles, layouts and information graphics. Everything." Art direction and design by Angelo Sardina, HGSO. Reprinted with permission from the Interlake Corporation.*

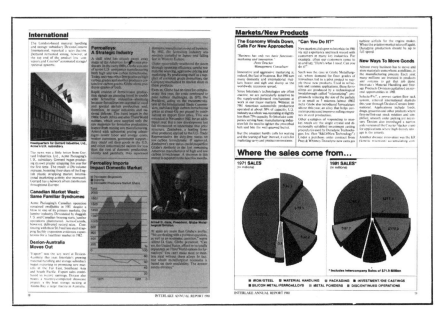

The solution? An annual report that was a direct copy of *Time Magazine.* Kahrs and designers made off with the nameplate, masthead, table of contents, typography, photographic and writing styles and *Time*'s entire stylebook. They filled the annual report with new campaign advertisements for the many new companies that were part of the Interlake aegis—a brilliant way to introduce the campaign to their target audience. This strategy was obviously bifunctional, since it not only mimicked the look of *Time* but reinforced the entire concept of bringing important company news to the reader. In this instance, the design was more than mere magazine emulation. It was out and out theft—insightful and functional format snatching. It was outrageously different and just as outrageously successful. Kahrs and Interlake received a silver medal from *Financial World*, which selects the best annual reports internationally each year.

These two examples remind us of what should be obvious at all times. Namely, that all publications should be designed with audience in mind. Too often we forget the audience by neglecting to notice that it has changed dramatically or is in the process of a major change. Or, we're so insulated that we don't measure what we publish by the most important touchstone—our consumers.

Finally, a quick word about intent *and* medium. Sometimes, intent isn't correctly aligned with medium or format. Closely examining what your intentions are might cause you to reconsider format.

Principles of Design

Most of us don't pay much attention to a design when everything is correctly ordered. In fact, the average person seldom sees design in anything at all. We read newspapers daily without noticing the skeletal framework that orders the headlines, photography, graphics, text and other style elements of a page. And we raise our wineglasses to toast without realizing that stems are designed to keep our hands from warming the wine. But the best design is like that: it exists, but doesn't call attention to itself. As a friend once remarked, "A good designer doesn't design for design's sake. The best design serves its purpose, period— without calling attention to itself."

Not only do the best designs go unnoticed, but the balance principle present in these examples is also overlooked. But make no mistake, it is there. If it wasn't, we wouldn't be able to set the wineglass down. We would lay aside the newspaper because it made us feel unsteady just to look at—and few of us have Dramamine delivered with the newspaper.

However limited our visual educations, we are generally astute enough to see when something is wrong with a design. And typically, imbalance is the first problem we'll spot.

Balance

Of all the principles of design, balance is probably the most obvious and understandable to us. If you've ever felt a small fishing boat or canoe adjust to your weight shift when you reached for the worms, you have a working knowledge of balance and what it entails.

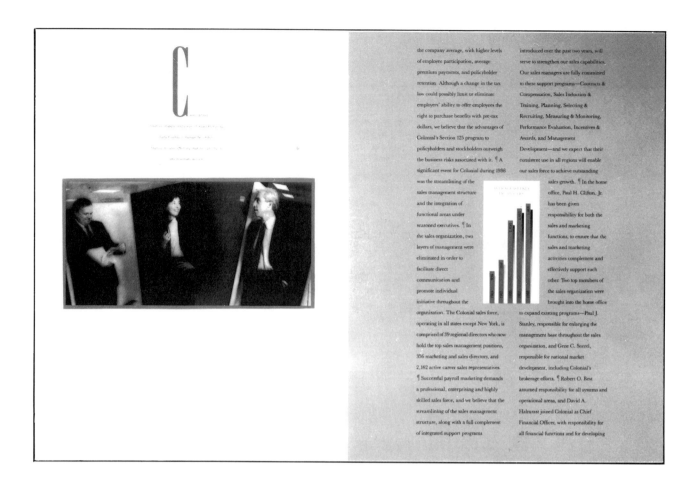

Balance involves equalizing the weight on one side of a vertical axis with the weight on the opposite side of that axis. Actually, you know that instinctively, because standing or walking involves equalizing *your* weight distribution. If you're carrying something that's heavier to one side, you have to either adjust that weight arrangement or adjust your position. Otherwise, you'll end up on your back. That same simplicity applies to design.

There are two approaches to balance. The symmetrical approach tends to be more ordered, simple and *formal*. The asymmetrical approach, also carefully ordered, is complex, yet *informal*. Either can be balanced—just as you may balance three packages squared up beneath your chin, or offset two lighter bundles in one arm with a heavier box under your other.

Symmetry is easier to work. Formal balance lines up all the elements so that when they're split vertically, each is distributed evenly to either side. What's to the left is equal to what's to the right. Everything—the typographical areas and visuals—is centered. A symmetrical layout, when blurred or abstracted, has a Rorschach look to it. One side mirrors the form or general shape of the other.

Symmetry also brings formality to the design. It solves the tightrope problem of balance in a rigid, structured fashion. Which is to say that the symmetry organizes the design by whacking each part in half, and arranging those halved portions appropriately. Although this provides a kind of basic structure for another design principle—namely, unity—it may limit yet another—proportion—because it halves the format and freezes the spatial dynamic, because the amount of space is equal. Consequently, neither is dominant or subservient and the halved areas deaden the space.

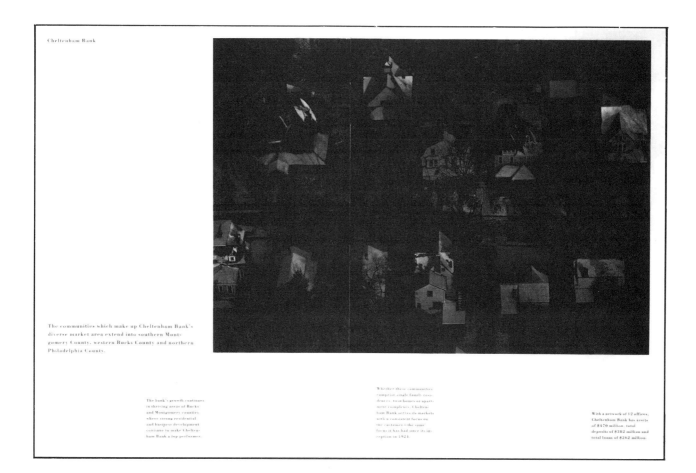

Cheltenham Bank

The communities which make up Cheltenham Bank's diverse market area extend into southern Montgomery County, western Bucks County and northern Philadelphia Counts.

The bank's growth continues in thriving areas of Bucks and Montgomery counties where strong residential and business development continue to make Cheltenham Bank a top performer.

Whether these communities comprise single family residences, town homes or apartment complexes, Cheltenham Bank serves its markets with a consistent focus on the customer—the same focus it has had since its inception in 1924.

With a network of 12 offices, Cheltenham Bank has assets of $479 million, total deposits of $382 million and total loans of $262 million.

Normally, when we think of balance, bilateral symmetry comes to mind, where the left or top parts of a design equal the right or bottom portions. But symmetry may also be radial. Its uniformity *radiates* from a central point outward. The symmetrical approach may also be derived from pattern instead of a vertical or horizontal split, employing a specific shape or configuration that repeats itself horizontally or vertically. Regardless of approach, all produce an ordered form of balance.

Symmetry has its advantages. To begin with, it's difficult to mess up when you're only juggling one ball. So long as you keep everything centered and squarely balanced, you can't go wrong or lose the stability of a layout. Furthermore, symmetry may furnish the precision appropriate to a conservative or traditional audience or a particular intent or image. Again, both intention and audience should weigh into your design overture.

On the other hand, **asymmetry** brings variety, tension, movement, surprise and informality to a page's architecture. It's one thing to hang all the visual elements evenly down the spine of a design. It's another to begin the drama and spectacle of balancing elements independently of one another. It involves the juggling of more than one ball—it's like tossing balls, clubs, sharp-edged objects and flaming beartraps. Obviously, working asymmetrically involves a certain degree of risk and requires a full understanding of optical weight.

Optical weight is a system of visual measure that establishes relative heaviness of an element, depending upon its position, size, shape, value, color and tonality. For example, large things weigh more than smaller ones, optically; odd shapes—due to their unusual configuration—are heavier than regular

Figure 2.8 _____

This Independence Bancorp annual report contrasts many of the design strategies seen in the previous report. For starters, its design is mostly asymmetrical. Major photography bridges the two-page layouts, as seen here, in vertical ground thirds arrangements. Designer Michael Gunselman uses the white space to frame Kevin Fleming's photography here in a strong L-shape. Each city or community section is beautifully photographed and set in the same basic design. Gunselman provides a clean and interesting solution in each instance, giving the reader a real sense of place as well as key financial and background information. This show-and-tell tactic is as inviting and informative as it is memorable. Reprinted with permission from Independence Bancorp and Michael Gunselman

shapes; darker areas carry more visual mass than light areas; color has more heft than black and white; and darker colors tend to be weightier than lighter ones, while bright colors usually outweigh flat hues.

Asymmetry generates visual tension and excitement through its playful or complex balancing of visual mass. It may suggest motion or a casual feeling to a design by seesawing different shapes, colors, sizes and tonalities. For instance, you can counterbalance something large and gray with a smaller dark area farther from the vertical axis, or vice versa. You'll soon notice that where something is located on that axis strongly affects balance. The closer the visual element is positioned to the axis, the less its visual mass or weight effect.

Since you already understand how real weight is distributed, learning optical weight and applying it to your asymmetrical layouts should come quickly. As in everything, practice makes perfect. You increase your applied understanding of informal (and formal) design by doing it—and by paying close structural attention to whatever you put your eyes on. From now on, you should be thinking about design when you're not thinking about design. Treat all publications as your supplemental texts. When you open a newspaper, magazine, or direct-mail piece, note its design particulars. Figure out why a page, poster or advertisement was planned and assembled as you see it. How do formality and informality reflect its intent, audience and medium?

Both formal and informal balance have their place in design. The former can be predictable and direct. The latter tends to be more dynamic and active, adding variation and contrast to a design. And although it may seem to possess an offhand quality, it is probably even more carefully planned, plotted and organized than its formal counterpart.

Proportion

Proportion is the spatial relationship that exists between design parts. It is a comparison of related components that examines how one element's area, size, line, weight, shape or location relate to another.

Everything we see is experienced by comparison. When we're asked to describe or identify someone or something, we use proportional visual connections. We measure everything against our inner visual yardsticks: darker, taller, broader, thinner, wider, greener, more beautiful *than* something else.

Our eyes note proportion involuntarily. Fortunately for us, our vision constantly relays proportional information that's crucial to comprehending our environment. The most basic spatial information we derive from proportion helps us survive. Without proportional savvy, we'd be nervous wrecks trying to make out the size and scale of our surroundings. We wouldn't be able to determine when it was safe to cross the street, or how far away a speeding truck might be.

Proportion also shows us what is important, dominant or subordinate in a layout or visual arrangement. Think about what stops you in your tracks, or how you make special note of what's around you. Our eyes are steered to bigger parts, brighter colors, unusual perspectives and whatever appears larger than life to us. That's why communicators often use disproportion as an attention-getting design tactic. Volkswagen was especially successful with a campaign that focused upon—among other things—disproportion as understatement. More often than not, though, disproportion is accomplished through overstatement.

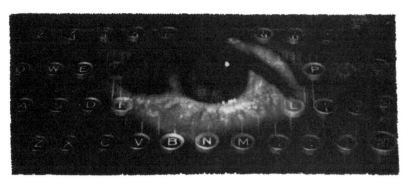

Vachss reaches deep into his life and work for writing material—a dangerous posture for someone who values his privacy. The books are his one unprotected flank.

sharp angles, like a predatory bird, the one good eye as intense as a candle flame.

I thought about kiddie porn. About selling little boys in Times Square. Rapists. Child molesters. Snuff films. The tape looped inside my head.
—Burke in *Blue Belle*

We make small talk about his well-received third novel, *Blue Belle*, then get down to Vachss's business. Investigating child-abuse cases. Keeping kids out of the hands of incorrigible slime. Pounding on the judicial system—literally—until it performs as it's supposed to.

"How I busted this is a perfect example," Vachss says with a rueful look at his hand. "You know the [Lisa] Steinberg killing? I had a kid with exactly the same injuries who, unfortunately, didn't die. My client was only 90 days old. And one of the things wrong with my client was a broken pelvis—both sides—okay? It was the doctor's position that this was caused by shaking the baby in the following manner [shakes his hands back and forth as though he were emptying a sack of flour] to make it stop crying. It was my position that the kid was beaten.

"So I said to the doctor, 'The pelvis was broken. Couldn't that have been done by a blow?' The doctor said, 'How could it be done by a single blow, because you have

two points to the pelvis.' So I said to her, 'This is my forearm. Would you please measure the width of the child's pelvis on my fist and forearm?' which she did. Then I turned around and smashed the hell out of the wall. And I said, 'Wouldn't that do it?' And she responded, 'Yeah, that would do it.'"

A Seamless Obsession

The same kind of intensity runs through Vachss's books—and for good reason. Their plots come straight from his work. Vachss says there's nothing in *Flood, Strega, Blue Belle,* or his most recently published novel, *Hard Candy,* that he hasn't run into: the baby rapist working the day-care center, the porn-photo sessions at the babysitter's, the incest, the pain freaks, the $25,000 for a transplantable, black-market baby heart—all too real. And for Vachss, the cases, the stories, the books are all part of a seamless preoccupation.

Which must make Burke, the narrator and avenging angel of the novels, a fantasy projection of Vachss himself. Right?

"I have to quote the honorable Elijah Mohammed," Vachss says with a rare trace of a smile. "'Those that know don't say, and those that say don't know.'"

Look, man, let's all be telling the truth here. The word's been out a long time—you got a

PURSUITS • SUMMER 1989

Figure 2.9 _____

Jeffery Newbury's multi-image photography makes for a dramatic ground thirds break on this page from Pursuits *magazine. Notice how the dark area of the artwork dominates the layout and weighs heavily upon remainder of the page. In addition, the photography has uneven and tattered edges to give it even more weight. Finally, the eye in the image holds our vision; its circular shape is repeated in the typewriter keys. Look ahead to* **Figure 2.14** *to compare this page to the article's two previous pages. Those responsible include: Deborah Hardison, art director, Tanya Roberson, design director and Frank Kuznik, writer. Reprinted with permission from* Pursuits, *copyright 1989, Whittle Communications L.P.*

We know that halved space has a frozen look. It's static and boring, lacking the energy and spatial dynamic that unequal areas bring to a design. This was noted long ago. Over the years, some thinkers have seriously sought theoretical and mathematical solutions to the problem of proportion.

One of these thinkers was Pythagoras, a Greek philosopher who is credited with creating the **Golden Mean** or **Golden Section**. Pythagoras suggested that in the proportional segmentation of a line the relationship of the small section of a line to its larger segment would equal the ratio of the large segment to the entire line. This concept was integrated into mathematics and geometry, and was literally used as the cornerstone for much of Greek architecture, as well as for Hellenic sculpture and painting. It is carried on still today throughout the realm of design.

Ground Thirds is lesser known and less scientific, but is a very practical law of proportion. It suggests that to provide a more dynamic ratio to your space, you divide it into one-third: two-third sections. It's remarkable just how often this spatial arrangement turns up in newsletters, advertisements, magazines, posters, other collateral publications and throughout the fine arts.

Visually, a halved format suggests little beyond the idea that the area of one half is exactly the same as its counterpart. It does nothing to suggest scale or spatial relationships. When area is evenly split, it doesn't establish largeness or dominance, smallness or subordinance of any one design component.

Avoiding an equally sectioned arrangement improves a design's proportion and emphasis dramatically. However, halved space may be effectively utilized to create symmetry, to supply a muted sort of straitjacket conformity, or to emphasize the "dead zone" appropriately. If you want to be deliberately monotonous, dividing the space in two will help achieve a static feeling by freezing any movement—and squelching any kind of proportional variety.

This brings us back to the question of formality. Evenly spaced divisions (twos, fours, sixes, etc.) tend to be formal, and lend themselves to a fixed, symmetrical look. Odd divisions—one-third/two-thirds or one-fifth/four-fifths—are more dynamic spatially. Furthermore, they bring variety, energy, excitement

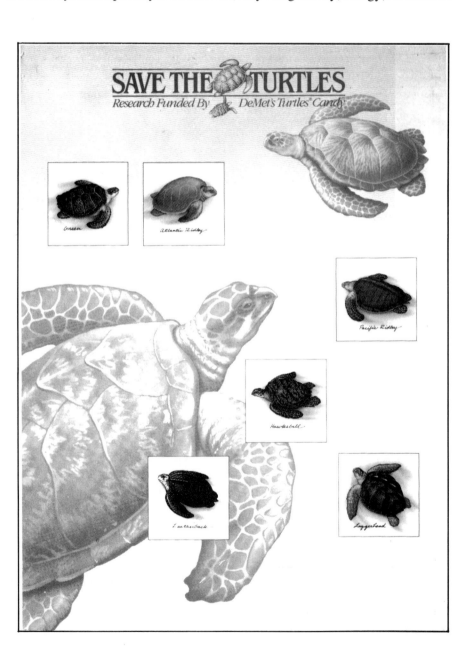

Figure 2.10_____

The design firm within Hill and Knowlton's Chicago office created this folder; it is double-pocketed inside. The larger (unboxed) sea turtles and type are printed in aquamarine and the smaller, individual turtles are run full color with aquamarine shadowing. Sequencing is exemplary here. Our vision enters at the lower left corner with the largest turtle and moves to the next largest-sized one (upper right) through the type and back down from upper left to the lower right corner—a classic Z-readout. Notice how the lowest three boxed turtles point upward, and how three of the boxed turtles make a strong diagonal line running parallel to direction of the largest sea turtle. Client: Save the Turtles Fund (research funded by DeMet's Turtle® Candy); designed by Kathy Keen and illustrated by Michael Carroll. Reprinted with permission of DeMet's Candy and Hill and Knowlton.

Figure 2.11 _____

*This is a complementary piece from Hill and Knowlton for Save the Turtles. It is used as both a response card and sticker. Other materials (letterheads, news release forms, cards, stationery and the like) carry design variations from the original piece. (See **Figure 2.10**.) It is important that all campaign materials bear a close resemblance to one another. See previous acknowledgements for credits. Reprinted with permission from DeMet's Candy and Hill and Knowlton*

and informality to their arrangements. Again, your choice should consciously tailor your design to your audience and your intent.

Design is an open-ended proposition. There is no perfect solution or best way to solve the problem at hand. Hundreds of equally creative and effective solutions to a visual problem exist, and each of them may be developed by employing the same design concepts and concerns. But that is the beauty of design. It's also the reason why a good grasp of design's basic tenets will afford you the understanding, vocabulary, syntax and composition necessary to fix an existing design or to create a new one.

Sequence

Sequence refers to visual direction, or how the eye of the reader flows through a page. Normally, the occidental eye runs left to right, top to bottom.

Certainly, it is how we *read* the written word. What may have never struck you as noteworthy, however, is how most publications order their designs. Typically, what we find is this:

- Headlines tend to sit atop copy blocks in most forms of printed material, including advertisements, newspapers, magazines, posters and newsletters. There are exceptions, but we'll note reasoning for those differences later.

- Copy follows heads or headlines, fleshing out their shout or calling attention to the gist of the story, message or pitch.

- Important stories or message parts sit higher than less important ones.

- The left side of a design (depending on whether it's a left- or right-hand page) has priority over its right counterpart. If you don't buy this, examine a typical newspaper or magazine page, and note what news goes where. Or, better yet, look closely at how advertising is positioned on a magazine page. Normally, the far left column on a left-hand page is a prime location for advertising—and, more often than not, the far right of the right-hand page runs a close second.

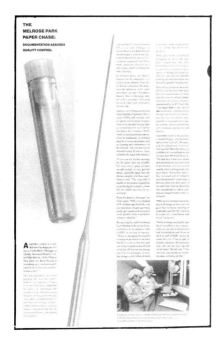

The Melrose Park Paper Chase:
Documentation Assures Quality Control

Figure 2.12

Sequence is worked hard in this layout. The vial in the color screen connects the headline to the lead paragraph and the piping bridges the wide column break, linking up the copy. Two color is used minimally here: in the screen and in the caption. The color screen also creates a vertical ground thirds, which makes the lithe 11" x 17" format seem even thinner. Note the bled notch created on the upper righthand edge of this right page to suggest page turn; the left pages for this publication have a triangle pointing right—it is similarly sized and positioned on the far left edge of the left pages. Hill and Knowlton designed this newsletter for LyphoMed. Printed with permission from LyphoMed and Hill and Knowlton.

- Everything has a general flow. Visuals—photography, illustration, artwork, graphics and informational graphics—typically follow the same pattern. With some exceptions, the best stuff sits high and left, the least important low and right.

- Optical weight can yank our visual patterns around. And very often a designer utilizes color, isolation, larger sizes, oddly shaped configurations, exaggerated formats or other such visual strategies to redirect our visual patterns.

Sequence is central to design as both a principle and strategy because it can carefully and correctly route the vision of your audience through the ideas, story, pitch or information on your page.

In any campaign—be it directing an African safari, or directing the marketing and advertising of African safaris—it is imperative that we're familiar with and understand the nature of the beast we're stalking. Make no mistake. We have basic visual patterns, tendencies, strengths, weaknesses and idiosyncrasies. Without a doubt, we are visually bent and have specific preferences, some of which have been noted, however briefly, earlier.

So, not directing your reader is misdirecting your reader.

Some researchers contend that we read pictorial communications differently from written communications. They suggest that our vision enters pictorial information from the lower left corner, makes an upward diagonal run to the right, cuts left and then sweeps in a Z-like motion downward. Most agree that we are visually predisposed to the lower left area, and that in most instances our vision exits from the lower right corner.

Normally, the visual exit point of almost any layout is its lower right corner. A quick glance through any publication shows that "signatures" or logotypes are positioned in the lower right corner of an advertising layout nine times out of ten. This is the advertiser's final opportunity to reinforce brand image, to "sign off" or otherwise provide a parting shot.

As a designer, you are responsible for controlling not only where your audience looks but how it tracks what you've visually ordered. In order to steer that visual traffic, remember that your audience reads the written word left to right and top to bottom and that its usual reading patterns may be redirected or maneuvered through visual shortcuts via principles of optical weight.

Remember the formal and informal considerations that exist concerning sequence. For the most part, we read top to bottom and left to right. That constitutes a normal or more formal readout. We read a layout more informally when optical weight reroutes our usual visual inclinations. Size, color, perspective, imbalance, angle, disproportion, darkness, shape, predictability and both positioning and posturing may *redirect our vision,* turning it away from its predisposed routing.

How the eye travels through the page is crucial to ordering any message. If you, as designer, writer or communicator, make bad ordering decisions about your design sequence, you'll short-circuit the information. No matter how thoroughly researched, cleverly or clearly written, dramatically illustrated and properly positioned that information is, a bad design sequence will make it only a holler in the dark.

Lost. A pitiful waste of your time.

Imagine a film without a director. A shootist without a target. A flight without a destination. Or an expedition without a compass. You'd be surprised at how often both sequence and audience direction is taken for granted—and astonished at the horrible rate of communication derailment that occurs because of bad visual sequencing.

Emphasis

Every design needs a focus. One element should dominate to create a fixation point on the page, advertisement, poster or cover. Confusion sets in when readers are confronted with a layout lacking emphasis, or contrast, a term some publications professionals prefer. However named, it makes the same point. Something needs to stand out.

Without a focal point, our eyes go into a holding pattern. But not for long. Because, for the most part, we possess very limited visual patience. If our vision encounters any barrier—illegible type, too much copy, visual disorganization, ambiguity, an overly gray page or a design lacking visual opposition or clear direction—we'll overlook it. Without a clear, inviting place to land, vision quickly moves on. Like it or not, our eyes make snap judgments and tend to be visually unforgiving. And, as all designers understand, if you make the audience hesitate, you're likely to lose the majority of it.

The point is this: *have* a point. And make it visually apparent.

The contrast or emphasis of your design acts as a bull's-eye of sorts. It provides a quick and obvious target to the audience, grabbing its attention, relating important information and establishing the heart of the design. But good visual emphasis also redirects vision through the design's inner composition. For example, good designers will use lines of force—the direction a subject

Figure 2.13 _____
Jeff Stoffer shot this Relief Nursery booklet cover at a wide aperture setting to limit the depth of field. By blurring the foreground and background, he achieves emphasis here and the face of the boy dominates the imagery. Notice how the designer uses both the front and back sides of the cover in his design. Using a front and back shot of the subject creates unity by spanning the two pages while concurrently providing sequence to facilitate our read. Art direction and design, Bill Ryan. Photography by Jeff Stoffer. Reprinted with permission of The Relief Nursery, Zack's mother and Bill Ryan.

Figure 2.14

Designer Tanya Roberson uses several devices to achieve emphasis for this two-page layout. As you know, our vision is involuntarily drawn to intersection points. The title here makes a dramatic intersection: AVENGER is reversed and stacked on a textured screen with THE riding above and a brief blurb below to flesh it out. The heavy optical weight of the reverse block snags our attention, as does the very black image on the adjacent page. A simple but very effective bit of designing. Frank Kuznik wrote "The Avenger," and Tanya Roberson designed it for Pursuits *magazine. Tanya Roberson directed the art and Jeffery Newbury's photography. (Also, see* **Figure 2.9** *to note continuity particulars.) Reprinted with permission from* Pursuits, *copyright 1989, Whittle Communications L.P.*

might be looking in a photograph or illustration—or diagonal lines to point your sight in a new direction, steering you through the design to establish connections between important points or elements of the layout itself.

Emphasis should be plotted specifically to attract your target audience. Using something large for the sake of largeness doesn't get it. It's not enough, say, to simply use a large, bad photograph to dominate a page or to arbitrarily provide the design emphasis. If it's a boring or inappropriate photograph, it *might* get a passing glance. (Or a laugh and a moustache.)

Emphasis may also indicate significance to the reader, literally to show where your priorities lie. A bad or boring photograph sends mixed signals. Size suggests importance, but inappropriate content short-circuits that logic, leaving the audience confused and possibly resentful.

Which is to say that emphasis is more than spatial fodder. It's important that you ask serious questions and make thoughtful decisions about the content, suitability and meaning of what you stress. While emphasis fixes vision and provides a simple and efficient logic to a design, it also suggests something about your sense of priority, import and judgment. And don't allow too much emphasis or contrast to dilute or diffuse the principle's effect. A newsletter or newspaper layout should have one dominant visual area, not two, three or ten.

There are a number of ways to obtain emphasis. Optical weight furnishes immediate and typical strategies; size, darkness, color, location and contrast tend to dominate a visual field. But there are other tactics.

• **Isolation** may convey emphasis by contrast, scale, space or detachment. It might employ optical weight, and often uses ground neutrally. (**Ground** refers to the background or subordinate areas in a design, as opposed to the **figure**, the dominant or featured shapes.) So, for example, an illustration might employ a stripped-out background, or a photograph might use a black background and foreground. This insulates the visual content from its format, making it stand out from the rest of the layout.

- **Imbalance**, although it borrows from a different design principle, steers visual attention to the tension and lopsidedness of its arrangement. It may provide a kind of visual imposition: a seemingly haphazard visual arrangement in an otherwise balanced and precisely ordered space. That in and of itself is enough to derail the eye from its usual course.

- **Ragged edges, unusual shapes** or **uneven borders** rail against conformity and the uniformity of a page's design. Although our eyes like order, something out of the ordinary, however simple and minimal, may attract attention.

- **Incongruity**, the art of transposition, pulls something out of its normal visual context and juxtaposes it against inappropriate or unsuitable surroundings. Visual incongruity gives us a feeling that "something's wrong with this picture." That a major visual piece of the design puzzle looks out of place is what brings strength and direction to this device.

- **Disproportion** is similar to incongruity, but like imbalance, it also has allegiances to a design principle other than emphasis. It calls attention to itself by disorienting our sense of scale or violating symmetry. Caricature and political cartoons often employ disproportion to emphasize specific physical characteristics of the subjects rendered.

- **Selective focus** is a compositional device unique to any medium using a lens. Wide aperture settings blur the foreground and background, leaving only what was focused on clear to our vision. It leaves our vision little choice but to lock on the sharp detail of the focused picture area.

Just as photographers emphasize composition in a portrait by neutralizing backgrounds or using selective focus, designers must produce a focus in the layout that emphasizes or contrasts one of the design's elements.

Figure 2.15 _____

This brochure for Cracker Barrel was designed by Thomas Ryan Design. Ryan has unified this piece in several ways: first of all, by the border; second, by the headline which straddles all five panels here; third by color; fourth, by the artwork which connects five panels as well; and fifth, by the typography itself. The muted color, antiquated guest check and old newspaper give this a nostalgic feel. Notice how the plate and eggs in the artwork act as a bullseye and how the newspaper routes your vision to the first panel. There is a special charm in this simple but meticulous design. Reprinted with permission from Cracker Barrel and Thomas Ryan. Design by Thomas Ryan. Photography by McGuire.

Customarily, in newspapers, magazines, posters, print advertising and other publications, the visual dominates. That shouldn't surprise us. Vision was our ancestors' first language, and we still carry their pictorial predisposition and attraction to visual simplicity.

Unity

Like our forebears, we also possess a penchant to see a composition's parts assembled. **Gestalt** investigations and applied theories have proven that we perceive the people and things around us as wholes before we begin dissecting them into parts. For example, when we look across the table at someone, we don't initially see ears, hair, eyes and other features of the person sitting there; we see and recognize a person. We continually process whatever we see into simple, harmonious wholes. That explains, in large part, why we seek visual order: to make sense of our environment.

Unity refers to the cohesion and overall coherence of a layout's parts, especially as each element relates to the rest. Headlines, copy areas, artwork and perhaps a variety of graphics should fuse, be in harmony, or at the very least be compatible with one another. Most of us sense unity fairly well, regardless of whether we've had formal training in design or visual studies. We bring an intuitive sense to what we see and can usually tell if a design is unified or not.

However, too often these instincts stop short of understanding why unity works. Which is sort of like saying that we realize a vehicle is dysfunctional when smoke pours out from beneath the hood and dash, and the automobile comes to a halt. But we haven't the foggiest notion of why it's on fire—or how to fix it.

Designs can be unified in a multitude of ways. Typically, we resort to the grid and rectangular shaping. Proportion has a lot to do with this. It is no accident that most newspapers, magazines and other publications are rectangular and share similar proportional and design characteristics. That's because proportion serves both aesthetic and functional purposes.

Piet Mondrian, a Dutch painter and the father of the *De Stijl* movement, studied and worked the rectangular format relentlessly. What is especially interesting was his fascination with the essential relationships between growth, represented as *verticality*, and stability, or *horizontalness*. He was intensely occupied with bare-bones design, especially with unity as it relates to proportion and balance. His "perpendicular" paintings fractured rectangles into more rectangles and squares, using evenly stroked horizontal and vertical lines. His proportional studies gave birth to a new sense of modular design that influenced painting, sculpture, architecture and communications. Indeed, the skeletal framework that supports most of the content of today's newspapers (and many magazines and newsletters) is Mondrian-inspired.

But there is more than one way to unify the design cat. Type is a logical, direct and necessary route to unity. Remember, our eyes and brain swim over a composition and order the splash of its parts into a whole, unified design. That compositing linkage, or Gestalt, is impaired by visual distraction, sometimes caused by small things we overlook. One such oversight, overloading the page or layout with too many typefaces, is a common and deadly distraction.

Parallel structure is another unifying design tactic. Using symmetry and formal balance, it shapes or sculpts half of a design and mirrors that configuration in the other half. Basically, this is an intra-design scheme, where one side of the design is aligned or matched to the other side. This method of unification has a neck and neck look to it. It is analogous and proportional, and helps our eyes immediately pick up on the corresponding parts to balance and tie them together.

This concurrent arrangement or look can be achieved by aligning columns, shape, typography or other elements. It may occur within a single page layout or in two-page designs, especially in double-truck newspaper advertising and, with magazines, in two-page opening designs and in two-page advertising. Recently, for example, Arrow shirts not only used parallel structure as a two-page unification strategy, but as design continuity for an entire advertising campaign—an award-winning one.

Grouping is probably the most common of all the different unifying techniques. Its wont is to show the relatedness of a design's parts by grouping them. This may be accomplished by lassoing a layout's elements with the help of a border. Fencing off one element within a layout clearly segregates it from the others and can effectively separate a story or advertisement from the rest of a page. Rules, lines, screens and tint blocks may be put to use similarly.

Color offers a spectrum of unifying options. A color layout on a gray page may provide a designer the perfect unifying solution. And a color page riding amid a sea of black and white pages might merge its elements clearly, while distancing itself from the rest of the publication. Color might also more subtly relate parts by employing a dominant hue from the artwork throughout its design. For example, if a full-color illustration is loaded with purple, maroon and reds, a designer might use a burgundy for all the dropped initial letters, rules, lines and other typographical marks within a two-page magazine design.

Simple color screens or color blocks can unify articles and pages, too.

Figure 2.16_____

Unity is accomplished by bleeding Amy Guip's illustration off both pages of the spread. The copy block was then dropped off-center on the left page; the tattered edges of the block add to the edgy feeling that today's industrial workers feel because of automation, robotics and computers. There is no doubt in our minds that these pages go together. Shoshana Zuboff's "Automation Anxieties" was excerpted from his book, In the Age of the Smart Machine *and appeared in* Best of Business Quarterly. *Bett McLean gets the honors for design direction and Tom Russell for art direction. Reprinted with permission from the* Best of Business Quarterly, *copyright 1990, Whittle Communications L.P.*

Establishing a connection or interrelatedness between parts, regardless of the unifying element, is what is crucial.

White space can also establish unity. (It often is concurrently employed for emphasis, but affects all the design principles.) Basically a grouping strategy, it accomplishes what borders, lines and blocks succeed in achieving, without roping off or delineating space. Because trapping space is a mortal sin in design, remember to keep white space to the edges. Bear in mind, also, that white space can divide or unify. It is another Winnie the Pooh proposition: what you achieve by using it depends upon how it is used. Just as the concepts of comparison and contrast are connected but opposite, so, too, are the principles of unity and contrast.

Unity, then, pays close attention to proportion. The size, weight and proportional arrangement of one part should relate fittingly to the other parts of a design. Unity also links to balance. A larger, lighter component might be off-balanced by a heavier, though smaller, darker one. And sequence steers vision through a page working independently from the other principles, while also employing optical weight for its own reasons. While contrast—although linked closely to sequence—is its own concept and works toward its end.

Unity links each of these concepts, and using compositional mortar, it bricks them into place. When any one of the principles is altered or moved from within its designed arrangement, it affects the others. Just as a brick pulled from a wall would affect the wall's overall structure.

In many ways, unity provides a common ground for all the design principles, utilizing their concerns while weaving their interrelatedness together.

Elemental Form

Structure can also harness a layout tightly in place through the use of elemental form. Essentially, **elemental form** orders a page's arrangement using a handful of basic letter shapes.

Despite our familiarity with the alphabet's parts, we seldom recognize its compositional scaffolding. In many ways, it's a forest from the trees conundrum. But letters use line as the basic language of design blueprints. Letters also bring an inherent sort of beauty and formal regularity to any composition. The strength of using a letter-shape organizational approach is this: the audience seldom recognizes the presence or shape of any letter, but does feel its underlying order.

Elemental form is used in publications design, photography and all of the fine arts. It can structure the visual elements within your page, or it may be used to compose each element separately. For example, you can use elemental form to plan a magazine page layout while you also shape your photographic compositions or other layout components with it. The insightful designer who

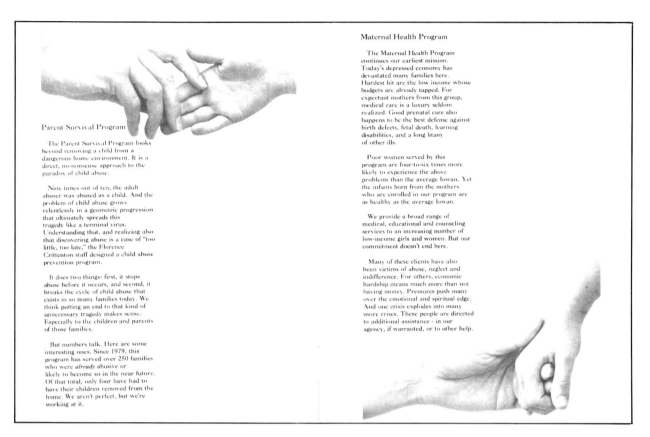

Maternal Health Program

The Maternal Health Program continues our earliest mission. Today's depressed economy has devastated many families here. Hardest hit are the low income whose budgets are already tapped. For expectant mothers from this group, medical care is a luxury seldom realized. Good prenatal care also happens to be the best defense against birth defects, fetal death, learning disabilities, and a long litany of other ills.

Poor women served by this program are four-to-six times more likely to experience the above problems than the average Iowan. Yet the infants born from the mothers who are enrolled in our program are as healthy as the average Iowan.

We provide a broad range of medical, educational and counseling services to an increasing number of low-income girls and women. But our commitment doesn't end here.

Many of these clients have also been victims of abuse, neglect and indifference. For others, economic hardship means much more than not having money. Pressures push many over the emotional and spiritual edge. And one crisis explodes into many more crises. These people are directed to additional assistance - in our agency, if warranted, or to other help.

Parent Survival Program

The Parent Survival Program looks beyond removing a child from a dangerous home environment. It is a direct, no-nonsense approach to the paradox of child abuse.

Nine times out of ten, the adult abuser was abused as a child. And the problem of child abuse grows relentlessly in a geometric progression that ultimately spreads this tragedy like a terminal virus. Understanding that, and realizing also that discovering abuse is a case of "too little, too late," the Florence Crittenton staff designed a child abuse prevention program.

It does two things: first, it stops abuse before it occurs, and second, it breaks the cycle of child abuse that exists in so many families today. We think putting an end to that kind of unnecessary tragedy makes sense. Especially to the children and parents of those families.

But numbers talk. Here are some interesting ones. Since 1979, this program has served over 250 families who were *already* abusive or likely to become so in the near future. Of that total, only four have had to have their children removed from the home. We aren't perfect, but we're working at it.

envisions elemental form throughout a publication often applies it to the arrangement of individual design parts.

Generally, we need more than design principles alone to shape and vary our pages. That is precisely what elemental form brings to design. Understanding how elemental form can add shape and organization to a publication will strengthen what you produce. But understanding its application also requires that you understand linear thought. A student of design must be able to break shape, volume, composition and other design elements into simple lines. A good way to acquaint yourself with the linear thinking of elemental form is to use a marker to black out artwork and graphics on newspaper and magazine pages. The skeletal remains reveal a layout's foundation and the form behind it. This is a good exercise for any beginning designer, because it cuts to the bone of the design and sharpens the eye.

Five letter shapes are normally used; other letter structures you might find are usually variations or combinations of these five. They are L-shape, T-shape, O-shape, /-shape and S-shape or C-shape.

L-shape

Vertical and horizontal lines dominate our environment. Buildings, streets, electrical poles, furniture, signs and most everything else around us run vertically or perpendicular to level ground. Likewise, vertical and horizontal lines dominate the outer and inner structure of publications. These arrangements bring order, stability and efficiency to layouts.

Probably the most widely used of the letter forms is the L-shape. It may be used to wrap visual, graphic or copy areas. Often, framing occurs with this letter form, because it encloses the element (or elements) within the design. In doing so, it adds emphasis, calling attention to the dominant design component. L-

Figure 2.19

In these examples, L-shape is accomplished by integrating the artwork with the copy. Not only is there a natural sequence in the photography , the elemental form links the pages together in this Florence Crittenton brochure. Art direction, design and photography, Bill Ryan. Reprinted with permission from Florence Crittenton and Ryan Design.

Figure 2.20 _____

shape framing provides structure to a composition while delimiting the space around it.

For example, a newsletter may feature a strong photograph on its cover and provide L-shape elemental form by running copy down the left (or right) side of the visual and along the bottom. In establishing these boundaries, you order and divide the space while injecting a hierarchy of visual priorities. Simply by dropping this form into the visual field you've established a framework by firmly supporting the bottom and one side of your design. .

This common and effective form may be inverted, flipped, rotated or combined. Because we read left to right and top to bottom, however, it is most commonly found running down the left side and across the base of a layout.

T-shape

Like the first form, the T-shape is often used to wrap or frame other design elements. A wonted function in this case is to use strong vertical and horizontal lines as edges to mark a boundary between one area and another. With an exaggerated visual, this shape might split a page vertically, or, thrown on its side, break it widthwise. And like the L-shape, it may be inverted, flipped, rotated or combined with itself or other letter forms.

The most common position—an inverted T-shape—is used for everything from classic portraiture to mug shots, from newspaper pages to magazine spreads. The secret lies in thinking lineally. A head shot of any kind reveals an inverted T-shape. In publications and most two-dimensional art, the inverted form is preferred by our eyes because the extensive base anchors the arrangement, providing more stability to designs.

Our eyes have a tendency to connect line endings or dots, just as you did with your connect-the-dots book when you were a child. A line may be real or implied. And, with the T-shape, our eyes often join the three line endings to form a triangle, making triangular composition common to this shape.

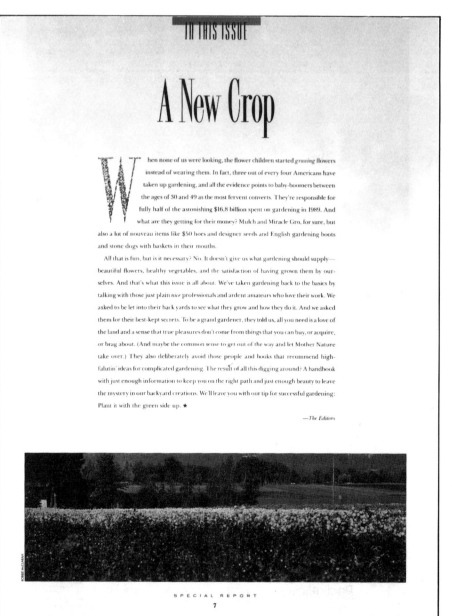

Typically, too, when T-shape and triangular composition are positioned in rectangular formats, they tend to hatch out other triangles. Our eyes are enlivened and engaged by this. Vision feasts on repetitious shapes. And triangles intersecting rectangles propagate more triangles, setting up an optical banquet. This further orders the composition and shakes out a visual echo through the diagonal lines and repetitions that are created.

Triangular composition brings strength and excitement to a design. In the case of bridges, buildings and other construction, deltoid girder systems are unsurpassed in their efficiency and rigidity. And the diagonal lines and visual thrust implanted within this three-cornered composition create an exciting spatial dynamic. (More on this on the /-shape.)

Figure 2.21 _____

Design firm Gunselman and Polite used O-shape elemental form throughout this annual report for The Children's Hospital of Philadelphia. All of the photography has been cropped circularly. The photographer has also framed the child in this shot and used intersecting lines (top, left and right) to further strengthen this image's composition. More memorable photography from Ed Eckstein. Designer, Michael Gunselman. Reprinted with permission from the Children's Hospital of Philadelphia and Michael Gunselman.

O-shape

More than anything else, the O-shape brings a special symmetry and dignity to a design. Its basic form contributes a unique kind of order, grace, strength and uniformity wherever it appears.

The circle possesses a singular geometry. It is composed of an unending line whose central point is equidistant from any of its outside points, or edge. It is

Figure 2.22 _____

*Tina Adamek again goes to a peach tint block (see **Figure 2.17**) in this layout, and, by completely wrapping her copy around the photography, achieves an O-shape elemental form for this* Senior Patient *sidebar. Executive art director, Tina Adamek. Reprinted with permission from* Senior Patient.

unlike any other shape in its smoothed regularity. And it is central to movement, literally and figuratively. The circle is the geometric passport to technology and the single shape upon which we judge civilization's development.

Just for a moment, think about what this shape represents visually, and how it's been used or is used in our lives. Circular forms have long been used to show continuity, regularity and unity. Coins are still used in financial transactions and suggest value. The circular form of wedding rings symbolizes unity and a special coupling. Halos bring sanctity to whomever is beneath their glowing circle. Bracelets, wreathes, rings, garlands, crowns and necklaces bring their own history, significance and meaning to our lives. Even the semicircle provides a marvelous realization of strength. Arches, too, are a watermark of civilization and early technology.

The circle's special power and unifying architecture allows it to literally encircle design parts or hold elements together by its configuration alone. In addition, the circular form is a common framing device. Its equidistant borders carry unequaled formal symmetry to their designs. Rounded form attracts our vision. We look inside and through it, as we do the windows, portholes and other circular openings from which we view the world. Finally, it is a targeting device. Our eyes go to the circle, the same as the archer's or marksman's do.

Figure 2.23 _____

A strong diagonal strip of artwork joins these two In View *magazine pages. Although this elemental form is less common, it can bring excitement, movement and attention to a design. Here, art director Lester Goodman catches our attention by boxing and running four of Melanie Acevedo's photos diagonally. Reprinted with permission from* In View, *copyright 1989, Whittle Communications L.P.*

Understanding these things, we can use the O-shape as a powerful visual tool in constructing designs that not only look and work well in publications, but are equally pragmatic and useful to message and audience alike.

/-shape

The diagonal shape brings a brisk, energetic feel to a layout, imbuing it with a sense of motion or movement. Think about how diagonal line is used in other media and how we normally process it. In both cinematography and videography, it implies direction and movement—especially via persistence of vision (a physiological phenomenon whereby a successive series of still frames, when run in rapid succession, appear to be moving). Think about how you read movement. If you're standing in the middle of the street and a Porsche 911 is bearing down on you a couple blocks away at 170 miles per hour, it's difficult to realize its speed—*or* your apparent danger. However, if you could see it from an angled or perpendicular perspective, you'd immediately know that it would be a good idea to engage your feet.

Angle and angular strokes are important to publications, too. For example, a slash striped across the lower right corner of a publication demands attention, immediacy. It implies that important, late-breaking news happened so recently the editors had no other alternative but to slash the corner of the cover to alert you that they'd caught it and put the story to page.

Diagonals bring movement to a design. Angularity provides directional steerage for our vision. It routes our sight, creating (or rearranging) sequence by

Figure 2.24 _____

Diagonals dominate this two-page spread. Everything has diagonal shaping or alignment—the folios (page numbers), artwork, captions, and the arrangement of the copy block. This playful design is loaded with movement and visual excitement. What you cannot see are the hot colors. Diagonal elemental form is especially appropriate for Leaf (Candy), Inc. Annual report designed by Greg Samata. Main photography by Mark Joseph. Dennis Dooley shot the product photography. Reprinted with permission from Leaf, Inc. and Samata Associates.

Figure 2.25_____

In this case, the elemental form in the illustration contrasts that in the type and overall design of the adjacent page. The illustration exudes S- and C-shape elemental form; that form slows and rounds out the diagonal lines of force. Notice how the newspaper in the illustration directs vision to the feature's title and copy. An introduction, atop right page, provides background and overview to the feature. The title is run the same column width as the intro, with EDITED and PAPER set in approximately twice the point size as the rest of the headline. Text wraps a blurb and by-line. Gary Sluzewski is art and design director at Cleveland Magazine *and is responsible for this lively layout. The illustration is another marvelous one from Sandra Hendler. (If you'd like to see another Hendler illustration, look at **Figure 5.22**.) Reprinted with the permission of Cleveland Magazine.*

setting up visual priorities. Oblique lines running through a visual plane shoot our eyes from one point to another. Visual elements that are positioned lower left-upper right (or vice versa) establish a diagonal path. Placing elements on a diagonal axis attracts visual attention and establishes or creates a bias.

Additionally, diagonals may provide a shortcut for our vision. Since we often look into visuals from the bottom, creating an angular incision diagonally from either corner would establish a controlling visual strategy. Using the lower corners diagonally is referred to by some as lead-ins, or lower lead-ins. By taking advantage of the eyes' normal patterns, a good designer directs or leads our vision into and through a visual field.

S-shape or C-shape

Much of what we've established as conventions of proportion and balance originates in the structure of the human body. Without a doubt, the human form provides an incredible mix of symmetry, variety and innate beauty. And so it isn't by accident that artists of all aesthetic concerns, styles and periods have turned to the human figure as content. The curved line inherent to that subject matter carries a special grace and feeling.

Designers, too, use the curved line. It blends aesthetics with practicality to bring a fresh and limber quality to any layout. Of all the elemental letter forms, the S-shape (or C-shape) is the most graceful. And, while it is quite distinctive and different from the others, it does share some similarities. It bears some resemblance to the O-shape's rounded edges and circular arrangement via its curved form. Also, however, it wears the diagonal slash or inclined lineal quality in its spine.

But more than structural similarities tie the S-shape and the /-shape. They are quite alike functionally as well. Both strongly affect direction, sequence, movement and spatial alignment. However, they do so in appreciably different ways.

The S-shape directs our eyes, but in contrast to the /-shape, it steers vision gently and smoothly. It softens directional movement and is a slower shepherd of our sight. Because of its undulant, more meandering stroke, it is less compelling and forceful than the diagonal. On the other hand, it is more inviting. Its visual track is not as direct nor as efficient as its counterpart, but is quite functional nonetheless.

As a lead-in device, the S-shape goes about its business in quite the same way. Not a rigid one-way sign, like the diagonal, this form tends to be more gradual, gentle and charming in leading the eye.

Space

In publications, space is primarily two-dimensional. And we usually deal with pages or layouts strictly in terms of length and width. Obviously, that vertical/horizontal quality and flatness are the most immediate design concerns. But it is important, too, to be aware that other dimensions exist.

Depth

All pages have thickness, however slight. And many publications, specialty pieces in particular, don textured papers that literally bring depth and shadow to

Figure 2.26 _____

Typography for the headline makes a strong T-shape. The headline and copy block frame up the pullout or blurb beautifully, all of this centered and squared up, including the byline. But it is Sluzewski's use of white space that makes the most of this design. A bouncing, soft focus diagonal line connects the two pages, but more importantly, they give the artwork—the balled up $50 and $100 bills—movement. If you don't buy that, cover up that line and see what happens. White space highlights all of the design elements, head, copy and art—and, it provides an inviting landing place for your eyes. The article was written by Connie Schultz Gard for Cleveland Magazine; *design and art direction, Gary Sluzewski. Photography by John H. Whaley III. Reprinted with permission from* Cleveland Magazine.

Figures 2.27 and **2.28** _____

Jack Anderson directed the art on this remarkable brochure ensemble for Print Northwest.
Space and depth figure into this design in real terms. The sleeve, for example, was designed to
accommodate a specific thickness. Scott McDougall created the N variations for the cover
with airbrush. The diamond motif on the envelope—die-cut on top and copy block at bottom—
is echoed in the forty-five degree angle treatment of the Ns and copy block on cover. This was
designed by Jack Anderson, Heidi Hatlestad and Jani Drewfs. Reprinted with permission from
Print Northwest and Hornall Anderson Design Works.

Figure 2.29

Georgia Deaver transforms words into art. She is a designer and calligrapher who has been exhibited internationally and is a member of the prestigious Society of Scribes and Illuminators. The word "Documentation" is foil-stamped on this two-page spread. It literally and figuratively reflects the high quality control standards described in the text. Die-cuts use space and depth in a design by integrating different pages and places in a publication. Designed by Hornall Anderson Design Works. Calligraphic elements created by Georgia Deaver. Reprinted with permission from Print Northwest and Hornall Anderson Design Works.

the paper. But the gauge of a page is important not only as a paper selection (which will be discussed later in the printing chapter) but as fabric.

Seldom do we think of our clothing as *merely* covering. Its fabric and style are tremendously important to us. How will it wear, feel, look, and how will others perceive it? As readers we do more than read; we scan, search, skim and study. We also note and examine texture. When we browse a publication, our eyes get a visual feel of a page from its typography and general look. We also understand this textural familiarity firsthand. Our fingers turn the pages and feel surface to connect visual with tactual. It might be rigid, smooth, frail or rough. Just as we read beyond the word, we read beyond tactual information.

Simply stated, texture affects message. It implies a great deal beyond its physical character. For example, the look and feel of newsprint carries a much different message than does an antique linen. However inside out, this analogy to clothing is fitting and appropriate to the point made. Namely, that publication space means more than a page's length and width.

Figures 2.30 to **2.33** _____

*Time and sequence are central to these pages. Notice how the hands attract attention and work as directional devices in **Figure 2.30**. Then, in **Figures 2.31** to **2.33**, the two hands begin reaching toward one another and finally come together on the last two pages. Florence Crittenton delivers various social services—everything from emergency shelter for abused women and children to adoption programs—for those who have nowhere else to go. The hands were used here to reflect the personal concern and special treatment clients receive at Florence Crittenton. Design, photography, typography and copywriting by Bill Ryan. Reprinted with permission from Florence Crittenton and Dakota Productions.*

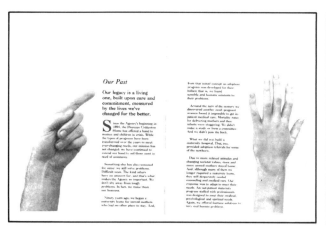

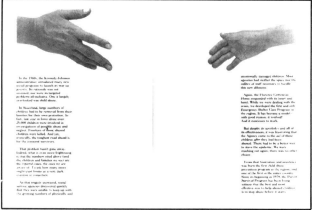

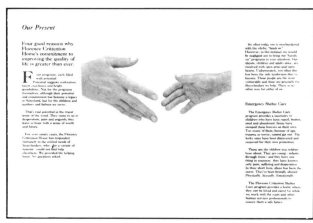

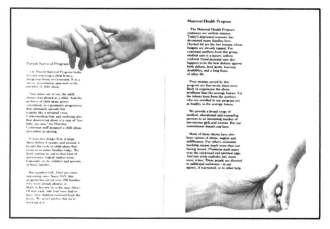

Although we tend to design and use pages one at a time, they do not, in fact, exist separately. A single page does not exist in a vacuum. It is affected by adjacent pages. More protracted, every page is part of a sequence. The cover, table of contents, articles and successive pages of newsletters, magazines, annual reports and other publications string together as a whole.

But publications have *depth* in still another way and should *not* be thought of only as vertical designs. Instead, think of articles as a series of pages that flow into your publication. They have a special kind of mass and thickness, and they should be planned start-to-finish as a unit. Previsualize horizontally, adjust and fit them to their allotted depth. If you can imagine your pages spread out horizontally from start to finish, you get a more realistic sense of a publication's depth and flow and will likely avoid a great deal of the fragmentation that often occurs from myopic design.

Time

Time—one of our most valuable resources—figures into the readout in several ways as well. It takes time to read and make sense of the words and graphics that compose our messages. Streamlining that temporal effort is mutually beneficial.

Normally, your readers run a crash course through a publication. They may steer their way through it in any number of ways. They might go directly to the table of contents to select the pieces most interesting to them, quickly flip through the pages or begin their read in the middle or from the back. Often, too, readers hop back and forth, perhaps referring to a statistical chart to better understand some numbers or to examine a photograph to flesh out a name. You can't orchestrate these idiosyncrasies, but you can eliminate bottlenecks and reduce reader frustration.

In any case, time is a very real publication dimension. Sadly, however, its importance is overlooked. In today's brisk, distracting and preoccupied world, providing a quick, lucid and logical read is central to any effective communication. Why waste the audience's time and energy by erecting unnecessary barriers that encumber a thorough read?

What follows is an incomplete but basic list of tactics that can help you conserve your readers' time and effort.

- Place the table of contents as close to the cover as possible. Try not to position it beyond the first three inside pages. Have you ever caught yourself rummaging through a publication looking for the contents page? It's infuriating. Burying such an important page may cause the reader to lay your publication to rest.

- Put departments, columns or regular features in the same place each issue. Columns and regular features develop strong followings. Varying their location forces an unnecessary search.

- Once you've established a design look, stand by it. Changing designs, *however minimal*, confuses the reader. Never buy into any design commitment without a thorough examination of your audience, current design, redesign and reasons for changing.

- Properly align visually supportive elements on the same page as its text citation—or an adjacent facing page—so your reader doesn't have to search for them. For instance, place a photo or pie chart on the same page as its initial reference. Of course this isn't always possible, but when you design horizontally (by spreading out all of an article's pages in front of you) rather than vertically (by planning one page at a time as you go) you can avoid the fragmentation that occurs due to shabby alignment.

- Eliminate or minimize jumps. As much as possible, keep articles, departments and sections intact, start to finish. Readers hate being referred elsewhere to finish a story. Putting jumped articles in a particular place on a page helps, as does putting all the jumped items on the same page.

- Show unity throughout a spread. If there's any doubt in your mind whether a piece is unified or that two pages connect, be assured that your readers will be confused.

- Establish a stylebook and stick to it. Fixed typographic guidelines bring order and unity to a publication. Copy, headlines, subheads, captions, crossheads, pull-outs and other type styles need to be consistent. Varying them can lead to chaos.

Readers carry recall of what they've already read and seen to subsequent pages—and issues, for that matter. So, along with a present, your audience brings an immediate past and a future to the publication. But, with that memory, they bring expectations.

We are all creatures of habit. Keeping that in mind, take note that your audience seeks creature comforts. Making sure they stay comfortable means keeping the design simple, consistent, clear and uncluttered. It's likely, too, it will mean keeping your audience as well.

White Space

White space—that area *not* taken up by visual or typographical elements—is an integral part of any design. Too often, though, it is incorporated into a layout by accident. It is not uncommon for a non-designer to fit the headlines across the layout, figure and place the copy and visuals into the page and attempt to symmetrize whatever space remains. Worse yet, that same person is likely to jam something else into that open area.

That's not passive use of white space. It's downright antagonistic.

Figure 2.35 _____

Once again, Steve Liska uses generous white space on one page to offset the fully bled photography on the opposite page to demonstrate Potlatch Quintessence paper color accuracy and precise clarity by printing four-color photo separations of black-and-white photography. Notice how the head of the dog is placed on the righthand page in approximately the same spot as the head of the man, and how it directs vision back to the left page. Left photograph: portrait of Francesco Clemente by Timothy Greenfield-Sanders for Comme des Garcons; right photograph by Jim Matusik. Design by Liska and Associates. Reprinted with permission from Potlatch Corporation and Liska and Associates.

Using white space *creatively* means considering its presence in a design before and while fitting the other elements into place. Think of your design elements in terms of page color; headlines are black, copy gray and white space white. Each is integral to the design; although they are distinct from one another, they have a lot in common. All three should work to make the design efficient, attractive and functional. Thinking of white space as surplus area, or residual space that needs a last minute reshuffling, is misusing a major design element.

White space can be utilized to provide a resting place for the reader's eyes. Indeed, inserting additional space between an article's major divisions (or providing extra space between paragraphs in an ad's copy blocks) opens the layout and breaks up the gray quality of copy-heavy pages.

White space contributes to the open look of a publication. Cramming doesn't get more on to the page. It gets more readers off the page. When an audience is confronted with elements that have been jammed together, a kind of visual claustrophobia sets in and we beat a hasty retreat. Openness contributes immensely to a good read. Next time you're paging through any publication, note how white space draws your vision.

Providing a contrast to the gray or color that abounds within all publications is a good tactic. White space works closely with the design principles of contrast and emphasis because of its propensity to isolate. To make an island of any element in a sea of white space is to give it notability.

White space is also an unobtrusive organizer. Most publications use white space to connect pages, separate items and show what belongs together. By its junctions and demarcations it shows what goes with what and what doesn't—quickly, gracefully and economically.

Changing horses midstream is no easy maneuver, but white space can help you drop a horizontal module into a vertically designed page. It can echo shape and contrast linear direction by providing an extra margin of white around the horizontal layout to make it stand out against the overall up-and-down feel of the page.

By increasing the white space within a design, you can suggest a feel of affluence, high image, quality and luxury. Generous use of white space as a separate element does this by itself, but there are lots of variations. Some quality products that play to prosperous audiences may increase the leading (or spacing between lines) in their copy. The same may be done with margins. (Next time you're browsing in an art gallery, notice how mats work as inner framing. Or, for that matter, pick up a magazine that is narrowly targeted at the affluent to learn a real lesson in using white space to this end.)

In many ways, we associate extensive space in advertising with wealth, and cramped designs with a lack of it. Applying that notion to design is natural. It's hard to imagine a millionaire scrutinizing the classifieds or busy appliance or grocery sales pages. Compare those jammed formats to a Nieman-Marcus, Bonwit Teller or Marshall Field's magazine advertisement.

White space unifies pages and inner elements, and where used appropriately, it can be the most cost-effective visual element. With white space, there are no extra charges for graphic marks, photography, overprinting or color. It is efficient, clean, clear and cheap.

Order the white space geometrically. Typically, it is best to work in neat, rectangular shapes, because that configuration echoes the shape of the layout itself. Other shapes work, but aren't as universally applicable. Readers mustn't think the empty area was an oversight, or that a halftone was lost somewhere on the way to the printer. When you've clearly indicated the space, it's likely that it won't be misread. Remember that it also affects balance, unity and proportion.

Keep the area open to the edge, which is to say, don't trap white space within the design's layout. Trapped white space attracts attention, but to no end. It is a dysfunctional use of space.

A disproportionate amount of white space surrounding an illustration or stripped out photograph is likely to give the visual a floating look. Normally, it's a good idea to stabilize the artwork somehow. Connecting it to a horizontal base, giving it a shadow or filling in a background helps anchor the visual and eliminates that hovering look.

Unity is still another principle that often works with white space. And it does so without the use of tint blocks, borders or rules. Indeed, it is probably the most common tactic used to unify magazine advertising—the borderless border.

Remember that margins, too, are created from white space. But it is *outer* white space, because it marks a boundary between the inner design area and

Figure 2.36_____
Generous margins and modular layout contribute to the simple but very ordered nature of this layout. The copy block meets the horizontal axis of the lower photograph to help counterbalance the upper image. If you look closely, you'll notice that the two upper areas of white space are about equal to the white space beneath the text.

This Special Report *page was designed by Doug Renfro and art directed by Doug Renfro; photography by Michael Carroll. Reprinted with permission from* Special Report — On Personalities, *copyright 1990, Whittle Communications L.P.*

three-dimensional space. It unpretentiously edges all publications by framing the content. (Content is also known as "type page" or "live matter.") It's important to keep inside margins wide enough not to interfere with binding, folding or reading. Top margins ought to be a *minimum* of a quarter inch, but may be as deep as you like. Being stingy with the top margin may jam more copy into a page but isn't necessarily design-smart. A glutted page discourages readership. The same holds true for outside and bottom margins, although lower ones are generally deeper.

The **progressive margin formula** proposes that the inside or gutter margins are smallest, the top one slightly larger, the outside margin larger yet and the bottom one largest of all. Progressive margins are more attractive and proportionally pleasing than standard versions. This approach works for all publications. Note, also, that there is no one way to execute margins and that designers take great liberty with white space where margins are concerned.

Generous margins will give a design better proportion. Generally, the more open the page, the more inviting it is. Liberal use of white space suggests high quality—that your product, service or message is special or unique. Think of the outside margin as a picture frame that showcases the message.

As margins collapse inward, reading becomes more laborious. Trim the margins off any publication to the copy's edge and try to read the page. You'll discover that reading becomes awkward and troublesome. Margins help us track correctly from line to line as we read. Severely restricting them atrophies readout. This teaches a final and invaluable lesson about actively employing space within the design—one that speaks as much to function and readability as it does to design and aesthetics.

Figure 2.37 _____

This design features T-shape elemental form (sideways), lots of white space and a grid for its layout. The far left portrait image (on upper horizontal axis) is counterbalanced by the far right photograph (on the lower horizontal axis). The small, mortised shot of the organ keyboard is on axis with the caption above the dominant image.

Robert Bailey Design, Portland, OR, fitted this modular layout tightly together for Rodgers Organ Company; design by Robert Bailey and Thomas Kitts. Major photography by Brian Peterson. Reprinted with permission from the Rodgers Organ Company and Robert Bailey, Inc.

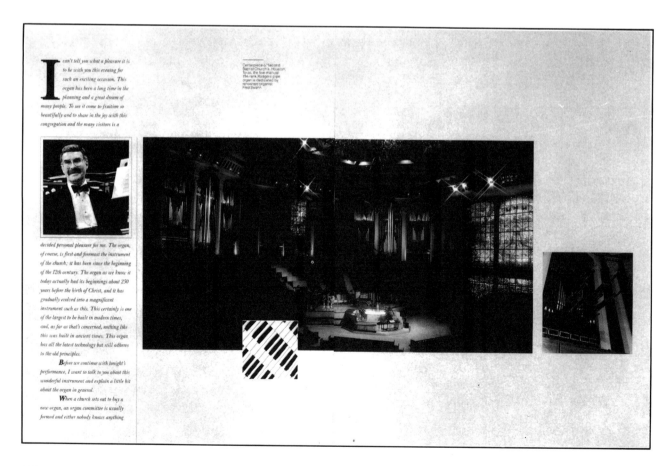

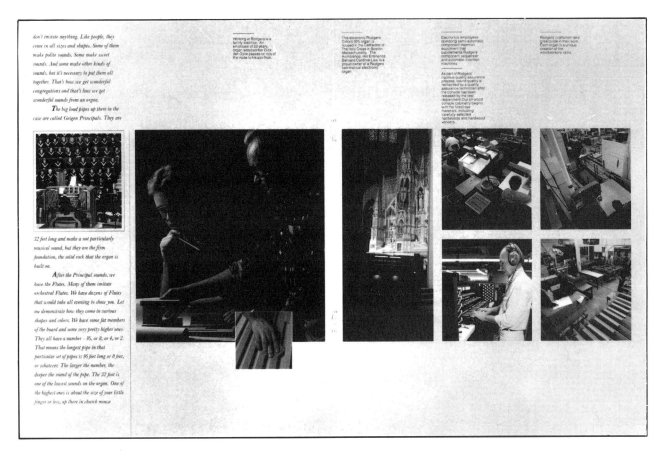

White space is one color available to you from your designer's palette. However minimal and basic it might seem, its application requires a skilled hand and an insightful eye. Think of white space as an element to shape the rest of the design, rather than being shaped by it. Use it actively. Not actively using it is a mistake. Misusing it might be disastrous.

Grids and Modular Layout

Simply defined, a **grid** is the subdivision of a space into horizontal and vertical modules. Actually, layout sheets are grids of sorts. In a true grid, however, each module echoes the rectangular layout's format, deftly ordering the design in other, smaller rectangles. It is a design strategy prevalent among contemporary newspapers, magazines, advertising and corporate publications. This modular approach to design is Mondrian-inspired. Essentially, his work was a form of geometric abstraction based on the grid, perhaps inspired by the rectangular divisions of the farms and canals on the flat lowlands of Holland. Mondrian's grid brings a stripped-down architectural framework to publications. It provides a precise geometry that is capable of neatly packing larger design space while it packages the rectangular design parts within. It brings order, simplicity and variety to a layout.

Counterchange is a tactic that alternates units and their alignments within the grid. Like Mondrian's paintings and most newspaper pages, counterchange involves all the design principles, but especially those of balance and proportion. For instance, a photograph is squarely balanced by a caption and two columns of copy below; it makes an individually gridded unit that interacts with other

Figure 2.38 _____

Here are two more pages from the Bailey design for Rodgers Organ. In this instance, designers Robert Bailey and Thomas Kitts split the large photo area into six units: one large square, four smaller ones and a rectangle approximately the size of two of the smaller modules. Compare this figure to the previous one to note how the far left and mortised images reinforce the earlier master grid. Major photography by Brian Peterson. Reprinted with permission from the Rodgers Organ Company and Robert Bailey, Inc.

Figure 2.39

Leo Burnett Advertising uses heavy black rules and tint blocks to demarcate space in its newsletter, the Burnettwork. The broad rules are only used horizontally; the modules are divided vertically through screens and tinted areas. But the rules are bifunctional, because they also carry article headlines and folios. This makes for a very clean design. Design by Robert Feie, Boller/Coates/ Spadaro, Ltd. Reprinted with permission from Leo Burnett Co., Inc., Chicago.

articles, visuals and combination copy and graphic packages plotted within the overall grid. Or a large gray area is counterweighted optically by a smaller, dark or color area. Obviously, optical weight plays a significant part in working gridded layouts.

A grid possesses an infinite variety of possibilities, but maintains Spartan simplicity by arranging only rectangular components inside the master rectangle. In some ways, it reduces design to blueprinting a series of different sized boxes within a given space. Some criticize the grid because it constrains the designer or forces boxed rigidity. Nonetheless, the grid is important for a number of reasons.

- It provides an efficient tool for shaping design space. Because it offers incredible variety, the grid is one of the most functional design devices. Column widths may be altered. Both vertical and horizontal components (or a combination thereof) are easily accommodated. And there is no end to how the modules within the grid may be shaped and sized.

- A grid can quickly organize the whole of a page or individual page parts. A logical readout is established by ordering content through the grid's economical use of space. The audience is comfortable with modular design and moves through it adroitly because optical weight plots a clear course or sequence for them.

- The overall look of modular design is clean. It's pleasing to the eye because of the intrinsic order it brings to any page. Its geometry instills simplicity, and the straight lines used to create that geometric continuity help border, frame and highlight the text and visuals.

- Orderly subdivision makes designing easier. Sometimes, the obvious escapes us. But for a moment, think of the grid as a sort of publications silverware tray. Modular designs define your space and subdivide it cleanly into cloned parts, as it were. In doing so, it provides a quick patchwork pattern of repetitions, clarity, harmony and asymmetry. Opening a drawer of disorganized spoons, knives, forks and other utensils is discouraging; the silverware tray makes ordering and using the silverware easy. What the case does for tableware, the grid does for design. The reader is able to see immediately what is important and what isn't and doesn't have to read everything to make a fair judgment.

- The grid provides a flexible format. Copy can be quickly edited or fitted into modules; photographs and graphics can be stretched or cropped to fit holes left for them. Grid areas might even be transposed to handle edits. An entire layout can be carefully predetermined but easily adjusted to fit a late-breaking article, last-minute addition or deletion.

- Grids are especially functional for blocking lengthy copy areas. **Blocking**, using white space as a border to separate or unite elements, is quite common in modular design. It allows the gridded arrangement to be even more finely tuned.

Used correctly, grids can offer a quick fix for a design. A layout disaster can be sculpted into an orderly collection of information in short order. Modules also enhance the look of a page while offering limitless variety in a layout's structure.

All of the other design principles addressed in this chapter work easily within the grid for a number of reasons. First, the outer edge of the grid tends to unify a layout. Secondly, because the rectangular fracturing of space forces the designer to deal with proportions and balance, they are worked out early in a kind of *design by process*. Third, by ordering the space and making size determinations you are, in effect, showing emphasis and contrast within the design. Finally, for the same reasons outlined in the third point, you give a visual sequence to the information. For example, the largest module on a page is likely to grab the audience's initial look, a somewhat smaller photo area may be the second strongest visual point and so on. Bringing order, aesthetics and function to a layout is what design is about. Grids help do just that.

Chapter 3

Typography
Part A: Basics

With thousands of faces to choose from, selecting typefaces for a newsletter, annual report, print advertisement or direct-mail piece is a monumental task. Now that desktop publishing has suddenly imposed printer's responsibilities on those who know little of printing and type, the average person working in communications must acquire a rudimentary understanding of type, its terminology and its organization. Finally, even writers, public relations directors, editors and copywriters find themselves sitting in front of computers and linked up to art directors, makeup departments, designers and printers. All of them need to understand typography and how to "spec" type.

Type Anatomy

In order to understand type and distinguish between typefaces, it is necessary to know something about a letter's anatomy. **Figures 3.1** to **3.4** provide a quick but thorough dissection of letter structure. The following list of terms supplement the diagrams and will help you flesh out the concepts and definitions.

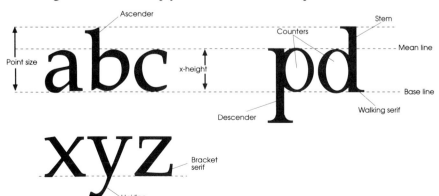

Figure 3.1

You must understand type anatomy in order to be able to distinguish typefaces. This example shows a type's major parts and measuring points—that is, the baseline, capline and mean or waist line.

Unkerned

Kerned

Figure 3.2 _____

Finished headlines require kerning; that means careful attention to adjusting the spacing between the letters of the words. Note the differences between the kerned and unkerned lines of type.

Figure 3.3 _____

Ligatures are letters that share a common stroke, usually two letters. Ligatures vary from face to face.

Figure 3.4 _____

In hot type, two or more unjoined letters on the same piece of type are referred to as logotype. See the definition.

Ascender The stroke of any lowercase letter that extends above the x-height or mean line, for example, *b, d, f, h, k, l, t.*

Axis An imaginary line that bisects the rounded portion of a letter. The axis in some lowercase letters (typically, *o*) can help determine if a roman typeface is old-style. Modern and transitional roman typefaces have a vertical axis, while old-style types slope slightly to the left.

Baseline An imaginary line upon which the letters rest.

Bracket That curved or diagonal area between the serif and the stem of a letter. Some like the strength, extra support or pinched styling that brackets bring to serifs. Brackets are generally found on old-style and transitional roman typefaces.

Counter The hollow or open area found inside the closed or nearly closed stroke of a letter, as in the *B, b, D, d, P, p.*

Descender The vertical or curved stroke of a letter that extends below the baseline, as in *g, j, p, q, y.*

Face Many printers and designers use this term interchangeably with typeface or the name of the type being used. It may also refer to the printing surface of type.

Hairline The thin stroke of a letter, most emphatic in modern roman typefaces.

Italic A slightly lighter weighted roman that is both pitched right and cursive. Aldus Manutius, a Venetian typographer and writer, designed italic; originally, its purpose was to conserve space. (To a printer anything underscored means put in italic.)

Kerning Adjusting the spacing between letters in a word to compensate for unequal letterspacing. Some typographers and designers prefer to reshape or compress words by tightening up the spacing between letters, especially in headlines. Sometimes they will kern to touch, that is, tighten the letterspacing until the letters actually touch.

Ligature Two or more letters combined by a common stroke, most common are lowercase *f* combinations, for example, *ff, fi.* Actually, today's *w* was originally a ligature. At one time the letter *u* was formed as a present day *v*, the ligature of two together formed a *double-u*—or *w.* Ligatures vary from typeface to typeface.

Logotype Two or more unjoined letters on the same type body, such as *Ta, Te, To, Va, Vo.* To compensate for unequal spacing between the letters, a typographer/designer adjusts the spacing appropriately and places the two letters on the same type body. Don't confuse this with business or corporate logotypes. (See *kerning.*)

Mean line An imaginary line that runs parallel to the baseline atop the x-height of lowercase letters. Mean line is sometimes referred to as **waist line.**

Serif The beginning or finishing stroke drawn at a right angle or diagonally across the arm or stem of a letter. The many serif variations include beaked serif, hooked serif, wedge serif, etc.

Slab serif A square-cornered serif, often used interchangeably with **square serif** or **Egyptian,** referring to that race or group of type.

Stem Any full-length diagonal or vertical stroke of a letter.

Walking serif Those serifs on the base of a letter, or any serif on the baseline; so named because they look like feet.

X-height The height of those lowercase letters that fit between the mean line (or waist line) and baseline; those lowercase letters without ascenders or descenders—*a, c, e, m, n, o, r, s, u, v, w, x, z.*

Understanding these terms and being able to dissect letters into individual parts will facilitate your understanding of typography and help you distinguish typefaces. In addition, it will improve your communication with printers and designers.

Categorizing Type

Scholars of typography and designers often differ on how type should be organized and categorized. What is important, regardless of how you sort and divide races of type, is that you have some understanding of how typefaces are grouped, how they relate and how they are different from one another. A **race** or group of type is a broad typographical categorization comprised of many different families that share common characteristics. **Family** refers to a specific typeface and all of its variations. **Font** is often misused in some typesetting and computer programs; often it is used interchangeably, but incorrectly with typeface. Font is the complete assortment of letters, numerals, punctuation

ABCDEFGHIJKLMNO
PQRSTUVWXYZ
abcdefghijklmno
pqrstuvwxyz1234567890;'.,?

Figure 3.5

A font is the complete assortment of letters, numerals, punctuation marks and other characters of a specific family at a given point size. See example; characters are different from one face and style to another.

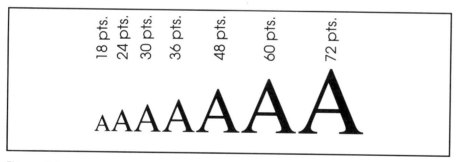

Figure 3.6

On the other hand, a type series is the range of sizes available for a given type. Desktop publishing programs provide a much broader selection of sizes than do other computer software or most phototypesetting systems.

marks and other characters of a specific family *at a given point size*. That may be very important if you need accented letters, special characters or graphic marks. On the other hand, a type **series** is the range of sizes available for a given type. (See **Figures 3.5** and **3.6**)

Type can be divided into six different races or groups: black letter, roman, square serif, sans serif, script and cursive, and miscellaneous or novelty type.

Black Letter or Text

Black letter takes its name from its heavy-handed style. Originally, it was boldly penned by cloistered monks and scholars; cloistered because they were hiding our written connections to antiquity, history and all of the arts and sciences from hordes of barbarian invaders. Black letter type is also referred to as **Gothic**, synonymous with rude or barbaric. The name is derived from the Goths, the Germanic tribe who overran the Roman Empire's northern borders. It is also often designated **text**, an especially appropriate term for a type that was copied directly from monastic inscription.

Because black letter borrows directly from medieval calligraphy, it is loaded with dark, oblique strokes and illegible ligatures that appear foreign to our eyes. There really are few uses for this type race, and what few applications that persist are largely pretentious. It's found atop the newspaper front page as a flag or nameplate, on diplomas, wedding invitations and graduation announcements and some heavy metal album covers. If you must use black letter type, don't use it all uppercase. It's difficult enough to read in upper and lowercase, all capitals makes it impossible. (See **Figure 3.7**)

This goodly
frame, the
earth, seems to
me a sterile
promontory;

Figure 3.7and **Figure 3.8**
Black letter type is also commonly referred to as "text," a fitting name for type that was directly cut from monastic inscriptions.

Roman (or serif) type's two common characteristics are serifs and the use of thick and thin strokes to form the letters—both traits were carried over from black letter.

This goodly
frame, the
earth, seems to
me a sterile
promontory;

Roman

Of all the races, the romans are most familiar. Their two most obvious characteristics are that they have serifs and the thick and thin letter strokes. Many feel that serifs better shape words and link letters. But one thing is certain: they are the overwhelming choice of most editors and designers as a copy face and are used for text in most magazines, newspapers, books and corporate publications. But romans are equally popular as a display type. Many use the term **serif** interchangeably with roman. ("Roman" also may refer to an upright letter posture.)

There are a number of ways to organize roman type.

Old-style romans

Type designers of southern Europe disdained the cryptic look and heavy angles of black letter, and stripped away most of the ponderous affectations. They eliminated the dark, somber letter quality by thinning the strokes, straightening letter stems and smoothing out the hard angles. (See **Figure 3.8**) As they uncluttered the black letter type, they opened up and widened its letters, using pointed, bracketed serifs and flattening the bottoms of the walking serifs. They also returned to the classic roman style. What they did keep that the original romans lacked were the arabic numerals and lowercase letters, at least in their stripped-down version.

In contrast to black letter type, **old-style roman** letters have high readability, as well as strength and elegance. They bring good typographic color and texture to a page. The thick and thin strokes are not especially pronounced in the old-style romans. Old-style serifs tend to be hooked by brackets that brace or fasten serifs to the stem of the main strokes of the letter. (See **Figure 3.9**) Their bracket-like appearance makes them look as though they've been pinched. Another characteristic is that often the axis of the rounded letters tends to slope to the left. This quality is only one of a number of structural nuances that make them especially endearing.

Figure 3.9
Brackets (also known as fillets) are more common to old-style and transitional romans. True straight serifs are generally found on modern romans.

This goodly
frame, the
earth, seems to
me a sterile
promontory;

This roman comes in formal and informal variations. The informal ones tend to carry more imperfections. Formal old-styles are more rigid (the uppercase *T* is one giveaway) and tend to have more contrast between the thick and thin

What a piece of work is man! how noble in reason! (Goudy)

What a piece of work is man! how noble in reason! (Garamond)

Figure 3.10 and **Figure 3.11**___
Designers of informal romans designed many of their original imperfections into them when they cut the type. Letter configurations of their formal counterparts are more rigid and precise.

strokes. (See **Figure 3.10**.) Caslon is an informal and Garamond a formal version of old-style type. (See **Figure 3.11**.)

Old-style romans, particularly the informal versions, have a warmth and special charm about them that stems from a number of imperfections—the slanted axis being one—that were integrated into their designs. Remember, the originals weren't cast or cut from metal. They were first brushed on and then carved into stone. So, both the character of the tools and their makers were transferred to the type when the designers cut the letters.

Not all of the old-style romans were created in fourteenth and fifteenth centuries. Caslon, for example, was designed by William Caslon in the eighteenth century; Goudy, by Frederic Goudy, in 1915, and others—like Stone Informal, designed by Sumner Stone at Adobe for computer typesetting—very recently.

Figure 3.12 _____
Because transitional serifs are a composite of old-style and modern romans, they are tougher to identify. They mix the more charming qualities of old-style design with the precision of the moderns. Often they'll mix serifs, using both bracketed and straight variations. Baskerville, a popular transitional shown here, is possibly one of the more elegant romans.

Transitional romans

Because **transitionals** are the trickiest romans to identify, they are often omitted as a separate subdivision of typefaces. As the name implies, these romans represent a type in flux. They tend to share characteristics from the two dominant roman subcategories: bridging old-style and modern.

In general, these faces show a more pronounced contrast between the thick and thin strokes of letter construction. In many instances, the hairline stroke of some old-style typefaces is really a misnomer; and although a top crossing stroke (as in the uppercase *T*) shows less weight than the vertical stroke, it might be light years from being a hairline.

Some majestic transitional faces make a marvelous marriage of the personal feel of old-style faces and the streamlined, very functional quality of the modern romans.

What a piece of work is man! how noble in reason!

What a piece of work is man! how noble in reason! how infinite in faculty! in form, in moving, how express and admirable! in action how like an angel! in apprehension how like a god!

Figure 3.13 a _____
Bodoni might best exemplify the clean, geometric precision of modern romans. Note the straight serif strokes and contrast between its thick and thin strokes.

One such type is Baskerville. (See **Figure 3.12**.) It is a face that says quality, grace and function. Its overall color and slim, very elegant serifs make it very inviting. At the same time, the remarkable weight shifts between its thick and thinner strokes make it highly readable. Many quality books are put to page with Baskerville. Indeed, it stands up well to most any publishing job. California, a recently created face, is another beautiful type, which, like most transitional faces, works as effectively for copy as it does display.

Modern romans

Of all the serifs, **modern romans** show the most contrast between their thick and thin strokes. This is a mixed blessing. At smaller point sizes, the hairline stroke in the letters virtually disappears or, if printed on an absorbent paper such as newsprint, it becomes tattered and uneven at its edges. Letter counters may fill or clot, too—that is, small counters like those of the lowercase *a* and *e* in a will fill in with ink when bolded or printed small. In addition to exaggerated stroke contrasts, modern romans have serifs that run perpendicular to the vertical stem(s) of the letter. Modern serifs also have minimal bracing and are neither

This the true joy in life, the being used for a purpose recognized

Figure 3.13 b _____
Here you see an interesting variation within the Bodoni family. It is the poster version of Bodoni.

bracketed nor wedged. The axes of rounded letters are vertical, while straight-lined letter strokes tend to give the letters a stiffer or more rigid appearance.

Modern romans have a uniform look to them. Not a single serif, stroke or stem appears out of place. Because their geometric quality suggests crisp, exact uniformity, they lack the warmth and humanistic touch of the old-style faces. The majority of modern roman faces function better for display purposes, and in bolded or more stylized versions, some make outstanding poster faces. They are attention-getting due to their contemporary or European flair.

The first modern roman was punch-cut in 1775 in France by Firmin Didot. (Didot was also the first type designer to offer *maigre* and *gras* fonts, or the equivalent of today's condensed and expanded types.) Bodoni, created by

Can Kids

Chad Barnes had been through three drug-treatment

programs by the time he was thirteen. None of them

On Drugs

worked. As a last resort his parents sent him to the

toughest program in Texas. But Chad vowed to beat it.

Be Saved?

BY SKIP HOLLANDSWORTH

At the Straight treatment program, Chad Barnes had to spend every day in a spare, windowless room, sitting erect in his blue chair. Teenagers who broke the rules were forcibly restrained by their peers.

Giambattista Bodoni, is one of the most popular of the modern roman faces. With its hairline thin strokes and beefy thick strokes, it makes a very dramatic and stylish statement on a page. (See **Figure 3.13**.) Bodoni is still a favorite among newspaper designers as a display typeface.

A final note: beware the readability *and* legibility of the modern Roman. Most make outstanding display faces, but they are a very risky text type.

Square Serifs

Some experts contend that **square serifs** should be grouped with the romans because their serifs are a common feature. Others argue that their uniform stroke makes them little more than an embellished sans serif; still other scholars feel they should be grouped with decorative types because they are predominantly used as a display face. Most, however, classify square serifs as a separate race.

Square serifs, which preceded sans serifs and played a hand in the latter's design, were very popular in the nineteenth century; the lettering we see on old WANTED posters and on newspapers, posters and trains from that period stereotype this group.

Square serifs are sometimes called **slab serifs** because of the rectangular shape of their finishing strokes. They are also referred to as **Egyptians**; first, because the letters have a boxy quality reminiscent of Egyptian architecture and a stiffness akin to hieroglyphics; secondly, square serifs were created in the midst of the tremendous British interest in ancient Egyptian culture.

Figure 3.14 _____

Notice how D. J. Stout, art director of Texas Monthly, *integrates roman (serif) and sans serif type in this page design. He further distinguishes the faces by running the roman headline in black and the sans serif subhead between the head lines in blue. Also, the byline and caption are set off in reverse blocks. Skip Hollandsworth wrote the feature, and D. J. Stout directed the art and design. Photography by Joseph Vento. Reprinted with permission from* Texas Monthly.

Whatever you call them, square serif faces feature letterforms constructed with equally weighted uniform strokes. (There are some exceptions—Clarendon, for example.) This uniformity gives the type an even texture, affording very little contrast between letters. Minor tapering may occur at the juncture of the stem and bowls, and at different branchings of the stroke, and, of course, the slab or rectangular-shaped serifs.

Because of their squared off serifs, heavy letter stroke and tendency for counters to fill when bolded or run in small point sizes, square serifs don't work well as a body type. Their architecture makes for a clunky read, and they receive low readability scores. However, because their architecture increases their legibility, they are easily seen. This makes them a good display type, especially when used with most romans. They don't mix well with sans serifs.

Sans Serif

As implied by the nomenclature (*sans*, French for without, serifs), this race does not wear serifs. Of all the races, these are the most geometric; there aren't any serifs to break off the inherent geometry of the letterform. By not having the edges that serifs produce, sans serif letters are more round, as in the uppercase *B, C, G, O, Q*; more rectangular, as in uppercase, *H, N*; and more triangular, uppercase *V, A*. They have a clean look, and they are considered very legible. This also brings austerity to the **sans serifs**, and a much cooler feeling.

Although most people think of sans serifs as a very contemporary race and associate it with its enormous success in the 1920s and the Bauhaus school, it was an innovation of the nineteenth century. In fact, it was none other than William Caslon, creator of Caslon, a classic old-style roman face, who designed it. Even then it was heralded as a typographic bridge to the future.

Some contend that of all the type designed during the nineteenth century, it is the sans serifs that best reflects that time. Spawned in England during the Industrial Revolution, they seem to have taken on the cold, machined feel of that era. The uniform width of the letter strokes also points to the sameness we so often associate with mass production and makes sans serif the most legible of all the races. (There are a handful of sans serifs that do have thick and thin strokes, Optima, for example, but they are the rare exceptions.)

The jury is still out on whether sans serifs are more readable than romans. Some supporters argue that the eye is a creature of habit, and that because we learn to read with serifs we are predisposed to them. A quick look at newspapers, magazines, books and corporate publications reveals that most editors, designers and publishers side with the serif for body copy.

It should be noted that sans serifs do give a page a flat look. Large areas of body copy set in sans serif lack the typographic texture and color that romans provide and often look gray and monotonous. But this, like other typographic issues, can be a matter of taste. In Europe, for example, **grotesques** (another name for sans serifs) are the norm for body copy, whereas in the United States, sans serifs are primarily used as a display type.

Today, some sans serifs are very "hot" faces. For example, Futura—often run in a bolded version with tight letterspacing—is enjoying a tremendous revival. It is also considered very stylish to use weighty versions of sans serifs as headlines. They are also used extensively in outdoor posters and billboards because of their high legibility.

This is the true joy of life, the being used for a purpose recognized by yourself as a mighty one; the being thoroughly worn out before you are thrown on the scrap heap; the being a force of nature instead of a

Figure 3.15
The uniformity of the letter strokes and squared serifs give square serifs good legibility. However, the stiff letter configuration makes for a clunky read; most designers avoid the faces of this race for body type. This example is set in Lubalin. A few scholars of typography suggest that William Caslon IV's "Egyptian" was probably the first sans serif. Most faces in both races (square serifs and sans serifs) have uniform letter strokes.

Figure 3.16
Helvetica, shown here, is the most popular face in the world. Most of the time, sans serifs are used as display type (Helvetica, Futura and Gilsans are three good examples), and although romans are still the overwhelming choice as a body face, more and more designers are experimenting with sans serifs for that purpose. Because of their even strokes and good legibility, sans serifs are logical choices for reverses.

feverish, selfish little clod of ailments and grievances complaining that the world will not devote itself to making you happy.
G.B. Shaw

Incidentally, many designers like to squeeze the letters in sans serif headlines closer together to give words better shaping. Remember, serifs better join letters and shape words. To compensate for this, designers and typographers tightly kern sans serifs, especially when used as a display type in uppercase. (See **Figure 3.17**.)

Script and Cursives

Everyday, colloquial writing strongly affected the development of letterform. Lowercase letters, for example, were in large part evolved through freehand efficiency. This led to the development of **script** and **cursive** types. Both of these faces resemble handwriting. What distinguishes them from one another is that script faces have connected letters, while cursive letters are generally printed separately.

Cursive and script styles were among the more popular faces from the late 1940s through the 1950s. Today, however, they are seldom used, and neither have much use in publication production. They have little application today because editors, designers, advertisers, publishers and their clientele realize their shortcomings. They have terrible readability—in fact, reading is often

I was a fresh new journalist and needed a nom de guerre;

Figure 3.18 _____

Script faces, because of their readability problems, are seldom used beyond a handful of decorative applications. Recently, however, some designers are integrating them into the page designs of annual reports and some upscale brochures. Most designers and typographers still avoid them like the plague. This type is Brush.

I was a fresh new journalist and needed a nom de guerre;

Figure 3.19 _____

Unlike script type, cursive letters are not joined. Like script, though, cursive type has limited application. Wedding invitations are likely places to find either of these races. Most cursives are little more than an exaggerated italic. This example is Zapf Chancery type.

Figure 3.20 _____

Most miscellaneous or novelty types are used for decorative purposes in retail advertising. And regardless of how you use type, they have minimal typographic application.

I WAS A FRESH NEW JOURNAL-IST AND NEEDED A NOM DE GUERRE; SO I CONFISCATED THE ANCIENT MARINER'S DIS-CARDED ONE, AND HAVE DONE

slowed to reading single words at a time. Because of this, they have no use as body copy and limited application as a display type. If you must use them as for display purposes, don't set them all uppercase. Neither script nor cursive were designed to be used to that end.

Although they are sometimes used to simulate a more personal or individual touch within a communication (say, in an endorsement letter in a magazine ad, or in a direct-mail letter), they do just the opposite and are perceived as being contrived, impersonal and fake. Unlike real handwriting, letter strokes and junctures of script types tend to be predictable and uniform in their construction.

There are uses for script and cursive faces, most often with specialty items. Although informality is linked to handwriting, just the opposite is the case with type. Scripts may be appropriately used in wedding invitations, graduation and coming-out announcements, reception cards and the like. Once in a blue moon, a designer finds some other fitting use for them—as dropped-initial letters, for example. But you are best advised to avoid them completely. If you *do* have a valid reason to use script in a design (perhaps as a handwritten note in print advertising, or as a *P.S.* in a direct mail letter), hire a calligrapher. Your message will prove much more credible, human and effective.

Cursive letters are not joined. These, too, have a very limited application, though some versions tend to be more readable than script type. It should be noted that a small number of type families have cursive variations. The majority, however, are really misnomers because they are not true cursives. In fact, more often they prove to be a variation of the family's letterform in a slightly more affected italic. Remember that while italics are a form of cursive lettering, they are *not* included in this group. (See the section on style in this chapter for more on italic type.)

Miscellaneous or Novelty

This category is to typography what the cloaca is to an amphibian: just about the worst of everything seems to end up here.

It is not a true race of type. Most of the faces in this group are orphans, derelicts or outcasts that don't fit anyplace else. They have no real typographical parents and so are the illegitimate offspring of other types. Some faces are made up to sell themselves or as something else. Still others are tasteless. (Imagine, if you will, carving one of the circus faces or a balloon type on your mother's tombstone.) Within this group are collected some of the most outrageous eyesores you could ever envision.

However, there are enough respectable faces here to make this group worth consideration. Some fat faces make respectable poster types when used appropriately. And a handful of ornamental faces spawned from square serifs function extremely well on the sides of locomotives and their tender cars or as logotypes for old-fashioned ice cream parlors. Still other faces perform correctly for the job at hand, regardless of aesthetics or decorum. These faces, in particular, must be used functionally. The majority of novelty faces seldom find daylight beyond a handful of applications, but when used appropriately they may be suitable for retail selling and other tasks. The most important thing is to fit the style and face to your need or your clients' needs.

Miscellaneous is an especially appropriate adjective because this catch-all grouping contains a myriad of miscellaneous types. Its typographic mishmash of typography includes shadow types, embroidered type and both outline and inline type, as well as stencil faces, variants to true faces with ornamental aberrations, cameo faces reversed atop toned backgrounds or patterns and ornamental affectations to suggest practically anything. The common denominators of this group are display, adornment and specialty. With very few exceptions, that is the purpose of miscellaneous and novelty typefaces.

Understanding Further Categorization

The previous section listed and characterized type races or groups. There is a further fracturing of type classification. **Family** refers to a specific typeface and all of its variations. Within each race of type there exist families—that is, all typefaces that share common characteristics. For example, Avant Garde, Futura, Franklin, Helvetica and News Gothic are all sans serif faces. While each is

Figure 3.21 _____
Family refers to a specific typeface and all of its variations. Each offering has specific uses and functions, as some of the names imply. At the very least, a family will have light, medium and bold variations. Also, the more popular a typeface is, the more variations you're likely to find within its family.

This is Helvetica condensed light
This is Helvetica normal
This is Helvetica bold

different, they have these characteristics in common: evenly stroked letters, no serifs and a more contemporary look. You, as a student of typography and publication design, could make similar analogies for each type group.

The next inner categorization calls attention to **style**, which varies from family to family. More realistically, it is dependent upon what type foundries or companies make available in each family of type they cut and market. Largely, their choice is based on demand.

Figure 3.22 _____
Typically, style offers you condensed, expanded and normal versions of the type. Here you see condensed, expanded and normal styles of Helvetica.

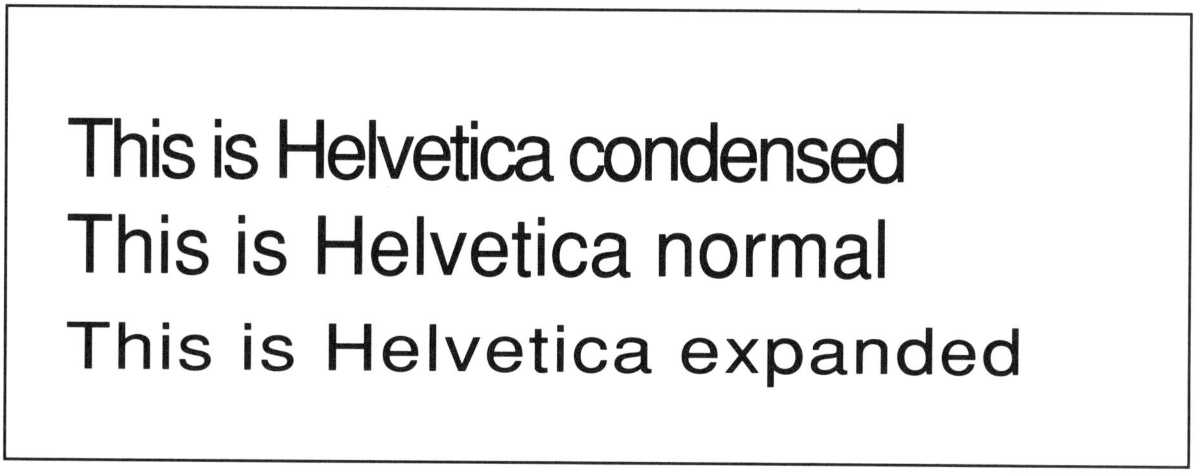

This is Helvetica condensed
This is Helvetica normal
This is Helvetica expanded

Hé Dieu! si
j'eusse étudié
Au temps de ma
jeunesse folle.

Francois Villon

Figure 3.23 _____

*Accent marks, special letters and characters unique to a language or special job make selecting a font very important. Here you see Goudy at 10 point. Also, see **Figure 3.5**.*

12 picas wide

Another rainy day,

—— Em dash

— En dash

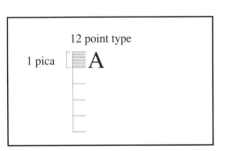

12 point type

1 pica A

Figure 3.24 and **Figure 3.25**____

Points and picas are printing's two basic units of measurement. Letter size is figured in points; line measure is always calculated in picas. Both ems and ens are used to standardize indentation or other typographic alignments. Ems, for example, are often used for paragraph indentation.

Style may offer **condensed, expanded, extended** and **normal** variations. Style is not a difficult concept, if you understand two things. First of all, style is a fickle business. What is popular and successful today may be doomed tomorrow. We tend to indulge on whatever is new, stylish and socially correct, until we tire of it. Then, we binge on the next "hot" typeface until it, too, becomes abused and a stylistic overdose. Styles generally include weight, posture and italicized versions of the above. Second, styles are dependent upon demand; if there is a high demand for an italicized version of a weight, it is incorporated into that style.

A **series**, the next level, consists of all those sizes that are available to each typeface style. (See **Figure 3.6**.) For example, a Garamond family, in its bold italic style, may have these sizes available to it: 6, 7, 8, 9, 10, 11, 12, 14, 18, 24, 30, 36, 48, 60 and 72 point. Those point sizes in that style of Garamond type, a roman face, constitute its series.

Font, the last type categorization, refers to the complete assortment of letters, numerals, punctuation marks and other characters of a family at a specific point size, such as Helvetica Bold. Many computer manufacturers, desktop publishing and word processing software companies and professionals use "font" interchangeably with typeface or family. Font is derived from the French *fonte*, which meant to pour a single casting of type, that is, all letters, numerals and punctuation marks at a single size. (See **Figure 3.5**.)

A font's characters are especially important to jobs that might require unusual symbols like accents or other letter marks, mathematical symbols, or graphic marks. Not only do these vary from size to size, they vary from style to style, and family to family.

Nothing is a given typographically. Always double-check font when your character needs deviate from normal character selection.

Type Measurement

Printing has two basic units of measurement: the **point** and the **pica**. A point is a printer's unit of measurement. There are 72 points to the inch, six picas to the inch and 12 points to the pica. Type size and leading are measured in points. Column width is generally measured in picas, but the depth of a column is usually measured in inches.

To understand this is to have a hand on the printer's measure. A typical typesetting series comes in these point sizes: 6, 7, 8, 9, 10, 11, 12, 14, 18, 24, 30, 36, 48, 60 and 72 point. In some instances, type is measured slightly smaller— to the agate (5 1/2 point)—or larger (96 point is the next standardized measure beyond 72 point), but it may run even larger. **Body copy** is normally set in 8, 9, 10, 11 or 12 point type. In rare instances it may be set smaller; very seldom is it larger than 14 point. **Display type** is 14 points or larger. Measurement is also used in establishing line spacing dimensions, or **leading**. Other terms common to type measurement include em, en, thin space and unit.

An **em**, generally used to establish indentation, paragraph indentation or other alignment arrangements, is the square of the point size. It's so called because an uppercase *M* was originally as wide as it was tall—hence, the square of its point size—for example, a 12 point letter's em would be 12 points x 12 points. It is often used as standard paragraph indentation.

An **en** is exactly one-half the size of an em. Its derivation is similar to the em; it originated from the width-to-height ratio of the uppercase *N*, because that letter's width was half its height. A 12 point letter's en-width would be six point, or one-half the em-distance. A **thin space** is approximately one-fourth that of an em, while a **unit** is about one-eighteenth of an em.

Readability and Legibility

These two terms are not interchangeable, but unfortunately, many people treat them as though they were. **Readability** refers to the readout of the type or how easily the words read. **Legibility**, on the other hand, relates to visibility, or how seeable the letters are.

Scholars of type have different theories about readability and legibility and why it is that some faces read better than others. Most feel that since our eyes are creatures of habit, we are more comfortable with familiar typefaces and so read them more quickly and efficiently. There are two staunch camps: one preaches that the readability of serifs is superior to that of sans serifs, the other that sans serifs are better.

Roman faces do join, align and shape words better than sans serifs. Walking serifs hint at a baseline of sorts, and align letters and words to one another. If you look closely at the serifs of any roman face, you'll notice that their horizontal reach suggests a juncture between the letters within a word. This is especially

They drew all manner of things—everything that begins with an M... such as mouse-traps, and the moon, and memory, and muchness—you know you say things are "much of a much-ness."

Lewis Carroll

Figure 3.26 _____

Unlike the vast majority of sans serifs, Optima is one face in this race that has variation in its letter strokes. If you want texture in your page, but lean toward sans serifs, this may be the face for you.

"A slow sort of country!" said the Queen. "Now, here, you see, it takes all the running you can do, to keep in the same place." Lewis Carroll

Figure 3.27 _____

Most designers and scholars of type would suggest that roman faces are more readable; quickly check the body faces of the newspapers and magazines you read. Because of the variation in serifs and thick and thin letter strokes, they bring more texture to copy-heavy pages. But it is precisely the uniformity in the letter strokes that make sans serifs more legible, that is, easier to see. Favored as display type, they used a lot in posters and outdoor advertising.

true in the beginning and ending strokes of most lowercase and uppercase letters. Serifs also further define the shape of each letter.

In addition, the thick and thin strokes bring more texture and variety to a full page of copy, while the uniform letter strokes of sans serifs tend to be monotonous when used in large areas. (A handful of sans serifs specifically designed to be more readable have thick and thin strokes. Optima is a fine example. (See **Figure 3.23**.) Finally, there are a lot more roman than sans serif faces to choose from.

But there is a lot to be said for sans serifs. Generally perceived as modern and stylish, they are more legible and easier to see. Style notwithstanding, they are an excellent selection for posters and outdoor media. When your audience is moving, or when the medium itself is moving, legibility is critical. Sans serifs' even letter strokes make them quickly visible. Similarly, they are a popular choice as a display type for the same reasons—good legibility and style.

Remember, the primary function of type is to be read. It is important to mate type properly with your audience, client, medium, and image. For example, Futura or Helvetica might be perfect for both the display and copy of a technical piece. On the other hand, for a newsletter, annual report or advertisement for a very conservative organization, you're liable to want a formal old-style roman.

Figure 3.28

Sometimes, typography replaces artwork. Here, for example, design director Jim Darilek and art director Mary Workman collaborated on the design and used a bolded white sans serif face, outlined it in black and placed it atop a bright red background. It probably suggests as much about vices as any montage could. What's more, it does so clearly and simply. Notice, too, the nice mix of typefaces. The high legibility of the sans serif really flags the reader, especially with the fire-engine red. The italicized roman face beneath VICES is used large enough so that it is easily read. It is run the same as the title, too: white type with black outlining. Reprinted with permission of Special Report — On Health, *copyright 1990, Whittle Communications L.P.*

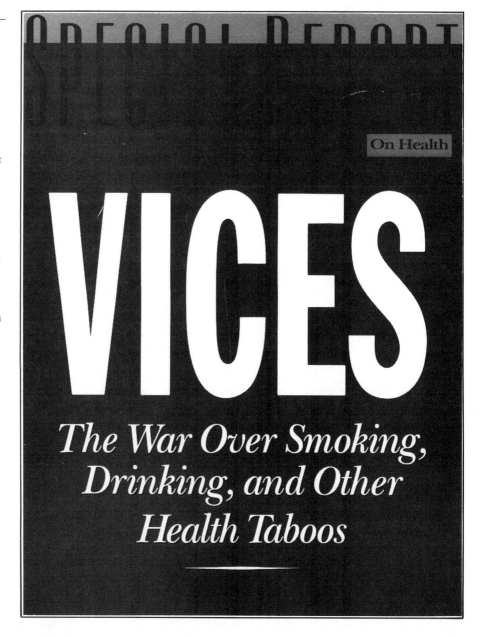

Mixing Faces

The easiest and most logical solution is to use one typeface and provide variety by altering its weight, posture and style. For example, you might select a 10-point medium Goudy leaded at 12 with a 26 pica line measure set ragged right. Your captions might follow the same specs but in an italic; your headlines may be set in 24, 30, 36 or 48 point Goudy bold. Remaining with a single family eliminates any possibility that you will lose unity and continuity within a publication. On the other hand, you may want to mix faces. You might run text in roman while running headlines or sidebars in an appropriate sans serif for contrast. Some designers will even integrate heads and subheads. Whatever you decide, make sure the two faces work together and use them consistently throughout the piece. Be aware that you risk exploding typographic unity by improperly mixing faces.

Integrating and mixing typefaces is largely intuitive. Be certain to see the combinations as they would appear together before you make a decision. It's one thing to compare a roman alphabet to a sans serif alphabet in a type catalog. It is another to actually see sample headlines, subheads and copy blocks using that combination. *Never choose a face without seeing some examples of sizes, weights, line lengths and other specifics similar to those in your publication's design.*

And don't forget: less is more. The fewer faces you use, the better.

Type Specification

Computer technology has made "specing" type no longer just the editor's or designer's responsibility. People in public relations, business communications and advertising now struggle with typographical decisions, either as the designer of a project, or as the one responsible for approving it. Journalists have taken on the same responsibilities.

Computer software programs force you to choose typefaces, point size, leading, style, weight, posture, line length and line arrangements. Not making decisions about these important nuances is making decisions. And backing into a decision is likely to be catastrophic; it's not easy to wiggle out of typographical parameters once they've been established. By learning the typical type specification basics that follow and understanding the reasoning behind them, you will

Figure 3.29

When selecting a type for copy, check the x-height first. Typically, the larger its x-height, the better its readability. If you're "speced in" to use a very small point size for the body, then x-height becomes even more important.

Figure 3.30

Although it's important that you get your material printed, it is even more important that it be read. If you run your copy too small, only the more industrious readers will bother to dig up a magnifying glass to read it. Additionally, keep audience in mind when assigning point size. Younger and older audiences do better with larger type, for different reasons. These selections are set in 8-, 10- and 12-point New Century Schoolbook.

Honor pricks me on. Yea, but how if honor prick me off when I come on? how then? Can honor set to a leg? No. Or an arm? No. Or take away the grief of a wound? No. Honor hath no skill in surgery then? No. What is honor? a word. What is that word, honor? Air. A trim reckoning! Who hath it? he that died o' Wednesday. Doth he feel it? No. Doth he hear it? No. It is insensible then? Yea, to the dead. But will it not live with the living? No. Why? Detraction will not suffer it. Therefore I'll have none of it. *William Shakespeare*

Honor pricks me on. Yea, but how if honor prick me off when I come on? how then? Can honor set to a leg? No. Or an arm? No. Or take away the grief of a wound? No. Honor hath no skill in surgery then? No. What is honor? a word. What is that word, honor? Air. A trim reckoning! Who hath it? he that died o' Wednesday. Doth he feel it? No. Doth he hear it? No. It is insensible

Honor pricks me on. Yea, but how if honor prick me off when I come on? how then? Can honor set to a leg? No. Or an arm? No. Or take away the grief of a wound? No. Honor hath no skill in surgery then? No. What is honor? a word. What is that word, honor? Air. A trim reckon-

Figure 3.31 _____

If you're going to run anything in reverse, size and legibility are especially important to reading. The type treatment here in this Andy Doerschuk feature suggests "big and heavy." Appropriately, the reverse says heavy and the uppercase roman head says big. Art director and designer Saroyan Humphrey used deep leading in the title and the text—both help the read in a reverse layout. To improve readability, he might've used a larger point size for the type, or even run it in sans serif on this opening page. Reprinted with permission of Drums & Drumming, *a publication of Miller-Freeman, Inc.*

be able to communicate clearly with production people or specify type by yourself. Included in each specification area, you will find additional remarks.

Type Size

You already understand printer's measure. Type sizes are measured in points, and there are 12 points to a pica and 72 points to an inch. To measure the type's size, you measure from ascender to descender, not the height of the uppercase letter.

Body copy is normally set between 6 and 14 point, and most often between 8 and 12 point. (Most newspapers set type between 8 and 10 point, for example.) When you must select a smaller point size, choose a typeface with a large x-height. In fact, it's a good idea to select a typeface with a large x-height for all body copy.

To use the right point size for the job at hand, *think of your audience first.* Understand their predisposition to typography and its nuances. Generally, large x-heights and larger point sizes work better for younger and older audiences. Children who are new to our marvelous system of abstract symbols need larger letters because they are still learning letter sounds in combinations and how to read words; older people appreciate them because as we age our vision deteriorates. Larger point sizes and crisp typefaces help readability for both these audiences.

Moderately larger point sizes may also facilitate a quick read in advertisements, charts, graphs and various information graphics or anything that expects an at-a-glance communication.

Any type 14 points or larger is usually considered **display type**. These bigger sizes are more likely to attract attention, one of the more obvious strategies of headlines. Normally, too, headlines are bolded. Be careful, though. Sometimes you don't want headlines to shout, or you discover that using big type alone is enough to call attention to a title or headline. If you decide to use boldface or any of its heavier variations, be sure to check the counters. A number of typefaces have counters that clot or fill up too much at some point sizes.

Larger point sizes are often needed for reverse blocks. Black backgrounds tend to swallow up white lettering; indeed, some paper stocks, like newsprint, will allow blotting and bleeding to occur. This causes serifs and hairline strokes to become lost or smeared. Using a larger size (or a sans serif face) will make reversed copy more legible.

THE BIG HEAVY PICTURE

NOTHING IS SACRED. EVEN HEAVY METAL music—the champion of sacrilege—has proven itself susceptible to the winds of change. Today it comprises a dizzying spectrum of splinter groups. In one corner stand the commercial Goliaths of metal; coiffed, posed, apparently born for MTV. Across the ring stand the hard-core element—themselves divided into subcategories—snarling and hurling wrenches into the machinery. And in between is everything imaginable.

Collectively, it's a movement to be reckoned with. And temptation leads us to search for common threads, shared traditions, clues to the origins of metal drumming and the depth of its subculture. We turn to a voice of experience, Whitesnake's Tommy Aldridge, who helped invent metal double-bass vocabulary in the '70s with Black Oak Arkansas. He's a survivor. He'll know what it's all about. →

BY ANDY DOERSCHUK

D&D AUG/SEPT 1990 **29**

Leading

The amount of space you allot between lines of type is called **leading**. It derives it name from handset type nomenclature, when printers would literally insert strips of metal (usually lead) between the lines of type. Incidentally, the term is pronounced LED-ing, as in zeppelin.

Proper leading is very important to readability. Most typographers and designers adjust leading from typeface to typeface. These fine-tuned adjustments are usually based upon the size of each face's x-height. Faces with larger x-heights tend to have short ascenders and descenders, so the space between the mean line and the ascender line and the space between the baseline and descender line are narrow. To brighten the look of a page and make the copy more readable, add more leading. The opposite is true of letters with small x-heights, because there is more space above and below the x-height part of the letters.

Insufficient leading creates a claustrophobic effect. Lines appear to be jammed together, darkening the texture of the page and making it uninviting to the reader. On the other hand, too much leading forces the eye to jump from one line to the next and tires the reader.

A good rule of thumb to figure leading for body copy is to simply add two points to the point size. If you were marking up 10-point type with 12-point leading for a printer, you would write it like this: 10/12. (Point size always precedes the leading figure.) If you've selected a face with a short x-height, adding one point might suffice: 9/10. **Solid leading** refers to leading that is set the same as the point size of the type: 11/11. **Minus leading** is using line spacing that is less than the point size used: 10/9.

Figure 3.32 _____

Leading is as important to your readout as the point size or typeface itself. Adding two points to the letter size is a healthy rule of thumb for optimum read on body copy. Here you see three different leadings of the same material in New Century Schoolbook. The left example is set 10/12. The middle is set solid, 10/10. And the right is minus-leaded, 10/8. Which is easiest to read?

Honor pricks me on. Yea, but how if honor prick me off when I come on? how then? Can honor set to a leg? No. Or an arm? No. Or take away the grief of a wound? No. Honor hath no skill in surgery then? No. What is honor? a word. What is that word, honor? Air. A trim reckoning! Who hath it? he that died o' Wednesday. Doth he feel it? No. Doth he hear it? No. It is insensible then? Yea, to the dead. But

Honor pricks me on. Yea, but how if honor prick me off when I come on? how then? Can honor set to a leg? No. Or an arm? No. Or take away the grief of a wound? No. Honor hath no skill in surgery then? No. What is honor? a word. What is that word, honor? Air. A trim reckoning! Who hath it? he that died o' Wednesday. Doth he feel it? No. Doth he hear it? No. It is insensible then? Yea, to the dead. But will it not live with the living? No. Why? Detraction will not suffer it. Therefore I'll have

Honor pricks me on. Yea, but how if honor prick me off when I come on? how then? Can honor set to a leg? No. Or an arm? No. Or take away the grief of a wound? No. Honor hath no skill in surgery then? No. What is honor? a word. What is that word, honor? Air. A trim reckoning! Who hath it? he that died o' Wednesday. Doth he feel it? No. Doth he hear it? No. It is insensible then? Yea, to the dead. But will it not live with the living? No. Why? Detraction will not suffer it. Therefore I'll have none of it. *William Shakespeare*

Generally speaking, minus leading is a practice to avoid, but today it is considered to be a very fashionable way to treat advertising headlines and custom heads, especially those with all uppercase letters. Bolded sans serifs that have been tightly kerned and minus leaded bring a sculpted look to a headline. Indeed, these heads have a monolith-like look to them. They suggest strength and power, but they won't win readability awards. In short doses, however, they can be very effective.

Minus leading is more self-defeating in heads using upper and lowercase letters, though, especially when applied to leggy romans. Here the minus leading

Figure 3.33 _____

*Minus leading is fashionable in
heads with bolded, uppercase sans
serifs. But minus leading tends to be
self-defeating in heads using upper-
and lowercase letters, particularly
when the ascender line is higher
than the cap line.*

EMPLOYEES RIOT, REJECT MANAGEMENT OFFER

Cap line
Employees Riot, Reject Management Offer

Employees Riot, Reject Management Offer While President Fiddles.

Employees Riot, Reject Management Offer While President Fiddles.

Figure 3.34 _____

*If you're set on running one column or your design calls for longer lines, use deeper leading
so your readers can track effectively. Note the claustrophobic effect in lines more tightly
leaded here.*

causes intersections between the descenders on one line and the ascenders on the line below. Despite poor readability and visual noise, some art directors continue minus leading with downstyle romans. **Downstyle** capitalizes only lead words and proper nouns.

As the length of your line increases, readability decreases. Longer lines make it more difficult for our eyes to track accurately from one line to the next. When reading single-spaced correspondence, you may find yourself reading a line, losing your place, reading the same line over and descending to the next line again. Correct for long line length by increasing the leading. Adding four or five points to the point size usually eliminates the problem.

If you are using any substantial amount of bolded copy, increase its leading as well. Weightier type makes for a darker page and a more difficult read. To air it out some and lighten the page's texture, add three or four points to the letter size to figure your leading.

Occasionally, designers of corporate publications or advertising like to apply lots of leading over relatively small amounts of copy. This provides a lighter texture to a page, and implies luxury, wealth and good taste. It also suggests that the advertiser can afford to waste space in this manner—but used sensitively that exorbitant amount of leading is anything but wasteful.

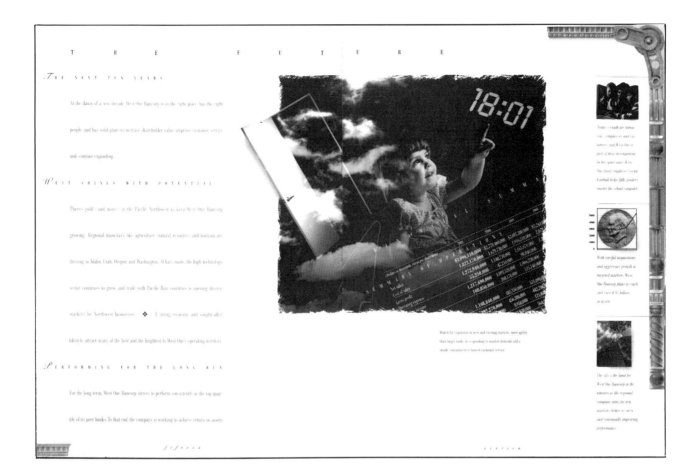

Line Length

Because we scan groups of words at a time when we read, it's important to establish line breaks that complement our reading rhythm. Longer lines, especially in any quantity, tire the eye. That's because when we read, our eyes are used to working in an even rhythm, whatever the reading speed. Line lengths can work with or against that rhythm. It is as simple as that.

Long lines stop us midstride, so to speak. They break that rhythm at the end of a line, especially when we stop to hunt out where to pick up that line on the left. The opposite is true of very short lines. They force our eyes to do visual wind sprints that are equally exhausting and very frustrating, because we're continually starting and stopping, and often lose our train of thought.

A number of different formulae can help you arrive at an **optimum line length**. One formula recommends doubling the point size of your type to determine the number of picas in your line. Using this approach, an 11-point type would suggest a 22-pica line. You can also calculate the measure of your typeface lowercase, *a* to *z*, then add exactly half of that measure to arrive at your line measure. Let's say the lowercase *a* to *z* measure is 18 picas. Half of that—9 picas—added to the original length gives you a line length of 27 picas. This same formula states that the minimum line length is the *a* to *z* measure itself—18 picas in this instance—and, the maximum width would be twice that *a* to *z* measure, or 36 picas. David Ogilvy in his fine text, *Ogilvy on Advertising*, suggests that the standard magazine format should employ three columns, each 35–45 characters across. A quick comparison shows that all of these formulae work out to approximately the same length.

Figure 3.35 _____

These pages work deep leading into the overall design—that is, in both the longer and shorter lines of copy, and one in between. Note, too, how the added letterspacing in the title and heads fit into this layout. The extra-wide letter spacing allows the title to bridge both pages with the art. Also, script initial letters are used in the heads. Art direction by Jack Anderson; he, Julie Tanagi-Lock and David Bates designed this annual report. Artwork: Jonathan Combs, illustration and Tom Collicott, photography. Reprinted with permission of West One Bancorp and Hornall Anderson Design Works.

Line Arrangement

There are a number of ways to arrange your copy. The two most logical ways are to set your copy ragged right—that is, flush (or "neat") to the left, save paragraph indentation, and ragged on the right side—or justified, with even line endings so that, excepting paragraph indentation and endings, the left side of the copy is parallel to the right. Less common but sometimes more appropriate are centered lines and copy set flush right. Each has advantages and inherent problems.

Ragged right—also known as **unjustified**, **flush left** or **neat left** copy—is characterized by an even left side and uneven line endings on the right. It is inherently more informal than justified copy. It has other advantages. Letterspacing and word spacing is always consistent and evenly textured because there isn't a specific breaking point for a line. Because letterspacing and word spacing are even, you never end up with gaps of white or rivers of white streaking the type's texture, regardless of how narrow the column measure might be. And it's easy for the reader to track from one line to the next, since the left side of the column is even and the unaligned right side complements a normal tracking rhythm.

Because ragged right text has a haphazard look, it has more of a laid back feel. Most designers and readers react to the loosely structured right side informally. Dr. Mario Garcia, designer and professor of graphic design at Syracuse University and the University of South Florida, suggests that you can tell how seriously a newspaper takes itself by noting if it sets its copy justified or unjustified.

Figure 3.36 _____

Strive to use type creatively. Typography figures into the sense of the title and this Glen Gibbons feature, "GPS and the Quake." In this instance, art director Lee Eide used a heavily bolded version of Futura oblique and cut into the title to deliberately misalign it to suggest a similar type of stratified shifts that cause earthquakes. Look, too, at how UAKE is set outside the color bar that holds the rest of the title; the color bar also breaks the artwork.

Art direction: Lee Eide. Photography from Earth Observation Satellite Company. Reprinted with permission from Aster Publishing Corp.

Ragged left copy, also known as **neat right** or **flush right** copy, is seldom used as a line arrangement because we have a difficult time reading it. Until recently, ragged left copy was almost never found in publication work. The only place you'd find it was in advertising copy blocks, usually to contour the type along the left side of the visual. Today, however, it is somewhat stylish to run some captions, credits, surprinted cover lines and contoured columns ragged left.

Although readability suffers some, it is all right to use reasonably scant amounts of flush right copy. In fact, the accepted current style for some publications is to run captions to the right or left side of the photographs, setting copy ragged left on the left side of the image and ragged right on the right. If you do arrange lines in this fashion, use a little extra leading to help the reader better track from one line to the next. If you have an extensive amount of copy, don't set it flush right. It won't get read—not by much of your audience, anyway.

Centered copy has the same disadvantages as its ragged left counterpart—it is difficult for readers to track. However, centered copy in short amounts is accepted practice. The great majority of it is found in advertising, on covers and on rare occasion in captions. It is more readable in very short doses such as headlines or subheads. It is less tolerable in copy blocks, and disastrous in anything exceeding a handful of paragraphs.

Justified copy is more formal. Its even right and left sides (discounting paragraph beginnings and endings) are much more rigid. They appear stiff to the eye of the reader and the typesetter. Indeed, they often prove to be a designing and typesetting nightmare where narrow column measures are employed.

There are problems inherent in justified line arrangements. Regardless of how sophisticated a spacing and hyphenation program you have built into your typesetting, you're bound to end up with some gapping, uneven letterspacing and inconsistent wordspacing. Narrow columns only make this worse. Horrible gapping, torrential rivers of white, and picket fence letterspacing take away not only the good looks of a design, but, just as importantly, good readability. Any newspaper, large or small, contains examples of each of the problems cited above. Therein lie the shortcomings of justification.

Figure 3.37 _____
Some of the advantages of lefted copy include fewer hyphenations, consistent letter and wordspacing, even typographic texture and an informal look.

To endure is greater than to dare; to tire out hostile fortune; to be daunted by no difficulty; to keep heart when all have lost it; to go through intrigue spotless; to forego even ambition when the end is gained—who can say this is not greatness? Bravery never goes out of fashion.
William Thackery

Figure 3.38 _____
Copy that is set neat or flush right is more difficult to read. Typically, you find it in advertising and text that contours artwork. These days it is also a stylish approach to captioning.

To endure is greater than to dare; to tire out hostile fortune; to be daunted by no difficulty; to keep heart when all have lost it; to go through intrigue spotless; to forego even ambition when the end is gained—who can say this is not greatness? Bravery never goes out of fashion.
William Thackery

Figure 3.39 _____
Centered copy is difficult to read. It's used commonly in headlines and in other places in small amounts, like captions, blurbs and magazine cover lines.

To endure is greater than to dare; to tire out hostile fortune; to be daunted by no difficulty; to keep heart when all have lost it; to go through intrigue spotless; to forego even ambition when the end is gained—who can say this is not greatness? Bravery never goes out of fashion.
William Thackery

Justification epitomizes order by tightly aligning columns on both the right and left sides. And, as Mario Garcia points out, justification mirrors how seriously we take ourselves. Most editors, publishers and writers take themselves quite seriously. So, too, do the presidents of corporations,

Figure 3.40 _____

Note some of the inherent problems of justified copy: gapping, hyphenations, rivers of white and uneven spacing are common. These become more exaggerated in narrow columns.

Still, justified copy is considered the proper arrangement for most of our print media. The great majority of books, newspapers, magazines, journals, annual reports, print advertising and other forms of publications set justified copy. Why, you ask, despite the inherent problems and high risks, do editors, designers, publishers and readers seem to favor justified copy? Or, to rephrase the question, is justification justified?

Most everything we see in print has roots to the past. Line arrangements are no exception. The monks and scribes who saved most of our cultural and historical connections to antiquity worked from fairly well-fixed margins. How they put words to page strongly affected early printing technology. What other models did printers have? Also, straight margins to either side helped printers order and align their type, an approach that has continued from Gutenberg's time to today.

Justification epitomizes order by tightly aligning columns on both the right and left sides. And, as Mario Garcia points out, justification mirrors how seriously we take ourselves. Most editors, publishers and writers take themselves quite seriously. So, too, do the presidents of corporations, public relations directors and everyone else who communicate through publications.

Finally, we are most comfortable with what we know best, and centuries of use have accustomed us to justifed columns. As the old saying goes, "if it works, don't fix it." But because many designers bristle at conforming to the norm, flush left or ragged right copy is slowly becoming more and more accepted in formal and informal situations alike.

Figure 3.41 _____

Because uppercase copy blocks are spaced evenly, they are difficult to read. All uppercase settings also take up a great deal more space. Compare the two blocks of type. Lowercase letters better shape words and improve readability.

Lowercase letters also better shape words. Ascenders and descenders give letters a functional architecture that connects them structurally to their uppercase counterparts, and lets our eyes glide easily over these subtle shifts in letterform. Because it's easier to recognize word shapes, we read quickly.

ALL UPPERCASE COPY BLOCKS SPACE EVENLY. VARIATIONS ABOVE THE MEANLINE AND BELOW THE BASELINE ARE NONEXISTENT. NO DISTINGUISHING SHAPE OR DELICATE PATTERNING IN THEIR CONSTRUCTION MAKES FOR A GROPING SORT OF READ. AND, BECAUSE OUR EYES AREN'T USED TO SEEING MORE THAN A HANDFUL OF WORDS WRITTEN IN THIS FASHION, IT IS DIFFICULT TO SCAN ANY QUANTITY OF UPPERCASE COPY. (SEE **FIGURE 3.30**.) IN ADDITION, ALL UPPERCASE LETTERS TAKE UP A LOT MORE SPACE. THERE IS MUCH TO LEARN FROM THIS.

Uppercase vs. Lowercase

When put to the test, we read upper- and lowercase type much more efficiently and effectively than we do all uppercase. That's because capital letters tell us one of two things. Either we are looking at a proper noun, or we've reached the end of one sentence and the beginning of the next. Both stop or slow our reading.

Lowercase letters also better shape words. Ascenders and descenders give letters a functional architecture that connects them structurally to their uppercase counterparts, and lets our eyes glide easily over these subtle shifts in letterform. Because it's easier to recognize word shapes, we read quickly.

All uppercase copy blocks space evenly. Variations above the meanline and below the baseline are nonexistent. No distinguishing shape or delicate patterning in their construction makes for a groping sort of read. And, because our eyes aren't used to seeing more than a handful of words written in this fashion, it is difficult to scan any quantity of uppercase copy. In addition, all uppercase letters take up a lot more space. There is much to learn from this.

Weight refers to the amount of ink or blackness a specific typeface carries. This varies from face to face. For example, one face's regular weight might be considerably heavier than another's. Most faces carry **light, medium** (or **regular**) and **bold** weight variations.

Weight refers to the amount of ink or blackness a specific typeface carries. This varies from face to face. For example, one face's regular weight might be considerably heavier than another's. Most faces carry **light, medium** (or **regular**) and **bold** weight variations.

Weight refers to the amount of ink or blackness a specific typeface carries. This varies from face to face. For example, one face's regular weight might be considerably heavier than another's. Most faces carry light, medium (or regular) and bold weight variations.

First of all, never set copy all uppercase. If you must set headlines in uppercase, keep them short, and use short words. Bolded uppercase letters may add power to a headline, but overstatement from bigness, boldness and combinations thereof alienate a reader. You needn't yell to get attention. It is best to use a downstyle approach—capitalize proper nouns and sentence beginnings only. Run everything else lowercase.

Let the words do their job and the typography do its job. Asking both to do the same thing usually results in one getting in the way of the other. Readers pick up on that redundancy quickly.

Figure 3.42 _____
Weight is important to type specification. Light faces, unless set at very large sizes, tend to be under-inked and fragile. Normal or regular weight is the most readable of these three. Bolded type is heavier and is often used for emphasis, in headlines or titles, for example.

Weight

Weight refers to the amount of ink or blackness a specific typeface carries. This varies from face to face. For example, one face's regular weight might be considerably heavier than another's. Most faces carry **light, medium** (or **regular**) and **bold** weight variations. However, more variations exist, depending upon available weight within a given face. The more popular a face is, the more weights that face will carry. A quick look at any type catalog will indicate which faces get the most use.

Studies and current practice suggest that regular weight is the most readable. (Sometimes regular weight is referred to as **normal** or medium weight.) Bolded copy, especially in any quantity, overweights a page. Be sure to closely examine the counters in any bolded weight of a face. Some have a propensity to close up.

A good rule of thumb is to use normal weight for copy. Display type might warrant heavier weights, but be careful not to over-ink. Don't mark copy up and then react to it, after the fact. If there is any question in your mind about how something will look, scrutinize it. Moderation is always best. Light faces, unless employed at very large sizes, tend to be under-inked and fragile. You can't see them. Bold versions of a face tend to say the same thing—only louder. Don't be redundant, know what you are up to.

The straight up and down posture is generally referred to as **roman**. *This is where confusion often sets in. In this instance, roman refers specifically to posture, not to serifs or an entire race of type. This posture is also called* **upright**, *a very specific and appropriate term.*

Obliques are often used in headlines or display type, or as a head variation in decks, crossheads, subheads and the like. They might also be used for emphasis in sidebars or special features. Their directional design gives them a sense of urgency or may suggest movement. Unlike italics, their weight and stroke is uniform, and they tend to read well. For that reason their popularity has increased dramatically in recent years.

Italic *is sometimes considered a style, sometimes a separate race, sometimes a type entity in and of itself. It is much more than type that is slanted to the right. True italic has a lighter weight, thick and thin strokes, a cursive affectation, serifs and a narrower width than upright letters.*

Figure 3.43 _____
We are most used to seeing roman or upright posture; for that reason, it is easier for us to read words set upright. Because of their directional design, obliques give type a sense of movement or urgency. Italics have a unique posturing situation, because they are not only slanted, but lighter and slightly cursive. They should not be confused with obliques.

Examining an alphabet and set of numerals in a type catalog tells you very little about a typeface. Know the weights, sizes, leading, faces, line measures and arrangements firsthand. Run sample galleys of them so you know how they'll look in print.

Posture

Basically, there are three postures, not all of which will always be available to you: roman, oblique and backslanted.

The straight up and down posture is generally referred to as **roman**. This is where confusion often sets in. In this instance, roman refers specifically to posture, not to serifs or an entire race of type. This posture is also called **upright**, a very specific and appropriate term.

In the **oblique** posture the letters are constructed or stroked as normal but pitched slightly to the right. Usually, however, oblique refers specifically to sans serifs. The oblique style is also commonly referred to as **forward**. Forward positioning should not be confused with italics, which are actually an entirely separate development in typography.

Obliques are often used in headlines or display type, or as a head variation in decks, crossheads, subheads and the like. They might also be used for emphasis in sidebars or special features. Their directional design gives them a sense of urgency or may suggest movement. Unlike italics, their weight and stroke is uniform, and they tend to read well. For that reason their popularity has increased dramatically in recent years.

Very seldom do we even see the third variation in posture, called **backslanted** or **raked** due to its letters' backward, to-the-left lean. Because the letter construction is much different from what we're used to seeing, and because its pitch goes against our natural reading flow, it is seldom offered as a letter posture.

Functionally, the normal, upright (or roman) posture is most readable. It is also used ninety-five percent of the time. Obliques can be very effective in smaller amounts to suggest emphasis. Most designers will tell you they've never used backslanted posturing.

Type Style

Although there may be some disagreement about what all constitutes type styles or where they fit into typographical organization, most scholars of typography would include **condensed, expanded, extended, normal** and **italics** as specific type styles.

Condensed type is characterized by slightly smaller, narrower letters. Not a good style to use for body copy, it is best worked in scant amounts. Many designers avoid condensed type because of its reduced readability. **Expanded** type uses wider-than-normal letters. It too is seldom used as a copy face because it takes up a great deal more space. However, it is commonly accepted as a display tactic, especially when a designer is looking to remain within a given family of type. In **extended** type, the letters have been stretched out vertically. Its application is limited, but when a design calls for a type to exaggerate slimness, it might prove a logical choice. Most computer drawing programs can stretch type in this fashion. **Normal** style is the upright, medium weight of type we are most used to seeing. It has high readability and serves many different functions.

Video meliora, proboque, deteriora sequor.
Ovid

Figure 3.44 _____
Italics were originally conceived and designed by Aldus Manutius, a fifteenth century publisher and designer. He'd planned to publish the Latin classics, and so wanted a smaller, readable type to cut back printing costs. Note the lighter weight, slant and cursive quality of the letterform.

Italic was originally created by Aldus Manutius, publisher, scholar, designer and businessman of fifteenth century Venice. What Manutius did was to integrate the cursive pitch, shaping and some of its ligatures from colloquial writing into a new face that blended both the roman and some of the cursive affectations from everyday writing. And so he conceived a familiar type style that would prove very readable to the educated, and a type that took up substantially less room, which made a great deal of sense to publishers planning to print most of Latin classic literature.

Italic was originally created by Aldus Manutius, publisher, scholar, designer and businessman of fifteenth century Venice. What Manutius did was to integrate the cursive pitch, shaping and some of its ligatures from colloquial writing into a new face that blended both the roman and some of the cursive affectations from everyday writing. And so he conceived a familiar type style that would prove very readable to the

Italic was originally created by Aldus Manutius, publisher, scholar, designer and businessman of fifteenth century Venice. What Manutius did was to integrate the cursive pitch, shaping and some of its ligatures from colloquial writing into a new face that blended both the roman and some of the cursive affectations from everyday writing. And so he conceived a familiar type style that would prove very readable to the educated, and a type that took up substantially less room, which made a great deal of

Figure 3.45 _____
Compare the readability and amount of space used by these styles. They are condensed, expanded and normal versions of Times Roman.

Italic is sometimes considered a style, sometimes a separate race, sometimes a type entity in and of itself. It is much more than type that is slanted to the right. True italic has a lighter weight, thick and thin strokes, a cursive affectation, serifs and a narrower width than upright letters.

Italic was originally created by Aldus Manutius, publisher, scholar, designer and businessman of fifteenth century Venice. What Manutius did was to integrate the cursive pitch, shaping and some of its ligatures from colloquial writing into a new face that blended both the roman and some of the cursive affectations from everyday writing. And so he conceived a familiar type style that would prove very readable to the educated, and a type that took up substantially less room, which made a great deal of sense to publishers planning to print most of Latin classic literature.

Today, most designers will tell you that italic isn't as readable as normal styled type because it is light, cursive, small and narrow. For the most part, they are correct. It's best to use italics sparingly, only where style dictates. For example, use italics with foreign words, book and magazine titles and the like. Because italic is graceful and fluid, it is tempting to integrate it into one's design.

As the name implies, **wordspacing** is the amount of space between words. Wordspacing is figured or measured in full and half units and may be set anywhere from very loose (+1 unit) to very tight (-1 unit). (Remember, a unit is one-eighteenth of an EM. Wordspacing may be used for a single line or for an entire galley of type. The reasons for its use vary, but the most common one is obvious: to squash a slightly

As the name implies, **wordspacing** is the amount of space between words. Wordspacing is figured or measured in full and half units and may be set anywhere from very loose (+1 unit) to very tight (-1 unit). (Remember, a unit is one-eighteenth of an EM. Wordspacing may be used for a single line or for an entire galley of type. The reasons for its use vary, but the most common

As the name implies, **wordspacing** is the amount of space between words. Wordspacing is figured or measured in full and half units and may be set anywhere from very loose (+1 unit) to very tight (-1 unit). (Remember, a unit is one-eighteenth of an EM. Wordspacing may be used for a single line or

Figure 3.46

You can control the amount of space between words with wordspacing. It is figured or measured in units. Compare the three justified examples. The first is set tight; the middle one is set with normal wordspacing; and the he last one is set very loose.

These days, it is also stylish to use italic in captions, credits and other short copy blocks. Use them wherever you should be using them, stylistically. But if you intend to incorporate italic into your publication's stylebook, do so understanding its shortcomings. Consider going to a version that is slightly heavier in weight or use a larger point size. However, whatever you do, don't use italic type in reverse blocks, unless the point size is 18 or larger.

Wordspacing

As the name implies, **wordspacing** is the amount of space between words. Wordspacing is figured or measured in full and half units and may be set anywhere from very loose (+1 unit) to very tight (minus 1 unit). (Remember, a unit is one-eighteenth of an em. Wordspacing may be used for a single line or for an entire galley of type. The reasons for its use vary, but the most common one is obvious: to squash a slightly longer story into a smaller space, or to stretch a slightly shorter story into a larger space. Wordspacing is a design tool in itself and may also be used to better isolate words. (To get a better idea of how wordspacing affects the look of your type, see **Figure 3.32**.)

Figure 3.47 _____
*Samata Associates used typography to help maintain an informal feel throughout this Leaf annual report. Notice how the diagonal, Z-readout on the captions reinforce the candid feel of this photograph; note, too, how the configuration of the type echoes the structural composition of the photo—a similar Z-readout from the boy's head to the toy airplane to arm, where the caption begins. Also see **Figures 9.33** and **9.34** from the same publication. Main photography by Terry Heffernan; Dennis Dooley made the product shots. Design by Pat and Greg Samata of Chicago. Reprinted with permission from Leaf, Inc. and Samata Associates.*

Letterspacing

Like wordspacing, **letterspacing** uses the unit system to fine-tune spacing distances—the amount of space provided between the letters of a word. This book is set in normal letterspacing, approximately minus one-half unit. Although letterspacing varies from typeface to typeface, this is the most common spacing, at least for *copy.*

Generally speaking, display copy, especially advertising heads, is set much tighter than copy. And these days it is considered very stylish to squeeze letters together with minus letterspacing. In the case of downstyle display type, heavy-handed minus letterspacing may make single words ligatures, that is, join or intersect the letter strokes. Especially tight letterspacing, however crowded, knits words and makes heads more distinctive-looking. But it may do so at the cost of readability. This is a risky tactic. Any time readability suffers, you are likely to lose readers. If you frustrate them too many times, you may lose them for good. With larger publications a single percent or even fractions of a percentage may translate to thousands of possible customers or members of your audience.

Typeface

The look of your typeface communicates before the reader makes sense of your publication's content. Without realizing it, the reader makes associations, judgments and connections to the type you've chosen for headlines, body and other particulars in your publication. Type affects your formality, credibility and

Letterspacing allows you to fine-tune the area between letters; you can perform this manipulation on a single word, line or entire article or book.

Letterspacing allows you to fine-tune the area between letters; you can perform this manipulation on a single word, line or entire article or book.

Letterspacing allows you to fine-tune the area between letters; you can perform this manipulation on a single word, line or entire article or book.

Figure 3.48 _____

Letterspacing allows you to fine-tune the area between letters; you can perform this manipulation on a single word, line or entire article or book. Here you see very tight, normal and loose handlings of letterspacing. Compare them for readability.

feel. It colors the mood of your communication. What's more, type generally makes up a disproportionate share of your message.

Before you even consider opening up a type catalog, assess your medium, your client, that client's image and your real target, the audience at large. Should you be communicating formally or informally? Are you publishing an annual report or a flyer? A newsletter to university biology researchers or a bowling team? Do you want the look of the publication to be more traditional or contemporary? Are they concerned with matters dealing with high finance or selecting an impulse item at the check-out line? However exaggerated, these questions are just as relevant to you in establishing type considerations as they were for considering your initial design.

Roman faces tend to be more traditional and direct, more trusted. They are also very readable. On the other hand, sans serifs are fashionable and more contemporary; they are also more legible. Juggling one or two of each within a publication design is a common solution for many designers.

This comes full circle to a point made earlier in the chapter. The purpose of type is to be read. It is not to dazzle, be clever, stylish or to win awards. Mind you, your typography ought to be both fashionable and communicative. But watch out when style overshadows function and content. Always think audience and your communication purposes first.

Before you select a typeface, study the type categorization section of this chapter, and all of the details on type specification. Each "type specing" area affords a full array of possibilities that should be tied to the audience, client, client image and strategy for the task at hand. There are no easy answers. But the successful ones come by careful and inventive means.

White Space and Margins

Too often white space is either overlooked, or seen as a gaping misjudgment, a blank oversight to be filled. The fact is that white space provides the reader that important visual relief that makes any length of copy more inviting. It also establishes unity, organization, division or emphasis.

Most of all, however, it is an essential ingredient to efficient reading. White space is closely linked to improved readability in wordspacing, appropriate letterspacing, leading, line length and margins.

Margins dramatically affect how well type reads, and determine whether we even read what is placed in front of us. Whenever we overload a page or design with type or other elements, we defeat its purpose. Which is to be read. The next time you page through a magazine, notice where you hesitate or stop. Most likely, it is to some open place where your vision is neither crowded by wall-to-wall typography, nor repelled by narrow column or page margins. Art directors and designers don't "open up" the first page of an article or feature to waste space or spend more money. They know that the sudden island of white will invite your eyes, tired after swimming through a sea of gray. Even artwork and photography use generous amounts of white or neutralized space within their borders and are heavily bordered by more white space.

What's more, margins help us track more accurately and easily from line to line. If you don't believe that, try this: Select a familiar magazine or newspaper

Figure 3.49 _____

Because the letter construction of nearly all sans serif faces are uniformly stroked, they are more legible and consequently more readable in reverse blocks. Compare the read of the sans serif on the left to the modern roman.

Letter from "Mark Twain."
(Special Travelling Correspondent of the *Alta*.)

Wherever we went, in Europe, Asia, or Africa, we made a sensation, and, I suppose I may add, created a famine. None of us had ever been anywhere before; we all hailed from the interior; travel was a wild novelty to us, and we conducted ourselves in accordance with the natural instincts that were in us, and trammeled ourselves with no ceremonies, no conventionalities. We always took care to make it understood that we were Amiercans—Americans!

Letter from "Mark Twain."
(Special Travelling Correspondent of the *Alta*.)

Wherever we went, in Europe, Asia, or Africa, we made a sensation, and, I suppose I may add, created a famine. None of us had ever been anywhere before; we all hailed from the interior; travel was a wild novelty to us, and we conducted ourselves in accordance with the natural instincts that were in us, and trammeled ourselves with no ceremonies, no conventionalities. We always took care to make it understood that we were Amiercans—Americans!

Times

A B C D E F G H I J K L M N O P Q R
S T U V W X Y Z a b c d e f g h i j k l m
n o p q r s t u v w x y z 1 2 3 4 5 6 7 8 9
0

Stone

A B C D E F G H I J K L M N O P Q R
S T U V W X Y Z a b c d e f g h i j k l
m n o p q r s t u v w x y z 1 2 3 4 5 6
7 8 9 0

Bodoni

A B C D E F G H I J K L M N O P Q R
S T U V W X Y Z a b c d e f g h i j k l
m n o p q r s t u v w x y z 1 2 3 4 5 6 7 8
9 0

Bookman

A B C D E F G H I J K L M N O P
Q R S T U V W X Y Z a b c d e f g
h i j k l m n o p q r s t u v w x y z
1 2 3 4 5 6 7 8 9 0

Futura

A B C D E F G H I J K L M N O P Q R
S T U V W X Y Z a b c d e f g h i j k l
m n o p q r s t u v w x y z 1 2 3 4 5 6
7 8 9 0

Garamond

A B C D E F G H I J K L M N O P Q
R S T U V W X Y Z a b c d e f g h i j
k l m n o p q r s t u v w x y z 1 2 3 4
5 6 7 8 9 0

Goudy

ABCDEFGHIJKLMNOPQR
STUVWXYZabcdefghijklm
nopqrstuvwxyz1234567890

Helvetica

ABCDEFGHIJKLMNOPQ
RSTUVWXYZabcdefghijk
lmnopqrstuvwxyz123456
7890

Korinna

ABCDEFGHIJKLMNOPQ
RSTUVWXYZabcdefghij
klmnopqrstuvwxyz123
4567890

Lubalin Graph

ABCDEFGHIJKLMNOPQ
RSTUVWXYZabcdefghi
jklmnopqrstuvwxyz12
34567890

Palatino

ABCDEFGHIJKLMNOPQR
STUVWXYZabcdefghijkl
mnopqrstuvwxyz1234567
890

and choose an interesting article or column. Tear out the page of the piece. Then, with a scissors, trim the top, bottom and both sides of the copy to the type. Which is to say, cut away the margins—all of them. Now read it.

It is highly likely that you will encounter a good number of tracking and realigning problems, and that you'll give up reading within a few minutes. Side margins help us track. The point is that white space has a specific function. It is not just aesthetic generosity, or compensation for a story that came in too short.

For more information on white space see **Chapter 2**.

Reverses

Typographically, reverses place white letters against a background page color; usually, this means putting white copy against black, although specific colors and screens thereof may also be used. (See **Figure 3.28**.)

Research strongly suggests that reverse lettering is considerably less readable than black type on white. The classic example cited by most designers and teachers of design comes from David Ogilvy, who recommended that an ad for

Figure 3.52 _____

Although photography dominates this spread, white space and type are used creatively to make a memorable layout. The photograph on left page is fully bled, its caption—run lower left corner of right page—and title (left, mid-page) are printed sans serif in red ink. Note, too, how the pullout, run larger but not in red, is placed in the opposite corner of the right page above the small image in the generous margin of white. Both photos were run as four-color black and white. Reprinted with permission of Texas Monthly, *D. J. Stout, art director. Photography by Wyatt McSpadden.*

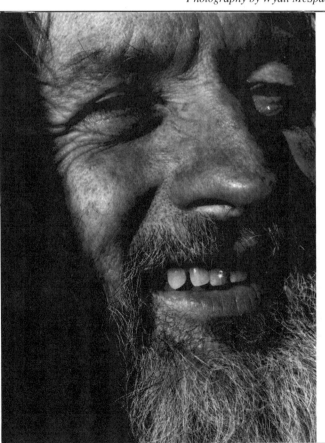

the Save the Children Federation be switched from reverse to black type and photography on white. They heeded his advice, and raised twice as much money as did the original reversed magazine advertisement.

While reverses may add drama and power to a design, they do so at the expense of readability. Reversed copy generally presents a tougher read, especially when copy is lengthy. In scant amounts, say, for headlines or in short reverse blocks, they work fine.

If you must use reverses, choose a legible type. Sans serifs stand out better than most romans. When romans are reversed, their serifs and thin strokes become difficult to discern. They are often swallowed up when cheaper printing methods or materials are used, because the fine lines and precision of the serifs become muddied in reverses. If you must choose a Roman for your reverse block, select an old-style version, one with minimal contrast between its letter strokes And try to avoid using an italic, unless you're running a large point size. Italic structure is lighter than its upright counterpart. Its tapered, cursive quality is flimsier and will blot, clot and fill in dark backgrounds.

A good rule of thumb is to increase your point size no less than two points wherever you've marked reverse copy. (If two points cannot be added, go to the next larger point size.) Reading smaller point sizes in a reverse field is particularly difficult. Imagine reading a novel in 6-point legalese. Reading even moderate amounts of normally sized copy in a reverse field has the same effect. If you must use a reverse for any copy block, keep the copy short and sweet.

The same principles of optical weight you learned in the second chapter of this book apply here. Black or dark areas weigh more than white or lighter toned or colored areas. This is as important to typographic decisions as it is to design decisions.

Figure 3.53 _____

Compare this two-page spread with the one on the opposite page. Although both are good solutions, the design approaches are as different as night and day. In this case, the photography is given a full bleed for both pages; even folio lines are surprinted atop the artwork. Then a tint block is figured into the left page and gear wheels and type are integrated into the title. Notice how the copy is sculpted around the dominating typographic arrangement. Reprinted with permission from Bass Player *magazine, a publication of Miller-Freeman, Inc. Photograph by Peter Figen, art direction by Paul Haggard.*

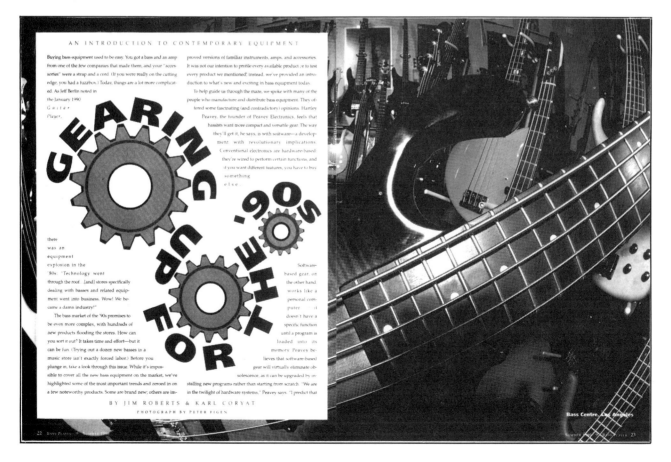

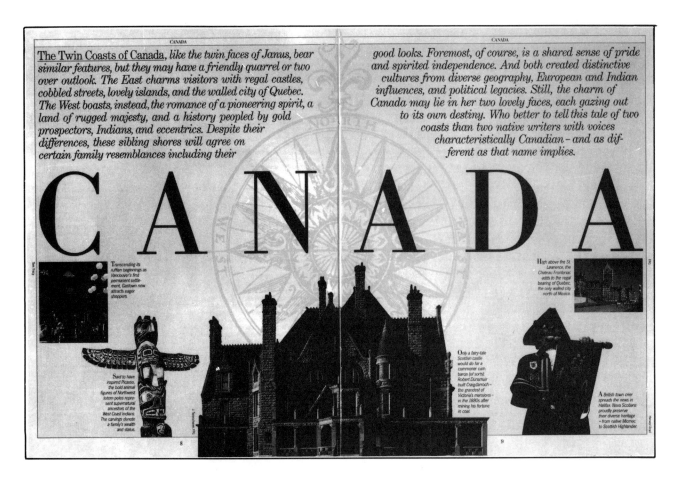

CANADA

The Twin Coasts of Canada, like the twin faces of Janus, bear similar features, but they may have a friendly quarrel or two over outlook. The East charms visitors with regal castles, cobbled streets, lovely islands, and the walled city of Quebec. The West boasts, instead, the romance of a pioneering spirit, a land of rugged majesty, and a history peopled by gold prospectors, Indians, and eccentrics. Despite their differences, these sibling shores will agree on certain family resemblances including their

good looks. Foremost, of course, is a shared sense of pride and spirited independence. And both created distinctive cultures from diverse geography, European and Indian influences, and political legacies. Still, the charm of Canada may lie in her two lovely faces, each gazing out to its own destiny. Who better to tell this tale of two coasts than two native writers with voices characteristically Canadian – and as different as that name implies.

Transcending its ruffian beginnings as Vancouver's first permanent settlement, Gastown now attracts eager shoppers.

Said to have inspired Picasso, the bold animal figures of Northwest totem poles represent supernatural ancestors of the West Coast Indians. The carvings denote a family's wealth and status.

Only a fairy-tale Scottish castle would do for a commoner cum baron (of sorts). Robert Dunsmuir built Craigdarroch – the grandest of Victoria's mansions – in the 1880s after mining his fortune in coal.

High above the St. Lawrence, the Chateau Frontenac adds to the regal bearing of Quebec, the only walled city north of Mexico.

A British town crier spreads the news in Halifax, Nova Scotia, proudly preserve their diverse heritage – from native Micmac, to Scottish Highlander.

8   9

Figure 3.54

This spread uses two small full frame photos and three silhouette photographs, a bridging title in red ink, an extensive summary which contours the compass (screened in yellow) and a tint block for its design. Despite all that, its design is simple, symmetrical and very inviting. Reprinted with permission from Skald *magazine and Pentagram. Art direction by Kit Hinrichs. Photography by Harvey Lloyd, Tom Tracy and Jay Taposchaner, FPG.*

Surprinting

To some, surprinting means printing black type atop a gray or colored area. It also refers to any typography placed atop artwork, photography or any form of illustration.

A common practice used by some designers for feature pages and magazine (and other publication) covers, surprinting is a typographical tactic used to hawk one's wares, benefits, nameplate, feature articles or most current model. It is to publications what a shout is to everyday conversations.

Photography and illustration are different than typography and each has its own job. Most editors would have heart attacks if other words (or images) were superimposed on top of their editorial material. On the other hand, no one seems to blink an eye when titles, decks, teases and blurbs are paved across a publication's photography or illustration.

Most designers won't pit one against the other. (Closely examine the best posters you find. In most cases, the typography does not interfere with the visual content of the poster.) There are many good alternatives to surprinting, but if you have to surprint, do so against blank or neutral areas of an image. Make sure, too, that there is sufficient contrast so that your dark type isn't absorbed by dark tones or colors.

Overprinting and surprinting are two entirely different things. **Overprinting** involves the integration of colors (or screened variations of colors) to give the feel of a third color. Printing blue with yellow would produce green; red with yellow would create orange, for example. By varying each color's screen percentage, you give the illusion that you are using more than two colors. When you use overprinting naturally—say, overprinting a photograph of a sunset in red and yellow—you end up with not just red, yellow and white, but various shades of orange, so that the reproduction of the sunset more closely resembles how it might appear using full color.

On the other hand, **dropouts** are either lettering or halftone areas that have been opaqued out. They are the opposite of surprinting.

Breaking Up the Gray: Working Strategies

Typographically, nothing is less inviting than a gray page, that is, a page without photos, illustrations or any graphic devices whatsoever. Visuals are the best way to open up a page, but sometimes you must find other graphic alternatives. Some of the better ways to offset the gray follow.

Initial and **dropped-initial letters** are a time-honored convention. They began as elaborate illustrations in illuminated manuscripts in the middle ages. While they usually refer to the first letters in the copy of an article or advertisement, often they are employed throughout a communication to show transitional or chronological breaks. Usually considerably larger than the copy point size, they may also be bolded or styled differently. Very often, too, they are letters from a completely different race. In this text, for example, the copy is roman and the dropped initials are sans serif.

Designers know that initial letters improve readability by breaking up the gray of a page, and invite readership by providing a clear entry point. They also dress out a page. Think of initial letters as a niche that funnels the eye into your copy, because that is exactly what initials do.

There are a number of different approaches to the initial letter. The standard initial letter (or **raised initial letter**) is simply a larger first letter in a word at the beginning of the top paragraph of a text or text section. (See **Figure 3.36**.) It is usually weighted or styled differently from the copy's face or from a different family or race altogether.

The **dropped-initial letter** is literally dropped into the body of the first paragraph. But it has a couple variations: the straitjacketed, contoured and stacked dropped-initial letter.

The **straitjacketed dropped-initial letter** runs an invisible line around the total unit space of the dropped-initial letter. Typically, straitjacketed dropped initials have a strong vertical drop along the full length of the letter parallel with the outside (or right) edge of the unit space, and an even horizontal space from that outside edge to the left margin. So, lines of copy make an even, perpendicular field to the right of the dropped-initial letter and also run beneath its unit space.

In the case of the **contoured dropped-initial letter**, copy runs parallel to the diagonal or curved right side of the letter. The copy edge echoes or visually reinforces the outside line of the letter. By contrast, a **stacked-initial letter** is placed atop the copy block. In some instances copy-sized type may run beneath the width of the lower stroke of the letter, or between the two lowermost strokes of that letter.

Today, both initial letters and dropped-initial letters are in vogue. But not too long ago, a client refused to allow the use of dropped-initial letters in an annual report because he felt that they were reminiscent of fairy tales. He was not about to have his new image positioning misconstrued as something out of Grimm's.

This drives home a number of points about typography and design. The first is that most stylistic typographic conventions come and go. Thankfully, much of what is really hot and timely today will be thought trite and "old hat" tomorrow. And some of what is widely accepted now has, in fact, been resurrected from the past. Secondly, we must remember that clients and editors have their own sense of style. They may need to be updated or reacquainted with a style's cyclical tendency, but not condescended to. Finally, if you can provide sound reasoning and explanations for your work and ideas, you will receive a lot less argument and a great deal more understanding. In other words, have rationales beyond "intuition" for your decisions. Solid reasons for how you use typography make for remarkable defenses of how you've envisioned or "speced" a job.

Figure 3.55 _____

Here are five variations of the initial letter. They are the raised initial letter, contoured initial letter, straitjacketed initial letter, stacked initial letter and a wrapped initial letter.

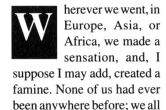

Wherever we went, in Europe, Asia, or Africa, we made a sensation, and, I suppose I may add, created a famine. None of us had ever been anywhere before; we all hailed

Wherever we went, in Europe, Asia, or Africa, we made a sensation, and, I suppose I may add, created a famine. None of us had ever been

Wherever we went, in Europe, Asia, or Africa, we made a sensation, and, I suppose I may add, created a famine. None of us had ever been anywhere

Wherever we went, in Europe, Asia, or Africa, we made a sensation, and, I suppose I may add, created a famine. None of us had ever been any

Wherever we went, in Europe, Asia, or Africa, we made a sensation, and, I suppose I may add, created a famine. None of us had ever been anywhere before; we all

Turn the situation around. Think how you might react in their respective positions to anything unfamiliar or unsettling. Especially when that publication bears your sign-off, established relationship with a client, or your company name and money.

- **Widows** are short lines at the end of a paragraph. Some designers disdain any kind of widow, especially the one-word variety. But widows can open up the gray of a page by lightening the darker texture with the white space left in their wake. And anything that brightens a page improves readership. Orphans—widows that appear at the top of a column—should be avoided.

- **Pull quotes** are strong quotations pulled from a story or article or succinct summaries of a paragraph or section of the text. When no other graphics or visuals are available, these make a logical strategy. Because they are set in a larger point size and perhaps even a different style, they provide graphic contrast to the gray type. If it is functional—that is, interesting, provoking, startling or enticing—the pull quote itself should attract readership. Pull quotes also help flesh out headlines, subheads or teases.

- **Crossheads** are one of the most functional of strategies. Normally, a crosshead is a terse phrase or statement that summarizes a point or section of information. A full page of copy might employ anywhere from a couple to perhaps a half-dozen of them. Typically, extra leading or white space is provided above and below each crosshead, and generally they are bolded. On occasion you'll find them sized up a couple of points.

Crossheads provide a thorough shake-up of the gray. Additionally, they impart the gist or sense of an ad, article or story, so even if readers don't delve into the text, they come away with some understanding of its message. What's more, well-written crossheads can entice readers to stop and read an article. Also effective in advertising and direct mail, they are a tool that communicators should take advantage of more often.

IN PROFILE

Chip Davis

The Man Behind Mannheim Steamroller Makes Arranging Look Like Magic

BY DEBORAH STARR SEIBEL

N THE MIDST OF ALL the electronic wizardry—a mind-numbing array of 20th-century synthesizers, samplers, and digital and computer technology—it comes as a jolt to know that one highly successful composer/arranger/producer/performer *never* enters the studio without his candle, teddy bear, and crystal wand.

"I have these good-luck things," says Chip Davis, the Omaha-based creative force behind classical-rock hybrid Mannheim Steamroller and the thematic "Fresh Aire" series of epic recordings known to new age enthusiasts and audiophiles everywhere. "I'm kind of superstitious." To this prolific composer, a simple candle offers a means of clearing the mind. "Flame has always mystified mankind," says Davis. "So when I have to totally compose something from scratch, I stare at it until my mind is a blank."

Also helping him clear the mental canvas of extraneous thoughts and worries is a fuzzy teddy bear. "My wife gave it to me six years ago when I went to record with the London Symphony Orchestra and I was really nervous. When I look at it, I know that someone is caring about how I'm doing."

But it's the magic wand with its cut crystal handle that helps clear Davis' path to the creative process and allows the artist to begin filling his musical canvas. "I get up really early when I'm composing," says Davis, "and I look through the handle at the moon." Calm, fearless, and inspired by the universe, Davis can begin the work of composing and arranging.

Despite his meditative creative method, Davis also is one of the most hard-nosed, cost-efficient producers in the business. He has been known to take a song from composition to computer print-out in less than two hours. But the studio in his basement—for all its 48 digital channels and MIDI bells and whistles—is just a highly sophisticated packaging tool for a single, all-important concept: the song.

"That's the most important thing," says Davis, who agrees with the notion that some music arrangers may be distracted, even confused, by the number of modern musical and technical options at their disposal. "I come from the standpoint that less is usually more.

"Take a song like 'Deck The Halls,'" suggests Davis, referring to a cut on Mannheim Steamroller's phenomenally successful 1985 holiday album, *A Mannheim Steamroller Christmas.* "The basic topic of that song is fun. You're not going to want an arrangement in a minor tone, or one that uses a lot of dark instruments. You try to follow what the song *means.*"

On a practical level, following the song's meaning for Davis involves establishing the chords, bass line, and melody to give the piece what he calls a "black and white framework," or solid foundation. "That basic framework should sound good," Davis says, "covering rhythm, tempo, and the brightness or darkness of the whole piece."

Then the "coloring" process begins, with Davis injecting what he calls the "textures and surfaces" of the music. "That's when I start adding strings," he notes, "and other instruments to enhance the mood and convey the

CONTINUED ON PAGE 21

Figure 3.56 _____

In this instance, a wrapped initial letter is centered beneath and printed slightly atop the artwork. Note the way the type has been contoured around the circular wrap and how the centered subhead and byline compliment this design. Reprinted with permission of EQ *magazine, a publication of Miller-Freeman, Inc. Art director, Saroyan Humphrey; Elizabeth Ledgerwood and Rick Eberly, graphics associates.*

Typography: Basics   115

Figure 3.57 _____

*This page from a house magazine
shows a number of stylistic devices,
including headline, subheads, pull
quotes, and lines.*

• **Subheads** don't have quite the strength or enticement of crossheads, but
they do work hard. As the name implies, they run after or beneath a
headline. Their function is to clarify a title or headline and, in many
instances, to tease the audience into reading the story. Normally, they are
set in some version of the headline's typography but are often from
another race of type altogether. On occasion they may be **decked**, that is,

---

Security is a full-time job for Dallas General Alarm

by Ellen Hart

Technology and common sense blend to provide a thoroughly modern security service

---

The sign on the door reads "Grade 'A' UL Central Station." To the people at Dallas General Alarm (DGA) and to the hundreds of businesses and homes they protect, this means the availability of some of the best alarm and intrusion detection systems in the country. In fact, almost every improvement made to DGA over the past few years has had as its goal the attainment of UL certification.

In 1924, Underwriters Laboratories, Inc. began offering a means of identifying burglar alarm systems that met acceptable minimum standards. The installing company can apply for investigation of their services and if found qualified, may be issued UL certification.

To the customer, this certification can mean a large reduction (sometimes up to 70 percent) in insurance premiums, depending on the exact grade and extent of the UL approved service used.

The over-a-thousand customers who either lease or by alarm or detection systems from DGA range from some of the biggest businesses in Dallas, to private residences. In addition, all of the schools in the Dallas area are monitored from the DGA central station against break in and vandalism.

The monitoring devices, located at the DGA central control, vary from a simple paper tape printout to actual voice communication with the premises being protected. For instance, the card-key system used by Atlantic Richfield Company allows access to certain areas through the use of a magnetic card inserted into a slot in the door. Access is forbidden to those lacking the proper clearance and the number and time of the attempted access are printed out at the DGA central station.

By far, the most impressive system is the "Hyper Guard Sound System" which allows the central station operators actually to listen into a building or home once the

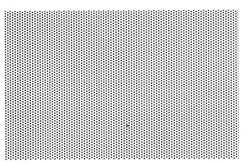

Dave Michaels of Dallas General Alarm sits in front of the main counsole from which dozens of businesses are monitored daily.

system is activated. If the building is entered, the sound sensitive system is activated causing an alarm to go off at the DGA central station. By the use of microphones installed on the premises, the DGA operators can then determine the presence of an intruder. The owners, of course, sign in and out verbally when they open and close. Most of these customers also carry the special "holdup" feature of this system

> ## "For the three or four dollars a day this system costs, they couldn't even afford a guard dog."

which allows them to trigger, unnoticed, an alarm in the event of a robbery.

"We tried out a lot of other sound-activated systems," says Michaels, "but the 'Hyper Guard' made by Associated Products Corporation is the best I've ever seen." Michaels says that the Hyper Guard system is probably 20 times more sensitive than most other brands DGA has tried. "And, in our business, sensitivity is a key component of a successful detection."

Once an alarm is received from any of

the hundreds of points serviced by DGA, it is only a matter of seconds before security guards, police, ambulance or fire department are notified and on their way. DGA maintains direct, no-dial lines to all of these agencies.

DGA currently contracts with Smith-Loomis which dispatches two or three security guards to each of DGA's calls. "Our average response time is under 4 1/2 minutes," says Dave Michaels. "Of course, we often have to wait on the owner to show up to let us in." Michaels says that if DGA keeps a key to the premises, another 10 percent often can be taken off on insurance premiums because it allows a faster response time and a higher apprehension rate. "Recently, we got two apprehensions in three alarms at a local pharmacy," he says. "We roll on every suspicious alarm. UL only allows one opening and one closing time per business unless prearranged," says Michaels. "This way, we know exactly when there should be nobody on the premises."

DGA offers a number of different systems. Some respond to motion, and some to sound. There are systems with silent alarms and systems on sight alarms fit to frighten the toughest intruder; and, DGA also handles smoke and heat detection systems. But, the key to a UL Grade "A" certified system, says Michaels, is the central control. "That's the added factor in a Grade 'A' system," he says. "We know immediately when something has occured, and we respond."

"We don't expect more than a couple of hundred customers for the UL system over the next few years," says Dave Michaels, "but that's all right. Our customers know their needs and they know that they can't get a better system for the price." Collins smiles. "For the three or four dollars a day this system costs, they couldn't even afford a guard dog."

22

Figure 3.58 _____

Dropouts are not to be confused with reverses. Typographically, a dropout is type dropped out to white on any halftone less than one hundred percent.

Figure 3.59 _____

Basically, reverses are dropouts run across a solid background: that is, any area run in one hundred percent of its color—black, blue, red, whatever color.

run as a series of short subheads. Decked subheads are not as popular today as they once were, but styles are always in flux.

- **Bullets** are generally employed here for design and organizational purposes, but they also bring a page more typographic color. Bullets or their typographic equivalents are effective when you have a number of unrelated points or ideas to make. They allow you to tick off those points cleanly and quickly. At a glance you can see where they begin and end. They also help organize the main points or features by breaking them out separately.

- **Screens** or **screen tints** are a common design strategy. Screens are halftone dot patterns, which are figured in percentages of black (or another color) from 10 percent to 100 percent. For example, a 20 percent screen is an unmodulated halftone dot pattern that shows 20 percent of whatever color you're printing—and 80 percent white (or whatever color the paper stock happens to be). Be careful if you're surprinting or running copy atop them. Too dark a screen could swallow or dim the type. Try not to run type over anything more than 20 percent; reading muddies up quickly with screens any heavier.

  The opposite is the case when using **dropouts**. Typographically, dropouts are type dropped out to white on any halftone less than 100 percent. **Reverses** are dropouts run across a solid background. Readability should guide you in selecting the proper contrast when using surprinting or dropouts. (See **Figure 3.58**.)

- **Rules** are lines that are used for graphic or decorative purposes. They may separate or join design elements. In the past they were available as strips of metal (letterpress). Today you're more likely to use them as rolls of adhesive tape or electronically via the computer. They're available in a great variety of styles (double lines of equal width or unequal width, triple lines, etc.) and widths. Normally, rule width is calibrated in points. Use them sparingly. Too many can turn a design into a super grid.

Typography
Part B: Computers

Probably the single most revolutionary breakthrough in computer technology, for publications people at least, has been the ability to set type. The advent of desktop publishing has been a blessing for some and curse for others. It all depends on who you are.

For years, art directors and layout artists struggled with "conventional" means for mocking up type. One tedious and time-consuming method was to sketch in type blocks and hand-letter display type (see **Figure 3.60**). Another method, press-down lettering, required the purchase of sheets of transfer lettering which was painstakingly placed on the mechanical, carefully spaced, and rubbed down and burnished.

With a little practice, *almost* anyone can set their own type for publication. While you can imagine the relief among designers and artists when computer-set type became available to everyone, computer-set type has not exactly pleased the typesetting industry.

Millions of dollars a year are spent setting copy in type. In fact, quite a large percentage of any print production budget goes into typesetting. Computer typesetting has cut down on cost and time. Before, you had to type your copy, spec it for copy fitting, mark it, take it to the typesetter, wait until it was typeset, proof the type, have the typesetter make any necessary corrections, and then paste it up. Now, typesetting, corrections and additions, and pasteup can all be done by one person at the same time. And costs can often be cut by a third or more.

Smart typesetters and printers have been quick to keep themselves in the production chain by offering valuable services such as Linotronic output or some other computer-assisted production function. Many printers and typesetters now accept computer disks or direct feeds from your computer.

Desktop publishing has probably been of the most benefit to the smaller or single-person office. What once took a number of intermediaries to accomplish can now be done by one person. Of course, you have to know something about writing, design and editing to have your publications look professional. Before, sending your copy out to a typesetter meant that a professional would be setting your type—someone with expertise and knowledge in type and typesetting. If you are going to take on this job yourself, you'd best become something of an expert in your own right. Fortunately, the basics of type apply to computer-set type as well as traditionally set type.

Figure 3.60 _____

Traditional type layout techniques. *Indicating type on a mockup the "old-fashioned" way meant developing a technique for "graying out" the areas designated as type blocks. This gave an illusion of type without actually having to set it just for the mockup or comp. Two of the most common techniques were lining in copy blocks or rendering them as rows of "squiggles." The headlines were usually set in press-down lettering.*

Digital Fonts

Digital fonts are computer-designed and -generated typefaces, and although type generated on the computer should be identical to type set the conventional way, it's not. First of all, computer-set type is standardized. That is, the eccentricities and flourishes of hand-designed typefaces are often sacrificed when the type is digitized. What this means to the true type afficionado is that many of the built-in irregularities that give typefaces their distinctive charm are missing.

For example, some of the older typefaces had different length descenders for different letter or word combinations or leading. For example, a *y* on a line above a word with an ascender such as a *d* might need to have a version with a shortened ascender, while set above an *o* it might need a longer descender. This slight irregularity from letter to letter within the same face is what adds charm to traditional type.

Bit-mapped and Outline Fonts

Your computer's printer also affects your finished product. Let's assume that for most publications, daisy-wheel and dot-matrix printers are ruled out. If you are outputting directly to a printer for final copy, you'll want to use a laser printer. And, you will most likely use one of two technologies—a printer based on Apple's LaserWriter or one based on Hewlett-Packard's LaserJet. Both will give you quick, clean copy, but each handles type differently.

The LaserJet-type printer stores type in its memory as bit maps (dot patterns) that restrict the printer to specific sizes. If the printer has information on 12-point Helvetica then it will only print 12-point Helvetica. It won't print 24-point Helvetica. If you want other sizes or other fonts, you have to provide them either through cartridges or software that is downloadable (can be loaded from your computer into your printer). The only problem with downloadable fonts—and it affects both types of printers—is that the more information you download to your printer, the less memory it has. A standard laser printer with 1 megabyte or less of RAM (Random Access Memory, which is what your printer or computer uses *while* you're working) will quickly run out of memory.

LaserWriter-type printers use an outline method of storing type shapes. That allows you to scale your type to any size, rotate it, distort it, print it backwards, or anything else you want. This is important to desktop publishers who need to have the flexibility to work with type in all its forms. But, recent advances in hardware and software have allowed the LaserJet-type printers to approximate the capabilities of the LaserWriter-type printers.

WYSIWYG

Another problem peculiar to desktop publishing is WYSIWYG (pronounced wizzy-wig), or "what you see is what you get." Many computers and computer monitors promise WYSIWYG, but when it comes to type, few deliver. The problem is that most monitors build images out of tiny squares called pixels. Computer type fonts appear on the screen as composites of these pixels regardless of whether you are using a LaserJet-type printer or a LaserWriter-type printer. The result is that you can't often tell from your screen what your type is going to look like—or how it's going to fit—until you print it out. This

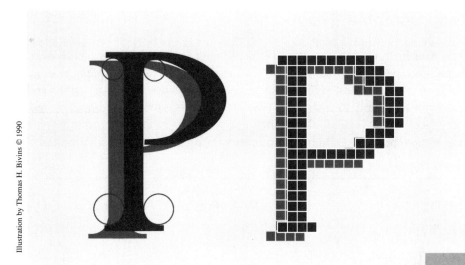
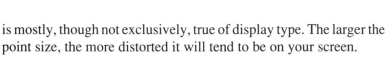

Illustration by Thomas H. Bivins © 1990

Figure 3.61 _____

Outline vs. bitmapped fonts.
Outline fonts (far left) are stored as
mathematic values allowing the
printer to perform adjustments of
almost any sort on the type. The
fonts print out "object oriented,"
that is, they appear as unbroken
curved and straight lines instead of
the ragged bit-mapped fonts (right).
Although on some laser printers,
bit-mapped fonts show up as near
letter perfect, under a magnifying
glass you will see the ragged edges.
When used as display type, the
raggedness is even more apparent.

is mostly, though not exclusively, true of display type. The larger the point size, the more distorted it will tend to be on your screen.

One method of cutting down on distortion at larger point sizes is to load screen font versions of your typefaces in the largest available sizes.

Screen and Printer Fonts

Type fonts for the Macintosh computer, for instance, come in both printer and screen versions. You have to have both to operate efficiently. Basically, the printer font version is loaded into (or is already resident in) your printer and becomes available when you use it. Depending on your system, fonts can be loaded in a number of ways. Placing them into the system file allows some programs to load them as needed (which frees up printer memory after each font is used). Manually downloading them as you need them ties up quite a bit of printer memory, which then can only be cleared by reinitializing the printer. Placing them in separate files for downloading later, storing them on a separate hard disk, or using printer cartridges are other options.

The screen font version has to be loaded into your computer system or program so that you can get a representation of that font on your screen. To save memory space, most people load a minimum of point sizes—usually 10, 12, and 14 points in each font. As long as some point size is loaded, you can scale up or down to any point size you need. However, unless you've loaded a screen font in the exact (or near exact) point size you ultimately scale to, your screen type is going to look extremely ragged.

The problem, of course, is WYSIWYG. It is impossible to kern, for example, with large point sizes on the screen. All you can do is do it, print it, look at it printed out, and do it again. But, help is on the horizon. Already there are several programs (including Adobe *Type Manager*) available that help reduce the disparity between the type you see on the screen and the type that comes out of your printer.

Figure 3.62 _____

Screen vs. printer fonts. Above left
is a 72-point screen font much as it
might appear on a Macintosh
screen. As you can see, the bit-
mapping at this size can cause you
trouble if you are trying to align
characters or kern. The printer-
produced version on the right (from
an outline-font printer) is proof that
what you see on your screen isn't
always what you get.

Using Computer Type

Once you have decided on how your publication is to look (see individual chapters on specific publications and **Chapter 4** for layout techniques), you can decide on the typefaces, styles and sizes you want to use. The precautions and guidelines that apply to traditional type also apply to selecting computer type. Some faces and styles go with certain types of messages, and others don't. Let's look at the typefaces commonly available as resident fonts in many printers.

Times	New Century Schoolbook
Helvetica	Palatino
Bookman	

In addition to these, there are several other faces appearing as "most used" on laser printers.

Avant Garde	*Zaph Chancery*
Garamond	Souvenir
Goudy	

The computer typographer can choose from among hundreds of faces available through dozens of software manufacturers in a range of prices. One word of warning. It is usually best to stick to the traditional faces manufactured (or digitized) under auspices of the original designers or their agents. For instance, of the hundreds of faces available from International Typeface Corporation (ITC), dozens of these have been packaged by Adobe Systems. As you become more familiar with type and aware of the vast array of faces available for the computer, you will undoubtedly be tempted to purchase some of the many cloned faces. These are basically altered copies of already existing faces. Since most typefaces are copyrighted, all you have to do is alter one letter slightly in order to market a clone.

The difference between an original typeface and its clone isn't readily apparent to everyone; however, such things as line thickness, legibility at smaller point sizes, and clarity of individual characters can be important to your final product. We're not saying to avoid everything but brand-name type, but at least consider the best for your publications. After all, a lot of design skill went into the original typeface. Use that to your advantage.

Copyfitting on the Computer

Copyfitting used to require patience, a ruler, patience, a calculator (or knowledge of math), patience, knowledge of type-fitting formulas and measurements, patience and more patience. With a computer, all you need is a little know-how. Under the traditional (read "old-fashioned") method, you decided on column width and type size and the typesetter gave it back to you set that way. Unless you had a lot of money to waste, your copy might as well have been carved in stone. If you suddenly decided you needed 18-pica-wide columns instead of 24-pica-wide columns, you paid to typeset the whole thing over again.

Now, all you do is pick a point size and column width and, *voila!*—it's done. And, if you don't like it, you can do it again. It only takes seconds. Naturally, some planning is necessary up front. It might be fun to sit in front of your computer for hours playing with column width and point size, but you're probably on a deadline. Once you have a basic design in mind and have set up the grid (see **Chapter 4** for details on grids), copyfitting becomes a breeze.

For most, but not all, page-layout programs, copy is imported directly from a word processing program and then positioned on your page. That's why it's important to choose a compatible word processing program and to follow a few, basic guidelines when writing your document.

- Use a program from the same system type. That is, don't write your story on a PC system and try to transfer it to a Macintosh system. It's usually too much trouble. If you're using *PageMaker* for the Macintosh, write your copy on a Macintosh-based word processing program such as *Macwrite or* Microsoft *Word* for the Macintosh.

- Keep formatting within your word processed document to a minimum. It is usually easier simply to write in word processing and format in your page-layout program. Some minimal formatting can be done, but most of it will be lost when you import it into your page-layout program.

- Don't justify your copy in your word processing program. It will seldom match your final column width and will probably only confuse you when you go to place it on the page. Usually, there is no need to hyphenate either. Remember, your final formatting will be done in your page-layout program.

- Don't worry about faces, styles, sizes, and so on. You can assign them in your page-layout program. If you do use a specific style (bold subheads for instance) you might lose it anyway when you import the copy or set a new global style from your page-layout program's style sheet (see below).

- Set headlines and subheads for articles and other copy right in with your word processed document. Even if their style is lost during the transfer process, they will serve as designators as you begin to format. You can always re-bold as you go along. Another option, is to set display type such as headlines for feature stories, separately in your page-layout program. It is then more easily manipulated since it is a separate element.

Once you've imported the copy, you can place it, fit it, and change face, style, leading, spacing and size till your heart's content. **Figure 3.63** illustrates just some of the adjustments you can make on your own, and as many times as you want.

A word about style sheets

If your page-layout program has them, use them. In a nutshell, style sheets are electronic menus in which you designate how you want your copy to appear in its various incarnations. It remembers each description and on command will change designated text to the selected style. For example, *PageMaker* includes a style sheet on which you can pre-set typeface, size, style, leading, tab sets, indents, alignment and a number of other designations for any of several categories such as *body text*, *headlines*, *captions* and *subheads*. You can also add categories, such as *pull quotes*, to suit your particular publication's needs.

To use a style sheet, you simply select the portion of text you want to set a certain style, and then choose that style from the **style menu**. In an instant, the original text conforms to your pre-set style.

Figure 3.63 _____

Placing type in a page makeup program. All of the modifications below were accomplished in under a minute. (clockwise from the top) 12-point Times justified with auto leading; the same with 11.5 leading; auto leading flush right; in Helvetica 12-point; at 18 points; and flush left.

I was a fresh, new journalist, and needed a *nom de guerre*; so I confiscated the ancient mariner's discarded one, and have done my best to make it remain what it was in his hands—a sign and symbol and warrant that whatever is found in its company may be gambled on as being the petrified truth.

Mark Twain

I was a fresh, new journalist, and needed a *nom de guerre*; so I confiscated the ancient mariner's discarded one, and have done my best to make it remain what it was in his hands—a sign and symbol and warrant that whatever is found in its company may be gambled on as being the petrified truth.

Mark Twain

I was a fresh, new journalist, and needed a *nom de guerre*; so I confiscated the ancient mariner's discarded one, and have done my best to make it remain what it was in his hands— a sign and symbol and warrant that whatever is found in its company may be gambled on as being the petrified truth.

Mark Twain

I was a fresh, new journalist, and needed a *nom de guerre*; so I confiscated the ancient mariner's discarded one, and have done my best to make it remain what it was in his hands—a sign and symbol and warrant that whatever is found in its company may be gambled on as being the petrified truth.

Mark Twain

I was a fresh, new journalist, and needed a *nom de guerre*; so I confiscated the ancient mariner's discarded one, and have done my best to make it remain

I was a fresh, new journalist, and needed a *nom de guerre*; so I confiscated the ancient mariner's discarded one, and have done my best to make it remain what it was in his hands—a sign and symbol and warrant that whatever is found in its company may be gambled on as being the petrified truth.

Mark Twain

Display type

Display type is handled pretty much the same way as body copy. You can manipulate each of these elements to suit your needs. There are some special considerations you should be aware of, however.

- Don't always assume that the typeface you use for body copy will be just fine at 24 or 36 points. Some faces are better suited to headlines than others. The key to the proper display type is clarity. If it's clear, *then* check out the aesthetics.

- Be aware that the larger the point size, the more obvious the leading will be if set at *auto*. For example, a stacked, 36-point headline with auto leading is going to look very "loose" to the trained eye. The trick is to reduce the leading until the stack tightens up somewhat. Be careful not to let descenders bump the tops of ascenders in the lines below.

TIP: Altering the leading on display type on a Macintosh or compatible screen will often result in letters that seem to have been chopped off at the top. This is simply a screen aberration. If it bothers you, just switch to a different page view ("fit in window" to "full page view" for instance) and back. The image will clear up. You can also try moving the headline and then replacing it.

- Don't justify headlines. In longer headlines, this will create unsightly spaces between words. To center them, use the alignment command for centering rather than manually placing a flush-left headline in the center of a column. Aligning each headline will ensure consistency.

- Designate in advance exactly where you want your headline to appear. In *PageMaker*, for example, if you want to extend it beyond your column width, simply place the text tool at the starting point and, by depressing the mouse button, drag a dotted square to the farthest right-hand point you want your headline to extend to. When you type, your headline will ignore

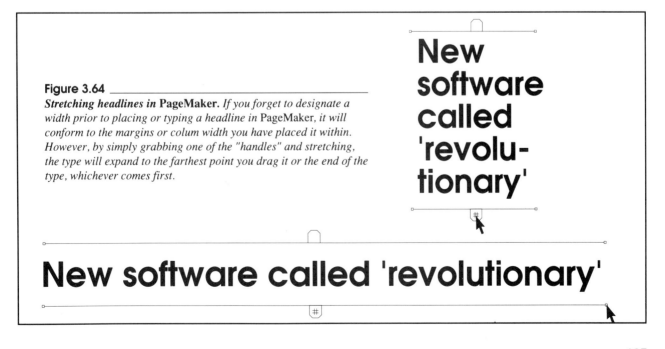

Figure 3.64 _____
Stretching headlines in PageMaker. *If you forget to designate a width prior to placing or typing a headline in* PageMaker, *it will conform to the margins or colum width you have placed it within. However, by simply grabbing one of the "handles" and stretching, the type will expand to the farthest point you drag it or the end of the type, whichever comes first.*

column indicators and continue to the designated point. Or, you can drag one of the handles (the small points at the ends of the copy lines) out to the needed width (see **Figure 3.64**).

It's best to set up style sheets for each of your categories of display type. It will save you time and frustration, especially if you are working on a multi-page document or setting up a template to be used from issue to issue. Suppose you're working on a 16-page tabloid full of headlines, subheads, pull quotes and captions. From page to page, you can't seem to remember if that second-level subhead was 14-point italic or 12-point italic bold. You have to keep "flipping" back to previous pages to check it out. If you set up a style sheet with each of these designations, you don't have to keep checking. For instance, you might have a headline style set for 36-point Helvetica bold, a first-level subhead of 18-point Times italic, a second-level subhead of 18-point Times italic underlined, and pull quotes of 14-point Helvetica bold italic. In addition, each of these elements will contain information on leading and alignment. Setting these up in advance will save you a lot of heartburn.

Kerning

Kerning, of particular concern when dealing with display type, refers to the amount of space between letters (or sometimes words). Layout problems usually account for a certain amount of automatic kerning between pairs of letters in any given typeface. For example, in some faces *o* and *e* will fit differently when paired than *t* and *e* . But, discrepancies in letterspacing at larger sizes are more apparent.

This was a problem with earlier versions of most page-layout programs. Headlines often looked awkwardly spaced. For instance, an upper case T might

Figure 3.65

Kerning*. At 72 points, the word* Toy *(top) has an unsightly spread between the* T *and the* o. *By manually kerning in* PageMaker, *we can tighten both the* o *and the* y *slightly (center). If we are not careful, however, or if we rely on the screen for accuracy, we might over kern (bottom).*

aesthetically fit closer to a lowercase *o* in a headline than the automatic-kerned setting allowed. The newer versions have compensated for this by adding manual kerning, which lets you tighten that space to your specifications. See **Figure 3. 65** for an example of how kerning works.

Figure 3.66 _____

Initial caps. Although programs such as Ventura Publisher *allow you to set guidelines for raised initial caps,* PageMaker *requires that you manually set the leading between lines. The procedure, which is simple, eliminates the problem seen in the top example. Raising the point size of a single letter set into a body of text increases the leading between the line it is on and the following line based on the point size of the raised letter, not the body copy. To avoid the gap, simply set the leading for the block manually.* PageMaker *calculates its auto leading at 120 percent of point size, regardless of the face. So 12-point Times will be auto-leaded at 14.4 points. Since* PageMaker *doesn't allow for increments of leading less than .5, you must set your manual leading at 14.5. This allow the lines to remain leaded properly despite the raised initial cap. Make sure that your leading is set to "proportional" not "top of caps" in the type menu under "spacing."*

I was a fresh, new journalist, and needed a *nom de guerre*; so I confiscated the ancient mariner's discarded one, and have done my best to make it remain what it was in his hands – a sign and symbol and warrant that whatever is found in its company may be gambled on as being the petrified truth.

I was a fresh, new journalist, and needed a *nom de guerre*; so I confiscated the ancient mariner's discarded one, and have done my best to make it remain what it was in his hands – a sign and symbol and warrant that whatever is found in its company may be gambled on as being the petrified truth.

A dorem ipsum dolor sit amet, consectetuer adipiscing elit, sed diam nonummy nibh euismod tincidunt ut laoreet dolore magna aliquam erat volutpat. Ut wisi enim ad minim veniam, quis nostrud exerci tation ullamcorper suscipit lobortis nisl ut aliquip ex ea commodo consequat. Duis autem vel eum iriure.

Figure 3.67 _____

Textwrapped initial cap. *Initial caps can be designed in an illustration program, imported, and treated as a graphic by using the textwrap function of* PageMaker. *This is probably the preferred method for those wishing to experiment with stretched or odd-sized letters as initial caps.*

Using initial caps

In most page-layout programs, initial caps can present some problems. In *Ventura Publisher* dropped caps are created and aligned automatically with a few key strokes. In other programs, such as *PageMaker*, using them is more difficult. You can either designate the actual first letter of your body copy by bolding it and raising the point size (which requires manually adjusting the leading between the line in which the cap appears and the line below it), or creating the cap as a separate piece of copy and placing it in the body copy (which requires moving the body copy to compensate for the space). See **Figures 3.66** and **3.67.**

Chapter 4

Photography
Part A: Basics

Photography is not only the most commonly used means of visual communication in publications, it has become, in one form or another, central to our experience. We use it to document both important and mundane events in our own lives. Photography has a marvelous power to fix our image and the images around us almost instantaneously. Its imagery links us to the world, and beyond.

Its highly graphic or representational nature is what makes it such a potent medium. Photography has such tremendous credibility that we often confuse it with truth, forgetting that photographs are *images* of reality and not the real thing. We believe something when we see it with our eyes, and so we believe photographs. Today, however, that credibility is strained, because photography is easily manipulated. Through computerized or digitized photography, images can be altered and overlaid with such precision that we cannot differentiate between the original and doctored imagery.

A second characteristic of photography is as fascinating as it can be troublesome. Photographic images are captured on film in split seconds. In a sense, they stop time, freezing it on a single frame of film. One of the charming things about photographs is that our images remain static over time even though we change. However, images recorded in fractions of a second can be quite deceiving. All of us have seen outrageous pictures of ourselves. Frames of film that caught us mid-word or while we blinked. Aside from not being flattering, these images are deceiving. Still another problem is that viewers tend to bring their own interpretations to the photographic image. That is why captions are so important. For these and other reasons, photography must be used with great care. Indeed, questions of ethics and photography arise often in journalism.

It is important to know up front the strengths and weaknesses of the medium, and, in at least two instances, to realize that photography's strengths and weaknesses are one and the same.

What Makes a Good Photograph?

Technically, good photographs should have the following characteristics.

- They are sharp—that is, clearly focused. Few things frustrate an art director more than receiving mushy or poorly focused photographs after photo selections have been made and layouts decided upon. Their detail should certainly hold up to standard enlargement, which is an 8" x 10" format.

- They are clean. There shouldn't be any dust, lint, abrasions, fingerprints or discoloration on the photographs. Proper cosmetics also include even borders and squarely printed photos.

- They have average contrast. Photographs are made under a wide variety of lighting conditions, but it is incumbent upon the photographer or lab technician to produce images that have average contrast. Images with too much contrast have no gray scale, and ones with too little-contrast reproduce flatly. (Incidentally, glossy photographic paper seems to work best for maximum contrast in the halftone, while matte surfaces deliver a softer or low-contrast halftone. Some production directors prefer working with semi-glossy photo paper because it provides average halftone contrast consistently.)

- They are properly and consistently printed. Each image in a given grouping of photographs should be tonally equivalent to the other photos.

Figure 4.1 _____

Greg Epperson's photography for NIKE's All Condition Gear catalog is a great working example of what makes an outstanding photograph. The images are razor sharp, clean, consistently printed and they have good contrast. In addition, the color has good saturation and the images are well composed. Notice how the inner page (left) adds to the feeling of verticality in the image of the rock climber on the left page. Reprinted with permission from NIKE, Inc. Creative direction by Ron Dumas. Photography by Greg Epperson. Design by Ron Dumas.

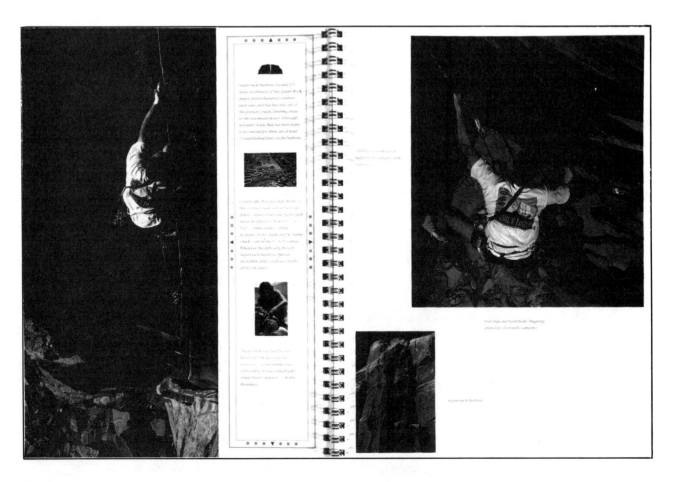

That means that in addition to being sharp, clean and properly contrasted, their gray scale and overall tonal range should be equal.

Good photographs also have structural requirements. (For a detailed discussion of design and composition, review Chapter 2.) One of the best approaches to learning photographic structure is to understand how to avoid photographic clichés. Probably the most glaring cliché is the centered image. Regardless of whether the camera's focus is split-image, overlapping or prismatic, most 35 mm cameras place their focusing systems in the middle of the viewfinder. It should come as no surprise, then, that experienced and inexperienced photographers alike position the most important element in their images in the center of the photograph. Unfortunately, because audiences see so much centered imagery, they become numbed by it.

Centering can sometimes be defended for symmetrical and other reasons. For example, centering a subject can make an image more confronting. Diane Arbus, who claimed she disregarded composition, used centering as a confrontational device in most of her work. However, in the great majority of cases, centering is the result of oversight or careless habit. Please note, though, in defense of camera designers, that long before photography had split-image focusing screens, photographers used ground glass to focus their images. All cameras still use ground glass in their viewfinders, which is to say that you have focusing alternatives. Use them. You can become accustomed to using ground glass for focusing in a short time.

Avoid over-centering by employing the **rule** or **principle of thirds**. It breaks space into thirds both vertically and horizontally. The ideal points for position-

Figure 4.2 _____

More memorable imagery; this time by Gary Nolton of Portland. This photography is from another NIKE project—a recent annual report. Both ground thirds (or a derivation therefrom) and rule of thirds have been used for structural reasons—to help establish scale and interesting proportion in the former case and for strategic placement in the latter instance. Our vision follows that of the subject here. And in the design of this text, this photograph was deliberately located on a righthand page, so the vision of the subject would lead you back to the lefthand art. Reprinted with permission from NIKE, Inc. Design by Ron Dumas. Photography by Gary Nolton.

ing are at or around where the lines intersect. Some refer to this concept as off-centering or strategic placement; both terms are quite fitting. Examining the work of your favorite photographers should illustrate and reaffirm this principle.

The second cliché is the overuse of the horizontal format. Unfortunately, some people believe that if God wanted us to make vertical photographs, he (or she) would have designed the camera differently. It doesn't occur to them to shift the camera a quarter turn to use a vertical format.

Before you even focus or meter your camera, respond to the linear structure of your image. If it is essentially a vertical image, adjust your format to accommodate its up-and-down line, and vice versa. Eliminating improper format means thinking in a linear fashion. Think *line* before you think *shape*, and shoot accordingly. Again, learn from the work of master photographers. Note how they've adjusted camera alignment to line.

One way to greatly improve linear vision is to shoot a few rolls of film of any subject with exaggerated vertical or horizontal lines, and then crop those images narrowly for your finished print. Narrow formats, incidentally, really tend to dominate a page. Their compact, exaggerated shapes call attention to themselves.

Cutting the field of the image in half is the third cliché. Perhaps it's our preoccupation with balance that makes us break images into halves: one-half

Figure 4.3 _____

Although Parker may discreetly display corporate logos in crown emblems on their pens, there is nothing particularly mysterious about how the Canadian Mapleleaf gold coin connects to the gold finish of their pens in this photograph. Terry Heffernan's meticulous studio photography employs most of the compositional devices discussed in this chapter. In addition, it says a great deal about Parker pens that words could never say. Dennis Dooley made the inset photography. Designed by Pat and Greg Samata. Reprinted with permission from Parker and Samata Associates.

TO EVERYONE WHO KNOWS
WHAT IT'S LIKE PRODUCING
BRILLIANT ADVERTISING.

Best of luck tonight from Ogilvy & Mather.

Figure 4.4 _____
Tracy Wong, then art director at Ogilvy & Mather, NY, deliberately uses symmetry here for its static effect. He says, "The original concept came from a National Geographic article on Japan. Since we couldn't get approval to use the existing image, we were forced to shoot it ourselves, which, ironically, turned out to our advantage. (The only sumo wrestler in town was actually an ex-sumo who was training to become a French chef.) By positioning him symmetrically and choosing tiny, tiny kids, we maximized his immobility."
Reprinted with permission from Ogilvy & Mather, NY and Tracy Wong. Art direction by Tracy Wong. Photography by David Langley.

sky, one-half ground; one-half background, one-half foreground. Handling proportion so mechanically creates a static spatial dynamic.

Unless you are deliberately trying to establish symmetry or imply a specific rigidity, avoid halving your space. **Ground thirds** offers a more practical way to handle proportion. By dividing space into one-third/two-third sections, one area will dominate, suggesting that it is more important. It isn't necessary to divide the design area exactly into one-third/two-third sections. Generally, uneven ratios work better than even ones. The idea is to fracture your dimensions appropriately to establish scale and show size, distance, or other spatial relationships between people, objects or areas of your photograph.

Fourth, too many publications suffer from posed photographs. You've seen these far too many times: sincere handshaking, dull ribbon cutting, official paper signing, or worse yet, speakers speaking, writers writing and committees doing what committees do—largely, nothing. If you can't come up with anything more innovative than the same old photograph, save yourself the time and money—don't make a photograph.

This is not to imply that you can't make interesting photographs of dull situations. It's not easy, mind you, but it can be done. The secret lies in using new angles and unusual perspectives, and, in being creative. Try to capture something spontaneous. Respond to candid moments that reveal personality, not stilted ones that stiffly pose your subjects. Loosen them up by talking to them before, during and after your shoot. The more at ease they feel with you, the less wooden they'll will appear.

Some of the best photographic opportunities for these kinds of situations exist before and after the posed shot, which brings to mind another important point. Shoot a lot of film, or be sure to direct whoever is responsible for the photography to make plenty of exposures. A good rule of thumb is to shoot *at least* two rolls of film for each photograph you expect to run in your publication. Indeed, if you're photographing a setup, shoot a minimum of three rolls of film per planned publication photograph. Also, design the setups before you unpack any photography gear.

Figure 4.5

Despite the limitations of black-and-white imagery, the candor and charm of Ed Eckstein's photography warms the pages of this Independence Bancorp annual report. Ed Haberman, pictured here, is a long-time testament to Lehigh Valley Bank in Bethlehem, Pa. Design by Michael Gunselman. Photography by Ed Eckstein. (Also, see their work in **Figure 9.1**.) *Reprinted with permission from Independence Bancorp and Michael Gunselman.*

How to Work with a Photographer

Take a photography course. Learn how to operate a camera and how to develop film and make prints. Learn composition by using it and become more visually literate. At the very least, read a basic photography text and teach yourself.

It is highly unlikely that this will make you a professional photographer. But you'll share a common vocabulary with the photographer and have a fundamental grasp of the medium. And you'll better understand some of its limitations and

Figure 4.6 _____

You've likely seen the work of Elliott Erwitt elsewhere. He is a master of composition and "decisive moment" photography; moreover, his photojournalistic style bridges photographic genres. Here, the broader motif—the texture and pattern of the cobblestone street—is reverberated visually in the fur coats of the women. (Also, notice the principle of thirds positioning of the subjects in the composition.) Liska and Associates of Chicago selected this Erwitt photograph to show off the tonal range of Potlatch's Quintessence paper through the four-color separation of this black-and-white image. Design by Steve Liska; photography by Elliott Erwitt/Magnum Photos, Inc. Reprinted with permission from Potlatch Corporation and Liska and Associates.

possibilities once you discover that photography consists of a great deal more than pointing a camera and squeezing the shutter release.

What then?

First, know who you're working with. There is a tremendous difference between a wildlife photographer and studio photographer. Examine or review portfolios; you may find a style, approach or arrangement that is exactly what you're looking for in a given situation.

Next, always discuss the story with the photographer—the more thoroughly the better. The editor or writer should provide a solid overview that includes the background, slant, characters and the rationale for the story, as well as anything else that may seem relevant. If any part of the piece has been put to page, share that, too. Of course you'll need to discuss where or with whom the photographer will be working: the lighting, physical layouts, personalities, and other particulars.

Figure 4.7 _____

Photography has no limitations— especially with the help of comput- ers and contemporary retouching techniques. This image of the Empire State Building began as a straight stock shot from the Image Bank. That's where all this became interesting. Tracy Wong, then art director at Goldsmith/Jeffrey, explains this visual's evolution: "A small segment of the building was stepped and repeated by computer, extending it to roughly three times its original cropped length. Areas of the blue sky were cloned to fill the new cropping. Clouds were then shifted to fill the gaps." The result is this highly acclaimed print advertisement for Crain Communication's New York Business. *Wong is currently art director at Goodby, Berlin & Silverstein in San Francisco. Reprinted with permission of Crain Communications and Tracy Wong.*

Discuss what you'd like to see. This includes providing the shooter a careful list of your proposed shots. Be specific and indicate angles, perspectives and whether the shot should be close, medium or long. Thumbnails with stick figures are appropriate and valuable. If you have swipe files of photography, you might be able to make what you envision even more specific. Being as concrete as possible will help you avoid open-ended photographic assignments. And if you can also explain why you'd like to see what you've suggested, so much the better.

Listen to the reactions and ideas of the photographer. Develop and clarify your ideas visually with thumbnails, doodles or more sophisticated means. Stick figures work fine. Remember, you're getting across important visual ideas, not putting the finishing touches on the Mona Lisa. The more explicit you are, the better the finished shots will be.

Again, shoot lots of film. Film stock is the cheapest part of any photography assignment. It is the last place to cut back your budget. Better to have a dozen strong images to choose from, than to be forced to decide between a reshoot and major plastic surgery on problem photographs. Similarly, when working with people pictures, have the photographer shoot the subject looking left, right and straight ahead. (Obviously, the photographer can move around to reposition the direction of a shot as well.) You may have a design that calls for a strong directional shot, or perhaps a last-minute change that moves a left page right. Publications work seldom runs smoothly and each issue or edition has its own share of adventure.

If photography is to play a strong role in a piece, *really* plan it. And do it with the assistance of your art director, photographer and/or other visual people. As the saying goes, plan your work and work your plan. Establish a theme or concept

Figure 4.8 _____

These images not only have power, they bear witness to the possibilities of documentary still photography, something easily forgotten in a world dominated by television.The main photograph (left) is centered, symmetrical and unpretentious. Although contrast exists tonally, its real contrast lies in its content: life and death. The latter—a dead bird—is held carefully in the hands of a girl. The photos were originally printed as four-color black and white. D. J. Stout art directed this project, "The Soul of East Texas," for Texas Monthly. *Keith Carter photographed these important images. Reprinted with permission from* Texas Monthly.

MAN WITH BLIND ROOSTER

FAMILY IN GARDEN

MEAGAN

and flesh it out with visual ideas. Suggest the composition of the dominant image and its complimentary photographs. Plan the entire design, start to finish, from specific images to how you'll use color, from type selections to directing vision through your layout. Again, swipe files and other visuals will clarify your vision and help the communication process.

Finally, photographers like to be appreciated not just for their compositional and technical skills but for their ideas. Contrary to what some believe, photographers can actually read and write. At the very least, use photographers to test captions; after all, they were there. Asking photographers to provide initial descriptions for all images being considered for publication offers a great starting point for building a caption.

Figure 4.9

Here, photographer Mark Klett uses the limestone outcropping to frame this photograph for a feature Texas Monthly *ran on the Big Bend Ranch of Texas, "Wild Forever." The pullout/caption reads: "Massive blocks of limestone look like upended ocean liners about to sink stern first into the sea"—a rather appropriate coupling of words and image. What compositional devices do you notice in this image? Does its description work for you? Art direction by D. J. Stout; photography by Mark Klett. Writing by Stephen Harrigan. Reprinted with permission from* Texas Monthly.

thralling—at the same moment it lifts your heart and fills you with apprehension.

But now, as we stood on the mesa, with the light growing softer and softer, some of the land's fierceness began to melt away. We walked back to the horses, scattering chips of lava with our boots. On the way down we let the horses pick their way along the rocky ground of the mesa slope. The brush was thick here, and I was glad I was wearing chaps to deflect the stout spines of catclaw and ocotillo.

I had borrowed the chaps from the tack house at the ranch. They belonged to Bob Armstrong, the former commissioner of the General Land Office. Armstrong had first laid eyes on Big Bend Ranch in 1970, and then and there vowed to acquire it for the state. He had gone to the ranch for a weekend of hunting, driving all night through

108 · DECEMBER 1989

Massive blocks of limestone looked like upended ocean liners about to sink stern first into the sea.

Publishing Your Photographs

Screening

Photographs are continuous-tone images, which is to say that they contain a full range of grays between black and white. Neither letterpress nor offset lithography can reproduce the gray, or continuous tones, by varying the tonality of the ink. They can only run ink where the image is and no ink where it isn't. In order for continuous-tone artwork to properly reproduce, it must be screened. (See **Figure 4.11**.)

Halftone screens convert continuous tones to a series of dots of varying sizes or concentrations. A charcoal or deeper shade of gray in an original photograph would be converted to a series of larger dots in a concentrated pattern. A light gray tone, however, would be configured with small blacks dots

JOHN P. COLE

Figure 4.10 _____
How does the landscape in this image compare to that in the previous photograph? Samata Associates designed, art directed and produced this page for Lincoln National Corporation's annual report. Marc Norberg borrows a page from David Hockney's composite approach to photography. It dominates the report photographically and suggests that the designers of corporate publications have a wide stylistic selection from which to choose. Designed by Greg Samata; photography by Marc Norberg. Reprinted with permission of Lincoln National Corporation and Samata Associates.

widely spaced apart. Our eyes optically mix the dots on the white field of the page to give the illusion of gray.

Because halftone screens reduce tonal contrast, expect to lose detail from your original work. That should suggest a number of things to you. To compensate, you need an average (or slightly greater than average) amount of contrast in the original photograph. Your image should also carry good tonal shifts. Without them, the halftone tends to run only slightly different tonal gradations together. Finally, to minimize the amount of detail you'll lose in the halftone transfer, make your original at least twenty percent larger than its reproduction size. Most production cameramen will tell you *not* to exceed fifty percent reductions; they also discourage enlarging from the original photograph to the halftone.

Continuous-tone copy—be it photography or illustration—is shot separately. Later its negative is combined with the negative from the **mechanical**, the camera-ready layout or **keyline**, which usually consists of typography and graphics that are not continuous tone. Combining the two negatives is referred to as **stripping** or **stripping in**.

Halftone screens come in varying degrees of fineness. A 130-line screen will produce 130 lines of dots for every inch. A 60-line screen will produce 60 lines of dots for each inch. In reproducing photos, newspapers generally employ 65- to 85-line screens; magazines use 100- to 150-line screens. The quality of the photography itself is a determining factor. If you begin with poor-quality photography, even a 30,000-line screen won't make it any better. By placing a magnifier atop halftones in a very finished corporate publication and a newspaper, you can see the varying dot patterns that fine and not-so-fine screens create.

Figure 4.11 _____

Halftone screens come in varying degrees of fineness. Here you see the same halftone reproduced at 60, 85, 100 and 150 dots (or lines) per inch. Because of the porous and uneven quality of newsprint paper, newspapers generally employ 60-to-85 line screens. Magazines and other upscale publications, however, usually work with much better paper and tighter photography; in these instances, 100-to-150 line screens are employed.

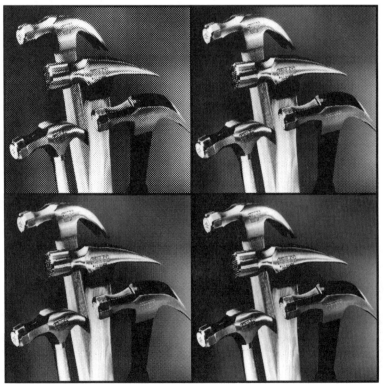

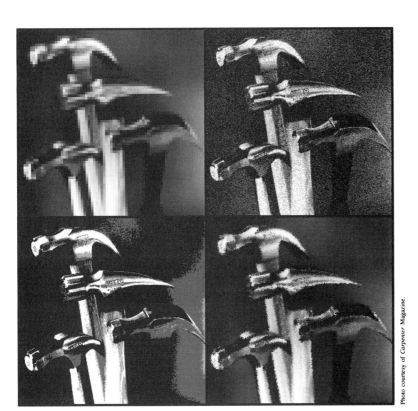

Photo courtesy of *Carpenter* Magazine.

Figure 4.12 _____

Halftone screens have another option in addition to fineness—or the amount of dots or lines per inch. Although generally less detailed, texture screens bring a specific pattern to the halftone. In fact, screens may make the halftone look much more like line art than photography. Compare these texture-screened reproductions to those on the previous page. These are mosaic, mezzotint, posterization and diffusion screens.

Paper stock and the type of printing used often dictate how fine a screen you may use. Coarser papers require 65- to 85-line screens because of their irregular surfaces. Newsprint and other absorbent papers are fine for newspapers but unsuitable for fine photography reproduction because they sponge up some of the ink. Some paper textures take ink well, while others take it unevenly. And generally speaking, the flexibility of its printing surface allows offset printing to use finer screens than letterpress. Gravure and offset printing may use up to 300-line screens. (See **Chapter 7** for particulars on printing.)

There are other halftone screens available. Their line conversions are patterned differently. Although **texture screens** tend to be less detailed, they can change the appearance of your photography or continuous-tone art. These screens not only convert the photo to halftone, they may even appear to change the medium. Mosaic, mezzotint, posterization and other texture screens provide quick-change art. For example, they can make photography look like illustration or a specific fine art medium. (See **Figure 4.12**.)

Finally, **screen tints** are halftone dot patterns figured in percentages of black (or another color). Photographs may be run over screen tints—in two-color work, the photo generally runs in black run over the other color. Remember that black is counted as a color in two-color printing. It is normally one of the two colors used in this process, although it's also possible to use two colors other than black.

Cropping and Scaling

Most photographs go through a series of croppings. Initially, the photo is cropped when the photographer making the image decides how to align the format, position the subject and utilize other compositional devices. Later, photographs may be printed full frame or cropped by adjusting the easel blades on the projected negative image. Finally, the enlarged print is more closely scrutinized and reconfigured with a cropping frame. (See **Figures 4.13** and **4.14**.)

In many ways, photography is the art of subtraction. Cropping is no exception. For the most part, it is a process of eliminating what doesn't contribute to the physical composition or mood of the image. It also allows you to reconsider placement, balance, proportion, sequence, unity and format within an image. Very often the hole or window in a predesignated layout will

determine how an image is cropped or fitted to that design. A **hole** or **window** is the physical area within the layout that has been reserved for the artwork. In this instance, the photographer is instructed to arrange and format specific shots for the preconceived pages. Other times the page's architecture is actually built around the format of a strong image. In many ways, cropping is one of the most demanding skills of photography because it takes a discriminating eye, an intuitive sense of composition and the ability to previsualize a finished image.

Scaling goes hand in hand with cropping because in addition to determining an image's format, you must make it fit the design perfectly. In fact, scaling is normally figured into the cropping process. It works something like this: you figure a close cropping that approximates the proportion of your hole, then figure your column width exactly and from that measure you determine the length of the image and its reproduction percentage. All of this is executed within a few minutes with the help of the cropping frame and a proportion or scaling wheel.

Operating the proportion wheel is a simple procedure. Begin by measuring the **cropped** area of the original photography or artwork. (Again, it must closely approximate the shape of the hole in the layout proportionally.) Then measure the column width for the reproduction—the hole. Now align the original art's measure, which is located on the inner wheel, with the reproduction's width, located on the outer wheel. Line up the original's dimension with the reproduc-

◀ **Figures 4.13 & 4.14** _____

Most photographs have an extensive evolution. Editing is as at least as important to the communication process here as it is elsewhere. And generally it begins early. A shooting script or outline is given to the photographer, who discusses the concept, content and particulars of the shoot with the creative director, editor and/or art director.

Normally, technical arrangements are also agreed upon at this meeting—like the locale and its problems, camera format, preferred lenses to be used, film stocks and lighting specifics. Designers and art directors also share compositional particulars with the photographer; these may include any number of the following: page design, the use of horizontal and vertical formats, color, contrast, distance, camera angle and perspective, depth of field, emphasis, the direction the subject faces. The list could go on and on.

In this instance, the original photograph (**Figure 4.13**) was shot on a 2" x 6" format camera. The image was spectacular, fitting the client's needs beautifully, but the space for the final layout (**Figure 4.14**) made it practically unusable. Tracy Wong, art director at Goodby, Berlin & Silverstein, discusses how the image was salvaged: "Fortunately, we were able to fill in the sky above and repeat the ocean pattern to fill in below. All on the computer. Without the technology, we would have been totally screwed in terms of budget and time."

In addition to the computer-finesse, the original image was flopped and cropped—in this case the crop was substantial, moving from the original's exaggerated horizontal format to a vertical one for the layout. This says something for the technology at hand; however, it says a great deal more for the insight and vision of the art director. Reprinted with permission from Goodby, Berlin & Silverstein and the Royal Viking Line. Art direction by Tracy Wong. Photography by Duncan Sim.

tion dimension, the latter above the former. The window (that is the hole cut in the inner wheel) will automatically give you the scaling percentage.

Essentially, the proportional scale sets up an algebraic equation: the width measure of the original is to the width of the reproduction as the length of the original is to that of the reproduction. Indeed, you can calculate measurements with that equation, and figure the proportion by dividing the reproduction width by the original width. A proportional scale can save you all that algebra and arithmetic, though. It also saves you the trouble of converting decimal measures to fractions.

Handling Photographs

Think of your photography as irreplaceable; in many situations it is just that. Follow these suggestions and you'll never damage your photographic imagery.

1. Whenever you must pass along or mail photography, sandwich prints between two pieces of cardboard. Corrugated cardboard works best.

2. Don't crop photography with a knife. Once you slash up a photo, you're stuck with it; which means that if you miscalculate the cut or the scaling, you're in trouble. You may also discover, too late, that you have another application for that image.

3. Keep food, drink and liquids away from the photos. Even water can spot photographic surfaces. Prevent this kind of accident by not inviting it to happen. If you're going to be handling prints, make sure your hands are clean. Glossy prints will pick up fingerprints, so keep your hands to the edges and back sides of prints. If moisture gets between resin-coated prints and is allowed to dry, you'll tear the emulsion off the photos trying to get them apart.

4. Retouched photographs are especially vulnerable. Think of retouched pieces as masterpieces. They are, after all, selected photos that have been repaired, refined and finished to your standards. Store retouched images safely away.

5. Keep all photography in the same storage area, file cabinet, etc. When photography is passed around or left unattended, it has a way of disappearing or getting lost.

6. Don't use paper clips to attach photography to layouts or mechanicals. They may mar the photograph's surface and appear in the production image. If you're bent upon using clips, place the photos in a 9" x 12" envelope and clip *it* to the layout.

7. Don't write on photographs. If you must write, use a nonreproduction felt marker and mark lightly.

Photographic Approaches

We're used to seeing pages framed by white margins. Margins unify a publication, provide structure and establish continuity. And they improve the readability of a page. It should come as no surprise, then, that there is much disagreement over the use of bleeds. Essentially, a **bleed** is any portion of a printed image that extends beyond the edge of a trimmed sheet.

Arguments against using them are functional as well as editorial. For starters, bleeds break standard page design by extending beyond the page's normal frame or layout area. In addition, a bled image calls attention to itself and may impede reading by blocking the visual flow of an article or story. In fact, many editors view bled photography or illustration as fine for advertising but not suited for editorial purposes. The opposite viewpoint might argue that when used with care, bleeds can add surprise and function to a design. Bleeds do make practical use of space; that is, they utilize an area otherwise left blank. The same argument that bleeds call attention to themselves can also be used in their defense. When correctly used, a striking photograph will have even more impact if bled. Although bleeds can impede visual flow, they can also stop a browsing reader. Advertising bleeds its imagery consistently to make full use of a page, to stop reading traffic and to call attention to itself.

Bleeds are most commonly used in advertising and on covers. Should you decide to adopt them as a design tool for the interior of your publication, use them correctly. Used indiscriminately, bleeds can lose their impact and make a mess of a publication. But when applied correctly and in small doses, they provide variety and add more visual punch. Don't call attention to mediocre imagery; and run most of your bleeds big. Remember, one strong image is better than five average ones—the same is true for bleeds. Largely, it comes down to stylistic choices and good taste. Extend your bleed no less than 1/8 inch beyond your trimmed page. Trimming is not an exact science, and the extra image area will ensure that you're not left with a border on your bled page or finished piece.

Figure 4.15 _____

Running a full bleed of this very tight shot is a great idea. Its larger than life proportions give it great power, while concurrently suggesting something about the potency of IMC's fertilizers. The hands also imply great strength. Photographer Terry Heffernan uses contrast to isolate the content here. But contrast is used in other ways; for example, the photography pages are printed on narrower pages of enameled paper, which contrast the wider format and textured paper of the other pages. Design by Pat and Greg Samata.

Reprinted with permission of International Minerals and Chemical Corporation of Northbrook, Illinois and Samata Associates.

Similarly, don't let crucial visual information straddle the edges of your imagery. If you do, you're likely to lose it.

A **full bleed** means that a photograph (or artwork) extends beyond all four edges. But bleeds need not be all inclusive. It is especially in vogue to run a single bleed to the right, left, top or bottom. If you quickly browse the more stylish publications, you'll find photography and artwork running bled from the top down into a page, from the left across the left onto the right page and bled. *Bled pages offer readers a quick point of entry.*

Silhouette photographs are images without backgrounds (and often foregrounds). They are silhouetted by artists, airbrushed away by professional photography retouchers or stripped out by printers. Today, computer software programs allow you to scan an image and remove or replace its background. It is a remarkably simple procedure, much easier than the other means of disposing of a photograph's detail. However, if you know you want to drop a silhouetted or **outlined** photograph into a design from the start, you are better off having the image shot that way. Studio photographers who make outlined photos regularly have white or neutral backgrounds specifically for such purposes.

Partially silhouetted photographs are often integrated into page design. This photographic approach is most typically applied by stripping away the upper one-third or less of an image's background. Less common are **partials** that strip out the bottom, right or left side of a photograph. Just as bleeds suggest that the image is too big or important to be placed on a single page, partial silhouettes impart the feeling that the visual image couldn't be contained within its rectangular format. Often designers echo the shape of the silhouetted portion of the photo by contouring the typography around or along the image's outline.

Figure 4.16 _____

*This image is bled on three sides—top, bottom and right. NIKE liked this photograph so much, it was used in its annual report (**Figure 4.2**) and here in this very dressy All Conditions Gear catalog. In this instance, the subject not only looks onto the adjacent page, he also looks directly into the inner page—regardless of which side it's turned. Compare the two croppings and how they are used in their respective formats. Creative direction and design by Ron Dumas. Photography by Gary Nolton. Reprinted with permission of NIKE, Inc.*

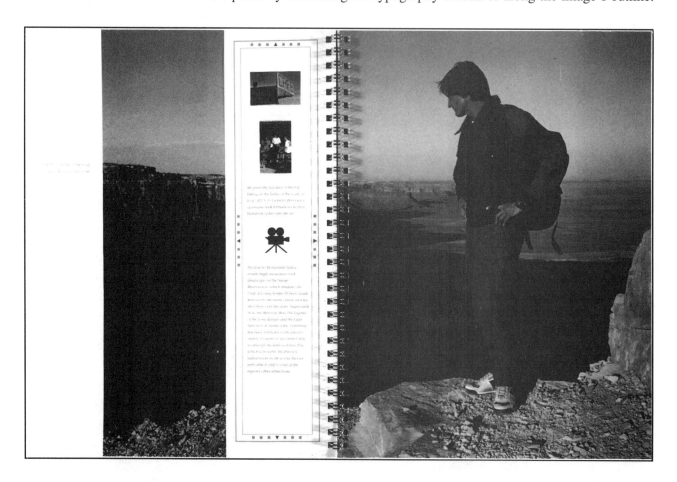

Vignettes, on the other hand, are halftones with shaped backgrounds, usually with graduated edges.

Photography is a subtractive art. Silhouettes, with their empty or stripped-out backgrounds, isolate the subject and in so doing direct your vision to the image. Silhouettes are used extensively for publication covers and as illustrative visuals. Along with streamlining visual direction, they bring a clean, orderly look to a design.

Duotones

You can extend your photograph's tonal and two-color possibilities by using **duotones**, a two-color process that uses two halftone negatives and consequently two press runs (unless you're printing on a multicolor press).

In order to create the duotone, your printer shoots two separate negatives of your original photograph. This process requires two exposures, each one different from the other. One negative is shot for the darker range of the image; normally this is the plate that receives the darker of the two inks used. The second negative is shot for the lighter highlights of the photograph and its plate usually

Figure 4.17 _____

This action shot is not bled, but framed off by the margins on the left, top and bottom and by the title and copy on the right. Notice how selective focus blurs the background out completely, and how you're drawn to the face of the lacrosse player. Note, too, how his vision directs your sight to this feature article in The Physician and Sportsmedicine. *Sports photography by Paul A. Sounders/ALLSPORT. Tina Adamek is the executive director of art and Steve Blom art director at* The Physician and Sportsmedicine. *Reprinted with permission of* The Physician and Sportsmedicine.

carries the lighter ink. Additionally, the shots are made at different screen angles. Normally, too, the second color is run at more than thirty percent. The end result of this process is a subtle tonality in the printed image—one with richer light and dark areas.

Duotones add continuity to a publication in a discreet fashion because the second color is somewhat difficult to discern, at least to the uneducated eye. That sophisticated use of color is one of the strengths of the process. When properly executed, duotones have a very finished, high-quality look that can dress out any publication.

Duotones are used commonly to approximate older photography that might have been sepia-toned or brown-toned. Running sepia, orange or lighter browns with black ink on a duotone also warms up your photography. Regardless of whether you make two press passes or one with a multicolor press, you'll be charged for the second color and plate. To save money, you can fake a duotone by overprinting black (or another color) atop solid or screen tint blocks, but you won't receive the same richness and subtlety in the image's tonality. Besides, the second color will be very apparent. **Fake duotones** are much more common than their authentic counterpart and can be quite effective in accentuating color in a publication.

Figure 4.18 _____

Silhouetted photography is very fashionable these days. By stripping out backgrounds, it's easier to emphasize the major element of an image, particularly when the background and foreground busy it up or compete with the main idea. Here, art director Paul Haggard isolates this image of bass player Mike Watt and wraps all four columns of type around the outline photograph. Z.Wolf shot this photograph for Bass Player *magazine. Art Direction: Paul Haggard, © 1990 Miller Freeman Publications, Inc. Reprinted with permission from* Bass Player *magazine.*

Figure 4.19 _____

*Although they aren't common design ploys, vignetted photographs are used effectively in some designs. (Circular crops are becoming more acceptable; see **Figure 2.21**.) This inverted keyhole-like shaping was used on a* Special Report *table of contents page in a recent issue on women in sports. If you look closely, you'll see that the edges of the elliptical part of the shape have been deliberately faded. Contrast it to the hard-edged rectangular area that works strongly as a base for the image. This shot and the cover photography by Frank Ockenfels 3 / OUTLINE. Jim Darilek is design director and Mary Workman art director at* Special Report. *Reprinted with permission from* Special Report — On Sports, *copyright 1990, Whittle Communications L.P.*

High-contrast Photography

There are a number of ways to create **high-contrast photography**. Whichever approach you choose, you produce a **dropout** effect in the finished image; that is, you have minimal-to-no tonal range. Most high-contrast imagery has no gray scale whatsoever—only black and white. High-contrast photography also eliminates a great deal of the detail in the finished image. Typically, it is only used for graphic effect; for example, a good many magazines and newspapers use it for their columnists' mug shots.

Basically, there are three ways to secure high-contrast images: on the film itself, on the print, or by using high-contrast graphic arts film.

You can make high-contrast imagery directly on continuous-tone black-and-white film by filtering your photographs with an yellow, orange or red filter. The contrast filter is screwed on the end of the camera lens and filters the light coming through the lens onto the film. Contrast filters alter the relative brightness of colors that would otherwise reproduce as approximately the same shade of gray, thus eliminating a good part of the gray scale or tonal range. The brighter the lighting condition, the more contrast is passed to the film. The result is a very contrasty film negative. Deep red filters provide maximum contrast using this filtration method.

If you use variable or polycontrast photographic paper, contrast may also be controlled on the print during the enlarging process. When using color (dichromatic) enlargers, you can dial in large amounts of magenta to increase the contrast. The more magenta you add, the more contrast you'll have in your photographic print. Using the same principles and printing paper, you can get the same amount of exaggerated contrast using a normal black-and-white (condenser) enlarger. In this instance, magenta filters (#4 and #5 give the most contrast) in the filter drawer of the enlarger increase the print's contrast.

You may also purchase papers with a fixed contrast to improve contrast. Contrast-graded papers (#4 or #5 or VH or UH) will achieve similar results. Finally, you may project your negative onto a special graphic arts film (Kodalith or Agfa Gevalith). It is a special high-contrast copying film that changes tonal ranges from continuous tone to black and white. One production advantage to working with litho-film is that it is camera ready and doesn't have to be screened. However, because of its highly limited tonal range, it would never work for standard pictorial imagery.

Figure 4.20

High-contrast photography tends to be dramatic and carry a great deal of power. This image exemplifies both of those points. Too often, we think of high-contrast imagery in terms of black and white, but this one is run full color in NIKE's All Condition Gear catalog. It sums up much of the early imagery nicely. It also serves as a rather graphic lead into the price list section of the publication. Photography by Gary Nolton. Ron Dumas worked as creative director. Reprinted with permission of NIKE, Inc.

The Last Word—Writing Captions

Captions, or cutlines, should neither rehash the obvious nor be unrelated to the photograph. Your words should provide the necessary information—such as names, places, situation (where appropriate), time and the significance of what is pictured. Remember, without the proper explanatory remarks your readers may misinterpret the image, because we tend to bring our own meanings to unexplained visuals. So, your comments must go beyond what is pictured.

4.21
The exaggerated horizontal format of the photography both dominates and anchors this page. And the high-contrast imagery and a smokey-looking backdrop give the photograph an interesting mix of tight studio work and candid portraiture. What's more, its deep leading, understated imagery and generous use of white space make it an impressive publication— especially when coupled with the gold ink edging on the photos. Photography by Robert B. Tolchin, typography by Typographic Resource. Design by Greg Samata. Reprinted with permission from Kemper Reinsurance and Samata Associates.

4.22

This delicate image makes a striking visual metaphor for a wedding invitation. Its beauty lies in its simplicity and form. It originally appeared as a duotone printed on smooth ivory stock. Photography by Claire Trotter. Design by Thomas Rubick and Jeanne Maasch. Reprinted with permission of Thomas Rubick.

- Imagine that you know nothing about the photograph you're using. (In many instances that's exactly what happens. Those responsible for writing the captions weren't present when the shots were exposed, and they may write in their own interpretations.) Succinctly fill in whatever blanks might exist. In a nutshell, that's exactly what captions should do. It's too bad photographers don't normally write captions, because they're the ultimate litmus test of the content and value of those accompanying words.

- Keep it short. You need to be concise and clear. Avoid the obvious and scrutinize every word you use. If the caption reads as well or better minus a word or phrase that doesn't take away from the integrity and meaning of a photograph, purge. Captions are almost always read before the copy, and sometimes before headlines, so make them appropriate, clear and succinct. Think of them, too, as a launching area. Ideally, they should deliver the reader to the story. The last thing you want to do is write an essay.

- Write the caption in an informal manner. On average, captions are much more conversational, written directly in everyday language. *They should communicate almost as quickly as the visual they are describing.* The real measure of success with a caption is: "Does it communicate clearly and efficiently?"

- Tense is largely a matter of your stylebook and the content of the photo itself. Some publications write in the present tense and others in the past. Generally speaking, use present tense for either candid or action photography and past for posed imagery. Present tense adds to the impact of photography.

- Be clear. If there is any doubt about the content, sequence or meaning of the photograph, trash the caption and begin again.

- Directional information is important, but if identification is obvious without it, don't use it. "Pictured above..." or "left to right" with two people in the photo isn't necessary. We don't need to be told read left to right; better sequential aids might include "moving clockwise" or "top" or "bottom" row, so readers know where to start and finish.

- Mugshots get straight identification. No less, no more.

- When a caption is written singly, it is best to place it beneath the image. Occasionally, a design may call for positioning the caption to the side of the image. Captions may also be clustered in photo spreads. In this instance, one caption block, often highlighted by a screen or box, provides remarks for each photo of the grouping. **Cluster captions** normally refer to the images in a clockwise fashion.

- Research shows that readers track first to the visual, then to the head, then the caption and finally the copy. Remember that words are meant to provide reassurance and explanations to readers, to fill in or further explain information that a photograph doesn't provide.

There are different schools of thought on whether *all* photographs need captions or identification lines. If you look carefully, you'll find very few photos that don't receive them; even most covers receive captions in cover commentary on the first page, in the table of contents or occasionally on the cover itself. Photographs that don't require them are few and far between, so we strongly recommend that you write them, period.

Until recently, even if you created your entire publication on computer, you still had to convert your photographs to halftones before they could be printed. Then along came **scanning**. Scanning is a term loosely used to describe a process whereby a continuous-tone photograph (or any artwork for that matter) is "scanned" electronically and is transferred into information that is readable by various computer software programs.

There are basically two types of scanners: **bi-level** and **gray-scale**. Bi-level scanners save information as bit maps like a computer "paint" program produces and works fine if you just want a bit-mapped reproduction of line art. But, if you want to produce a photograph with a simulation of grays, you're going to have to use a gray-scale scanner. Gray-scale scanners run the gamut from expensive to cheap, from "this is okay for layout" to "this is almost magazine-quality."

If you're serious about getting some functional mileage out of a scanner, buy one that will give you at least 64 levels of gray. You can get by on 16 levels of gray, but only if you're producing a comp or if you're just using your scanned images as "locators" for final artwork in your mechanical. If you ever plan to use your scanned photos for a higher-quality comp or for a final ad, you might as well start with a higher-quality scanner. Don't assume that higher quality means higher price. You'll be surprised at what you can get for under $2000.

Even if you pay a fortune for your scanner, you're still only going to get a maximum of 256 levels of gray out of it. The only real difference between full gray-scale scanners is in the way they compute the levels of gray—a subject we don't need to get into here. However, you do need to understand something of how a scanner, computer and printer produce those "miracle" halftones.

The Method

Photographic halftones are made up of actual dots. The *levels* of gray derive from dot size. Laser printers and other computer output devices can't reproduce dots of varying sizes. They only print "dots" of one size. In fact, these "dots" aren't really dots at all but individual, rectangular cells composed of even smaller cells which, depending on whether they are turned on or off, simulate dot size. (Most of us can't tell, even with a magnifying glass, that these are cells instead of dots.) This is known as **dithering**. To keep confusion to a minimum, we'll call the larger cell the **cell/dot** and the smaller cells that compose the larger cell **printer dots**.

The size of the cell that replicates a halftone dot is important. Cell size depends on how many printer dots are in that cell. A 4 x 4 cell has 16 individual printer dots. A cell this size will yield 17 possible shades of gray ranging from all 16 printer dots turned on (black) all the way down to all the printer dots turned off (white).

A Brief Glossary of Terms

Bi-level scan—A bi-level scan produces bit maps at roughly 300 dpi. Although bi-level scanned images look okay at greatly reduced sizes, they plainly show the bits when enlarged. They don't print well on a Linotronic since the 300 dpi is "locked in" during scanning and will print at that figure regardless of output device.

Cell/dot—The "dot" produced by a computer output device that replicates a halftone dot. This cell is itself composed of smaller **printer dots**. These smaller dots determine the number of grays in an image by their configuration and by how many are turned on or off. When you send your image to a printer, it determines how many gray levels will be produced by dividing the number of dots per inch (dpi) the printer can print by the number of lines per inch (lpi) in the image (as defined by your software or the printer's default setting).

DPI—Dots per inch. This figure represents **resolution**. The greater the dpi, the higher the resolution. Some typesetters, such as the Linotronic 300, are capable of producing up to 2500 dpi while the most the LaserWriter can produce is 300 dpi. Since resolution decreases as the number of gray levels increases, an output device with an ability to produce 2500 dpi is about the only way you're going to get anything approximating 256 levels of gray. Dpi can be set on most scanners as **sampling rate**. For magazine-quality images, scanning at 150 dpi seems to be adequate. For images that will be enlarged later, scanning at a higher rate is recommended.

EPS—*Encapsulated PostScript*. The format in which graphics created in illustration programs such as *Freehand* are transported into page-layout programs such as *PageMaker*. EPS creates large and unwieldy files when used to save photographs. It is best to avoid this format for anything but illustration.

Gray-scale scan—Depending on the scanner, a gray-scale scan can produce up to 256 levels of gray. Although many scanners allow you to set resolution as you scan, gray-scale scanned images depend on the output device for their final resolution. A Laser-Writer, for example, can only produce images with a maximum of 48 levels of gray; while a Linotronic 300 can give you in excess of 256 levels of gray in addition to excellent resolution.

Halftone—The traditional method of rendering a continuous tone photograph into a series of dots of varying sizes that can then be printed. This process is replicated on a scanner by the creation of **cell/dots**.

Line screen—The frequency at which dots (or cell/dots) appear in a printed image. This figure is controlled by the number of lines in the screen used to produce a traditional halftone or the setting of the output device in a scanned photograph. Most output devices have a default setting: LaserWriters default to a 53 lpi screen at a 45-degree angle. The Linotronic 100 defaults to a 1250 dpi screen at a 45-degree angle. A typical newspaper photo uses about an 85 or 90 lpi screen while a typical magazine photo is run at 133 lpi.

LPI—Lines per inch. This is normally representative of the screen you use in the halftone process; however, lpi is a determining factor in scanned image quality as well. See **line screen**.

Moire effect—A shimmering effect resulting from scanning an image previously halftoned, such as an image from a magazine. You can reduce this effect by scanning in the negative mode (if your scanner allows) and returning the image to a positive in a photo manipulation program such as *Image Studio*.

Output device—The device by which you print your document. It can be any type of printer (e.g., Laser-Writer) or typesetter (e.g., Linotronic) or any number of graphic plotters or other such instruments.

PICT—A picture-type, object-oriented format common to many draw programs. It uses *PostScript* to print out on most output devices.

Resolution—Resolution is determined by **dpi** or dots per inch and can be set as you scan (see **sampling rate**), reduced during importation into a photo manipulation program, or enhanced or limited by your output device.

RIFF—*Raster Image File Format*. The working format in *Image Studio*, it takes up less room than a standard TIFF file and can be converted to TIFF, or other formats, if need be. At this writing, it can't be used as-is in many other programs.

Sampling rate—The number of dots per inch scanned into your image file (sampled) as a result of your scanner's setting. Many allow up to 300 dpi while newer models are offering 400 dpi. Theoretically, the higher the sampling rate, the better the resolution (see **dpi**). Lower settings (such as 72 dpi) are sufficient for locator graphics used only for placement in your layout. Most high-quality publications can use 150 dpi images quite well. Line art and images that will be enlarged later should be scanned at 300 dpi or higher.

TIFF—*Tagged Image File Format*. One of the most common file formats for saving scanned images. It is usable in almost all page-layout programs, photo manipulation, and illustration programs. Its major drawback is the amount of file space it takes up. An image scanned in TIFF can be reduced by lowering the resolution as you scan or as you import it into a photo manipulation program.

The basic difference between a bi-level-scanned image and a gray-scale-scanned image is the ability of the individual cells to vary their sizes. In a bi-level scan, all the printer dots in any given cell are either on or off. That is, the cell is either all black or all white. This arrangement is determined at the time of the scan and can't be altered no matter what type of printer you use.

In a gray-scale image, the individual cells simulate varying degrees of gray depending on how many printer dots are in the cell and how many are turned on. This number, in turn, depends on the ability of the output device (printer or typesetter). The output device's interpreter calculates how many printer dots will be turned off or on. The printer interpreter divides the number of dots per inch the printer can print by the number of lines per inch in the halftone. The resulting number defines the size of the cell/dot.

For example, if you print out a photograph on a LaserWriter, the number of grays you will be able to simulate will be decided by the size of the cells the LaserWriter can physically produce. There is a relatively easy formula for determining how many gray levels you will get from a given output device.

$$(\text{dpi} \div \text{lpi})^2 + 1 = \text{number of gray levels}$$

dpi = dots-per-inch your printer produces
lpi = lines-per-inch screen you are using. Either you designate this before you print by using your software program or it defaults to the printer. In the case of a LaserWriter, the default line screen is 53 lpi (regardless of the fact that other sources including Apple place it at 60).

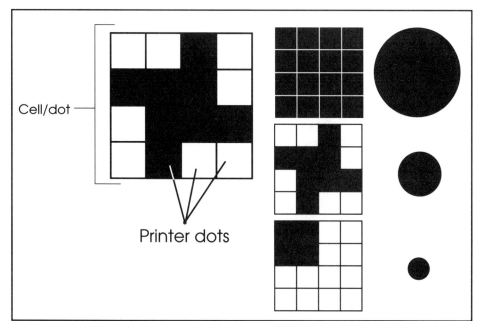

Exhibit 4.23 _____
Cell/dot. *The cell/dot (left) is itself composed of smaller "printer dots" unlike a typical halftone dot which is both the largest and smallest unit. Seen here (right) are dots and corresponding cells at 100%, 50%, and 25%.*

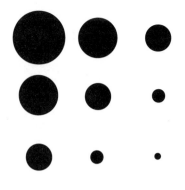

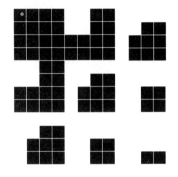

Let's assume that you set your line screen in *PageMaker* to 75 lpi before you print. So, knowing that a LaserWriter produces 300 dpi, your formula would look like this:

$$(300 \div 75)^2 = 16 + 1 = 17 \text{ levels of gray}$$

This means that your printer will produce a 16-dot cell (4x4). Adding one to that number represents the cell with no printer dots turned on—or white—giving you 17 possible gray levels.

If you let the printer default to 53 lpi, you get more levels of gray. Thus:

$$(300 \div 53)^2 = 32 + 1 = 33 \text{ levels of gray}$$

This brings up an interesting point. You would think that by increasing the resolution (number of lines per inch) you would automatically get a better looking photo. Not so. As you can see from the results of the above examples, the finer the screen (the more lines per inch), the fewer the gray levels. The reason is not so complex as it might seem.

The size of the cell determines not only the possible number of grays that will result, but also the resolution of your image. A 4 x 4 cell composed of 16 printer dots yields 17 levels (including white). An 8 x 8 cell composed of 64 printer dots yields 65 levels of gray (including white). However, *resolution decreases as number of gray levels increases*. Why? Because the size of the individual cells increases as the number of printer dots in them increases. The result is that the cells take up more room. A larger cell/dot means a larger screen size because certain size cells will only accommodate certain screen settings (lines per inch). When a finer screen is applied, the larger cell/dots are broken up, thus reducing again the number of possible grays.

One way around this problem of increased resolution versus decreased gray levels is to use an output device that produces smaller cell/dots that can contain a more complete gray-scale. Although the number of printer dots within the cells depends on the above formula, the actual physical size of the final cell/dot can change depending on the printer you are using. A Linotronic 300, for example, produces a much smaller cell/dot than a LaserWriter, thus allowing for more dots per inch. In fact, the Linotronic 100 can produce up to 1270 dpi (the Linotronic 300, twice that many). That means that a cell/dot printed on the Linotronic 100 at 150 lpi (the Linotronic can actually print much higher in lpi than that) only takes up 1/150 of an inch. If you remember, the LaserWriter default screen is only 53 lpi, so each cell/dot will take up a whopping 1/50 of an inch. You can see what this means for resolution. Obviously, printing to an output device that allows for higher lpi will give your scanned photograph a much higher resolution and take advantage of as many gray levels as possible.

Again, don't expect that even with line screens of magazine quality (133 lpi) you're going to get 256 or even 64 shades of gray just because that's what you scanned your photo at. For example, supposing you run a photo on the Linotronic 100, screened at 133 lpi. Then:

$$(1270 \text{ dpi} \div 133 \text{ lpi})^2 = 91 + 1 = 92 \text{ levels of gray}$$

As you can see, you only (*only*?) get 92 levels of gray. For most of us, that's plenty; but to the trained or discerning eye, there will be noticeable problems. The most common problem is "banding"—an unsightly demarcation between gray levels in which not enough differentiation has been made. The obvious solution is to either increase the dpi (go to a Linotronic 300, for instance) or decrease the lpi.

Exhibit 4.25 _____

Cell/dot size. *The 4 x 4 printer cells in the cell/dot on the left will produce up to 17 different combinations representing 17 different levels of gray. When cell/dot size is raised to 8 x 8, the number of potential gray levels goes up to 65 (64 with varying degrees of black and one solid white).*

The Process

Let's suppose you have a scanner, or access to one. Here's how the process works.

1. Place your original photograph on the scanner. You should start with a good original. Here's why:

   - When you scan photos that have already been published or printed, you are laying one dot pattern over another. There is literally no way you can align your scanner so that your scanning pattern will match the original halftone screen. You'll often get a disturbing *moire* effect—the result of superimposing two incompatible patterns on each other—usually most noticeable in backgrounds and solid gray areas where it will give your image a sort of mottled look.

   - Since a typical halftone darkens with each generation it goes through in the publication process, it is best to start with a low-contrast (flat) photo. Printers and lithographers will tell you that the best results are obtained from a scanned photo in which the lightest areas are at least 10 percent gray and the darkest areas are no more than 90 percent.

     Few scanners allow you to set this kind of detailed assignment of light versus dark areas. However, photo retouching and manipulation programs such as *Digital Darkroom* and *Image Studio* now include techniques for making these adjustments once you import the scanned image. See below for more on these programs.

2. Set the **sampling rate** for your scan. Most of the better scanners let you indicate how many dots per inch you want to store from your photograph as information in your computer. Current wisdom recommends scanning at a rate roughly analogous to the line-screen density or lpi you plan to use when you print. Both *PageMaker* and *Image Studio* recommend scanning at 150 dpi. When you scan at 150 to 300 dpi, you're really covering your bases pretty well. If you're using a scanner capable of recording 256 levels of gray to scan a photo at 150 dpi, you're creating an image that will give

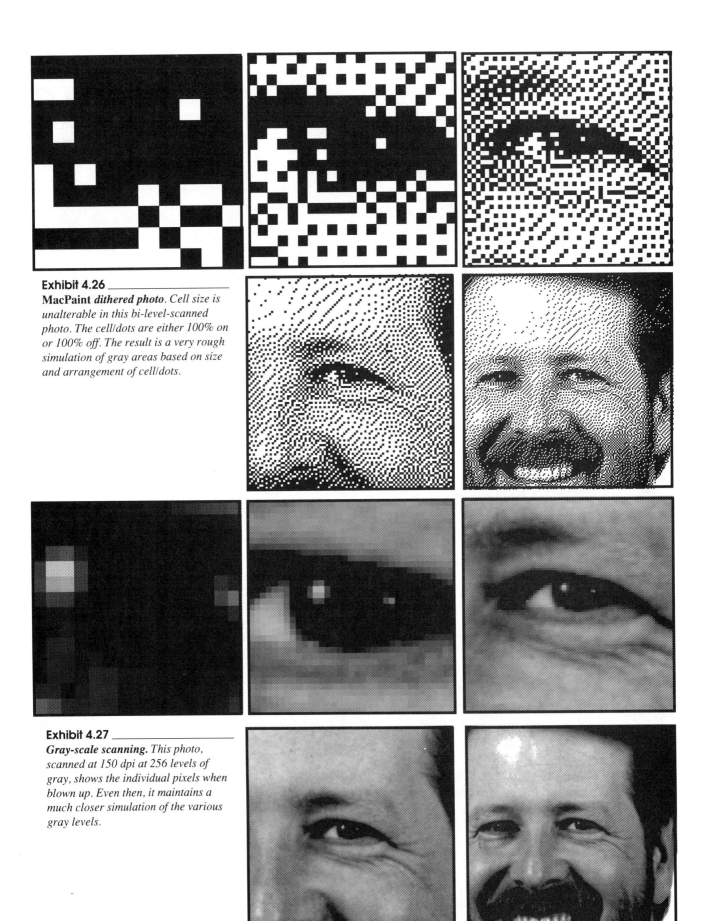

Exhibit 4.26
MacPaint *dithered photo. Cell size is unalterable in this bi-level-scanned photo. The cell/dots are either 100% on or 100% off. The result is a very rough simulation of gray areas based on size and arrangement of cell/dots.*

Exhibit 4.27
Gray-scale scanning. This photo, scanned at 150 dpi at 256 levels of gray, shows the individual pixels when blown up. Even then, it maintains a much closer simulation of the various gray levels.

Exhibit 4.28 _____

LaserWriter vs. Linotronic. The LaserWriter printout on the left is usable in some newsletters and for proofs. It contains 33 shades of gray because that is all the LaserWriter can produce at the default setting of 53 lpi and a 45-degree angle. Although other combinations are possible, this setting is the optimum. The photo on the right is run on a Linotronic set at a 133-line screen with a 45-degree angle at 1250 dpi.

you at least 72 gray levels on a Linotronic 100 and more than 256 levels on a Linotronic 300. If you print to a LaserWriter, use the default setting. You're not going to get any better image than that produced with a 53-line screen at 300 dpi. Keep the following guidelines in mind when determining sampling rate.

- *PageMaker* recommends scanning any images for use in its program at 150 dpi, regardless of the output device. This is good advice. This dpi is high enough to give you excellent resolution off both the Linotronic 100 and 300 and won't hurt your output to the LaserWriter if you use its default screen.

- In some cases—photos with sharp diagonal angles, for instance—scanning at a higher dpi can *help* final resolution since at a lower dpi these edges appear jagged. Don't scan any higher than twice the final screen lpi, however. You're wasting disk space after that. But remember, if you designate a lower screen value in your output program, you void the higher sampling rate. That is, if you print to a Linotronic with a designated screen of 150 lpi and you scanned at 300 dpi, you're only going to get one dot every 1/150 inch—no matter what. This means that you effectively lose 150 dots, or half your stored information.

- Use a higher resolution sampling rate such as 300 dpi to scan black-and-white line art. It will take up more space, but it will give you much cleaner images.

- If you plan to enlarge your scanned image after you place it in your page-layout program, use a higher sampling rate. For instance, if you scan at 100 dpi and enlarge 200 percent, your dpi drops to half the original or 50 dpi. The reverse is also true. If you plan to reduce, you can scan at a much lower dpi. A 100 dpi scan reduced 50 percent will give you a 200 dpi image.

- Some photo software programs like *Image Studio* will allow you to scale your image by lowering the resolution as you load it into the program for touch up or manipulation. For example, if you are importing an image scanned at 300 dpi, you can lower the resolution to 150 (50 percent) as you load it into *Image Studio*. This also shrinks the size of the image file.

3. Choose the proper format for saving your image. Most scanner software allows you to save into the most common photo formats: TIFF (*Tagged Image File Format*), EPS (*Encapsulated Postscript*), and *MacPaint*. Both TIFF and EPS files take up a lot of space. In fact, a complex, 8.5" x 11" photo scanned at 300 dpi could take up over 1 megabyte of space! Unless you've got a lot of memory, you're going to be concerned about file size. Here are some ways to save space.

- Saving to RIFF (*Raster Image File Format*) can cut your file size by 30 or 40 percent. Programs such as *Image Studio* use RIFF as an operating format (even though you can still save in TIFF, EPS, and *MacPaint*), but unless your layout software accepts RIFF, you're not going to be able to use it.

- As mentioned above, you can open your file into *Image Studio* at a reduced resolution, say 150 dpi instead of 300 dpi. This will seriously cut down the amount of file space your photo will take up. We've found, for instance, that TIFF files created at even 150 dpi can be formidable in size. But, when opened at a reduced resolution of as much as 50 percent the original loses very little when run on a Linotronic 300. Most photos will be reduced or cropped when placed in the final publication layout. An 8" x 10" photo scanned at 150 dpi, reduced 50 percent, to 75 dpi, then reduced in physical size to 2.4" x 3" (70 percent reduction), will still give you a 127 dpi image and a potential Linotronic output of up to 250 lpi screen.

- Scale your image as you scan it. If you know that you're not going to use an 8" x 10" full size but rather at 50 percent, scan it at 50 percent and save half the disk space.

- Reduce the sampling rate. Remember, you rarely have to sample any higher than 150 dpi for any gray-scale image.

- If your scanned images will only be used for placement or rough layout, scan them at a very low resolution such as a 72 dpi *MacPaint* file. This saves you space and makes manipulating the images in your page-layout program faster.

150 dpi 256 gray scale   *150 dpi 16 gray scale*   *72 dpi 256 gray scale*

Line art   *Dithered MacPaint*

Exhibit 4.29 _____

Sampling rates and formats. *With 256 gray-scale images, scanning at above 150 dpi is usually a waste unless you plan to enlarge the image later. (Clockwise from the top) scanned at 150 dpi at 256 gray-scale setting; 150 dpi at 16 gray-scale setting; 72 dpi at 256 gray-scale setting; scanned as a dithered* MacPaint *image; scanned as line art.*

4. Use a photo software program such as *Image Studio* or *Digital Darkroom* to edit, crop, touch up and do virtually anything to a photo that a trained darkroom specialist can to.

5. Use a page-layout software that allows you to manipulate your scanned images further. *PageMaker*, for instance, has an image control menu that allows you to set line screen and angle (best stick with 45 degrees) brightness and contrast. In fact, if you don't set your line screen in your page-layout program, it will default to the printer settings automatically. Be aware, however, that in order to save file space, *PageMaker* only stores a screen image of your photograph. It won't look very good, but it will give you a good idea of how to place it, adjust it and crop it. When printing, you'll have to "link" the photos to the file in which the original resides. *PageMaker* documents will ask you for this information each time you open them. Once you've linked the photos, however, *PageMaker* will remember where they are unless you move them to another folder or disk.

6. Once you've placed your image into your page-layout program, you can make a number of adjustments. Some programs allow gray-scale image adjustments to brightness or contrast. Most programs allow for cropping

and scaling. The adjustments you make depend on whether you're going to be using your placed image as final art or just for placement. Here are some things to keep in mind.

- Cropping can be done in any one of the several stages prior to placement in your page-layout program. Some scanners allow for cropping before you scan; however, cropping as you scan prevents you from changing your mind later on. Although you can further crop the photo, what you crop out as you scan is gone until you scan it again. Photo software programs such as *Image Studio* allow cropping as well as many other subtle adjustments. Using this type of program also finalizes your cropping once your image is placed in your page-layout program. You should always save your original photo as well as your adjusted version just in case.

  The beauty of cropping in your page-layout program is that you can crop your whole photo to your heart's content. If you don't like it, just uncrop it. The adjustment isn't cut in stone. The only problem is that the original size of your image is always resident in the page-layout program file, whereas a precropped image only uses the memory it needs to represent that size.

- Scaling is the single most attractive feature of using a computer to generate photos for your layouts. In the traditional layout approach you had to measure the exact amount of space you allowed for your photo, measure your photo, scale it using a proportional wheel or calculator, indicate cropping to your printer or lithographer, and have your photo shot and screened in the appropriate size.

Exhibit 4.30 _____

Cropping and Scaling. The advantage of sizing your images to your exact needs without going through the painful steps of figuring sizes mathematically can't be overstated. As quickly as you can think of a size, you can scale to it in PageMaker *and many other programs. Scaling won't solve all of your problems, however. If you have to fit a specific sized area, you may have to crop, or scale and crop both. As you can see, scaling alone won't make the original conform to a horizontal space when it is vertical. Of course, you could distort the image, but that won't make the subject of your photo very happy. The best answer is often to crop to the space you have to fill.*

Now, all you do is place it, and scale it until you get it the way you want it. If it won't fit proportionally, crop it to the proper proportions and then scale it again.

Remember, if you know in advance that you are going to scale a photo down, say 50 percent, either scan it at 50 percent at the resolution (sampling rate) you intend to use for your final printout, or scan it at a lower sampling rate since resolution will double when you scale the photo in your page-layout program.

- Take advantage of any fancy layout techniques your software allows. for example, *PageMaker* has a text wrap function that allows you to literally wrap your text around your photos or other scanned images. This is very helpful if you are using silhouette photos that you have cropped in a photo manipulation program.

   One reminder, however: don't get carried away. Just because your program allows you to wrap text (or something else) doesn't mean your message supports that sort of look. Be sure of your intended message and its "look" before you experiment too much.

   One of the great benefits of computer layout is the ability to make changes, change the changes, change them back again, and make some more. If you're careful and systematic, you won't lose any of your best ideas.

- Save frequently! Although some programs save automatically, don't rely on them too much. After each major change or addition, save your file. And, if you aren't sure of which page arrangement you like, save each version under a slightly different name using a "save as" function.

7. Don't take what you see on the screen at face value. Most Macintosh screens only show a 75 dpi dithered image. This means that you're not going to see a real gray-scale image until you print it out. And, if you're viewing a 300 dpi image on a 75 dpi screen, it's going to look much larger than it actually is. Both of these conditions will lead you to make a number of sample copies of scanned photos before you get them just right.

   And, even if you do get them to your satisfaction off the laser printer, they won't come close to what they'll look like off the Linotronic. Using a high-resolution monitor will help. The Mac II monitor or one of the larger layout monitors such as *Radius* will give you a complete range of grays. In fact, the monitor image will often be better than even Linotronic output. Here are some things to consider when preparing for your final output:

   - If you're using your scanned photos for a simple, not too flashy newsletter, scan at 150 dpi or lower and use laser printer output as your final image. You'll be surprised at how clear it really is.

   - If you're looking for a more sophisticated, near-magazine quality look, scan at 150 dpi or greater (depending on whether you plan to enlarge or reduce the final image) and run it on a Linotronic with a 100- to 133-line screen.

   - Bottom-of-the-line 256-level gray-scale scanners will produce a very good image, but it will darken considerably when it's run on a phototypesetter like the Linotronic.

> **TIP:** *In* PageMaker, *"saving as" will compress your file and clear up a lot of disk space.* PageMaker *files with a lot of graphic elements take up a lot of space. Each move, crop, scale, delete, place and wrap stores in your file, whether you need them or not. "Saving as" will save only the final version of each of these, not every little indecisive move.*

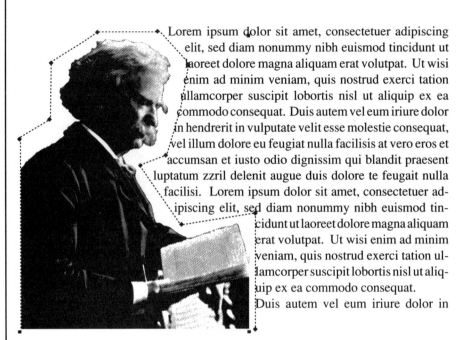

Lorem ipsum dolor sit amet, consectetuer adipiscing elit, sed diam nonummy nibh euismod tincidunt ut laoreet dolore magna aliquam erat volutpat. Ut wisi enim ad minim veniam, quis nostrud exerci tation ullamcorper suscipit lobortis nisl ut aliquip ex ea commodo consequat. Duis autem vel eum iriure dolor in hendrerit in vulputate velit esse molestie consequat, vel illum dolore eu feugiat nulla facilisis at vero eros et accumsan et iusto odio dignissim qui blandit praesent luptatum zzril delenit augue duis dolore te feugait nulla facilisi. Lorem ipsum dolor sit amet, consectetuer adipiscing elit, sed diam nonummy nibh euismod tincidunt ut laoreet dolore magna aliquam erat volutpat. Ut wisi enim ad minim veniam, quis nostrud exerci tation ullamcorper suscipit lobortis nisl ut aliquip ex ea commodo consequat.

Duis autem vel eum iriure dolor in

Exhibit 4.31 _____

Text wrapping. One of the more creative aspects of newer page-layout programs is the text wrap function. In PageMaker, *it is accomplished by moving individual "handles" which then inscribe an outline about your image. Text flows automatically around this outline instead of over your image. At the bottom, the image showing how it would look printed. Above, with the text wrap function selected.*

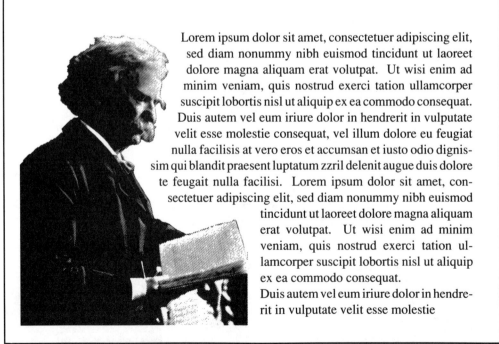

Lorem ipsum dolor sit amet, consectetuer adipiscing elit, sed diam nonummy nibh euismod tincidunt ut laoreet dolore magna aliquam erat volutpat. Ut wisi enim ad minim veniam, quis nostrud exerci tation ullamcorper suscipit lobortis nisl ut aliquip ex ea commodo consequat. Duis autem vel eum iriure dolor in hendrerit in vulputate velit esse molestie consequat, vel illum dolore eu feugiat nulla facilisis at vero eros et accumsan et iusto odio dignissim qui blandit praesent luptatum zzril delenit augue duis dolore te feugait nulla facilisi. Lorem ipsum dolor sit amet, consectetuer adipiscing elit, sed diam nonummy nibh euismod tincidunt ut laoreet dolore magna aliquam erat volutpat. Ut wisi enim ad minim veniam, quis nostrud exerci tation ullamcorper suscipit lobortis nisl ut aliquip ex ea commodo consequat.

Duis autem vel eum iriure dolor in hendrerit in vulputate velit esse molestie

The solution is to learn to manipulate your images with the software so that your final product will match your desired product. This may require setting density ranges at 10 and 90 as mentioned above, altering brightness and contrast, or changing screen resolution. The trick is to experiment. Some scanners, such as the *Apple Scanner*, produce test strips using various settings. You can produce a test strip of your own by varying the settings on a page full of the same photo (or section of a photo with the most representative contrast) and having it run on the Linotronic. Be sure to indicate the exact settings above each photo.

• Don't fall for what you read about it taking 30 minutes or an hour to run one scanned photograph on a Linotronic. Sure it will if you run a 8x10 photo scanned at 300 dpi unaltered. If it takes up 2 MGB of disk space, it's going to take forever to print out. But, if you reduce the file size by one of the methods cited above, you won't lose any noticeable resolution, and it won't take much time at all to run a photo.

Our experience has been that a photo scanned at 150 dpi, manipulated in *Image Studio* to reduce file size, physically reduced to the final placement size, and printed on a Linotronic 300 along with a complete 8.5" x 11" page of copy only takes from 4 to 6 minutes. In fact, we've run tabloid-sized pages with as many as five photos in 6 to 7 minutes per page. Remember, the size of the image file affects how long it will take to run the scanned image. And, unless you are certain your final product will come out right the first time, keep experimentation to a minimum. Experimenting on the Linotronic can be expensive, and every test photo you run will decrease the cost effectiveness of the process.

• If your final product will be offset printed, consider running your pages directly off a Linotronic as negatives. Although most of us are familiar with Linotronic paper positives (very much like PMTs), it also produces negatives that can then be used to make the printing plates.

If your Linotronic service doesn't charge any more for negatives than positives, this alone can save you money by eliminating a step in the printing process—shooting the negatives from your camera-ready mechanicals.

Another reason for going with negatives is that the photos produced on a Linotronic positive at anything over 100 lpi screen will be too fine a halftone to be reshot as a negative. The result will be a "muddy" image. Printing directly to negative film will save this step and maintain clarity.

Chapter 5

Illustration

Part A: Basics

To printers and publishers, anything that is not typographic is referred to as art. For our purposes, illustration consists of all visual art, excluding normal photography. That includes line drawings, painting, air-brushing, pastels, etching, technical renderings, charts, locator maps, information graphics and more.

Commercial art is a common name for illustration. Sometimes disdained, it is a very fitting term for a sizeable chunk of today's illustration, which is commercial in the sense that it is specifically designed or created for editors, art directors, publishers and corporate designers. It is also commercial in that it is original work created by staff or freelance artists who happen to be paid, regularly or irregularly, by the company comptroller. And contrary to what some high-minded aestheticians might suggest, it isn't really sinful for artists to accept money for contracted services. The same design and composition principles and technical skills which produce artwork that hangs in galleries also go into the creation of commercial art. Indeed, *Communication Arts*, a graphic arts magazine, publishes an illustration annual that showcases what its jury of art directors, artists and designers have deemed the very best illustration of that particular year. It is a dazzling array of commercial art.

Good designs are conceived in their entirety right from the start. Words, type and visuals should be preconceived, shaped, refined and reconfigured, so that every element will mesh and work together to produce the planned effect. The best illustration begins at the point where the initial ideas are hatched.

Because we have less time today and because we tend to be more impatient, publications are becoming more visual. We relish encapsulated summaries and when we do read for information, it tends to be in small bites. Most of us scan newspapers, magazines and other publications quickly, seldom reading from cover to cover. And so, both editors and designers employ illustration for a number of good reasons, some of which overlap and work in combination with one another. What follows is a thorough but not exhaustive list.

Figure 5.1

This Joseph Salina artwork is a dazzling example of illustration that is not only flawlessly executed but beautifully tailored to the article. "Appetite for Destruction" is a special report on how the deregulation of the savings and loan industry created a long litany of fraudulent and highly questionable management practices. Beyond that, of course, the S & L problems were spawned from greed, arrogance and other stripes of immorality. Salina's insightful illustration acts as a lucid visual metaphor here, working directly with the title and content of the feature. Also, the graphic affectations—on the wrapped initial letter, byline and special report box—are strongly reminiscent currency engravings; fittingly, they are colored a light gray-green.

Tom Russell is art director at Best of Business Quarterly, *where this piece was published. The article originally appeared in* Regardie's *under the title of "A Confederacy of Greed." Reprinted with permission from the* Best of Business Quarterly, *copyright 1989, Whittle Communications L.P.*

- Visuals—be they illustration or photography—attract attention. Because seeing is a painless and effortless endeavor, our eyes favor pictorial or graphic information over the written word.

- Illustration tends to stop the audience. Even if readers are only paging through a publication, they'll scan a visual. They may browse on, but the visual provided an unscheduled stopover, however brief.

- Visuals tend to be more memorable. When image, corporate identification, recall and brand awareness matter, visuals serve a good purpose.

- Illustrations give the reader a resting place. Plant them strategically. Non-stop visual information becomes overkill and generally does not allow the visuals to function as planned resting points for your audience.

Figure 5.2

Bill Sanderson illustrated this piece and several others which appeared in a special report "A Yen for Power" in a recent issue of Best of Business Quarterly. *(See more of Sanderson's work in* **Chapter 8**.*) It illustrates Clyde Haberman's article, "The Presumed Uniqueness of Japan," which chronicles Japan's feelings of "specialness" and examines its aloofness as a global citizen. It mirrors the gist of Haberman's piece, literally and figuratively. Compare this illustration with Sanderson's other work and notice how the elaborate line work and style mesh. Joannah Ralston directed the art. This article first appeared in* The New York Times Magazine. *Reprinted with permission from the* Best of Business Quarterly, *copyright 1989, Whittle Communications L.P.*

Figure 5.3

Stephen Pietzsch gives us this remarkable cover image of Bill Moyers, a microphone firmly gripped in his right hand and a pen raised in his left. Mimi Swartz penned the feature article on Moyers' rise from "small-town Texan to TV superhero" for Texas Monthly; *D. J. Stout, art director. Reprinted with permission from* Texas Monthly.

THE MYTHIC RISE OF BILLY DON MOYERS

*From Marshall, Texas, he set off on a heroic
journey to become LBJ's protégé, the conscience of TV news,
and the prophet of a brand-new faith*

BILL MOYERS stood in the wings at the University of Texas cavernous performing arts center last spring while the faithful poured in, their hopes caged like anxious doves, waiting for release. Though he had felt this fervor many times before, at times had even cultivated it, Moyers ambivalence showed in the tiniest widening of his eyes behind the trademark aviator glasses and the slight but impatient pursing of his thin lips. Still, augustly dressed in business attire, he took his place at stage left, and clasping his hands comfortably on the table in front of him, he set about doing what he does best: giving the people what they want.

Tonight they wanted Moyers to do what he had done in his most successful television series to date, to carry the word of Joseph Campbell. In *The Power of Myth*, six stunningly successful one-hour interviews on PBS last year, Moyers had elicited from the once-obscure elderly Sarah Lawrence professor the message that anyone could be a modern-day Odysseus; all you had to do was follow the path blazed by the heroes of the world's great myths. Find your purpose, and devote your life to it, Campbell had urged. "Fol-

At 55, Moyers has chosen television over politics as his pulpit for preaching American values.

low your bliss." Though his blue eyes were cloudy and his gravelly voice was ground to a gentle rasp, Campbell, with Moyers acting as a simultaneous interpreter for the New Age, had unwittingly provided sustenance to a spiritually starved America. Millions of viewers heeded the call to become the heroes of their own lives.

Since Campbell's death in 1987 it had fallen to Moyers to continue his work. Moyers was no stranger to such duty; it was in fact his bliss to carry the word of others, and this role had made him a modern-day hero. Once the brightest boy in Marshall, Texas, Moyers had set out to carry the word of God as a Baptist minister, and then carried the word of Lyndon Johnson as the president's chief aide. More recently, as a television journalist, he carried the word of the nation's foremost thinkers in his documentaries and interviews. At 55, Bill Moyers had emerged as the secular prophet of American values. Over time, his role had grown but never changed; he had always been the willing, at worst the wary, standard-bearer of the best we see in ourselves.

This night was no different. The audience for *The Power of Myth in Everyday Life*, as Moyers presents

BY MIMI SWARTZ

MOYERS AS SIR LANCELOT

Illustration by Ian Pollock

MOYERS AS ODYSSEUS

Illustration by Phillip Burke

MOYERS AS ROBIN HOOD

Illustration by Anita Kunz

◀ Figure 5.4 _____

Because Swartz gives us different facets of Moyers, D. J. Stout, art director of Texas Monthly, *chose to provide his audience differently styled visuals. He used four illustrators for the same feature article—an unusual tactic, but an appropriate and very effective one. Ian Pollock illustrated this version, Moyers as Sir Lancelot. Reprinted with permission from* Texas Monthly.

◀ Figure 5.5 _____

Here, Bill Moyers is portrayed as Odysseus. "After smiting the enemy at CBS, Moyers had to battle PBS station owners to bring the word of an unknown mythology professor to his viewers. Illustration by Phillip Burke.

◀ Figure 5.6 _____

Finally, we see Moyers as Robin Hood. The caption reads, "On the air, Moyers showed how the powerful dominate the powerless. Behind the scenes, he shrewdly maintained a power base of his own." Illustration by Anita Kunz. Compare the four illustrations and their respective styles for this feature. Stout brings us a very creative and unusual solution, one which connects visually to Moyers' various traits. Reprinted with permission from Texas Monthly.

Figure 5.7 _____

Stout once again chooses several different artists to illustrate a single feature in "Cowboy Songs"—five to be exact. The subhead relates as much to the art as the songs themselves: "Five classics from the open range as you've never seen them before." Richard Mantel is the illustrator for "Little Joe, the Wrangler" in the opening pages of the spread. Anne Dingus wrote the article. Stout epitomizes the art director who is eclectic, open-minded and knows his illustrators as well as he knows his audience. Reprinted with permission from Texas Monthly.

▼

Figure 5.8 _____

Northern Telecom of Nashville, Tennessee begins this report with background remarks on Fort Knox, the U.S. Gold Depository, and how it has been the emblem of monetary strength and value. But, we are told, "Today's currency is information... a whole new economy based on the exchange of information." Interestingly enough, the interspaced, expensive black pages hold scant amounts of copy set in metallic gold ink with varnish atop the copy area to give the words a subtle emphasis and sparkle. What's more, the art is also printed on black—in copper, silver and gold ink. And it illustrates how information and information networks are commodities of today and the future. Design by Thomas Ryan. Illustration by David Wariner; copywriting by Richard Fulk. Reprinted with permission from Northern Telecom and Thomas Ryan Design.

- Visuals establish a particular mood or feeling. Artists may use diagonal lines to imply movement or motion, incorporate textures that send our eyes playing braille with the imagery or infuse warmth through the reds and oranges of an illustration.

- Illustration may simply flesh out or show what a headline says.

- Visuals may illustrate a facet of the story or article that isn't readily apparent to the reader, or tell a pictorial and written story with good graphic information and a caption. Sometimes, captions may link further with subheads, decks or pullouts.

- On occasion, a number of captioned visuals work collectively, and may by arrangement—clockwise, left to right or via their optical weight—direct the reader through a story or show sequence or chronology.

- Illustration style may serve as a connective device. In this instance, a particular style of illustration may help unify a single story or even provide a visual continuity for an entire publication. (See **Figures 5.3** through **5.6**.)

Don't use illustration as filler. Visuals should be purposeful, directly connected to the writing, design, space and sense of the piece. When you're considering how to use and execute illustrations, ask yourself a few questions first. What is the relationship of the visual to the story, headline, subhead or pullout? Will this type of illustration attract your audience? Is the style of the

With the demise of gold as a financial standard, money has become a security, backed by a new, *intangible* commodity — the credit of others. And the transactions by which we exchange value have themselves become more and more intangible.

We have moved from gold coins and gold certificates to silver-standard currency, and even to non-currency transactions such as checks and credit cards. Finally, we have further reduced even these paper representations, so both the medium and the transaction itself have become increasingly *transparent*. Today commercial exchanges are frequently computed, processed, and stored as bits of electronic information on a computer disk or chip, visible only as lighted digits on a computer screen.

In short, *today's currency is information*. Yet information is more than just a new currency. It is the foundation for a whole new economy based on the exchange of information.

In this new **Information Commerce**, local, national, and international economies are structured around information transactions: information as *product*, information as *service*, information as a form of *payment* — all equally intangible and transparent.

A New Measure of Value

The global, electronic infrastructure that serves today's financial community, in fact, demonstrates how thoroughly information technologies have transformed the world's trade, finance, and monetary systems. Geo-political boundaries seldom impede today's electronic payments. Information about capital and credit — the new money — flows intangibly across national borders. Banking and finance have seized the power of information technology to beat international floating exchange rates, transcend time zones, and overcome geographic barriers. They have even been surprised on occasion by the dimensions of these same technologies. The global stock market crash of October 1987, for example, was directly attributed by some analysts to the instantaneous flow of information around the world.

---

illustration appropriate to both the story and the publication's format and formula? Do you have a style in mind that you want to be dominant? In a comparatively small publication, it may be a good idea to choose one illustration or photographic style and stick with it. That usually means working with a single illustrator, artist or photographer.

And don't sell the visual short. The average reader is likely to page over even the best story if its graphic presentation is mediocre or missing. To be sure, not all stories need illustration, but they do require something, even if it's as minimal as an island of white space. Where illustration is warranted or especially fitting for your work, use it. But do so carefully and skillfully by making it the focus of your layout where warranted—and part of your plan from the very beginning.

Working with the Artist

Read a couple books on art history and contemporary art. Know what impressionism, realism, art noveau, art deco, abstract expressionism and other styles look like. Learn more about composition and visual communication. Subscribe to a good design or graphic arts publication; *Communication Arts, Print, Graphis, How* and *Step-by-Step Graphics* are a handful of good ones. And don't open a publication unless you have a pair of scissors at arm's reach. Most art directors, creative directors and designers maintain an extensive collection of swipe files.

Figure 5.9 _____

Illustration is a well-traveled avenue to continuity. And David Wariner's illustration helps knit the concept, message, look and feel of this report tightly together. Although we normally tend to think of woodcuts as being an older medium, they bring an element of surprise here: their content is updated and their style fresh. (Actually, this illustration medium is scratchboard.) In addition, the simplicity and well-demarcated areas of the medium make for clean production. Something good designers keep in mind. Wariner's illustration is Spartan in look and design. The typography and page arrangement are equally clean and simple, which makes for an elegant but easy read. Design by Thomas Ryan. Reprinted with permission from Northern Telecom and Thomas Ryan Design.

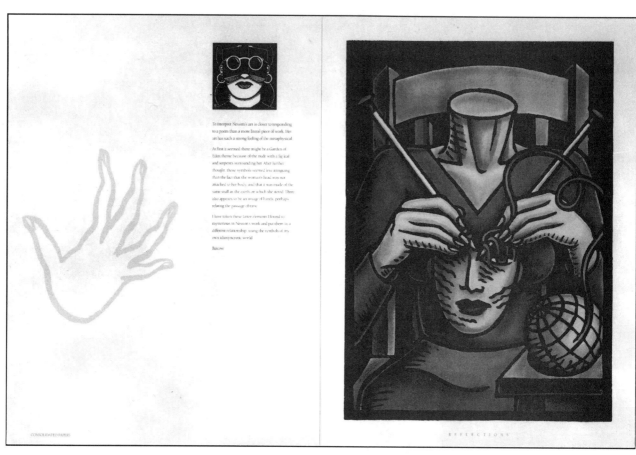

Figure 5.10 _____

Consolidated Paper and Liska and Associates of Chicago chose to show off Consolidated's Reflections line of paper by having an artist "reflect visually" on a cover photograph. His interpretation was subsequently passed to seven other artists. The sequential illustrations were published along with a statement from each artist. The artwork shows off the paper by demonstrating its halftone dot definition, uniform inking and color brilliance. This illustration is the work of Bascove, linocut with watercolor and colored pencil. Steve Liska designed and art directed this publication. Reprinted with permission from Consolidated Papers and Liska and Associates.

Following the suggestions below won't turn you into Andrew Wyeth, but you will have a richer visual sense and feel much more comfortable working with artists.

- Have a strong idea of what you want, but be willing to examine other visual ideas. More important, be willing to acquiesce and accept an idea that's visually better than yours. A swipe file is very important and may save you time, money and a lot of misdirection. For example, you may have a perfect example of the sort of art you'd like to use. That gives you something tangible to work with when discussing your illustration needs with the artist. Don't misunderstand; the intent of swipe files is not to plagiarize. Obviously, you won't want your clipped art copied line for line, but it can serve as a working example of the medium, style, composition and design you're after. Or, if you intend to leave this decision up to the artist, make sure that the artist understands your audience, publication, limitations and the story or article to be used.

- Whenever possible, have the artist or illustrator read the manuscript first.

Discuss the story with the artist by providing an extensive briefing of it. The more your artist understands about the slant, characters and thrust of the piece, the less chance you'll end up with misleading artwork. Most visual misdirection doesn't occur because the artist is a prima donna. More often, it's a result of bad communication or the artist not knowing *enough* about the story.

- Work with the artist. Whatever you do, don't think of the artist as just a "wrist." Think of whoever produces the art—illustrator or photographer— as a member of your staff. Get their input, ideas and reactions to your ideas before they begin. Listen carefully not only to their ideas but to their sense of the story. Remember, it is in your best interest not only to hire the best person you can afford, but to help them do the best job they can. And the great majority of the time, the artist wants to exceed your expectations and standards. After all, it's in their best interest to produce something better than they've ever produced—for you, for their portfolios, for their own self-esteem.

- Few artists have equal command of media. Someone who is marvelous with pen and ink might be a horrible painter. So it is important that you have a fairly good idea of which medium you intend to use and why you

Figure 5.11 _____

Simpson Paper Company decided to show off its "sensitivity to the marvels of nature" by creating EverGreen Text and Cover paper. Because it is recycled paper and reflects their ecological mission, Simpson decided to use a sample paper book that featured important American naturalists from John James Audubon to Jack London. In **Figure 5.11,** *illustrator Ward Schumaker celebrates Johnny Appleseed. The illustration was originally printed in black plus three matched colors and two matched fluorescent colors. Kit Hinrichs of Pentagram is responsible for the art direction. Reprinted with permission of Simpson Paper and Pentagram.*

Figure 5.12

*William Duke's photographic
multiple image has more of a
painterly or illustrative look than it
does a photographic one. Originally
it was printed as a duotone in black
and flat green. Duke's photo
manipulation gives us a quick visual
overview of the article, reflecting
the stress and pressures that are
commonly associated with making it
to the top of the corporate heap.
Duke brings the same softened edge
to three portrait shots which are
also included in the article. Robert
S. Boyton wrote the article; art
direction by Joannah Ralston of*
Best of Business Quarterly. *This
piece originally appeared in*
Manhattan, inc . *Reprinted with
permission of the* Best of Business
Quarterly, *copyright 1990, Whittle
Communications L.P.*

intend to use it. Keep a filing system that lists artists' media strengths, and, as long as they agree to it, even a photocopy or two of their work. Make sure the copies are representational of what they do. This gives you a quick picture, sort of a visual swatch, of their style and preferred medium.

- Share the layout with the illustrator. Format should be a given, but too often it is overlooked or isn't specific enough. Provide the artist all the necessary design information. Is it a vertical, horizontal or square layout? What is the exact size? Will it be running on a left or right page—and if it's going to be less than a page, is it running on the right or left side? Or does it run across two pages? If so, the artist should work carefully not to put important visual information in the gutter or crease.

Once again, the importance of the overall plan cannot be overstressed. The design comes first; it should be tailored to the concept, story and publication. If titles and type are agreed upon and the story size is established, the typographic elements fit neatly into place. Then, the artwork can top off the design. It can literally be rendered to size, or be proportionately oversized and later scaled down.

That brings up another point. Be sure to tell the artist if you don't intend to use one-for-one art. In fact, you'd be wise to calculate exact sizes for the original art. This is not meant to be condescending, but the simple fact is that very few artists (or writers) know much about publication production. It only takes a minute to figure original sizes from a hole in a design, but it might save you a lot of stress and time later.

- Don't decide on the artwork until you've seen a series of thumbnails. After the initial meeting with the artist, arrange a follow-up meeting a few days later to examine and discuss the rough visuals. Select one or two for further development, or have other quick examples rendered and make sure you understand one another. Again, *showing is always better than telling*. Swipe file examples may come in handy again.

- If you intend to feature a color let the artist know what hues and values you expect integrated or stressed in the artwork. Let's say that you intend to incorporate cobalt blue in dropped initial letters and in a series of bullets and rules in a layout. If it is important that cobalt blue or other colors be present in the art, make that clear up front, and give the artist a color sample or two to work from.

- Establish a deadline that is comfortably ahead of your real deadline. Some creatives seem to thrive on the adrenaline that fuels that last-minute work mode, which is to say that they don't necessarily share an editor's or art director's sense of the importance of deadlines. Impress upon them that meeting the deadline is crucial to your printing schedule and to their compensation and future work.

The most stressful job in the cosmos is that of the printer. Publishing runs a very close second. Establishing fair deadlines and making everyone live up to them can help eliminate some of the given stress.

Figure 5.13 _____

Compare the montage effect that illustrator Melissa Grimes applies here for Mac Margolis' piece from World Monitor, *"Brazil's Bad Dream," to the previous photo-composite of William Duke. To be sure, there are similarities, but here the artist uses silhouetted photography, jewelry, money and illustration atop map sections of Brazil to build her artwork. Poverty and ecological rape contrast greed and affluence in an interesting fashion: the lines from the gold beads (lower right) contrast the lines in the eroded soil (upper left). In the illustration, lush color and larger form dwarf the flat hues and diminutive forms in the upper left corner. This article was reprinted and redesigned in* Best of Business Quarterly. *Joannah Ralston directed the art. Reprinted with permission of the* Best of Business Quarterly, *copyright 1990, Whittle Communications L.P.*

Figure 5.14

Joannah Ralston elected to use the illustration of Joseph Salina for an article in the same issue of Best of Business Quarterly *that was related to the article, "Appetite for Destruction," that you saw earlier. (See **Figure 5.1**.) Although unrelated in the sense that this was a book excerpt (*The Trouble With Money*) and from a different writer (William Greider in this instance), the excerpt examined another facet of the thrift crisis. Salina's artwork is insightful, graphic and perfectly matched to the title and gist of the article. Although either photography or illustration might have been employed here, it's difficult to imagine a better visual solution. Note how Ralston not only reemployed the same graphic nuances but copied the layout exactly. There's no mistaking the connections. Reprinted with permission of the* Best of Business Quarterly, *copyright 1990, Whittle Communications L.P.*

Illustration or Photography?

There is no clear guideline that indicates whether you should use photography or illustration for a given situation. Traditionally, art directors have selected photography for nonfiction because of its literal and documentary characteristics, and illustration for fiction because of its more personal, creative qualities. This is not to say that photography can't be personal and creative, nor does it suggest that illustration cannot be highly realistic.

Photography has more credibility than illustration. In fact, we not only accept photography as being truthful, we sometimes confuse it with reality because of its highly documentary and literal nature. We also tend to associate illustration with fine art, often because we are unfamiliar with the medium itself. After all, we know photography firsthand from our own experience, but watercolor, oils and engravings are another matter. We are more in awe of the imagery and execution—shapes, textures and color that seem to flow from the hands of artists who are skilled and talented in those media.

Illustration has a tremendous range of styles and approaches. Extremely fine-lined work may have an etched quality that would be well suited for a fifty-dollar bill, a magazine that is largely editorial, or for portraits of chief executive officers in an annual report. That same style would be inappropriate for the cover of *People* or *American Photographer*. Comic or cartoon art might be effective for *TV Guide* or *Mad*, but outrageous on a presidential poster, *The National Review* or *National Geographic* covers. You get the point. It is impossible to make blanket statements about where and how to use illustration and photography.

Most good art directors either experiment with illustration themselves or are open to such experimentation. The best are first to understand and apply the possibilities of new styles and media. Generally, these are the same people who are liberally educated and find visual innovation in areas other than publication. Like other media, illustrative style is always shifting and changing, discarding what seemed appropriate yesterday and perhaps picking up what fell from grace fifty years ago. (See **Figure 5.11**.)

Illustration is another one of those "it all depends" propositions. Some art directors may design a stylebook that stipulates that no photography or illustration will be used, or that no illustration will be used. They might also be very rigid about style and content, so that a magazine or annual report is truly fixed stylistically. This might lend a great deal to a publication's formality, continuity and conservative look. On the other hand, a designer or art director might run with a very flexible format, using both illustration and photography, employing different type races for headlines of different articles, perhaps even running some stories ragged and others justified, all to add to the spontaneity, informality and open feel to the publication. Another art director might sit somewhere in between, perhaps using illustration for covers, editorial material and column mugs, while using only photography elsewhere.

There are benefits and constraints to any approach. But choosing between photography and illustration is less important than making sure that whatever you use is excellent work, and that it is appropriate for your audience and publication image.

Figures 5.15 and **5.16** _____

In both of these instances other formats were basically borrowed and reapplied to the literary magazine Prologues. *BIG KONG WRITING TABLET borrowed its format from the old-style writing tablet. TIGER CRACKERS took its format from the labeling of a typical firecracker package; it was run in two color (orange and black) and overprinted with various screens to give the tiger a full-color look. The animals are significant because both* Prologues *issues focused on endangered species. The artwork in both instances came from stock art, engravings selected from Dover's Animals collection. Concept, design and art direction Bill Ryan. Reprinted with permission of* Prologues *and Bill Ryan.*

Figure 5.17 _____

In this case, the stock art originated from Dynamic Graphics clipper service. The artwork is a well-executed air-brushing that you may have seen elsewhere. Compare its softened image to that in Duke's photography composite; there are definite similarities. This poster design was also used as fictitious advertising in the satirical publication, The Rational Enquirer, *and received awards for its design and concept. Concept, design and art direction by Bill Ryan. Reprinted with permission of* The Rational Enquirer *and Bill Ryan.*

Finding Illustrations

Finally, good illustration is largely a matter of tastefully but realistically aligning your publication and its needs and image with your budget. Every publication, regardless of its size or sophistication, can afford some sort of illustration; none can afford not to use it. There are three basic sources of illustration available to you: stock art, freelanced work and in-house art.

Stock Art

Stock or *clip art* collections may be used for general use in a publication. Its quality ranges from poor to excellent, and clip art is highly reproducible for most all offset printing situations. (One of the pluses of working with offset is that just about anything can be shot by the printer and reproduced cleanly and cheaply for your publication.) It doesn't require much work from the publisher or the printer.

Basically, there are four main sources of clip art.

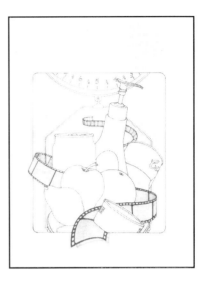

- **Public domain** Artwork that exists in the public domain, which has no copyright or has an expired copyright, is available for use to everyone. A word of caution, though, don't get mixed up in copyright problems. If you're not sure whether a piece of work is in public domain, check with the publisher or owner before you print it.

- **Published collections** Some publishing houses sell large collections of line drawings, etchings and engravings for a set fee. Typically, these collections focus on a particular subject. For example, Dover Publications' *Animals* contains over fourteen hundred wood engravings of mammals, birds, reptiles, fish, insects and invertebrates, and costs about ten dollars. (See **Figures 5.15** and **5.16**.) Dover has many other collections in its Pictorial Archive series. Other publishers who furnish quality line art collections are Hart Publishing, Art Direction Book Company (this is the same publisher that produces *Art Direction*) and Sutphen Studio.

Figures 5.18 and **5.19** _____
Compare and contrast the rough version of this Oregon Food Journal *cover which was done in graphite, pen and ink (above) to its finished stage. In the latter case, the art was air-brushed. This issue of the magazine examined how the feature film had impacted the grocery store industry through videotape sales and rentals. The dark, curved line of the film stock snakes its way through the other products to add its weight on the scale. The film calls attention to itself through optical weight and by breaking out of the cover window. Reprinted with the permission of the* Oregon Food Journal. *Art direction by Diana Ball. Illustration by Jarrett Jester; cover design, Bill Ryan.*

This art has wide application. It may be used for illustration, logotypes, posters and just about anything else you can think up. But there may be limitations on how much of the art you may print within a single issue of your publication. Dover, for example, allows that "you may use the designs and illustrations for graphics and crafts applications, free and without special permission, provided that you include no more than ten in the same publication or project." More may be used if you secure permission.

- **Monthly or regularly published clipbooks** Other graphics companies provide clip art on a monthly basis. Payment is normally arranged on a sliding scale, so publications with very large circulations pay more for their graphic subscriptions than do smaller ones.

Cost may also vary because these companies offer a number of different services and graphics. For instance, some companies provide a creative or general service, which consists of seasonal art, portraits, landscapes, sports and the like. Their retail or promotional service offers organized sections with artwork of food, clothing, appliances, automobiles, and the like. Both normally include splashy graphics, sale tags and other artwork in an assortment of sizes.

Dynamic Graphics, Metro Creative Graphics, Stamp-Conhaim and PMS are a few of the larger graphic services companies. Subscriptions are normally sold on yearly contracts, payable monthly, that range from $300 or $400 to $3,000 or $4,000 per year, depending upon services received and the size of a publication's circulation. The basic limitation is that despite the art's quality, you still may not be able to use it. No matter how well executed the line drawing, if you can't use it, it becomes useless. Also, it's easy to become caught up in the graphic work, select a drawing and work backwards. Tailoring your copywriting or lead paragraph to

Figure 5.20 _____

*In this article, "Survival of the
Foulest," writer Michael Lewis
gives "a wickedly funny account of
the highs and lows of the Salomon
Brothers' corporate culture in the
mid-1980s." In attempting to
capture that same flavor for the
article's illustrations, Tom Russell
called upon Steve Brodner and his
distinctive illustrative style.
Although mildly reminiscent of
Ralph Steadman, Brodner's work is
more in control while still bearing
his personal "fear and loathing"
version of caricature and satirical
humor. Notice how Russell's design
breaks the vertical rule on the right
with Brodner's artwork and how the
typography contours it . This
excerpt was pulled from Lewis'
book,* Liar's Poker, *and appeared in*
Best of Business Quarterly.
Reprinted with permission from the
Best of Business Quarterly,
*copyright 1990, Whittle Communi-
cations L.P.*

match the graphic instead of coupling the graphic to a finished story is a
clumsy arrangement that can be limiting and usually ends up costing you
precious time. Finally, anyone can subscribe to these clipper services,
which means you may find your annual report clip art graphic showing up
in an advertisement for someone else's fire sale. If you're thinking about
using a clip art service, most companies will provide you with past
monthly catalogs for examination.

In a pinch, however, the services may prove invaluable. Although the
media used to produce the art varies, the overall quality of the clipper
services is quite good. (See **Figure 5.17**.)

- **Computer clip art**   Today computer clip art is just beginning to bloom,
it is quite likely that within a few years it will be the dominant clip or stock
art service. Most of the larger monthly clip art services already have
computer clip art services. In fact, all recent purchasers of Apple Macintosh
systems with one megabyte of memory or more, and either two 800K disk
drives or just one disk drive and a hard drive, receive a *HyperCard*
software system free when they purchase the Macintosh computer.

HyperCard is a very powerful information storage and retrieval
software system that comes with a rather extensive array of clip art. The
majority of it isn't up to most publication standards, but manufacturers are
likely to be providing more sophisticated graphic work designed for use
with a *HyperCard* system.

Computer graphics are available on both disk and CD-ROM and are
accessible via modem. Dynamic Graphics, Metro and Stamp-Conhaim

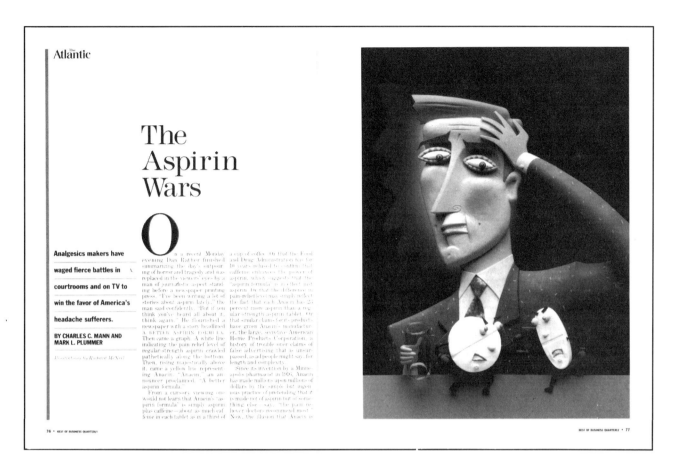

have desktop-publishing graphics available as pixel art on a one-time buy, or more sophisticated graphics that are available in the encapsulated post script format. See the **computer applications** section of this chapter for more specific information.

Freelancing

Freelancing by definition is the selling of one's artwork, writing or designing to a publication on an irregular or occasional basis. There are a number of inherent advantages and disadvantages both for the client and freelancer. The advantages to buying freelanced work are many. For starters, having freelancers produce your artwork may bring real economic benefits. Not having another full-time employee means not having another full-time check to sign, and not having to be responsible for a long litany of fringe benefits, including workman's compensation, medical insurance, sick leave, paid holidays and vacations. You also don't carry any of their overhead or equipment costs, which can become substantial.

For another thing, new artists bring fresh ideas and unique approaches to illustration. Too often, artists—and art directors, for that matter—become too predictable or cautious, taking the easy way out. While there is something to be said for the standard treatment, fresh ideas and young talent can make for exciting illustration. (See **Figure 5.21**.)

Figure 5.21 _____

This illustrative style might resemble something from a PeeWee Herman nightmare done in Claymation. Along with being eye-catching and quite distinctive, it has a marvelous show and tell quality to it and quickly communicates to us that analgesic manufacturers are waging fierce battles "to win the favor of American headache sufferers." This Best of Business Quarterly *feature first appeared in* The Atlantic. *Richard McNeel rendered the illustration and Joannah Ralston did the art direction. Charles C. Mann and Mark L. Plummer wrote the piece. Reprinted with permission from the* Best of Business Quarterly, *copyright 1989, Whittle Communications L.P.*

Best of all, you have a unique opportunity to assemble a group of professional illustrators and artists from which you may select the right artist for the appropriate job. Artists seldom have more than two media strengths. Getting an artist who is terrific at line drawings and airbrush (or whatever) is a good find, assuming those two skills are what you're after, of course. But if you've seen enough artists' work, you're in a position to have a painter, an engraver, someone skilled at airbrush, another proficient with scratchboard and three photographers just a phone call away. Few advertising or publication shops have all that talent under one roof.

There is also a downside to working with freelancers; initially, anyway. The most obvious problem is that you take on a considerable risk because you don't know them. How dependable are they? Will they meet your deadlines? Will the work be up to the standards of your publication? Is the artwork going to be what you expected? Will the art fit the format and hole you've designed? Questions like these are endless.

Fortunately, because most freelancers are out to make a name or situation for themselves, they are apt to try harder, work longer and go to greater lengths to get a foot in your door. Look for consistently good work in portfolios, and note which freelancers are most dogged about checking back with you. If you have a pesky one whose work is strong, give that artist a fitting assignment.

One of the art director's more important jobs is to assign artists work in their strongest medium and handle them properly, smoothly and efficiently so there are no bruised egos, missed deadlines or substandard work. The best art directors are good public relations people, who manage to stay out of the way while keeping everyone happy with a minimum of direction, compromising or

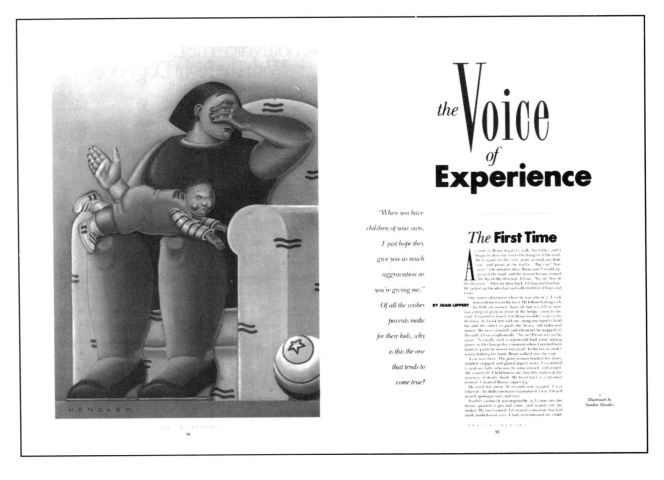

Be a howling success.

Feel as if you've been thrown to the wolves? Let an Apple Macintosh soothe your academic nightmares.

A Mac can transform the hairiest of assignments into a smooth presentation. And since a Mac is so simple to use, you'll soon be leader of the pack.

Now the cost of a new Macintosh won't make you howl. Enormous discounts are being offered to UO students, faculty and staff. And with Apple's Loan-To-Own Program, you can pounce on some easy financing.

So stalk on over to the Microcomputer Support Lab and sink your teeth into an Apple.

But don't wait for the next full moon.

Think Big.
Apple Macintosh

Microcomputer Support Lab / Room 202 Computing Center / M-F 9 am - 5 pm / 686 - 4402

Leave a big impression.

Why struggle with monstrous projects, when you can be king of the jungle with an Apple Macintosh computer.

A Mac can take your hairiest projects to new heights, making them and you more polished.

And now you don't have to be the top banana to own a Macintosh. Massive discounts are being offered to students, faculty and staff. And with Apple's Loan-To-Own Program, you don't have to monkey around with financing.

But don't be tricked by misleading advertising. There's only one authorized university program. And it's on campus.

So swing over to the Microcomputer Support Lab and snatch yourself up a Mac.

But be ready for a really big deal.

Think Big.
Apple Macintosh

Microcomputer Support Lab / Room 202 Computing Center / M-F 9 am - 5 pm / 686 - 4402

Swamped with work?

Green at the gills in a sea of paperwork?

With an Apple Macintosh there's no need to be bogged down with monstrous projects and papers. A Mac can transform your academic nightmares into the most polished presentations.

And now owning a Mac doesn't cost you an arm and a leg. Gigantic discounts are being offered to students, faculty and staff. And with Apple's Loan-To-Own Program, you won't be scared off by financing, either.

But don't be hooked by fishy advertising. There's only one authorized university program. And it's on campus.

So splash your way over to the Microcomputer Support Lab and snatch up a Macintosh.

Don't be left floundering.

Think Big.
Apple Macintosh

Microcomputer Support Lab / Room 202 Computing Center / M-F 9 am - 5 pm / 686 - 4402

Take a bite out of the Big Apple.

With an Apple Macintosh it's easy to make an impression in the big city.

A Macintosh lets you turn a frightening mass of information into the most professional presentation. And it can take the horror out of preparing your papers and projects, too.

And now the cost of a new Mac shouldn't scare you out of owning one. Monstrous discounts are being offered to students, faculty and staff. And with Apple's Loan-To-Own Program, financing a Mac won't make your stomach growl.

So if you're ready for the thrill of owning a Macintosh, stomp your way over to the Microcomputer Support Lab. That's where you'll find the only authorized University program on campus.

Think Big.
Apple Macintosh

Microcomputer Support Lab / Room 202 Computing Center / M-F 9 am - 5 pm / 686 - 4402

Figure 5.23 _____

These illustrations are an interesting blend of computer-generated art and pen and ink. The backgrounds and framing for all of these were rendered on a Macintosh with the Aldus FreeHand™ program. Notice how the moon in the upper right area of the illustrations acts as a targeting device and directs your vision from the illustration's character to the copy block. These advertising pieces were specifically aimed at college and university students. Then University of Oregon students Greg Brown and Susan Pierson did the illustration and copywriting respectively. Creative direction by Bill Ryan. The concepts for the Apple Macintosh Monster campaign belong to Greg Brown and Bill Ryan. Reprinted with permission from Bill Ryan and Greg Brown.

Figure 5.24 _____

Matt Bertolone-Smith rendered this stunning design in its entirety. He is responsible for the design, art direction, illustration and typography. This artwork is a compli-cated overlayering of illustration parts executed on a Mac II with the Aldus FreeHand™ program. It reveals the possibilities and detail of computer-generated art and what talented hands can do with it. Reprinted with the permission of the University of Oregon Outdoor Program and Matt Bertolone-Smith.

M O U N T A I N   B I K E

RIDE GUIDE

Oregon's South Willamette Region

shouting matches. They understand both sides of the street and know when to be patient and when to throw someone out.

Most art directors or editors use anywhere from one or two artists to twenty of them. Because the strongest illustrators are the busiest, a large stable lets you assign work to the best creatives available. Most directors prefer to work rather steadily with a handful of artists whose work and work habits are well known. They're a lot less likely blow a deadline or show up with shabby artwork.

Normally, the size, payment and importance of assignments is commensurate with how long the freelancers have worked for you and how well established they are. If you've never worked with artists previously but feel their portfolios are strong, check their references. You'll quickly discover how dependable, fast and good they really are. Test their mettle on a smaller, less important assignment the first time out and work from there. If you happen to wander onto talent whose work is as remarkable as it is timely, hang on to that person.

Freelancers create a substantial share of the artwork and writing you find in publications today. Working with them isn't always easy, but the advantages of hiring freelanced art far outweighs its disadvantages. Organization and long-term planning can increase the likelihood of working with the artist of your choice—and decrease tranquilizer consumption.

Creating Your Own Art

If you choose not to work with freelanced artwork and don't like the idea of purchasing stock art, you have two other choices. You can forget about artwork completely, or you can create your own. Many house organs (or in-house publications) forgo illustration entirely; others produce exciting work largely due to the design power and sophistication that computers bring to smaller publications through desktop publishing.

Should you decide to produce artwork in house, you'll need someone to work as an art director. But in many instances, small company publications can barely afford to carry an editor at a decent salary. And company decision-makers

Figure 5.25 _____

Computers extend the possibilities of Nigel Holmes' information-graphics revolution. Using Toy Manufacturers of America as his research source, Dale Glasgow gives the audience an at-a-glance info-graphic that works not only as a clear, ten-year measure of the increased revenue of the toy industry but as another entry point to the page. This Doug Stewart article originally appeared in Smithsonian. Dale Glasgow did the illustration/info-graphic. Reprinted with permission from the Best of Business Quarterly, copyright 1990, Whittle Communications L.P.

often feel that desktop publication should enable editors to do the designing as well as make all the art decisions even though they have very little or no design or art background.

What should you do?

You owe it to your editor, publication and your image to hire on someone with the right mix of artistic, design, computer and production skills. At the very

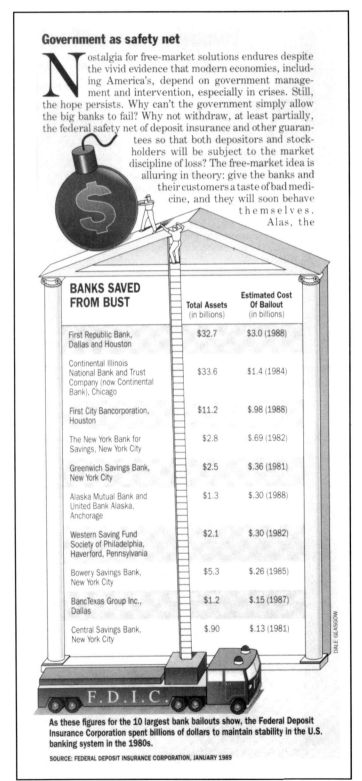

Figure 5.26 _____

This information-graphic has a strong computer-generated USA Today *look to it—with good reason. Glasgow used a computer and a standard info-graph style to illustrate and assemble this piece. His source of information was the Federal Deposit Insurance Corporation. Many of today's younger illustrators bring a mix of design, statistics, journalism, liberal education and computer literacy to the workplace. This graph appeared in* Best of Business Quarterly *for Greider's "Farewell to Laissez-Faire." (See* **Figure 5.14.**) *Illustration Dale Glasgow. Art direction Tom Russell. Reprinted with permission from the* Best of Business Quarterly, *copyright 1990, Whittle Communications L.P.*

least, try to match up your applicants with three of the four job descriptors—or two, if they're especially strong in both areas.

First and foremost, you need someone who is a good designer. Someone who can make beautiful layouts, convert verbal ideas into visual ones, mark up and work type, and *understand*, not necessarily be adroit in, basic media. In other words, you're looking for someone who's visually literate with good aesthetic instincts. Second, it would be highly beneficial if this person was also skilled—technically and compositionally—in photography and one other medium, because photography dominates publications and advertising, and is central to the offset production process.

The third attribute is a toss-up between computer literacy and publication production. These aren't third in terms of importance necessarily; normally, however, basic desktop skills and publication savvy are easier to pick up than becoming proficient at design or highly skilled in a single medium. (Multiplying loaves and fishes while walking on water would also be beneficial.)

Today, computers are bringing many of these art director job descriptors closer and closer together. Thanks to desktop publishing programs, a publication can be roughed out in thumbnails and designed and laid out precisely on the computer. Moreover, the copy, heads and all other typography can be marked up, set, edited, checked and placed with a computer. Elemental graphics (bullets, screens, endmarks, rules, boxes, shadows and lots of other visual glitter) can be created and placed to enhance the overall design. Photography may be scanned, scaled, cropped and set into the holes or windows of the pages. If you don't like how it looks, you can move, resize and manipulate to your heart's content. Finally, you can bring finished layouts to the printer on a disk or two that fits in your jacket pocket. That means no more wax or glue, no X-acto knives and border tape and no expensive typesetting.

This isn't the epilogue of *Future Shock*. Many publications are put together that way today. Among other things, computers own a major chunk of the technology and design of publications. If anything, they'll command an even stronger role in the future.

Creating exciting visual ideas that make words come to life is important to designing and central to your communication. Some of the best art directors aren't especially talented artists, but they are gifted at fleshing out concepts with lucid visualizations—or dreaming up both concepts and visualizations. They can pitch their ideas and designs and coordinate the visual end of the publication. That probably means overseeing an art department, examining freelancers' portfolios and coordinating assignments and deadlines. In all likelihood, the art director is also producing art for a number of projects as well.

Information Graphics

Normally when we think of illustration, we don't think of information graphics. Today they play an increasingly important part in publications. They dress out statistics and numbers in annual reports, newspapers, magazines, newsletters and most other publications. **Information graphics** may be taken to be anything from maps, charts and graphs to compact visuals that illustrate, explain or visually relate some process.

When properly used, they *show* what words have great difficulty communicating or explaining. Information graphics cater to our pictorial and graphic

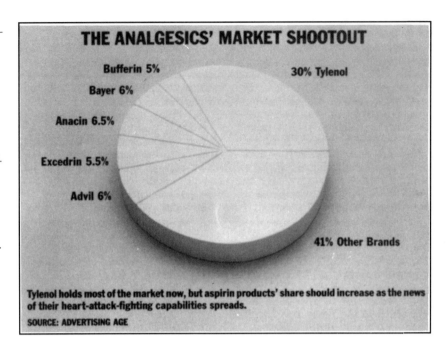

preferences, which we quickly turn to whenever we run up against difficult, abstract or complex information—or sometimes not so complicated information. That's exactly what maps do. If you've ever requested directions somewhere, you know how a handful of lines scribbled on paper compare with a written or verbal set of instructions.

But graphics can do much more than provide illustration or simple direction. A carefully designed and executed chart or graph can, at a glance, tell a story, suggest patterns and trends, explain change or a process. And information graphics may impart sophisticated mathematical, philosophical or statistical information—without extensive written explanation.

Some subjects or kinds of information readily lend themselves to information graphics. Maps make remarkable examples. Imagine the course of history without them. Or for that matter, imagine yourself trying to get around in a large city without a map; you ask someone directions and in return receive a nearly blank sheet of paper marked only with a dot and the inscription, "You are here."

Information graphics also have a propensity for concretely dealing with numbers and statistics with great clarity and dexterity. Most of us are afflicted with acute math anxiety. We avoid numbers in general and statistics in particular—at any cost. In fact, some of the finest and most experienced writers are encumbered when it comes to clearly expressing information such as financial or statistical data.

For these and other reasons, it should come as no surprise to us that information graphics have become increasingly important to publications, because they impart a sizeable chunk of information quickly by taking advantage of our graphic predisposition.

Although information graphics will never replace words, they serve an important need and have a rightful place amid the written word. Besides, despite the efforts of our educational systems, some of us don't read well—and many don't read at all. Some of those people may be an important part of your audience. In any case, your job is to facilitate communication, be it with words or graphically.

Although once considered cute or visual dressing, today's information graphics have found their way into the most serious publications. They may help show divestiture, percentages, gains, process, growth, location or long-term improvements . Regardless of application, what information graphics do best is show and tell, quickly. They translate complex mathematical and statistical information into bright, easily understood charts and graphs; they make comprehensive comparisons immediately clear, explode an abstract panel of gray copy into a concise message in a fresh and memorable manner. What's more, visuals improve recall tremendously.

Streamlining communication is a formidable task that editors and designers struggle with daily. Among the various tools at their disposal is the information graphic. Use it where appropriate as a tasteful visual bump to accompany a major point, as an expedient means to express statistics, numbers, process or location. Incorporate them in your logotype or among your typographic affectations. But remember that information graphics, where appropriately applied, can be just the eye candy your reader needs to appreciate a tasteful design or to help sweeten the bitter crunch of numbers.

Illustration

Illustration is one of the hardest publication elements to accomplish on the computer. But the beauty of computer-generated illustration is that it can be manipulated at will and used over and over again. In essence, you create your own clip art each time you commit an illustration to computer.

Computer illustration can be broken into four categories:

- Art created from scratch by an artist using computer software, or scanned art or photos manipulated in some way after scanning
- Scanned art used as is after scanning
- Clip art (created in either of the above two ways)
- Technical illustration.

Let's look at these one at a time.

Illustration Programs

For artists or illustrators, the computer is just one more tool at their disposal. Earlier illustration programs were fun and easy to learn and use, took up very little file space, and looked just like computer-generated art when printed. For the non-artist, they were little more than toys; however, for the artist or illustrator, they opened new doors into the world of computers—a world heretofore left primarily to the number-crunchers and newly initiated word processors.

Programs like *MacPaint* and *MacDraw* (once put out by Apple and now by Claris) were pioneers in the field of computer illustration. *MacPaint*, a bit-mapped, freehand art program, allowed even the novice to play artist on the computer screen. The only problem with these programs was the final product. Unless severely reduced when printed, the bit maps showed the end product to be typical computer art.

Object-oriented illustration programs such as *MacDraw* were next on the scene. Object-oriented art used *PostScript* to create precise angles and straight lines for the printer. The result was illustration that had a pen-drawn rather than a computer-drawn appearance—sort of. Although newspaper illustrators took programs like *MacDraw* to their artistic limits, the flexibility wasn't there for the dyed-in-the-wool perfectionist or the technical illustrator.

Then, along came Adobe *Illustrator* from the people who had invented *PostScript*, the language that allowed object-oriented art and computer type-setting to enter a new age. Adobe *Illustrator* literally rocked the illustration and computer world. It could create lines, Bezier curves, geometric forms; and scale, distort, rotate and reflect any shape you created. *Illustrator* was to the graphic artist what *PageMaker* had been to the layout artist. It was based on a whole new technology and wasn't for the faint-hearted. Even those with previous computer-

Figure 5.28 _____

Bit-mapped vs. **PostScript***.*
Although in trained hands paint-
type programs provided a creative
outlet on the computer, the
resolution of the final printed
product suffered from bit-mapping.
Unless severely reduced, the bits
clearly showed, even on a laser
printer. Once PostScript illustra-
tion programs became available,
clean lines and multiple gradations
of shadings could be reproduced
with excellent resolution. Above,
Lincoln drawn from scratch in
Macpaint, *drawn from scratch in*
FreeHand, *traced from the*
Macpaint *original in Adobe*
Streamline, *transferred to* Free-
Hand *and shaded.*

art experience were at first uncomfortable with *Illustrator*; however, once mastered, it became *the* computer tool for artists.

Illustrator, and later its competitor Aldus *FreeHand*, are still the preferred methods for creating computer-generated art that doesn't look like computer-generated art. The two basic methods for doing so are to scan an original and manipulate it in the illustration program, or draw it from scratch.

For the novice or non-artist, scanning and manipulating art may be the best approach, although learning a program as complex as *Illustrator* or *FreeHand* just to use scanned art is a bit like learning to fly a 747 just to use your family car on the weekends. In any event, the method is simple enough.

• Scan the art you wish to use as **line art**. If you are going to trace it in your illustration program (a function now offered by both *Illustrator* and *FreeHand*), it's best to scan it as a TIFF file rather than a paint file. The jagged, bit-mapped lines of a paint file will trace out as jagged, bit-mapped lines as well. In addition, don't try to trace gray-scale scans. Neither illustration program distinguishes between the gray levels well. If you absolutely have to trace a gray-scale photo, make it as high contrast as possible by using a photo software program such as *Image Studio* or *FreeHand* itself, since it allows for image control much the same way *PageMaker* does.

- Once the image is scanned, you can work with it to make it look less like a computer-generated drawing. Unless you have one of the new trace programs designed for use in conjunction with an illustration program, doctoring your traced image will be somewhat frustrating and time-consuming.

For the experienced graphic artist, drawing from scratch is always rewarding and instructional. The best way to learn an illustration program inside out is to experiment; and nothing tests your skills better than creating from scratch. Both *Illustrator* and *FreeHand* provide a great deal of guidance by way of manuals and tutorials.

Figure 5.29

Draw-type programs produced object-oriented, geometric patterns excellent for design and certain types of newspaper graphics (especially charts and graphs). They were, however, difficult to work with and provided no true FreeHand drawing tool. The only rough equivalent produced a sort of polygon which could then be "smoothed." Below are some technical drawings produced using McDraw.

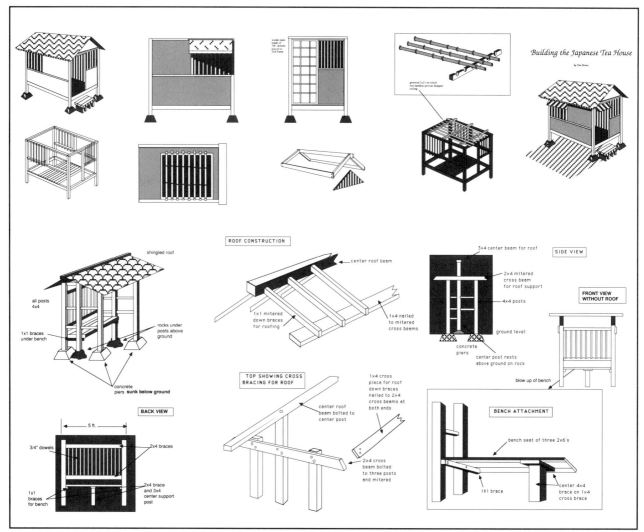

Illustration by Thomas H. Bivins © 1990

Scanned Art

Reworking scanned art is one way of using an illustration program. However, you can also use scanned art as is by scanning a piece of art directly into your page-makeup program for use as a **locator** for finished art or as finished art itself.

When using scanned art, keep a few guidelines in mind.

- When scanning anything other than pure line art, use as many gray scales as your scanner will produce and a 300 dpi resolution. This will allow you to reproduce any art with gradations of coloring or gray areas, including pencil drawings, pastels and paintings.

I was a fresh, new journalist, an
needed a *nom de guerre*; so I
confiscated the ancient mariner'
discarded one, and have done m
best to make it remain what it w
in his hands – a sign and symbol
and warrant that whatever is
found in its company may be
gambled on as being the petrifie
truth.

Mark Twai

Figure 5.30 _____

Scanned and traced photos. *In order to utilize the trace function in* Illustrator *or* FreeHand *(these were done in* FreeHand*) you must start with a high contrast photo or extremely clean line art. Once the tracing is complete, you still have to do a great deal of touch-up to remove the innumerable points created by trace function as it attempts to pick up shading and cross-hatching. The best method is to simply eliminate roughly every other point.*

Figure 5.31 _____

Drawing from scratch. *This illustration, created from scratch, is an example of the complexity of* Aldus *FreeHand. All of the text, display type, and illustration are created in* FreeHand*, as are the various shading patterns. One advantage* FreeHand *has over* Illustrator *is the ability to work with graduated fills and to see them on-screen as you work.* Illustrator *only allows you to work in a "preview mode" in which only the outline of your drawing is visible.*

O • F • C O M P U T E R

D E S I G N

W hat a piece of work is a man!
How noble in reason!
how infinite in faculty!
in form, in moving,
how express and admirable!
in action how like an angel!
in apprehension how like a god!

- For the best reproduction of lines, even in line art, scan to a TIFF or other photo format at a 300 dpi resolution. To eliminate any graying of background areas or lines, adjust your scanner (if it's adjustable) to a higher contrast or use your page-layout program to do it.

- Watch out for file size. A complex piece of line art (say, one with a lot of cross-hatching) can easily take up as much disk space as a large gray-scale photograph. Scaling during scanning, or reducing resolution at scanning or in a photo manipulation program can help.

- If disk space allows, scan at a larger size than your final artwork will be. Reducing scanned line art greatly enhances its crispness, although reducing fine lines will tend to muddy the image.

- Using scanned art and photos as place holders or locators for finished art lets the layout person fit copy and graphic elements exactly, leaving spaces for stripping in finished art. If you're using scanned art for this purpose, there is no need to take up valuable disk space with high-resolution gray-scale images. Unless you're fitting copy around art, scan at a low resolution (72 dpi *MacPaint* format is just fine) and import it into your page-makeup program for placement.

Clip Art

Dozens of manufacturers now offer computer-generated clip art services. Originally, these were based on the bit-mapped technology of the early paint programs or the clumsy but clean draw programs. Today you can purchase clip art in either bit-mapped format or object-oriented format (usually referred to as *PostScript* art) that can be placed directly into your page-makeup program or loaded and manipulated in either *Illustrator* or *FreeHand*. Clip art usually comes on disk or CD ROM (Compact Disk Read Only Memory), a compact disk that is accessed by your computer in order to retrieve information only. Because it can store millions of kilobytes of information, clip art that might fill twenty or thirty double-sided, double-density disks to house can be placed on one compact disk.

Much of what passes for clip art now, however, is a mixed blessing. In any given collection, you will find both superb and amateurish examples. The individual pieces may have been created by dozens of artists using any number of methods ranging from

Figure 5.32 _____

The dinosaur above was rendered by hand first, scanned as line art, traced in Adobe Streamline *(an amazingly fast tracing program for converting line art to computer art), then shaded in Aldus* FreeHand. *The process is much less time consuming than cutting in a rub-down shading pattern by hand. The duck on the left is simply scanned at 300 dpi and full 256 gray-scale from a pencil drawing and placed directly in* PageMaker.

Figure 5.33

TIP: Don't blow up bit-mapped clip art. Enlarging the individual pixels (cells) makes them truly look "computerized." Avoid clip art of any kind that comes with several illustrations to a page or file. Instead, purchase bit-mapped clip art in large originals that you then scale down. The larger the original, the cleaner the art.

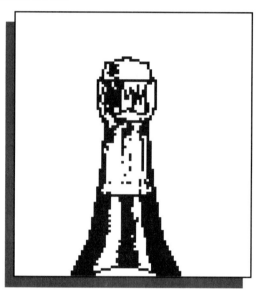

Illustration by Thomas H. Bivins © 1990

Figure 534

One of the real beauties of using computer graphics is the ability to place, size, and basically use them at any time—without having to redraw them. Encapsulated PostScript art can also be enlarged many times its original size without any loss of definition. Unlike bit-mapped graphics (above).

Figure 5.35 _____

TIP: *If you're using the text wrap function in* PageMaker, *you'll run into a small problem when you remove the locator art for placement of finished art: the words that wrapped so neatly around your locator image rush back in like the Red Sea over the Egyptians once you remove it. By scanning your locator art as a gray-scale image at a low resolution, you can use* PageMaker's *image control function to turn the brightness all the way up until the image disappears. Now you can run off your final proof with a dropout ready for your final art.*

scanning original clip art with little or no modification to art created from scratch on the computer. The latter is usually the preferred format for serious clip art users since it is usually divisible (*ungrouped* in the language of illustration programs) into its various original components and thus highly manipulatable using an illustration program. Scanned images don't ungroup because they were scanned as whole images instead of drawn from scratch.

When using clip art, consider the following rules of thumb.

- Decide in advance on the format you want to use. If your layout requires excellent and sharp reproduction, choose *PostScript* clip art. If you are publishing a daily or weekly newsletter that won't suffer from less-than-magazine-quality artwork, use bit-mapped clip art. It can be cheaper and often is available in greater variety than *PostScript* art because of the disk space requirements. Some very excellent bit-mapped clip art is available.

- Don't use it in its original size. Clip art isn't usually intended for use as a 3" x 4" or 1" x 2" piece of illustration. Nothing offends the artistic sensibilities more than a layout peppered with tiny illustrations. Experiment with sizes and different croppings. Make a number of thumbnails or quick layouts until you're satisfied with your illustrations.

Technical Art

Technical art is best left to technical artists. It is a highly specialized area and, like drafting, isn't usually the forum for the typical illustrator. But as a publisher, you need to be aware of two approaches to technical art.

   CAD (computer-assisted drawing) has become a buzzword in the desktop publishing business. Architects, designers, and drafting people alike sing its praises. Basically, CAD programs combine the precision of an illustration program with the needs of a designer to work in three dimensions. CAD software allows you to create three-dimensional images, rotate them, enlarge or reduce them, and manipulate them in dozens of ways. For technical artists who have labored hundreds of hours recreating the same part of a complex machine over

Figure 5.36 _____

Charts and graphs don't have to be dull to make a point. As you can see from the illustrations on this page created in FreeHand, *the points are graphically brought home in a clear and interesting manner.*

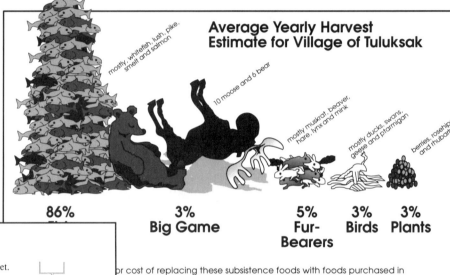

Average Yearly Harvest Estimate for Village of Tuluksak

mostly whitefish, lush, pike, smelt and salmon

10 moose and 6 bear

mostly muskrat, beaver, hare, lynx and mink

mostly ducks, swans, geese and ptarmigan

berries, rosehips and rhubarb

86% | **3%** Big Game | **5%** Fur-Bearers | **3%** Birds | **3%** Plants

...r cost of replacing these subsistence foods with foods purchased in ...erson.

How big is an acre?

One acre contains 43,560 square feet. This is enough land to contain:

3/4 of a football field...

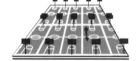

9.1 basketball courts...

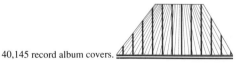

484 mid-sized automobiles...

40,145 record album covers.

J U P I T E R

The largest planet in our solar system, Jupiter is really a huge gas-giant, weighing as much as 330,000 earths.

Illustrations by Thomas H. Bivins © 1990

and over again for each individual version of a drawing, computer-assisted design is heaven sent. But, unless you are an illustrator (technical or otherwise), you'd best stick to clip art or hire out.

Graphing programs (graphic spread sheets) have multiplied over the past few years. In the old days, you analyzed a pile of raw data, plotted it as a chart, and painstakingly drew it out to the exact dimensions needed. Now, you can do it with a single keystroke. Unfortunately, many of these programs are bit-mapped. The final printout is okay if it's going into a report, but if you want to wow your audience with this year's corporate earnings' statement, you're going to have to find a flashier program. Fortunately, more programs are now available in a *PostScript* format that provide clean charts and graphs.

For the desktop publisher whose graphics needs are usually a lot less precise, it is often advisable to create the graphs in an illustration program or right in your page-makeup program. And don't forget freelancers. Hundreds of graphic artists around the country make a healthy living creating unusual ways to graph information. We see the creative results every day in our newspapers and magazines.

Finally, if you can't produce an instantly readable graph or chart, don't use one. It's self-defeating to muddle your message with an undecipherable chart, and can be distracting as well. Although one picture can be worth 10,000 words, it may add more verbiage than you're looking for.

Chapter 6

Layout
Part A: Basics

Buildings have architects—so, too, do publications. Buildings have a structural form that is held together by a foundation, footings, beams, trusses and girders, all of which are carefully planned, calculated and integrated into the design by the architect. At its functional best, that form is a marvelous blend of pragmaticism and aesthetics. Its plan or blueprint is explicitly documented and shared with carpenters, masons, electricians, plumbers and others who make the architect's plan a reality.

Designers are the architects of publications. They are responsible for the publication's permanent master plan, which is carefully tailored to the budget, audience, image and editorial needs of the publisher. Please note that design is not a cosmetic makeover, but a skeletal inner architecture upon which all else is supported. Along with structure, designers bring a tasteful aesthetic to the

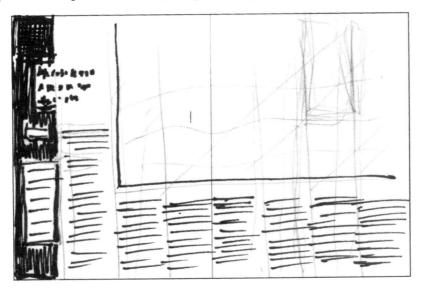

Figure 6.1 _____

Lee Eide, art director at Aster Publishing Corp., uses his own printed thumbnail outlines to work from; Rina Boodman created these "Eidetic" windows, as she refers to them. Here is his thumbnail version of a two-page spread for GPS *(Global Positioning System) magazine. However minimal and quickly rendered, the thumbnail should create a good visual frame of reference, as Eide has done with this one. Reprinted with permission from Aster Publishing Corp.*

publication, by utilizing composition and the basic principles of design, choosing appropriate and hard-working typography, and developing a suitable format. Think of **design** as the *form* of the publication, the permanent visual arrangement that dictates the shaping of the contents. It establishes identity, continuity, regularity and visual flow.

On the other hand, a **layout** is more specific. It is a particular problem-solving process that takes one part of the content—a story, for example—and molds it to fit a given space within a publication's design. It fleshes out the *form* of a magazine, newsletter or brochure, by living up to design specifics of format, typography and visual elements. It also employs the very same design principles as the overall design.

Basic Design Principles—A Common Ground

To reacquaint yourself with approaches to composition and design, review the material in Chapter 2. A succinct review of the principles of design that influence the look of a publication and its layouts follows.

- **Balance** is a matter of equalizing the weight on one side of a vertical axis with that on the opposite side of the axis. We understand balance in a very personal way because we use it to equalize our own weight distribution when we walk, run, ride a bicycle or move around in a small boat. And we are likely to notice a design that is flawed by improper balance immediately, whether or not we've received any graphic arts or design education.

Figure 6.2 _____

*Compare the next stage of layout, the "rough," to the thumbnail which inspired it. (See **Figure 6.1**.) You acquire a lucid sense of Eide's design at this stage. Roughs may vary from being crude enlargements of the thumbnails to the fairly finished pieces. The rough should give a good idea of typography, overall design and artwork for the layout. Here you see a four-column layout which employs L-shape elemental form, a bridging illustration and a bold color bar on the far left column to indicate the start of a new feature. Bolded Futura is used for the head, dropped initial letter and crosshead and Times Roman is used for text. Reprinted with permission from Aster Publishing Corp.*

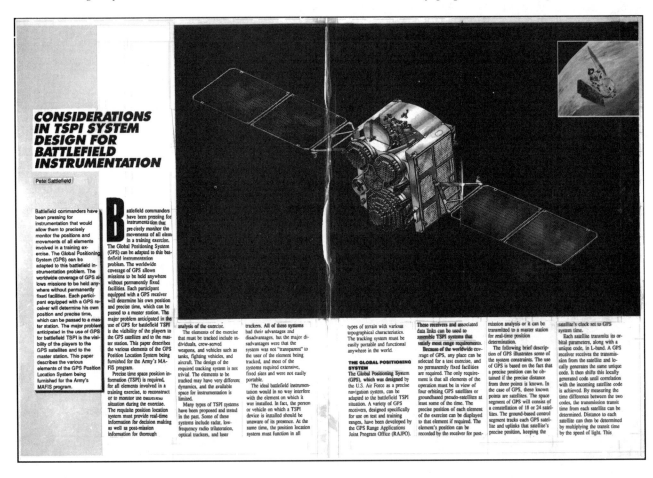

There are two approaches to balance. Formal balance employs symmetry to establish its order. Normally when we think of symmetry we paint a mental image of **bilateral symmetry**. When a space is divided equally in two this symmetry produces reciprocal halves; that is, one side is a mirror image of its opposite half. It is the easiest of the two approaches to arrange in a layout because creating this type of balance is simply a matter of centering and stacking everything—visual, headline, subheads, copy and other elements. Although they impose a rigid order and precision to a page, symmetrical layouts tend to be stiff and much more formal than asymmetrical ones. If your publication, audience or company is conservative, then this traditional use of balance might be a fitting solution.

Asymmetry is a more complicated matter because it involves a certain degree of risk and a full understanding of optical weight. Its weight distribution isn't centered; instead, one side offsets the other much like a seesaw. And like a seesaw, the closer the visual element is located to the axis, the less its visual mass or weight. Asymmetry brings an inherent visual tension and energy to a layout. Like a quick sleight of hand, informal balance stirs our curiosity and forces us to figure it out optically. If motion, excitement, energy or a casual look happen to be what you're looking to impart through a layout, asymmetry may be the answer—or certainly part of it.

- **Proportion** is the dynamic of spatial relationships—how one part or element of your layout compares in size to the rest of its parts—or how one element relates to the whole. Proportion helps us understand and measure distance, size and the relevance of what we see. Something is larger, smaller, closer, wider, darker, thinner, more narrow or heavier *than* something else.

  In addition, proportion directs the sequence of our vision and affects our interpretation of spatial priority. Size implies a visual hierarchy to us: typically, larger sizes suggest importance, dominance, attention or priority over their smaller counterparts. The largest part of any design normally commands our attention, especially larger *visual* portions—they're irresistible and vision tracks to them involuntarily. Generally, avoid working with halved layouts. Half-visual and half-word arrangements are liable to confuse us because they suggest no particular priority and present a static spatial dynamic—visually, anyway. Additionally, fractured space seems more formal and exacting in even portions and more informal and exciting in uneven ones.

- Visually, **sequence** refers to the order of the readout, or what we see first, second, third, and so on within a layout. Normally the Western eye reads from left to right and top to bottom. However, optical weight may redirect our sight, altering customary sequential patterns. So, big areas dominate small ones; color has more attraction for us than black and white; bright colors outweigh flat hues and so forth.

  Some generalizations regarding sequential organization follow:

  - Headlines are normally positioned atop copy blocks, regardless of medium.
  - The more important something is, the higher up its placement in a layout.

Figure 6.3 _____

This page was one of a series of prototype pages created for the redesign of the Oregon Food Journal. *It uses symmetry and a standard three-column format for its mostly traditional audience; for similar reasons, roman type is used throughout. Bill Ryan designed it. Reprinted with permission from the* Oregon Food Journal *and Bill Ryan.*

Figure 6.4 _____

In this instance, the director's photograph was scanned using a diffusion tool. The department designation, rule and text are all centered. The mugshot offsets these, making the page design asymmetrical, despite the former formal elements. Reprinted with permission of the Oregon Food Journal.

- Typically, the left side of a layout carries more priority than its right counterpart. In most publication pages, the most important elements usually sit higher up and, more often than not, on the left.
- Optical weight can rearrange our visual patterns; some of the more common tactics are isolation, color, larger sizes and exaggerated formats.
- Normally our eyes exit a design in the lower right quad.

Sequence is an essential design principle in layout because you are responsible for effectively routing the vision of your audience through a page. Not properly directing them is misdirecting readership. Remember, you're responsible for controlling not only where readers look but how they track what you've visually ordered. Poor sequencing is likely to make us overlook important elements, short-circuiting communication.

- **Emphasis** suggests that a single element should be isolated, contrasted or featured within a layout. When nothing is contrasted or emphasized (tonally, proportionately or otherwise), our vision is forced to guess which part of a layout is important. Proper emphasis provides a clear entry point for the audience and grabs their attention while relating important information and making succinct connections to other elements on the page. The trick is not allowing the audience to hesitate; if you do, you'll likely lose them.

Don't forget that an isolated element or a large visual indicates significance to the reader and shows where a layout's priorities lie. It's important that you ask realistic questions and make thoughtful decisions about the content, suitability and meaning of what you feature. Be sure that

Figure 6.5 _____

Sequence is central to these prototype pages, also created for the Oregon Food Journal. *This simple ragged-bottom, four-column format has a playful feel to it. Notice how the use of rules and photography contribute to sequence and unity of the two pages. The Innovation department features new products and services for the food industry. Design by Bill Ryan. Reprinted with permission of the* Oregon Food Journal.

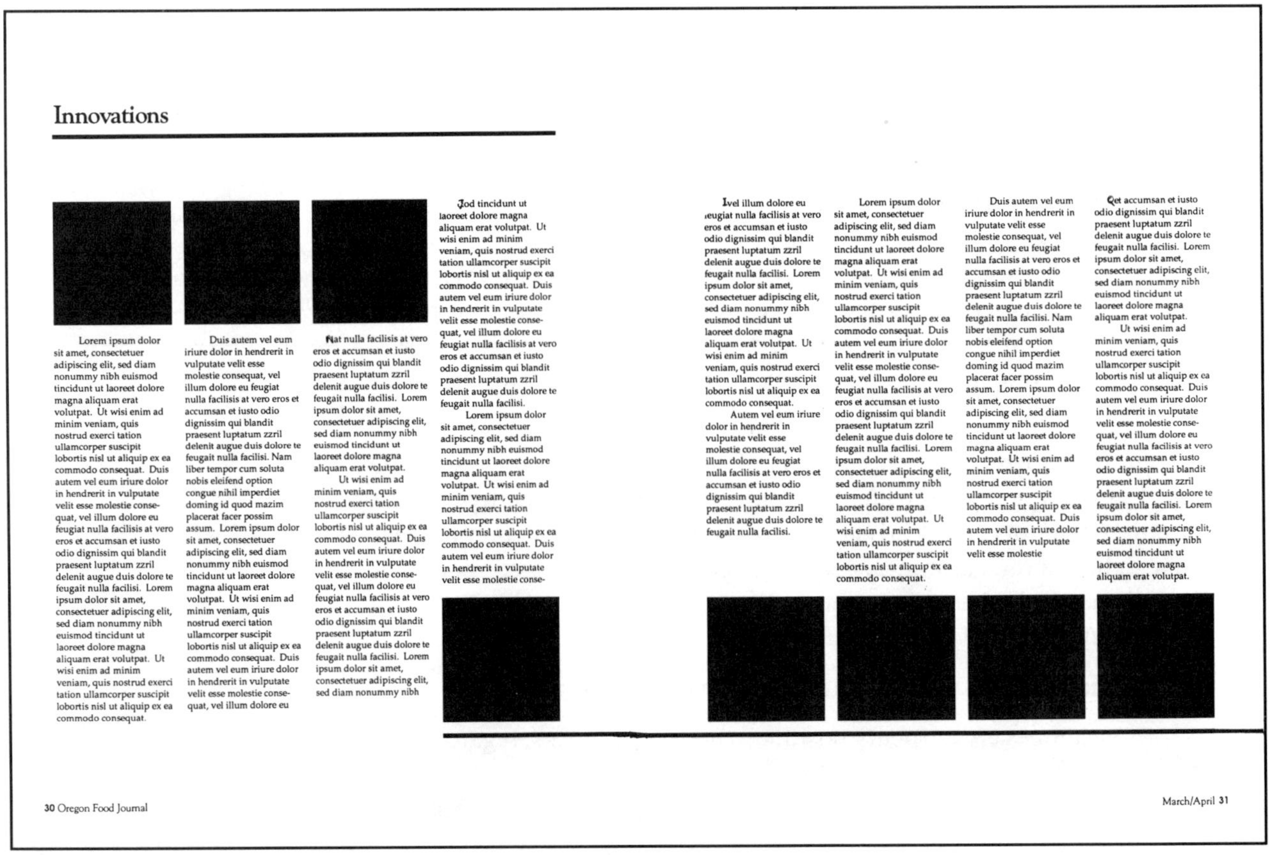

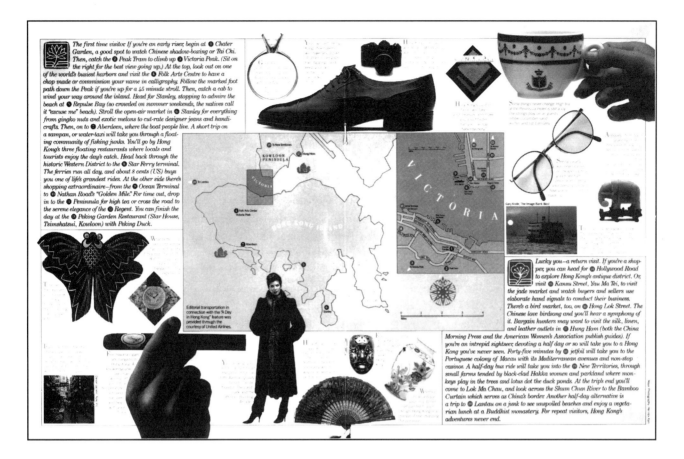

The first time visitor: If you're an early riser, begin at ● Chater Garden, a good spot to watch Chinese shadow-boxing or Tai Chi. Then, catch the ❷ Peak Tram to climb up ● Victoria Peak. (Sit on the right for the best view going up.) At the top, look out on one of the world's busiest harbors and visit the ● Folk Arts Centre to have a chop made or commission your name in calligraphy. Follow the marked foot path down the Peak if you're up for a 45 minute stroll. Then, catch a cab to wind your way around the island. Head for Stanley, stopping to admire the beach at ● Repulse Bay (so crowded on summer weekends, the natives call it "excuse me" beach). Stroll the open-air market in ● Stanley for everything from gingko nuts and exotic melons to cut-rate designer jeans and handicrafts. Then, on to ● Aberdeen, where the boat people live. A short trip on a sampan, or water-taxi will take you through a floating community of fishing junks. You'll go by Hong Kong's three floating restaurants where locals and tourists enjoy the day's catch. Head back through the historic Western District to the ● Star Ferry terminal. The ferries run all day, and about 8 cents (US) buys you one of life's grandest rides. At the other side there's shopping extraordinaire—from the ● Ocean Terminal to ● Nathan Road's "Golden Mile." For time out, drop in to the ● Peninsula for high tea or cross the road to the serene elegance of the ● Regent. You can finish the day at the ● Peking Garden Restaurant (Star House, Tsimshatsui, Kowloon) with Peking Duck.

Editorial transportation in connection with the "A Day in Hong Kong" feature was provided through the courtesy of United Airlines.

Lucky you—a return visit. If you're a shopper, you can head for ● Hollywood Road to explore Hong Kong's antique district. Or, visit ● Kansu Street, Yau Ma Tei, to visit the jade market and watch buyers and sellers use elaborate hand signals to conduct their business. There's a bird market, too, on ● Hong Lok Street. The Chinese love birdsong and you'll hear a symphony of it. Bargain hunters may want to visit the silk, linen, and leather outlets in ● Hung Hom (both the China Morning Press and the American Women's Association publish guides). If you're an intrepid sightseer, devoting a half day or so will take you to a Hong Kong you've never seen. Forty-five minutes by ● jetfoil will take you to the Portuguese colony of Macau with its Mediterranean avenues and non-stop casinos. A half-day bus ride will take you into the ● New Territories, through small farms tended by black-clad Hakka women and parkland where monkeys play in the trees and lotus dot the duck ponds. At the trip's end you'll come to Lok Ma Chau, and look across the Shum Chun River to the Bamboo Curtain which serves as China's border. Another half-day alternative is a trip to ● Lantau on a junk to see unspoiled beaches and enjoy a vegetarian lunch at a Buddhist monastery. For repeat visitors, Hong Kong's adventures never end.

what you emphasize warrants emphasis. Blind or dead-ended visuals also will abort a communication. Making an inappropriate visual larger for emphasis only makes the mistaken judgment more apparent to the reader.

A layout that contains too much emphasis is as much a problem as one that has none. It creates visual anarchy, with visuals and other elements fighting one another. Simple is better. Every layout should emphasize or contrast one element or idea.

- **Unity** refers to the cohesion and overall coherence of a layout's parts, especially as each portion relates to the rest. Normally layouts consist of headlines, artwork, copy blocks and perhaps another element or two—for example, a graphic, logotype, chart, graph or the like. All of these must fuse or fit comfortably together.

Regardless of whether we've had formal design training, we sense when something is out of place or doesn't quite assimilate. For example, borders are considered appropriate unifiers, but the frilly affectation of an embroidered border on a contemporary advertisement shatters whatever other unity might be present.

Typography is also critical to unity. One strategy you might employ to maintain typographical unity is to avoid overusing faces, a common temptation for someone new to design or desktop publishing. Another is to work with a single face and employ different weights, sizes and postures within a design—or, for that matter, within a publication.

Other ways to unify a layout include color, parallel structure, appropriate use of white space, contrast and the other design principles we've already discussed in **Chapter 2**.

Figure 6.6 _____

This exciting spread on Hong Kong pushes design principles to the limit. The asymmetrical balance is a wild mix of art (mostly silhouette photography) and type. The hand in the lower left balances and directs vision concurrently, while its upper right counterpart balances a cup of tea on its caption. Sequence links the text by joining the two copy areas with a map of Victoria Harbor. Borders, typography, tint blocks, graphics and art that cross the gutter help unify the pages. In this case, the artwork reinforces the emphasis of the map by intersecting and framing it . Elemental form (L-shapes) is established through the white areas that contain the art and captions in the areas above and below the map. In fact, the copy areas are chunky versions of the same elemental form. Kit Hinrichs art directed these lush pages for Skald *magazine; Karen Berndt coordinated the art, and Henrick Kam was responsible for the major photography. Reprinted with permission from* Skald *and* Pentagram.

Layout Stages

There are three different layout stages: thumbnail sketches, roughs and finished layouts. Certainly, variations within each stage run the gamut from very rough to painstakingly finished, so what constitutes a rough to one designer, might be closer to a finished piece to another. The important thing to remember is that every layout should evolve, from thumbnail to camera-ready layouts.

Novices are often likely to slam together a rough version of a layout without ever giving thought to creating a series of **thumbnails**, miniature replicas of what the life-size layout will look like. Thumbnails need not be detailed, because their function is to provide a preliminary overview of a layout's structural possibilities. They should be carefully considered graphic experiments or possible solutions to the problem at hand. Extensive swipe files provide a great variety of artwork to consider when developing thumbnails.

To get a real feel from your strongest thumbnails, make them proportionate to the finished size. (A scaling wheel can help you with explicit scaled down sizes.) Be sure to work in the approximate tonal values and color that you intend to use in the finished version, and render these quick-study sketches on the same color paper you'll be using in your publication. Keep the size, shapes and location of layout elements fairly proportional to the finished design. Finally, use traditional means or a computer to figure out the approximate area of your copy. (See the back section of this chapter for particulars on copyfitting.)

Remember, the function of a thumbnail is to provide a *rough* idea of your layout possibilities. Don't make two of them and presume you're finished. The

Figure 6.7 _____

*Lee Eide provides a variation of this basic feature design in this rough. (Compare this rough layout to that in **Figure 6.2**.) Although he maintains the four-column feature arrangement, he uses one of those columns on the left page for the artwork which bridges the two pages. Still another left column is used for the color bar, which is color-keyed to the photography. Reprinted with permission of Aster Publishing Corp.*

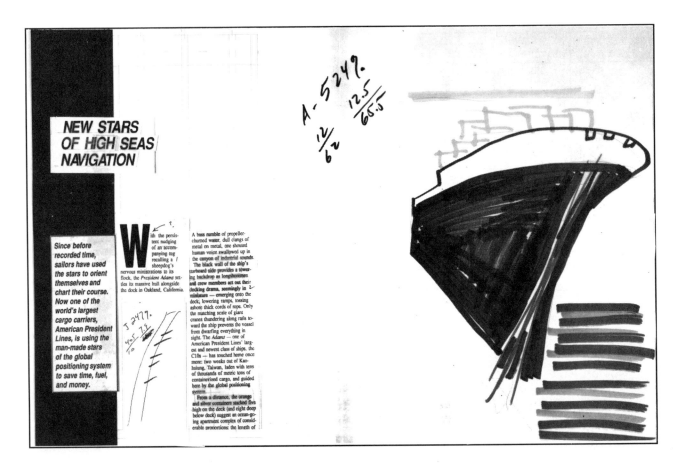

more you produce, the more likely you are to arrive at a solution that's as functional as it is attractive.

When you're satisfied that you've sketched enough thumbnail sketches, select the strongest two or three for additional development. At this point, you want a closer look at the layout.

Rough layouts are always rendered at reproduction size, except when working with outdoor or poster design. (See **Figure 6.8**.) Many layout artists use tracing or layout paper for roughs because it allows them to trace visuals or lettering quickly.

Begin the rough by lining in the dimensions of your layout. Then transfer a refined version of each element proportionally to the full-size sketch. It's important that you capture the look and feel of the type you've chosen, so be sure to letter in the headlines carefully. Chisel point pencils produce a broad stroke and a fairly hard edge, so you can put down lettering quickly and cleanly.

If you intend to run a 48-point headline, letter it in at that size, using the weight, posture and positioning you intend to use for publication. Type specimens are available in type books or various texts. One easy way to approximate line size is to measure the letters to be used one word at a time, then figure positioning from those estimates. Or use a typeset or laser printed headline, because it leaves positioning less to chance and because it's easy to have heads printed out. If copy for the project is complete, have it set as it would be for the finished layout, in the correct typeface and point size, weights, leading, column width and other typographical particulars. That way you can line in the copy exactly. Remember, the closer the rough is to the finished version the better. Apply color and other particulars to flesh it out.

Figure 6.8 _____

How closely do designers follow their design strategies and guidelines? In most cases, very closely. Of course, working with real copy and artwork helps flesh out a page very near to its completed form, as evidenced with this two-page layout executed by Lee Eide, art director for GPS *magazine. The point, however, is clear; namely, that rough layouts have a specific purpose: to connect the designer's original idea to production. Reprinted with permission of Aster Publishing Corp.*

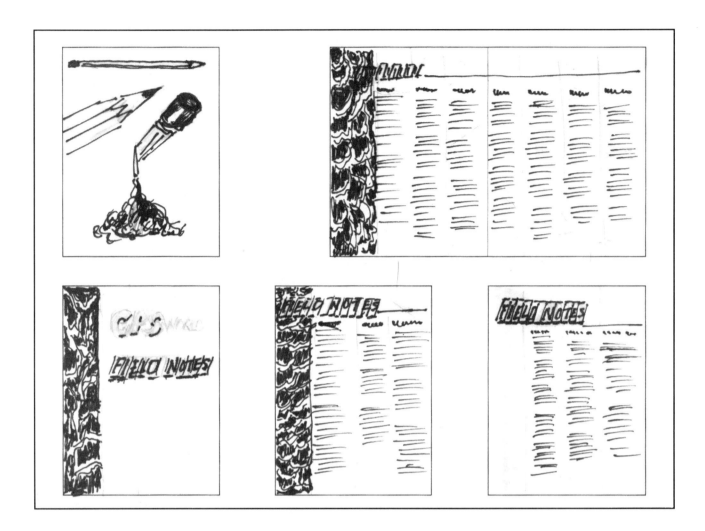

Figures 6.9, 6.10 and 6.11_____

Thumbnail sketches need not be detailed, because their function is to provide a preliminary overview of a layout's structural possibilities. These thumbnails—and variations thereof—led to the development of both a magazine department as well a collateral publication for GPS. The reticulated black-and-white background is reminiscent of a composition notebook and was used here for Field Notes.

Using the smaller designs as a yardstick, compare them to the publication's rough and finished stages. Thumbnails, rough and finished pieces created by Lee Eide. Reprinted with permission from Aster Publishing Corp.

If you don't like the full-size rough as much as you did its miniature counterpart, return to your thumbnails or sketch a variation or two from the rough. Returning to the smaller layout permits you to rearrange elements and work a kink or problem out of the layout quickly.

Finished layouts further refine the idea. Don't even think about them if you haven't resolved every single question or problem raised by the rough. Finished layouts take a good deal of time and effort, so you need to be confident of what you've come up with.

Some designers or production people use the term **comprehensive** or **comp** interchangeably with finished layout. Comprehensives should always simulate the quality of the finished piece. Like the other stages, there is a wide range of finish or detail to this stage, too. How detailed they should be depends largely on the client or your needs. The less a client knows about this process, the more finished your comprehensive should be. Very often headlines, copy and other typographic elements are typeset and laid out with the artwork and photographed or photocopied. In this instance, the comprehensive isn't the original work.

Very often the comps are mounted and matted for presentation. Sometimes a presentation will include slides of the comprehensive, its evolution and specific parts so clients have a larger than life view of the work and understand its development. Pinning up an 8" x 10" finished layout and discussing it fifteen feet away doesn't do it justice. Using a poster-sized layout in this situation isn't the best way to present it, either. If you can afford it, make color copies of the

FIELD NOTES

JANUARY

INTRODUCTION

Because of the worldwide coverage of GPS, any place can be selected for a test exercise, and no permanently fixed facilities are required. The only requirement is that all elements of the operation must be in view of four orbiting GPS satellites or groundbased pseudosatellites at least some of the time. The precise position of each element of the exercise can be displayed to that element if required. The element's position can be recorded by the receiver for post-mission analysis or it can be transmitted to a master station for real-time position determination.

The following brief description of GPS illustrates some of the system constraints. The use of GPS is based on the fact that a precise position can be obtained if the precise distance from three points is known. In the case of GPS, these known points are satellites.

IMPACT OF GPS

The elements of the exercise that must be tracked include individuals, crewserved weapons, and vehicles such as tanks, fighting vehicles, and aircraft. The design of the required tracking system is not trivial. The elements to be tracked may have very different dynamics, and the available space for instrumentation is limited.

Cost of Installing the GPS tems have been proposed and tested in the past. Some of these systems include radar, low-frequency radio trilateration, optical trackers, and laser trackers. All of these systems had their advantages and disadvantages, but the major disadvantages were that the system was not "transparent" to the user of the element being tracked, and most of the systems required extensive, fixed sites and were not easily portable.

TECHNOLOGICAL

Because of the worldwide coverage of GPS, any place can be selected for a test exercise, and no permanently fixed facilities are required. The only requirement is that all elements of the operation must be in view of four orbiting GPS satellites or groundbased pseudosatellites at least some of the time. The precise position of each element of the exercise can be displayed to that element if required. The element's position can be recorded by the receiver for post-mission analysis or it can be transmitted to a master station for real-time position determination.

The following brief description of GPS illustrates some of the system constraints. The use of GPS is based on the fact that a precise position can be obtained if the precise distance from three points is known. In the case of GPS, these known points are satellites.

GPS FOR HYDRO SURVEYING

GPS Impact on Chart Users. cise that must be tracked include individuals, crewserved weapons, and vehicles such as tanks, fighting vehicles, and aircraft. The design of the required tracking system is not trivial. The elements to be tracked may have very different dynamics, and the available space for instrumentation is limited.

Many types of TSPI systems have been proposed and tested in the past. Some of these systems include radar, low-frequency radio trilateration, optical trackers, and laser trackers. All of these systems had their advantages and disadvantages, but the major disadvantages were that the system was not "transparent" to the user of the element being tracked.

Table 1. Definition of terms

The following are some of the terms frequently used in contact lens

Head 2
preclinical lens material/solution interaction study that examines lens surface tendencies (parameters, discoloration, uptake, wettability)
what a lens is subjected to when the prescribed regimen is followed one time
a means of killing residual bacteria or other microorganisms
a protein cleaner used to remove tear protein and debris that may be deposited on the lens surface
the four FDA hydrogel lens groups are Group 1 (low water, nonionic); Group 2 (high water, nonionic); Group 3 (low water, ionic); and Group 4 (high water, ionic)
the process of decomposing hydrogen peroxide into a non-toxic, non-irritating solution
a prescribed set of regular lens care procedures, usually involving surfactant cleaning, disinfection, and enzymatic cleaning
a detergent-like cleaner used to remove normal biofilm and debris from lenses

LITERATURE

There are many factors to consider when using a GPS receiver. Antenna placement and design to assure sufficiently received L-band signal strength, since the spread spectrum GPS signal is only 136 dBm, is a major consideration in GPS tracking system design. Data link antenna design and placement are also important to assure reliable transmission position data to a master station. In addition, the required pseudo range measurements can be made either in parallel or sequentially. The dynamics of the vehicle to be tracked determine which mechanization is used. A slowly-sequencing receiver is adequate at up to 1g. A fast sequencing receiver can handle up to 4g, and a parallel receiver with an associated inertial reference unit can handle up to 10g.

POSITIONS

There are several ways to determine position without being in view of four orbiting GPS satellites. This makes it possible to extend the windows of use of the GPS during time of limited satellite availability. A pseudo-satellite, or GPS ground transmitter, can substitute for one or more satellites. Also, if a precise time standard is available to the receiver, only three satellites or pseudo-satellites are required for a position determination once the clock is set to GPS system time. Militarized rubidium oscillators combined with disciplining electronics can hold time to within 10 nsec over a 2-hr period.

Peter Kielland
Canadian Hydrographic Survey

There are many factors to consider when using a GPS receiver. Antenna placement and design to assure sufficiently received L-band signal strength, since the spread spectrum GPS signal is only 136 dBm, is a major consideration in GPS tracking system design. Data link antenna design and placement are also important to assure reliable transmission position data to a master station. In addition, the required pseudo range measurements can be made either in parallel or sequentially.

PRODUCTS

The accuracy required detertest and training ranges, have been developed by the GPS Range Applications Joint Program Office (RAJPO). These receivers and associated data links can be used to assemble TSPI systems that satisfy most range requirements.

1) Calibrating Existing Survey coverage of GPS, any place can be selected for a test exercise, and no permanently fixed facilities are required. The only requirement is that all elements of the operation must be in view of four orbiting GPS satellites or groundbased pseudosatellites at least some of the time. The precise position of each element of the exercise can be displayed to that element if required. The element's position can be recorded by the receiver for post-mission analysis or it can be transmitted to a master station for real-time position determination.

2) Calibration of Loran C Using tion of GPS illustrates some of the system constraints. The use of GPS is based on the fact that a precise position can be obtained if the precise distance from three points is known. In the case of GPS, these known points are satellites. The space segment of GPS will consist of a constellation of 18 or 24 satellites. The ground-based control segment tracks each GPS satellite and uplinks that satellite's precise position, keeping the satellite's clock set to GPS system time.

3) Instrument Recovery. orbital parameters, along with a unique code, in L-band. A GPS receiver receives the transmission from the satellite and locally generates the same unique code.

TIP OF THE MONTH

TOUGH JOBS	There are several ways to determine position without being in view of four orbiting GPS satellites. This makes it	possible to extend the windows of use of the GPS during time of limited satellite availability.
COMPUTERS	pseudo-range rather than range because the individual clock biases in the satellites are not precisely known. To ob-	tain GPS system time, pseudo-range from a fourth satellite is measured and used to correct the receiver's
STUFFY OFFICES	A pseudo-satel-lite, or GPS transmitter, can substitute for one or more satellites. Also, if a precise time standard is available to the receiver, only	three satellites or pseudo-satellites are required for a position determination once the clock is set to GPS system time. Militarized

Calibration is normally done close to shore using a short range microwave positioning system. This normally means that the survey ship loses a lot of time steaming back and forth to the calibration site

Figure 1: GPS Calibration Sharp Increased the Productivity of Offshore Surveys.

Calibration is normally done close to shore using a short range microwave positioning system. This normally means that the survey ship loses a lot of time steaming back and forth to the calibration site

---

FIELD NOTES

MAY/JUNE

ARTICLES

GPS World's May-June issue will feature GPS applications in railroad system management, marine navigation and positioning, geographic information system-based work or toxic waste monitoring, photogrammetry, and timing.

■ "On Track with GPS" will focus on Burlington Northern Railroad's plans to use a GPS-based Advanced Railroad Electronics System (ARES) designed by Rockwell International. After years of testing on a trial system in the Mesabi Iron Range, BN is moving toward implementation of a major capital works program that will bring ARES on-line in the next few years.

■ "Northern Lights: GPS Shines on Canadian Coast Guard." David Jackson, manager of the operational requirements division in the DOE's Fleet Systems Directorate, describes his agency's use of GPS-equipped ships for icebreaking, buoy-tending, and search and rescue.

CALL FOR ARTICLES

An enthusiastic satisfied business is your company's best representative. Your customers are a good part of your GPS-related creative applications or new applications that have been tried and proven. Join the crowd promoting the GPS technology-related articles.

■ "GIS Applications of the Global Positioning System." Environmental scientist Terrence Stonecliff writes about the Environmental Protection Agency's use of GPS with GIS to evaluate and quantify the spatial accuracy of digital map data for toxic EPA successful sites.

■ "A Practical Example of Photogrammetric Control by Kinematic GPS." The National Oceanic and Atmospheric Administration reports on use of kinematic GPS techniques to establish photogrammetric control experiments.

■ "GPS — It's about Time!" presents an overview of how GPS satellites' atomic clocks can meet precise timing and time transfer needs.

■ Columns. Our innovative editors discuss the GPS satellite signal and Washington View reports on the latest meeting of the Civil GPS Service steering committee.

NEWS FROM THE RESEARCH DEPT.

A recent subscriber survey conducted by GPS World showed that 68.5% of GPS World readers plan to purchase GPS equipment.

half of these readers are planning to purchase equipment within the next year. To find out the actual number of units each of these people plan to purchase, **contact Art Rosenberg at (201) 549-3000.**

68.5% will purchase

"TOP 10" SALES LEAD GENERATORS

Magellan	390
Ashtech	249
Trimble	227
US Avionics	222
Racal-Survey	166
Geotronics	121
Wild Leitz	118
SKI	117
Plessey	111
Navstar	98

As of March 8, GPS World has generated over 4,300 sales leads for its January-February advertisers. Here are the "Top 10" producers (includes advertising and "I-applicable-product/literature leads).

MAY ISSUE FEATURES BONUS DISTRIBUTION AT FIG XIX

The benefits of worldwide circulation will be clearly demonstrated to advertisers in the May issue of GPS World. The 30,000+ worldwide circulation will be enhanced with bonus distribution at FIG XIX in Helsinki, Finland.

AD CLOSING IS APRIL 16.

To reserve your advertising space, call Art Rosenberg at (201) 549-3000 for more information.

GPS party meets locals near Turkish-Iranian border.

INDUSTRY NEWS

EDO NAMED ASHTECH'S CANADIAN REP

Ashtech Inc. of Sunnyvale, California, announced that it has selected EDO Canada Ltd. of Calgary, Alberta as its exclusive Canadian representative for sales and leasing of Ashtech GPS geodetic survey equipment. Formerly JMR Instruments Canada Ltd. EDO has background in both the survey and navigation markets.

EDO has established a complete maintenance and training depot for Ashtech equipment at its Calgary manufacturing facility, where an extensive pool of Ashtech precision geodetic GPS receivers is available for leasing. Analytical engineering support and training will also be conducted on a regular basis. Under this agreement Ashtech and EDO will conduct joint development activities related to integrated navigation systems and azimuth determination systems using GPS.

STC SUPPLIES SIMULATOR TO ESA

STC of London has furnished a GPS satellite simulator to the European Space Agency for use in the precisely received space-related program. ESA will use the six-channel STR-type simulator in the development and testing of its new breed of spaceborne navigation equipment. The system will be used to simulate the GPS space segment in a laboratory environment.

GPS systems of the future, such as Navstar, use a constellation of satellites to provide accurate data to users anywhere on earth at any time of the day or night. The simulator provides the frequencies and the modulation to truly represent these signals as received during operation. For relevant operating conditions, the simulated motion of the dynamic motion of the receiver and the spacecraft.

The simulator, valued at more than £300,000, was manufactured at STC's factory in Paignton, Devon, United Kingdom, and has been installed in the European Space Research and Technology Centre at Noordwijk in the Netherlands.

TIP OF THE MONTH

GUIDELINES FOR PRODUCT AND LITERATURE SUBMISSIONS

Our readers are eager for news of your products. That's why GPS World's Product and Literature sections are so popular. The Reader Service Numbers allow readers to find out more about your product and enable you to make contact with potential buyers. But to present your product in one of those sections, we need material from you.

For the Product section, we need a press release that includes:
■ Product brand name and model number
■ Generic description of the product type
■ Standard and optional features
■ Capabilities
■ Applications
■ Company contact and locator

Releases accompanied by a four-color transparency or print of the product are more likely to be published

For the Literature section send a press release that includes:
■ Brochures
■ Catalogs
■ Information packets
■ Data sheets
■ Newsletters

Literature material can feature one product, a series of products, or your company's entire product line, and it should have a cover that will reproduce well in black and white.

For information call Guy Maynard (503) 343-1200

Here is your first installment of GPS World's newsletter. In addition to upcoming editorial features and marketing opportunities, we'll be bringing you market research results, tips on preparing product and literature releases, and industry news. Let us know what you'd like to see in the newsletter. Send ideas and press releases for the newsletter to GPS World P.O. Box 10460, Eugene, OR 97440

The seventh Block II NAVSTAR GPS satellite was scheduled to be launched no sooner than March 21, 1990. The sixth Block II satellite was launched January 24, 1990, and set "available" on February 14. Four more satellites are scheduled to be launched during 1990.

comprehensive for everyone attending the presentation. Slides can be effective in crowded situations, but be sure to have first-generation mechanicals, photographs or the original itself at the presentation.

Modular Layout

Grids reinforce the rectangular format common to most publications by ordering layout elements in smaller rectangles. In fact, layout sheets are grid maps which offer you a wide variety of rectangular options, vertical and horizontal. They stratify your layout space with a multitude of column and module sizes, offering two, three, four or more columns per page on the same layout sheet.

Layout sheets come in as many different sizes as there are formats. Many sheets that are custom-designed for publications come complete with registration marks, outer margin lines and usually are hashed or lined in inches and picas and points. These sheets come printed in a light turquoise, which is nonreproducible because the film used to shoot layouts is insensitive to that color. Layout artists and designers often mark up their layouts with nonrepro blue pencils and markers because, although obvious to the naked eye, these

Figure 6.12 _____

Using an Apple Macintosh computer and Aldus PageMaker desktop publishing program, The Bailey/Warner Group and designer John Williams created these immaculate-looking roughs for ABC's newsletter, As Easy as ABC. *The five-column pages are based on the grid and use the outside columns for supportive information: teases, contents, logotype, pullouts and captions and photos that extend beyond the designated copy area. This very simple but functional basic grid format was created by John Williams and The Bailey/ Warner Group for ABC Technologies. Reprinted with permission from ABC Technologies and The Bailey/Warner Group.*

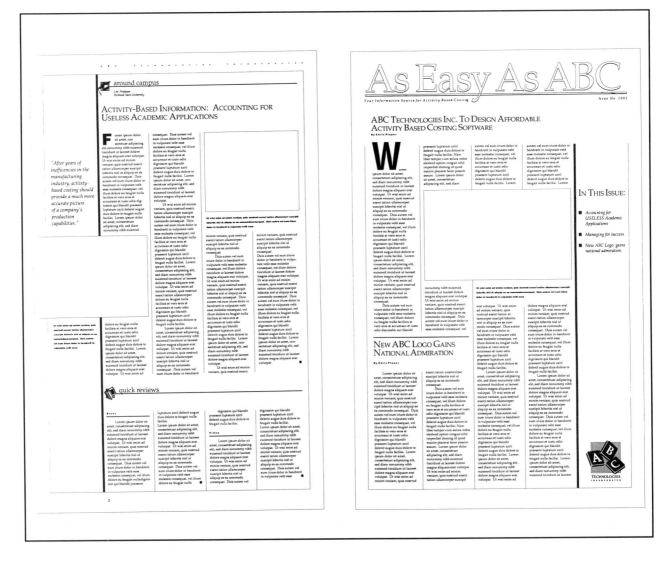

scribblings aren't picked up by the camera. Don't write on a final layout unless you're using these special pencils. Some designers and printers don't like finished layouts to be marked up or written on at all. In those instances, use self-adhesive notes for the layout.

Grids are also available to you electronically. All of today's desktop programs use video grids for both layout and design purposes; their use will be explored in the second half of this chapter.

Although a Spartan model of simplicity, the grid offers you an infinite possibility of choices. Modular layout orders space clearly and cleanly. It also establishes a hierarchial treatment of the layout elements, or individual stories and their respective parts. Modular arrangement neatly wraps headlines, body copy and artwork together. In many instances, borders demarcate space and hold a module in place; on other occasions borderless screens clearly distinguish the module. Usually, the various modules themselves highlight one another through their self-containment. Because mod-layouts are preplanned and adjustable, they are easier to execute. What's more, they may be modified without destroying the entire layout—something paste-up and production people greatly appreciate. That quality allows the layout artist a flexible but precise way of handling layout particulars.

Figure 6.13 _____

Compare this finished publication to its "rough" version—Figure 6.12. Although minor differences exist— for example, a mug shot appears on the back page where none existed in the rough—the finished version nearly mirrors the rough. Two very important things that computers bring to the design process are an incredible immediacy to facilitate feedback and graphic and typographic precision that rivals the finished product. The finished publication used the logotype and icons designed for the rough as well as a second color—maroon in this case. Designed by The Bailey/ Warner Group and designer John Williams. Reprinted with permission from ABC Technologies and The Bailey/Warner Group.

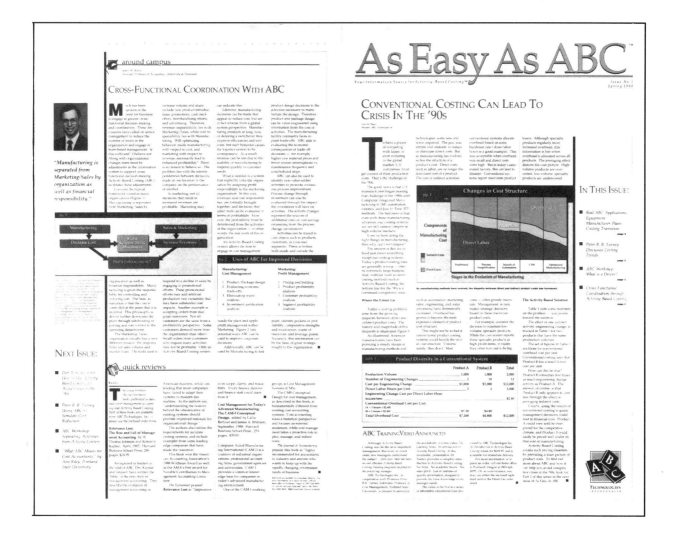

Figure 6.14 _____

Another place that grids and modular design dominate is the table of contents page. Probably ninety percent or more of all table of contents designs are modular. This prototype page, created for the Oregon Food Journal, *is no exception. It was designed by Bill Ryan on a Macintosh II and Aldus PageMaker™. Reprinted with permission from* Oregon Food Journal *and Bill Ryan.*

A few years back, it was fashionable to use horizontal modules to break up the vertical grid. Today, the dominant vertical approach is again in vogue, but there is something to be said in favor of horizontal layouts. For one thing, they look a lot less imposing. Besides offering a modular format some variety, they are reader-friendly, that is, their approach to a layout is easier to read. Also, although they take up more room, horizontal layouts tend to look more ordered and make better use of two pages in running layouts.

Photo Arrangement in the Layout

How you arrange photographs is also determined by the principles we've already outlined. Consider the following additional points.

- In any grouping of photographs, one should dominate. Try to place it somewhere in the middle of others, so that it radiates or connects clearly to the others. Individually, each photograph should have only one dominant element as well.

- People in your photographs should look into the page—not off it. We follow tend to follow vision almost as closely in design as we do in real life. When you notice someone looking intently upward (or whatever direction), your curiosity steers your vision the same direction. The same is true for photographs. Understanding that, don't direct your reader off the page.

- Use directional devices to your advantage. Run those photographs that look, point or move to the right on the left side of the grouping (and vice versa). These internal leads will direct the eyes of the reader to the middle, featured image.

- Bigger images attract more attention than small ones. It should go without saying that if you have a truly important or remarkable photograph, you should run it large. If you must run photographs at postage stamp sizes, why use them at all? At such miniature sizes no one will be able to see them. Time and again, newsletters jam a group shot of a dozen people or so into an area half the size of a playing card. The captions for these images sometimes take up more space than photographs themselves. If space forces you to run photographs at postage-stamp sizes, you're probably better off to leave them out.

- When you're running an action image, don't cut it short. If the object or person in an image is moving to the right, leave space in the photograph's right side. Action images need a margin of space to grow or move into. When you cut them short, you stifle the illusion of movement within the frame.

- Bleeds suggest that something cannot be contained on a page. Bled images need not be totally bled. Often an image can be successfully bled on one, two or three sides. All other things being equal, a partially bled image commands more impact or power in a grouping of pictures. In fact, if your sizes are restricted, you can make an image dominate a group by bleeding it to one or more sides.

- We're used to seeing photography straitjacketed into the same format as its negative. But since we seldom use the entirety of a negative image in the print, why should we remain shackled to the format? Exaggerated formats can compliment the verticality or horizontal quality of the space you're using.

  Accommodate line more fully by cropping narrowly where appropriate. Better yet, plan your original layout with the exaggerated format in mind. Accenting the use of line in a layout makes it appear slimmer and more stylish, and offers the reader a refreshing change. This is especially true when exaggerated formats are bled.

- Remember, one good photograph is worth 10,000 lousy ones. Edit your photographs ruthlessly; if you have doubts about the value of an image, trust your instincts and purge it.

Final Observations

Here are a few final layout generalizations to keep in mind. Please note, though, that they are not hard and fast rules.

- Ground thirds is an important proportional device; it is not by accident that most magazines, newsletters and annual reports use this principle. This approach lends a more dynamic ratio to your space, and it provides logical divisions: one-column copy to a two-column visual and vice versa. You

Figure 6.15 _____

Unusual camera angle, the grid and elemental form (O-shape in the image itself and L-shape in the overall page design) add to the success of this layout. Although the main photograph isn't bled, its targeting device and repetitive shapes help it dominate both pages. Additionally, the red of the football players' jerseys is reinforced in the blurb and caption. Note how the left-hand page image is bled to that side; that strategy provides the designer an additional entry point on the page, a smart and effective move by Texas Monthly *art director D. J. Stout. The photography shows off the talent of Robb Kendrick. Reprinted with permission from* Texas Monthly.

Can't Win for Losing

On the verge
of becoming Texas' worst
football team ever,
underdog players at an underdog high school have
one last chance to break a
six-year losing streak.

by
Skip Hollandsworth

The co-captain: Rene Bocanegra (left) had a B average.

It was already Wednesday afternoon, the game of the year was just three days away, and an all-too-familiar sense of doom was sweeping over the practice session of the Memorial High School Minutemen. The offense broke out of the huddle with a clap, senior center Louis Hernandez bent over the ball, and on the proper count, he snapped it between his legs into what he thought were the waiting hands of the quarterback. Unfortunately, the quarterback, Edward Romo, wasn't there. He was waiting for the hike seven yards away in the back

The huddle: As they get together for Thursday afternoon football practice, San Antonio's Memorial   High Minutemen carried the burdens of 51 straight losses, an impoverished neighborhood, too little school pride, and too much awareness that life can be unfair.

Figure 6.16 _____

Stout makes remarkable use of Kendrick's photography through gridded positioning, sensible photo sizes and bleeds. Artwork that is positioned to the outside is bled off the edges on these two pages. By panning with the action at slower shutter speeds, the photographer partially blurs the image and contributes to the feeling of action and movement within the images. Kendrick's style and Stout's keen editing add to the visual continuity and intensity of Skip Hollandsworth's article for Texas Monthly, *making this layout a memorable and exemplary one. Reprinted with permission from the* Texas Monthly.

can also use ground thirds vertically. A visual makes up the upper two-thirds of a layout and the head and copy the lower third.

• Don't scatter related photographs or illustrations on a page. They'll have more impact if you group them, and it's likely that they'll strengthen the page's unity.

• Elemental form may serve as a strong framing device in a layout, particularly the L- and T-shapes and variations thereof. Work this concept in headline arrangements, photography and overall page design. It can work as effectively with modular design as it can working alone.

• It's a good idea to frame black-and-white photographs with borders. Most photographs have white areas on the edges, making it difficult to see where the photograph ends and the white space begins. Framing the photograph with a hairline or one point line is unobstrusive and will help unify the image.

• Use white space as a visual element. Too often, it is used in a layout by accident—as leftover space. Remember that white space may be incorporated into any of the design principles. What's more, it invites readership by providing a resting place for the eyes, while organizing, demarcating and otherwise further structuring the layout.

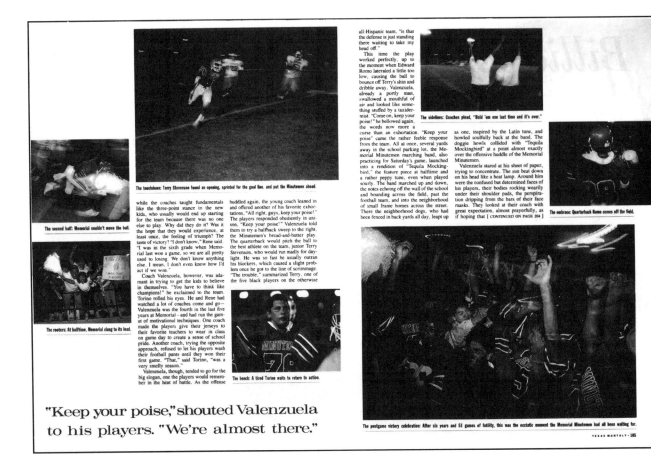

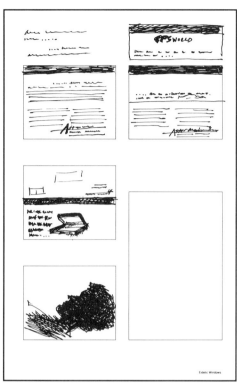

Figure 6.17

Even though these thumbnails are reproduced at slightly less than half their original sizes—practically postage stamp dimensions to begin with—you still come away with a good visual idea of what they'll look like. Thumbnails by Lee Eide. Reprinted with permission from Aster Publishing Corp.

Figure 6.18

Thumbnails are central to any design process, regardless of whether you're producing automobiles or publications. This finished piece was spawned from a series of thumbnails, some of which appear in the previous figure. These two-color collateral pieces were created for Aster Publishing's Marketing Services by art director Lee Eide. Reprinted with permission from Aster Publishing Corp.

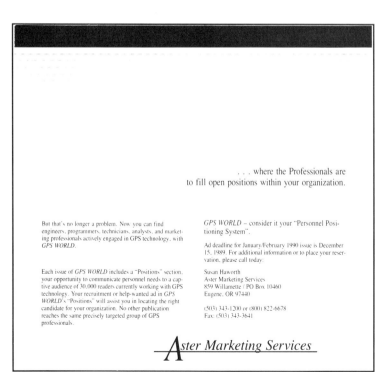

Figure 6.19

Not only must all print materials live and die by design principles, they are created by designers who also pay very close attention to different media nuances. What's more, art directors and designers must evolve the different publications thoughtfully throughout all layout stages. For example, although Eide created these materials for GPS magazine, they more closely resemble a card or folding brochure. Nonetheless, he used the same set of design principles and layout stages to create them. Reprinted with permission from Aster Publishing Corp.

One of the key changes desktop publishing has brought about is the speed with which any publication can be laid out. That's because in computer layout, all your tools are in your computer and your drafting or layout table and pasteup board are on your computer screen.

This section will discuss computer layout techniques for thumbnails, roughs, comprehensives and mechanicals. The techniques are based primarily on Apple Macintosh hardware and Aldus *PageMaker* page composition program, but may be roughly transferrable to other systems and software. However, our point is not to detail the use of one system over another, but to demonstrate the versatility of the computer in publication layout.

The Advantage of Computer Layout

There are a number of basic advantages to computer page layout that you need to be aware of before you plunge into designing and formatting publications on your computer.

Placing Text and Graphics

The primary advantage of computer page layout is the ability to place text and graphics right on the page from word processing or illustration programs. Although other page-layout programs require you to create a *frame* in which you then place text or graphics, *PageMaker* allows you to place these items directly on the page, anywhere you want them. Once there, they can be manipulated in a number of ways. You can also place text one column at a time or in *PageMaker*'s *textflow* mode which allows it to flow uninterrupted from page to page until it is completely placed. Text can be confined to any size column or stretched across columns by a simple movement of the mouse. Once on the page, text can be made longer or wider by manipulating the *handles* that are part of each *PageMaker* element.

Figure 6.20 _____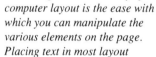

Stretching text. *The beauty of computer layout is the ease with which you can manipulate the various elements on the page. Placing text in most layout programs is as easy as designating the space and importing the existing text copy. In* PageMaker, *you don't even have to designate the space in advance.*

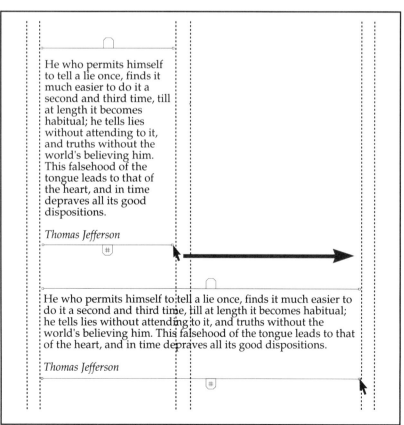

He who permits himself to tell a lie once, finds it much easier to do it a second and third time, till at length it becomes habitual; he tells lies without attending to it, and truths without the world's believing him. This falsehood of the tongue leads to that of the heart, and in time depraves all its good dispositions.

Thomas Jefferson

He who permits himself to tell a lie once, finds it much easier to do it a second and third time, till at length it becomes habitual; he tells lies without attending to it, and truths without the world's believing him. This falsehood of the tongue leads to that of the heart, and in time depraves all its good dispositions.

Thomas Jefferson

Graphics, such as those imported from Aldus *FreeHand*, are placed in roughly the same way. By moving the mouse pointer to the position on the page where you want the graphic to appear and holding down the mouse button while dragging diagonally, you may designate the size you want the graphic to be when it is placed. This will then constrain the placed element to that area (in the case of text) or size (in the case of a graphic).

Once placed, the graphic may be sized, cropped, or otherwise adjusted depending on the software used to produce it. Graphics placed from PICT or EPS formats can be sized proportionally in *PageMaker* by simply holding down the *shift* key while dragging a corner handle. Paint-type graphics can also be sized without loss or compression of shading patterns if you hold down both the *command* and *shift* keys as you drag. If you don't hold down the *shift* key or *command* and *shift* keys while executing these maneuvers, the images will distort. Many programs also now include a text-wrap function that allows you to literally wrap text around a placed graphic.

Figure 6.21 _____

Placing graphics. *Graphics placement in* PageMaker *can be restricted to a specific place on the page or a specific size. Keep in mind, however, that stretching the graphics block without holding down the shift key will result in a distorted graphic.*

Illustration by Thomas H. Bivins © 1990

Using Lines and Boxes

Today, even word processing programs now allow you to create boxes and lines, but not all that long ago this was one of the primary selling points of a page-layout program.

Boxes

Although it is possible to import or place boxes and other such simple patterns from other programs, it is easier to create them in the page-layout program. Boxes do have to be moved each time you make an adjustment to type or format, but it's easier to move them in a computer program than on a pasted-up piece of paper.

Drop shadows are easy to create and can be effective if they are not overused. In *PageMaker*, drop shadows are produced by adding a darker shaded box slightly diagonally and to the rear of your original box. Be sure your top box is not transparent, and delete the line around the shadow. Experiment with different shades and don't assume that black is the best for a drop shadow.

Tint blocks, boxes that are filled or shaded, should also be used with care. Very small type or type with thin serifs won't print well over a tint block, especially on a laser printer. Use a light shade (no more than 20 or 30 percent) and a type size of at least 12 point. If your final product will run on a Linotronic, be aware that fills or shades will appear darker than on a laser-printed copy. A 40 percent fill that looks fine on a LaserWriter will be too dark for a copy block on a Linotronic.

Figure 6.22 _____

Creating a drop shadow. To create a drop shadow in a program such *as* PageMaker, *simply draw a box, duplicate it by copying and pasting; place one box slightly at a diagonal to the other and overlapping; shade the lower box; delete the line around it; fill the top box with white and make sure it's brought to the front.*

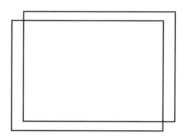

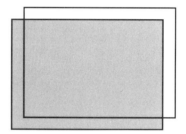

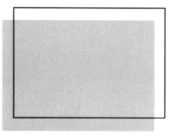

Figure 6.23 _____

Tint blocks. Tint blocks are useful graphic devices for attracting attention; however, remember that shaded boxes will darken when run on a Linotronic. *As you can see below, the darker the box, the more difficult it is to read the copy. Clockwise from the top, the shades are 10%, 20%, 40% and 30%.*

Lorem ipsum dolor sit amet, consectetuer adipiscing elit, sed diam nonummy nibh euismod tincidunt ut laoreet dolore magna aliquam erat volutpat. Ut wisi enim ad minim veniam, quis nostrud exerci tation ullamcorper suscipit lobortis nisl ut aliq

Lorem ipsum dolor sit amet, consectetuer adipiscing elit, sed diam nonummy nibh euismod tincidunt ut laoreet dolore magna aliquam erat volutpat. Ut wisi enim ad minim veniam, quis nostrud exerci tation ullamcorper suscipit lobortis nisl ut aliq

Lorem ipsum dolor sit amet, consectetuer adipiscing elit, sed diam nonummy nibh euismod tincidunt ut laoreet dolore magna aliquam erat volutpat. Ut wisi enim ad minim veniam, quis nostrud exerci tation ullamcorper suscipit lobortis nisl ut aliq

Lorem ipsum dolor sit amet, consectetuer adipiscing elit, sed diam nonummy nibh euismod tincidunt ut laoreet dolore magna aliquam erat volutpat. Ut wisi enim ad minim veniam, quis nostrud exerci tation ullamcorper suscipit lobortis nisl ut aliq

Lines

Like type size, line thickness is usually given in points. This is convenient since line width is much narrower than you would want to measure in inches. The standard seems to be 1 point; however, experiment with line thickness and use what seems most appropriate to your purpose. For example, some programs designate "hairline" as well as .05- and 1-point line thicknesses at the narrower end of the range. Hairlines are excellent for the lines used in coupons or fill-in-the-blanks forms. You'd be surprised how thick a 1-point line looks in these forms. On the other hand, a 2-, 4-, or 6-point line is quite a bit thicker-*looking* than a 1-point line. Use the thicker settings sparingly.

Grids, Master Pages and Templates

Once you're familiar with your page-makeup program, you can experiment with actual publications. You can be producing simple publications in no time once you've mastered three devices that can be used to add consistency to your publications page by page and issue by issue: **grids**, **master pages** and **templates**. The creative use of these devices can save you time and frustration and further streamline a process already greatly speeded up by the computer.

Grids

Grids are guides around which you build your publication. Their importance to layout can't be overstressed. Grids are not, as some graphic artists will tell you, confining. They do not stifle creativity or limit your imagination. They do aid you in balancing your publication page by page or from spread to spread.

A grid is composed of a series of non-printing horizontal and vertical lines. They can appear directly on the page you are working on or remain invisible until you call them up. They are variably adjustable and can be moved about to suit your needs.

For longer or regularly produced publications such as a weekly newsletter or monthly house magazine, grids are indispensable. Even for smaller publications such as brochures, grids keep your margins consistent and your layout balanced.

Master pages

Master pages are created (on *PageMaker*) at the beginning of your layout process and consist of any elements you want to repeat from page to page—not just grids, but also page headers, numbers, rules and other graphic elements. Every page is then overlaid by the master page elements unless otherwise overridden.

Master pages also hold the basic grid on which each page is built, including columns, margins and other space dividers. Some programs, such as Letraset's *ReadySetGo*, set up grids as a series of vertical and horizontal rectangles instead of columns.

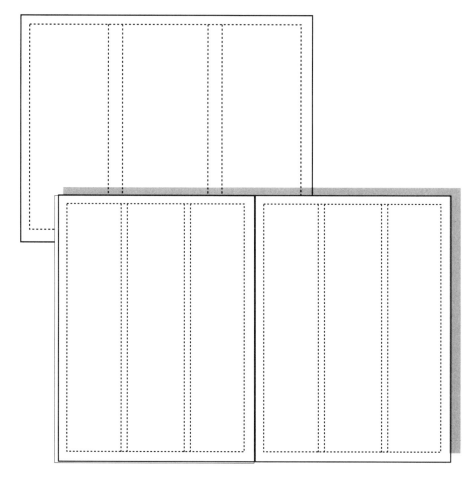

Figure 6.25 _____
Grids. *The most common grids for publication layout are the three-column magazine page (bottom) and the three-column brochure page (top).*

Templates

Templates are probably the most useful tool for the editor who publishes a large periodical publication on a recurring basis. Templates allow you to save all of the grid elements, master pages and style elements that will be reused each time, saving you hours of frustration. Templates were originally developed as tutorials for page-layout programs and later as specialty offerings packaged as guidelines for certain types of publications such as memos, newsletters, brochures, etc. Aldus packaged several early sets for newsletters and business publications and now includes a number of these with their *PageMaker* program.

Pre-packaged templates

For the less-experienced publication editor, pre-packaged templates can be a great help if they are designed for the program you are using or have access to. The key to making the most of a template is to decide in advance whether you are going to use it as-is or only as a base from which to experiment. Not every template is flexible enough for experimentation, but if you are aware of the limitations of the templates you are using and comfortable enough with your own skills, you can work both within and outside the established format as you wish.

A template includes the basic grid for the publication, and a number of **place holders** and **spacers**. Place holders are usually samples of display or body type executed in the face, style and size pre-set for that template. They appear exactly or approximately in the location on the page in which you would use them if you made absolutely no format changes. Again, the flexibility of your prepackaged templates depends a lot on your abilities and willingness to experiment.

Creating your own templates

Once you have the experience, creating your own custom templates is simple enough. The more you know about your page-makeup program, the easier it will be. Although your program will dictate the exact way in which you build your template, the following process—based on *PageMaker*—can be transposed to other software programs.

1. Establish page size, orientation and margins in your *page setup* function. For example, if you are developing a template for a tabloid-sized newsletter, indicate *tabloid*, margins, number of pages and beginning page number. Most templates are composed of two or three pages—a cover page and sample inside pages. If you have certain sections or departments with special heads or boxes, you can include these as well; however, try to keep your template to as few pages as possible and add special features when you begin to construct your actual issue. Normally you'll want to set up your front page separately from the inside pages with masthead and other recurring elements already in place.

2. Set the measurement system you wish to use. Most prepackaged templates and most professional layout artists use points and picas. You may use whatever you are most comfortable with; however, since you will undoubtedly be working with printers and typesetters, you might as well get used to their measurement system.

3. On your *master pages,* establish column number and width as well as any recurring elements that you want to appear on succeeding pages. For

Figure 6.26

Working with a template. The template (below) is representative of the basic template found accompanying programs such as Page-Maker. Using this template, the newsletter page (inset) was created. You will find that adjustments will usually have to be made to type face and size.

APC Action

A revolution in the making

New software may turn the tide in education

Lorem ipsum dolor sit amet, consectetuer adipiscing elit, sed diam nonummy nibh euismod tincidunt ut laoreet dolore magna aliquam erat volutpat.

Ut wisi enim ad minim veniam, quis nostrud exerci tation ullamcorper suscipit lobortis nisl ut aliquip ex ea commodo consequat.

Duis autem vel eum iriure dolor in hendrerit in vulputate velit esse molestie consequat, vel illum dolore eu feugiat nulla facilisis at vero eros et accumsan et iusto odio dignissim qui blandit praesent luptatum zzril delenit augue duis dolore te feugait nulla facilisi. Lorem ipsum dolor sit amet, consectetuer adipiscing elit, sed diam nonummy nibh euismod tincidunt ut laoreet dolore magna aliquam erat volutpat.

Ut wisi enim ad minim veniam, quis nostrud exerci tation ullamcorper suscipit lobortis nisl ut aliquip ex ea commodo consequat.

Duis autem vel eum iriure dolor in hendrerit in vulputate velit esse molestie consequat, vel illum dolore eu feugiat nulla facilisis at vero eros et accumsan et iusto odio dignissim qui blandit praesent luptatum zzril delenit augue duis dolore te feugait nulla facilisi. Nam liber tempor cum soluta nobis eleifend option congue nihil imperdiet doming id quod mazim placerat facer possim assum.

Lorem ipsum dolor sit amet, consectetuer adipiscing elit, sed diam

nonummy nibh euismod tincidunt ut laoreet dolore magna aliquam erat volutpat.

Ut wisi enim ad minim veniam, quis nostrud exerci tation ullamcorper suscipit lobortis nisl ut aliquip ex ea commodo consequat.

Duis autem vel eum iriure dolor in hendrerit in vulputate velit esse molestie consequat, vel illum dolore eu feugiat nulla facilisis at vero eros et accumsan et iusto odio dignissim qui blandit praesent luptatum zzril delenit augue duis dolore te feugait nulla facilisi. Lorem ipsum dolor sit amet, consectetuer adipiscing elit, sed diam nonummy nibh euismod tincidunt ut laoreet dolore magna aliquam erat volutpat.

Ut wisi enim ad minim veniam, quis nostrud exerci tation ullamcorper suscipit lobortis nisl ut aliquip ex ea commodo consequat. Duis autem vel eum iriure dolor in hendrerit in vulputate velit esse molestie consequat, vel illum dolore eu feugiat nulla facilisis at vero eros et accumsan et

APC moves up	**Page 2**
A penny for your thoughts	**Page 3**
More on software	**Page4**

Masthea

36pt. headline placeholder

18pt. subhead placeholder

24pt. column headline placeholder

This is a 12pt. bold byline placeholder

This is a 12pt. body text placeholder composed of Times Roman set flush left

A spacer allows you to place a predetermined amount of space (in this case, 1 pica) at even intervals between elements on your page. Here, the body copy is placed 1 pica beneath a graphic element.

This is a 12pt. caption placeholder of Times Roman italic

example, if you establish a three-column format, it will repeat on every page thereafter unless suppressed on a page-by-page basis. In addition, most programs, including *PageMaker*, also allow you to indicate page number placement, which then automatically numbers your pages. Other elements, such as boxes or rules, can be included here as well. You may either lock these elements, including margins and column guides, or leave them and adjust them on a page-by-page basis. Remember, what you put on your master pages will appear on every page after that, but it can be either suppressed, altered, or changed at any time.

4. Create your *style sheet*. Establish all of the parameters for each of the type styles that you want to remain consistent from issue to issue. For instance, you might set your body text style at 10-point Times, justified with auto leading; your headline style at 24-point Avant Garde bold, centered with 25-point leading; your pull quotes at 14-point Avant Garde bold italic, centered with auto leading; and your captions 10-point Times italic, flush left with auto leading. You may also set such parameters as tabs, indents (both for paragraphs and whole subsections), hyphenation, and so on. The beauty of a style sheet has already been explained, but when combined with a template, it becomes an indispensable tool for the publication's editor or designer.

5. Create **place holders**. Place holders combine the advantages of a style sheet with a visual representation of where elements are usually placed in a given publication. For example, to create a headline place holder, simply type in the word "Headline" in the size and style that you wish your finished headline to be. To insert your finished headline, just place your text cursor, highlight the place holder word, and type in your headline. It will appear in the size and style of the place-holder. Place holders can be used in place of or in conjunction with a style sheet. Some people prefer just to use a style sheet because of the flexibility. Place holders tend to pre-establish a design in your mind and are better for those who *need* a design pre-established.

6. Certain graphic elements such as imported art or special boxes can sometimes be placed on the *desk top* beyond the edges of the pages, cut and placed in the *clipboard* file (held only so long as your computer is on) or placed in a *scrapbook* for later use. Admittedly, elements saved this way take up more disk space; but if you use them a lot, yet don't want to lock them into any particular place on your layout, try "putting them to the side."

7. Once you have constructed your template, be sure to save it as a template. If you save it as a regular publication, any subsequent changes you make to it while laying out an issue will remain. If saved as a template, it will open only an untitled copy each time. Changes made to that copy can then be saved as a separate issue of your publication.

Remember, templates aren't cut in stone—they're only etched on your computer's memory. But templates exist to bring continuity and consistency to a publication. One of the pitfalls of computer layout is the ease with which changes can be made. *Resist the urge to change your publications just because it's easy.* Make changes infrequently. Make sure each change has a legitimate rationale, and then make sure you can live with the change once you've made it.

Creating Thumbnails on the Computer

Thumbnails are usually accomplished by hand. Since they are very rough and very small, most artists and designers can quickly sketch five or six in just minutes. A computer can't match a good sketch artist's ability, but it can greatly aid the not-so-adept or beginning designer, *and* the finished product is much easier to judge for design potential than a hand-sketched thumbnail. A number of computer-assisted shortcuts can add consistency to the process and open up some clogged creative arteries.

Size

The first step is to create the master page you will reduce for your thumbnails. You will need to create it in the exact size you want your thumbnail to appear. A number of software programs create thumbnails; *PageMaker* can produce good thumbnails complete with reduced copy (normally greeking) that can be set in any way normal copy can be set. Whatever the size, be sure to work in dimensions you feel comfortable with. You can work full size if you wish, but a smaller dimension lets you place many more thumbnails on a single page and make comparisons on the screen instead of printing them out as you go.

Scaling

Depending on the size and page orientation of your finished publication (*landscape* [horizontal or *wide*] or *portrait* [vertical or *tall*]), you will need to scale down proportionally to the thumbnail size. To make sure your reduced page is scaled properly, you can use a couple of different methods, depending on the computer hardware and software you are using.

First, decide on the size of the final publication. Suppose, for instance, that you will be producing a standard two-fold brochure. Your finished product will be 8.5" x 11" laid out horizontally. When you open your file for the first time, simply select *letter* from the page setup menu and *wide* for the orientation.

After your file opens, access the master page or pages and set up your templates there. That way, each succeeding page will have your template guidelines already on it. Choose the diagonal tool from your screen tool box and draw a diagonal line (a hairline will do) from the top right corner to the bottom left corner of your page. Now, choose the tool for making boxes and draw another box so that the upper right and lower left corners both touch the diagonal line. No matter what size you make your box, the box will be some incremental reduction of your original folder size if these two corners intersect the diagonal line. The easiest size to work in is roughly 5.75" x 4.5" placed one on top of the other on a vertically oriented page.

Now you have a reduced version of the folder in which to place your elements. You can copy just the box portion of your folder at any time and paste it for another thumbnail. In fact, you might want to do that right away and arrange the full page of thumbnail templates in rows before you begin to add the various elements of your folder. At this juncture, resetting the original page setup to a long orientation will allow you to stack two half-page layouts on top of each other. That way, you can lay out both the outside and inside panels on one page.

One final note. You will probably want to leave your template unshaded (not white) so as to cut down on having to move items to the front and to the back constantly. Of course, if you want to experiment with different backgrounds, you can add shading as you go along.

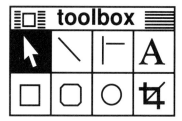

Figure 6.27 _____
The **PageMaker** *toolbox.* Page-Maker *provides its users with an assortment of tools including (clockwise from upper left) a pointer for selecting and adjusting elements, a diagonal for drawing lines, a horizontal/vertical line tool, a text tool for writing and editing, a cropping tool for photos and illustrations, a circle, a rounded-edge rectangle and a rectangle.*

Figure 6.28 _____

Scaling for thumbnails. This method should be familiar to older hands at design. It works the same way on a computer as on a drawing board.

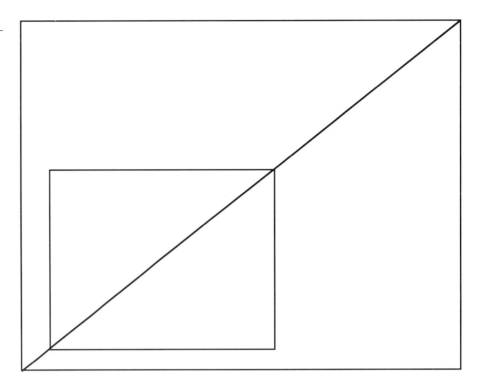

Visuals

Visuals for thumbnails are a matter of taste. Some designers don't care to mess with detail on a thumbnail, but a computer lets you use a reducible visual again and again with no extra trouble. For instance, the thumbnails on the following pages use illustrations created on Aldus *FreeHand* and exported to *PageMaker* in *Encapsulated PostScript*. They can now be placed, sized, cropped and stretched to suit the designer's needs.

If you don't have pre-made visuals on the computer, you can easily substitute geometric patterns or lines to approximate the shape of the intended visuals.

Headline

Even in small sizes, thumbnails can look quite polished if they use legible, reduced lettering. For example, if you are working with the sizes shown on these pages, your headline can vary from 14 points to 24 points and still replicate fairly accurately what the finished product will look like. Remember, all a thumbnail has to be is close. Exactness comes later.

Body copy

In a traditional thumbnail sketch (and even in rough full-size layouts) body copy is typically **greeked**—that is, indicated by ruled lines or lines of squiggles made to look like columns of copy. Greeking also refers to copy that is nonsense or unintelligible. With *PageMaker*, you can represent greeked copy with actual lettering. If you have the actual copy written—great. If not, use the greeking that comes with *PageMaker*. Aldus refers to it as *Lorem ipsum* after the first two words of the greeked copy. For years, the only way to get this type of greeked body copy was to buy it as rub-down lettering in the size and font that represented what your real copy would look like or cut it out of magazines and glue it in place. Now, with a computer, you can make your own, or, if you use *PageMaker*, use *Lorem ipsum*.

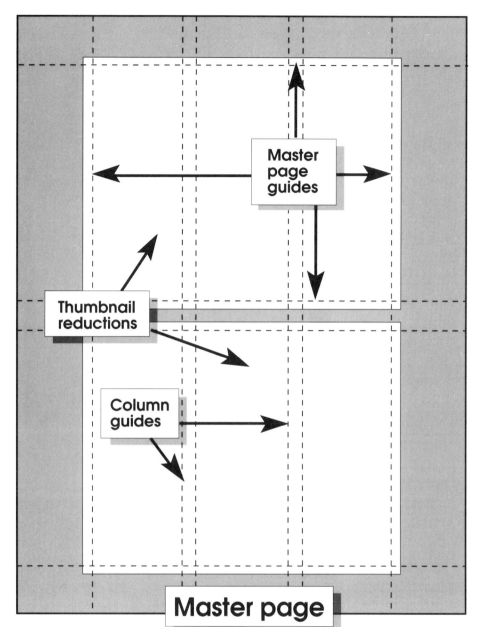

Thumbnail reductions

Master page guides

Column guides

Master page

Figure 6.29 _____

Setting up columns. Setting up columns for a thumbnail version of a folder can be tricky. The best way to do it is to scale your thumbnail templates to half-page size then use the PageMaker *column setup to suit your reduced page. You will need to adjust the space between columns to something around a pica. Then pull in outside guides from your master page to use as the outside margins on your thumbnail.*

You can place your greeked copy directly onto the thumbnail and size it as small as you need. You can also approximate columns (justified or unjustified, flush right or left, or centered). In fact, you can replicate any style or experiment with any alignment you would use in the finished product—only in thumbnail size! This is the reason for carefully placing column guides on your thumbnails. Greeked copy won't fit properly without them.

Creating Roughs on the Computer

The next stage is the rough. Many designers simply skip the thumbnail stage and go right to the rough, which gives them a feel for the full-size folder and lets them work in broad strokes without having to render details. Some designers create as many roughs as they normally would thumbnails. The only difference is size.

Figure 6.30 _____

Indicating visuals on thumbnails*.
As you can see, the top layout
includes an illustration done on
FreeHand, exported in Encapsulated
PostScript, placed and sized in
PageMaker. The bottom layout uses
black rectangles to indicate the
truck. For thumbnails, geometric
shapes serve as well as a completed
illustration to indicate placement in
relationship to other elements in the
brochure.*

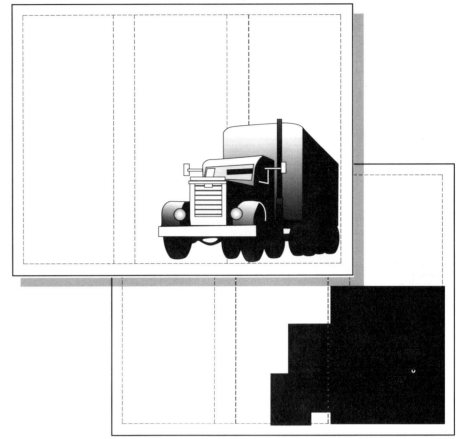

Figure 6.31 _____

Copyfitting thumbnails*. The
beauty of computer-generated
thumbnails is the ability to use real
or greeked copy in exactly the
same way you would on a full-size
brochure. The top brochure layout
(an inside spread) uses greeked
copy fit around a* Freehand
illustration. With PageMaker *3.0,
you can wrap copy around a
graphic using the text wrap
function. The bottom layout (an
outside spread) uses a standard*
PageMaker *pattern to indicate
copy. Simply use the box tool
filled with horizontal lines to
indicate copy blocks, then delete
the outside line.*

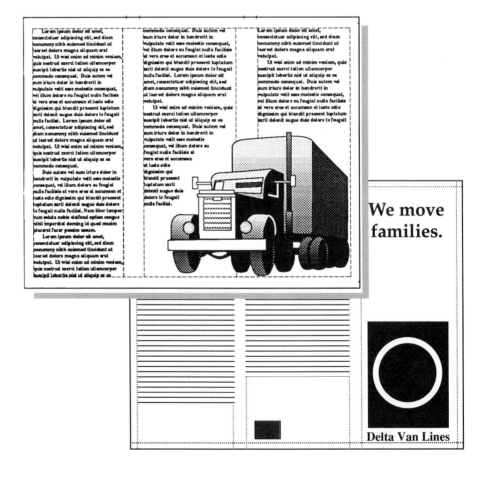

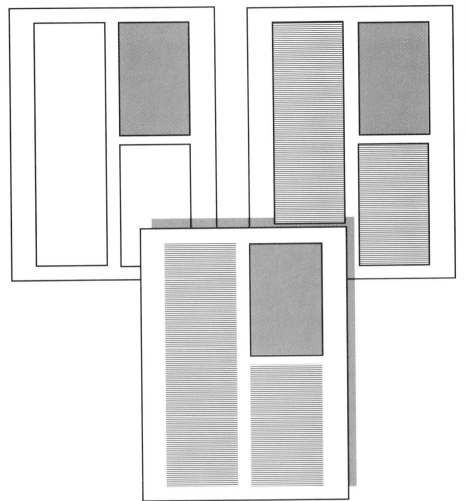

Figure 6.32 _____

TIP: For even quicker thumbnails, indicate text blocks with actual squares by using the box tool common to many page-layout programs. Just indicate the column width and length with a box, fill the box with a horizontal line pattern, and delete the line around the outside of the box. The result looks like justified, greeked type.

If you like to look at a number of sketches simultaneously, thumbnails offer the most flexibility; however, you can lay out as many roughs side by side as you have room for.

The rough is simply a full-sized version of the thumbnail with copy indicated (usually by horizontal lines or squiggles) and artwork roughed in. Like the thumbnail, it is only used to give the designer several creative approaches to the layout. Time is usually the limiting factor here. A rough can be accomplished much faster than a comprehensive.

The computer can be enormously helpful in letting you can place all the elements of the brochure just as you would for the final product. While most roughs only indicate copy, a computer-generated rough can use either the actual copy or greeked copy instead of lines and squiggles; and, if the visual has been duplicated or created originally on a computer, it can be used as well. If not, rely on shapes and patterns just as you did in the thumbnails.

Creating Comprehensives on the Computer

The next stage in the evolution from thumbnail to finished publication is the comprehensive or comp, the stage you will ultimately show to the client for approval. With computer-generated artwork, headlines and body copy, you can come very close to a finished product with none of the costs normally associated with a complete comprehensive.

The comps on these pages were designed and laid out completely on a computer. Artwork was accomplished on Aldus *FreeHand* and layout was done using *PageMaker*. The technique involves creating the artwork (line work and shading) in *FreeHand*; exporting the finished artwork in *Encapsulated PostScript* for placement in *PageMaker*; placing the artwork and sizing it in *PageMaker* (it can be reduced, enlarged, or cropped to suit your needs, but it pays to work in *FreeHand* in some increment of your final product); and adding the copy elements in *PageMaker*, which manipulates text more flexibly than *FreeHand*. As you can see, the final product is very polished.

Creating display type in other programs, such as Adobe *Illustrator* and *FreeHand*, does have its advantages. The latest version of *FreeHand* provides for automatic kerning of all the letters in a single word or text block by simply grabbing a *handle* and stretching the block. In addition, headlines exported to page-layout programs such as *PageMaker* can be stretched, sized, or distorted—something you can't do with display type created in *PageMaker* itself.

Figure 6.33 _____

Finished comprehensive. Below is a page from the book you are reading now. You see it here exactly as it appeared in comprehensive form only scaled for presentation on this page.

Color comps

Most clients expect color comps, and the newer software programs (*FreeHand* and *PageMaker* especially) take advantage of this. Color separations as well as spot color can be programmed into your layout, and separations can be printed off and combined for a finished product through the normal printing process.

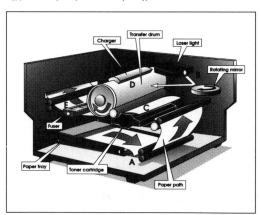

As we stated in **Chapter 3**, most laser printers today are based on one of two technologies – the Apple *LaserWriter* or Hewlett-Packard's *LaserJet*. The basic difference between the two is that the *LaserWriter* (and printers based on its technology) uses *PostScript*, a programming language that allows entire pages of both text and graphics to be sent to the printer at one time. Type can literally be produced at any available size and even extremely complex graphics can be printed out, restricted only by the resolution of the printer. However, as already mentioned, software/hardware packages are now available that will turn a printer based on *LaserJet* technology into a printer that accepts *PostScript*.

Keep in mind that, although prices have come down considerably on laser printers, they still can cost you quite a bit – ranging roughly from $1000 to $5000 depending mainly on the amount of memory the printer comes with.

Some of the newer laser printers – especially those that accept PostScript – come with at least 1 MGB. These are variously upgradeable to as much as 12 MGB or more and some accept external hard drives boosting the memory even higher. The greater the memory, the less time it takes to print, the more pages the printer can store at one time, and the more printer type fonts it can handle. For example, upwards of 30 type fonts come "packaged" now on some laser printers, and with expanded memory, dozens more can be added. In fact, some font manufacturers sell hundreds of fonts on their own hard drive ready for installation on your system. The difference in printer memory size can mount up in dollars, however, so be ready to pay for what you get.

Figure 1 _____
The laser-printing process

A. As the paper enters the printer from the paper tray, it is given a positive charge. As the paper moves along the paper path to the transfer drum, The rotating drum receives a negative charge from the charger.

B. Meanwhile, the computer image is transferred to the rotating transfer drum from the printer's memory via the laser light. The laser light bounces its image onto a rotating mirror and onto the drum. The light "draws" a picture by neutralizing the spot where black will be, leaving the surrounding area negatively charged where white will be.

C. The toner cartridge provides a negatively charged powder. As the drum rolls through the toner powder, the negative toner avoids the negative surface of the drum, but sticks to the neutralized dots created by the image drawn on the drum's surface by the laser light.

D. Since the toner is negative and the paper positive, when the paper passes over the drum, the dots stick to the paper.

E. The fuser unit "fuses" toner onto the paper using temperatures of up to 400 degrees Farenheit.

Although laser printers are definitely the ideal, you can get along without one. Many quick printers and photocopy stores can run laser copies of your files right off your disks. Many such outlets carry the most common software applications. If you're in doubt, just call. It pays to at least have a dot matrix printer, however, to run drafts. These won't exactly match your laser output copies, but they will give you some idea of what to expect.

Pre-mechanical printing

Depending on what stage in the layout process you are will determine what kind of print job you need. Word processed documents or manuscripts can be proofed from almost any type of printer. If cost per page is a factor, consider drafts run on a dot matrix printer. Every copy you run off a laser printer just to edit manuscript pages will cost you more than it's worth. With the cost of toner cartridges running over $100 each, every copy you make will probably exceed a normal photocopy cost.

Illustration by Thomas H. Bivins © 1990

But, you don't need to go this far for comps, if (and this is a *big* if) you have access to a color laser printer.

Color laser printers can actually produce full-color comps based on your instructions in your illustration or page-layout program. The problem is that color laser technology is very expensive. The only other quick and dirty option is to try out one of the new color copying systems using your laser-printed color separations much the same way a printer would. If you limit yourself to large areas of color and don't get too fancy, the outcome can be adequate. Registration may be a problem, for there is no way to register accurately on a color copier of any type.

Even without a color laser printer, you can still execute professional color comps by simply using oil-based design markers to color your laser-printed comps. The oil-based markers won't smear the toner used in most laser printers. Or, if you don't like the smell of markers, try soft, colored pencils. The beauty of this method is that, because *FreeHand* illustrations are already shaded, all you have to do is apply a base color to the illustration.

Preparing the Mechanical

The final stage of layout is the mechanical, the finished layout that goes to the printer. Again, the computer has revolutionized this process. If you are diligent, exact, and working with a limited range of graphics, you can literally present your printer with a mechanical in one piece—*with no pasted-up parts*! We have,

Illustration by Thomas H. Bivins © 1990

Figure 16.34

Finished comprehensive. This finished comp can be shown to the prospective client as a laser-printed, black-and-white mockup or color can be added by hand. The alternative is to complete the comp using a color laser printer—very expensive but also very impressive.

in fact, sent whole publications directly to our printer's Linotronic 300 typesetter via our computer network and had the camera-ready mechanical handed back to us for inspection within a few hours. You can even go directly to negative film from a Linotronic, saving the cost of shooting negatives from a positive mechanical—but only if you are completely satisfied with your layout.

Assuming you are working in black and white, there are several ways to construct your mechanical.

1. You can have it run *entirely* off a Linotronic, either from your computer disks or through a network or phone line hookup. This implies that all of the elements on your mechanical are computer generated—word-processed text and display type; borders, boxes and rules produced in your page-makeup program; photos scanned, cropped and sized in either a photo manipulation program—such as *Image Studio*—or right in your layout program; illustrations created in a paint, draw, or illustration program and imported or placed in your layout program; and any color separations already accounted for by your software.

2. You can run the basic mechanical (text, display type, rules and boxes) on a Linotronic and have photos and art shot separately and stripped into the negative before the printing plate is made. If you don't have a scanner or access to electronic clip art, this is probably the closest you'll get to having the whole thing done in one step. Even at this level, the savings in typesetting and pasteup alone are worth it.

3. You can run your mechanical on a laser printer at either of the above two levels. This assumes you either don't have access to a Linotronic, or you don't feel that the extra quality is needed for your particular publication. Some very nice newsletters and brochures can be offset printed directly from laser-printed mechanicals. The difference to the trained eye (or anyone with a magnifying glass) is the type. It bleeds badly at larger point sizes and can even look fuzzy at smaller sizes. But if you're on a shoestring budget, this is a great compromise.

Adding color

Today, full color on the computer is tedious and fairly imprecise. Although there are color monitors, full-color scanners and photo programs to work with them, and processes to make and print the requisite separations—the end results are not as satisfying as the mechanical process now used. At the speed at which computer technology is advancing, however, it won't be long before full-color photography can be handled cost-effectively and with good results.

Many page-layout programs support spot color, and many more are developing color capabilities. Both page-layout programs like *PageMaker* and illustration programs like *FreeHand* have the ability to add color and make separations for printing. In fact, at this writing, *FreeHand* contains a complete Pantone library of colors as well as the ability to mix your own, and the newest version of *PageMaker* will have full-color capabilities including the Pantone library.

The only drawback is the exactness of the color separations—they are *too* exact. If you opt not to have your colors overprint (a wise choice unless you're intentionally trying for a special look) both *FreeHand* and *PageMaker* knock out the shape of the colored object on the object beneath it. Ideally, this allows one color to print in a white space designed exactly for it. In reality, printers usually provide for a tiny overlap between the knockout and the color printed over it. Without this overlap or shadow, and if registration isn't absolutely exact, you'll most likely end up with tiny slivers of white space where the top object didn't quite fit into the knockout below it.

If all you're doing is adding some spot color, both programs, and many others, will do just fine. Just remember, working with color has always been a difficult proposition. Working with it on a computer can be rewarding and exciting, but it is also confusing and occasionally frustrating.

One final word of warning. If you are thinking of investing in color capabilities for your computer be aware of the WYSIWYG problem (what you see is what you get). Color monitors are the greatest thing since sliced bread, but they're hardly accurate. Don't expect the color you see on the screen to replicate on your new $8,000 color printer or look the same in your finished job. One problem is that color monitors use light-mixed colors that just don't look the same as colors mixed with real ink. What can you do?

- First, set up your monitor with a color card. They are usually provided with the monitor. Some software programs, such as Aldus *FreeHand*, provide a color card based on the Pantone system. Get as close as you can to these color cards and check the adjustment every so often to make sure it hasn't wandered.

- Once you have set up color in a publication, check it against what your printer is using. Don't expect a color comp run on a color printer to match anything the printer has. Be ready to get a close match, or re-spec your color based on printer samples. If you use Pantone or another coded system, you can easily check out what you thought was Reflex Blue on your screen by taking a quick look at your printer's Pantone book.

- Finally, be prepared for disappointment if you rely too heavily on your color screen for the final word. Use your monitor and software programs to their fullest, but be sensible and talk over your choices with your printer and *look at samples.*

Remember, the closer you can get to a finished mechanical on a computer, the more cost effective your production process is going to become. With the possible exception of scanned photos, the rest of the process saves money. Once scanned photos reach the quality of photographic halftones and the printing process quickens, prices will drop. Then you won't see any more traditionally done photos in publications.

Chapter 7

Printing

Part A: Basics

To help your publication reach its full potential, you must know enough about printing and production to communicate intelligently with your printer. Unfortunately, many who deal with printers put their heads in the sand, solemnly turn over their materials at the printing deadline and hope for the best. Having a common vocabulary is a good start, but there are other obvious reasons why you should understand printing processes and know something about their materials.

Let's begin with this premise. If you have no idea of your printing possibilities, it is unlikely your publication will reach its full potential. It is also likely that you will learn little from your failures and that what success you do receive will, as much as anything else, be the result of happy accidents or a kindly printer or production boss who is watching out for you.

Most printing professionals are kept as busy as the air traffic controllers at O'Hare Field. They will have little time for your project, and even less for educating you about printing. The point is that it's important to understand the process so that you can select the correct printing method, paper and ink for your publication. We're not suggesting that you become a printer's devil, but you must understand that different publications have different needs, problems and requirements, and that different printing processes vary in quality, application, cost and more.

Different printers have different strengths and weaknesses, consistencies, standards of excellence, craftspeople and printing processes. When you select a printer, you should know these differences as intimately as you know the numbers of their respective bids. Know their work. See it and hold it. Also, find out how dependable and honest they are. Printers will provide you references, and you should seek out others on your own. You should be as familiar with printers and their work as you are with your own needs and budget limitations. With printing, the more you leave to chance, the more you welcome catastrophe.

Printing Processes

There are three basic printing processes: letterpress, gravure and offset lithography. A handful of less-used approaches are noted later in this chapter, along with specific computer applications for desktop publishing and printing.

Letterpress

Letterpress printing has three basic press variations: platen, flatbed and rotary. Of those **platen** is probably the least complicated and most frequently used. It utilizes two surfaces. The printing surface, commonly referred to as the bed, is inked and closed against the platen—its other surface, which presses the paper against the bed (see **Figure 7.1**). Paper is fed to the platen either by hand or by machine. Sometimes known as a "job" press because it is hard-working and highly adaptable, the platen letterpress is also used for scoring, perforation, die-cutting and embossing.

Scoring produces a crease in the paper so that it is easier to fold. This is accomplished through a round-edged steel rule. In some instances a sharper edge actually cuts partway through the paper surface. On the other hand, **perforation** punches a series of holes in the paper so that part of the page may cleanly ripped from the publication. **Die-cutting** uses basically the same procedure and materials as does scoring; in this instance, however, the steel rule is razor sharp, not rounded on the impact edge. **Embossing** molds the paper by forcing it between a concave and convex die and counter. Embossing may produce a relief or raised

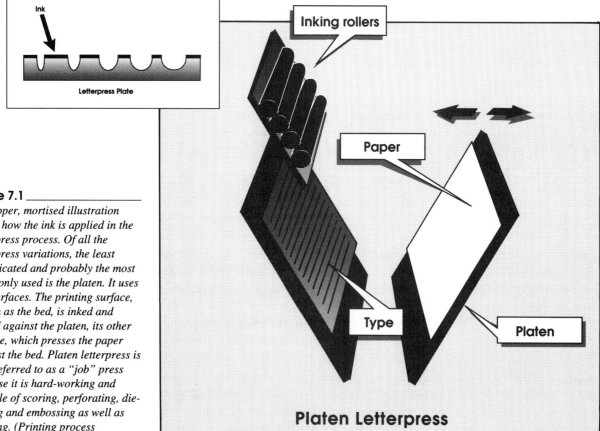

Figure 7.1 _____
The upper, mortised illustration shows how the ink is applied in the letterpress process. Of all the letterpress variations, the least complicated and probably the most commonly used is the platen. It uses two surfaces. The printing surface, known as the bed, is inked and closed against the platen, its other surface, which presses the paper against the bed. Platen letterpress is also referred to as a "job" press because it is hard-working and capable of scoring, perforating, die-cutting and embossing as well as printing. (Printing process illustrations by Tom Bivins.)

surface on a printed or unprinted (blind embossing) surface. Each of these printing procedures will add to your publication costs because they require additional handling, materials and separate press runs. One of the beauties of working with the platen press is that it does so much so well.

The **flatbed** press is so named because its printing surface or form is fitted to a flat bed that slides back and forth beneath the impression cylinder. Usually the paper is sheet fed, gripped by the crimps on the impression cylinder and rolled across the image-making surface in the flat bed, that is, slid under it and back again (see **Figure 7.2**). Many flat-bed presses are also capable of scoring, die-cutting and perforation.

Rotary letterpresses work with two cylinders which roll the paper between them; the printing plate cylinder passes over ink rollers and around to complete the revolution and transfer the image to the paper which is pressed against it by the impression cylinder below. (See **Figure 7.3**.) They are web-fed, which means that a continuous roll of paper feeds into the press and is cut into sheets before exiting. Rotary presses tend to be more cost effective for running large jobs like newspapers and magazines at tremendous speeds without a lose in quality.

Despite recent trends, it is unlikely that the letterpress will ever be entirely obsolete. It is flexible and does everything from standard printing jobs to embossing and die-cutting, from full-color magazines to business cards. And its reputation for high letter quality and sharp image resolution is well deserved. But quality has its price. Expect to pay more for halftones and line art—referred to as **photoengravings** with letterpress.

Figure 7.2 _____

This illustration clearly shows why the flatbed press is so-named. As you can see, its printing surface is fitted to a flatbed that slides back and forth beneath the impression cylinder. Usually the paper is sheet fed, gripped by crimps on the impression cylinder and rolled across the image-making surface in the flatbed; that is, it is slid beneath it and back again.

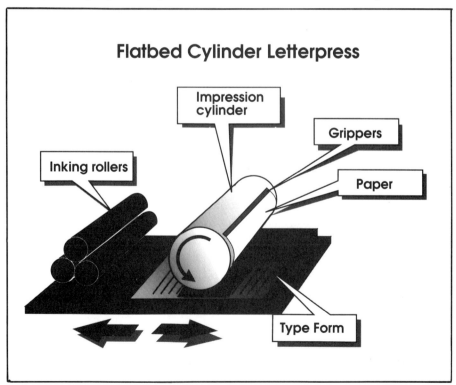

Flatbed Cylinder Letterpress

Impression cylinder

Grippers

Inking rollers

Paper

Type Form

Figure 7.3_____

Of all the letterpress variations, the rotary letterpress is most cost effective for very large jobs like newspapers and magazines, because it can be run at tremendous speeds without affecting their quality. The rotary letterpress uses two cylinders to roll the paper between them. The printing plate cylinder passes over ink rollers and around to complete the revolution and transfer the image to the paper which is pressed against it by the impression cylinder below.

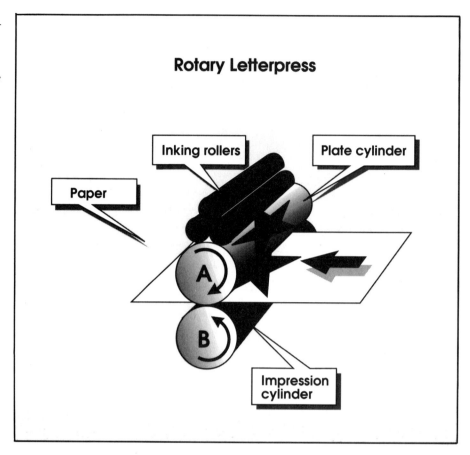

Gravure

At first glance, the **gravure** process appears almost identical to that of the rotary letterpress. Despite the roller-drive similarities, the process is exactly the opposite: whereas letterpress printing is relief, in gravure or **intaglio** printing, the type and image are recessed on the printing plate. The plate cylinder first runs through an ink trough, which presses ink into the well areas on the plate. Then the doctor blade scrapes ink from the outermost surface of the plate. Finally, the impression cylinder pushes paper against the plate, which transfers the ink from the wells to the page (see **Figure 7.4**). When this process is web fed it's called **rotogravure**.

The gravure process screens everything—type, graphics and artwork. Despite the exclusive use of fine screens (typically 150-line or more), the type has a fuzzy look to it that makes most designers wince. But there are advantages to gravure printing. Strangely enough, gravure produces remarkably finished photographic reproductions. The fine screens produce a look that closely resembles the original continuous tone photograph or art. In this case, the "fuzzing" characteristic of gravure nicely blends tonal shifts and subtle changes in gradation, producing richly toned photographic imagery.

But there are additional advantages. The inks used in gravure dry quickly—beneficial when quick turnaround is important, or when you need fast, high-quality photographic reproduction for up-scale catalogs, magazines and quality color advertising inserts. Another advantage is that proofs for gravure are made on the production press, which means that color in those proofs is truer to your

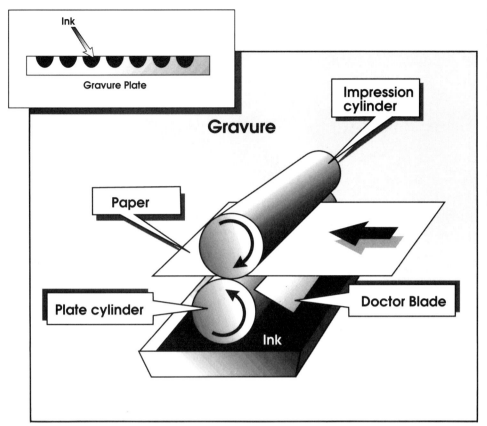

Figure 7.4

Note the inking illustration; it shows that gravure is intaglio printing—that is, the type and image are recessed on the printing plate. In the gravure process, the plate cylinder first runs through an ink trough, which presses ink into the well areas of the plate. Next, the doctor blade scrapes and cleans the ink from the plate's surface. Finally, the impression cylinder pushes the paper against the plate to transfer ink from the wells to the page.

final printed piece than proofs made on a proof press. The strong suit of gravure, though, is its tight photographic reproduction.

Ironically, the disadvantages of gravure are linked to its strengths. The chief drawback is economic. Creating plates for the process is expensive—platemaking must be sent out—and somewhat difficult. And compared to other printing methods, neither line art nor type reproduce especially well.

Offset Lithography

This process is the most contemporary of the three, although it owes its technology to two older media: lithography and photography. **Lithography**, because the process itself is a lithographic one based upon the principle that oil and water don't mix. The nonprinting area of the offset plate accepts water, but not ink. The exact opposite is true of the image area, which is "greased" or treated chemically so that it takes the ink but repels the water. **Photography**, because after the original layouts are shot by production cameras and the halftones are stripped in, the composite negatives (called **flats**) are then printed on photosensitized metal plates. These plates don't have to carry a reversed image because of the offset process. **Offset** gets its name from the indirect, "offsetting" printing process, which is to say that the printing plate doesn't directly put the image and type to page; instead, its image is "offset" to a rubber blanket which sets the ink on the paper.

Figure 7.5 _____

A quick glance at this illustration reveals the offset lithography's main differences from the other processes. Offset gets its name from the indirect, "offsetting" printing process, which is to say that the printing plate doesn't directly put the image and type to page. Instead, its image is "offset" to a rubber blanket which puts the ink on the paper. See how the type and image go from positive to negative to positive again.

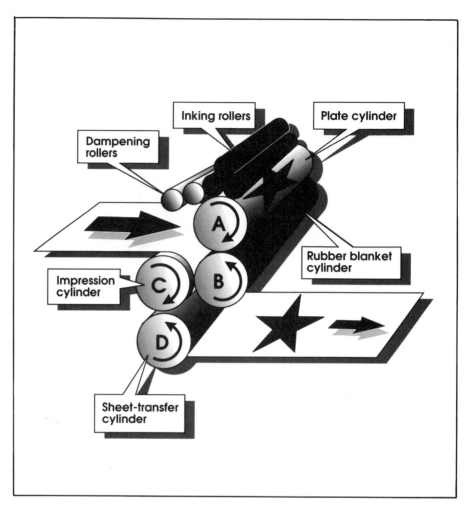

Here's how the process works. Offset uses three separate printing cylinders: a plate cylinder, a blanket cylinder and an impression cylinder. The printing plate is mounted to the plate cylinder, which also has ink and water systems fitted alongside it. With each revolution the plate on the printing cylinder is dampened and inked. That inked image is transferred from the printing plate to the rubber blanket (located beneath the plate cylinder), which in turn transfers the ink to the paper as it passes between the bottom cylinders (see **Figure 7.5**).

Offset has quite a bit going for it. It is a relatively inexpensive, high-quality process that is suitable for large and small jobs alike. It is also the only printing process of the three that allows the printers to make their own plates, a cost savings in itself, especially when you consider that both letterpress and gravure plates are expensive to begin with. Because the image plate never comes in contact with the paper, the plates wear well and maintain their printing quality over long press runs. Additionally, the rubber blanket reduces plate pressure while its flexible surface delivers ink clearly and cleanly to the paper, even to the rough or recessed areas of textured paper. Offset also uses less ink, which decreases drying time and minimizes smudging. The fact that the flats store easily and can be used over and over again also adds to the cost effectiveness of this printing method.

Letterset Printing

As its name suggests, **letterset** is an interesting bastard child of the letterpress and offset printing processes. Because dampeners aren't used in this printing approach, it is also known commonly among printers and designers as "dry offset." Like letterpress, it uses a relief or raised printing plate, but with one big difference: the letters and imagery aren't reversed. Like offset, it uses a blanket to transfer the image to page.

There are two advantages to letterset. First, this process uses a faster-drying ink, which provides printer and client alike faster job turnaround and quicker successive runs. Second, the ink tends to hold a brighter gloss. In addition, images and type fade less and tend to be more evenly inked, which is sometimes a problem with offset.

Screen Printing

Also known as **stencil printing, screen printing** is used more in art studios and sign shops than in printing houses. This process is very simple. Friskets or stencils are bonded to a framed screen material—silk screens are the most common—to mask off the area that won't be inked. After the screen is placed atop the paper, ink or paint is applied to one end of the frame and squeegeed, by hand or machine, across the length of the screen. When more than one color is used, separate screens are made and closely adjusted for registration; each color is inked separately and given time enough to dry properly between runs. Screening is celebrated because, in addition to paper, it can print on just about any material you can think of, from glass to fabric.

Although its publication use is limited, screen printing provides unique opportunities for special covers, packaging, T-shirts, posters, banners, outdoor billboards and the like. You can, for example, use screen printing to put your logo

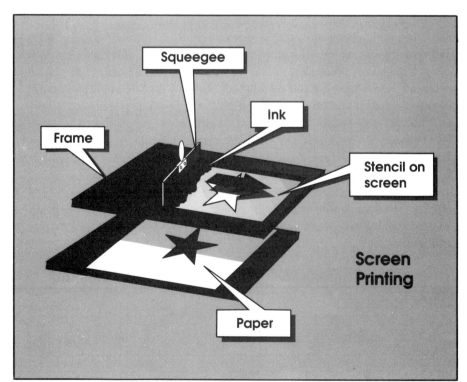

Figure 7.6 _____

Screen or stencil printing bonds friskets or stencils to a screen material—typically a silk screen—to mask off the area that won't be inked. After the screen is placed atop the paper (or other printing surface), ink or paint is applied to one end of the frame and squeegeed across the length of the screen. Because of its flexibility and relatively moderate cost, screen printing is used for a wide assortment of printing needs.

or design atop bottles, plastic or boxes. Or you can produce a very small number of package designs or promotional materials that require special handling or attention, and have them look professional. Screen printing might be exactly what you need for a special cover, or to show off a packaging design for a prototype product.

Flexography

Flexography is actually a variation of letterpress printing. Rather than using rigid printing plate surfaces such as metal or wood, flexography uses rubber for its relief surface—hence, its name. Because rubber is more flexible, flexography doesn't hold letter or image integrity as well as its letterpress counterparts. It employs a liquid ink, not the paste version you find in the three main processes, that is fast drying and a little less opaque but given to minor distortion problems. Not anything you'd notice while reading the contents of your candy bar, but distortion you'd shudder over in a magazine or annual report. Flexography is generally accomplished with web-fed rotary presses and used extensively for printing that is less formal than most publications tend to be.

While a good number of paperback publishers run flexographic printing presses, flexography is typically used for all kinds of packaging: bags, boxes, containers, wrappers, cartons and cellophane. It is also used extensively for printing atop consumer products. It is not a high-quality printing process, but the flexible nature of its printing plate makes it well suited for some jobs. It is inexpensive, uncomplicated and technology is improving its image quality and expanding its application.

Photogelatin

This process is capable of reproducing continuous-tone imagery without using a halftone. Like offset lithography, the **photogelatin** process uses thin metal plates for transferring ink, and it does so in a remarkably similar way. A photosensitive emulsion is painted on the plate. After the plate has been allowed to dry, a negative is placed atop it and exposed. Also, like offset, photogelatin plates are first dampened and then inked; unlike offset, however, the image is transferred directly to the paper via either flatbed or rotary presses.

Photogelatin—which is also known as **collotype**, the photographic process discovered by William Fox Talbot—delivers remarkable imagery. It is a high-quality process used almost exclusively for photography and continuous-tone artwork that doesn't carry a terribly high price tag. One shortcoming is that its printing plate surface is short lived, seldom providing more than a few thousand impressions before going bad. On the other hand, it is a special purpose printing process, comfortable with anything from artbook reproductions to pseudo-photographs.

Color Printing

Color brings an added dimension to any publication, whether it's as simple as a second color to help accent, unify or dress out a publication, or as complete as full color. Using color may help brand or identify your company with your

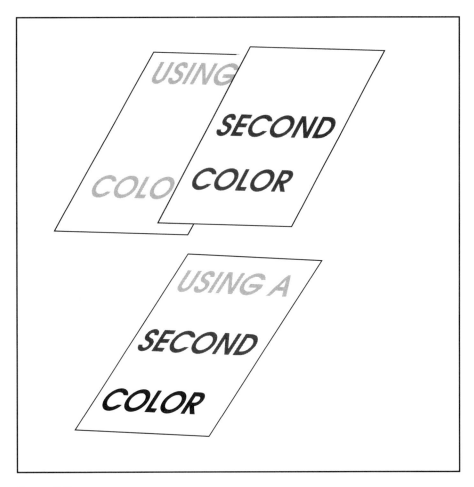

Figure 7.7 _____

Two-color separation. *The base color (bottom page at the top) is overlaid with a second color (top page). Areas of overlap create a third color.*

publication. It may also suggest a mood or feeling—remember, warmer inks and papers make a publication more personal and informal, while cooler materials tend to depersonalize or formalize it. To use color effectively, you should have a rudimentary understanding of how the different color processes operate.

Spot Color

Spot color, which is also known as **two color** or **flat color**, is the placement of a second color (black—or whatever the primary inking color—being the *first*) in a publication. (Note that in printing, black is counted as a color.) Unless you're using a multicolor press, applying the second color means an additional press run. That translates to more ink, materials, handling and press time and money.

In two-color printing, two sets of printing plates are made, one for each color run. Often, a designer will use the second color for the art and graphic affectations—say, dropped-initial letters—and use the black (or other first color) for the type, overprinting, and so on (see **Figure 7.6**). By combining screens of the two colors, you can give the illusion that additional color has been used. Because most printing inks are transparent, they may be layered on top of each other, so, for example, red and yellow overprinted produce orange—how light or dark an orange would depend upon the amount of red and yellow used. By selectively mixing and screening two color, you can produce more than two colors. Carefully screening black and orange for the halftone or lineart of a tiger would produce a tonal range of ruddy browns and sepias in addition to the full black, orange and white. Through overprinting, the printed tiger would have a full-color, natural look, without the more expensive full-color treatment.

Duotone is another creative use of flat color or two color. For more information on its use and connection to the two-color process, see **Chapter 5**.

Selecting the Second Color

There are a number of ways to select a second color. The most used and most predictable one, though, and the one professional designers and printers use is **PMS**, the **Pantone Matching System**. It is a standardized color system which uses ten basic colors that, when correctly mixed according to their respective formulae, are capable of consistently producing over 500 different colors.

To use it, you select or match the needed color from a sample book that contains each of the PMS colors on both coated and uncoated stock. You can indicate color to the printer either by writing down the PMS color number or by ripping off that swatch of color and attaching it to your layout. Writing down the PMS color is the safest bet. Swatches can be lost or mismatched by accident. Designers also keep Pantone's *Color/Tint Overlay Selector* at arm's reach to evaluate normal overprinting or mixes of different colors or color tints. By overlaying the acetate sheets, designer and client alike can see exactly what a mixed color combination will look like.

Process Color

Process color or **four color** is used for reproducing full-color artwork or photography. This illusion of full color is accomplished by optically mixing the three primary colors yellow, red (actually **magenta**) and blue (called **cyan**) along with black. Four color plates are shot, and the screened halftone of each color blends through overlaid dot patterns. The semitransparent inks are blended by our eyes—for example, when we see minute dots of red and blue together, we mix them optically and see violet. Each color plate is shot at a slightly different screen angle to enhance color alignment. In addition to coloring black areas of the image, the black plate provides the contrast and spatial anchoring required for the full-color effect.

Color plates may be created in a variety of ways. The most common use either photographic or electronic (laser) scanning. Both methods employ black-and-white photography color filters to isolate the hues sought. These film negatives are printed to positive transparencies or as the printing plates themselves. Color corrections are almost always made to adjust for color imbalance and the filtering process and to ensure that its finished image is a decent reproduction of the original. Corrections may be done via photography or scanning during the color separation process. Color proofs check corrections and provide designers and client alike a preview of the production color. Today, designers and art directors use **matchprints** as final proofs.

There are two types of color proofs. **Overlays** stack each color separation individually on a single sheet of acetate; when the yellow, red, blue and black sheets are overlaid, you see the full-color proof. Overlays are a cheaper color proof that give a flat look to the color. **Integrals** shoot the four separations onto a single photo. These proofs bear a closer resemblance to the real thing, and don't gray out like overlays tend to do. Despite their higher cost, designers and art directors prefer the second type of proof because it is closer to the publication's reproduction image.

On press, each color is applied separately, one plate at a time and one color atop the others. The quality of this four-color overprinting method largely depends upon the quality of the original work, the quality of the cameras, plates and printing press used, and upon the skills and professionalism of those who operate the equipment. Sometimes five-color or six-color (or more) process is used. Normally, the additional colors are metallic inks or varnishes used in specialty or high-quality color projects. With each additional color or run, costs increase.

Printing Materials

Just as an artist needs to know his media and materials intimately, so, too, must the designer. You already know that no two printing processes produce the same definition, color, image or tonal shifts. Letterpress produces immaculate type that jumps from the page. Gravure and photogelatin reproduce photography and continuous-tone artwork so closely that the untrained eye might have a tough time differentiating it from original work. To know the process is one thing, but to understand its materials is another, equally important matter. For example, with one process a particular paper might provide you meticulous precision; with another, it might have the opposite result.

You need to know processes and materials separately—and you need to know how they work together. Each printing material has its own characteristics, limitations, quality range, definition of detail, image and cost. But choosing them requires thoughtful consideration. The entire list of printing possibilities— printing process, typesetting, artwork, color, paper and ink—has a logical mapping. Misdirected, they are capable of turning the best writing, photography and layouts into publication disasters. Unfortunately, such disasters happen regularly. What's more, their cost cannot be figured precisely in dollars and cents.

Paper

Paper is important, if for no other reason than because it constitutes somewhere in the neighborhood of one-quarter to one-half your total publication costs. This gets more interesting all the time, doesn't it?

It's also important because printing processes limit many of your paper choices. Some processes don't reproduce successfully on certain paper stock. When the printing process and paper are improperly matched, you end up with poor print quality. The wrong choice of paper might lead to jamming or binding the press operation, or cause breakage or tearing. The paper you choose should be runnable, period. It should also be printable, that is, take and hold ink exactly the way you want it to. It's amazing how many production problems disappear when you follow this strategy. To choose wisely, there are a number of paper characteristics you need to know about.

Paper is more than a material that receives the ink and carries your message. It communicates before the words on it are read. When you pick up a publication, your eyes and hands notice certain things about the paper stock. You can feel its surface and texture, note its reflectance, color, weight and rigidity. What follows is a brief discussion of paper characteristics.

- **Grain** refers to the alignment of the fibers in the paper. Normally, the direction of the grain runs parallel to the papermaking machine. This structural feature of paper is especially important if your materials will be folded, as in the case of most direct-mail or brochure pieces. Paper folds evenly and much more easily if the crease is made with the grain or machine direction. Similarly, paper is more rigid, or stiffer, in the grain direction.

  You can quickly assess the direction of the grain in a paper by tearing it. A fairly clean and straight rip indicates that the grain direction runs parallel to the tear; if it tears diagonally and unevenly you're going against the grain.

- Paper **weight** is figured by the weight of a ream (500 sheets) of a basic size. So, for example, let's say that a ream of 25" x 38" coated stock weighs 70 pounds. Its basis weight (based on a ream of that paper) would be 70 pounds. However, size varies from paper to paper, but sizes are noted in the paper specifications. Don't go by weight number alone; examine the paper carefully to make sure it's right for your job. In fact, your evaluation of it will be more accurate if you can see and feel printed samples.

  Note, though, that the significance of paper weight extends well beyond its aesthetic and functional characteristics. If you are mailing your publication and paying postage by the pound, weight will be very important to you. Choosing paper weight may mean balancing the look and heft of a paper stock against your budget.

- **Bulk** is simply the thickness or **caliper** of a paper. It's of interest to a designer because it figures physically into the design of a publication. Additionally, it is a factor separate from weight; for example, there is a tremendous range of bulk in 60-pound (or any other weight) papers. Bulk may be calibrated with a micrometer, but you can estimate the thickness of your publication from the paper manufacturer's **PPI** (pages per inch). Bulk may also be important to you because it affects opacity.

- **Opacity** is the "show through" quality of paper. If the reader is able to see the type and imagery on the opposite side of the page being read, the paper has light opacity; if the opposite is true, the paper has heavy opacity. The more transparent a paper stock is, the more difficult it will be to read because our eyes are receiving visual information from both sides of the page concurrently. Opacity is affected by the bulk, weight, fillers, dye and coatings of a paper. Few publications use opaque paper, but most use paper that is dense enough to ensure a good read.

- **Brightness** is the reflective quality of a paper. The brighter and more reflective a paper is, the more contrast and snap it brings to the photography and graphics printed on it. Typically, high-quality corporate publications or those with lots of artwork use bright paper.

- The **finish** of a paper affects the look of the printed image. Usually printers break finish into two subcategories, **coated** and **uncoated** stock. Uncoated (sometimes referred to as **uncalendered**) paper is literally less finished, which is to say it has had fewer passes beneath the rollers or calenders of the paper-making mill. Its top side is the smoother of the two sides. As a paper is calendered, it becomes smoother and more finished; its bulk properties are also decreased.

- A paper's **texture** may be the result of minimal calendering or rolling; because it hasn't been pressed out, it carries a raised fiber and a natural texture. However, texture may also be rolled or pressed into a paper through rotary embossing machines. In the latter instance, literally any texture—linen, pebble, leather—can be pressed into the paper's surface. Coated papers are more finished and consequently have a smoother surface.

  Smoothness is a high priority for anyone whose publications include finely reproduced photography. Because of the additional handling, machining and fillers, most coated papers are more expensive than uncoated stock. They also tend to have more brilliance, opacity and sheen. As a result, coated stock takes ink extremely well and is especially suitable for high-quality black-and-white and color photographic reproduction. Letterpress, gravure and photogelatin printing process all demand smooth paper; offset lithography, flexography and letterset do not because of the more flexible nature of their respective processes.

- **Glossy** or **enameled** papers are specially treated coated papers, normally "cast-coated" with an enamel finish. Some printers and designers like to use an enameled paper for photography because it adds to the illusion of depth in a halftone. But the exaggerated reflective quality of this group of papers makes for a strenuous read. If you have a copy-heavy publication, you may do well to avoid glossy stock.

- Finally, different paper finishes influence how the paper receives, holds or reacts to the ink. Make sure that your paper is compatible with the printing process you're using. For example, if you're printing with offset, your paper should be resistant to water. **Picking** is the tendency of some inks to pull (or even lift) the paper surface. It is a problem common to offset, so papers used in this process should be pick resistant as well as water resistant. Paper and ink need to be compatible not only to the printing process that you're using, but to one another.

- **Paper color** refers not only to the hue of the paper but to the subtle toning that affects the whiteness of a page. Minute amounts of browns and yellows added to a paper warm it up; these are the "creamy" stocks like ivory, or bone white. Warmer whites bring a more personal, friendly feel to paper. Blues and blue-grays are used to cool a paper. Although this tends to depersonalize the feel of the paper, small amounts of blue add brilliance or sparkle to paper and increase its contrast slightly.

Papers are also classified in a general way according to function or use. A typical **paper grade** classification includes newsprint, book, cover, bristol board or cardboard and tag.

- **Newsprint** (24" x 36"), the cheapest grade of paper, is very absorbent and unstable; it stiffens and discolors easily. Its use is pretty much restricted to newspapers and tabloids.

- As the name implies, **book** (25" x 38") is used extensively for textbooks. (This paper is a book paper.) But it is also used for magazines, brochures, newsletters, posters and the like. The broadest paper grade of the bunch, it is further stratified as uncoated, coated, antique, offset or gravure. Some of these names suggest their primary use. Printers can furnish you with countless examples, textures, colors and finishes for each of these. While you're examining these possibilities, ask your printer to show you examples of how each prints halftones and responds to different colors.

- **Cover** papers (20" x 26") are also available in a tremendous number of colors, textures, coatings, finishes and weights; in fact, you'll frequently be able to match them exactly to the book paper you're using. Cover stock is stiffer and heavier because it's normally used for covers of books, magazines, catalogs and the like.

- **Bristol** paper (22 1/2" x 35") is layered and bonded together. Much heavier and tougher than cover stock, its construction makes it especially tailored for high-speed folding, laminating, stamping and die-cutting. Furthermore, it takes ink well and is suitable for high-quality photographic and art reproduction. Some common uses include greeting cards, record album covers, menus and posters.

- **Tag** (24" x 36") takes its name from its most common application: being used to make tags and tickets. It doesn't have the same quality as some of the bristols, but, like them, it provides a tough but flexible surface perfect for a variety of printing purposes.

Ink

It's important to correctly match ink to the paper and printing process you're using. Each process, because of its specific method of applying ink and running paper, has different inking demands and its own peculiarities. Depending upon the process, inks may be applied thinly and thickly, dry quickly or very slowly, carry light or heavy amounts of pigment, and react differently when they are applied to paper.

Tack is the inherent sticking tendency of an ink. Too much tack and not enough paper strength results in the paper surface tearing or picking. Inks used with offset lithography need to be somewhat tacky and dense in color in order to produce sharp imagery and solid letters. They also need to be both water and alcohol resistant. Letterpress inks aren't quite as tacky, as a rule. Generally, both the letterpress and offset presses use very dense, thick inks. On the other hand, inks for gravure and flexography printing are very fluid, quick-drying inks that use solvents to assure even application of ink and to speed up the drying process.

There are other, more specialized inks. For example, metallic inks use metal powders and are sometimes used in full-color printing as a fifth color; in fact, they may be used as color samples for automobiles and other products. Magnetic inks employ magnetized pigments which the banking industry uses for high-speed electronic reading on your checks.

Whenever you select inks, double-check with the printer to make sure your choices are runnable, printable and aesthetically appropriate. If you're printing on color paper, examine paper/ink samples so you'll have no surprises with color shifts. Finally, to make sure that you and the printer share the same expectations, ask to see samples of work using the same inks, paper and process as your publication—samples your printer has created.

Binding

There are two general approaches to binding: lightweight binding for brochures, magazines, pamphlets and catalogs, and bookbinding for larger, more permanent publications.

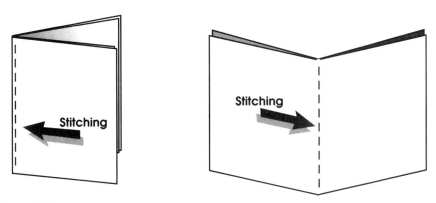

Figure 7.8 _____

Side and Saddle Stitching. *Signatures for side stitching (left) are place on top of each other and stitched a quarter-inch from the edge. The cover is then glued on. With saddle stitching, the signatures and cover are laid open on top of one another and the spine is stiched.*

Most binding begins by organizing the publication's signatures. A **signature** is a single sheet of paper, both sides of which have been printed in a prearranged grouping of single pages. (Signatures are usually printed in multiples of sixteen pages, but they may be smaller depending on the format and number of pages in the publication.) In lightweight binding, the signatures are folded, arranged into sections of four, collated, stitched and finally trimmed. If a publication has but one signature, it is trimmed and folded (or vice versa), or simply folded if no trimming is necessary. When the weight or stiffness of the paper encumbers this process, printers first score the signatures. Scoring—impressing an indentation on the paper via a steel rule (or string) so that it folds easily—is often standard procedure with publication covers because their paper stock is heavier.

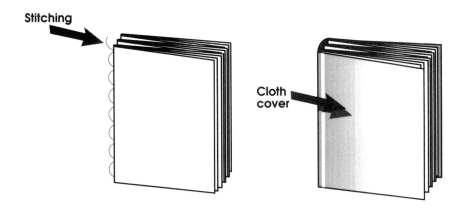

Figure 7.9 _____

Edition or Case Binding. *Signatures are stitched individually and stacked. The spine is covered and glued, while enpapers are glued to the last sheets of the outside signatures. A board and cloth cover is added later.*

After signatures have been collated, they may be side stitched or saddle stitched. **Side stitching** is generally used with larger or bulkier publications. In this case, the folded signatures are placed atop one another and the stitching is driven through the sides of all the signatures approximately one-quarter inch from the edge of the publication. Covers are normally glued on afterwards, which helps further bind the already stitch-bound signatures. Side-stitched publications are sturdier than their saddle-stitched counterparts, but they are clumsier and won't stay open flat. That is not the case with saddle-stitched publications. **Saddle stitching** is a simpler, less expensive procedure that nests the signatures atop one another and drives two to three staples through the spine and cover of the publication. Saddle-stitched publications, as you probably know, come apart more easily than do side-stitched ones.

Publications that are expected to receive a great deal of use and/or be around for a while are more likely to be bookbound. There are three major ways to bookbind a publication: edition binding, perfect binding and spiral binding. In **edition** or **case binding**, the signatures are first folded, collated and stacked. At this point endleaves are bonded to the last page of the bottom signature and the first page of the top signature. Then the separate signatures are sewn together and trimmed, and the spine is glued. Later the spine is rounded so that the cover (or casing) will fit snugly, and open and close easily. Finally, a super—or cloth strip—is glued to the spine; it extends to the left and right of the backbone of the book because it later will be used to attach to the book's cover. A casing-in or cover machine glues the endleaves and presses the cover to the rest of the book.

In **perfect binding**, the backs of the collated signatures are trimmed or ground off and dense adhesive is applied. While it's still sticky, a bonding/lining is placed atop the adhesive and the cover is glued on. The adhesive maintains its flexible bonding strength for a long time. Most paperback books and some hardcover books are bound in this manner, which is cheaper than edition binding.

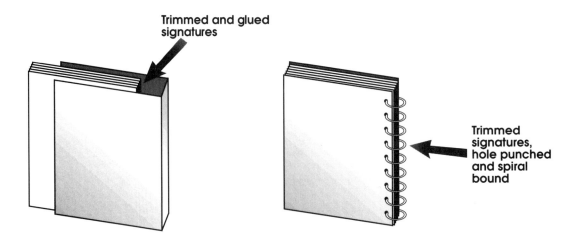

Trimmed and glued signatures

Trimmed signatures, hole punched and spiral bound

Figure 7.10 _____

Perfect and Spiral Bindings. *Both of these bindings usually require that the signatures be trimmed. In perfect binding, they are then glued to the cover. In spiral binding, they are hole-punched along with the cover and bound with wire or plastic.*

Spiral binding doesn't have the same aesthetic as any of the other binding methods, but it has become the binding of choice for designers of many manuals and notebooks because it opens flat. After the signatures have been collated and trimmed, holes are drilled or punched through the gutter of the publication and either wire or plastic is inserted or "spun" through the holes. If you choose this binding method, be sure you have sturdy covers and heavy enough paper for the pages. The metal or plastic spiral will tear up lightweight pages in short order.

Working with Postal Regulations

If your publication is going to be mailed, consult the United States Postal Service before designing it. Many publications—direct-mail pieces, newsletters, brochures or envelope panels for return mail, etc.—require special designing for bulk rate postage or any mailing. Anyone who has designed or printed direct mail pieces has at least one horror story to tell.

Generally, our postal system is most accommodating, and they provide the best service in the world, often despite outrageous situations. That is easy to forget if you happen to have a run-in with them over a seemingly minor detail. The fact of the matter is that their rules are established for the greater good and to keep the system modern, well-greased and efficient, so that the service and convenience we're accustomed to is maintained.

If you're contemplating a large mailing, consider bulk mailing. The savings third-class bulk rate offers over first-class are considerable. To begin with, there is an annual charge. In addition, there are three methods to pay postage.

1. **Precanceled stamps**. You must possess an approved application in order to use this bulk method. Be sure that your postal area or envelope brochure panel carries both a return address and that either NONPROFIT or BULK RATE is printed on the top line of the stamp design, the area referred to as the **indicia**. (NOTE: The nonprofit or bulk-mail designation may be placed adjacent to the stamp design if it isn't included within the stamp.)

2. **Meter stamps**. Should you choose this alternative, you must buy or lease a meter. Again, the NONPROFIT or BULK RATE aegis must appear next to the metered postage. If using a third-class bulk mailing, it's a good idea not to date your mail. Dating metered stamps requires that the date be correct and that your entire mailing reach the post office that same day. It complicates mailing without really offering much in return.

3. **Permit imprint**. Should you have large and/or frequent mailings, the bulk-rate permit imprint method may prove most beneficial. It requires a separate annual fee and a substantial deposit, which is placed in an account used later to cover postage. Permit imprint may be used only on mailings with identical pieces. Content need not be the same, but each publication must be identical in size and weight.

Current regulations require that the stamp or indicia be positioned in the upper right-hand corner of the envelope panel. Both your return address and your stamp, or permit imprint designs, must be parallel to the bottom of the publication or envelope. Obviously, the type, rules and printing accents must be crisp. (It is interesting to note that the postal service asks customers not to use script, italic or flamboyant typefaces. These type styles are not only difficult for your audience to read, they are unreadable by current scanning technology.) Finally, the post office suggests you "use black ink on a white background for best results." Good contrast on an even background is key.

Other third-class bulk requirements dictate the minimum number of pieces allowable per mailing, the limitations you have establishing some of the publication's physical properties (weight, dimensions, thickness), the uniformity of mailing pieces, and so on. While some of these may seem petty or constraining, they are important to your design and, obviously, to the postal service's automated scanning and sorting technology.

For a complete picture of how design and printing can be affected by the post office, consult postal authorities regarding current regulations before beginning designs for anything that will be mailed.

Printing
Part B: Computers

When computers were new, we were so happy to be working on them instead of typewriters that printing was just gravy. It wasn't long, however, before we began to appreciate the nuances between such terms as *letter quality* and *near letter quality*. If all we did was churn out correspondence, then either would suffice, so long as the end product didn't look like it had been hand-lettered by someone suffering from a caffeine overdose. Then along came the desktop publishing revolution, and choosing the right printer became serious business.

Roughly speaking, printers can be broken down into three types.

- **Daisy wheel** printers use a type element that looks like a wheel. Each character is present on the wheel, which rotates into place as it is chosen by the computer/printer memory. Daisy wheel printers provide letter-quality printing but are slow—usually somewhere between 15 and 70 characters per second—and limited as to type size, weight and style. Bold, for example, is accomplished by simply striking over a letter several times.

- **Dot-matrix** printers also form letters by striking an inked ribbon; however, the letters consist of a series of dots rather than a single character. Most dot-matrix printers allow you to run everything from extremely rough drafts to near-letter-quality jobs. They are faster than daisy wheel printers (between 60 and 300 characters per second) and have the added advantage of being able to produce type in different weights, styles and sizes. They can also print graphics—a giant step above daisy wheel printers.

- **Laser printers** are the desktop publisher's answer to typesetting. They are quieter than impact printers (there is no ribbon to strike) and faster, printing lines per minute rather than characters per minute. At upwards of 600 lines per minute, laser printers typically print six to eight pages every minute. These printers literally assemble entire pages in memory before they print them. The real breakthrough, however, is the laser printer's ability to print documents that are near-typeset quality.

Most laser printers today are based on one of two technologies—the Apple LaserWriter or Hewlett-Packard's LaserJet. The basic difference between the two is that the LaserWriter (and printers based on its technology) uses *PostScript*, a programming language that allows entire pages of both text and graphics to be sent to the printer at one time. Type can be produced at any available size and even extremely complex graphics can be printed out, restricted only by the resolution of the printer. Software/hardware packages that will turn a printer based on LaserJet technology into a printer that accepts *PostScript* are now available, and new LaserJet printers are now coming on the market with built-in *PostScript* capability.

Keep in mind that, although prices have come down considerably, laser printers can still cost you quite a bit—ranging roughly from $1,000 to $5,000, depending mostly on the amount of memory the printer comes with.

Some of the newer laser printers—especially those that accept *PostScript*—come with at least 1 megabyte of memory. These are variously upgradeable to as much as 12 megabytes or more and some accept external hard drives boosting the memory even higher. The greater the memory, the less time it takes to print, the more pages the printer can store at one time, and the more type fonts it can handle. For example, upwards of thirty type fonts now come packaged on some laser printers, and with expanded memory, dozens more can be added. In fact, some font manufacturers sell hundreds of fonts on their own hard drive ready for installation on your system. The difference in printer memory size can mount up in dollars, however, so be ready to pay for what you get.

Although laser printers are definitely the ideal, you can get along without one. Many quick printers and photocopy stores carry the most common software applications, and can run laser copies right off your disks. If you're in doubt, just call. It pays to at least have a dot-matrix printer, however, to run drafts. These won't exactly match your laser output copies, but they will give you some idea of what to expect.

Pre-mechanical Printing

The kind of print job you need depends on where you are in the layout process. Word-processed documents or manuscripts can be proofed from almost any type of printer. If cost per page is a factor, consider drafts run on a dot-matrix printer. With toner cartridges running over $100 each, every copy you run off a laser printer just to edit manuscript pages will cost you more than it's worth.

For the same reason, don't use your laser printer to run multiple copies of multi-paged documents. On the average, toner refills for a photocopier are cheaper than toner cartridges for laser printers. And the wear and tear on a laser printer (which runs hotter than a photocopier) should be taken into consideration. It is much simpler, and cheaper, to take your original laser copy and run multiple copies on a photocopier.

Save the laser printer for drafts that need to be checked for page layout, type alignment and design considerations. Here are a few tips for running drafts on a laser printer based on *PostScript*.

- If you've run previous drafts on a dot-matrix printer, don't count on the laser-printed version being the same. Alignment is a good bit different on these two types of printers, as is letterspacing, sizing, and so on. Get your original draft in the best shape you can before you run a copy on the laser printer. Be prepared to make adjustments.

- Prior to running a second laser draft, make as many adjustments to your first draft as you can. For example, don't just adjust the kerning and run another copy when you could have also reset the column width and changed the headline type. Learn to economize and make each copy count.

- Don't expect completely clean copies from your laser printer. These printers are temperamental. Toner quality and distribution vary from

Figure 7.11 _____

The laser-printing process.

A. *As the paper enters the printer from the paper **tray**, it is given a positive charge. As the paper moves along the **paper path** to the **transfer drum**, the rotating drum receives a negative charge from the **charger**.*

B. *Meanwhile, the computer image is transferred to the rotating transfer drum from the printer's memory via the **laser light**. The laser light bounces its image onto a **rotating mirror** and onto the drum. The light "draws" a picture by neutralizing the spot where black will be, leaving the surrounding area negatively charged where white will be.*

C. *The **toner cartridge** provides a negatively charged powder. As the drum rolls through the toner powder, the negative toner avoids the negative surface of the drum, but sticks to the neutralized dots created by the image drawn on the drum's surface by the laser light.*

D. *Since the toner is negative and the paper positive, when the paper passes over the drum, the dots stick to the paper.*

E. *The **fuser unit** "fuses" toner onto the paper using temperatures of up to 400 degrees Farenheit.*

Illustration by Thomas H. Bivins © 1990

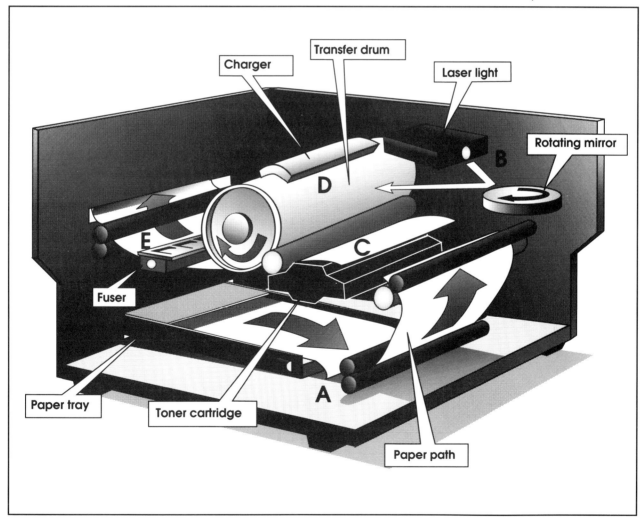

cartridge to cartridge, new cartridges take a few copies to "kick in," lightness versus darkness adjustments are tricky, and larger black areas are just not going to print out solid, no matter what you do.

Some printer manufacturers recommend removing the cartridge and shaking it to spread the toner more evenly. This often works. Don't try it unless you know how to remove the cartridge and put it back. And don't do it in white clothing.

• Read your printer and software manuals' sections on printing. Each program deals a little differently with print specifications. Don't assume that each program will use the same commands or even the same menus. Be aware, for instance, of paper size limitations. Many printers will run letter- and legal-sized documents only. Some allow for different paper trays for each size, while others require hand-feeding anything other than letter-sized paper.

Some software programs allow you to *tile*. Tiling breaks larger pages, such as 11" x 17", into four overlapping pieces. You can cut and paste these together for a rough layout. Other programs limit the actual area on a given paper size that will be printed on when using a specific type of printer. For example, *PageMaker* reduces the print area of legal-sized pages to 6.8" x 12" when printing on a LaserWriter; however, when printing to a Linotronic typesetter, it will run full-size pages including bleeds and crop marks to indicate trim size (more on this below).

Most laser printers will only print to within a quarter-inch of the paper edge. This limits your ability to use bleeds, or at least see them on drafts printed on laser printers. But it doesn't restrict your final copy if run on a phototypesetter.

• If you are using bleeds, or if you want to run a tabloid-sized page so you can see it whole—without tiling—try reducing it. Most page-layout programs will allow you to set a reduction value before you print. For instance, an 11" x 17" page can fit onto an 8.5" x 11" page at a 70 percent reduction. In most cases, it will still be legible. When reducing, indicate the edges of your document with crop marks, or simply add an unshaded box around the outside edges of your page before you print.

Selecting Paper for Laser Printing

Paper is probably the least thought about part of laser printing. Most of us simply opt for whatever is handy. The fact is, some papers are made specifically for laser printers, and some papers definitely should be avoided.

Ask yourself three questions when you pick laser printer paper.

• Will the laser copy be used as a finished piece or for reproduction?
• Does the paper say what you want it to say? In other words, what is its look and feel?
• Does it run well in your printer?

Keeping in mind the paper specifications presented earlier in this chapter, the following rules of thumb should help you select the proper paper for your needs and your printer.

- Brighter paper reproduces well on laser printers. (This doesn't mean *whiter* paper. There are varying degrees of brightness even among white papers.) Brighter papers are also good for reproduction masters. In fact, several paper manufacturers make papers specifically for laser printer output that will be used for reproduction. Also, since it's hard to predict the degree of darkness of your printer, the brighter the paper, the more contrast you're likely to have between the print and the paper. In general, avoid colored paper. However, some interesting effects can be obtained with lighter colors such as gray and beige.

- Stay away from heavily textured paper. The heavier the texture, the more broken your type will look, because it will be harder for the toner to adhere to the paper's surface. Texture also affects any large, dark areas such as screens and display type. Some texture, like that found in bond paper and linen stock, is fine. The trick here is to experiment.

- Avoid heavy papers like cover stock, generally 90 pounds or more, unless you like removing jammed paper from your printer. On the other hand, extremely light papers, such as onion skin, may stick to the rollers or jam as they feed into the printer. Don't experiment much here. Just settle for a text-weight paper (generally around 60 pounds) and consign covers to your commercial printer.

- Use a fairly opaque paper, especially if your laser-printed copy is to be your final version. If you use a paper with high opacity, be sure it isn't also heavily textured.

- Don't expect heavily textured papers to retain their texture. Unlike offset presses, laser printers flatten the paper as it moves through the printer. In most cases, any texture will be lost.

- By the same token, don't use embossed or engraved papers in your laser printer since they might jam the mechanism and will flatten out anyway.

- Make sure your paper is heat resistant. Since laser printers work in temperatures of around 400 degrees Fahrenheit, certain letterhead inks may melt or stick and any metal or plastic will certainly ruin your printer. Above all, don't use acetate in your laser printer unless it has been specifically designed for your particular printer.

Printing the Finished Piece

Printing specifications vary greatly depending on whether you're printing a draft or a final product—a mechanical that will be reproduced by a commercial printer, or a report or presentation. Depending on your particular needs, a mechanical might be printed right off your laser printer. For quick-print jobs or "daily tidbits" publications, this is probably the cheapest way to go. Remember, though, that a LaserWriter only prints at 300 dots per inch. This is okay for body copy and most display type below 64 points, but for complex gray-scale photos and very large type, you might consider another method. If you do go with laser-printed originals, the following tips might be helpful.

- Make sure your printer's toner is new or in good shape. If you can't get truly dark originals, try having your laser originals re-copied on a good photocopier. Just remember, each generation of copying deteriorates the image further.

- Use a strong typeface with solid serifs or sans serif and a good x-height. Pick a size that's easily readable (generally 10 or 12 point). And don't work with display type larger than 36 point, since it will tend to show the ragged edges even at 300 dpi.

- Large black areas and wide rules will tend to "gray out" on a laser printer, even one with a new toner cartridge. Try to avoid them.

- If you must use photographs, select those with few heavy black areas and a good contrast level. Remember, they are going to print out at 300 dpi, which will give you only about 33 shades of gray. If possible, work with line art or high-contrast photos instead.

- Use a bright, fairly slick paper for your reproduction master.

To get the best possible camera-ready pages, run your mechanical on a computer-compatible photo typesetter or page compositor, such as the Linotronic 300. At 2500 dots per inch, the quality rivals (some say surpasses) traditional typesetting methods. Display type that looked ragged on your laser printer will look crisp and black; shaded areas will look dense and smooth; large, black areas will be uniformly black; illustration will be crisp; and photos will appear in a full range of grays. Clearly, there are advantages to using this method; and now that the price of a page of copy on a Linotronic is roughly five dollars, cost is one of the major ones.

If you are going to use a Linotronic, here are some tips.

- First, consider whether you need a positive or a negative run. Negatives will save you a step in the printing process, although they can't be checked for accuracy easily. In fact, positives containing photos are best run as negatives since the photos will probably muddy if shot a second time.

- Understand the parameters of your output device before you send anything to be run off. Are you running your pages on a Linotronic 100 with a 1250 dpi capability or a Linotronic 300 with a 2500 dpi capability? If you are using a Linotronic 300, is it actually set for a 2500 dpi default, or has it been set down to save running time? In most cases, printing at 1250 dpi produces more than enough resolution and your final product will run in less time than if printed at 2500 dpi. Lower resolution does mean fewer gray levels; however, this usually isn't problem since most of us can't easily distinguish between 95 levels of gray and 256 levels of gray anyway.

  Also, ask about the default line screen. It can be variously set on many typesetters. If you don't designate a line screen with your software, your gray-scale images will default to the typesetter's settings. If you're running magazine-quality photos, use 120–133 line screen setting. For newsletters and newspapers, use 85–90.

- Although you can obtain extremely fine reproduction by printing scanned images on a phototypesetter, many images will need further adjustment. In fact, you will often find it cheaper to have halftones shot separately and stripped into your negative. See the section on computer applications of photography in **Chapter 4** for more information on scanning.

- Remember, the limitations of print area imposed by your laser printer don't necessarily apply here. The Linotronic 300, for example, can print widths up to seventeen inches and any length. This allows for bleeds and over-sized pages. Don't forget to indicate that you want your pages run with crop marks, however.

- If you're running color separations, be sure to request registration marks— and carefully check your final output for proper registration.

- Make sure you include the type of program you used, copies of the original scanned photos on disks, and anything your printer needs to know to run your pages for you. Printers are likely to charge you even if the pages don't look like you thought they would—especially if it's because of something you didn't tell them.

- If your final product doesn't look like what you laid out, trace the problem to its origin. Computer programs are notoriously fluky, and trading disks between your machine and your printer's machine and thence to the Linotronic allows for many a slip. Among other things, make sure that you are both using the same version of your page-layout program. If you've included any illustrations to be placed by them, make sure they have that program as well. Specify any screens or other vital photographic information. And make sure the typefaces you used are carried by your printer or typesetter. Nothing is more frustrating than having to completely reset your publication because your Linotronic operator doesn't have Helvetica Narrow.

Color Printing

There are basically two ways to consider color: as used in creating a comprehensive, thus produced in house, and as a final print job. In the latter case, color separations are developed, either through your software program and run on an output device, or by your commercial printer in the traditional way. For our purposes, we will discuss only the possibilities of in-house color printing.

There is a great deal of difference between what you see on that $2,000 color monitor and what comes off your color printer. That's because screen colors are light mixed. That is, they produce virtually all the visible colors the human eye can behold by varying the amounts of red, green and blue light. The better color monitors now available can apply up to 256 shades to each of these primary colors, giving us a possible color palette of nearly 17 million combinations. Most color printers (as well as commercial printers) replicate this palette by mixing yellow, magenta and cyan (yellow, red and blue) inks or pigments; and what you mixed with light just isn't going to look the same when mixed with ink.

The issue is further complicated by the technology itself. Just as monochrome laser printers print with cells instead of dots, so color printers are limited by their inability to vary density. In traditional color printing, variations in density are implied by variations in dot size. Color printers, like monochrome printers, use dithering to produce either colors or shades of gray. As we saw in **Chapter 4**, the greater the number of gray levels, the lower the resolution. For the same reasons, the greater the number of colors, the lower the resolution. Since each color is *simulated* by printing dots of various colors next to each other to form a specific color or shade, the more colors you indicate, the more dots you require, thus lowering resolution.

Let's go over the three most common types of color printers available today: **ink-jet printers**, **thermal transfer printers**, and **film recorders**. Of course, most dot-matrix printers can also print in color, but the range and quality is very limited.

Ink-jet Printers

Ink-jet printers are great if all you want to do is add some spot color to a presentation and don't care much about high quality. These printers use small jets to spray colors from bottles or cartridges inside the machine onto paper spinning on a rotating drum. The colors are mixed from yellow, magenta, cyan

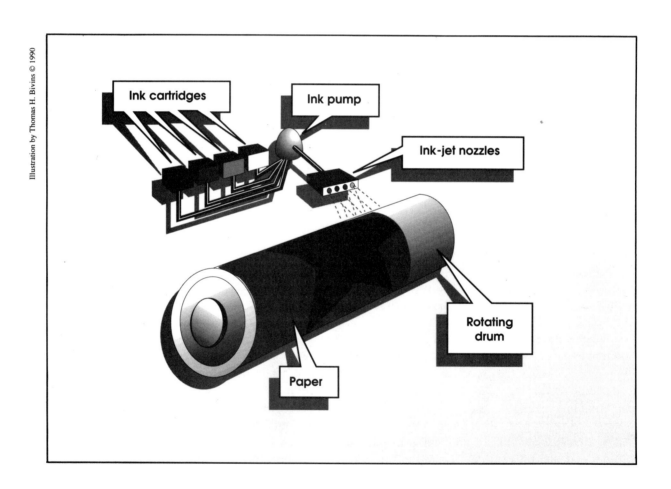

Figure 7.12 _____

Ink-jet printing. During this process, the paper adheres to a rotating drum onto which four colors of ink are sprayed by a head moving parallel to the drum. The ink is drawn by a pump from ink resevoirs or cartridges holding yellow, magenta, cyan and black pigments.

and black and reproduce best on special paper. Although at the bottom end of the line these printers are relatively inexpensive, the best quality comes from those in the $60,000 to $70,000 range. In the $1,500 to $2,000 range, you can find several models that are useful for rough color comps and limited presentations.

Thermal Transfer Printers

Thermal transfer printers literally transfer color to paper via a transparency film and lots of heat. They also provide pretty good resolution (200–300 dpi). But they dither the output much the same as a dot-matrix printer would, making it unsuitable for camera-ready art but certainly good enough for most comps. Thermal printers are relatively fast (about a minute a page) and relatively inexpensive (about fifty cents a page).

Although at around $8,000 the Tektronix color printer is already quite an investment, you still only get bit-mapped images—passable for graphics but not so good for type. On the other hand, you can get *PostScript*-type images (no jagged, bit-mapped edges) for a mere $20,000 plus by investing in something

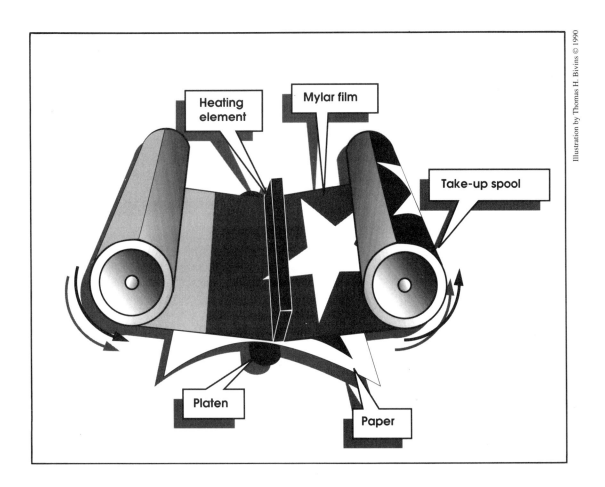

Illustration by Thomas H. Bivins © 1990

Figure 7.13 _____

Thermal transfer printing. *Thermal transfer uses sheets of Mylar film coated with yellow, magenta and cyan pigments. A thermal head scans the page, transfers the proper sheet into place, and melts small dots of color onto the page. The result is very good for comps but the dithered appearance isn't camera-ready and the finished layout is very slick (light reflective) because of the transfer method.*

like the QMS Colorscript 100 (although, at this writing, both Tektronix and QMS have introduced a *PostScript* color printer for *just* under $10,000). If you need to proof color separations before sending them to a Linotronic, for example, a *PostScript* compatible color printer could be very helpful. Whether you use one or the other, the basic problem of WYSIWYG still applies. The disparity between your monitor, your color printer, and your commercial printer's inks is going to make you crazy if you depend on your layout and output devices to provide you with accurate colors.

Film recorders

Film recorders actually take a picture of what's on your monitor. At $6,000 to $12,000, they'd better be good photographers! They use a 35mm slide format to record exactly what you set up on your high-resolution color monitor. The output is excellent for generating color separations but not as good for color comps.

In short, in-house color printing hasn't reached the point at which it's worth the investment to *most* people. However, if it's like the rest of the computer industry, it won't be long before it's cost effective and aesthetically satisfying.

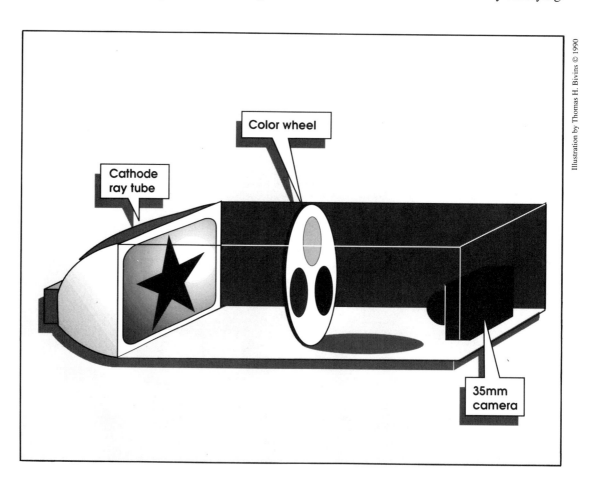

Figure 7.14

Film recorder. From the outside, film recorders look like a simple, plastic box. That, in fact, is exactly what they are. Inside the box, a 35mm camera takes a series of multiple exposers of a CRT (cathode ray tube) through a color wheel—one exposure for each of the red, green and blue filters on the wheel. A light beam eminating from the CRT exposes the film as the filter wheel moves into place for each color.

Part Two

The Basic Publications

Magazines

Annual Reports

Brochures

Newsletters

Chapter 8

Magazines

Part A: Writing

W hen we speak of magazines most of us think of our favorite consumer publication (*Time, Newsweek, National Geographic,* the *Atlantic,* etc.); however, for our purposes, we are speaking primarily, but not exclusively, of the **house publication**. Recent research has shown that house publications are the *least* looked to form of organizational communication. Guess what's first? Face-to-face communication.

That's not surprising, but it doesn't mean that the house magazine is dead. What it does mean is that it should *contribute* to open communication rather than be relied upon as the sole source. In addition, it plays another role. Unlike most print media an organization might have access to, the house publication is a totally controlled medium—the organization producing it has sole editorial control. The company can go on record through its house organ, state its position on a controversial issue, or simply tell its story its way. The house organ is still a good public relations tool, especially when read by those outside the organization.

The typical house organ is meant for an internal public—usually employees, shareholders, and retirees. Sometimes, though, it is offered to the external public. A publication like *Exxon USA* stresses a broader emphasis with articles often dealing with the industry as a whole and subjects of interest to those outside the company. Because the house organ is, at bottom, still a public relations piece, its thrust remains company oriented. Even a seemingly unrelated story will, in some way, eventually relate to the organization.

The house publication is usually in either magazine or newspaper format (or sometimes a hybrid called a "magapaper"). Both communicate with their various publics efficiently. Unless the company is large enough to produce a slick, in-house publication, the house organ will be sent out to an agency for design and printing. Sometimes the agency will even provide writers to work up the stories; however, the best articles still come from writers inside the company who know and work with the people they write about.

Content and Format

Like their smaller cousin, the newsletter, house magazines usually present the following editorial mix:

- 50 percent information about the organization—local, national and international
- 20 percent employee information—benefits, quality of working life, etc.
- 20 percent relevant noncompany information—competitors, community, etc.
- 10 percent small talk and personals

How you organize these elements is important, since the organization will lead your reader through your magazine in a logical order, and one that is pleasing and most interesting to him or her.

There is no single organizational format for house magazines. What is important is that you find a place for all of your intended information, a place inclusive enough to house similar information from issue to issue.

Before you even start (or if you're overhauling an existing publication) you need to set some objectives. You should review the sections in **Chapter 1** dealing with objectives because they are relevant here as well. To make sure your reasons for publishing a house magazine are realistic, ask yourself some questions.

- Are my goals and objectives consistent with the goals and objectives of the organization itself? What am I really trying to get out of this? The temptation is very real, especially for creative people, to produce a magazine for simple ego gratification. Don't succumb to it. Have good, solid reasons for publishing.

- Can I attain these objectives through another, more effective, method? Can I achieve good downward communication through an existing newsletter or more frequent meetings?

- Can I attain these objectives in a more *cost-effective* way? House magazines are expensive to produce. As usual, your budget restrictions will have the final say.

Once you have answered these questions satisfactorily, and you have satisfied yourself that your prospective audience will benefit from your publication, you can decide on its proper organizational format.

Most house magazines contain very much the same type of editorial information as newsletters. The following items are listed in the approximate order in which they might appear (allowing for overlap in the case of articles).

- **Table of contents**: Usually run on the front page.
- **Masthead**: Gives publication information (editor, publisher, etc.) and usually run on the table of contents or second page.
- **Editorial**: Can be in the form of a "President's Column," a signed editorial from management or the publication's editor.
- **Letters:** If the publication is designed for two-way communication, a letters column is a common addition.

- **News Notes**: A quick (and brief) look at what's happening around the organization. You can get a lot of these in two or three pages. This is a good place for employee information as well.
- **Articles:** News and feature articles make up the bulk of the magazine and should have a consistent order of their own. For instance, the cover story should always appear in the same approximate location each issue.
- **Announcements**: Usually boxed, but sometimes run as regular columns for job placement, promotions, etc. This is another good place for employee interest pieces.
- **Calendar**: Upcoming events of interest to readers.

Remember, there is no hard and fast rule for formatting your magazine; but stick to whatever method you choose. Your readers look for consistency. If your format changes every two issues, you'll quickly lose them.

Writing Articles

House publication articles range from straight news to complete fiction, and include everything in between. Most, though, are either straight news or feature. Since straight news has been covered in **Chapter 1**, we will concentrate on feature writing here.

As you probably already know, a feature can be construed as almost anything that isn't straight news. In fact, *feature* has several meanings. As used in the term "feature story," it simply means the main story or cover story in the publication. In its broader sense it means an article that features something as its central point or theme. This something may not necessarily be the message of the story or, in some cases, the publicity angle. It is most often the story itself. For example, you've been asked to do a story on a new product—say, a plastic lining that can be used as a bed for soil or sod to keep it from eroding or slipping. Instead of doing a straight news story on the product itself, you opt to do a feature story on a user of the new product. Maybe you find a golf course that's using the new underliner to rebuild its greens and the focus of the story becomes the golf course. The publicity angle or the message about the new product becomes almost secondary. Featuring the golf course adds an extra dimension to your product story and sets it in context. In fact, the most useful element of a feature story approach is that it presents a context. Not every straight news story can do that.

A vast array of writing styles can justifiably be called "magazine writing." Articles or ideas for articles that don't seem to fit one particular magazine format, or even one section of a magazine, may well fit into another. For example, let's say you interview an employee on a job-related topic such as benefits. In the course of your conversation you discover that he builds model ships for a hobby and, in fact, has won several competitions. You actually gather enough information for a how-to article on building model ships as well as enough for a feature on the employee. Neither of these ideas may fit into the story you originally set out to do; however, they may fit into another section on employees or one on hobbies. The lesson, of course, is never discard information just because it doesn't fit into your present assignment. Even if the tone or style of the article or information doesn't seem to fit one category, it may well fit another.

Although several standard types of feature articles are appropriate for magazines, the most common is the **profile**.

The Profile

The profile is most typically a feature story written specifically about a person, a product or service, or an organization or some part of it. It literally profiles the subject, listing facts, highlighting points of interest, and—most importantly—tying them to the organization. Regardless of the subject of your article, you are writing for a specific organization and the article must have some bearing on it—direct or indirect.

The personality profile

Personality profiles are popular because people still like to read about other people, whether these people are just like them (so they can easily relate) or very different (so they can aspire or admire). Of course, a personality profile should do more than just satisfy human curiosity, it should inform the reader of something important about the organization itself by putting it in the context of a biographical sketch. For example, this lead was written for a brief profile on an award-winning engineer:

> When Francis Langly receives the Goodyear Medal this spring, it will represent the symbolic crowning of a lifetime of dedication to the field of chemistry. Awarded by the Rubber Division of the American Chemical Society, the Goodyear medal is the premier award for work in the field of specialty elastomers—an area that Langly helped pioneer. When Langly makes his medalist's address to the gathering in Indianapolis in May, his comments will be a reflection of almost 50 years of innovation and development which began in 1938 when he joined Rogers Experimental Plastics Company as a research chemist.

What does this say about the organization? It implies, for one thing, that the company is obviously a good one to have such a well-respected person work for it for so long. A profile like this calls attention to the merits of the organization by calling attention to someone who has something to do with it—or, in some cases, to someone who benefits from its services or products. Consider the following lead:

> Guy Exton is a superb artist. His oils have hung in galleries all over the country. But, for nearly five years, he couldn't paint anything. In order to paint, you typically need fingers and a hand, and Guy lost his right hand in an auto accident in 1983. But now, thanks to a revolutionary new elastomer product developed by Rogers Experimental Plastics Company, Guy is painting again. He can grip even the smallest of his paint brushes and control the tiniest nuance through the use of a special prosthetic device designed by Medical Help, Inc. of Franklin, New York. The device, which uses REP's "Elastoflex" membrane as a flexible covering, provides minute control of digits through an electro-mechanical power pack embedded in the wrist.

One of the most common types of personality profiles is the Q & A (question and answer format). This style typically begins with a brief biographical sketch of the person being interviewed, hints at the reason for the interview, and sets the scene by describing the surroundings in which the interview took place. For the remainder of the piece, speakers are tagged Q or A. Sometimes, the interviewer is designated with the magazine's name (for example, *The Corporate Connection* might be shortened to *CC*). Likewise, the interviewee might be designated by her or his last name.

The descriptive narrative tells the story of the individual being profiled from a second-person point of view. Naturally, quotes from the subject may be included, but sometimes a successful profile is simply a biographical sketch, and won't necessarily need them. The following profile is a mixture. Although there are some brief quotes, most of the profile is simple biography.

The product or service profile

Profiling a product or service means describing it in a way that is unusual in order to draw attention to the product and the organization. This is often done in

Figure 8.1 _____

Personality Profile. *Notice that the biography and the story itself serve as a vehicle for mention of several products.*

A Lifetime of Service

When Francis Langly receives the Goodyear Medal this spring, it will represent the symbolic crowning of a lifetime of dedication to the field of chemistry. Awarded by the Rubber Division of the American Chemical Society, the Goodyear medal is the premier award for work in the field of specialty elastomers—an area that Langly helped pioneer. When Langly makes his medalist's address to the gathering in Indianapolis in May, his comments will be a reflection of almost 50 years of innovation and development which began in 1938 when he joined Rogers Experimental Plastics Company (REPC) as a research chemist.

Born in Brooklyn, New York, in 1915, Langly received his BA in chemistry and his PhD in organic chemistry from Cornell in 1939. His first position at REPC was in the Chemical Department at the Experimental Station near Ravenswood, Vermont. At the outset of World War II, he was working on the synthetic rubber program addressing the problem of an adhesive for nylon tire cord for B-29 bomber tires. These studies eventually culminated in the development of the vinyl pyridine adhesives so widely used today.

Langly's background in organic chemistry led to his transfer to the Organic Chemicals Department at the Johnson Laboratory in Stillwater, Oklahoma, where he discovered the first light-fast yellow dyes for cotton; and during the next 10 years, he led the task force that developed dyes for the new synthetic fibers that were fast becoming a mainstay of American fashion.

From his work in dyes, Langly moved onto work in fluorine chemical research. The small research team he headed is credited with the discovery of a family of new elastomers. The team at that time had, what Langly calls, "a very special business in fluorine chemicals," but no solid applications yet for these quickly developing products. Langly and his group knew that they had something distinctly different and new in the field of elastomers. To an inventor, of course, the invention comes first. It didn't seem to trouble him that there was little or no market at that time for these products. "There was no surprise in development," Langly says. "We understood the properties of the products we were developing and were sure that markets would eventually open up."

Chief among these early fluorelastomers was "Axon," a polymer that could resist extremely high temperatures, toxic chemicals, and a broad range of fluids. Other products, however, were gathering attention in industry and defense and the company was eager to market these already-accepted materials. In fact, the *Axon* project was sidetracked in the early 1950s when it was thought that the Langly research team could be better utilized in work on an already existing product. In a way, this turned out to be a profitable diversion. Although the proposed research turned out to be a dead end, a small pressure reactor system that had been designed to build EP rubbers was converted to make fluoropolymer and used as a pilot plant to produce *Axon*.

According to Langly, "you rarely have a chance to fill a vacuum with something entirely new." And *Axon* was entirely new. The Air Force had been searching for some time for a product that could withstand very low and very high temperatures and was impervious to oil for use as engine seals on jet aircraft. *Axon* fit the bill perfectly. The Air Force quickly adopted it for use in jets, and the product went commercial for the first time in 1959.

When interest in space exploration led the United States into the space race in the late 1950s, *Axon* gained another and larger market for use in rocket engine seals. Because of its ability to seal against "hard" vacuum, *Axon* was one of the first rubbers that could be used in space.

As the markets for *Axon* continued to expand—to automotives, industry, and oil exploration uses—Langly progressed through a series of promotions. When the Elastomer Chemicals Department was formed in the mid-1960s, he was transferred to corporate headquarters in Freeport as Assistant Director of Research and Development.

Until his retirement in 1979, Langly continued to develop his interest in the field of elastomers. To date, he has 35 patents issued in his name and some 15 publications. In the 25 years since the birth of "Axon," Langly has seen the product grow to its present status as the premium fluoroelastomer in the world with a new plant recently opened in Belgium which provides the product to a hungry European market.

But, Langly numbers the discovery and development of *Axon* as only one in a long line of accomplishments attained during his half-century of work in the field of chemistry. Since his retirement, he has remained active in the field, working in art conservation, developing new techniques for the preservation of rare oil paintings. In a year and a half of work with the City Museum in New York, he set up a sciences department for the conservation of paintings. He is currently scientific advisor for the Partham Museum in Baltimore. He continues to consult, working closely with industry. He serves as expert testimony at court trials involving chemicals. And, he has given a speech before the United Nations on rubber.

Yet, Langly remains low key about his accomplishments and his current interests. "I'm just trying to keep the fires going," he says. Despite this modesty, it is apparent to others that when Francis Langly receives the Goodyear Medal this year it will represent, not a capstone, but simply another milestone in a lifetime of service.

subtle ways. For example, the personality profile lead on the artist Guy Exton is really a way of mentioning a product. Clearly this doesn't detract from the human-interest angle, but it does accomplish a second purpose (probably the primary purpose) which is publicity. The same techniques you use in other article types can be used in profiling products. For instance, the following Q & A covers a new product through an interview with the company president—coincidentally the person who came up with the original idea. The Q & A, most typically used for personality profiles, doubles here as a way to profile a new product through a personal interview.

Figure 8.2

Product profile as Q&A—Notice that even though this is an interview, it is cleanly written. This usually means it has been edited for grammar and a certain amount of style. This can typically be done only if the person being interviewed is the person paying for the article (i.e., your client).

New Software 'Brainchild' of APC President

Ever wish you could talk to a historical personality? If you were one of the thousands of lucky students in test markets all over the U.S., you could! That's right. With the newest educational software developed by the Electronics Division of APC you can "talk" with Benjamin Franklin, explore the inside of an atom, or view the age of dinosaurs.

Corporate Connections sat down with APC President, James P. Sutton to talk about the revolutionary new software. It was his original concept which eventually became InfoQuick (IQ).

CC: Mr. Sutton, I understand that this new educational software, InfoQuick, that APC has developed is an entirely new concept. How so?

SUTTON: Well, it's new in that it is so expansive. That is, it covers so much curriculum over so many grade levels. We designed it to be used with children all the way from the first grade through high school. Educational software isn't exactly new, but IQ is like a textbook company providing all the textbooks needed for a child through his entire educational career.

We cover everything from spelling to higher math, including calculus and algebra. Our programs also have the advantage of being interrelated because they're produced by a single company.

CC: Do you see that interrelatedness as being a problem? I mean, doesn't that amount of interrelatedness lead to a sort of tunnel vision— like being taught the same courses by the same teacher all your life. Wouldn't you tend to see only one side of everything?

SUTTON: Not really. What we've done is to hire the top programmers and educators in the area of software curriculum development to work on our project. Each discipline— history, math, science, etc.— is covered by a number of experts in the field, not a single person. What I'm talking about when I speak of interrelatedness is our ability to reference across a number of courses by computer. In other words, the student using one program in the IQ series will be guided to related topics in other subject areas, much the same way you are guided by cross-references in the library card catalog.

CC: You've obviously spent a lot of time and money on this project. Why do you think it will be su*CC*essful— especially in the light of the recent drop-off of interest in video games?

SUTTON: Part of the reason is that we are "selling" (if that's the right word) our curriculum to schools and educators. We have to first convince them that the IQ system of learning is easy and fun. Which brings me to another point. One of the reasons for developing IQ in the first place was to take some of the load off the teacher.

We have statistics showing that an average teacher in, say, a fourth-grade class of 30 students, spends approximately only 10 minutes a day with each student individually. Students who need more than that 10 minutes either have to take up time outside of class or try to get the needed in-depth information from their textbooks—or their parents. IQ helps provide that needed personal attention because of its interactive format. Look at it this way: what is the reason for questions at the end of a chapter in a standard text book? They're supposed to stimulate the student to "interact", in a sense, with the book. But the book doesn't really respond in the truest sense of the word. It merely houses the answers to the questions while the student carries out any action that is taken.

On the other hand, when a student works with a computer loaded with an IQ program, he or she is interacting with it. The computer not only asks questions, it provides the student with hints, advice, and guidance. IQ programs explore various facets of each subject by quickly leading the student through an assignment, for instance. It can actually teach, ask questions, and guide the student in his or her search for the answers.

CC: Could you give me a concrete example of what you mean?

SUTTON: Sure. We have a program already developed called Meet Mr. Franklin in which the student will actually carry on a computer initiated conversation with Benjamin Franklin.

CC: You mean, they actually hear Ben Franklin talk?

SUTTON: No. Although simulating a voice on the computer is not beyond the realm of possibility. What happens is that the computer introduces Franklin to the student as if it were the person himself. The program is designed for younger students, fourth to sixth grade, and makes heavy use of computer graphics. Graphics have become very sophisticated today. The Franklin program opens with a picture of Ben Franklin who introduces himself on the screen. From that point on, the student is actually involved in a conversation with him.

Franklin tells him about his life and the times in which he lived, punctuated with graphic displays of objects, maps, and documents of the period. At certain points throughout the lesson, the student is prompted to ask questions of Franklin. Depending on the question selected, from a list on the computer screen, Franklin will then respond.

Again, what's most exciting about the entire package is its interrelatedness. On the Franklin program, for instance, the student will be referred to other programs in the history series for that age group. You can go from the Franklin program to one on Washington, or Jefferson, or Adams and begin to get different perspectives on the same historical era.

CC: To change the subject slightly—I understand that APC is now involved with the National Education Association in a joint project concerning computers.

SUTTON: Yes, and again, we're very excited by the prospects of working with such a large and important group. As I've said many times before, we're strong an education here at APC—and that's not just PR talk. I wouldn't be where I am today without my education and I want to do everything I can to see to it that today's children get the chance to get the best education possible.

We've given the NEA a rather large grant to get them started on a program of teaching seminars all over the country. They'll set up a speaker's bureau of educators in the area of computer learning who will travel to requesting schools and explain the benefits of computer education.

They'll hold workshops for teachers and students and provide the computers needed to get started on their own programs. Part of our donation will help pay for these computers.

CC: Is this tied in with your software marketing effort?

SUTTON: Not directly, no. But, of course, they're related. I'd look like a fool if I told you that they're not. But the money APC's donated to the NEA is a no-strings-attached grant. We're not requiring that they use our software or even mention it in any way. The money is a gift. We're not even asking for sponsorship identification.

CC: Why this sudden push by APC in education, especially computer education?

SUTTON: Because we live in a different age than we did when I grew up. Kids today need to know how to cope with the "information age." They need to know how to work with computers. I don't want this generation to be replaced by these machines— I want them to learn to master them.

I believe our joint project with the NEA will give them that chance. I also believe our new software will teach them the same basics I learned as a kid while showing them the wave of the future. We're committed to this course. We've pumped a lot of

The organizational profile

In the organizational profile, an entire organization or some part of it is profiled. The organizational profile and the personality profile are accomplished much the same way, except that you need to interview a number of key people in the unit you are profiling in order to obtain a complete picture of that unit. The following two profiles look at an entire company providing a unique service, and a department within a large corporation.

Figure 8.3 _____
Organizational and departmental profiles—Notice the similarities between the two profiles. The nature of a good profile is to set a scene or context and present the pertinent information within that context.

DGA Wins UL Certificate

The sign on the door reads "Grade 'A' UL Central Station." To the people at Dallas General Alarm (DGA) and to the hundreds of businesses and homes they protect, this means the availability of some of the best alarm and intrusion detection systems in the country. In fact, almost every improvement made at DGA over the past few years has had as its goal the attainment of UL certification.

In 1924, Underwriters Laboratories, Inc. began offering a means of identifying burglar alarm systems that met acceptable minimum standards. The installing company can apply for investigation of their services, and if found qualified, may be issued UL certification.

To the customer, this certification can mean a large reduction (sometimes up to 70 percent) in insurance premiums, depending on the exact grade and extent of the UL-approved service used. However, Dallas General Alarm doesn't sell only UL service. "We sell and lease our systems on the merit of the system and the particular need of the customer," says Dave Michaels, director of quality control for DGA. "Of course, those who do have the UL Grade 'A' system installed can usually pay the extra cost entailed with the savings they make on insurance alone."

What makes this Grade "A" system so effective that insurance companies charging sometimes thousands of dollars a year in coverage are willing to cut 40, 60 or even 70 percent off their premiums?

"The UL people are really tight on their standards," says Michaels. "They conduct a number of 'surprise' inspections of DGA on a regular basis. If we fall down in any of their requirements, we get our certification cancelled."

DGA has its own tight security system consisting of television monitors on all doors and verbal contact with people entering their offices. The central control room is always manned and locked. A thick, glass window allows the operators on duty to check personally all people entering the premises. Other UL requirements are extra fire proofing for the building itself and a buried cable containing the thousands of telephone lines used to monitor the various alarm systems which run out of the building. The cable is unmarked, preventing the adventurous burglar from cutting it and thus disabling the hundreds of systems served by DGA.

The over-a-thousand customers who either lease or buy alarm or detection systems from DGA range from some of the biggest businesses in Dallas to private residences. In addition, all of the schools in the Dallas area are monitored from the DGA central station against break in and vandalism.

The monitoring devices, located at the DGA central control, vary from a simple paper tape printout to actual voice communication with the premises being protected. For instance, the card-key system used by Atlantic Richfield Company allows access to certain areas through the use of a magnetic card inserted into a slot in the door. Access is forbidden to those lacking the proper clearance and the number and time of the attempted access are printed out at the DGA central station.

By far, the most impressive system is the *Hyper Guard Sound System* which allows the central station operators actually to listen into a building or home once the system is activated. If the building is entered, the sound sensitive system is activated causing an alarm to go off at the DGA central station. By the use of microphones installed on the premises, the DGA operators can then determine the presence of an intruder. The owners, of course, sign in and out verbally when they open and close. Most of these customers also carry the special "holdup" feature of this system which allows them to trigger, unnoticed, an alarm in the event of a robbery.

"We tried out a lot of other sound-activated systems," says Michaels, "but the 'Hyper Guard' made by Associated Products Corporation is the best I've ever seen." Michaels says that the Hyper Guard system is probably 20 times more sensitive than most other brands DGA has tried. "And, in our business, sensitivity is a key component of a successful detection."

Once an alarm is received from any of the hundreds of points serviced by DGA, it is only a matter of seconds before security guards, police, ambulance or fire department are notified and on their way. DGA maintains direct, no-dial lines to all of these agencies.

DGA currently contracts with Smith-Loomis which dispatches two or three security guards to each of DGA's calls. "Our average response time is under 4 1/2 minutes," says Dave Michaels. "Of course, we often have to wait on the owner to show up to let us in." Michaels says that if DGA keeps a key to the premises, another 10 percent can often be taken off on insurance premiums because it allows a faster response time and a higher apprehension rate. "Recently, we got two apprehensions in three alarms at a local pharmacy," he says. "We roll on every suspicious alarm. UL only allows one opening and one closing time per business unless prearranged," says Michaels. "This way, we know exactly when there should be nobody on the premises."

DGA offers a number of different systems. Some respond to motion, and some to sound. There are systems with silent alarms and systems with on-sight alarms fit to frighten the toughest intruder; and, DGA also handles smoke and heat detection systems. But, the key to a UL Grade "A" certified system, says Michaels, is the central control. "That's the added factor in a Grade 'A' system," he says. "We know immediately when something has occurred, and we respond."

Frank Collins, president of Southwestern Gemstones, Inc., has had his Grade "A" system since September. "I was robbed last year of over $400,000 worth of merchandise," he says, "and I was uninsured. That won't happen again." Collins is impressed with his system.

From his office in the Calais Building, Collins can watch everyone who enters his showroom via television monitor. A telephone allows visitors to identify themselves from outside the front door before entry. The showroom itself has an impressive array of precious gems and gold and a great many antique art objects, frequently hand-made turquoise and silver pieces. "I got the complete works," Collins says, "audio sensors, motion sensors, TV monitor, everything," resulting in a good-sized cut in his necessarily high insurance premiums.

For the many high-risk businesses served by Dallas General Alarm, the UL Grade "A" system seems to be the answer. "We don't expect more than a couple of hundred customers for the UL system over the next few years," says Dave Michaels, "but that's all right. Our customers know their needs and they know that they can't get a better system for the price." Collins smiles. "For the three or four dollars a day this system costs, they couldn't even afford a guard dog."

The Legal Department at APC

Sitting behind a cluttered desk, boxes scattered around the office—some still unopened—is the new head of the Law Department at Associated Products Corporation, Ed Bennett. Ed is a neat man, both in appearance and in speech. As he speaks about the "new" Law Department, he grins occasionally as though to say, "Why take the time to interview someone as unimportant as a lawyer?" That grin is deceiving because, to Ed and the other attorneys who work for APC, law is serious business.

Questions of law are rarely debated around APC. According to Ed, when something is not legal, it simply is not legal. No vote is taken by anyone; no decision needs to be arrived at. For this reason, "house counsel" (those attorneys who work for and in companies rather than for individuals) are often thought to be against all suggestions—paid to say no to projects or suggestions. This isn't so, says Ed. "It just so happens that a number of things that people wish to do must meet certain requirements. In most cases," he says, "it's not a question of 'you can't do it' but rather a matter of 'you have to do it this way.'"

According to Ed, this often puts the bearer of this news in an awkward position—much like the messenger who brings the Chinese Emperor bad tidings and has his head cut off for his efforts. It is a lot better in Ed's mind to make the adjustments to a particular project now than to wait until they can no longer be made and find out that the entire project is unworkable.

In APC's Law Department, each attorney handles a specific area dealing with particular projects. Like many of the other departments in APC, Law is experiencing a period of transition. Consequently, specific areas of assignment are only tentative. Still, the four-man legal staff now employed by APC is specialized to the extent that each member has an area of expertise in which he or she works a majority of the time.

Dennis Silva, newly arrived at APC from work with the State, is involved primarily with local and state government matters. Gary Williams is involved primarily in contractual matters, often between APC and other large companies. Keith McGowan has been handling research and certain other issues, frequently dealing with the Federal Government.

Ed, recently elected Vice President and General Attorney, describes his role as that of a player-coach. Aside from his specific responsibilities, he must also present the legal overview of the company's actions, and accept the consequences of his advice. "Along with responsibility, comes accountability," he says.

Ed, who has been with APC for nearly two years, was Assistant Center Judge Advocate at Walter Reed Army Medical Center prior to coming to APC. He received his Juris Doctor from the University of Pennsylvania Law School and graduated from the College of William and Mary. Before coming to work for APC, Ed was a Judge Advocate Officer at the Headquarters, U.S. Army Fort Dix, New Jersey 1972 to 1975.

Together with the three other attorneys, Ed helps comprise a relatively small department. Despite its size, it may well be one of the most important functions within the company. "The myriad of legal and regulatory requirements, particularly in a business like this,

creates a jungle," Ed says. "It is impossible to get to the other shore of this particular river by rowing in a straight line. There are cross currents and tides, with the wind blowing from a hundred different directions."

The metaphor may be mixed, but the point is clear. According to Ed, the various State and Federal regulations governing our operations are, by no means, consistent. Neither, frequently, are the goals of the company as expressed by the input of each of the departments. Consequently, it is also the responsibility of the Law Department to make uniform, or parallel, the various desires of the company.

"The end is always the same though," says Ed. "It is not to turn out neat legal briefs which, though often well researched and executed, are not useful if a manager can neither understand nor conform to them. It is to strike a balance between our own professional conscience and the utilitarian nature of the work."

"Of course," says Ed, "we'd like to spend six months on each item, carefully researching it, but by then we have lost the element of timeliness which is often equally important."

The people who make up the Law Department are, in the highest sense, professional. In fact, they have a professional responsibility quite separate from the company. Every attorney is a member of a bar association, and thus is answerable to the Code of Professional Responsibility unique to his profession. "We are not exempted," says Ed, "simply because we are 'house counsel,' from the dictates of that Code." Thus, their advice has to be correct, or as correct as it can be under prevailing circumstances. All of APC's attorneys are members of at least one bar and some are members of up to four.

The role of the APC attorney is similar to that of the "outside" attorney in that they are here to represent the company in legal matters. But APC's Law Department does more than that. It not only represents the company when it gets into difficulty, but expends a great deal of time and effort in keeping the company out of difficulty. To that end, the house counsel of APC must maintain sufficient contact with the company, its people, and its activities in order that it may render timely advice and thus prevent difficulties.

In a way, the modern attorney is still much like his medieval predecessor, who, hired to represent his client on the field of combat, used every honorable devise in his power to win. Perhaps the armor and shield have been replaced by the vested suit and briefcase, but the same keen edge that decided many a trial-by-combat is still very much apparent. Never draw down on an attorney. They are still excellent swordsmen.

Writing the Story

Magazine articles, unlike straight news stories, must have a definite beginning, middle, and an end. Developing these elements is not easy. It takes patience, practice and organization.

The Lead

Always start at the beginning. A good lead is just as important to a magazine piece as it is to a news story. You must hook your reader into reading further and you must keep his or her interest through to the end.

In your lead, you must tell the reader what the article is about. You don't have to cram everything into the lead; however, you should include enough information so that the reader doesn't have to search for the topic. Consider the following leads.

A lead for a horse-racing trade:

> For some time now, the sound of heavy machinery has been echoing through the rolling green countryside and heavily forested groves of Eastern Maryland. But that sound will soon be replaced by the sound of galloping horses as they take to the newly banked turns and straightaway at what is being billed as "the most innovative thoroughbred training and sports medicine facility in North America."

One for the hospital industry:

> The scene is a standard hospital room designed with fire safety in mind: a very low fuel load, floors of asbestos tile, walls of gypsum board on steel studs and a ceiling of fiberglass panels. The hospital is built in accordance with the National Fire Protection Agency Life Safety Code and has received the Joint Commission on Accreditation of Hospitals maximum 2-year approval.
>
> Late in the evening, a patient ignites the contents of his trash can which, in turn, ignite the bed clothes and, eventually, the mattress. The ensuing fire is a disaster, and despite the correct operation of all fire systems, multiple fatalities occur and the entire hospital wing is a total loss. Why? There are no fire standards on the upholstered furniture in this hospital and the mattresses meet a federal code designed to retard fires from smoldering cigarettes, not open flames.

A lead for a new product aimed at highway engineers:

> You're traveling along at high speed—the familiar "clackety-clack" of the rails beneath your feet. But wait a minute. You're not on a train, you're in an automobile, and that familiar sound beneath your feet is the result of deteriorating pavement joints that have been repaired with the usual "hot pour" method.

And an article for golf course superintendents:

> Valleyview Country Club had a problem—the twelfth hole was sinking again. For almost 40 years, the facilities people at Valleyview had been rebuilding the green. In fact, it had been rebuilt three times over that period of time, but each time with the same results—in a matter of a few years, the green would begin to sag again. This time, it was almost bowl-shaped and was acting as a funnel for rainwater that was draining from its outer edges into its concave center.

Although you may not have guessed it, each of these leads comes from articles announcing new products or new applications for established products. Remember, even the most mundane subject can benefit from a creative treatment. Your readers will only read your story if they like your lead.

The Body of the Article

The body of your article should contain all the information your reader needs to understand what you are trying to say. Obviously, it's in your best interest to present your ideas clearly. Working from an outline is the best way to ensure that you have covered all your key points in a logical order. (Several methods for organizing an outline were presented in **Chapter 1**.)

The body of the article must support your main point (hopefully already made in the lead) and elaborate on it. You should anticipate questions your reader might have, and answer them satisfactorily. Remember to utilize logical transitional devices when moving from one point to another. Subheads, while technically sound, don't alleviate the need for thoughtful transitions. Back up your statements with facts and support all generalizations with specifics. Although magazine articles seldom use footnotes, they are not completely inappropriate. Usually, however, citation can be taken care of in the body of the text.

Articles for house publications tend to be shorter than consumer magazine articles or even trade journals. The average length of most house publications (magazine format) is around twelve pages. Article length runs about 1,000 words or less for features (about four typed pages). Considering that magazine column width is about 14 picas for a three-column spread, and that articles are usually accompanied by photographs or artwork and headlines, subheads and blurbs—a 750-word article may cover several pages.

In **Figure 8.4** notice the organizational concept and transitional devices that move the article from point to point, and the contributions of the lead and ending.

The Ending

The most powerful and most remembered parts of your article will be the beginning and the end. Good endings are as difficult to write as good beginnings. However, there are only a few ways to wrap up an article and bring your readers to closure (a sense that they are satisfactorily finished): summarize your main points (summary ending), refer back to the beginning in some way (referral ending), or call for action (response ending), although this last is rarely used in magazine article writing. Consider the following leads with their respective endings.

Posing a question in the lead/summary ending

Lead:

Name the oldest civilization in North America. If your anthropological information is such that you pinpointed the Aleut peoples of Alaska, you are both well-informed and correct.

Ending:

"Intellect and knowledge, technical skills, helpfulness, and concern for the truth are still the hallmarks of Aleut culture," observes the Connecticut anthropologist, Laughlin. Such virtues are valuable assets, ever more useful as the 21st century approaches, and the bedrock on which the best that is Aleut may find permanence and continuity.—Richard C. Davids for *Exxon USA*

APC's Answer Man

You might have noticed, if you've been in the new headquarters building at Associated Products Corporation long, a rather harried figure dashing madly up and down the halls. That man with the worried expression is Dave Martin. Dave, in a sense, is the ombudsman for APC's new building. He's the man who fields all the complaints, large and small, that have to do with everything from desk positioning to major malfunctions.

Dave's official title reads: Manager, Headquarters Facilities and Services. This constitutes a promotion for Dave who was Manager, Technical Services. It also constitutes quite a lot of "heartburn."

The job was almost a matter of evolution for Dave, who became associated with the project through working with Bob Allen, Project Manager for the new building. Dave continually found himself involved with planning of space allocation, since this was a natural carry over from his former job. He cites the speed at which the building was completed as one of the major factors for his almost sudden immersion in the project.

An undertaking of this magnitude usually takes years to complete. The space layout itself, which usually takes six to eight months, only took six to eight weeks. Dave and the planners worked night and day setting up seating arrangements for each department. These arrangements had gone through each department weeks before but had to be thoroughly scrutinized by the architects and planners before implementation.

Dave realizes, of course, that not everyone is going to be completely happy with his or her particular arrangement, but no major changes can be made until after the first of the year. There are several reasons for this. "The move itself will take up to 60 days to complete," says Dave, "during which time furniture will constantly be arriving." According to Dave, each piece has been designated for a particular spot in the new building, and last minute changes would only serve to confuse further what will doubtless be a confusing move as it is.

Telephones have already been assigned to particular individuals and can't be moved, and the special ambient lighting fixtures built into the desks provide light for a specific grouping of furniture. Moving a desk would mean disrupting the lighting scheme for a particular area which would affect more than just one person. All of these factors lead Dave to stress acceptance of the new floor plan, at least for the time being. According to Dave, psychological adjustment to new surroundings normally takes about 30 days. A great deal of complaints handled prior to that time are likely to be adjustment oriented. Those are the complaints he would like to avoid initially.

The lead paragraph incorporates many of the basic elements of a news-type lead including who, what, where and how. It also delays the discovery of the topic until the second sentence by setting the scene first.

The second paragraph is the "bridge" from the lead to the body of the story. It begins with a factual statement and ends with another teaser.

Paragraphs 3 through 6 follow a sort of chronological order based on the construction of the new building, and provide background information

---

Figure 8.4 _____

Organization of article. *Even a short article such as this deserves considerable organizational thought.*

Dave's new position will have him on the fourth floor as part of the Industrial Relations Department, where he will be in charge of the expanded reproduction facilities as well as Office Services, which handles supplies, PBX operation, mail service, and messenger service.

Dave is going to be monitoring almost every aspect of the new building. He will handle the janitorial contract, the plant contract (yes, Virginia, there will be greenery inside too) and snow removal. As Dave says, "If the building has a problem during the day, I'll hear about it first." Dave's only concern right now is that he will receive too many complaint calls like "I don't want to sit next to Joe," or, "I can't see the window from here." With all of the major problems involved in a move of this magnitude (by the way, he's also in charge of getting everybody into the building) Dave doesn't need to hear the "personal" problems each employee is bound to have.

So, if you see this man with the harried expression in his eyes rushing around the halls of APC's new headquarters building, have a heart. Remember that Dave, like a modern-day Atlas, bears the weight of six floors on his shoulders. Just say "hi," give him a smile, and learn to live with your new desk for a while.

> *Paragraphs 7 and 8 come back to the subject (focusing on the human angle) and expand on his position and point of view.*

> *The closing paragraph refers to the opening paragraph as a technique for gaining closure.*

Setting the scene in the lead/referral ending

Lead:

For one emotion-filled moment on July 28, when the Olympic torch is lit atop the Los Angeles Memorial Coliseum, this sprawling California city will be transformed into an arena of challenges and champions. But that magic event, shared with two billion television viewers around the world, will mark more than the beginning of the XXIII Summer Olympic Games.

Ending:

For GTE employees worldwide, perhaps some of that special thrill can be shared by just watching the Games on television, and knowing that whenever gymnastics, fencing, water polo, volleyball, yachting or tennis are televised, those images and sounds will have passed through the hands of 425 fellow employees—GTE's Team at the Olympics.—Bill Ferree for *GTE Together*

An anecdotal lead/summary and referral ending

Lead:

In 1737, Benjamin Franklin wrote in the Pennsylvania Gazette of an auroral display so red and vivid that some people thought it was a fire and ran to help put it out.

Ending:

Although the effects of auroral activity on the lower levels of the earth's atmosphere are more apparent, the effects on the upper atmosphere are not, and we are only now beginning to understand them. With more understanding, we may eventually view the aurora with a more scientific eye, but until that day comes, it still remains the greatest light show on earth.—Tom Bivins for *National Bank of Alaska Interbranch*

Writing Headlines

Writing headlines for magazines is much like writing headlines for newsletters, but there are some exceptions. First, some definitional differences. A **headline**, strictly speaking, is for news stories, while a **title** is for features. For example, a news story on a new product might read like this:

> ### New software will 'revolutionize education' says APC president

Now, contrast that headline with the following title:

> ### Talking to the past—
> ### Learning about the future

The headline tells something about the story, so that even the casual reader can glean some information from reading it alone. The title, on the other hand, entices the reader or piques his or her interest. Therefore, a basic rule of thumb for writing headlines and titles is: use headlines for news articles and titles for feature articles. And, as with all writing, try to be clear. If your headline or title confuses the readers, they won't read on.

Editing Your Article

Magazine articles probably get, and deserve, the most editing of the various types of writing discussed in this book. Length has something to do with it, but more than that, it's the freewheeling attitude of some article writers (especially novices) that contributes the most to this need. Since many writers of basic company publications end up dealing with pretty dry topics, an assignment to do an article for the house magazine might be seen as an invitation to creativity. This usually leads, in turn, to a looser style, wordiness, and lack of organization. Whatever the reason, even the best-written article can benefit from intelligent editing.

A quick word here about the term "intelligent editing." This implies that you are being edited by (or are yourself, if you're doing the editing) someone who knows something about writing—both grammar and style. Unfortunately, as many of us who have worked on in-house publications for years know, editors are often chosen because of their position within the organizational hierarchy (or the obligatory approval chain) and not for their literary talents. One of the best (if perhaps a little cynical) rules of thumb for dealing with "inexpert" editing is to ignore about 80 percent of it. You quickly get to recognize what is useful to you

The Legal
Department
at APC

Sitting behind a cluttered desk, boxes scattered around the office— some still unopened—is the new head of Associated Products Corporation's Law Department, Ed Bennett. Ed is a neat man, both in appearance and in speech. As he speaks about the "new" Legal Department, he grins occasionally as though to say, "Why take the time to interview someone as unimportant as a lawyer?" That grin is deceiving because, to Ed and the other attorneys who work for Associated Products Corporation (APC), law is serious business.

Questions of law are rarely debated around APC. According to Ed, when something is not legal, it simply is not legal. No vote is taken by anyone; no decision needs to be arrived at. For this reason, "house counsel" (those attorneys who work for and in companies rather than for individuals) are often thought to be against all suggestions— paid to say no to projects or suggestions. This isn't so, says Ed. "It just so happens that a number of things that people wish to do must meet certain requirements. In most cases," he says, "it's not a question of 'you can't do it' but rather a matter of 'you have to do it this way.'"

According to Ed, this often puts the bearer of this news in an awkward position—much like the messenger who brings the Chinese Emperor bad tidings and has his head cut off for his efforts. It is a lot better in Ed's mind to make the adjustments to a particular project now than to wait until they can no longer be made and find out that the entire project is unworkable. In APC's

Law Department, each attorney handles a specific area dealing with particular projects. Like many of the other departments in APC, Law is experiencing a period of transition. Consequently, specific areas of assignment are only tentative. Still, the four-man legal staff now employed by APC is specialized to the extent that each member has an area of expertise in which he or she works a majority of the time.

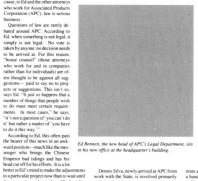

Ed Bennett, the new head of APC's Legal Department, sits in his new office at the headquarter's building.

Dennis Silva, newly arrived at APC from work with the State, is involved primarily with local and state government matters. Gary Williams is involved primarily in

contractual matters, often between APC and other large companies. Keith McGowan has been handling research and certain other issues frequently dealing with the Federal Government.

Ed, just recently elected Vice President and General Attorney, describes his role as that of a player-coach. Aside from his specific responsibilities, he must also present the legal overview of the company's actions, and accept the consequences of his advice. "Along with responsibility comes accountability," he says.

Ed, who has been with APC for nearly two years, was assistant center judge advocate at Walter Reed Army Medical Center prior to coming to APC. He received his Juris Doctor from the University of Pennsylvania Law School and graduated from the College of William and Mary. Before coming to work for APC, Ed was a judge advocate officer at the Headquarters, U.S. Army Fort Dix, New Jersey 1972 to 1975.

Together with the three other attorneys, Ed helps comprise a relatively small department. Despite its size, it may well be one of the most important functions within the company. "The myriad of legal and regulatory requirements, particularly in a business like this, creates a jungle," Ed says. " It is impossible to get to the other shore of this particular river by rowing in a straight line. There are cross currents and tides with the wind blowing from a hundred different directions."

The metaphor may be mixed, but the point is clear. According to Ed, the various

21

Figure 8.5

Even relatively short articles can take up a considerable amount of space when accompanied by photographs, pull quotes, headlines and proper white space. These two profiles on the legal department and Dallas General Alarm together take up three full pages and are approximately 1,000 words each.

---

our operations are, by all means, consistent. Neither, frequently, are the goals of the company as expressed by the input of each of the departments. Consequently, it is also the responsibility of the Law Department to make uniform, or parallel, the various desires of the company.

"The end is always the same though," says Ed. "It is not to turn out neat legal briefs which, though often well researched and executed, are not useful if a manager can neither understand nor conform to them. It is to strike a balance between our own professional conscience and the utilitarian nature of the work."

"Of course," says Ed, "we'd like to spend six months on each item, carefully researching it, but by then we have lost the element of timeliness which is often equally important."

The people who make up the Law Department are, in the highest sense, professional. In fact, they have a professional responsibility quite separate from the

"The legal requirements in a business like this create a jungle."

company. Every attorney is a member of a bar association, and thus has imposed upon him the Code of Professional Responsibility unique to his profession.

"We are not exempted," says Ed, "simply because we are 'house counsel,' from the dictates of that Code." Thus, their advice has to be correct, or as correct as it can be under prevailing circumstances. All of APC's attorneys are members of at least one bar and some are members of up to four.

The role of the APC attorney is similar to that of the "outside" attorney in that they are here to represent the company in legal matters. But APC's -more Law Department does more than that. It not only represents the company when it gets into diffi-

culty, but expends a great deal of time and effort in keeping the company out of difficulty. To that end, the house counsel of APC must maintain sufficient contact with the company, its people, and its activities in order that it may render timely advice and thus prevent difficulties.

In a way, the modern attorney is still much like his medieval predecessor, who, hired to represent his client on the field of combat, used every honorable devise in his power to win. Perhaps the armor and shield have been replaced by the vested suit and brief case, but the same keen edge that decided many a trial-by- combat is still very much apparent. Never draw down on an attorney. They are still excellent swordsmen.

Security is a full-time job for Dallas General

by Ellen Hart

Technology and common sense blend to provide a thoroughly modern security service

The sign on the door reads "Grade 'A' UL Central Station." To the people at Dallas General Alarm (DGA) and to the hundreds of businesses and homes they protect, this means the availability of some of the best alarm and intrusion detection systems in the country. In fact, almost every improvement made to DGA over the past few years has had as its goal the attainment of UL certification.

In 1924, Underwriters Laboratories, Inc. began offering a means of identifying burglar alarm systems that met acceptable minimum standards. The installing company can apply for rivestigation of their services and if found qualified, may be issued UL certification.

To the customer, this certification can mean a large reduction (sometimes up to 70 percent) in insurance premiums, depending on the exact grade and extent of the UL approved service used.

However, Dallas General Alarm doesn't sell only UL service. "We sell and lease our systems on the merit of the system and the particular need of the customer," says Dave Michaels, director of quality control for DGA. "Of course, those who do have the UL Grade 'A' system installed can usually pay the extra cost entailed with the savings they make on insurance alone."

What makes this Grade "A" system so effective that insurance companies charging sometimes thousands of dollars a year in coverage are willing to cut 40, 60 or even 70 percent off their premiums?

"The UL people are really tight on their standards," says Michaels. "They conduct a number of 'surprise' inspections of DGA on a regular basis. If we fall down in any of their requirements, we get our certification cancelled."

DGA has its own tight security system consisting of television monitors on all

doors and verbal contact with people entering their offices. The central control room is always manned and locked. A thick, glass window allows the operators on duty to personally check all people entering the premises.

Other UL requirements are extra fire proofing for the building itself and a buried cable containing the thousands of telephone lines used to monitor the various alarm systems which run out of the building. The cable is unmarked, preventing the adventurous burglar from cutting it and thus disabling the hundreds of systems served by DGA.

The over-a-thousand customers who either lease or by alarm or detection systems from DGA range from some of the biggest businesses in Dallas, to private residences. In addition, all of the schools in the Dallas area are monitored from the DGA central station against break in and vandalism.

22

The monitoring devices, located at the DGA central control, vary from a simple paper tape printout to actual voice communication with the premises being protected. For instance, the card-key system used by Atlantic Richfield Company allows access to certain areas through the use of a magnetic card inserted into a slot in the door. Access is forbidden to those lacking the proper clearance and the number and time of the attempted access are printed out at the DGA central station.

By far, the most impressive system is the "Hyper Guard Sound System" which allows the central station operators actually to listen into a building or home once the system is activated. If the building is entered, the sound sensitive system is activated causing an alarm to go off at the DGA central station. By the use of microphones installed on the premises, the DGA operators can then determine the presence of an intruder. The owners, of course, sign in and out verbally when they open and close. Most of these customers also carry the special "holdup" feature of this system which allows them to trigger, unnoticed, an alarm in the event of a robbery.

"We tried out a lot of other sound-activated systems," says Michaels, "but the 'Hyper Guard' made by Associated Products Corporation is the best I've ever seen." Michaels says that the Hyper Guard system is probably 20 times more sensitive than most other brands DGA has tried. "And, in our business, sensitivity is a key component of a successful detection."

Once an alarm is received from any of the hundreds of points serviced by DGA, it is

only a matter of seconds before security guards, police, ambulance or fire department are notified and on their way. DGA maintains direct, no-dial lines to all of these agencies.

DGA currently contracts with Smith-Loomis which dispatches two or three security guards to each of DGA's calls. "Our average response time is under 4 1/2 min-

"For the three or four dollars a day this system costs, they couldn't even afford a guard dog."

utes," says Dave Michaels. "Of course, we often have to wait on the owner to show up to let us in." Michaels says that if DGA keeps a key to the premises, another 10 percent often can be taken off on insurance premiums because it allows a faster response time and a higher apprehension rate. "Recently, we got two apprehensions in three alarms at a local pharmacy," he says. "We roll on every suspicious alarm. UL only allows one opening and one closing time per business unless prearranged," says Michaels. "This way, we know exactly when there should be nobody on the premises."

DGA offers a number of different systems. Some respond to motion, and some to sound. There are systems with silent alarms and systems on sight alarms fit to frighten

the toughest intruder. The most impressive smoke and key to a UL says Michaels the added thing has Frank C ern Cement system sing year of ov dise," he won't happ with his sy From his Collins ca showroom phone allo from outsi The shows of precious antique art turquoise complete sensors, m rything," necessarily the many Dallas Ger Alarm, to be the m than a comp UL system Dave Mich customers that they c prise." Co four dolla couldn't e

Dave Michaels of Dallas General Alarm sits in front of the main counsole from which dozens of businesses are monitored daily. The slightest sound will set off an alarm at this console and, if a burglary is deemed to be in progress, police or security officers are dispatched within minutes of the alarm. The sound-activated system is manufactured by the Electronics Division of APC.

23

and what is not. Basically, editing that deals with content balance and accuracy is usable. Most strictly "editorial" comment is not. A vice president's penchant for ellipses or a manager's predilection for using *which* instead of *that* are strictly stylistic preferences (and often ungrammatical). In many cases, even if you do ignore these obligatory edits, these same "editors" won't remember what they said when the final piece comes out. A rule of thumb for most experienced writers is to try to avoid being edited by non-editors. If you can't, at least see how much you can safely ignore.

As for editing yourself, there are several methods for cutting a story that is too long, even if you don't think you can possibly do without a single word.

- Look at your beginning and end to see if they can be shortened. Often we write more than we need by way of introduction or closing when the real meat is in the body of the article.

- If you used a lot of quotes, cut the ones that are even remotely "fluff." Keep only those that contribute directly to the understanding of your story.

- Are there any general descriptions that, given later details, may be redundant? Cut them.

- Are there any details that are unnecessary given earlier general descriptions? Cut them. (Be careful not to cut both the general description *and* the details.)

- Are there any people who can be left out? For instance, will one expert and her comments be enough or do you really need that second opinion?

- Finally, look for wordiness—instances in which you used more words than you needed. This type of editing hurts the most since you probably struggled over that wording for an hour and went through your thesaurus twenty times.

Your goal is to get the article into the size you need without losing its best parts or compromising your writing style. Good luck.

The following article shows how some of these guidelines can be applied.

Figure 8.6

Editing an article. Take a close look at this article and notice to what degree the edited
sections add to the article. If they add indispensable information, they shouldn't be edited out.

DGA Wins UL Certificate

The sign on the door reads "Grade 'A' UL Central Station." To the people at
Dallas General Alarm (DGA) and to the hundreds of businesses and homes
they protect, this means the availability of some of the best alarm and intrusion
detection systems in the country. In fact, almost every improvement made at
DGA over the past few years has had as its goal the attainment of UL
certification.

In 1924, Underwriters Laboratories, Inc. began offering a means of
identifying burglar alarm systems that met acceptable minimum standards.
The installing company can apply for investigation of their services and, if
found qualified, may be issued UL certification.

To the customer, this certification can mean a large reduction (sometimes
up to 70 percent) in insurance premiums, depending on the exact grade and
extent of the UL-approved service used.

These four paragraphs, although adding additional information, can be cut without loss to the overall information impact of the story since they deal with details that we can actually get along without. Naturally, given enough space, we would opt to leave the story intact.

However, Dallas General Alarm doesn't sell only UL service. "We sell
and lease our systems on the merit of the system and the particular need of the
customer," says Dave Michaels, Director of Quality Control for DGA. "Of
course, those who do have the UL Grade 'A' system installed can usually pay
the extra cost entailed with the savings they make on insurance alone."

What makes this Grade "A" system so effective that insurance companies
charging sometimes thousands of dollars a year in coverage are willing to cut
40, 60 or even 70 percent off their premiums?

"The UL people are really tight on their standards," says Michaels. "They
conduct a number of 'surprise' inspections of DGA on a regular basis. If we
fall down in any of their requirements, we get our certification cancelled."

DGA has its own tight security system consisting of television monitors
on all doors and verbal contact with people entering their offices. The central
control room is always manned and locked. A thick, glass window allows the
operators on duty to check personally all people entering the premises. Other
UL requirements are extra fire proofing for the building itself and a buried
cable containing the thousands of telephone lines used to monitor the various
alarm systems which run out of the building. The cable is unmarked,
preventing the adventurous burglar from cutting it and thus disabling the
hundreds of systems served by DGA.

The over-a-thousand customers who either lease or buy alarm or detection
systems from DGA range from some of the biggest businesses in Dallas to
private residences. In addition, all of the schools in the Dallas area are
monitored from the DGA central station against break-in and vandalism.

The monitoring devices, located at the DGA central control, vary from a
simple paper tape printout to actual voice communication with the premises
being protected. For instance, the card-key system used by Atlantic Richfield
Company allows access to certain areas through the use of a magnetic card
inserted into a slot in the door. Access is forbidden to those lacking the proper
clearance and the number and time of the attempted access are printed out at
the DGA central station.

continued on next page

By far the most impressive system is the *Hyper Guard Sound System* which allows the central station operators actually to listen into a building or home once the system is activated. If the building is entered, the sound sensitive system is activated, causing an alarm to go off at the DGA central station. By the use of microphones installed on the premises, the DGA operators can then determine the presence of an intruder. The owners, of course, sign in and out verbally when they open and close. Most of these customers also carry the special "holdup" feature of this system which allows them to trigger, unnoticed, an alarm in the event of a robbery.

"We tried out a lot of other sound-activated systems," says Michaels, "but the 'Hyper Guard' made by Associated Products Corporation is the best I've ever seen." Michaels says that the Hyper Guard system is probably 20 times more sensitive than most other brands DGA has tried. "And, in our business, sensitivity is a key component of a successful detection."

Whatever you do, don't edit out the purpose for writing the article in the first place. In this case, it's mention of a product.

Once an alarm is received from any of the hundreds of points serviced by DGA, it is only a matter of seconds before security guards, police, ambulance or fire department are notified and on their way. DGA maintains direct, no-dial lines to all of these agencies.

DGA currently contracts with Smith-Loomis which dispatches two or three security guards to each of DGA's calls. "Our average response time is under 4 1/2 minutes," says Dave Michaels. "Of course, we often have to wait on the owner to show up to let us in." Michaels says that if DGA keeps a key to the premises, another 10 percent often can be taken off on insurance premiums because it allows a faster response time and a higher apprehension rate. "Recently, we got two apprehensions in three alarms at a local pharmacy," he says. "We roll on every suspicious alarm. UL only allows one opening and one closing time per business unless prearranged," says Michaels. "This way, we know exactly when there should be nobody on the premises."

DGA offers a number of different systems. Some respond to motion, and some to sound. There are systems with silent alarms and systems with on-sight alarms fit to frighten the toughest intruder. DGA also handles smoke and heat detection systems. But, the key to a UL Grade "A" certified system, says Michaels, is the central control. "That's the added factor in a Grade 'A' system," he says. "We know immediately when something has occurred, and we respond."

Frank Collins, president of Southwestern Gemstones, Inc., has had his Grade "A" system since September. "I was robbed last year of over $400,000 worth of merchandise," he says, "and I was uninsured. That won't happen again." Collins is impressed with his system.

From his office in the Calais Building, Collins can watch everyone who enters his showroom via television monitor. A telephone allows visitors to identify themselves from outside the front door before entry. The showroom has an impressive array of precious gems and gold and a great many antique art objects, frequently hand-made turquoise and silver pieces. "I got the complete works," Collins says, "audio sensors, motion sensors, TV monitor, everything," resulting in a good-sized cut in his necessarily high insurance premiums.

Here is a good example of an extra character who can be deleted without substantial loss to the story. Although this kind of testimony adds credibility to any story, in this case, the story is about DGA and their spokesperson actually provides the first-person credibility we need for our purpose—which is to get one of our products mentioned.

For the many high-risk businesses served by Dallas General Alarm, the UL Grade "A" system seems to be the answer.

"We don't expect more than a couple of hundred customers for the UL system over the next few years," says Dave Michaels, "but that's all right. Our customers know their needs and they know that they can't get a better system for the price." Collins smiles. "For the three or four dollars a day this system costs, they couldn't even afford a guard dog."

tors can then determine the presence of an intruder. The owners, of course, sign in and out verbally when they open and close. Most of these customers also carry the special "holdup" feature of this system which allows them to trigger, unnoticed, an alarm in the event of a robbery.

"We tried out a lot of other sound-activated systems," says Michaels, "but the 'Hyper Guard' made by Associated Products Corporation is the best I've ever seen." Michaels says that the Hyper Guard system is probably 20 times more sensitive than most other brands DGA has tried. "And, in our business, sensitivity is a key component of a successful detection."

Once an alarm is received from any of the hundreds of points serviced by DGA, it is only a matter of seconds before security guards, police, ambulance or fire department are notified and on their way. DGA maintains direct, no-dial lines to all of these agencies.

DGA currently contracts with Smith-Loomis which dispatches two or three security guards to each of DGA's calls. "Our average response time is under 4 1/2 minutes," says Dave Michaels. "Of course, we often have to wait on the owner to show up to let us in." Michaels says that if DGA keeps a key to the premises, another 10 percent often can be taken off on insurance

premiums because it allows a faster response time and a higher apprehension rate. "Recently, we got two apprehensions in three alarms at a local pharmacy," he says. "We roll on every suspicious alarm. UL only allows one opening and one closing time per business unless prearranged," says Michaels. "This way, we know exactly when there should be nobody on the prem-

> ### "For the three or four dollars a day this system costs, they couldn't even afford a guard dog."

ises."

DGA offers a number of different systems. Some respond to motion, and some to sound. There are systems with silent alarms and systems on sight alarms fit to frighten the toughest intruder; and, DGA also handles smoke and heat detection systems. But, the key to a UL Grade "A" certified system, says Michaels, is the central control. "That's the added factor in a Grade 'A' system," he says. "We know immediately when something has occured, and we respond."

Frank Collins, president of Southwestern Gemstones, Inc., has had his Grade "A" system since September. "I was robbed last year of over $400,000 worth of merchandise," he says, "and I was uninsured. That won't happen again." Collins is impressed with his system.

From his office in the Calais Building, Collins can watch everyone who enters his showroom via television monitor. A telephone allows visitors to identify themselves from outside the front door before entry. The showroom itself is an impressive array of precious gems and gold and a great many antique art objects, frequently hand-made turquoise and silver pieces. "I got the complete works," Collins says, "audio sensors, motion sensors, TV monitor, everything," resulting in a good-sized cut in his necessarily high insurance premiums. For the many high-risk businesses served by Dallas General Alarm, the UL Grade "A" system seems to be the answer. "We don't expect more than a couple of hundred customers for the UL system over the next few years," says Dave Michaels, "but that's all right. Our customers know their needs and they know that they can't get a better system for the price." Collins smiles. "For the three or four dollars a day this system costs, they couldn't even afford a guard dog."

Figure 8.7 _____

As you can see from these layouts, the unedited version of the DGA story takes up approximately one and a half pages including pull quote, photo and caption. The edited version (following page) takes up only a single page including a reduced photo, edited caption, and the full-sized pull quote.

Security is a full-time job for Dallas General Alarm

by Ellen Hart

Technology and common sense blend to provide a thoroughly modern security service

The sign on the door reads "Grade 'A' UL Central Station." To the people at Dallas General Alarm (DGA) and to the hundreds of businesses and homes they protect, this means the availability of some of the best alarm and intrusion detection systems in the country. In fact, almost every improvement made to DGA over the past few years has had as its goal the attainment of UL certification.

In 1924, Underwriters Laboratories, Inc. began offering a means of identifying burglar alarm systems that met acceptable minimum standards. The installing company can apply fo rinvestigation of their services and if found qualified, may be issued UL certification.

To the customer, this certification can mean a large reduction (sometimes up to 70 percent) in insurance premiums, depending on the exact grade and extent of the UL approved service used.

However, Dallas General Alarm doesn't sell only UL service. "We sell and lease our systems on the merit of the system and the particular need of the customer," says Dave Michaels, director of quality control for DGA. "Of course, those who do have the UL Grade 'A' system installed can usually

pay the extra cost entailed with the savings they make on insurance alone."

What makes this Grade "A" system so effective that insurance companies charging sometimes thousands of dollars a year in coverage are willing to cut 40, 60 or even 70 percent off their premiums?

"The UL people are really tight on their standards," says Michaels. "They conduct a number of 'surprise' inspections of DGA on a regular basis. If we fall down in any of their requirements, we get our certification cancelled."

DGA has its own tight security system consisting of television monitors on all doors and verbal contact with people entering their offices. The central control room is always manned and locked. A thick, glass window allows the operators on duty to personally check all people entering the premises.

Other UL requirements are extra fire proofing for the building itself and a buried cable containing the thousands of telephone lines used to monitor the various alarm systems which run out of the building. The cable is unmarked, preventing the adventurous burglar from cutting it and thus disabling the hundreds of systems served by

DGA.

The over-a-thousand customers who either lease or by alarm or detection systems from DGA range from some of the biggest businesses in Dallas, to private residences. In addition, all of the schools in the Dallas area are monitored from the DGA central station against break in and vandalism.

The monitoring devices, located at the DGA central control, vary from a simple paper tape printout to actual voice communication with the premises being protected. For instance, the card-key system used by Atlantic Richfield Company allows access to certain areas through the use of a magnetic card inserted into a slot in the door. Access is forbidden to those lacking the proper clearance and the number and time of the attempted access are printed out at the DGA central station.

By far, the most impressive system is the "Hyper Guard Sound System" which allows the central station operators actually to listen into a building or home once the system is activated. If the building is entered, the sound sensitive system is activated causing an alarm to go off at the DGA central station. By the use of microphones installed on the premises, the DGA opera-

Dave Michaels of Dallas General Alarm sits in front of the main counsole from which dozens of businesses are monitored daily. The slightest sound will set off an alarm at this console and, if a burglary is deemed to be in progress, police or security officers are dispatched within minutes of the alarm. The sound-activiated system is manufactured by the Electronics Division of APC.

23

22

continued on next page

Security is a full-time job for Dallas General Alarm

by Ellen Hart

Technology and common sense blend to provide a thoroughly modern security service

---

The sign on the door reads "Grade 'A' UL Central Station." To the people at Dallas General Alarm (DGA) and to the hundreds of businesses and homes they protect, this means the availability of some of the best alarm and intrusion detection systems in the country. In fact, almost every improvement made to DGA over the past few years has had as its goal the attainment of UL certification.

In 1924, Underwriters Laboratories, Inc. began offering a means of identifying burglar alarm systems that met acceptable minimum standards. The installing company can apply for investigation of their services and if found qualified, may be issued UL certification.

To the customer, this certification can mean a large reduction (sometimes up to 70 percent) in insurance premiums, depending on the exact grade and extent of the UL approved service used.

The over-a-thousand customers who either lease or by alarm or detection systems from DGA range from some of the biggest businesses in Dallas, to private residences. In addition, all of the schools in the Dallas area are monitored from the DGA central station against break in and vandalism.

The monitoring devices, located at the DGA central control, vary from a simple paper tape printout to actual voice communication with the premises being protected. For instance, the card-key system used by Atlantic Richfield Company allows access to certain areas through the use of a magnetic card inserted into a slot in the door. Access is forbidden to those lacking the proper clearance and the number and time of the attempted access are printed out at the DGA central station.

By far, the most impressive system is the "Hyper Guard Sound System" which allows the central station operators actually to listen into a building or home once the

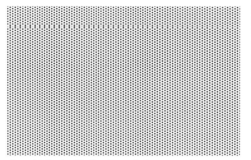

Dave Michaels of Dallas General Alarm sits in front of the main counsole from which dozens of businesses are monitored daily.

system is activated. If the building is entered, the sound sensitive system is activated causing an alarm to go off at the DGA central station. By the use of microphones installed on the premises, the DGA operators can then determine the presence of an intruder. The owners, of course, sign in and out verbally when they open and close. Most of these customers also carry the special "holdup" feature of this system

> ### "For the three or four dollars a day this system costs, they couldn't even afford a guard dog."

which allows them to trigger, unnoticed, an alarm in the event of a robbery.

"We tried out a lot of other sound-activated systems," says Michaels, "but the 'Hyper Guard' made by Associated Products Corporation is the best I've ever seen." Michaels says that the Hyper Guard system is probably 20 times more sensitive than most other brands DGA has tried. "And, in our business, sensitivity is a key component of a successful detection."

Once an alarm is received from any of

the hundreds of points serviced by DGA, it is only a matter of seconds before security guards, police, ambulance or fire department are notified and on their way. DGA maintains direct, no-dial lines to all of these agencies.

DGA currently contracts with Smith-Loomis which dispatches two or three security guards to each of DGA's calls. "Our average response time is under 4 1/2 minutes," says Dave Michaels. "Of course, we often have to wait on the owner to show up to let us in." Michaels says that if DGA keeps a key to the premises, another 10 percent often can be taken off on insurance premiums because it allows a faster response time and a higher apprehension rate. "Recently, we got two apprehensions in three alarms at a local pharmacy," he says. "We roll on every suspicious alarm. UL only allows one opening and one closing time per business unless prearranged," says Michaels. "This way, we know exactly when there should be nobody on the premises."

DGA offers a number of different systems. Some respond to motion, and some to sound. There are systems with silent alarms and systems on sight alarms fit to frighten the toughest intruder; and, DGA also handles smoke and heat detection systems. But, the key to a UL Grade "A" certified system, says Michaels, is the central control. "That's the added factor in a Grade 'A' system," he says. "We know immediately when something has occured, and we respond."

"We don't expect more than a couple of hundred customers for the UL system over the next few years," says Dave Michaels, "but that's all right. Our customers know their needs and they know that they can't get a better system for the price." Collins smiles. "For the three or four dollars a day this system costs, they couldn't even afford a guard dog."

22

Continuity is the most important element of magazine design. Readers are creatures of habit who expect not only to recognize your publication's cover, but to feel comfortable with what's inside. Plan and execute your design thoughtfully, because once you've adopted it, you must live up to it regularly.

Logistics are also important. Readers want to page quickly to their favorite column, department or writer, without searching or receiving rude surprises. Before configuring the particulars of a blueprint, an architect must determine what goes where. And so should you. As a designer, you are responsible for establishing an efficient magazine floor plan to route the audience. That means knowing how many departments, columns, features, editorials and other special sections you have, and where you're going to put each of them.

The first step is to organize. Put like things together. It sounds obvious, but this sorting process is often neglected. There are a multitude of possibilities. One common approach is to group departments so that they follow one another, and then similarly arrange other groupings like features, columns and editorials. This procedure will help establish your magazine's organizational framework.

Figure 8.8 _____

This two-page layout would stop any reader. Artwork dominates through the large, exaggerated horizontal format of the main photograph and through the smaller, rebus-like images that are contoured by type. The pages obviously go together; they are unified by borders, photography that crosses both pages, a tinted text block and the smaller stripped out photos. Art director Kit Hinrichs also uses ground thirds here to establish emphasis and to give this design a pleasing proportion. Terry Heffernan is responsible for the photography. Reprinted with permission from Skald *and* Pentagram.

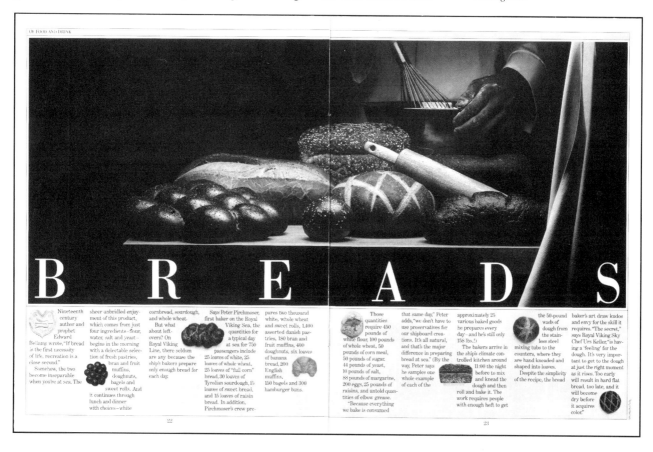

Figures 8.9 and **8.10**_____

It's no easy task designing a cover that is as creative as it is functional, especially when it's the cover of the Art Center College of Design's magazine, REVIEW. *Both of these covers not only call attention to the main feature through exciting photography, they also serve as a table of contents for the magazine. Title descriptors are run in red ink to stand them off.* **Figure 8.9** *was designed by Kit Hinrichs and Terri Driscoll, Pentagram; photography by Steven A. Heller.* **Figure 8.10** *was designed by Kit Hinrichs and Lenore Bartz, Pentagram; photography by Henrik Kam; Walid Saba executed the pencil illustration. Art direction by Kit Hinrichs. Reprinted with permission from Pentagram and the Art Center* REVIEW.

Typically, a magazine has a cover, table of contents, departments and features. Of course, there are variations—a magazine may feature fiction and nonfiction or include an editorial section, for instance. To better understand how the magazine will function as a whole, let's examine its parts individually.

The Cover—Your Undercover Agent

Covers preoccupy everyone who works on a magazine. The editor knows.that books are judged by their covers, the doors to the inside of the magazine. Publishers realize that covers, when linked properly to image, audience and magazine positioning, spark curiosity, newsstand sales and subscriptions. Magazine sales executives want the cover to convey a specific identity to uphold an image, sales and their commissions. Designers use covers to reflect the image and content of the magazine and mirror their sensibility and aesthetics. (Well-designed covers may also provide readers a preview of what lies inside.) Writers hope their pieces will be featured, directly connect to cover art or be listed among surprinted titles or teases. The entire staff realizes it is a publication's most important page.

The reason covers receive a disproportionate share of attention extends beyond vanity and money, however. Covers are, after all, a magazine's best side—what readers generally see first and last. They are a visual representation

of the inside of the magazine and must attract the reader, project the correct image and communicate quickly and clearly. What's more, they must do all this without words and within a few seconds. Nameplate, cover blurbs, other surprinting and (on rare occasion) the slash are made up of words, but artwork communicates first. Cover art is the hook, the visual metaphor, the photograph or illustration that often determines whether a magazine is picked up or passed over. In the case of company or in-house magazines—where advertising is nonexistent and the publications are subsidized—the cover may be even more important, because content lacks the variety and sparkle of other magazines.

Typical cover elements include art, nameplate and incidental information (indicating date, volume, number, price), surprinted blurbs or titles, slashes and splashes and the design itself. **Slashes** are diagonal strips that run on one of the corners of the publication (usually the lower or upper right) to announce a timely article, important story development or a special theme for the issue. **Splashes**, on the other hand, are blurbs printed atop an exploded area.

Art—A Picture Is Worth 10,000 Words Department

Photography dominates magazine covers. To begin with, it is as graphic and representational as it is flexible. It is also a lot more predictable and reliable. Art directors can see the final image when they choose from proof sheets, color transparencies or a group of finished photographs.

Figure 8.11 _____

Here, Saba's artwork from the front page of the REVIEW *is prominently figured into this two-page NEWS spread. Bolded, uppercase sans serif type and heavy-handed rules work as headings to show where one story begins and another ends. Artwork is woven into the design by a grid of sorts—"woven" in that much of the artwork is contoured by the type. Again, we are treated to the design work of Kit Hinrichs and Lenore Bartz of Pentagram; illustration by Walid Saba and John Mattos; photography by Steven A. Heller. Art direction by Kit Hinrichs. Reprinted with permission of Pentagram and the Art Center* REVIEW.

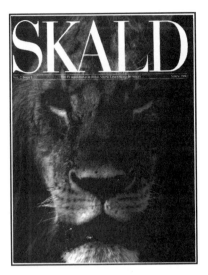

Figure 8.12 _____

Research shows that people's faces, children and animals pull best on magazine covers. Keeping that in mind, look closely at this cover and the one in the next figure. Skald magazine is a publication devoted to the interests of travelers of the Royal Viking Line. This issue featured a series of pieces on traveling Africa. Notice how clean and inviting the cover is; the nameplate is the only other cover element. Photography by Comstock, Inc. Design director: Kit Hinrichs; art director: Terri Driscoll. Reprinted with permission from Skald and Pentagram.

Photography is also a relatively fast medium. If an image proves unworkable or wrong, other photography from the shoot can be considered. Or a reshoot can be ordered and new prints developed in a fairly short amount of time. In addition, one needn't possess drafting skills to shoot good photographs. This is not to say that aesthetics aren't common to photography, that composition isn't central to effective imagery, or that photographers aren't artists. It only suggests that photography's representational properties and quick turnaround make it expeditious in most deadline situations. Finally, photography is more credible than other media. If a picture is worth 10,000 words, an exceptional cover shot may be worth thousands of dollars. Indeed, it often is.

Illustration offers advantages, too. Depending upon the availability of artists, who is hired out, and the medium chosen, it can be cheaper than photography. Also, illustration offers an immediate flexibility. The only limiting factor in securing unlimited angles, landscapes, content and perspectives is the artist's imagination. Sometimes executing an idea from the mind's eye of an art director can be more easily and successfully executed by illustration. Or, a painterly or lithographic look may be more appropriate for a given issue or publication. Some magazines, notably *The New Yorker*, have done quite well using illustration as their sole approach to magazine covers.

Stock art and photography companies may provide another solution. Most of these services are available on a yearly or one-shot basis. Remember, though, you are not buying exclusive rights to a piece of art. Indeed, you may see the same illustration or photograph in a number of publications or different media, including newspaper or other advertising. Hiring a good freelance artist or photographer may be your best bet. This way you receive original work for a reasonable fee. What's more, if you establish a good relationship, you may end up with full-time benefits without full-time costs and commitments.

There is room enough for each of these approaches to cover art, but your choice should be determined by function. Who is your audience? What is the image and intent of the publication? Why does one medium appear to be the better choice? How does the cover relate to content? Audience? Positioning of the magazine? Good answers to these questions will help you properly align image, intent, and magazine positioning on your covers.

Establishing some sort of continuity is almost as important to your covers as it may be for the rest of your magazine. Most magazines adopt a cover format and live or die by it. *The New Yorker, LIFE, Saturday Evening Post, National Geographic, Communication Arts* and many other magazines adopt both a consistent design format and a consistent approach to artwork. There is no mistaking their identity. In fact, these magazines reaffirm their image and identity with each successive issue. Other magazines adopt a format but vary their art. Today's widest-read magazine, *TV Guide*, maintains its design but varies its visuals, feeling as comfortable with photography as it does illustration.

Figure 8.13 _____

Although each issue of Skald *is a smorgasborg of features on faraway places, normally there is a focus. In this instance, the place highlighted was Canada. Herman Hines of Masterfile made this image of a child of the Inuit—the original inhabitants of Canada. Both covers are simple and inviting. This fully bled photography dominates for good reason: it is appropriate to the publication; it is interesting and it well executed.*

With the exception of the photography (Herman Hines shot the photograph), credits are the same as the previous figure's. Reprinted with permission from Skald *and Pentagram.*

The Indian Ocean is the last of earth's great imponderables. We could name craters on the moon more easily than deal with Farafangana on Madagascar or Silhouette in Seychelles. But some names haunt with memories of places unseen, experiences never lived except through good books or bad movies: Mombasa, Zanzibar—as provocative as perfumes. Filled with the scent of spices, inhabited by unearthly creatures, and infused with mysterious pasts, it is a world more imagined than real.

AFRICA

RARE
EXPERIENCES
ALONG THE
INDIAN
OCEAN

One last word of advice. A single, strong photograph or illustration does a better job of attracting attention than a more fractured design employing a number of images.

Nameplate—Your Sign on the Dotted Line

The **nameplate** or **flag**, which is your publication's cover name or logo, should also remain consistent from issue to issue. Maintaining the same nameplate is one way to help establish cover continuity. (Incidentally, nameplates are often *incorrectly* referred to as mastheads. **Mastheads** are the information blocks which generally appear alongside or below the table of contents or on some other early page in the publication. Normally they list information regarding submission policy, subscriptions, costs, addresses and a hierarchical chart listing names and positions of everyone from Editor-in-Chief to administrative staff.)

Remember, the nameplate is your magazine flag. It should be appropriate, legible, memorable and consistent throughout your communication materials: logo, letterheads, stationery, business cards, billing slips, press releases and whatever else might bear your aegis or symbol. Generally, because it is your public identity, your nameplate should be carefully selected and professionally designed and executed. Your audience associates it directly with you, so choose it wisely. It represents who and what you are in the eyes of your public and staff. Remember, once you've chosen the nameplate you must live with it—at least for a few years.

Figure 8.14 _____

On the left page, elemental form (T-shape) brings a delicate balance through stripped out photography and the creative use of type. Opposite, a mortised image of a rare African plant is placed atop an equally rare white rhino. With the exception of a brief introductory blurb, title and caption, photography carries the first two pages of this eight-page feature in Skald. *Design direction: Kit Hinrichs; art direction: Terri Driscoll; photography: Comstock, Inc. Reprinted with permission from* Skald *and Pentagram.*

Figure 8.15 _____

A magazine's nameplate should be simple, legible and memorable. Additionally, it should be appropriate both to its audience and for the image of the publication and/or the organization it represents. In this case, an old-style roman was selected—bolded Goudy to be precise, which reflects a conservative audience and organization. Designed by Bill Ryan. Reprinted with permission from the Oregon Food Journal *and Bill Ryan.*

Figure 8.16 _____

A closer examination of the Oregon Food Journal *nameplate reveals a number of formal affectations: the old-style serif type, its optically centered arrangement and its symmetry. Also, look at how the top stroke of the* F *supports the letters above it, and how the upper serif of the lowercase* d *contours and suggests support for the letters above it. With the exception of the original sketches, this nameplate was designed on a Macintosh computer. Reprinted with permission from the* Oregon Food Journal *and Bill Ryan.*

Magazines don't make a habit of changing their image or nameplate on a regular basis. You don't change magazine identity like you do socks. When inconsistencies exist at this level, readers, employees, or shareholders will note them. Mixed signals will only generate confusion and suspicion from your audience.

Whatever you do, don't mix your old image with your new one. One of the authors of this book once designed direct-mail materials, a fund-raising brochure, and a new letterhead and logotype for a company that will remain unnamed. While visiting their offices, I noticed that they were stuffing new stationery and direct-mail pieces into envelopes bearing their old logotype. Aghast, I asked why and discovered that they believed they were saving money by using up the old envelopes. Should you decide to put on a new face to change image or look, do so uniformly.

Normally, nameplate design is farmed out to a designer or graphic artist. But this is not a place to cut corners. Be sure to carefully impart how you're currently perceived by your audience, shareholders, employees, etc., how you now wish to be perceived, and why. Indicate, too, why you need an image overhaul. It might not be a bad idea to have the designer examine your competitors' logotypes before discussing the image you desire. Ask for reactions, and ask to see a dozen rough ideas or thumbnails along with sample art from the designer or artist.

Other information may also be important to the person changing your publication's logo. At the very least, discuss budget, company colors, sizes, printing limitations and materials. Explain which ancillary items should appear with the nameplate, including corporate or magazine slogan, dates and volume numbers, price and whatever else you normally incorporate into your cover. If you use cover lines—blurbs or titles—say so and indicate how many. **Cover lines** consist of anything (excluding the nameplate publication dates, etc.) that appears on the cover; **blurbs** are short subheads or story summaries; **titles,** of course, are descriptive headings of the articles and magazine content.

Many software graphics programs also provide the basic tools for creating very sophisticated logotypes. However, like any other tool, the craft and beauty of the design comes not from the tool itself but from the designer who uses it. If you learn your lessons well and know your tools intimately, the computer can literally bring a wealth of graphic and design resources to your fingertips.

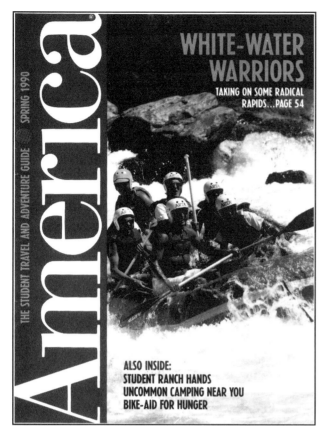

Figure 8.17 _____

If you must surprint on your covers, this issue of America *magazine best exemplifies how to do it. There are two surprinted areas: top right and bottom middle—each uses good contrast so the message is clear (bright lettering on a dark background in the former case and just the opposite in the latter instance) and each places the cover lines away from the crucial parts of the visual. Cover photography by George Olson. Design direction by Ken Smith; art direction by Brad Zucroff. Reprinted with permission from* America, *copyright 1990, Whittle Communications L.P.*

Figure 8.18 _____

This Texas Monthly *cover frames Mark Klett's landscape photography, leaving the image clear and clean the way the artist meant it to be seen. Cover lines exist, most of them related to the photograph, but not at the expense of trashing Klett's color imagery. Art direction tastefully executed by D. J. Stout. Reprinted with permission from* Texas Monthly.

Typography is your nameplate's most important element. Choose an appropriate face and style; see the typography section in **Chapter 3** for a review. Adopting the same face and styling for the magazine's interior logos, departments or special sections will help maintain its continuity. Should you desire this, instruct your graphic artist to create additional interior thumbnails.

Normally, the nameplate runs across the top of a publication. It should flag your audience and stand out from the rest of your competition in news and magazine racks. If your magazine won't end up on the newsstands, your options are wide open. But because we read top to bottom and left to right, nameplates are usually fixed near or at the top of the cover. Normally, too, they are centered or set flush left. There are exceptions to positioning nameplates left and center, but they are few.

Cover Lines—To Surprint or Not to Surprint. That Is the Question

How you handle cover blurbs, titles and teases depends a great deal on how you distribute your magazine. Magazines that are largely dependent upon newsstand

▲ **Figure 8.19**

The background of Jean Moss' cover shot for Special Report *was neutralized by the studio backdrop she used to begin with, so the surprinting doesn't ambush the subject in her photograph. Instead, the cover was specifically designed to accommodate the cover lines and the photo planned to fit the type. Design direction: Jim Darilek; art direction: Sara Christensen; photography: Jean Moss; logotype: Dennis Ortiz-Lopez. Reprinted with permission from* Special Report—On Families, *copyright 1990, Whittle Communications L.P.*

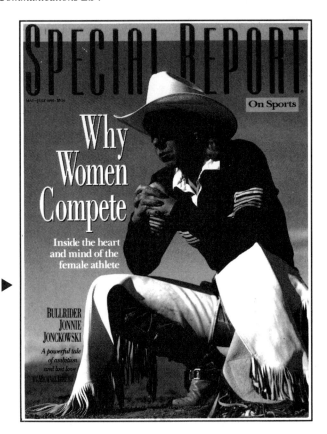

Figure 8.20

This Special Report *cover design takes on a strategy similar to the last figure. The background is mostly neutralized by selective focus and a low camera angle that utilizes the sky as backdrop. Then, cover lines wrap and contour the left edges of the subject in the image, and bullrider Jonnie Jonckowski looks into the main cover title. Jim Darilek is design director and Mary Workman is art director. Cover photography by Frank Ockenfels 3/Outline. Reprinted with permission from* Special Report—On Sports, *copyright 1990, Whittle Communications L.P.*

sales will use surprinted blurbs, titles, splashes and slashes to compete with the hundreds of other magazines displayed together. Most effective consumer magazine covers sell the magazine's content through unusual, attention-getting, relevant and effective artwork. They're likely to show exciting photographs of someone from the magazine's feature piece or interview. Illustrations and photographs of people tend to pull better than images which are peopleless. Newsstand magazines are also apt to flash a good number of blurbs and other cover lines. Additionally, the blurbs are likely to be brightly colored: canary yellow, electric lime, adolescent pink, blood red or florescent lavender.

Their strategy is simple and direct. To capture the audience's attention, they lead with a striking visual image, followed by tantalizing cover lines that are properly contrasted against their backgrounds. Next time you pass a magazine rack in a bookstore, grocery market or airport, glance at it quickly and note where your vision is led. It is likely to stop on a cover featuring an individual you hold in very high or low esteem. The cover is also likely to use good contrast between the lettering and background, and bold colors. The cover blurbs tempt us to look inside. At this point, the cover has done its job. It is, for the most part, expected to do little more than that.

Surprinting is a good tactic; if it weren't, it wouldn't be so widely and successfully employed by newsstand magazines. For many other kinds of publications, however, surprinting is unnecessary. Nonetheless, some editors persist in running similar cover-line tactics. Especially in noncompetitive or subsidized publications, it is a good idea to let the cover art do its job unencumbered. Allow the photography or illustration to shine in its complete space, without being overlaid with a veil of surprinting. If you must use cover lines, place them in a contrasted area away from strong image content. Too often even the slickest consumer magazines forget about the legibility of their cover lines and run them atop a mottled background where contrast between the blurbs and photography is minimal. The result is that the type is swallowed up; it becomes camouflaged and tough to see, much less read.

There are alternatives to surprinting. You can designate a specific cover area for the blurbs. This lets photographers and artists know from the start that a given location—typically lower left or right side—should be reserved for cover lines. With that in mind, they can compose or design their imagery using that general area as neutral space. This way color blocks or neutralized areas are predesignated as locations for the written word. By avoiding surprinting (atop artwork, anyway), your typography doesn't clash with the visual or compete for your readers' attention. Instead, it reinforces, informs and fleshes out the art as a separate cover element, complimenting artwork instead of fighting it.

If you decide to use a single cover line, it should connect directly to the visual. However, should you insert more than one title or blurb, the art may link to either or possibly both descriptions. In the case of thematic magazine issues, the artwork may relate to all cover lines. One of the advantages of theme issues is that covers and articles may be planned well in advance and cover artwork determined and assigned long before press deadlines.

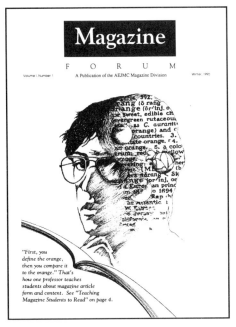

"First, you define the orange, then you compare it to the orange." That's how one professor teaches students about magazine article form and content. See "Teaching Magazine Students to Read" on page 4.

Figures 8.21 and 8.22 *_____*
Magazine Forum is a low-budget magazine which is published twice a year for the Magazine Division of AEJMC. It was designed on a Macintosh computer and reproduced through quick-copy. Although it's not meant to compete with slick, dressed-out publications, it is cleanly designed and has a solid look. Note how the department interior logo, Head Lines, is a subtle variation of the publication's nameplate. Editor: Ken Metzler. Design and art direction and logotype by Bill Ryan. Cover illustration by Jarrett Jester. Reprinted with permission of Magazine Forum *and Bill Ryan.*

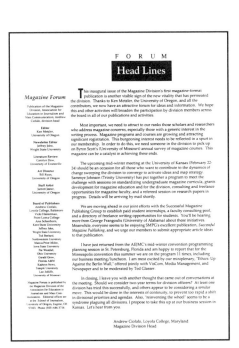

Figure 8.25 _____
Here you see the end result—the final GPS *cover—after the production staff have heeded the art director's instructions and reversed the surprinting and part of the nameplate that doesn't take the PMS color, and reversed and trapped that area of the nameplate which does take the specified color.* GPS *fully bleeds its cover photography. Art direction: Lee Eide; photography by Richard A. Cooke III. Reprinted with permission from Aster Publishing Corp.*

It is in your best interest to keep the type family the same throughout your cover notes. (Of course, this does not necessarily include the magazine's nameplate.) The more you vary cover typography, the more you will fracture its unity and effectiveness. Try not to split the type into more than two dominant cover locations. Also, avoid surprinting atop continuous tone black-and-white or mottled areas.

If you run reversed type, set it larger than you normally would. Bolded sans serif will provide a more legible read. Modern roman type is normally not a good choice for reverse blocks because the thin strokes and some of the serifs get swallowed up in the background, especially at small and middle point sizes. This is even more a problem when you're using textured paper stock or cheaper production methods. If you use a roman face, choose an old-style or traditional serif, one with little contrast between its thick and thin strokes, and one with bracketed serifs.

Design Format—The Final Put Down

Studying the design framework of a magazine cover is a good way to see how all of its elements work together. To uncover it, take a wide, black art marker and stratify magazine covers by their graphic parts. Black out the nameplate area. Draw a heavy line around the artwork, including mortises or overlapping photos. **Mortises** are "cut-in" areas; generally, they are copy boxes or other photographs that cut into other art. Line in all cover lines. Do the same thing to previous issues of the same magazine prior to blacking out other magazines. Blacking in and outlining design element areas brings home a point that cannot be overstated; namely, that most designs are simple and efficient, and that a format's success depends largely upon the successful execution of each cover part. They should relate quickly and clearly.

You'll find that visuals, or art areas, dominate. Nameplates are the next most likely element to be noticed; blurbs, titles and other cover lines follow. You've discovered the basic cover design layout formula, which goes like this:

1. Nameplate and ancillary information
2. Art
3. Cover lines

Although visuals attract the most attention, the nameplate generally runs first because it must be visible on magazine racks that cover the bottom two-thirds to one-third of a publication.

Your blackened covers will also reveal just how often diagonal lines within the artwork direct the visual flow upward to the nameplate and down again. That's because magazine covers are especially given to the basic Z-form or elemental diagonal structure. Triangular formations in the artwork and cover lines act as arrows to move our eyes to and from main cover elements. Typically, when we wed visual and written components, our eyes land on the dominant visual element, jump to the nameplate and read it left to right, look to the visual again and read the cover lines, exiting at the lower right side of the design.

Despite the fact that this spot is the last one normally noted on the typical visual scan, the lower right corner is a strategic design point. And rightfully so. If you don't concur, make a quick examination of every print advertisement you come across in any magazine. Count the number of times advertisers choose to place their company signature in the lower right corner.

More Cover Notes

Many magazines print their covers separately. If you plan to run full color only for this section, want a heavier or special paper, a gatefold or other special handling, a separate cover is the answer.

Self-covers are printed on the same paper as the interior pages of the publication. If your paper is flimsy or lightweight, your cover will also be flimsy and cheap looking. So if you're using a good grade of paper that is heavy enough and suitable for a cover as well, a self-cover might be to your advantage. If you're

Figure 8.26 _____

A good table of contents page works as a menu of sorts, listing magazine departments or major sections, followed by entreés or titles and where to find them. Best of Business Quarterly has a very functional and attractive contents page: departments and features are clearly organized and listed on the left page, and the magazine background and special features are provided on the adjacent page. Art direction, Tom Russell; design direction, Bett McLean; illustration by Bill Sanderson. Reprinted with permission from the Best of Business Quarterly, *copyright 1989, Whittle Communications L.P.*

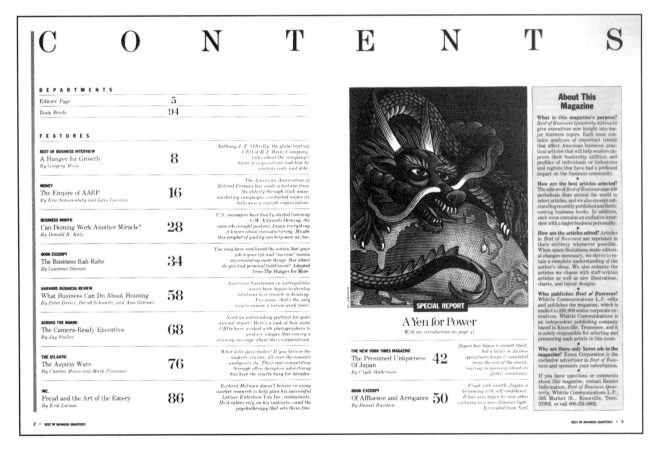

going to use a self-cover, though, remember to figure it into your signature. As you recall, a **signature** is any grouping of pages printed together on both sides of a single sheet of stock—normally sixteen or thirty-two pages. By designing a self-cover into the signature, you save the additional printing and special handling costs. What's more, if you plan to run color on the cover, you can add it to the rest of that signature for very little additional cost.

Full bleeds tend to make your artwork appear larger, even if it is only the background that bleeds. Pushing visuals off the page suggests that the subject or idea stretches beyond the physical limitations of the magazine format. These days bled photos happen to be very stylish as well.

Table of Contents

The table of contents acts as a menu of sorts, listing magazine departments or major sections, then specific entrées or titles beneath each section. The contents page should be well ordered and organized so that readers can quickly and easily discover what the magazine contains, what articles are about and where they can be found. What's more, the table of contents itself should be easy to find. Typically it is located somewhere in the first five pages of the publication. In the past, it was most commonly run on the first, third or fifth page, but today the second or fourth page is just as appropriate. In larger magazines, it may be designed across two pages. Whichever you choose, be consistent and stick with that format each issue. If you have ever been seduced by a cover blurb or tease and then had to search out the article blindly because you couldn't locate the table

Figure 8.27 _____

Like Best of Business, America *also uses a two-page contents. Its generous white space is very inviting. (See how the type, specially designed rules and photography link the two? What you cannot see is how designated color—red titles, red page numbers and a very large, red dropped-initial letter also bond the pages.) Along with information about the magazine, this publication places its Editor's Note and a masthead on right page. Design direction: Ken Smith. Art direction: Brad Zucroff. Photography by Skeeter Hagler. Reprinted with permission from* America, *copyright 1990, Whittle Communications L.P.*

Figure 8.28

This one-page contents page for Special Reports *uses elemental form (a quarter-turned T-shape), white space and a single photograph as its design formula. Other issues use the same format. It is clean, easy to read and attractive. Design direction by Jim Darilek, art direction by Doug Renfro and photography by Rocky Schenck. Reprinted with permission from* Special Report—On Personalities, *copyright 1990, Whittle Communications L.P.*

Figure 8.29

Kit Hinrichs uses a very unusual seven-column, single-page table of contents for Skald *magazine. This mostly symmetrical design features the cover photography (sans* Skald *nameplate) and then partially wraps it with a very clean and elegant blend of titles/descriptors and small photography and illustration. Page numbers are run in red and are easy to find and align. Art direction by Kit Hinrichs. Reprinted with permission from* Skald *and Pentagram.*

of contents, you know firsthand how frustrating it is to work without one. Almost as irritating is not being able to locate the featured cover piece on the contents page because its title is ambiguous or much different from that on the cover.

Good contents pages fracture out the departments or magazine sections clearly, so that the readers can find the department or section heading and title they're looking for at a glance. A good organizational strategy is to immediately categorize the magazine parts with general headings—for example, features, fiction, departments and editorials. Entries beneath each are normally arranged chronologically and are further detailed by some or all of the following.

A **title** gives the audience a general idea of the article's content. **Subtitles** may further clarify what the entry is about or the slant of the piece. **Content blurbs** summarize, tease or sensationalize the listings. **Folios** or **page numbers** are mandatory; they indicate to the reader where to find each article. **Bylines** may follow the title or blurb of each piece. Sometimes publications provide **art** and **design credits** in addition to the bylines. However, it is not uncommon to list writers separately. On occasion, a magazine will carry brief **entry descriptors** to clarify whether the piece is fiction, humor, nonfiction, opinion or the like.

Visual previews or teases are also included on some contents pages. *Also, if your publication is strong visually, make it apparent from the start. Lead with a strong visual table of contents.* Cover credits give the full story behind a cover photograph or illustration, and the table of contents is the most logical place for them. They might consist of brief credit line for the cover's creator and a brief description or a longer explanation of how the artwork relates to the current issue.

Other components of the table of contents page may include:

- Nameplate or logo, publication date, volume and issue numbers
- Masthead and credits box to list magazine staff
- Company, association, or magazine affiliation, usually noted by name and logo or aegis

- A preview box to promote content highlights and photography of the upcoming issue

Departments

Most magazines have at least a couple departments. Typical departments might have a news, opinion, legislative or educational designation.Sometimes they are created by default; that is, they are whatever isn't listed as feature, non-fiction or fiction.

Departments better structure the magazine by aligning related material. Normally they have common visual characteristics and styling; that is, the type and graphic arrangements are essentially the same. That way they are easily distinguished from features and advertising, but in terms of design, are still visually connected to one another. On occasion, departments are linked to the nameplate through typography, styling or graphics. Once planned and used, they remain a regular part of the magazine.

You may also wish to distinguish departments from other content by altering typography, line arrangement and the number of columns per page, or even stylizing the photography or graphics differently from the nondepartment content. For example, *GPS* magazine uses four columns for features and three for departmental material. The trick is to make the departments connective enough to link to your overall design and maintain unity, while distinguishing them from the rest of the publication. This should be accomplished through minor, not major cosmetic surgery. The best approach might be to make two or three simple variations from the styling of the rest of the magazine.

Figure 8.32 _____

*Compare this feature layout to several other designs by Kit Hinrichs. (See **Figures 8.8-8.14** and **8.29**.) Are there any compositional or design devices that seem to reoccur? Is the anything vaguely reminiscent about any of the content? This is another well-anchored design that reveals a playful kind of symmetry, which although striking and beautiful is very functional. Notice how the copy is coded to the map. Design director: Kit Hinrichs. Art director, Karen Berndt. Still life photography by Barry Robinson; other images by Nancy Simmerman and Tim Thompson/AlaskaPhoto and by Harvey Lloyd. Reprinted with permission from* Skald *and* Pentagram.

Figure 8.33

Running a feature vertically down two pages that are normally read as horizontal pages may be risky business, but then so is running the rapids of California's Tuolumne River. Is George Olson's photographic image and Cherie Spino's feature article worth the quarter-turn the reader must make to see and read this? In a word, Yes. One of the basic things to remember when working designs for features is that there really are no hard and fast rules—at least none beyond stylesheet or stylebook guidelines. Most publications don't harness designers with specific type specs when it comes to featuring features. Even those that do ought to be flexible enough to allow a design the creativity to present a feature uniquely, appropriately. Art direction by Brad Zucroff, designed by Allyson Adden, design direction by Ken Smith. Photographs by George Olson. Reprinted with permission from America, *copyright 1990, Whittle Communications L.P.*

Featuring Features

Features generally receive the greatest amount of attention from readers, designers and editors. After all, they are the magazine's main draw. Besides, editors and designers usually invest more money, time and energy in them.

In some respects, feature pages function as inside covers because they flag and stop the reader. Like the cover, their artwork usually dominates the page. Sometimes the main feature even resembles the cover, because it is a slightly different version or rehashing of the cover art—often by the same artist or photographer. This high visibility helps the feature stand apart from all the other editorial material and advertising. And it is the best way to arrest the attention of the reader. Nothing mandates that art be used in features, but very few run without it.

Keep the artwork simple and isolated so that only one element dominates. If you use photography, isolate it through contrast, lighting, depth of field and

Figure 8.34 _____

The following page of America's *white-water story—seen here—gives the reader a marvelous sidebar which tells the reader everything from where this stretch of river is located (complete with maps) to how to get there, where to lodge, eat and hang out after you've dried out. It also lists other white-water treks in the immediate vicinity and at large. Sidebar researched and written by Elizabeth Robbins; see credits in* **Figure 8.23**. *Reprinted with permission from* America, *copyright 1990, Whittle Communications L.P.*

On the Tuolumne we usually tried to avoid the rocks. But occasionally we'd "sheboing"—a rafting term for hitting a rock and hopping it bounces you off in the right direction.

Figure 8.35 _____

Notice how the free-spirited design from the previous example is continued. Your vision is dumped into the read through the diagonal elemental form of the partially bled, upper left photo. The type is contoured to fit the playful angle of the art. Mid-page, a pullout echoes the diagonal thrust of the top photo by zigzagging the type downward. It is printed atop a bubbly-looking texture screen in light blue and white. This design reinforces the excitement of white-water rafting. Reprinted with permission from America, *copyright 1990, Whittle Communications L.P. Note credit acknowledgements in previous figure.*

careful cropping. Often silhouetted images are the answer. If you use illustration, arrange its composition to your best advantage through similar strategies.

Your headline should be succinct. It should complement or connect to the visual so that these two elements work much the same as the poster. Typography for the headline may be fairly rigid and standardized, or it may be totally different from the rest of the type in your publication. You can find successfully designed magazines that use both approaches; however, they seldom break from their preference once it's established. A more conservative or traditional publication may be more comfortable using limited typography that is predetermined and

Figure 8.36 _____

Assignment? Design a two-page, feature spread that uses type creatively to call attention to the growing problem with Alar-tainted fruits. University of Oregon magazine design student Matt Bertolone-Smith turned in this computer-designed layout. It is successful for a number of reasons, among them are the creative title, the dark ground thirds layout, the reversed title and inserted copy block. It is also immaculately executed. Bertolone-Smith is currently art director at Media Index Publishing, Inc. in Seattle. Reprinted with permission from Matt Bertolone-Smith.

perhaps use symmetry and even proportions. In contrast, a more contemporary magazine may favor typefaces that reflect the art and feeling of the article. Less traditional publications are also more likely to use asymmetry and odd proportions in the design.

Body type typically remains the same, but some designers take liberties with a feature piece by stretching the line length, using a different face for dropped-initial letters, adding leading, increasing point size for the first paragraph or changing the number of columns on the page. Sometimes, too, the typography contours the right or left edge of the artwork. Don't get too complicated; simple is still best. Again, beware typography that calls attention to itself.

Positioning the feature is an entirely different matter. Will your feature begin on a right-hand or a left-hand page? Should you bridge the art across two pages? On a two-page spread, do you use the left page for artwork only? These questions relate to the logistics of the design and don't have pat answers.

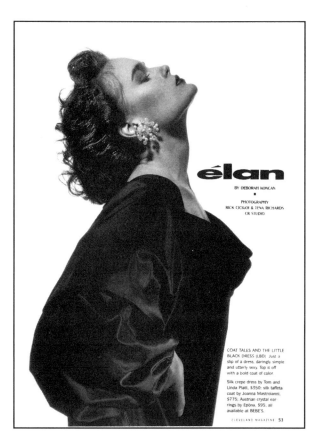

élan

BY DEBORAH KONCAN

•

PHOTOGRAPHY
RICK CICIGOI & TENA RICHARDS
CR STUDIO

COAT TALES AND THE LITTLE
BLACK DRESS (LBD) Just a
slip of a dress, daringly simple
and utterly sexy. Top it off
with a bold coat of color

Silk crepe dress by Tom and
Linda Platt, $350; silk taffeta
coat by Joanna Mastroianni,
$775; Austrian crystal ear-
rings by Epóna, $95, all
available at BEBE'S.

CLEVELAND MAGAZINE 53

Figure 8.37

*Righthand openers have a couple of inherent problems; first,
we are predisposed to whatever appears on the left—
remember, we read left to read—and secondly, right pages
must compete with lefthand pages, which usually contain
advertising. Here, design director Gary Sluzewski literally
has the model turn her back on the adjacent page and direct
our vision to the title and text for this* Cleveland Magazine
*feature. Rick Cicigoi and Tena Richards set up and shot this
striking photography for Deborah Koncan's fashion article,
"élan." Reprinted with permission from* Cleveland
Magazine.

Figure 8.38

Compositional ploys abound in this intriguing Cleveland
Magazine *layout. Strong diagonal lines of force lead our
vision from the lower left corner to the intersection point in
the upper righthand corner of the left page, then shift us
directly to the copy block on the right page, as does the gaze
of the model. Contrast—black fashion in a sea of white
space—makes this design really stand out. Indeed, opposites
do attract. See previous acknowledgements for credits.
Reprinted with permission from* Cleveland Magazine.

NIGHT DETAIL The LBD
attracts attention to details

Jet and gold crystal necklace
by Epóna, $265, available at
BEBE'S. Satin shoes by Mario
Gordano for Enzo Russo,
$557; grosgrain handbag by
Luc Benoit, $480; Isotoner
gloves, $200, all available at
MONTRACHET COUTURE.

OPPOSITES ATTRACT The
straight and narrow of the
LBD is broken by a big bow in
high contrast white

Silk dress by Bernard Perris,
$2,695, available at MON-
TRACHET COUTURE.

Right-hand openers have some problems and limitations. In many magazines, the right-hand feature competes with material on the opposite page—usually advertising, but sometimes another article, department or a jump page. (A **jump page** picks up stories continued from earlier pages.) The design and look of the right page must be different to distinguish it from the left, especially since our vision alights on the left page first. Finally, there is an entirely different dynamic with a right page; you must be careful not to redirect the vision of the reader back to the left or off the page entirely.

You should consider position in whatever you're designing; that is, will what you're designing be located on the right or left side? That is one reason why it was suggested that you shoot your photographs with subjects facing right, left and center. In doing so, you bring more flexibility when placing the art within your design.

The majority of designers would recommend running strong art on the right-hand opener. But you should avoid any kind of photographic layout that might be misconstrued as advertising. Some feel that a powerful image—be it photography or illustration—would be wasted if it can't be stretched into a two-page spread or even bled into the margins. But better a somewhat slighted piece of art than a lost feature.

Another common ploy for right-hand feature pages is to build an extra margin of space into the left side of the design through the use of vertical ground thirds. In other words, use a one-third or two-third block of color, white space or art to push your copy away from the left-hand page. The idea is to clearly separate the two pages while highlighting both the design and content of the right page. It also incorporates proportion, sequence, emphasis and unity into the

Figure 8.39 _____

There is long litany of design strategies that make this feature especially inviting. Symmetry, deep leading, exaggerated horizontal photography, generous white space and spread type in the title, to name a few.

D. J. Stout art directed this for Texas Monthly. *"FENCE ME IN" was written by Melanie Young. Beryl Striewski executed the photography of these unusual Texas fences. Reprinted with permission from* Texas Monthly.

design, and it is an especially useful tactic when you don't have strong artwork. Still another compositional approach would be to employ elemental form into the page's design through framing with L- and O-shapes.

On the other hand, left pages offer considerably more possibilities. (Because they are preferred advertising locations, however, there are fewer of them.) Vision tracks to this side first, and there is always the possibility of running a two-page spread. In fact, some magazines don't use a right opener, period, while others make it their stock in trade with gray pages and advertising opposite.

Standard left-hand page features tend to work a little harder than right-hand features. Many designers prefer to use a great deal of white space around the artwork to set it off—generous borders make it stand out. There is very little copy on the opening left page, so we are able to move directly into the story's copy on the opposite page. Because readers don't have to jump to a continuation many pages away or even turn the page, they are more likely to stay with the story. So, a left page start makes good sense to the designer and editor both.

Full spreads do much more than any single-page opener. For starters, they afford an alternative to the vertical designs that are the preferred format for almost all magazines. Because full spreads are horizontal, designers can straddle the two pages by running artwork, graphics or type across the gutter. That ties the pages neatly and emphasizes the horizontal format. Others push the unusual magazine format even further by dropping in exaggerated horizontal artwork. This very narrow, connective approach gets high marks for attracting attention and stopping the reader. However, all too often the horizontal format is treated as two vertical pages—typically, the left page is fully bled and the right carries the title, credit particulars and the copy. While this is acceptable—and sometimes it is the best answer because of artwork's horizontal limitations—it isn't especially inspired. Full-page spreads have incredible power to dominate the entire magazine when treated horizontally. And in addition to providing variety, horizontal layouts read well and suggest movement better than their vertical cousins.

It should be noted that the quality of any artwork used for a full spread must meet a high standard—and it should have an obvious horizontal flow. When you plan the pages, make sure that the artist or photographer knows what you're up to so that their linear treatment of the subject will work for your design. The more carefully planned and plotted your advance work is, the better your finished product will be.

Chapter 9

Annual Reports

Part A: Writing

A nnual reports are probably the least read of all house publications. Recent research indicates that about half the shareholders who receive them spend less than 10 minutes looking at them. And, 15 percent of all stock analysts don't read them at all. So why is corporate America spending $5 billion a year producing annual reports?

Part of the reason is that the federal government requires it. The Securities Exchange Act of 1936 required publicly traded companies to provide their investors with a yearly financial statement. This law also requires that an annual report be delivered to stockholders no later than 15 days before the annual meeting. Quarterly reports also had to be filed.

Beginning in 1980, the Securities and Exchange Commission (SEC) mandated that additional information be added, including financial data covering the past five years, and an expanded discussion and analysis of the company's financial condition. It's not surprising, then, that annual reports increase in size and complexity each year—so much so, in fact, that a few years ago General Motors asked the SEC to allow them and other companies to develop and file an abbreviated, "summary" annual report.

In 1987, the SEC ruled that companies could indeed publish such a report as long as they included all of the elements required by law as either appendices to the abbreviated report or in another formal document, such as the already required Form 10-K. Critics worry that this new flexibility allows companies to selectively cut bad news from its most visible communication vehicle. They argue that most stockholders will read *only* the annual report, believing it complete. Although some companies have experimented with the "summary" annual report, at this writing, most companies still produce the lengthy report already familiar to stockholders.

Annual Report Audiences

When you produce an annual report, you're writing for a primarily internal audience, one with a vested interest in the well-being of your organization. That's why many annual reports gloss over the bad news, even though research shows that most stockholders would feel a lot better about a company if it were open and honest with them.

However, stockholders aren't the only audience for annual reports. These organizational summaries are excellent information sources for media people, especially financial reporters. They also provide valuable background for financial analysts, potential stockholders, nonshareholding employees and customers, and opinion leaders such as legislators and community leaders.

Before you write an annual report, you must first decide which of these audiences you are writing for. Don't ever assume that you are talking only to shareholders; rank the other potential audiences in order of their importance to you and be sure to address them, too.

Annual Report Contents

No two annual reports are alike; however, the SEC does require certain elements be present including:

- Certified financial statements for the previous two years

- An explanation of any difference between these financial statements and statements filed in another form with the SEC

- A summary management analysis of operations for the past five years

- Identification of the company directors' principal occupations

- Stock market and dividend information for the past two years

- Notice of Form 10-K availability

- A brief description of both business and line-of-business in the "audited footnote." This all appears in the footnote itself.

- Any material differences from established accounting principles reflected in the financial statements

- Supplementary inflation accounting

The form this information takes is what makes annual reports different from each other. To accommodate the SEC guidelines, annual reports have developed certain standard mechanisms for housing the required information.

- A description of the company including its name, address (headquarters, subsidiaries and plant sites), its overall business, and a summary of its operations, usually in both narrative and numerical form.

- A letter to stockholders including an account of the past year's achievements, an overview of the industry environment and pertinent markets, and a discussion of future business and investment strategies.

- A financial review as set forth by SEC regulations listed above.

- An explanation and analysis of the financial review that outlines the factors influencing the financial picture over the past year.

- A narrative report covering anything from a discussion of subsidiaries to details on corporate philanthropy. Many companies use the annual report as a forum in which to discuss social issues or beat their own public relations drum, as it is one of the best publicity tools available.

Writing for Annual Reports

There are generally two ways to produce an annual report: you can write it in house, or you can farm it out to an agency. Frankly, agencies—including those that specialize in annual reports—produce the bulk of these publications. However, with the advent of desktop publishing, more organizations are considering in-house writing and production.

No matter who writes it, the bulk of an annual report is taken up with tables, charts and flashy photographs. In fact, critics charge, annual reports often try too hard (and too blatantly) to sweeten a bitter financial pill with a lot of pretty sugar coating. Many annual reports do stand guilty of this, but countless others perform a valuable informational service to shareholders and members. In fact, because they *are* good message vehicles, a great many nonprofit organizations are now producing annual reports even though they don't really have to. The modern annual report has become a major tool in any organization's public relations arsenal.

Writers produce only a small portion of the annual report, but it is the portion most read by shareholders—the president's letter and the narrative report.

The President's Letter

There are some really awful president's letters in annual reports. The reason most cited is the SEC guidelines telling them what they have to talk about. Fortunately, these guidelines don't tell writers *how* to talk about what they *have* to talk about. There is no reason these letters have to be crashingly dull, wordy and confusing. What impresses the everyday shareholder is honesty, a straightforward writing style, and no fluff.

Both of the following examples opt for the "numbers up front" approach on the mistaken belief that readers want it that way.

> [Company name] expanded its financial base in 19__ and substantially increased the number of property interests in its investment portfolio. A $47 million common stock offering, completed in June, plus a $40 million public offering of mortgage notes and common stock purchase warrants in December 19__ were among the financial resources which permitted [company name] to increase the number of its property interests to 191 by adding 99 real estate investments during the year.

> ●

> The year 19__ was a successful one for [company name]. Net income was up substantially, over 27 percent greater than 19__'s results, to a record $305.6 million, as the economy moved into a strong recov-

ery. On a per share basis, our earnings were $9.50, an increase of 13 percent, reflecting both the issuance of additional common stock during this past year, as well as the preferred stock issued during 19__.

The next example at least begins with an interesting image of a "corporate renaissance."

> We are in the midst of a corporate renaissance and 19__ was a strong reflection of the growth, diversification, and enthusiasm that typifies [company name].
> We had a record performance in 19__ in many areas. For the first time, net income exceeded $1 billion, at $1.2 billion. Sales reached an all-time high of $13.4 billion—up more than $2 billion from the 19__ level. The list of records also included earnings per share at $6.47; and operating income, which at $2.3 billion was up 69 percent from the previous record.

And what about bad news? This letter buries it under a barrage of industry buzzwords such as " maximizing profitability."

> [Company name] continued its strategy of maximizing profitability in basic markets and businesses in 19__. All these areas of the Corporation had a truly excellent year. Unfortunately, the property and casualty reinsurance lines of the Insurance Group, which are not a part of our basic long-term strategy, incurred continuing heavy losses, significantly lowering our overall profitability. Reflecting this impact, [company name]'s consolidated net income of $106.3 million was about flat with 19__, although earnings per share increased marginally to $4.02 from $3.96 reflecting a slightly reduced number of common shares outstanding.

Finally, here's a letter that approaches a mixed year with an interesting, number-free narrative approach.

> External forces produce both opportunities and challenges—and 19__ had its share of both for [company name] and its businesses.
> During the year, some of the external forces facing our four business segments served to expand revenues and growth. Others had a dampening effect, calling for effective counter-measures.
> The mix of forces at work included... [bulleted list follows]
>
> We worked to take advantage of those external forces that offered opportunities, and to overcome the challenges posed by others.

If you can write the letter yourself, and simply route it for the president's approval, you'll get better results than you would if the president drafts it. When you do it yourself, keep in mind a few points. Because most of the rest of the report is numbers, it's best to keep numbers in the letter to a minimum. Keep your letter short, and keep its language friendly and simple. This way, you'll be able to cover the SEC bases without boring your readers.

The Narrative Report

The body of the annual report is your only chance to write anything without numbers—or, at least, with a minimum of numbers. Here is where you get to describe the company, its operations, its people (a favorite focus of many reports), and its future in detail. The only problem is one of space. Remember, you can't leave out anything required by the SEC. And you don't want to leave out anything that really makes your company look good.

One of the best ways to decide on content is to have the people in charge of the various divisions or subsidiaries submit brief lists of the year's highlights from their "down in the trenches" perspective. Make your needs known in plenty of time to get responses from your contacts. And leave the final compiling and writing to one person so that the entire report has a single style.

A quick word about that style. Depending on a company's image, the style of an annual report can vary greatly. Some are formal to the point of being stiff. Others are too informal and leave shareholders with a feeling that the company is being loosely run. The best and most appropriate style is somewhere in the middle.

As with the president's letter, you don't have to begin your narrative report with numbers. In fact, it benefits greatly from a little introduction. There is no reason why annual reports have to be boring reading. The following introductions to the narrative report sections of two different annual reports are fairly good examples of what can be done to lend a modicum of interest to an otherwise often dull subject.

> To come up with a winner in global competition, you have to provide the highest quality... the greatest number of choices... and the most innovative solutions to a customer's needs, regardless of location.
>
> In meeting that challenge, [company name] uses a system of "global networking" to choreograph its worldwide response by product, function, and geographic area. Networking teams enable [company name] to draw upon its resources around the world and to respond quickly no matter where customers may be headquartered.

●

> There are many ways to define shareholder value... and many ways that companies strive to create it. But at [company name[, the strategy has been three pronged:
>
> - Utilizing existing resources within the company to diversify into four separate businesses.
> - Acting on opportunities to build and strengthen these existing businesses.
> - Keeping abreast of trends that hold promise for the future.

Use numbers to *augment* your narrative—don't let numbers be the entire focus. Although annual reports are intended to spell out a company's financial environment, they communicate more often with average people than financial analysts. Financial analysts won't rely on an annual report as their sole information source. Many shareholders will, so it has to be written in a style they will understand.

Striking just the right tone, in both writing and design, is the most important ingredient in producing an annual report. In fact, so much depends on design that many annual reports emphasize the form the expense of its function.

Design for design's sake is still common. Be careful not to let your "look" overpower your written information. Ideally, form and function should work together to achieve a real sense of the company that readers care enough to own part of.

A standing joke among those who've worked on annual reports is that should they go to hell they'll be creating annual reports for all eternity. It reflects the frustration created from the mandates of the Securities and Exchange Commission regarding what annual reports shall contain, where and how those contents will appear and when the report must be published.

Some creatives feel fettered by annual reports. There are constraints. Certain items will always appear: a letter from the president or director of the organization, financial statements, sales and other financially related records from at least

Figure 9.1 _____

Here, the Independence Bancorp annual report features the average customer throughout its pages. The report focuses on different banks and their respective customers. In this example, security officer James Giles is profiled similarly to how the Third National Bank is profiled— as "a community leader." This award-winning report uses a no-frills, direct style that is both refreshing and informative. It also gives its readers slice of life insight about Independence Bancorp beyond the proverbial bottom lines. Michael Gunselman's design and Ed Eckstein's photography shine. Reprinted with permission from Independence Bancorp and Michael Gunselman.

Figure 9.2 _____

See the previous figure and compare this cover shot of Chad Deakyne to the Giles' image. Designer Michael Gunselman boldly sets the theme and its simple approach with his understated, minimal annual report cover. "In his dreams," we are told, "he's (Chad Deakyne, that is) either at third base on a major league baseball team or behind a saxophone at a jazz club." Also, we learn that he opened a saving's account at Freedom Valley Bank, "where his savings are growing with him." Simple is better. Just ask Michael Gunselman, designer or photographer Ed Eckstein. Reprinted with permission from Independence Bancorp and Michael Gunselman.

While internal growth has been a strong part of our success, we have outlined in our 1990–92 goals to continue acquiring stable financial institutions with strong market positions. In 1989, Boulevard Bancorp acquired Northwest Financial Corp., a one-bank holding company for National Security Bank of Chicago. National Security's stability is evident by the foundation they've established in Chicago's west town community, in addition to their strong customer relationships, such as the Gonnella Baking Company. They have maintained a close, significant relationship with Gonnella for over 80 years. National Security joining Boulevard Bancorp is a good representation of accomplishing our goal of acquiring secure, stable institutions. Going forward, we plan to acquire selected business partners who contribute to our financial objectives as well as complement and support our corporate values. Boulevard Bancorp is solidly positioned for the challenge of the future. As we stride ahead we're confident that our established corporate values support our direction for future growth. Success for Boulevard Bancorp means success for our customers, employees and shareholders.

GONNELLA

BAKING COMPANY

George Marcucci & Robert Gonnella

Figure 9.3 _____

Samata and Associates of Chicago adopted a completely different strategy to produce this exemplary annual report for Boulevard Bancorp, Inc. Here, we see banking and Boulevard Bancorp as a successful business partner to middle- to large-sized businesses. Marc Norberg's photography is friendly and sometimes amusing. Although the shots are set up (complete with props that work as metaphors of what these businesses and businessmen do), they are believable, something central to any annual report. George Marcucci and Robert Gonnella of Gonnella Baking Company are featured here. Design and production by Samata and Associates, Greg Samata, designer. Reprinted with permission from Boulevard Bancorp, Inc. and Samata Associates.

the past two years, budget statements. Furthermore, the SEC has a say on some matters of typography, as the following excerpt from a recent letter from John C. Brousseau, Attorney-Advisor to the SEC, shows.

> An annual report to shareholders must contain the financial and related information required by Rule 14a-3(b) (1), (b) (3) and (b) (4) as well as the information specified by Rule 14a-3 (b) (5) through (b) (10). Rule 14a-3 (b) (2) requires that financial statements and notes must be in roman type and as large and legible as 10 point modern. The financial statements may be in roman type as large as (sic) legible as 8 point modern if necessary for convenient presentation. All type must be leaded at least 2 points.

By no means is this complete. The Attorney-Advisor's remarks continue for two more pages and, though intended to be direct, clear and helpful, merely outline the SEC's rules and regulations for annual reports in a very sketchy fashion. And because the remarks were prepared by an attorney interpreting a document prepared by other attorneys, they are less than clear. Few designers keep a full set of the Securities and Exchange Commission's regulations between their PMS color guide and current *Communication Arts* issues. However, they are expected to live up to the letter of law when creating annual reports and, what's more, to do so in a fresh and informative manner.

But let's not throw rocks at the SEC. It is entrusted with a monumental task to protect all of us. After the stock market crash of 1929, the government created a number of agencies to protect the general public, many of whom lost fortunes in failed banks and a stock market that had gone to hell in a handbasket. The SEC

Figure 9.4 _____

Notice how the exaggerated format of Marc Norberg's photograph fits Greg Samata's design exactly. This thin spatial arrangement accentuates the publication's lean, fashionable look. In this case, the CEO's photograph is cropped and fitted to the exact dimensions of the copy's column size. Note, too, the photography's continuity. (See **Figure 9.3** *for comparison and credits.) Reprinted with permission from Boulevard Bancorp, Inc. and Samata Associates.*

Figures 9.5 and **9.6**

This annual report for Cracker Barrel Old Country Store has a distinctive "down home" flavor to it—from a more relaxed time when everything was less complicated, when "...television had not yet jaded our time span or sensibilities." The art —a mix of smaller snapshots for the center of the left page and large full-page set-ups—is done in muted color, while the copywriting resurrects warm memories that are seasoned with home-cooking and old friends. The 40s' snapshot quality was further enhanced by running the color slightly out of registration. But there's lots more that contributes to its nostalgia, including type that smacks of the 30s and 40s, paper with edges that look aged and ribbons from the state fair, 4-H and many other places.

In this example, Mom's apple pie receives a second place from the Ladies Church Bazaar, 1940. This wonderful report was produced for the Cracker Barrel folks by Thomas Ryan Design of Nashville. Design by Thomas Ryan and Kathy Wayland; photography by McGuire; copywriting by John Baeder. Reprinted with permission from Cracker Barrel and Thomas Ryan Design.

was one of those agencies. Its mandate is to provide some guarantees for our public investment and shareholdings by monitoring corporate America.

Among other things, the SEC mandates that any company that has shareholders make a public accounting of itself each year. How much money did the company spend? Where did it come from? How is each of these fractured out in terms of categories of expenditure, other company assets, debts. There are more financial records and figures that must be present, all of which must not only be accurate to the penny but audited and certified.

Accountability extends beyond the numbers, however. Annual reports list all connected to the company from the president and board members to attorneys and the company's accounting firm. In fact, presidents, boards, accounting firms and others typically have statements to accompany their lists of numbers and statistics.

But corporate America isn't the only filer of annual reports. They are also issued by many nonprofit institutions. They may be used for fund-raising purposes and included along with grant proposals to help their readers put a face and personality on the organization. In fact, today the nonprofit company that doesn't issue a yearly report is the rare exception.

It's easy to use SEC regulations as a patent excuse to work an annual report at arm's length and forget creativity. That's too bad, because of all the publication formats, this one probably deserves the most creative thought and innovation. In fact, it offers organizations the perfect stage to stretch the medium and shine among other, more conservative offerings. But much of that is changing. Each year *Financial World*'s prestigious international competition singles out the writers and designers of the finest annual reports. Companies like Samata Associates, Pentagram, Hornall Anderson, Thomas Ryan Design and Taylor and Browning of Toronto, who specialize in conceptualizing, writing and designing annual reports, have brought a renaissance to this publication form.

Figure 9.7

What better way to bring the news to your shareholders than by using a news magazine format? Creative director Kirk Kahrs helped change perspectives by borrowing the Time *magazine look; but to further illustrate that Interlake was more than just a iron and steel company, he showed their diversification by inserting advertising for the material handling, ferro alloy and conveyance subsidiaries of Interlake. Angelo Sardina directed the art for it. HGSO of Oak Brook produced this annual report; Kirk Kahrs, creative director and copy; Angelo Sardina, art director and designer. Reprinted with permission from the Interlake Corporation.*

Great Expectations

The annual report is expected to accomplish a great deal. Although it is perceived as a nuts and bolts publication which provides a simple financial overview of a company, its functions are many. Its primary purpose is to provide stockholders with a yearly checkup on their organization's financial health. But generally, annual reports are driven by an unwritten agenda that may be much more important than jumping through the SEC hoop. When thoughtfully conceived, precisely targeted and meticulously executed, an annual report can be a marvelous piece of information, advertising and/or public relations.

The following sections examine some of these other uses. While not every purpose is explored here, we want to point out that annual reports can handle plenty more than bean counting.

Information vehicle

Although all annual reports are informational by nature, a good percentage of them appear to be anything but informative. A quick trip through the jungle of annual reports makes this point clear. Most do little more than go through the financial calisthenics mapped out by the SEC. For starters, their numbers stand like monuments to intuitive accounting without much, if any, explanation. Histograms and fever charts provide little graphic relief, and usually have about the same amount of written information as the accounting sheets.

Figure 9.8

Some of the best annual reports adopt magazine formats. That's the tactic taken for this striking Plum Creek Annual Report. The CEO provides a brief but thorough overview on the inside cover in much the same way as an editor might highlight an issue or make an editorial statement. Note the very sophisticated table of contents page on the right. Hornall Anderson of Seattle produced this exemplary report. Jani Drewfs directed the art and, along with Paula Cox and Denise Weir, designed it. Cover photography by Kevin Latona. Reprinted with permission from Plum Creek and Hornall Anderson Design Works.

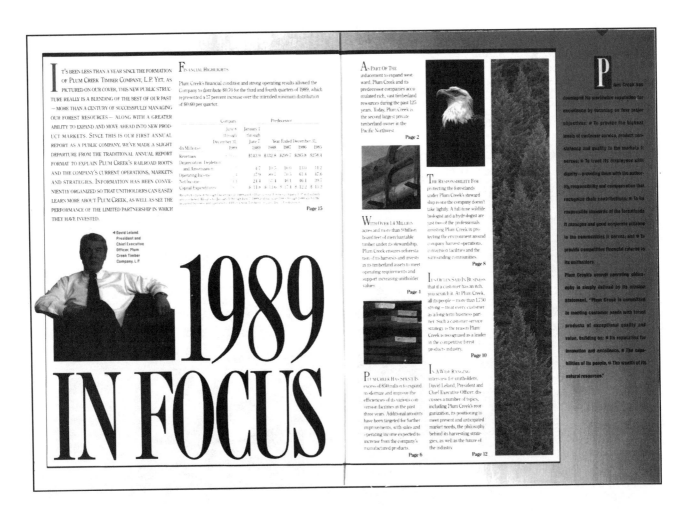

Figure 9.9 _____

Jay Jacobs is one of the West's leading clothing retailers. Mostly, they sell upscale fashions. This annual report reflects that in several ways. To begin with, this Hornall Anderson design is equally upscale and fashionable. The text blocks on the first page of the report have been crafted to accent and contour the diamond cropping on the photograph here. (Also note the diamond endmarks.) A pullout on the far middle right of the right page calls attention to the fact that sales had increased 11%, which surpassed their $100 million milestone. The fold-over (on left) holds a very positive quotation from the California Apparel News, *and its jagged line on the fold-over between the blue and mauve repeats the same pattern established by the die-cut on the edge of the left page. This is another beautiful design and production from Hornall Anderson; it was designed by Luann Bice, Jack Anderson and Mary Hermes. Art direction by Jack Anderson and Luann Bice. Photography was shot by Kevin Latona, Sylvia South, Phillip Dixon and Dan Lamont. Reprinted with permission from Jay Jacobs and Hornall Anderson Design Works.*

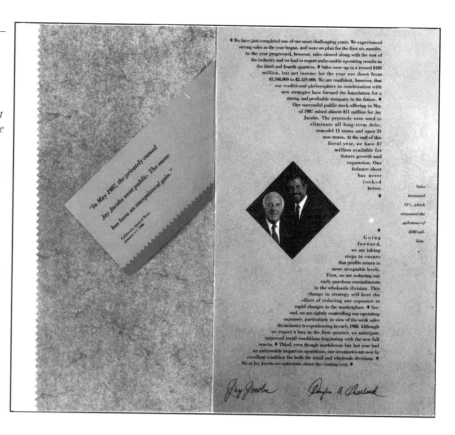

Figure 9.10 _____

The left copy block is bi-functional: it continues the triangular text-shaping established on the first page, and it works as a directional device, pointing our vision to artwork and copy on the opposite page. Furthermore, the rich color, meticulous arrangement and fashion photography make these pages look more like they came from a spendy fashion magazine than an annual report. See the previous credits for acknowledgements. Designed by Hornall Anderson. Reprinted with permission from Jay Jacobs and Hornall Anderson Design Works.

Figure 9.11 _____

Design is central to how you're perceived by your public. Often, new investors know you by little more than word of mouth, financial news, daily returns and your annual report. High fashion is communicated again here in this Jay Jacobs cover. Compare its elemental form strategies to the two previous figures; also find the appropriate credits there. Design by Hornall Anderson of Seattle. Reprinted with permission from Jay Jacobs and Hornall Anderson Design Works.

Figure 9.12 _____

Here the diamond-shaped, outer cover points to the quotation noted earlier—as do the die-cut edges of the second cover, which also bears Jay Jacobs' signature. The point of seeing the cover opened, partially opened, etc. is so you can fully examine the functional and aesthetic characteristics of this memorable design. It was designed by Luann Bice, Jack Anderson and Mary Hermes. Art direction by Jack Anderson and Luann Bice. Photography was shot by Kevin Latona, Sylvia South, Phillip Dixon and Dan Lamont. Reprinted with permission from Jay Jacobs and Hornall Anderson Design Works.

What few words do exist border on cryptic. The reader is staggered by professional jargon, left reeling from parochialism and slugged into unconsciousness by out and out boring writing. Getting through reports like these is nearly impossible.

Some annual reports take the opposite tack. These are pretentious "snowjobs" that attempt to disguise an off year with graphic glitz and glitter. But burying the truth is not part of the SEC's master plan for annual reports. Graphics and a good design should not mislead or gloss over the facts. What's more, good design isn't superficial or cosmetic. Its structure and function should make the truth more understandable, not cover it up with a trendy veneer.

News

Annual reports have a remarkable opportunity to bring new information to their audience. In the best of worlds this news would always be the good kind; and, indeed, corporations and organizations commonly have good news to tell. Often companies don't seize the opportunity to inform their publics of timely developments. What better time exists? How better can you target an audience? If you have relevant information for your investors that is also timely, lead with it.

But news need not be all good. Typically you'll have mixed news. While most reports lead with the good and don't dwell on the bad, bringing bad news to your audience can be to your advantage as well. However much that makes you wince or seems convoluted, it's likely your stockholders will get this news even faster than the good news

Figure 9.13

This Potlatch annual report epitomizes using the annual report as an information vehicle. Readers will not only learn about economic and financial highlights, they'll get an education on logging. The cover features loggers, cat drivers, skidder operators and others. Design by Jonson Pedersen Hinrichs & Shakery. Photography by Tom Tracy. Reprinted with permission from Potlatch Corporation and Kit Hinrichs.

Figure 9.14

It is fitting that the large stripped out image of the logger dominate this layout about loggers. The photograph not only supports the content, it brings emphasis, proportion, balance, sequence and unity to the spread. It also helps establish a loose grid of sorts. These pages bring you everything you ever wanted to know about a logger—from what he eats to what he chews. In addition, the clothing and equipment of loggers from Arkansas, Idaho and Minnesota are compared—lower left. A sidebar—upper right—also shares some colorful logger titles with us. A most informative and interesting two pages. Design by Kit Hinrichs; photography by Tom Tracy; camp cook photo from the Minnesota Historical Society. Illustrations by Justin Carroll, Will Nelson and Colleen Quinn. Reprinted with permission from Potlatch Corporation and Kit Hinrichs.

▼

Financial Highlights   Potlatch Corporation and Consolidated Subsidiaries

(Dollars in thousands—except per-share amounts)	1983	1982	1981
Net sales	$906,745	$820,180	$880,493
Net earnings	40,467	22,533	57,804
Per common share:			
Net earnings	$ 2.03	$ .87	$ 3.25
Cash dividends paid	1.48	1.48	1.42
Common stockholders' equity	35.48	34.93	35.55
Working capital	$ 92,587	$112,244	$112,082
Depreciation, amortization and cost of			
fee timber harvested	60,083	57,096	54,640
Capital expenditures	54,188	54,156	217,911
Long-term debt (noncurrent portion)	299,718	344,417	348,887
Common stockholders' equity	545,398	535,020	544,297

Founded in 1903 in Potlatch, Idaho, Potlatch Corp. is an integrated forest products company with 1.4 million acres of timberland in Arkansas, Idaho and Minnesota. Our manufacturing facilities convert wood fibers into two main lines of products: solid wood items (lumber, plywood, oriented strand board, particleboard and wood specialties) and bleached fiber products (bleached kraft pulp and paperboard, printing and business papers, packaging and household tissue).

Potlatch's business philosophy is to maintain a growing profit and reasonable rate of return, achieved by talented, well trained and highly motivated people, properly supported by a sound financial structure and a keen sense of social responsibility to all of the publics with whom the company has contact.

anyway, with or without you. By including it, you'll at least have the chance to explain the reasons for the bad news and provide them the full story.

Whether you take the straight informational approach or the news approach, remember that annual reports afford you a tremendous forum to tell a meaningful story to your stockholders in order to help them make intelligent decisions. If you keep that in mind, your design will become more functional and appropriate to your report.

Image

It's not by accident that so much talent, money and attention is put into creating corporate reports. Your annual report will be closely inspected not only because it provides hard numbers but also because it supplies a sense of who you are. It gives you a face and a personality, and does so collectively, through numbers, words and image.

A company's image campaign should begin with those most familiar with it—its stockholders and the more financially astute public that studies the corporate environment, provides the lion's share of its financial backing and freely enters the stock market crapshoot. Companies can use their reports to strengthen how they are perceived by this audience, reinforce established loyalties, attract new investors or shake up predisposed presumptions. They may even entirely reposition themselves in the market place. All via image.

Design is central to how you're perceived by your public. Often, investors know you by little more than word of mouth, financial news, daily returns and your annual report. However, the latter is most lasting, most easily retrievable and best remembered because it provides a fairly detailed picture of who you are. It holds you in your strongest light, and it may be your strongest public relations card. Don't sell it short.

Figure 9.15 _____

This layout uses symmetry and a simple grid for its layout of the Potlatch Operations page. Here, wood products are featured; the photograph uses diagonal elemental form. As a student of design, ask yourself why the designer and photographer chose to include the hammer in this photo? Credits cited earlier. Reprinted with permission from Potlatch Corporation and Kit Hinrichs.

Cosmic calling card

Annual reports are a kind of inked hotline to who you are and what you're up to financially. Regardless of the tales you may hear that only jaded or jaundiced eyes see your annual pages, take heart. Good investors look for tangible reasons why they should purchase your stock or not sell off. Your annual report can help clarify those reasons.

Because your audience wants *tangible* reasons why they should align with you, work them visually. A good calling card connects quickly and memorably. And it is turned over again and again in the mind's eye. The best calling cards are not only those that aren't thrown away, they're the ones that carry positive associations. Your report should have that kind of physical and mental visibility. It should identify changing trends, analyze fiscal worth, present sensible and understandable information and do so distinctively.

Here's the cosmic part. The average stockholder sees dozens of reports over the course of a year. Corporate investors see hundreds. Yours should stand out visually and connect to the past, the present and the future. Thread all three to the report visually, memorably. It's easy to stand on past achievement, show a current success or make promises about a bright and prosperous future. But if you expect to be successful, you must relate all three in a sensible and credible fashion. Good investors don't direct smart money to past laurels, hot seasons or inflated promises.

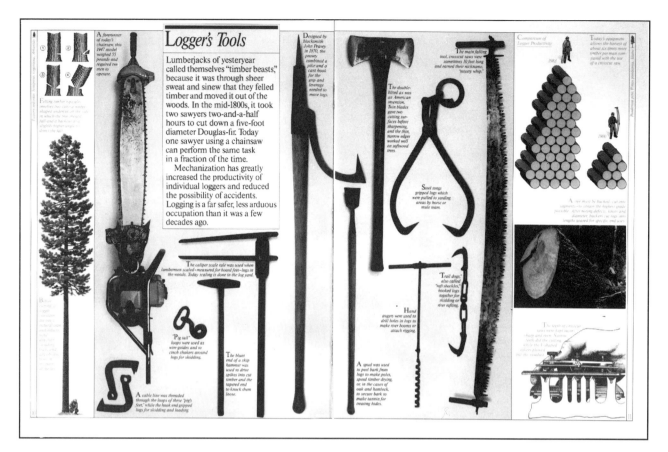

Figure 9.16

Designer Kit Hinrichs chose to treat the tools here vertically. Notice how he used the modules to either side of the tools spread: on the left we learn something about how to use them, while on the right we're given an information graphic comparing logging production from the turn of the century to today. Form follows function. Design by Jonson Pederson Hinrichs & Shakery. Photography by Tom Tracy. Illustration by Justin Carroll, Will Nelson and Colleen Quinn. Reprinted with permission from Potlatch Corporation.

Recruitment kit, or you want us

Annual reports should be able to stand alone as respectable, hard-working publications. And, although it is very important to set your sights on a particular audience and write and design to that target, some of today's corporate reports are being written and designed to do more than one thing.

Along with recruiting the stockholder's investment, annual reports may also turn up another kind of recruit. Yearly reports flesh out the whole of one financial season at a single reading, provide bottom lines, top priorities and middle-of-the-road politics. They give the long and short of expenditure and investment. They succinctly outline company history and honestly examine current problems, missions and direction. They present an interesting picture, painting part of the corporate canvas in broad strokes, while detailing other portions with painstakingly meticulous precision. What better way to woo corporate investment or recruit prospective employees?

It is in vogue to adapt yearly reports to a less rigid publication format. In this case, many of the charts and graphs are often replaced by striking photography that graphically plots a company's social commitment, community involvement or revolutionary innovation. Covers can be fitted with pockets to carry cover letters, literature explaining company health and insurance benefits, two decades of company stock earning information, retirement packages or the successes of research and development projects.

Have an Idea

Usually, an annual report adopts a theme, central concept or some other common denominator that becomes its internal unifying element, its inner touchstone. Likewise, there are countless ways to establish continuity through the typography, design, photography and general visual style of the publication. These unifiers are external and may apply to your design in a functional or superficial manner.

But remember the philosophy of the Bauhaus: form always follows function. Design is not a flimsy quick-change to be slipped in and out of like a disguise. It is the structure that connects the central idea of any publication to its audience. The primary concern and focus of the Bauhaus was that successful design facilitate communication, not become a barrier to it. Proponents linked conceptual, visual and written ideas so that they reflected and reinforced one another.

Let's say, for example, that your annual report's theme is ecological. In it you provide statistics about how your company has cleaned up not only its immediate environment but the larger one around it. In addition, you've decided to run a number of before and after photographs that show and tell your story memorably. One way to integrate the concept into your design might be to provide generous white space and run a classic roman typeface with a clean, fresh look. (Of course, the writing would be equally clean and efficient.) To take the concept even further, you might consider using recycled, biodegradable paper and chemically safe inks. This brings the design logic full circle, because it, too, shows and tells a tremendous amount about your sensibility and commitment to an ecologically balanced environment.

Certainly it would be in our best interests for all of us to use environmentally safe printing materials. That goes without saying. But this example shows how design extends beyond the drawing board and into the hands of the reader. In this instance, it put the commitment of the company in black and white.

Design—Helping It All Add Up

Although you are not responsible for your report's statistics, projected expenditures, accounting records and financial statements, as a designer you are obligated to help your audience make quick sense of them. That's why organization is imperative. Take it

Figure 9.17

*Compare this more recent Potlatch Annual Report Operations page to one that was produced two years earlier. (See **Figure 9.15**.) Credits are the same as those listed in **Figure 9.13**. Design by Jonson Pederson Hinrichs and Shakery. Photography by Tom Tracy. Reprinted with permission from Potlatch Corporation.*

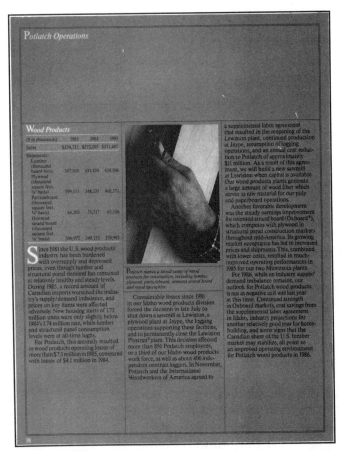

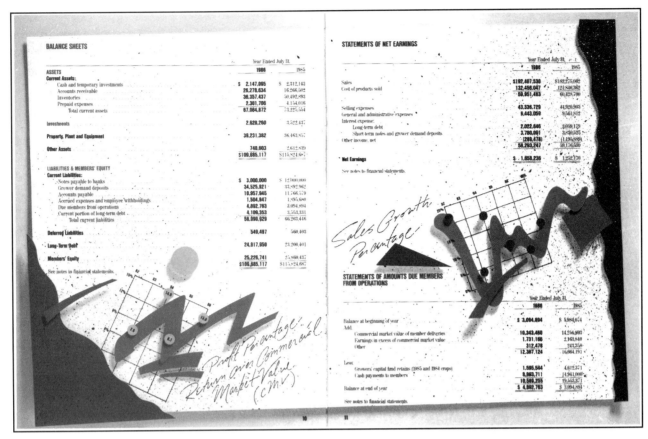

Figure 9.18

Numbers take up a disproportionate amount of space in the annual report. In order to best communicate their message, you need to combine words and images to interpret, explain and provide both meaning and relevance. Bruce Hale used computers to create dropped shadows and add a three-dimensional quality to these charts. John Hornall and Luann Bice directed the art and designed this flashy report. Bruce Hale created the illustration. Reprinted with permission from Tree Top and Hornall Anderson Design Works.

seriously; your readers do. If your report takes a chronological approach, make sure you're logged in properly and haven't transposed or juxtaposed figures and information. If you're working by subject or department, check to see that your figures and information are properly aligned. Also, check and double-check your master plan to make sure you've covered all the SEC questions and requirements. Do your answers to those questions show up where they're supposed to show up? Have you omitted anything?

Some information must appear in a specific typeface, point size and leading indicated by the SEC; other information must be supplied but where you put it is your decision. With that in mind, establish your priorities. Not all of the statistics and numbers included in the average annual report have equal billing. Some are more important; others don't lend themselves to any kind of meaningful graphic interpretation. Besides, you don't have the rest of your life to invent and execute a graphic design for every single statistic and accounting sheet in the report.

Here's another graphics principle you should never forget: if the numbers speak for themselves, don't butt in. Your job is not to make the obvious condescending—it's to facilitate communication.

Graphics—Working Figures Figuratively

Numbers take up a disproportionate amount of space in the annual report. After all, this kind of report is a formal discussion of an organization's financial activity over the course of a year. Right?

Well, yes and no.

To be sure, annual reports publicly air a company's financial laundry. And bottom lines read best in black and white. Too often, though, numbers don't carry the same significance to the average report reader that they do to the accountant or financial analyst who prepared them. In order to best communicate their message, you need to combine words and images to interpret, explain and provide both meaning and relevance.

Sometimes numbers need to be expressed in a variety of ways to be meaningful. Not all of us are sufficiently schooled to interpret figures much beyond basic arithmetic. Often, too, it takes pictographic imagery to simplify or extrapolate figures. That's why percentage, statistics, pie charts, histograms and fever charts are as important to understanding numbers as they are to understanding these publications. In an annual report, if the numbers get fuzzed up or their meanings confused, you've failed.

Not even accountants and economists take numbers at their face value. They look beyond their unit measure by interpreting tables, indices and financial reports to align that information with economic theory and marketing strategies. Economics is more than something simply adding up.

Figure 9.19 and **9.20** _____

Pie charts show proportion and percentages well. They may also compare figures clearly, as this Interlake report page demonstrates. In the lower example, the upper ground thirds area is used for both sidebar and graphic purposes; the graphics on the left page are illustrated, those on the right are stripped-in photography. Art direction and design by Angelo Sardina of HGSO; creative director, Kirk Kahrs. Reprinted with permission from the Interlake Corporation.

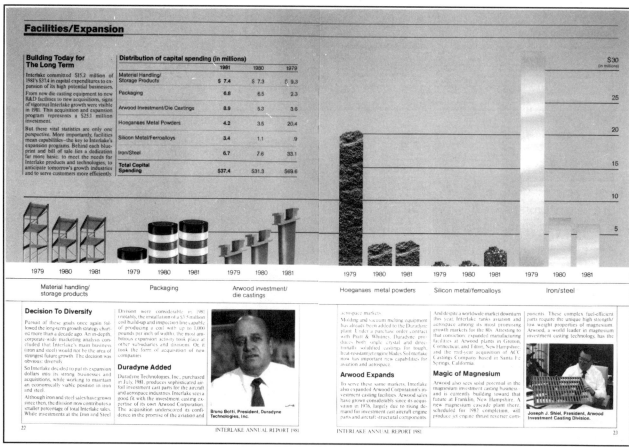

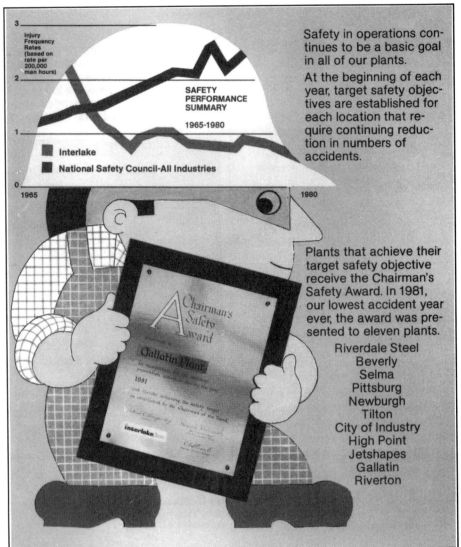

Within the figure:

Injury Frequency Rates (based on rate per 200,000 man hours)

SAFETY PERFORMANCE SUMMARY 1965–1980

3
2
1
0

1965   1980

■ Interlake
■ National Safety Council-All Industries

Safety in operations continues to be a basic goal in all of our plants.

At the beginning of each year, target safety objectives are established for each location that require continuing reduction in numbers of accidents.

Chairman's Safety Award

Gallatin Plant

1981

Plants that achieve their target safety objective receive the Chairman's Safety Award. In 1981, our lowest accident year ever, the award was presented to eleven plants.

Riverdale Steel
Beverly
Selma
Pittsburg
Newburgh
Tilton
City of Industry
High Point
Jetshapes
Gallatin
Riverton

Figure 9.21 _____

Nigel Holmes, who works as design director at Time, *has had a tremendous visual influence on newspapers and magazines around the world. But information graphics are now also common to the annual report. This one from an Interlake report compares their safety record to national figures. Creative director: Kirk Kahrs; art director: Angelo Sardina. HGSO designed and produced this annual report. Reprinted with permission from the Interlake Corporation.*

What do the numbers really mean? That is a fair and good question that your report should answer. Your facts and figures must be correct, clear, understandable and quickly digestible. The best measure of how well you answer questions is this: can the reader both understand and communicate the information easily to others?

Get the Right Tool for the Right Job Department

It would seem outrageous to see someone attempting to drive nails with a saw. And yet charts and graphs, both amazing tools of graphic design, are misused regularly. It's very important to select the correct chart or graph for the problem your numbers and statistics present. If you don't, you're likely to confuse or misinform your audience. That's why effective graphics are best performed by those who understand statistics as well as they understand illustration and design.

Charts and graphs shouldn't merely illustrate. They should be used to clarify information, facilitate understanding and streamline communication. If information graphics are blatantly redundant, they're pointless.

Different charts and graphs chart and map differently. Know the basic distinctions and specific applications of each.

Because **pie charts** show proportion and percentages so well, they are a standard charting tool of designers. Readers can use them to quickly compare individual parts to one another as well as to the whole. Be careful not to present them at odd angles that distort the proportions. On the other hand, both **bar** (horizontally oriented) and **column** (vertically oriented) charts make quick studies in individual comparisons. Designers choose between them depending upon whether the graphics they incorporate have vertical or horizontal direction. Although they only provide one-directional information, they are an effective and widely used charting method. **Fever charts** reveal temporal fluctuation. They are especially suited to annual reports because of their association with the Dow-Jones' approach of mapping out money and time in a meaningful way, be it the course of action over one day's or one year's time. Fever charts are bidirectional and measure two variables concurrently. **Histograms** (or **step charts**) are actually a variation of bar and column charts. They differ from the latter in that histogram columns touch. Because they measure two variables, you might wish to think of them as a perpendicular version of the fever chart. **Pictographs**, most commonly seen in *USA Today*, integrate bars, lines and "straight" chart or graph parts with pictorial representation. They may be incorporated into any type of chart or graph. Although they are less precise, they are memorable and

Figure 9.22

There are a number of ways to explain numbers' meaning. One of the best, however, is to have whoever is responsible for preparing them give a succinct explanation of what they mean in a sidebar. Here the controller and treasurer give a written accounting of their financial statements. Copywriting and creative direction by Kirk Kahrs. Art direction by Angelo Sardina. Reprinted with permission from the Interlake Corporation.

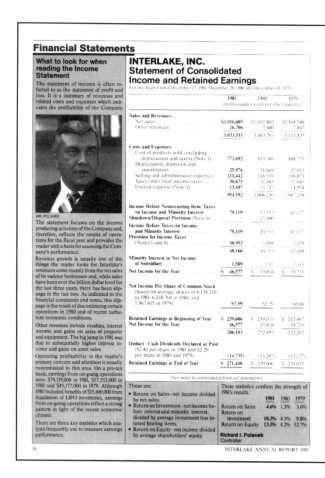

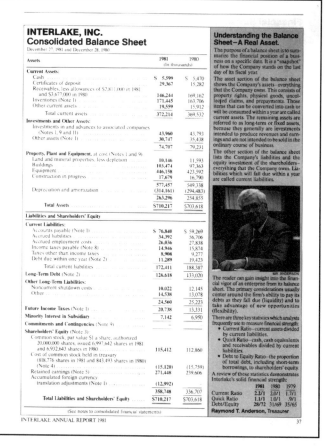

bring a special human touch to numbers and statistics. Don't defeat your purpose by making pictographs so involved and complicated that they confuse rather than simplify. **Flow** and **illustrative charts** best demonstrate process or assemblage. Flow charts tend to be more publication-oriented while illustrative charts are standard for instructions. Flow charts may map a natural chronology or process. Illustrative charts take you by the hand and walk you through the construction of anything from a model airplane to a sophisticated stereo receiver. For a remarkably insightful discussion and thorough demonstration of these graphic forms, see Jan V. White's *Using Charts and Graphs*.

Bringing Meaning to Charts and Graphs or Personalizing Statistics

Many of us find statistics frightening. When we are faced with a page of numbers and percentages, our senses numb and reasoning quickly leaves us. We have a pictographic preference. Pictures are capable of simplifying numbers, complex information, abstract ideas and simple process through illustration and visual association. We reveal such preferences in everything from a simple magazine or newspaper read to assembling toys Christmas night. When pushed to the limit, we read the dreaded directions. And should they prove to complex or cryptic for us, we resort to the modern hieroglyphics of pictographic diagram. No doubt you've had this experience.

In annual reports, too, charts and graphs help clarify statistics and economic trends. Our eyes follow the quickest path to understanding and we give pictures a high visual priority because they communicate quickly to us. When pictures,

Figure 9.23 _____
This very dramatic sidebar for First Florida Banks, Inc. speaks to their broad spectrum of successful investment options; the montaged illustration on the adjoining page helps flesh out those words. First Florida Banks annual report designed and produced by Hill and Knowlton/Chicago. Art direction by Andrew Brown and design by Kathy Keen. Frank Miller executed the illustration. Reprinted with permission from Hill and Knowlton and First Florida Banks, Inc.

statistics and numbers can be combined in a meaningful way, they can be quite an efficient communication model.

Today's readers process more information but have less time and less patience with reading. Realizing this, Nigel Holmes continues to perfect the art of information graphics. A few years ago, he revitalized *Time* magazine through his graphic genius, and impacted the entire world of publications, changing the look and structure of magazines as well as newspapers. His graphic style strongly influenced *USA Today* and its propensity for locater maps, computerized diagrams, charts and sophisticated graphics. Annual reports, too, reflect today's move toward using information graphics.

Holmes points out that successful information graphics must be accurate, relevant, suitable, simple and clear. And the designer or illustrator must also have an intimate knowledge of the audience. Remember, too, that graphics have a marvelous capacity to editorialize, something that annual reports have tremendous potential to do. But don't

Figure 9.24 and **9.25** _____

The cover for this stylish NIKE Annual Report prints copy and artwork atop a light grey 1989 run on its side. Note how the vertical slash partially underscores it. (Like some of the trim on NIKE sportswear, the slash is run in bright, dayglow orange.) Cover photography by Aaron Jones, Steve Wilkes, Gary Nolton and Pete Stone. Designed by Ann Schwiebinger.Note how the inside copy area is nearly identical to the cover. Also, all inside pages have the lower right edge trimmed diagonally from the lower right corner to mirror the effect established by the report cover. A very interesting design ploy which adds to the excitement of this NIKE report. Designed at NIKE by Ann Schwiebinger. Inside image of Andre Agassi by Steve Wilkes. Printed with permission from NIKE, Inc.

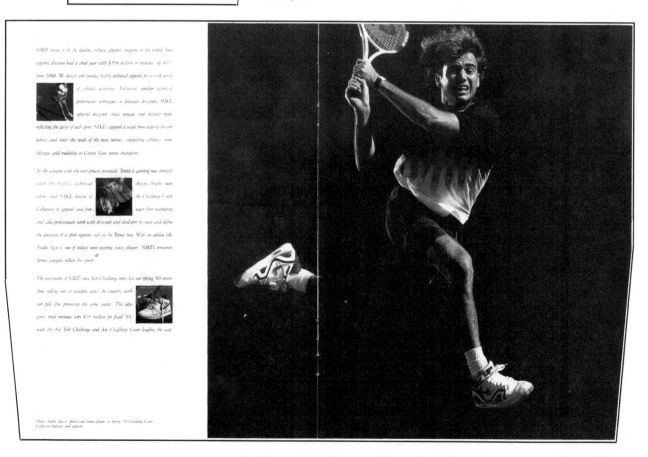

misuse pictographic approaches. Too often, Holmes warns, designers and editors use them for decorative purposes. Think function first in all you do.

Sidebars—Explaining the Bottom Line

This author has an unwritten law that anyone who turns in a page of numbers to a designer or editor must also hand in a brief, understandable explanation of them. Along with those comments is expected a handful of sentences demonstrating the numbers' relevance and a short list of visual ideas. Those documents are duplicated. One set goes into a file and the others are passed on to the project's visual people, who find them a good starting point.

Sidebars based on these explanations can solve all kinds of problems inherent in the tables and budget sheets that must be included in the annual report. They fit the editorial mold. And we're used to seeing supportive material brace and align related stories in magazines and newspapers. We also like the humanistic touch that sidebars add. In annual reports, accounting statements and other tables are often the main story. But their numbers stand alone, naked in their cold and hard reality without explanation or any real human connection. So why not have the person responsible for the numbers, explain them? Who better to interpret and explain the numbers than their creator?

If your president, fiscal officer or other appropriate spokesperson can articulate the meaning behind the figures, sidebars will add credibility to your report. Normally, they incorporate a mug or environmental portrait within their layout, so the reader can see who compiled this year's record earnings or projected next year's increases. Dropping the sidebar into a ground thirds design via tint blocks provides emphasis, sequence and proportion. (See **Figure 9.22**.)

Figure 9.26 _____

It is important to establish continuity throughout the report. Michael Jordon, whose NIKE endorsement is familiar to all of us, is photographed here in more of a fashion than athletic shot. Photography, again, by Steve Wilkes. See how the copy area echoes what we've seen in previous pages from this report? Design by Ann Schwiebinger. Reprinted with permission from NIKE, Inc.

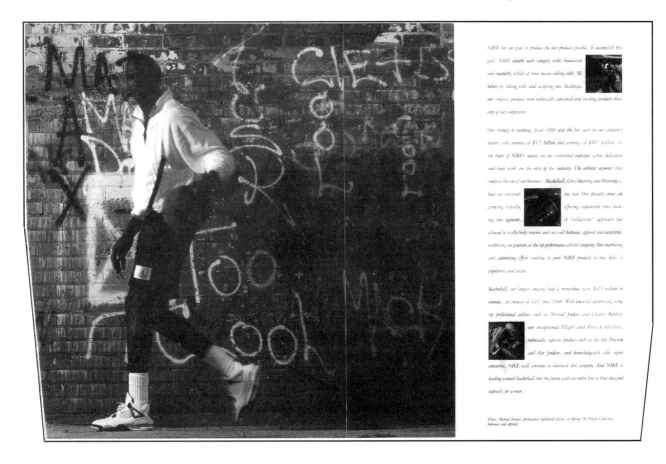

Integrating Your Information to the Theme

Figure 9.27 and **9.28** _____

You see one of several thumbnails sketched after the client decided not to run a montaged timeline as the artwork. The hands were used to suggest the personal care Florence Crittenton clients receive. Thumbnail sketch by Bill Ryan.

Here is a rough of the thumbnail above. This designer prefers to work with a combination of Xeroxed art possibilities and real type—that is, the speced out heads, subheads, text, etc. that will be used in the publication. That makes for few surprises with the type. It also forces writers to come to terms with copy earlier. See earlier credit. Reprinted with permission from Florence Crittenton and Ryan Design.

Like most magazines, an annual report should establish its theme or concept on its cover. This is what your shareholders and other audience members see first and last. And it is probably what will come to mind when they think of the report. Along with establishing or communicating the theme, covers should attract attention, serve as a window to the inside and project your organization's image.

Remember, too, that the cover carries more than artwork. If color is expected to play a significant role in the design, apply it adroitly on the cover. Color can establish a mood, reinforce your organization's identity, or suggest cool objectivity or excitement. It can warm your audience or underscore your image. Its importance is second only to the overall visual idea. So make it a priority when previsualizing and arranging your photography, illustration and type. Use it in the dress of whoever peoples your photography, as well as in the backgrounds and environs of the art. Use it thoughtfully in tint blocks, screens, dropped initial letters, rules and other typographical decisions.

Normally, the annual report cover consists of artwork, a title and/or company logotype or nameplate and a few coverlines. Nameplates and logotypes have prescribed typography; some of which are commonly borrowed for other cover parts.

The guts of the report, your inner pages, should continue the theme visually. Continuity can be further reinforced by sticking to a single photographer or illustrator—that individual's style will make the visual imagery appear more unified. Make sure you employ color, graphics style, artwork and type consistently throughout the publication. Obviously, the theme's elements—visual and nonvisual alike—should be equally consistent.

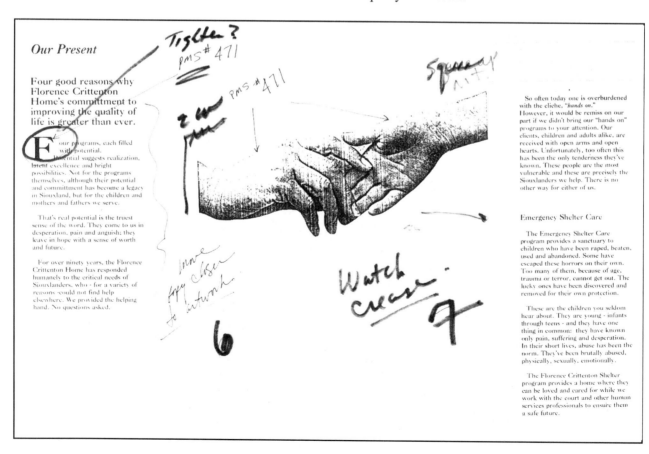

Photography is by far the preferred approach to artwork in annual reports. Because it is highly representational and documentary, its inherent ability to visually record imagery explicitly gives it tremendous credibility—something central to the success of the report. When coupled with the appropriate photography, clear, objective language and detailed financial analyses become not only more understandable, but more believable. Although good illustration can tackle most problems this publication form presents, it cannot match photography's credibility. That's why it is not used nearly as often, and seldom as the sole visual medium of the report.

Generally speaking, appropriate visuals help connect the concept or theme to the report; they work as visual metaphor. Through illustration, style and analogy, they bring added form to your report's content. Thematic visuals provide both unity and continuity. Third, they improve communication, increase credibility and make your report more memorable.

The Planning and Layout Process

Most designers and photographers prefer to work with a combination of thumbnails, rough layouts, xerography and snapshots to lay out the design and visual particulars of the report. Ideally both use their swipe files to plug clippings and predisposed ideas into the layouts.

The average design begins with grid variations that establish the architecture and look of the report. Will it be formal or informal, traditional or contemporary, conservative or flamboyant? How many columns and column variations will there be? Is the layout basically a vertical or horizontal one? How do margins and

Figure 9.29 _____

The sequencing in the photography was altered to extend the idea of the two hands coming together. (See previous figure to compare art.) Two color was used for this report. Sepia—PMS #471—was run on a linen, ivory-colored paper to enhance the personal feel and to warm up the black and white photography. Only the art and dropped initial letters were run in sepia. (The other color was black.) Bill Ryan wrote, designed and photographed this award-winning piece for Florence Crittenton. See credits from previous figure. Reprinted with permission from Florence Crittenton and Ryan Design.

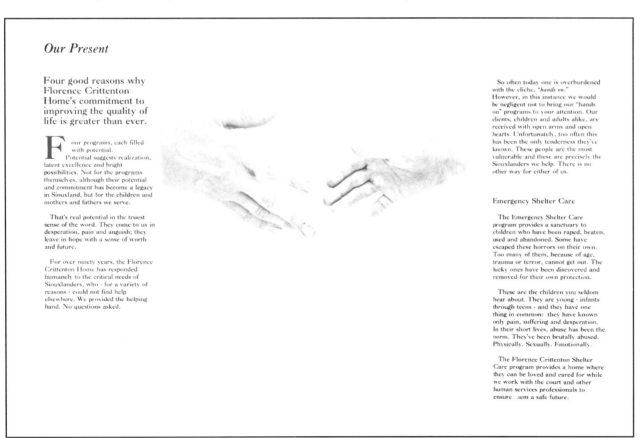

Our Present

Four good reasons why Florence Crittenton Home's commitment to improving the quality of life is greater than ever.

Four programs, each filled with potential. Potential suggests realization, latent excellence and bright possibilities. Not for the programs themselves, although their potential and commitment has become a legacy in Siouxland, but for the children and mothers and fathers we serve.

That's real potential in the truest sense of the word. They come to us in desperation, pain and anguish; they leave in hope with a sense of worth and future.

For over ninety years, the Florence Crittenton Home has responded humanely to the critical needs of Siouxlanders, who - for a variety of reasons - could not find help elsewhere. We provided the helping hand. No questions asked.

So often today one is overburdened with the cliche, "hands on." However, in this instance we would be negligent not to bring our "hands on" programs to your attention. Our clients, children and adults alike, are received with open arms and open hearts. Unfortunately, too often this has been the only tenderness they've known. These people are the most vulnerable and these are precisely the Siouxlanders we help. There is no other way for either of us.

Emergency Shelter Care

The Emergency Shelter Care program provides a sanctuary to children who have been raped, beaten, used and abandoned. Some have escaped these horrors on their own. Too many of them, because of age, trauma or terror, cannot get out. The lucky ones have been discovered and removed for their own protection.

These are the children you seldom hear about. They are young - infants through teens - and they have one thing in common: they have known only pain, suffering and desperation. In their short lives, abuse has been the norm. They've been brutally abused. Physically. Sexually. Emotionally.

The Florence Crittenton Shelter Care program provides a home where they can be loved and cared for while we work with the court and other human services professionals to ensure ..tem a safe future.

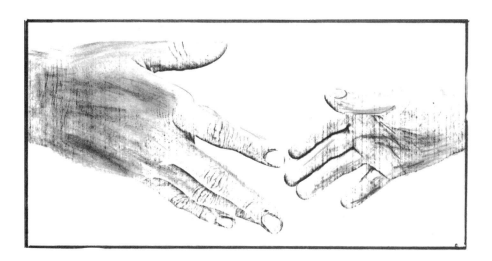

Figure 9.30, 9.31 and 9.32 _____

*Here are three of many photo-
graphic sequences for the report.
The designer insisted upon
photography because of its
credibility. It was decided that using
models (full view) would have
compromised the truth, while
working with clients might have
risked individual privacy; consequently, tight shots of the hands
were used for the art.*

*Among other things, counsel-
ors and social workers at Florence
Crittenton bring people together.
Certainly, it is one of the most
exciting parts of what they do.
Hands—reaching, accepting and
finally loving—expressed those
concepts and more. Additionally,
there was no faking up the photography. Art direction and photography by Bill Ryan. Reprinted with
permission from Ryan Design.*

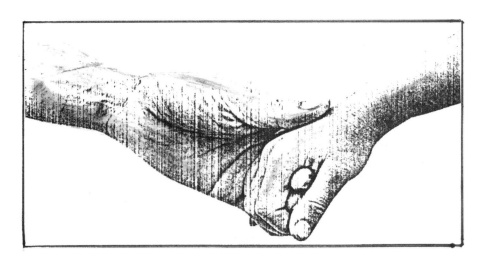

white space figure into the look? Along with being a blueprint of any project, the grid can serve as a quick visual sampler to help you clarify direction. This is the point where you should create a fairly extensive dummy. A **dummy** is a collection of page roughs for a magazine or annual report; usually, they are arranged chronologically to offer the editor a designer a quick overview of the publication. Often, the dummy pages are crudely executed thumbnails.

This experimental layout process helps define what the style will be and how it will be refined and executed. These rough layouts give everyone a quick compositional overview, while providing a fairly clear, initial idea of content. Although both style and content may change considerably, you establish a starting point. This also provides the flavor or feel of the report's pictorial essence. By beginning with a variety of visual possibilities, the designer and artist/photographers can begin planning all of the report. It's important that they share how the visuals will strengthen the text and bring explicit and inferred meaning to it. (It is important, too, that you—or whoever is appointed visual coordinator and sign-off person—not only have initial and final approval, but have a say in the project throughout its progress.)

Initial layouts also help establish how space will be worked out between the text and pictorial elements of the report. You need to budget space early. The most obvious element is typography. How much space will be needed to accommodate borders, white space, typeface selections, point size, leading, style, line length and arrangement and other stylebook considerations? What about your charts, tables and other graphic information? How prominently will the artwork factor into the design? Writers need to be told that they have a specific amount of words to work with for the president's report, financial statements, sidebars and the like. Graphic artists need to know sizes and scale for charts, information graphics, artwork and all other report elements.

Report page flow charts for pages and dummies are then created and approved for the overall layout. Sample galleys, using the type specifications of the annual report's stylebook, are then greeked and finessed into the layout and what will ultimately become the final design. However boring or tedious it might seem, this budgeting process is central to the success of the designer's vision, the photographer's imagery, the writers' words and the graphic artist's work. If the designer's formula is substantially off, the architecture of the annual report will be in a state of flux.

Create a work plan. It should indicate responsibilities, meetings, long- and short-term goals, and a schedule that maps out all important dates, times and deadlines. That means exactly what it says: deadlines for everything from initial layout approval to the first copy review, from final paste-ups to when the report is due at the printer's. Work plans are created to facilitate this process so that your report is developed logically and smoothly. Live up to the plan and its timeline, and your report will more likely reach its full potential.

Ultimately, the designer must make any required adjustments. Keeping this type of juggling to a minimum is highly desirable. Foul-ups mean rewriting, needless editing, reapportioning visual space, compromising the design itself and sometimes reconfiguring production particulars. (Like changing the number of pages in a report, shrinking or expanding borders and white space, or moving type onto previously blank pages.) They also mean that all sorts of additional pressures will be forced on you in order to meet established deadlines. Although some trouble and last minute chaos are expected in any report, major surgery and widespread changes are resented by everyone.

Do You Need Professional Help?

There are three basic approaches to designing and executing an annual report.

1. You can complete the project in house. That means putting a designer to work, yours or one you entrust the entire project to for its duration. It also requires assigning your own art people to the report, or letting your art director or designer hire the art out. Finally, it mandates that you employ your own writers and graphics/statistical people.

2. You can employ an advertising agency or public relations firm to coordinate all of the above. Most likely, they'll be able to complete at least half the work on their own, while spreading the remainder out among copywriters, artists, photographers and graphic designers they know.

Figure 9.33 _____

Samata Associates designed and produced this annual report for Leaf, Inc., an international candy company. And they make no bones about how they approach it. (The cover reads, "We Make Good Fun.") Not even president and CEO Erkki Railo is safe from the impishness. He's not seated in a chrome and leather chair, nor is he looking across the city from a teak-paneled office. Instead, he is surrounded by gumballs with diagonal credits below. This award-winning annual report is a masterpiece of design and photography. Designed by Pat and Greg Samata; photography by Mark Joseph. Reprinted with permission from Leaf, Inc. and Samata Associates.

3. You can turn everything over to a business communications agency that specializes in annual reports. Although some work may be sent out, this type of agency designs, writes and produces both graphics and art for yearly reports—or works regularly with those who do.

Many organizations feel most comfortable generating their own copy—even if it's only the original version—as well as the initial concept of the report. But art and photography are a different matter. Even if a company has a designer and/or artists on staff, those creatives may not have the time, style or situation to work on a project this size. Consequently, it isn't unusual for professional photographers, artists and graphic designers to be brought in to work in their respective areas—photographers being the most common hire.

A major concern in selecting a photographer or illustrator is not that they are competent or highly skilled (that should be a given), but that their style and medium meet your needs. If you've reviewed the work of freelance designers, photographers and illustrators, you've probably kept files and photocopied examples of their work. This is the best starting point for searching out creatives. Remember, though, that you need to keep track of who's available from the freelance pool of talent. Because the best and most stylish are going to be more in demand, they are generally more difficult to employ.

If you haven't an immediate candidate, advertise your needs, specifying content and media preferred for your report. Examine portfolios. Ask to see published examples of their work. And request references in every instance. It's important not only to be sure your artist or photographer is properly fitted stylistically to your project, but that he or she is dependable, easy to work with and can make deadlines.

Before meeting with any freelancers, have a written statement that directly expresses your needs and expectations. Make sure it is written simply and concretely. Thumbnails and swipe files will help articulate your ideas. If you don't feel comfortable speaking the visual language, bring pictures. Having a fixed idea of how you envision the look or spirit of the project is crucial. It should serve as both a yardstick against which to measure the style and skills of your artists, as well as a good visual starting point for the project itself. The point is this: you're likely to be much more successful if you *show* your visual prospectives (or staff) what you have in mind.

Good advertising agencies know the talent. Generally, they can quickly arrange a sampling of photography or illustration for you. You'll pay not only for the talent but for the agency's coordination and finding fees. However, their working knowledge of the artistic talent may save you considerable time and anguish if you don't know the players, their strengths and fees.

Chapter 10

Brochures
Part A: Writing

What most people refer to as brochures are technically called folders, but since the term "brochure" has fallen into common usage, we'll stick with it here. Brochures are usually formed of a single sheet of paper folded one or more times. The folded brochure may be stored conveniently in a pocket, making it literally pocket sized. However, it doesn't have to be. Part of the fun of designing a brochure is choosing its size and number of folds. Although writing for a brochure implies that you already know what size and shape the finished product will be, you can also write first and then determine the size and shape that fits your copy. As with any in-house publication, you can work it either way, fitting copy to design or design to copy. You should take the approach that works best for you, though you may need to cut costs by trimming your copy, or accommodate mandatory information by expanding it. Longer copy is best suited to other formats such as booklets or pamphlets. In any event, brochure copy is usually abbreviated.

Exactly how abbreviated, no one seems to know, for the length of a brochure varies enormously. Information is the key. Most brochures are used to arouse interest, answer questions, and provide sources for further information. Even when used as part of a persuasive campaign, brochures are seldom persuasive in and of themselves; they are support pieces or part of a larger media mix. Brochures can serve as stand-alone display rack literature, as a component of a press kit, or as part of a direct-mail packet. They can vary in length and size and are usually limited only by budget, talent and imagination.

Before you begin to write, you need to determine exactly what your message is. Are you trying to inform or persuade? Is a brochure the best medium for your message? Who is your intended audience? Your format and your style must match your audience's expectations and tastes.

Writing for Brochures: Parameters

Who Is the Intended Audience?

You can refer to **Chapter 1** for detailed information on target audiences. But you can begin by assuming that your audience will be seeking or processing an abbreviated amount of information. Most readers understand that brochures aren't intended to provide long, involved explanations.

There are several audience-centered considerations you should make before you begin writing.

- Is your audience specialized or general? If it is specialized and familiar with your subject, you can use the trade language or jargon familiar to them, no matter how technical it might be. For example, in a brochure on a new chemical product (a copolyester, let's say) you can deal with durometer hardness, temperature-related attributes, resistance to pollutants and weather, and stress characteristics. None of these concepts should be new or surprising to a specialized audience of chemical engineers or designers who use polymers. On the other hand, if your audience is a lay audience, you will have to deal in generalities.

  Here are two examples of a piece on an imaginary copolyester—one for a technical audience (engineers) and one for a less specialized audience (retailers of a manufactured product made from the raw product).

  Technical:

  > The results of laboratory testing indicate AXON II® polyester elastomer is resistant to a wide variety of fuels including leaded and unleaded gasoline, Gasohol, kerosene and diesel fuel. With a hardness range of 92A to 72D durometer, tests show the most fuel-resistant type of copolyester to be the 72D durometer with the other family types also showing an impressive amount of fuel resistance.

  General:

  > AXON II® polyester elastomer offers design potential plus for applications in a variety of industries. On the toughest jobs, AXON II® is proving to be the design material of the future. Its unique properties and flexibility in processing make it applicable in areas previously dependent on a range of other, more expensive, products.

- Are you persuading or informing? If you are persuading your audience, you can use the standard persuasive techniques covered in **Chapter 1** including emotional language, appeal to logic, and association of your idea with another familiar concept. As with print advertising, the tone of the brochure (whether persuasive or informative) is set in the introductory headline. For example, here are two cover titles or headlines from two brochures on graduate programs in journalism. The first is persuasive and the second informative.

  Persuasive:

  > Is one graduate program in journalism better than all the others?
  > Yes.
  > The University of Northern Oregon.

  Informative:

  > Graduate studies in journalism
  > at the University of Northern Oregon.

Regardless of your intent, the brochure copy should always be clear on what you expect of your audience. If you are trying to persuade, state what you want the reader to do—buy your product, invest in your stock, vote for your candidate, support your bond issue. Persuasion only works if people know what it is you want them to be persuaded about.

- How will your audience be using your brochure? Is it intended to stimulate information on a topic for which detailed information can be obtained in another form? Are you going to urge readers to send for more information? Is it meant to be saved as a constant reminder of your topic? Many health-oriented brochures, for example, provide information meant to be saved or even posted for reference, such as calorie charts, vitamin dosages and nutrition information. If your brochure is designed to be read and discarded, don't waste a lot of money on printing. On the other hand, if you want it to be saved, not only should you make the information valuable enough to be saved, but also the look and feel of the brochure should say "don't throw me away." The same is true of any publication. Newspapers, by their inexpensive paper and rub-off ink, say "read me and then throw me away." A magazine like *National Geographic*, on the other hand, says "throw *me* away and you'd be trashing a nice piece of work."

What Is the Format?

Format refers to the way you arrange your brochure—its organizational characteristics. As with everything else about brochures, format can go two ways: you can fit format to your writing or you can fit your writing to a predetermined format. For instance, if you are told to develop a Q & A (question and answer) brochure, you'll have to fit both writing and design to this special format. On the other hand, if you are writing a persuasive piece, you might decide to go with a problem-solution format, spending two panels of a six-panel brochure on setting up the problem and three on describing the solution.

Some organizational formats work well in brochures, some don't. Spatial organization (up to down, right to left, east to west), which can work well in book form or in magazine articles, doesn't seem to fit in a brochure. Neither does chronological organization. The reason for this may be the physical nature of the brochure itself. Magazine and book pages are turned, one after the other; and each page contains quite a lot of information. A brochure demands a more concentrated effort, one that is less natural than leafing through pages. Because each panel is limited in space, development has to take place in "chunks." Organizational formats that require continuous, linked development or constant referral to previous information aren't suited to brochures.

Pick a format that is suited to brochure presentation, or design your brochure to suit your format. Creative brochure design is part of the fun of working with this type of publication. For more on the potential of designing the brochure to suit your needs, see the second part of this chapter.

Support or Stand Alone?

Is your brochure to be used as part of a larger communication package (a press kit, for instance), or is it meant to be a stand-alone piece? If it is part of a larger package, then the information contained in the brochure can be keyed to information elsewhere in the package. If it is a stand-alone piece, it will need to be fairly complete—and probably longer.

The only other consideration to make here concerns writing style. The brochure needs to mimic the style of the package of which it is a component. Obviously, this doesn't mean that it should read like a magazine because it is packaged with a magazine, but it should resemble the companion pieces as closely as possible. If the other pieces are formal, the brochure should be formal; if they are informal, the brochure should be also. The key is consistency.

Length

Succinctness is an art. Almost all writers are able to write long, but very few can write short without editing down from something originally longer. Your information will probably be edited a number of times to make it as spare and succinct as possible, because short copy is the ideal for brochures.

Your copy must be short because of space limitations, in order to leave enough white space for aesthetic value, for type size considerations (for example, a brochure for senior citizens must utilize a fairly large typeface), or for cost considerations. Whatever the reason, you must learn to write short and edit mercilessly.

The copy in **Figure 10.1** was originally written for a brochure explaining the entire program of the Public Relations Student Society of America in detail. Clearly, a brochure written this way would be aimed at those who are already aware of the program and its basic offerings and now want more detail. As you read through it, notice that parts are in italics. This is text that could be edited out to produce two, slightly different versions of the same information.

While both versions could be viewed as informational, the edited version is slightly more persuasive. Its intent is to pique the reader's interest so he or she will send for more information. The long version assumes that the reader has already achieved the "aware" level common to the adoption process (see **Chapter 1**) and is now in the interest stage, while the edited version makes that awareness its chief objective. The copy shown here is used as an example of editing. In a real situation, you would have to create two distinctly different brochures in which information, if repeated at all, is done so in a completely different way.

Obviously, the longer copy is much longer and would need a larger format to accommodate everything and still appeal aesthetically. It was designed to fit a three-fold, 8.5" x 22" format. The shorter version will fit into a more open format, possibly a one- or two-fold that contains some white space (see **Figure 10.2**).

The key to editing the longer copy is to realize exactly how much a prospective graduate student would need to know about your program. If you include too much in a piece designed to merely attract attention, you may lose your readers. On the other hand, if you don't provide enough basic information, you may never pique their interest. Although the edited elements may in fact influence the final decision-making process, they may not be important in the awareness stage of the adoption process. Once you have decided on the purpose of your brochure, writing and editing become a much easier job.

Fitting It All Together

Whether you write for a specific size or you fit the size to the amount of information you have (especially if your boss simply can't live without that

<u>A professional association</u>

The Public Relations Student Society of America (PRSSA) is the student-run wing of the Public Relations Society of America (PRSA), the largest professional public relations organization in the nation. There are more than 4,300 students in 150 chapters at colleges and universities all across the United States.

The primary goal of PRSSA is to provide students with learning experiences that support coursework taken in public relations and related areas. Although PRSSA is a student-run organization, PRSA still plays an important and active role in its activities.

Each PRSSA chapter is counseled by a professional advisor and a faculty advisor (both members of PRSA) and is sponsored by a professional chapter. Here at the University of Oregon, PRSSA receives the full support of our parent chapter in Portland as well as a national network of professional and student services.

<u>Keeping in touch with your peers</u>

Members of the University of Oregon PRSSA attend a number of events each year including the national conference (where members from all 150 PRSSA chapters meet to exchange ideas and attend seminars and workshops), the annual PRSSA Assembly, local and regional workshops and seminars sponsored by PRSA and PRSSA, and the yearly District Conference here in the Northwest.

We belong to the Northwest District along with PRSSA chapters from Central Washington University, Washington State University and the University of Idaho. Each year, we gather for a three-day conference where we exchange ideas and attend workshops and seminars given by public relations professionals.

<u>Keeping in touch with professionals</u>

PRSSA members also make invaluable contacts with public relations professionals all over the Northwest through field trips, professional workshops on subjects such as resume writing and portfolio presentation, PRIDE internships (which carry national recognition) and the Professional Partners Program, in which students are matched with public relations professionals in the Portland, Salem and Eugene areas.

<u>Professional Partners Program</u>

Some things just go together, like peanut butter and jelly, apple pie and ice cream, baseball and hot dogs. One of the best combinations around has to be membership in PRSSA and participation in the Professional Partners Program.

(continued on next page)

Example 10.1 _____

Brochure copy. *The copy in italics may be edited out for a shorter format.*

The Professional Partners Program matches PRSSA students with PRSA members in an informal, information-sharing partnership. *The Oregon Chapter's professional advisor, Liz Cawood of Cawood Communications in Eugene, solicits the cooperation of senior PR professionals in Eugene, Salem and Portland.*

Students interested in the program fill out a form indicating their area of interest (i.e., special events, corporate PR, agency PR, etc.). The student is then matched with a partner practicing in that area.

The student is required to initiate the contact. Throughout the school year, the student and his or her professional partner meet informally to discuss the field of public relations, the professional's work, the student's particular interests and public relations in general. The usual method is through lunch meetings in the city in which the professional works, occasional visits by the professional to Eugene, and PRSA monthly luncheons in Portland. In addition, professional partners frequently share a workday in which the student gets to observe his or her partner in action on the job.

The Professional Partners Program offers PRSSA students ample opportunity to develop their knowledge of public relations through close relationships with practicing professionals. All students are encouraged to become involved in this and other activities offered through membership in PRSSA.

Becoming involved in Professional Partners is a great first step on the road to professionalism. There's no mistaking a winning combination.

PRIDE

One of the most exciting programs within the Public Relations Student Society of America is PRIDE.

PRIDE stands for Public Relations Internships to Develop Expertise. The School of Journalism has its own internship program under which students in all the areas of journalism can receive up to three credits for on-the-job-training. However, PRIDE internships are specially designed for members of PRSSA only.

A student undertaking a PRIDE internship needs to have already taken J359: Principles of Public Relations and J465: PR Writing to be eligible. This means that only majors with two years of college are eligible. In addition, the internship sponsor must be a public relations manager or executive who will oversee the student's work throughout the minimum 10-week internship. The PRIDE internship also requires a contractual agreement between the student and his or her internship supervisor and the student's faculty advisor.

The contract simply states the role of the supervisor, the duties of the student, and the obligations of the faculty advisor. Usually, this means that the faculty advisor meets several times with the supervisor during the course of the internship to check on the student's progress. In addition, the student is required to turn in samples of his or her work performed on the job.

At the end of a successful PRIDE internship, the student's contract is sent to PRSSA national headquarters in New York, which then sends the student a certificate of completion. Although more complex than a stan-

(continued on next page)

dard internship, PRIDE internships offer a more formalized insurance that the student will be working on coordinated projects specifically related to public relations.

PRIDE offers PRSSA students an opportunity to develop their knowledge of public relations through close relationships with practicing professionals. All students are encouraged to become involved in this and other activities offered through membership in PRSSA.

The Jack Ewan Award

Each year, an outstanding senior PRSSA member is honored as the recipient of the Jack Ewan Award. The award – named in honor of the first advisor of the University of Oregon chapter of PRSSA and 20-year faculty member, Jack Ewan—includes a $250 cash gift from the Columbia River Chapter of PRSA (our parent chapter). Seniors who have a 3.0 GPA and have been active in PRSSA are eligible for the award.

Joining PRSSA

Joining PRSSA is easy. All you have to be is interested. You'll receive a membership certificate, a reduce-price subscription to the most widely read professional publication in public relations, Public Relations Journal, and a chance to become a member of PRSA at a reduced fee when you graduate .

So, if you think PRSSA has something for you--or even if you just want to know more about us--let us know. Just talk to any member or come by a meeting. It could be the most professional move you'll ever make.

Benefits of joining PRSSA

- *Gives you a chance to experience public relations first hand through projects and work with real clients.*

- *Allows you to interact with PR professionals through the PRIDE and Professional Partners Program.*

- *Provides you with a professional environment in which other students are as interested in PR as you are.*

- *Gives you the opportunity to attend PRSSA and PRSA conferences, workshops and seminars around the Northwest and the nation.*

- *Connects you with the largest public relations professional society in the world, PRSA, and allows you to join it at a big reduction after graduation .*

- *Helps you "flesh out" your resume and portfolio through professional experience and guidance for the time when you go out into the "real world."*

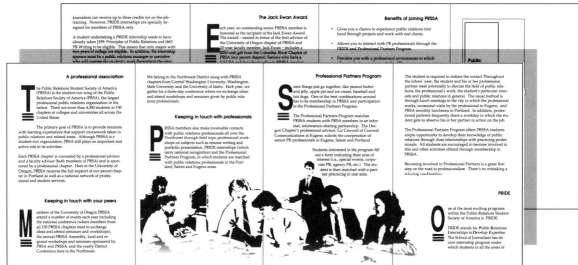

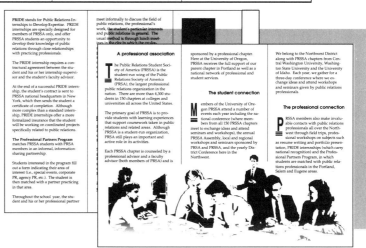

Figure 10.2 _____

Longer copy is best suited for other formats such as pamphlets (left) while shorter, or edited, versions may well fit into a folder, leaving attractive white space and plenty of room for photos.

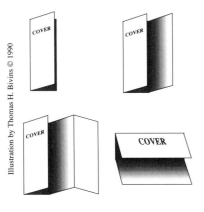

Illustration by Thomas H. Bivins © 1990

Figure 10.3 _____

Typical folds. *These are the most typical of brochure or folder folds. The creative designer, however, is limited only by imagination and money. Typically, the greater the copy, the more folds there are.*

detailed explanation of how beneficial your new widget is to Western technology), your copy will have to fit that unique characteristic of the brochure—the number of folds.

Brochures are designated by how many folds they employ. A two-fold, a sheet with two creases, has six panels—three on one side and three on the other. A three-fold has eight panels, and so on. Each fold adds two or more new panels. Although some very interesting folds have been developed, the usual configuration consists of panels of equal size (see **Figure 10.3**).

Each panel may stand alone—present a complete idea or cover a single subject—or may be part of a larger context revealed as the panels unfold. Either way, in the well-designed brochure careful attention is paid to the way the panels unfold to insure the information is presented in the proper order. Good brochures do not unfold like road maps, but present a logical pathway through their panels (see **Figure 10.4**).

Research indicates that the first thing a reader looks at in a direct mail package is the brochure. The last thing is the cover letter. Exactly how you present the brochure may determine whether it gets read or gets thrown away.

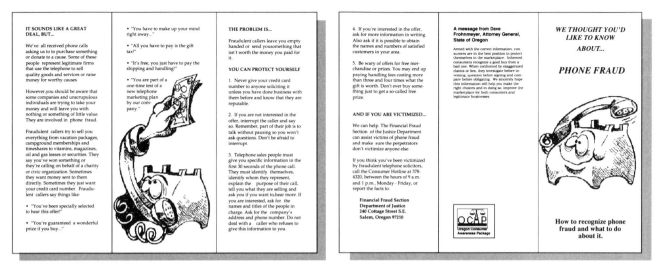

Panel 2	Panel 3	Panel 4	Panel 5	Panel 6	Panel 1

The first thing you must do is establish where the front panel is and where the final panel is. The first panel or front cover need not contain any information, but it should serve as an "eye catcher" that draws the reader inside. It should employ a "hook"—an intriguing question or statement, a beautiful photograph, an eye-catching graphic, or any other device that will get the casual peruser to pick up and read the complete brochure.

Brochures should be constructed much like good print ads. The opening section should explain the purpose of the brochure and refer to the title or headline. This is usually accomplished on the first panel or shortly following it if the first panel is devoted to a visual (see **Figure 10.4**).

If you begin your printed matter on the front cover, its headline or title becomes very important. Most informational brochures use a title simply to tell what's inside. After all, most people looking for information don't want to wade through a lot of creative esoteria. A brochure headline should be to the point. "Blind" headlines are of no use in a brochure. For example:

> ## Reaching for the stars?

Is this headline for a product (maybe telescopes)? A service (astrology)?

> ## In the Air Force, you can reach for the stars!

Now, both the intent and the sponsor are clear. For the information-seeking reader, a blind headline *might* work; however, if you really want to be sure—and if you want to pick up the browser as well—avoid them.

The second panel, at least in a two-fold brochure, is the first panel of the inside spread. Its job is to build interest. It is usually copy heavy, and may contain a subhead or crosshead. In fact, panels may be laid out around crossheads. But make sure the reader knows which panel follows which. Never let your copy run from panel to panel by breaking a sentence or a paragraph, or (worst of all) a word

Figure 10.4 _____

Typical two-fold. On a two-fold, like the one here, the information is easily enough presented. The order of progression moves from the front panel (panel 1) to the inside spread (panels 2, 3, and 4). Panel 5, although seen when the folder is first opened, still logically follows panel 3 inside. Panel 6 is used for a generic message (part of a series) and the logo.

in half. Try to treat each panel as a single entity with its own information. This isn't always possible, but it's nice to strive for.

The rest of the inside spread (panels three and four) carries the main load. It may be constructed to present a unified whole with words and graphics bleeding from one panel to the next, or the panels may retain their individuality.

The back panels (panels five and six) serve various purposes. Panel five may be used as a teaser or short blurb introducing the inside spread, or it may be incorporated into the design of panel two (especially useful since this panel is often folded in and seen as you open the front cover). It may also simply continue the information begun on panels two, three and four. Panel six may be left blank for mailing or contain address information. It doesn't usually contain much else.

Most of us are used to seeing two-folds folded so that the far right panel (inside panel four and outside panel five) is folded in first with the far left panel (outside panel one and inside panel two) folded over it. But this has always presented problems. For instance, what do you put on panel five? It is the first panel you see when you open the cover, yet it is technically on the back of the brochure. You can use it as a teaser, or simply as the informational panel that follows the inside spread. Or, you can experiment with the fold (See **Figures 10.5** and **10.6**). So much depends on the presentation of your information, and because they are folded, brochures are among the hardest collateral pieces to present properly. If readers are even slightly confused, you've lost them.

Crossheads

Crossheads should be used liberally in a brochure. They help break up copy and give your brochure a less formidable appearance. Studies have shown that copy formed into short paragraphs, broken by informative crossheads, gives the reader a feeling that he or she can read any section independently without being obligated to read the entire piece. While in some instances this may be self-defeating, reading one pertinent paragraph is often better than reading none; and, if you run your copy together in one long, unbroken string, you're going to limit readership to a hardy few. Aesthetically, your brochure will simply look better with the increased white space crossheads can add. And, white space encourages readership as well.

Copy Format

As you create your brochure, you may have to present the copy to others for approval. It helps to place it into a format that conveys the look of the finished product. Obviously, the best way to show anyone how a finished piece will look is to mock it up; however, copy often must be approved prior to any mockup, so indicating headlines, visuals and copy blocks in the order in which they appear is an important visual aspect of the brochure copy format. Indicating headlines and visuals will enhance continuity between the writer and the designer if they are different people (See **Figure 10.3**).

Figures 10.5 and **10.6** _____

Typical two-fold and modified two-fold. *(following two pages) Brochures are unique writing challenges in that often the writing has to follow the design. In this case, the order of presentation is altered radically in the second example (over page); yet, confusion over the function of panel five of the traditional brochure is cleared up.*

This is as far as most writers go; however, if you work for a small firm or nonprofit agency you may be solely responsible for producing collateral pieces from writing to layout.

Remember, you can write first and then develop a length and size to fit your editorial needs, or you can limit your copy to a pre-set design and size. Either way, you have to be aware of copyfitting requirements. Once you know how much you must write, stick to your guns. If you find that you have written more than will fit your original design concept, you can increase the number of folds and, thus, the number of available panels, or edit your copy.

The standard two-fold brochure places the cover on the far right panel of the outside spread. Panel five (inside panel four) folds in first (see below).

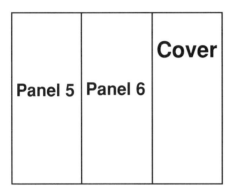

Outside spread

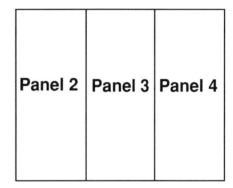

Inside spread

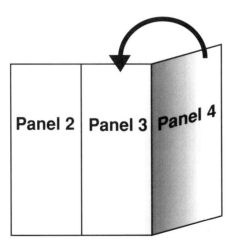

This traditional fold requires two "unfolds" to access the inside spread – the cover and panel five; however, panel five may or may not be intended as part of the inside spread. More often, it follows panels two-four, yet it appears as the first panel seen when the brochure is opened.

If your supervisor isn't clamoring for every ounce of information you can provide in 93.5 square inches of space, stick with editing your copy. The best brochures are almost always the short ones.

Three approaches that are *not* options for squeezing in extra information are decreasing the proposed point size of your typeset copy, eliminating planned white space or graphics, and reducing the size of your margins. Any one of these will severely reduce the aesthetic value of your brochure and deter or prevent the reading of it.

The standard two-fold brochure is redesigned here placing the cover in the center of the outside panel. This allows panel two to fold inside (see below).

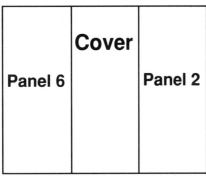
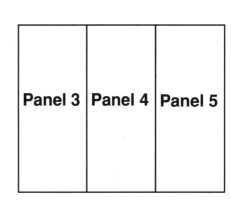

| Panel 6 | **Cover** | Panel 2 |

Outside spread

| Panel 3 | Panel 4 | Panel 5 |

Inside spread

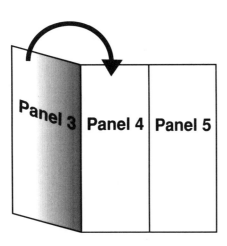

Outside panel two (inside panel three) folds inside becoming the first copy panel seen when the brochure is opened. Panel six folds over it to become the back (or mailer). This presents the center outside panel as the cover and sets up two "unfolds" to get to the inside spread; however, there is no doubt that panel two (even though it is folded inside) is the first panel to be read. This fold alleviates the "panel five" problem of the traditional fold.

Remember, simplicity, conciseness and succinctness are the keys to success. Come to the point quickly, elaborate only to the degree absolutely necessary, and get out—leaving your reader with a feeling that he or she has read something that means something.

Figure 10.7 _____
Brochure copy format. The format for brochure copy can be applied to advertising, posters, flyers, booklets or virtually any publication in which headlines, body copy and graphic elements are combined. The clarity of the format comes from the left margin notations guiding the reader through the panels one at a time.

```
"Phone Fraud"
3-fold folder
Attorney General

PANEL 1
HEADLINE:       WE THOUGHT YOU D LIKE TO KNOW ABOUT (graphic splits head
                line here) PHONE FRAUD

VISUAL:         Stylized graphic of telephone

SUBHEAD:        A consumer guide to your rights and obligations when
                dealing with telephone sales

PANEL 2
SUBHEAD:        WHAT IS PHONE FRAUD?

COPY:           We ve all been asked to purchase something or donate to a
                cause over the phone.

                Most of the people who contact us represent legitimate  firms that use the
                telephone to sell quality goods and services or raise money for worthy
                causes.

                However, there are companies that are involved in telemarketing fraud.
                According to the Federal Trade Commission, telemarketing fraud is the use
                of telephone communications to promote goods or services fraudulently.
                And this can cost you money!

VISUAL:         Cartoon drawing of telephone receiver

SUBHEAD:        WHAT ARE THEY TRYING TO SELL YOU?

COPY:           Fraudulent sales callers try to sell us everything from vacations and time-
                share condominiums to vitamins and magazines subscriptions.  They say
                they represent film clubs, vacation resorts, charities, magazine and book

                clearing houses, and even churches.  Sometimes they want money sent
                to them directly, or sometimes they just want your credit card
                number. (This is especially dangerous because they can charge any
                amount they want with your number.)

SUBHEAD:        WHAT DO THEY SAY TO YOU?

COPY:           Although fraudulent sales callers may have vastly different products or
                services to sell, there are frequently similarities in their  pitches.  These
                pitches often sound very professional. Sometimes, you are even transferred
                                          -more-
```

from person to person to make it sound more like a business setting. Do the following lines sound familiar?

-- You've been specially selected to hear this offer! (How was the selection process made?)

-- You'll get a wonderful prize if you buy... (How much is this prize worth?)

-- You have to make up your mind right away... (They make it seem like this is a now or never opportunity.)

-- It's free, you just have to pay the shipping and handling! (If they get only $7.00 shipping and handling per person and con 100 people into paying up front, they make $700!)

-- But first, I'll have to have your credit card number to verify... (To verify what and why?)

PANEL 3
SUBHEAD: WHAT HAPPENS THEN?

COPY: If it is a fraudulent sales call, you sometimes actually receive the merchandise--but it is often over priced, of poor quality, or the wonderful prize you won is usually a cheap imitation.

Or, if you've been asked to invest in something, it may turn out to be non-existent.

Or, you find out the worthy cause you donated to only got a tiny part of your actual donation while the caller got the bulk of it.

Or, unauthorized charges start appearing on your credit card bills.

PANEL 4
SUBHEAD: HOW CAN YOU PROTECT YOURSELF?

COPY: 1. First of all, always find out who is calling and who they represent. Ask how they got your name. Ask who is in charge of the company or organization represented. Get specific names and titles. Ask for the address and telephone number of the firm calling you. Be extremely cautious if the caller won't provide that information.

2. Be cautious if the caller says an investment, purchase or charitable donation must be made immediately. Ask instead that information be sent to you.

3. Be wary of offers for free merchandise or prizes. You may end up paying handling fees greater than the value of the gifts. And, don t ever buy something just to get a free prize.

4. If you re interested in the offer, ask for more information through the mail. Also ask if it s possible to obtain the names and numbers of satisfied customers in your area.

5. If you re not interested in the offer, interrupt the caller and say so. Re member, part of their job is to talk without pause so you can t ask them questions. Don t be afraid to interrupt.

-more-

```
PANEL 5
SUBHEAD:      WHAT DO YOU DO  IF YOU RE VICTIMIZED...
              Report the facts to :


                         Financial Fraud Section
                         Department of Justice
                         240 Cottage Street S.E.
                         Salem, Oregon 97210


KICKER:       REMEMBER, YOU HAVE RIGHTS.  DON T BE VICTIMIZED BY
              TELEPHONE FRAUD!

PANEL 6
HEADLINE:     HOW TO RECOGNIZE PHONE FRAUD AND WHAT TO DO ABOUT
              IT, FROM THE STATE OF OREGON ATTORNEY GENERAL S
              OFFICE
```

Figure 10.8 _____

Layout for "Phone Fraud" Brochure. *As you can see, all the copy fits nicely on a two-fold with ample room for illustrations and plenty of white space.*

Brochures

Part B: Design

One of the collateral formats least written about is the brochure. Strangely enough, it is also one of the most frequently used informational formats in advertising and public relations. In fact, you'd be hard pressed to find much beyond a handful of pages in most design publications, and barely a few paragraphs in public relations or advertising texts. Yet the brochure is the most frequently used advertising or public relations publication.

And they're everywhere. Brochures—also known as folders—appear regularly in your mailbox as part of the daily direct-mail onslaught, in press kits, at travel agencies, and on just about every counter in America. They preach the merits of candidates, automobiles, annuity programs, insurance benefits, corporate merchandising, retirement systems, tourist attractions, and anything else you can think of. They persuade, inform, reassure, sell, show, introduce, promote and educate. But what they do best is *show and tell,* in the truest and most literal sense of the words. That is especially appropriate since the brochure

Figure 10.9

Brochures (or "folders") are multi-faceted; they may be self-sufficient or a part of something else. In this instance, NIKE has designed a single-fold, special advertising section. It is triple-punched so that it can be saved and easily retrieved. This piece is inserted in sports medicine and research publications. Design-wise, it has a very formal, research journal look to it. Designed and produced by NIKE. Creative direction by Ron Dumas; design by Laurie Rickson. Reprinted with permission from NIKE, Inc.

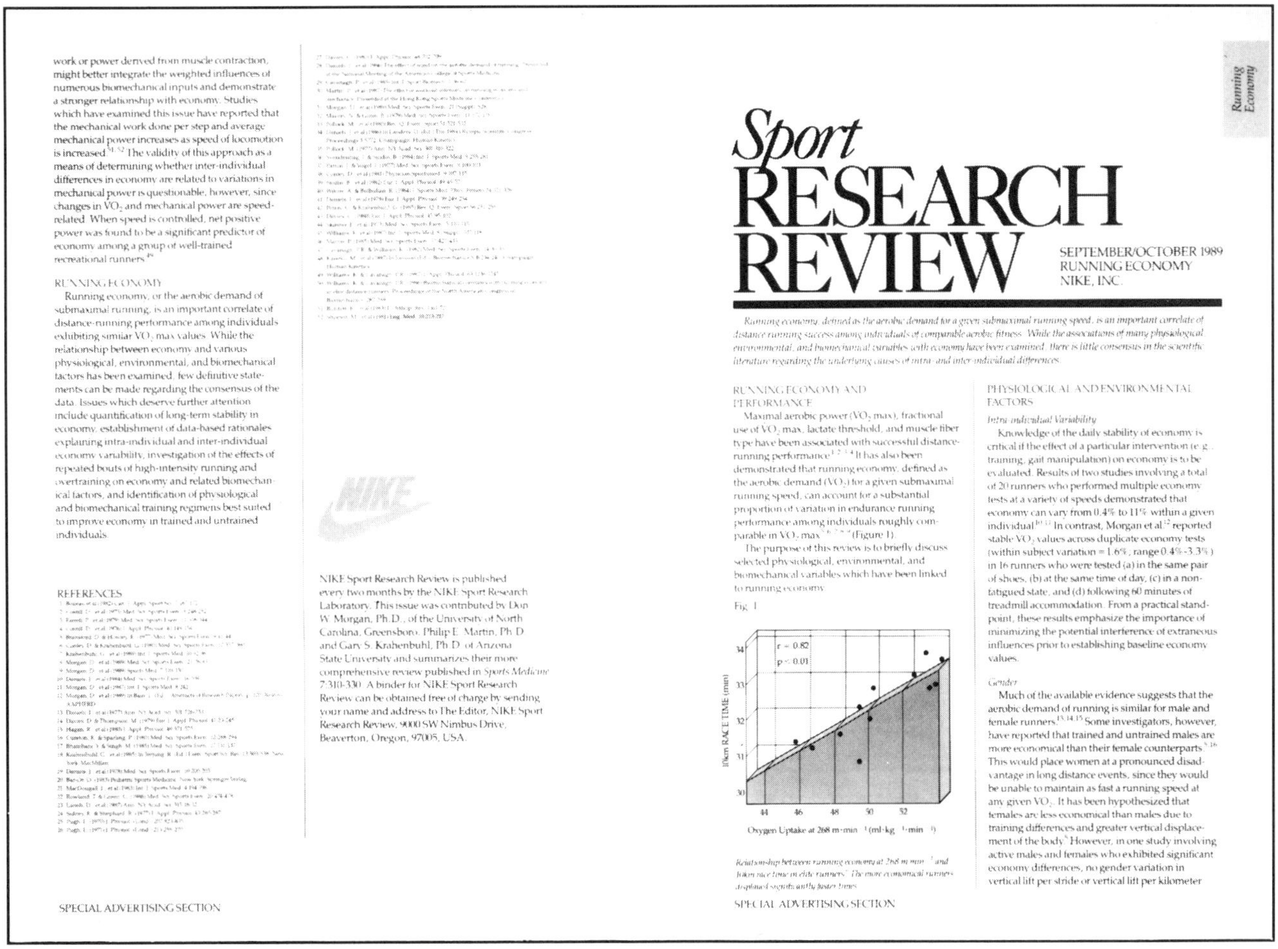

work or power derived from muscle contraction, might better integrate the weighted influences of numerous biomechanical inputs and demonstrate a stronger relationship with economy. Studies which have examined this issue have reported that the mechanical work done per step and average mechanical power increases as speed of locomotion is increased.[51,52] The validity of this approach as a means of determining whether inter-individual differences in economy are related to variations in mechanical power is questionable, however, since changes in VO_2 and mechanical power are speed-related. When speed is controlled, net positive power was found to be a significant predictor of economy among a group of well-trained recreational runners.[48]

RUNNING ECONOMY

Running economy, or the aerobic demand of submaximal running, is an important correlate of distance-running performance among individuals exhibiting similar VO_2 max values. While the relationship between economy and various physiological, environmental, and biomechanical factors has been examined, few definitive statements can be made regarding the consensus of the data. Issues which deserve further attention include quantification of long-term stability in economy, establishment of data-based rationales explaining intra-individual and inter-individual economy variability, investigation of the effects of repeated bouts of high-intensity running and overtraining on economy and related biomechanical factors, and identification of physiological and biomechanical training regimens best suited to improve economy in trained and untrained individuals.

REFERENCES

SPECIAL ADVERTISING SECTION

NIKE Sport Research Review is published every two months by the NIKE Sport Research Laboratory. This issue was contributed by Don W. Morgan, Ph.D., of the University of North Carolina, Greensboro, Philip E. Martin, Ph.D. and Gary S. Krahenbuhl, Ph.D. of Arizona State University and summarizes their more comprehensive review published in *Sports Medicine* 7:310-330. A binder for NIKE Sport Research Review can be obtained free of charge by sending your name and address to The Editor, NIKE Sport Research Review, 9000 SW Nimbus Drive, Beaverton, Oregon, 97005, USA.

Running Economy

Sport RESEARCH REVIEW

SEPTEMBER/OCTOBER 1989
RUNNING ECONOMY
NIKE, INC.

Running economy, defined as the aerobic demand for a given submaximal running speed, is an important correlate of distance running success among individuals of comparable aerobic fitness. While the associations of many physiological, environmental, and biomechanical variables with economy have been examined, there is little consensus in the scientific literature regarding the underlying causes of intra- and inter-individual differences.

RUNNING ECONOMY AND PERFORMANCE

Maximal aerobic power (VO_2 max), fractional use of VO_2 max, lactate threshold, and muscle fiber type have been associated with successful distance-running performance.[1,2,3,4] It has also been demonstrated that running economy, defined as the aerobic demand (VO_2) for a given submaximal running speed, can account for a substantial proportion of variation in endurance running performance among individuals roughly comparable in VO_2 max[5,6,7,8,9] (Figure 1).

The purpose of this review is to briefly discuss selected physiological, environmental, and biomechanical variables which have been linked to running economy.

Fig. 1

Relationship between running economy at 268 m·min⁻¹ and 10km race time in elite runners. The more economical runners displayed significantly faster times.

SPECIAL ADVERTISING SECTION

PHYSIOLOGICAL AND ENVIRONMENTAL FACTORS

Intra-individual Variability

Knowledge of the daily stability of economy is critical if the effect of a particular intervention (e.g., training, gait manipulation) on economy is to be evaluated. Results of two studies involving a total of 20 runners who performed multiple economy tests at a variety of speeds demonstrated that economy can vary from 0.4% to 11% within a given individual.[10,11] In contrast, Morgan et al.[12] reported stable VO_2 values across duplicate economy tests (within subject variation = 1.6%; range 0.4%-3.3%) in 16 runners who were tested (a) in the same pair of shoes, (b) at the same time of day, (c) in a non-fatigued state, and (d) following 60 minutes of treadmill accommodation. From a practical standpoint, these results emphasize the importance of minimizing the potential interference of extraneous influences prior to establishing baseline economy values.

Gender

Much of the available evidence suggests that the aerobic demand of running is similar for male and female runners.[13,14,15] Some investigators, however, have reported that trained and untrained males are more economical than their female counterparts.[5,16] This would place women at a pronounced disadvantage in long distance events, since they would be unable to maintain as fast a running speed at any given VO_2. It has been hypothesized that females are less economical than males due to training differences and greater vertical displacement of the body.[5] However, in one study involving active males and females who exhibited significant economy differences, no gender variation in vertical lift per stride or vertical lift per kilometer

Figure 10.10

This reply mail brochure provides "no postage necessary" panels to potential customers. It is part of a "Software Developers Club" kit for Miller-Freeman Publications. Each response card uses the magazine nameplate/logotype in the address area. A smart ploy to reinforce identity. Concept and design by Andrea McHone, Miller-Freeman. Reprinted with permission from Miller-Freeman Publications.

has characteristics that make it possibly the most flexible of all collateral publications.

Brochures may be the most flexible of all collateral publications. They offer the designer and client incredible possibilities. Their panels can be folded and arranged in a variety of ways. And they can be planned and designed to meet as many different budgets as they can needs.

As a subject of design, the brochure is unique. Its very exaggerated format is usually vertical, sometimes horizontal; on occasion, it takes on a square shape. Examined panel by panel, it has a natural one-column format that invites strong vertical composition. But it is arranged in a series of panels that may be folded two, three, four or more times. The panels may be evenly or unequally sized, and the designer must plan how the brochure will open. Its narrow vertical format is different from most other publications. And the fact that it folds out into a series of panels makes it unique. Add to that the necessity that the brochure must establish continuity—a natural or logical sequence, balance, unity, emphasis and proportion—and you begin to grasp not just its special advantages and applications, but also its disadvantages and special design problems.

Sequence

The reader must be able to open and move through the brochure in an orderly fashion to understand what's being read. Unsuccessful brochures are often ripoffs of other print formats, which lose their messages, power or meanings when quickly slammed into a brochure straitjacket. Heads or headlines may be unwittingly split inappropriately between panels. Photographs and artwork may be hacked to pieces through thoughtless cropping. When deciding how to sequence a brochure, remember that it requires a careful and functional arrangement of its parts to be effectively read and understood.

Balance

Either symmetrical or asymmetrical balance may be appropriate in a brochure design. It is difficult to go wrong with a symmetrical format, but you may better match your audience or client needs with a more informal, more dynamic approach in the design. A good designer will develop thumbnails that experiment with both.

Symmetry and asymmetry aside, brochures present balance problems that don't exist in other print formats. Most magazine, newspaper, poster, outdoor and other collateral publications stand alone. That is, their parts or elements are planned, designed, written and arranged to work together within their respective perimeters. This is not the case with most brochures.

Indeed, in some ways brochures more closely resemble moving film or video stills in that their parts, frames and panels are designed to work as a collective undertaking. Just as one frame of film relates to those frames that precede and follow it, so does a given panel relate to its preceding and following panels, except that the panel itself is less apt to be static. Further, just as moving frames of film require a smooth, fluid continuity, so do the panels within the brochure. They must connect, relate, show a continuity *and* maintain their balance.

Brochure panels must not only carry specific nuances in continuity, but must interrelate compositionally. That is, they must be balanced *individually and*

Figure 10.11

The flip sides of the response cards run horizontally; each contains a nameplate, a halftone of the magazine cover and an application blank with lots of room for completion. Design by Andrea McHone. Reprinted with permission from Miller-Freeman Publications.

collectively. No easy task, but one necessary to effective brochure design. What makes this even more difficult is that the brochure doesn't move at twenty-four frames per second. It must snare the viewer's attention in a split second, and then be intriguing enough to make that reader spend the next five or ten minutes reading it.

Unity

Unity refers to the interrelatedness of the brochure's design elements. Its fractured sort of format has inherent sequencing problems, because it is composed of separate panels and has two sides—so the stakes for maintaining unity are high.

Our eyes like order in what we see. Disorder confuses, frustrates and steers the reader away. Some think that parading a catalog of type styles in a single publication piece thrills an audience. Nothing could be further from the truth. A good rule of thumb is to not use more than three typefaces, type weights or styles in a given job. Consider also whether your typographical nuances properly reflect the audience. Have you chosen a typeface that mates up with the artwork or photography, connects logically to the reader, and properly conveys the mood and image of the brochure?

Other unity considerations may include using just photographs as artwork, or keeping the illustration style consistent. Consistency in type, artwork, column width and every other design element will help establish and maintain unity in your brochure's design.

Emphasis

Something within your design must dominate the brochure, brochure panels, and the *unfolded panel sections.* It might be artwork, photography or typography. It

Summer
Architecture
Academy

June 25-August 3, 1990

Figure 10.12

This inviting brochure for the University of Oregon's Summer Architecture Academy is both attractive and self-sufficient. Probably its most notable draw is the beautifully composed seascape photography of Kim Maynard. Reprinted with permission from Kim Maynard and the University of Oregon.

Figure 10.13 _____

*The previous brochure opens into a double-panel layout, which then opens fully to all four inside panels. Maynard's inviting square photograph suddenly becomes an even more-inviting exaggerated horizontal image. Note how the images change structurally and how the emphasis in the composition is different from the earlier format in **Figure 10.12**. The cover panel contains the summer announcement, dates and tells you who's sponsoring the academy. Its back is a mailer-panel. Reprinted with permission from Kim Maynard and the University of Oregon.*

Summer
Architecture
Academy

June 25-August 3, 1991

School of Architecture & Allied Arts
University of Oregon

might even be color, headlines or the copy blocks themselves. (Usually, for example, it is the artwork or photography that dominates the front panel of a brochure, or a dynamic graphic that illustrates or demonstrates.) Without emphasis or contrast, a layout suggests that nothing in its contents is special or unique, which neither entices nor invites the eye.

Size, color, shape, framing, angle, isolation, and other compositional devices may attract vision. Understand and apply optical weight within your design. You must learn not only to subordinate and stress different visual elements, but learn, too, *which* of those to highlight and how best to express them visually within the panel or series of panels you are planning.

Emphasis is closely linked to sequence. As a designer, you are responsible for directing and routing a reader's vision. If your reader doesn't know where to focus, where to go first, you're not in control.

Proportion

Proportions help establish spatial relationships. They may define scale, acting as a spatial frame of reference for the reader. In addition, proportions modify space and affect other design elements. For example, a large photograph or reverse block not only fixes a proportion, it also creates, via its optical weight, an emphasis that dominates smaller design components. Sometimes altering an element's size offsets balance. That's why it's important to remember that although design principles are distinct from one another, they are interrelated.

One design problem or cliché common to poorly proportioned brochures (and other collateral pieces, for that matter) is that of halved space. Visually, a

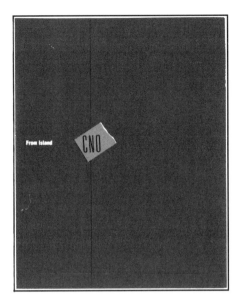

For additional copies or information contact

Corporate Networks Operations
2390 Mission College Boulevard
Regency One, Suite 1300
Santa Clara, California 95054
(408) 496-5654

Figure 10.14 and **10.15** ____

Thomas Ryan Design designed this multi-folding brochure for CNO (Corporate Networks Operations). Its textured, charcoal exterior is sealed with a dayglow gold seal, inscribed with the CNO logotype. The back cover gives little hint of its colorful insides. Design by Thomas Ryan; photography by Robert Tolchin; illustration by David Wariner. Reprinted with permission from CNO and Thomas Ryan Design.

Information Management — The Competitive Edge

Today's enterprise operations are characterized by widely distributed resources - people, factories, products, vendors, suppliers, distributors, and customers.

A common need, however, is the communication of information in all its forms — text, data, voice, and image. *Each enterprise operation must access, transmit, and manage information rapidly, accurately, and efficiently.*

Corporations have invested heavily in information systems to automate and accelerate conventional business transactions.

- Desktop computers and powerful workstations
- Computerized inventory, payroll, and accounting systems
- Databases for sales, service, and manufacturing operations
- Widely distributed facsimile machines
- Computer assisted design and manufacturing systems

Businesses have achieved unprecedented automation and acceleration of tasks within individual operations. But these automated systems have not always provided full connectivity and interoperability. Nor have they always reduced costs, promoted productivity, and increased profitability to the degree managers anticipated.

What has been created is a prevailing environment of automated islands of information.

These islands of automation are the legacy of the first generation of the information age. Now a new generation of information management systems must be created to transform these islands into fully integrated enterprise networks.

Figure 10.16 and **10.17**_____

The text and simple information-graphics of the left page are printed in brown ink on ivory-colored, enamel paper. Opposite, there's no mistaking the two-color treatment of the photography. Florescent orange lines begin a progression that begins with one person and expands to a middle shot of the earth networked with the same bright gold lines. Reprinted with permission from CNO and Thomas Ryan Design.

The CNO Process: The Evolution of an Architecture

Corporate Networks Operations works directly with you to develop an Enterprise Information Architecture founded on your existing information network and on your company's strategic business objectives.

In a preliminary executive briefing, CNO's experts meet with your strategic and technical thought leaders in a mutual fact-finding, interactive discussion. The focus is

- Your business issues and strategic business plan
- Current developments in information technology
- Technology requirements to achieve your plan

Following this briefing, CNO initiates an assessment of your present system. Over several weeks, select teams of skilled business and networking experts from Northern Telecom and Hewlett-Packard visit your locations and meet with your functional business managers and MIS and telecommunications professionals.

Through the interview process, these skilled experts analyze your business information flow to identify near- and long-term business opportunities and their inhibitors. This evaluation includes these results.

- A comprehensive assessment of the effectiveness of your installed information networks and current system applications and of the suitability of the existing network to your particular business objectives.
- A priority list of recommendations that identify immediate cost reductions, productivity improvements, and emerging opportunities for competitive advantage, building on existing network assets to protect and maximize your current investment.
- A long-range vision that details the evolution of your current network to a standards-based Enterprise Information Architecture.

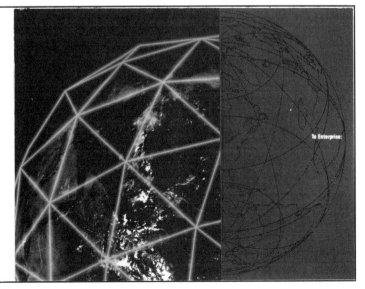

To Enterprise:

Figure 10.18

At first glance, this lean, fashionable cover for Miller Cascade gives no hint of its foldout structure. Its format and depth suggest that it's an upscale newsletter with few surprises. It was created by: Jack Anderson, art direction; Anderson and Cheri Huber designed the publication, and Gary Jacobsen executed the illustration. It is reprinted with the permission of Miller Cascade and Hornall Anderson Design Works.

halved format suggests little beyond the idea that the area of one half is equal to its counterpart. That is, it does nothing to suggest scale, compare size or show emphasis.

This is not an ironclad design rule. To be sure, any design principle provides general direction—not an itemized itinerary. Halved space may be used to deliberately act in a dormant manner, to help establish symmetry, to create a muted sort of balance, or to confront a reader or viewer. Generally, however, splitting space in equal portions is not recommended. One way to eliminate it is to employ the principle of ground thirds.

Brochure Parts

Front Panel

A successful front panel or cover is central to a brochure's success. It is the first thing your audience sees, and it might be the last as well if you aren't careful.

An effective front panel communicates visually: quickly, correctly and effectively. That means the reader is stopped by the looks of the brochure, has a sense of what the piece might contain and picks it up. It should give the browser the gist of what's inside and be compelling enough to get your audience to the inner panels. The visual, title and other written information should correctly indicate what the brochure is about. Finally, it should establish a theme, image or design style that runs consistently throughout the publication. This can be accomplished via artwork, photography, typography, color, graphic affectations, subject, format or any combination of these.

If this seems like a lot to accomplish in a relatively small space, roughly 3" x 8 1/2," you're getting the idea. Most brochures don't succeed because they fall short on one or more of the above.

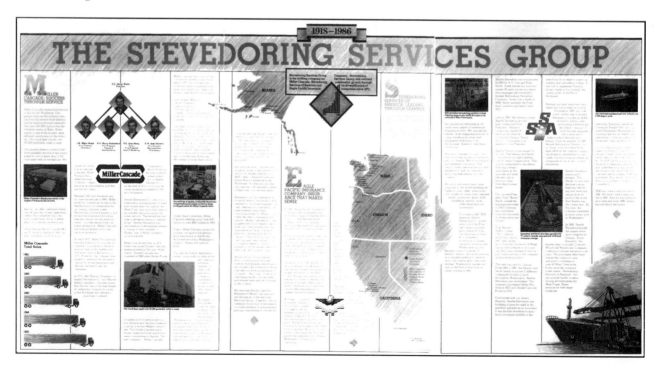

Folder or brochure covers have a great deal in common with outdoor advertising or billboards. Like a brochure cover, a billboard must communicate quickly. It must stop a moving target audience, establish image and succinctly implant a message that makes the receiver want more. The best outdoor and brochure front panels have other characteristics in common as well.

- Tight artwork or photography

- Exaggerated format and use of space (Typically, the outdoor format is exaggerated horizontally, the brochure cover exaggerated vertically)

- Dominant visual component

- Short head, headline or title

- A visual element that shows what the head or title says, and vice versa

- Immediate brand or image identification

Any element that doesn't efficiently and effectively contribute to the whole of either medium should be deleted.

Normally, the front panel consists of two or more of the following elements: strong artwork (photography, illustration, color panel or visual bump), logotype (sometimes accompanied by slogan, address or minor visual), cover panel headlines or titles, and continuity—to hold the brochure together.

Any one of these might dominate a cover panel, depending upon the goals, image and intent of the brochure's designer. More questions must be asked to determine which element should be emphasized. For example, what visual/head combination will best arrest the audience's attention and get them inside the publication? How can the cover design's style be extended throughout the brochure?

The best advice for these questions? First, know your audience intimately. If you don't have a good intuitive sense in this department, you're working in the dark. Secondly, understand the design principles discussed earlier in this book and this chapter. You needn't be Saul Bass or John DeLorean to design effectively. If you do no more than avoid flamboyant urges and continually be aware of clean, streamlined and functional design, it's difficult to go wrong. It's hard not to do a credible job if you keep the brochure simple and minimally designed. And be a ruthless critic. If any element doesn't contribute to the whole, purge it.

Some front panel designs don't use strong visuals; instead, they use some color and a reverse head or title. These generic-looking brochures are usually directed to an audience that is seeking out the brochure. You see quite a bit of this in government information pieces. That doesn't mean that they can't or shouldn't be improved visually. A little aesthetics and careful attention to design goes a long way.

◀ **Figure 10.19** _____

But there is more beyond the layout of this bold, five-color cover with its explosive graphics. Like this six-page design without the inserted page. Like lavish, multi-color illustrations that bridge pages, duotone images with metallic ink, and more—all of which are connected by a much larger than usual fold-over design. This newsletter was designed for Miller Cascade by Hornall Anderson of Seattle. Art and design direction by Jack Anderson and Cheri Huber (design only); illustration by Gary Jacobsen. Reprinted with permission from Miller Cascade and Hornall Anderson Design Works.

Figure 10.20 _____

The right, inside page provides the Stevedoring Services Group's philosophy, and it is appropriately more traditionally designed. Symmetry is established through squared up title sections, photography and graphics. See the credits and acknowledgements from the previous figure. Reprinted with permission from Miller Cascade and Hornall Anderson Design Works.

Inside Panels

The inner panels carry the substance of your communication, the content of the brochure. Typically, they are dominated by copy, but illustration, information graphics, charts, graphs and photography may also play a strong role. If you employ visuals, keep all previously discussed design principles in mind. Maintain an overall balance. Be sure the materials are properly sequenced. Use a simple design whose typography, artwork and other visual affectations are consistent. If you don't, your publication will appear haphazard and lack unity.

Consider ground thirds when adding visuals to a single panel and when working collectively with the panels. Establishing pleasant proportions is important. Give the middle panels an emphasis. If copy dominates, break it up with dropped initial letters, tint or reverse blocks, pullouts and occasional breaks in the copy. Breaking up the gray not only improves the overall look of the publication, it makes the copy more inviting and less intimidating. It tells the reader that there's breathing room below, that a diving bell isn't required for a full reading.

To help give your copy a visual texture, think about setting titles and crossheads in boldface and allowing for extra leading above and below them. You might also consider inserting pullouts in type larger than the body copy, perhaps dressing them out by setting them italic. You can also implant left column rules or feature vertical tabs that stand alone or work as reverse fields for dropped initial letters.

Don't overwork your panels. When copy is the dominant element, the panels should be unique but clean. Experiment. Pour your copy into panels that feature different design textures, invent your own variations and choose what works best for your format and material.

When at-a-glance information is important, or when abstract ideas or difficult content needs to be simplified, informational graphics or illustrations may help. Anytime visuals can better communicate your idea, show them. Don't waste the reader's time and your time attempting to say something that can't be explained without a sea of words. You'll drown the reader every time.

Remember: brochures are publications that *show and tell*. Making your information clear, memorable and easy to read is central to effective communication. Visuals that simplify and clarify your message may determine whether your brochure is read or used for wrapping fish.

Choose comfortable inner margins for your panel format, and then stick to them. Uneven margins and general lack of alignment hurts the look of your publication, giving the impression it was slapped together. Good design means attention to detail in each stage of the publication's development.

Panel Formatting

There are a number of formatting options open to you. Most often, each brochure panel is treated and designed separately, so that it has the same margins, size and format. A second approach combines panels, expanding two or more of these into a larger multiple-panel format. Even more sophisticated is the multi-panel design that makes one of the top folds work as part of both the top and bottom panels. This is difficult to execute because it throws additional technical and design elements into the formula, requiring very delicate registration and exacting folds that cannot be the least bit off. It also costs a good deal more.

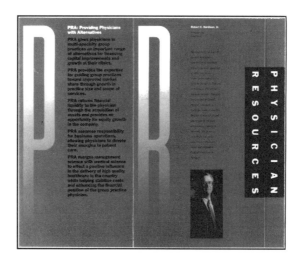

Figures 10.21, 22, 23 and **24** _____

Accordian fold brochures can be elegant and functional, as this Thomas Ryan design demonstrates. This slick brochure features bold, reversed tabs which act as a logical and handy index for the reader. Huge, graduated letters run from the top to the bottom of the page. They make up the acronym (PRA) for the Physician Resources of America. Each panel gives the identification, title and biography for the physican or executive featured. The strength of the design lies in its thorough content, simplicity and clean lines. What is especially interesting is that the opposite side has exactly the same design, except that the enameled paper is a different color. Thomas Ryan directed the design; McGuire made the photographs. Reprinted with permission from PRA and Thomas Ryan Design.

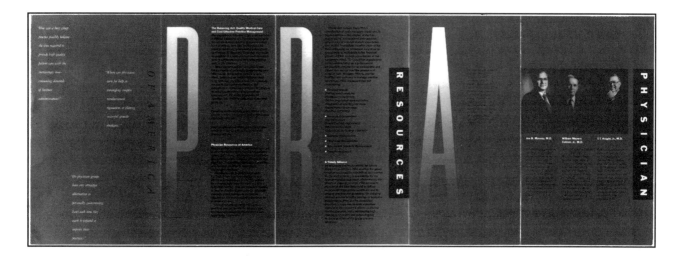

Figures 10.25 and 10.26 _____

This Intel computer enhancement brochure uses humorous blend of retouched photography and a good question to get the reader inside. Once there, the question is well answered above the visual of the accelerator board and demonstrated graphically on the left inside panel.

Bob Bredemeier and Harold Hutchinson are responsible for the photography. Design by Thomas Kitts, Sr. Designer at Robert Bailey Inc. Reprinted with permission from Intel and Robert Bailey, Inc.

Figure 10.27 _____

Fully unfolded, the middle and far right panel boldly suggest that you call their toll-free number and that the system is very affordable. Crossheads work hard here, providing clear benefits and descriptions for the text. A colored sidebar (far right) details the product's specifications. This is a well-designed, hard-working brochure that is interesting and effective. Design by Thomas Kitts, Robert Bailey, Inc. Reprinted with permission from Intel and Robert Bailey, Inc.

Figures 10.28 and 10.29 _____

Here are two other direct-mail pieces that Bailey conceived, designed and produced for Intel. Both of these use the same type of humor, strategy, inside demonstrations, content and design that made the first one so successful. Compare them, their continuity is exemplary. Like the previous pieces, these brochures were designed by Thomas Kitts. Bob Bredemeier and Harold Hutchinson are responsible for the photography. Reprinted with permission from Intel and Robert Bailey, Inc.

Sequence is probably the most important brochure design principle. Losing the audience anywhere in the unfolding process usually means losing that audience, period. To make sure that the information flow and readout are logical, try your dummy designs on an outside audience, preferably one similar to your real one. Watch carefully how they go through the brochure. What are their reactions? Can they move through it from start to finish without a hitch? If they ask you questions at any point, note them. Finally, incorporate what you learn in a new design that alleviates the problem and refines your original.

The best resource for seriously studying the brochure format is other brochures. Swipe files can be especially beneficial. Begin with brochures from your competitors. What is their overall strategy? Is it successful? What do they emphasize? What are their shortcomings? How do they approach the audience, and how is that reflected in the design of the materials? Have they taught you anything about your audience? Did you discover something you might have taken for granted? Which design element is the strongest? Why? Which is weakest? Why? How much did they spend? How was it distributed? You can learn a tremendous amount by asking and answering all of these questions.

But don't stop there. Isolate each design element and study it. Make notes and attach them to the materials. Examine brochures from outside your professional areas and divide them into three groups: those you feel are effectively designed, those you feel are poorly designed, and those you feel indifferent toward.

Studying the first group will provide you with some good ideas about brochure design. Make notes on their technical and design strengths. If there are items you feel you could improve upon, write those down, too. Attach your notes to each brochure from this group.

The second group will teach you what *not* to do. Itemize their weaknesses and you will learn at least as much about effective designing as you did from the first group.

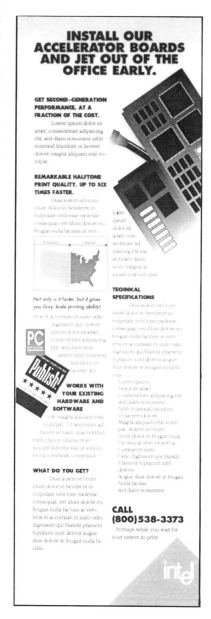

Figure 10.30 _____

Thomas Kitts produced this very tight rough—type, graphics and art—completely on a Macintosh. The head, crossheads and most of the graphics are finished; the text has been greeked in. This extreme vertical version was scrapped in flavor of the finished formats shown on the previous page. Reprinted with permission from Intel and Robert Bailey, Inc.

Figure 10.31 _____

Die-cutting accentuates the rocky Oregon coastline in this brochure for the Inn at Otter Crest. Note how the different top panel cuts stack up behind the cover panel. Design by Susan McFarlane of Ad Group. Photography by David Loveall and Lloyd Slonecker. Reprinted with permission from Ad Group and the Inn at Otter Crest.

Consider the last group a creative exercise. Examine each brochure, isolating and analyzing design elements. Write out a list of recommendations and sketch a series of quickly rendered thumbnails. (We aren't talking Rembrandt-like sketchbooks; we're talking rectangular shapes that represent brochure panels with columns of lines to represent copy and darkened spaces and stick figures to indicate photography or artwork; use bolder lines to suggest headlines or titles.) This group may prove to be the most rewarding of the bunch, because you can apply your own creativity, insights and intuition.

By the time you've finished, you'll probably have a decent collection of swipe files and some specific ideas about your own brochure's concept, formatting and design.

Layout: Front and Back

Because brochures can contain any number of panels, and because those panels can unfold in many different ways, the layout configuration differs from one brochure to another. The number of panels you decide to use depends on a number of factors.

- How much copy do you have? The longer the copy is, the more panels you'll need for the layout. Determine column widths, type styles, point sizes, leading and line arrangement, then print out a galley of the copy, heads, titles, crossheads and other particulars. (This is another reason computers and desktop publishing are invaluable. Not only do they provide tools for writing and saving those documents, they format, edit, design and provide your own typography.) Measure it. This will provide a good starting point and give you some idea of your panel needs. Ultimately, you may elect to shorten or lengthen the line measure, change leading, point sizes and other particulars to accommodate your space needs. Again, one of the biggest advantages of working with computers and desktop publishing is being able to flow copy directly into your format. Computers—equipped with the proper software—offer immediate feedback on fitting copy and art to a layout.

- How much room will your visuals require? Measure them closely and leave yourself some extra space. It is better to end up with a little extra space than to come up short.

- Is your brochure a self-mailer? If so, one panel will be used for mailing. This is usually the back middle panel, but varies depending upon the number and arrangement of folds. Designing this panel is serious business. (You, not the printer, are responsible for any postal problems that might arise from a design flaw. More information on tailoring your mailing design to U.S. postal regulations appears in **Chapter 7**.)

Once you've determined how many panels you'll be using, and once you've established your margins, you can begin the panel layouts. To find the design arrangement you favor, create a folded dummy. Write the panel numbers on each section, noting cover panel, back section and so on. Spread the design out and you'll see what the panel configurations for both the front and back look like. If you're including a response form, check its opposite side to make certain it doesn't contain information you want your reader to keep. Putting it opposite the mailing panel is a good strategy.

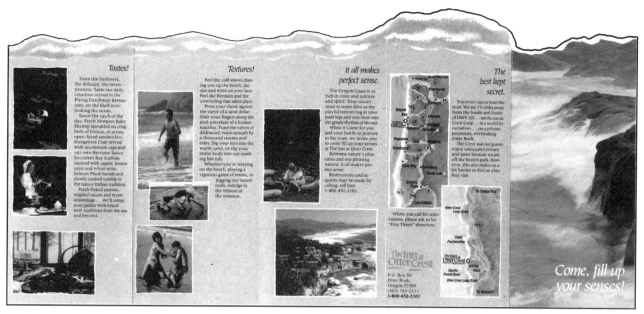

Double-check the panel positioning and location from the dummy brochure to the actual layout. Problems like juxtaposed panels, omissions, improper scaling and broken copy are far too common to be taken for granted. Use at least two different people for editing and layout checks.

Brochure as Poster

Posters are generally considered a miniaturized version of the outdoor billboard, but actually, modern outdoor advertising evolved from the poster format. In fact, some outdoor boards are referred to as posters. In either case, the format is commonly thought of as one-sided. The brochure version of the poster is an exception to that notion.

Figures 10.32 and **10.33**_____

Fully opened, the die-cut is equally functional. On the inside panels, what had been colored as sky against the rocks on the cover panel works as ocean and beach. The backside works exactly the same, with the exception of the last two right panels: the far right panel is the cover; the second one to the right serves as the brochure's back panel. It works logistically, carrying a full map of the Oregon coast as well as an exploded view. Design by Susan McFarlane. Photography by David Loveall and Lloyd Slonecker. Reprinted with permission from Ad Group and the Inn at Otter Crest.

Figure 10.34

Notice in the central photograph how the diagonally mortised stereo and audio components complete the fashionable living area to help form the perfect picture. Remote control and high tech make the room complete. Design by Liska and Associates. Reprinted with permission from NEC Technologies and Liska and Associates.

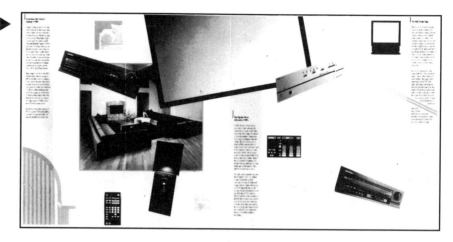

Figure 10.35

Liska and Associates designed and produced this stylish, two-color brochure for NEC Technologies. Long vertical screens carry the copy and work overtime to begin and end this spread. (See screened copy blocks to the far left and right.) Their inside counterparts help divide the panels. Notice how the designer uses diagonal elemental form and lots of white space to drawn attention to the artwork and to direct vision from panel to panel; in fact, the art cuts through them. Red is over-printed in the panels to help stand them off. Most of the photography is stripped out, and a few non-NEC images (for example, chairs, lamps, etc.) are screened. Steve Liska designed this work. Photography from NEC-file. Reprinted with permission from NEC Technologies and Liska and Associates.

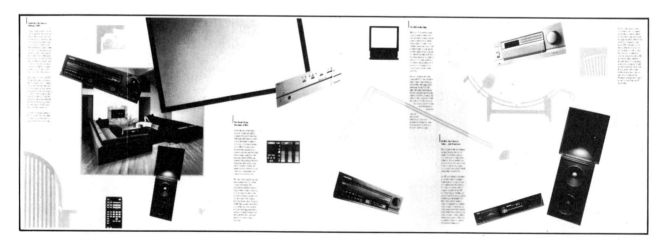

▲

Figure 10.36

Red, black and white make a powerful statement. Full color might have been used here, but the overprinting of delicate screens and the use of diagonal lines of force make these two-color panels more inviting and distinctive than had full-color had been employed. NEC materials by Liska and Associates. Notice how the diagonal lines route your vision through the format. Reprinted with permission from NEC and Liska and Associates.

A brochure that is intended to be posted uses one side for graphic display, while its opposite side may be utilized for any number of functions: other visuals (generally at least the front panel), copy blocks of information, an envelope panel, a response panel, charts and graphs. The list of possibilities is a long one. What is important to remember is that although the elements for the nonposter side of the piece follow the same design principles and layout, the poster side does not.

Posters are designed to be "posted" and read easily by a moving audience. In the case of a panel attached to a bus or taxicab, the audience is static and the poster moves. Or the poster may be read while both the reader and poster are fixed and the vehicle is moving, as in the posted interiors of buses, subway cars or taxis. Since the poster is seen by people on the move, it must be designed with that notable difference in mind. A moving audience spends less time on this medium, so the poster must communicate quickly and effectively. Keep these guidelines in mind when designing the poster half of your brochure.

1. Make sure that your head and visuals are large enough to be seen clearly at the expected viewing distance of your audience. Normally, this distance should be ten to fifteen times your format's width; for example, if your unfolded poster is two feet across, it should be readable from twenty to thirty feet away.

2. One element should clearly dominate. It might be the headline (or title), logotype, typography or artwork. And, unless art and type are fused, there should be only one element emphasized or contrasted.

3. The art should show what the head suggests and vice versa.

4. Your head should be visual. Use concrete language, active verbs that don't require modification and lucidly say/show what you mean. If any word can be stripped away without altering your message, eliminate it.

5. Keep written communication short, simple and to the point. The best posters use language that is direct, descriptive or suggestive.

6. Arrange your elements so that the readout is logical and efficient. Remember, we normally read visuals from the bottom-left upwards (or at least have a strong visual preference for the lower left) and written communications from left to right, top to bottom. It's crucial to route your viewer/reader quickly through your message.

7. Isolate your elements. Your audience has to be able to *see* your head or visuals clearly before they can read them, so play up contrast. Place light elements on dark fields, and put dark items atop light areas. Avoid mottled or continuous toned backgrounds; they tend to swallow or lose your message. Be especially wary of surprinting.

8. You needn't show all of the product, model or subject in the artwork. Tight cropping and a close connection between written and visual elements are more important. One doesn't have to see the whole of something to feel its essence.

9. Keep the design and message simple. The more complicated your message or design is, the more difficult it will be to communicate.

10. Bolder, more intense colors work better at a distance. Primary colors—the bolder the better—seem to be most effective in attracting attention. More sophisticated products or services tend to do better with less intense color.

Figures 10.37 and **10.38**_____

This direct-mail brochure uses different symbols to set the graphic style of the supermarkets. Although the art dominates, the individual logos play off the larger Tradewell logotype. Jack Anderson's thumbnail (above) gives a solid foundation for the stages to come. The finished inside of this mailer/poster (below) uses a natural fade by creating mezzotints for offset. Compare its slick, stylish finish to the thumbnail. Jack Anderson directed the art; he and Julie Tanagi-Lock teamed up for the design. Hornall Anderson produced the illustration. Reprinted with permission from Tradewell and Hornall Anderson Design Works.

Figure 10.39 _____

Formats for brochures need not always be vertical. This exaggerated horizontal layout for the design firm of Robert Bailey Incorporated of Portland makes an unusual and dramatic statement to prospective clients. This side is run in two-color with duotones. Design by Thomas Kitts and Robert Bailey. Reprinted with permission from Robert Bailey, Inc.

Figure 10.40 _____

However, the inside panels are a different matter. They are run full color, and showcase the full range of Bailey's services through the finished designs of many clients—including numerous logotypes, package designs, publications and advertising pieces. See previous acknowledgements. Reprinted with permission from Robert Bailey, Inc.

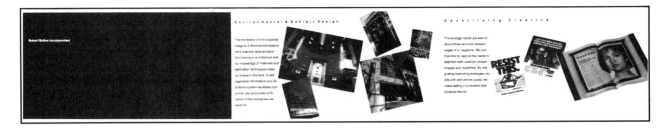

Figure 10.41 _____

These panels show and tell Robert Bailey's major strengths: designs that are extensions of careful marketing strategy and production that is a powerful blend of experience and state-of the art technology. The cover (left) is a very effective use of two-color: the exclamation point is run bright red and the firm name is reversed white on black. This is simple but impressive. Design by Robert Bailey. Reprinted with permission from Robert Bailey, Inc.

Once you've designed your poster, try this test. Walk past the proposed designs quickly and ask yourself (or your sample viewer) these questions.

- What did you see?
- What did it say?
- What did it mean?

If your audience can't identify what they saw, or express, simply, the content or meaning of the message, you'd better start over.

Figure 10.42

Fold-out formats may serve as simple folders, posters, direct-mail pieces, extravagant brochures or they may become part of something else. However trendy and exciting, this Tree Top annual report inside cover looks like a standard opener at first glance. Art direction and design by Jack Hornall and Luann Bice. Bruce Hale did the illustration. Reprinted with permission from Tree Top and Hornall Anderson Design Works.

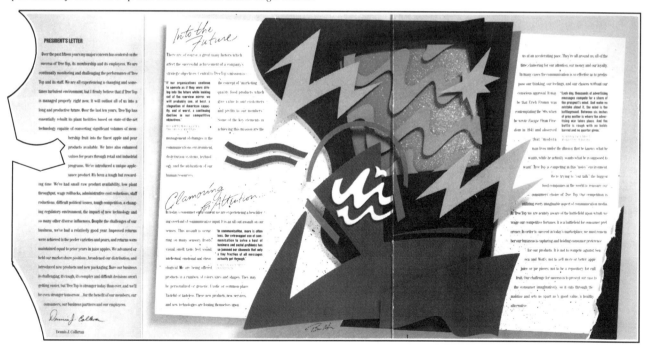

Figure 10.43

But the die-cut fold-out flips from the chairman's opening letter to the president's. The uncovered section also flows from the front cover's handwritten message: "Technology + Knowledge + Creativity = Change." Atop the unfolded area of the inside cover page reads: "Into the Future" in the same handwriting. This clever, progressive piece was born at Hornall Anderson, Seattle. Most of it was designed on a Macintosh computer. Please see previous credits for attribution. Reprinted with permission from Tree Top and Hornall Anderson Design Works.

Direct Mail: Books That Are Judged by the Cover

Today, selective mailing lists, credit card information, specific demographic breakouts and the computer make direct mail a well-respected and hard-working medium for advertising and public relations alike. If for no other reason, direct mail is an opportunistic medium because it allows its user to fine-tune testing on material designs, products, different audiences and to evaluate different promotional ploys. In fact, testing applications of direct mail are only as limited as the user's imagination.

The brochure is the heart of direct mail's packaged components. Indeed, when you mention brochure or folder, some form of direct mail usually comes to mind. It is the most commonly used format for direct marketing. In a self-mailer, it is the mailing piece itself; that is, the brochure is designed with an envelope panel and *mailed directly* to the audience. It may also be part of a direct-mail package, which may consist of a cover letter, individual advertising or promotional brochures, a return card or form and/or a postage-paid envelope.

Designing the direct-mail brochure is exactly the same as plotting any brochure, with two exceptions. First, you have to include a mailing or envelope panel. Second, the cover panel should be designed to get the recipient inside, and make no mistake about it, *whatever is inside is going to be judged by what is outside*. So it's critical to conceive an innovative cover panel that rises above the flood of direct mail that inundates us all.

Figure 10.44 _____

Direct mail is not only judged by its cover but by its outer skin. The design of some direct mail begins working to catch your attention before you ever open it up—with its envelope. A good strategy because a large share of direct mail goes into the trash unopened. This envelope for LAN *magazine uses an automobile license plate format and suggests that you take a test drive. At the bottom you're told that there's a free disk offer inside. This was designed for* LAN *and Miller-Freeman Publications by Bob Scott, San Francisco. Reprinted with permission from* LAN, *a publication of Miller-Freeman, Inc.*

Direct Response

Direct mail that elicits a prompt reply is also direct response in nature. Typically, a direct response brochure will use either a toll-free telephone number or postage-paid card or envelope to prompt reaction. Everyone likes getting something for nothing and that includes not having to stamp an envelope for an order, reply, subscription, inquiry or request for information. Unstamped cards or envelopes are considerably less effective, and do not pull well at all.

Figure 10.45 _____

The actual backside of the LAN *envelope is a mailer. It's indicia (far right), RSVP (middle) and return address (far left) are printed on the seal-fold. Notice the racing gloves at the bottom of the artwork. Designed for* LAN *and Miller-Freeman Publications by Bob Scott, San Francisco. Reprinted with permission from* LAN, *a publication of Miller-Freeman Inc.*

Direct-mail/direct response brochures offer the receiver the most personal and unobtrusive pitch of any advertising or promotion. Generally unsolicited, it arrives amid bills, shoppers, magazines, letters and general bad news. If designed properly and tailored to the correct audience, it may, indeed, be the most remarkable piece of mail arriving on any given day.

To ensure that your brochure pulls a decent response, the overall design should call attention to your reply card. And the reply card itself should make responding to your offer as easy as possible. It consists of two parts, each of which is a major design component that deserves careful thought: the postage-paid return mail panel and the order form.

The postage-paid return mail panel should follow the same basic guidelines as the envelope panel. (Please note that prepaid mailings are a separate issue to be worked out with the postal service. See the section on working with the post office later in this chapter.) The panel itself should be handsome. Generally, it is smaller in size and consists of a logotype, the return address, a postage-paid

Figure 10.46 _____

Once inside, a separate but related battle is waged for your attention and subscription. Using converging yellow roadblock diagonals, the recipient is instructed to "Listen to LAN"—*and specifically to listen to quotes from related publications and interviews from experts in the field LAN-operating systems. Design by Bob Scott and copy by Roy Beauchamp. Reprinted with permission from* LAN, *a publication of Miller-Freeman, Inc.*

indicia indicating that return postage is unnecessary, and computer line codings. Postal scanners will use some of these to route and cost out your reply mail, but you may also design some additional coding to help measure or evaluate the results of your mailing.

You might also wish to include graphics, a slash to announce special savings, reminders or other visual strategies. It is likely, too, you will need to arrange for special perforations to facilitate the removal of the reply card. In these instances, special dies or semi-cuts will need to be prescribed for the printer.

Directly *behind* the postage-paid panel is the return or order form panel. It is without a doubt *the* orphan of all design. And it is neglected not just in brochure layouts but in any media format requiring completion: subscription blanks, credit card applications, interest or premium returns, registration applications and more. (This could truly be a litany, with the completion format named and everyone chanting "pray for us.")

After you've devoted hours to planning and designing the brochure, spending money spent on artwork, typography, selective mailing lists, printing and mailing, it's appalling to include an order section only an elf scribe could fill out. What's the point of getting the readers completely through the brochure—no small undertaking—only to provide them an unusable order blank. Why frustrate, antagonize and alienate the very person you're trying to steer into your camp, sell a widget to or get to support your cause? Three simple rules will help you design an effective order panel.

1. Use type large enough to be read, and make the directions clear and scant. Nothing will scare a reader away more quickly than four paragraphs

Figure 10.47 _____

Inner page systems actually fall into the realm of brochure design. Here, is an especially effective example that is as aesthetically pleasing as it is functional. Along with being small, the inner page (right) is designed and printed on a different color paper. Note how the designer kept the inner page open in the middle so the view of the professor in the second photo on the left page could look unencumbered into the right page. This was designed by Michael Gunselman. The marvelous portrait was photographed by Ed Eckstein. Reprinted with permission from The Tatnall School and Michael Gunselman.

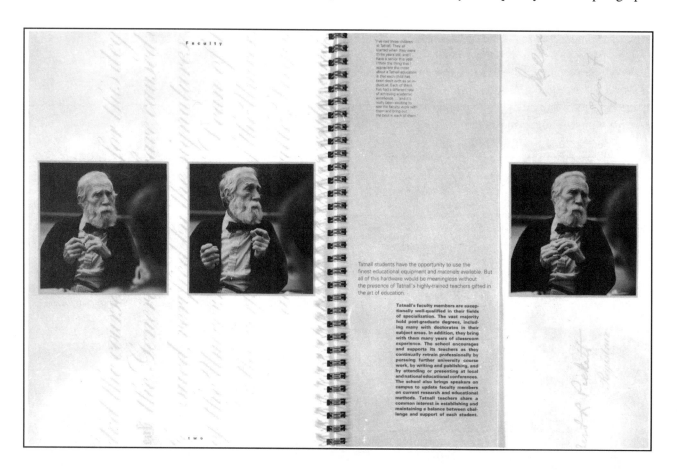

of explanation and disclaimer. If they can't read it, they won't complete it. No revelation here, but it's amazing how often this area more closely resembles a cipher than an understandable form to be completed.

2. Design simply and functionally. The function of this panel is to have your reader complete it as quickly and easily as possible. It need not have the impact of a Milton Glaser poster or the vibrant color and structure of an Ellsworth Kelly canvas. It should, however, be clean and uncluttered. Choose a crisp, clear typeface, one with a large x-height. Highlight important parts using boldface, spot color, a slightly larger point size or a reverse block. Don't confuse using a reverse block to set off directions with actually putting the coupon or order form in reverse. Designing a reverse order form would be catastrophic, sending readers on a hopeless quest for white ink.

Order the space so that the readout is logical and the sequence clear to the reader. Above all else, this panel should look inviting and be easy to fill out.

3. The last rule is the most important. *Allow your respondent ample space to write, print or type.* Space for whatever information you must have: name, address, phone, credit card number, signature, title, profession, company, profession, etc. Everyone detests being forced to write so small they can't write or print legibly. And it's infuriating to run out of room when you've only half-completed a line. Always allow enough room to get good information clearly and comfortably. A good rule of thumb is to allow two lines for the address. You'd be surprised how many forms have only one for that entry.

Figure 10.48 _____

*The look of this two-page spread— with the inner page turned over—is completely different. Compare this to **Figure 10.47**; note how changed the photography appears. Notice, too, how the designer has added a new dimension to the point being made—student/faculty rapport—by including a back shot of the students facing this professor (upper area of inside page). Elemental form (T-shape), generous white space and intersecting lines help make this design especially memorable for The Tatnall School of Delaware. Design by Michael Gunselman; photography by Ed Eckstein. Reprinted with permission from The Tatnall School and Michael Gunselman.*

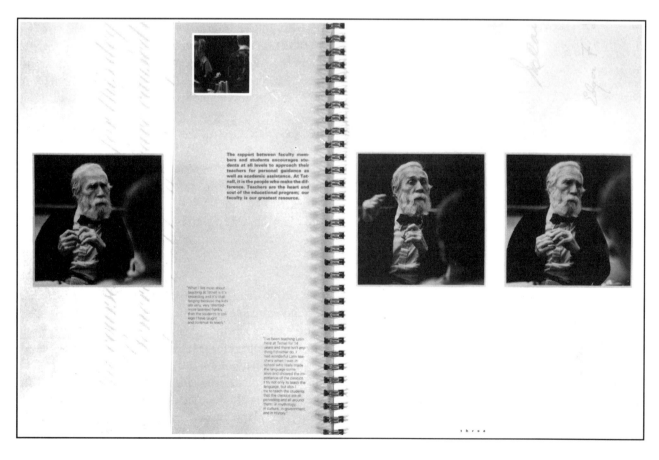

Figure 10.50 ⟶

Here, the inside die-cut cover and the now fully revealed photography work well off one another. Designer Michael Gunselman chose to leave the first page free of other elements, save a brief caption below Bowen's image of an Atlantic charter jet. On the other hand, the inside page (left) plays two copy areas off the axes of the die-cut. Reprinted with permission from Atlantic Aviation and Michael Gunselman.

Figure 10.51 ⟶

Generous white space and deep leading make the copy side of this layout very inviting. The art side of the layout is equally enticing. A wide, even border around the art adds to its direct simplicity. A centered caption below the photograph mirrors the first page's design format. Its simple, clean, uncomplicated and efficient design suggests similar traits for Atlantic Aviation. There is no pretension here—only an appropriately thoughtful mix of minimal artwork and words. See previous credits. Reprinted with permission from Atlantic Aviation and Michael Gunselman.

Figure 10.49 _____

This Atlantic Aviation brochure cover incorporates the inside art with its exterior face through the use of a square die-cut. (See following figure to secure a glimpse of the first page an a full view of Paul Bowen's meticulous photography.) The diagonal direction of the cropped photograph leads your vision to Atlantic Aviation's logotype in the lower right corner. Design by Michael Gunselman Incorporated. Reprinted with permission from Atlantic Aviation and Michael Gunselman.

If you're still wondering why your direct mail isn't pulling, take a close look at your order form or response blank.

Better yet, try filling it out yourself.

If you remember nothing else, remember this one rule: leave the people who have to fill out the form enough room to fill it out. Help them find it quickly and read it clearly and easily. Don't give them a nervous breakdown trying to complete the blanks or detach it.

Brochure Elements: Looking Inside the Insides

Brochure elements include typography, artwork, photography, copy, information graphics and logotype. Not all brochures utilize each of these, but most use at least four. Each element should be functionally integrated within the panels and follow the design principles discussed earlier in the book.

Typography

Type's primary function is to be read, so you should first judge it by that criterion: is it easy to read? Choosing exotic typefaces, a common mistake made by novices and designers alike, suggests that a typeface's stylistic affectations, its decorative qualities, are more important than its readability. Nothing could be more wrong. While creating a certain look or feel to suggest an image or to project a mood is important, communicating the message is your first job. If what you have to say can't be read, all you'll create is confusion and lost sales.

When choosing a typeface, think function and communication. Ask yourself about your audience's personality and its tastes. If you assemble a collection of

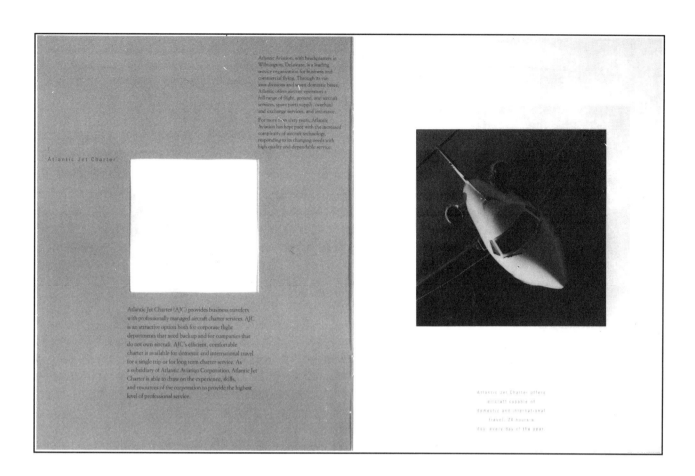

Atlantic Jet Charter

Atlantic Aviation, with headquarters in Wilmington, Delaware, is a leading service organization for business and commercial flying. Through its various divisions and seven domestic bases, Atlantic offers aircraft operators a full range of flight, ground, and aircraft services, spare parts supply, overhaul and exchange services, and insurance.

For more than sixty years, Atlantic Aviation has kept pace with the increased complexity of aircraft technology, responding to its changing needs with high quality and dependable service.

Atlantic Jet Charter (AJC) provides business travelers with professionally managed aircraft charter services. AJC is an attractive option both for corporate flight departments that need backup and for companies that do not own aircraft. AJC's efficient, comfortable charter is available for domestic and international travel for a single trip or for long term charter service. As a subsidiary of Atlantic Aviation Corporation, Atlantic Jet Charter is able to draw on the experience, skills, and resources of the corporation to provide the highest level of professional service.

Atlantic Jet Charter offers
aircraft capable of
domestic and international
travel, 24 hours a
day, every day of the year.

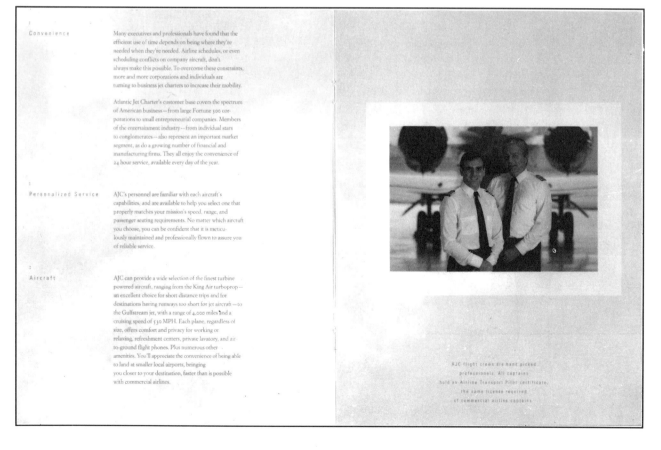

Convenience

Many executives and professionals have found that the efficient use of time depends on being where they're needed when they're needed. Airline schedules, or even scheduling conflicts on company aircraft, don't always make this possible. To overcome these constraints, more and more corporations and individuals are turning to business jet charters to increase their mobility.

Atlantic Jet Charter's customer base covers the spectrum of American business—from large Fortune 500 corporations to small entrepreneurial companies. Members of the entertainment industry—from individual stars to conglomerates—also represent an important market segment, as do a growing number of financial and manufacturing firms. They all enjoy the convenience of 24 hour service, available every day of the year.

Personalized Service

AJC's personnel are familiar with each aircraft's capabilities, and are available to help you select one that properly matches your mission's speed, range, and passenger seating requirements. No matter which aircraft you choose, you can be confident that it is meticulously maintained and professionally flown to assure you of reliable service.

Aircraft

AJC can provide a wide selection of the finest turbine powered aircraft, ranging from the King Air turboprop—an excellent choice for short distance trips and for destinations having runways too short for jet aircraft—to the Gulfstream jet, with a range of 4,000 miles and a cruising speed of 530 MPH. Each plane, regardless of size, offers comfort and privacy for working or relaxing, refreshment centers, private lavatory, and air-to-ground flight phones. Plus numerous other amenities. You'll appreciate the convenience of being able to land at smaller local airports, bringing you closer to your destination, faster than is possible with commercial airlines.

AJC flight crews are hand picked
professionals. All captains
hold an Airline Transport Pilot certificate,
the same license required
of commercial airline captains.

Figure 10.52 _____

NIKE announces its 1990 spring collection with this exuberant fold-out cover design. Closed, the NIKE cover's wrap-around piece fits neatly into a die-cut insert slot. It is run in three color: a deep teal blue, bright fuscia and black. Although nearly impossible to discern here, a spot varnish is run as well. This in-house NIKE project's creative director was Ron Dumas. Major design by Vallerie Taylor-Smith. Reprinted with permission from NIKE, Inc.

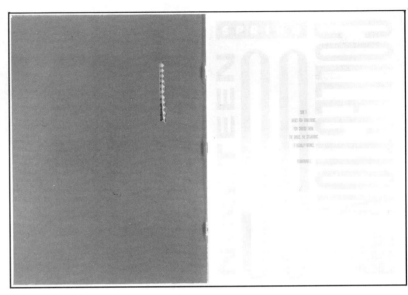

Figure 10.53 _____

The cover maintains a sleek and minimal look with the wrap-around section opened. Creative direction by Ron Dumas. Vallerie Taylor-Smith, designer. Reprinted with permission from NIKE, Inc.

Figure 10.54 _____

You don't see the fuscia ink until you turn the cover around. This is the publication's fully opened, rear view. The Roman numeral one, in SIDE I, is where fuscia is used. The enamel paper and elaborate production features make this cover very slick but understated—an appropriate fashion statement for the sensibility of the 1990s. Creative direction by Ron Dumas. Design by Vallerie Taylor-Smith. Reprinted with permission from NIKE, Inc.

Figures 10.55 and 10.56_____

Centerfold 52open each major section inside the NIKE spring collection catalogue. The large, two-color treatment of the sans serif type continues throughout the publication. In fact, the photography is duotoned (violet is used as the second color here). Fully opened, you see that the artwork has received a gradual screen, which leads you to the copy and the full-color photos. These images are presented as snapshots; they are also informally arranged and contribute to the casual, spontaneous look of the layout. Ron Dumas is NIKE's creative director. Design by Vallerie Taylor-Smith. Photography by Gary Nolton. Reprinted with permission from NIKE, Inc.

its newspapers and magazines, you'll probably discover an interesting typographical pattern that you might even borrow from. Typically, the more rigid or conservative its tastes are, the more formal your audience tends to be.

Formality suggests a more traditional typeface, possibly a roman type. Other typographical touches that might lend themselves to a sense of formality would include centering headlines, using justified rather than ragged columns and employing a kind of symmetry to any typographic designs.

Figure 10.57 _____

This NIKE catalogue has an entirely different look and approach. The photography—style, content and composition—unifies this publication; other than the captions, it is the only thing on the publication's large pages. It is run in lush, saturated color—full color, that is. The designer worked a simple grid for the layout with selective bleeds on the art and just the right amount of white space. Like the earlier Gunselman design, this one also uses small, very narrow inner pages. Note how perfectly they crop their respective pages when turned. Ron Dumas, creative director and designer. Photography by Greg Epperson. Reprinted with permission from NIKE, Inc.

Photography: Reality Frozen in Time and Space

It's no accident that photography is the dominant visual vehicle in brochures. Photography is also as immediate as it is detailed, providing an infinite array of visual representation quickly and at high art quality, if warranted. It can produce a gesture, mood, sensibility, sense of place or feel of nostalgia. It can evoke the deepest emotions, surface old memories or make an abstraction or reality incredibly clear.

We know that when we read a visual statement, our vision often enters from the bottom, usually the bottom left. Understanding that concept, it makes good sense to use a strong diagonal line from the bottom to move your viewer's vision up and through the photograph. That streamlines the visualizing process and takes the audience directly to the heart of the imagery. A good lead-in runs vision directly to the visual substance and back out again.

Photography can help unify a brochure's design in a number of different ways. Working exclusively in color or in black and white establishes continuity. A specific theme or subject used throughout the photo work provides consistency and unity. For that matter, a photographer's style may unify both the

photography and the publication. And, of course, a particular process (exaggerated grain or high contrast film) or photographic affectation can imply oneness. Here are some other suggestions for using photography in brochures.

- Use photographs to flesh out your writing. Integrate the photos neatly into your design by contouring the text where appropriate.

- Think exaggerated format because that's the brochure panel format. Single panels normally require vertical formatting, but exaggerated horizontal photography can connect a series of adjacent panels and smooth out the reader's transition from panel to panel.

- Crop your photography tightly, especially on the cover panel.

- Apply all design and composition concepts to photography.

- Use a common theme, subject or style to help unify both the photo work and the brochure itself.

- Be sure to isolate your main idea, subject or object. This can be achieved by working against blank or neutral backgrounds, or by using selective focus. Busy photographs fail because there is too much visual information and too little emphasis. Your eyes don't quite know where to land, where to begin or end, so they leave the picture confused. A photographer's main responsibility is to direct the vision of the audience by proportioning the image, establishing scale, creating an emphasis, framing, isolating, recording textures, repetitions, contrasts and lead-ins where they exist.

Figure 10.58 _____

*The inner page added to the verticality of the right page in **Figure 10.57**. Here, it sets off the barrier to the left page and opens up the art on the right. Notice how the designer has used the inner pages to carry the text. These pages contrast the larger, full-color ones in a number of ways: 1. The paper is a different color—a very lightly speckled ivory; 2. They are simply but graphically bordered; 3. Although they also run artwork, it is illustrated in the first case and run as a duotone in the second; 4. A copper metallic ink is run on the illustrations and on the little triangle graphics in the border. But there is continuity between the inner and full-sized pages. The inner pages are run with the same type specifications as the large pages, and the silhouetted landscape illustrations are related to the color art. This design is magnificent; one of the most startling this author has ever seen. See previous credits. Reprinted with permission from NIKE, Inc.*

Logotypes: Signing Your Work

Artists and artisans have been signing their work and companies have been imprinting corporate identification on their products for ages, and for good reason.

Logotypes are often synonymous with your trademark, company mark, service mark or insignia. Logotypes or signatures suggest a number of things. They assure consumers that they are getting the real thing. They establish a kind of standard. They identify and distinguish your product or service from all others, and they imply quality. Artists and craftspeople who take care enough about what they produce to sign it, put their names *on the line* as it were. They express pride in what they've produced. It's important that your audience know your signature or service mark, not only for the above reasons, but so they're able to identify your product or what you do clearly from your competitors' wares and services. Similarly, logotypes project or imply image and put you on the commercial map. They also serve as an aegis, an emblematic sign that unifies all of what you do or what you make and promises that it meets a specific level of quality and consistency.

The small company stamp that appears lower right in advertising, publications and on packaging communicates loud and long to all that see it. Many consumers tend to be loyal. If they've had a favorable experience with your product or company, it is likely they will continue their association with you and be predisposed to whatever else bears your imprint. Obviously, this is important in maintaining a clientele and for marketing or introducing new products or ideas. It follows, then, that your logotype should also be an important part of your brochure.

Brochures can showcase or show off a logotype in any number of ways. Some companies boldly splash their signatures across the front panel; for example, American Express runs its logotype diagonally via a larger than life photograph of its credit card. (Other design strategies and particulars differ from audience to audience, but the huge diagonal American Express visual remains the same on all of their current brochures.) Signature tactics for the cover may also include employing a small signature atop or in a lower corner, using company typography or company colors, or having tightly cropped photography show the product, and, of course, the logotype. You may even choose to fly the logo as the cover art.

Normally, the logo or company mark appears at least two or three times within the brochure. It may appear within the artwork or photography, on the return address of the envelope panel, on the response pitch, on the address of the order card, at the end of the copy as a signature, or emblematized on product packaging. The approaches taken to perpetuate and reinforce the company aegis vary, just as audience, product, image and marketing strategies vary. What is important is that you utilize the logotype in the brochure and other collateral materials thoughtfully. Company imprinting within the brochure may appear any number of ways: tasteful, brazen, subtle, loud or sophisticated.

Your identity should be as consistent as it is unique, positive and memorable. Maintain its consistency on all company materials. Identification inconsistencies cause confusion and put chinks in your image armor.

Your signature is your word. Indeed, it signifies your honor, integrity and commitment. It is also your brochure's parting shot. Don't miss.

10.59

These intricate logotypes represent three of many finished roughs created by designer Jarrett Jester for the Allergy and Asthma Associates allergy clinic. Jester has appropriately integrated artwork into the type design of each of them. These exemplify what logos should be: simple, distinctive, fitting and memorable. Reprinted with permission of Jarrett Jester.

Chapter 11

E very day in the United States thousands of newsletters are published and distributed to hundreds of thousands of readers. It is estimated that some 50,000 corporate newsletters alone are published each year in this country. Most newsletters are internal publications in the sense that they reach a highly unified public—employees, shareholders, members, volunteers, voting constituencies and others with a common interest. In fact, if you ask any self-respecting communications professional for the most effective means of reaching a primarily internal audience, the response will most likely be the newsletter.

Determining the Focus and the Need

Newsletters are as varied as the audiences who read them; however, they do break down into two categories, each based on *distribution*. Which category a newsletter falls into usually determines its focus. Newsletters that are distributed within a corporation are usually considered **vertical** publications because they are intended for everyone from the mailroom clerk to the CEO. Newsletters that are distributed to a more narrowly defined group with a common interest (such as newsletters on management techniques within a certain industry, or technical publications within an industry) are called **horizontal** publications.

Vertical Publications

There are three main types of vertical publications.

- **Association newsletters** help a scattered membership with a common interest keep in touch. Profit and nonprofit associations and almost every trade association in the United States publish newsletters for their members, often at both national and regional levels (see **Figure 11.1**).

- **Community group newsletters** are often used by civic organizations to keep in touch with members, announce meetings, and stimulate attendance at events. The local YWCA or Boys Club newsletter might announce their schedules, while a community church group newsletter distributed throughout surrounding neighborhoods might be a tool for increasing membership.

- **Institutional newsletters**, perhaps the most common type of newsletter, are usually distributed among employees. Used by both profit and non-profit organizations, they are designed to give employees a feeling of belonging. They frequently include a balanced mix of employee-related information and news about the company.

Horizontal Publications

There are also three main types of horizontal publications.

- **Publicity newsletters** often create their own readers. They can be developed for fan clubs, resorts (some resort hotels mail their own newsletters out to previous guests), and politicians. Congressional representatives often use newsletters to keep their constituencies up to date on their activities.

- **Special interest newsletters** developed by special-interest groups tend to grow with their following. *Common Cause*, for instance, began as a newsletter and has grown into a magazine representing the largest lobbying interest group in the United States.

- **Self-interest or "digest" newsletters** are designed to make a profit. The individuals or groups who develop them typically offer advice or present solutions to problems held in common by their target readers. These often come in the form of a sort of "digest" of topics of interest to a certain profession. In the public relations profession, for instance, you'll find PR *Reporter, PR News, Communicate, O'Dwyer's Newsletter, Communication Briefings*, and many more. If you have the money to produce it, and an audience willing to read it, you can probably sell it.

Why a Newsletter?

Why indeed? Most newsletters address an internal public, with the exception of those that target single-interest groups—such as professionals and executives—outside a formal organizational structure. The goal of most newsletters, then, is communication with a largely internal public.

Downward and Upward Communication

In the ideal organizational structure, communication flows vertically (upward and downward) and horizontally. The newsletter is a good example of downward communication. It fulfills part of management's obligation to provide its employees formal channels of communication. Upward communication provides employees a means of communicating *their* opinions to management. Ideally, even downward communication channels such as newsletters permit upward

Figure 11.1

Association newsletter. *Most associations produce a newsletter to maintain contact with a scattered membership. The four-page newsletter below is an example of a publication produced for a local chapter of the Public Relations Society of America. The national organization also publishes its own newsletter and its own magazine.*

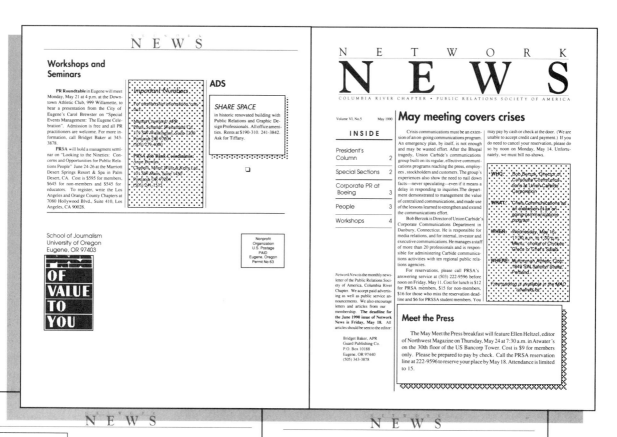

communication through letters to the editor, articles written by employees, surveys, and so forth. Newsletters can also provide horizontal communication, but this type of newsletter is rarely produced *within* an organization; rather it originates from outside.

Newsletter or Something Else?

But, why a newsletter instead of a magazine, booklets, bulletin boards, or (heaven forbid) more meetings? There are several questions you can ask yourself when deciding whether a newsletter is the publication that best suits your purpose.

- What *is* the purpose of the publication? Is it to entertain? Inform? Solicit?

- What is the nature and scope of the information you wish to present? Longer information is probably better suited to a longer publication such as a magazine; shorter, to brochures or folders. If your information is strictly entertaining or human interest, it may also be better received within a magazine format.

- Who, exactly, are you trying to reach? All employees from the top down? A select few (the marketing department, the credit department, the vice president in charge of looking out windows)?

- How often do you need to publish it to realize the objectives you set in answering the previous questions? Newsletters are best suited to situations requiring a short editorial and design lead time.

Keep in mind also that newsletters are best for small publication runs and information that needs a quick turnover. They handle information that is considered necessary but disposable (much like a newspaper, which in a sense the newsletter mimics). However, this is *generally*, but not *universally* true. Many fine newsletters are designed to be kept. Health and financial newsletters, for instance, are often hole-punched so that the reader can save them in ring binders. For the most part, though, they are considered disposable.

Setting Objectives and Strategies

Newsletters, like any well-managed publication, will achieve best results if objectives are set and all actions follow logically from them.

Newsletter Content

To determine a newsletter's content, you must first know your audience. Is it totally internal, or a combination of internal and external? Your audience and its interests will dictate, to a large extent, the topic and direction of your articles.

Depending on the type of newsletter you are publishing, the focus will be broad or narrow. For example, when you write for an internal, employee public, you must carefully balance information with entertainment. You must please management by providing information it wants to see in print and you must please the employees by providing information they want to read. Otis Baskin & Craig Aronoff, in their book *Public Relations: The Profession and the Practice*, present a rule of thumb for an appropriate mix in an internal publication (not necessarily a newsletter) aimed primarily at an employee audience.

- 50 percent information about the organization—local, national and international
- 20 percent employee information—benefits, quality of working life, etc.
- 20 percent relevant noncompany information—community news, etc.
- 10 percent small talk and personals

Given that most newsletters are fairly short, such a complete mix may be impractical; however, a close approximation will probably work. Remember, though, that this mix is only appropriate for vertical publications such as institutional newsletters.

By comparison, most horizontal publications tend to focus on items of interest to a more narrowly defined target public. For example, a newsletter for telecommunications executives may concentrate on news about that industry, omitting human interest items, small talk or industry gossip. In fact, almost every newsletter targeted to executives contains only short, no-nonsense articles. The reason, of course, is that busy executives simply don't have the time to read the type of article that interests the average employee.

Figure 11.2 _____

Tabloid size newsletter. Although most newsletters are 11"x17" folded into a four-page format, tabloid formats allow greater flexibilty and more room. However, they are usually published less frequently.

How to Set Objectives

Objectives relate to your publication's editorial statement. Editorial statements shouldn't be pie-in-the-sky rhetoric; they should reflect the honest intent of your publication. If your intent is to present management's story to employees, then say so up front. An editorial statement can be an objective, or it can serve as a touchstone for other objectives.

For example, from the editorial statement in the previous paragraph you could reasonably derive an objective such as "To raise the level of awareness of management policies among all employees by 'X' percent over the next year." Or, "To provide an open line of upward and downward communication for both management and employees." Whatever your objectives, make sure they are measurable. Then, you can point to your success in reaching them over the period of time you specified. You should also have some means by which to measure the success of your objectives. If your objective is simply "To present management's message to employees," how will you measure its success or failure? Don't you want to find out if just presenting the message was enough? How will you tell if anyone even read your message, or, if they did, whether they responded in any way?

Make your objectives realistic and measurable, and once you have set them, follow them. Use them as a yardstick by which to measure every story you run. If a story doesn't help realize one of your objectives, don't run it. If you just can't live without running it, maybe your objectives aren't complete enough.

Writing for Newsletters

Most newsletters are journalistic in style. They usually include both straight news and feature stories and range from informal to formal depending on the organization and its audience. Usually, the smaller the organization, the less formal the newsletter. Large corporations, on the other hand, often have a very formal newsletter with a very slick format combining employee-centered news with company news.

The responsibility for writing the newsletter is almost always handled in house, although some agencies do produce newsletters on contract for organizations. In-house personnel tend to be more in tune with company employees and activities. Sometimes the writing is done in house and the production, including design, layout, and printing, is done by an agency.

If you do produce your own newsletter, you are limited only by money and imagination. A standard newsletter is usually 8 1/2" x 11" or 11" x 17" folded in half. It averages in length from two to four pages and is frequently folded and mailed. Many are designed to include an address area on the back for mailing (see **Figure 11.3**).

Length of articles varies. Some newsletters contain only one article, while others include several. An average, four-page newsletter uses about 2,000 words of copy. Depending on the focus of the newsletter, articles can range in length from "digest" articles of less than 100 words to longer articles of 600 words for newsletters that cover only one or two topics per issue. The trend today is toward shorter articles, especially for the newsletter aimed at the businessperson or corporate executive. Even for the average employee, newsletter articles usually need to be brief. Most newsletters make use of simple graphics or photographs. While most are typeset (or, increasingly, desktop published), many are simply typed.

Because newsletters inform and entertain, articles should be written in an entertaining way. Usually, news about the company or strictly informational pieces utilize the standard news story style, except that there is no need to use the inverted pyramid because newsletter stories are seldom edited for space from the bottom up. Employee interest pieces tend to use the feature story style. Feature-type articles for newsletters should be complete, with a beginning and an ending.

Defining News

If you deal with the media on a fairly regular basis, you probably already know what they consider news. This journalistic definition can be very useful if you're attempting to provide *news* to a target public. Journalists all seem to agree on several major criteria for judging whether something is news or not.

- **Consequence.** Does it educate or inform? Is it important to lifestyle or the readers' understanding or ability to cope with current events? Does it have any moral or social importance? Basically, is it something your readers would want to know?

- **Interest**. Is it unusual, entertaining information? Does it arouse emotions? Does it have human-interest value? People like to read about other people like themselves.

- **Timeliness**. Ever wonder why news is called news instead of olds? People like to read about topics with currency. If it isn't new itself, it should take a new angle on an old topic or, at the very least, add something to a current issue.

- **Proximity**. Does it have a local interest angle? This is especially important for in-house newsletters. The information presented should usually pertain to events affecting the employees and occurring locally (i.e., within the organization).

- **Prominence**. Does it concern people or events well known by the readers? Like it or not, readers respond to celebrities or events that are already in the news. Focusing on a prominent person or event can serve as an angle to call attention to other news.

If your stories contain any of the above elements, they are probably news-worthy (at least from a journalistic perspective), which means they will stand a good chance of interesting your target audience.

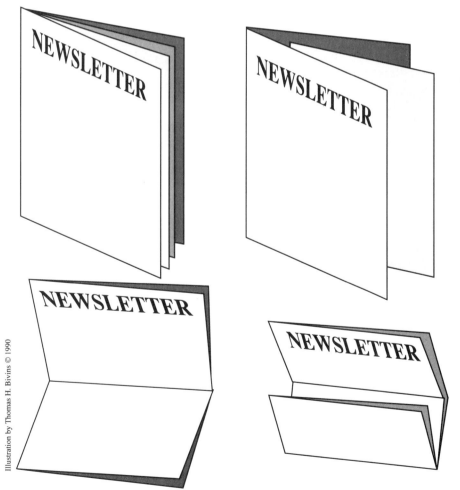

Illustration by Thomas H. Bivins © 1990

Figure 11.3 _____

Newsletter folds. Clockwise from upper left: standard 11" x 17", four-page folded and stapled; standard 11" x 17", single fold with one-page loose insert; standard 11" x 17" folded in thirds for mailing as-is or inserted into business envelope; standard 11" x 17" folded in half for mailing.

Where Do Stories Come From?

No one can tell you where or how to come up with acceptable ideas for articles. Sometimes you might receive ideas from employees or management. Sometimes a news release or a short piece done for another publication will spark enough interest to warrant a full-blown newsletter article. Whatever the source of the idea, you must next evaluate the topic based on reader interest and reader consequence.

If you're familiar with your audience's tastes, you can quickly determine their interest. To evaluate consequence, ask yourself whether they will learn something from the article. Although light reading is fun for some, an organizational publication isn't usually the place to engage in it.

Every newsletter editor will tell you that getting story ideas isn't all that hard. Finding someone to write them is. There are a couple of methods for enlisting writers. If you are putting out an in-house publication, try assigning "beats" just like a newspaper. If you're lucky enough to have a staff, assign them to different types of stories—perhaps by department or division, or by product or service. If you don't have a staff, rely on certain people in each department or division to submit stories to you. Sometimes the simple promise of seeing their name in print is enough inducement.

You can also send employees a simple request form, spelling out exactly what you are looking for. The return information will be sketchy, but you can flesh it out with a few phone calls (see **Figure 11.4**). This is an especially good method of gathering employee-related tidbits that don't deserve an entire story but should still be mentioned. Another method for organizing your shorter stories is to group them according to topic. For example, group all stories relating to employee sports, or all stories about employee community involvement, or promotions, and so on.

Of course, if your publication is a narrowly focused horizontal publication, you may end up doing most of the research and writing yourself. Many such newsletters are truly one-person operations. Because desktop publishing allows a single person to act as reporter, editor, typesetter, and printer, this type of publication is enjoying a rebirth.

Whatever system you use to gather stories, as editor you will probably be doing most of the writing as well as the editing.

Researching Stories

If you write most of your own stories, you know that every topic must be researched thoroughly. The first step in a normal research process is to do a "literature search" to determine whether your article has already been written. If it has, but you still want to explore the topic for your specific audience, then try another angle.

Next, gather background information. Try to get specifics. You can't write about something you don't know a lot about personally. It also pays to get first-hand information. Interview people who know something about your topic. Not only will you get up-to-date information, but you may end up with some usable quotes and some new leads. (See **Chapter 1** on interviewing tips.)

Don't forget the library. Many a fine article has been written based on a library visit. Library research is among the most valuable, and one of the cheapest, forms of research. In any event, most articles will be fairly complete and accurate if you do a little background research and conduct an interview or two. Since newsletter articles are usually short, this is about all the information you can use.

Figure 11.4 _____

```
            Employee Information Form
              For Newsletter Articles


     Employee Name: _____
     Deaprtment: _____
     Position: _____

     Do you have any information pertaining to promotions,
     awards, service recognition, etc. that might be of
     interest to fellow employees?  If so, please give details
     below.
     _____
     _____
     _____
     _____
     _____
     _____
     _____
     _____


     Do you have any story ideas for the employee newsletter?
     Please list your suggestions below.
     _____
     _____
     _____
     _____
     _____
     _____
     _____
     _____


     If you are directly involved in any of the above
     information, would you be willing to be interviewed?


     Would you be willing to write any or all of an article
     relating to any of the ideas mentioned above?



     Please return this form to the Corporate Communications
     Department, #302.
```

Employee Information Form.
Even a brief form such as this can provide enough initial information to spark a story or fill in some missing blanks in an existing one.

Writing the Lead

Now that you've got story ideas and done some research, where do you go next? Always start at the beginning. A good lead is just as important to a newsletter piece as to a news story. It's still the hook that entices the reader into reading the complete piece.

Although to a great extent newsletters depend on design to attract readers, the well-written article is what draws them back. Like any good story, the newsletter article should have a definite beginning, middle, and end. Of course, if the article is written like a straight news story (inverted pyramid) it will begin with a tight lead and taper off as it progresses. In both cases, the lead is the key.

Your lead must tell the reader what the story is about. It is not necessary to cram everything into the lead; however, you must include enough information so that the reader doesn't have to search for your topic. For straight news articles, the lead needs to come right to the point with the facts up front. For a feature, the delayed lead may be used. In this type of lead you create ambience, then place your story within the environment you have created. Other techniques include leading with a quote and placing it in context, or using metaphor, simile, analogy, anecdote and other interest-getting devices. Although most of us forgot these literary tools the minute we left freshman composition, we shouldn't assume that good writing can get along without them. Look over the following literary uses of metaphor, simile and analogy and then compare them with the newsletter article leads that follow them.

- A **metaphor** literally says that one thing *is* another:

  ...cauliflower is nothing but a cabbage with a college education. (Mark Twain)

  Tree you are,
  Moss you are,
  You are violets with wind above them. (Ezra Pound)

- A **simile** says that one thing is *like* another:

  Though I must go, endure not yet
  A breach, but an expansion,
  Like gold to airy thinness beat. (John Donne)

  In time of peril, like the needle to the lodestone, obedience, irrespective of rank, generally flies to him who is best fitted to command. (Herman Melville)

- **Analogies** make hard-to-understand ideas easier to grasp by placing them in reader context; or, in the following example, by making a point of view more understandable through humor:

  Soap and education are not as sudden as a massacre, but they are more deadly in the long run. (Mark Twain)

The following leads show even the most mundane subject is of interest to someone and deserves the most interesting treatment possible. Pay particular attention to the number of scene-setting or descriptive words used in these leads.

Leading with a quote:

"Steelhead trout are an elitist fish; they're scarce, big, beautiful and they're good fighters," says Bob Hooton, Fish and Wildlife biologist responsible for steelhead on Vancouver Island. (*Salmonid*, newsletter of the Canadian Dept. of Fisheries and Oceans)

Leading with an anecdote:

When teachers, lawyers and other well-seasoned professionals tell you to leave work at the office, take their advice. If you don't, you will end up sleeping with your work—and only with your work—every night. (*PReview*, newsletter of the University of Delaware PRSSA)

If past experience is an indication, the telephones at our Client Services Center in Laurel, Maryland, will rarely stop ringing on December 16. That day the Center begins accepting calls for appointments to review diaries from the Fall 1982 radio survey. (*Beyond the Ratings*, national newsletter of Arbitron)

April 1st marks the beginning of a new era in banking—and a new dawn of satellite communications. On that day a clerk in Citicorp's Long Island, N.Y. office will make history by picking up the phone and dialing a Citicorp office in California. *(Telecommunications Week,* newsletter published by Business Research Publications, Inc.)

Leading with an analogy:

Your living room may be a high-crime area—if that's where you watch TV. A study to be published in October by The Media Institute finds that TV crime is far more violent than real life crime... (*Business and the Media,* national newsletter published by The Media Institute)

You've heard the adage "two heads are better than one." What about 40? The Division's plants, more than 40 of them, are "putting their heads together" in the form of a Division-wide information sharing project recently released. (*Action Connection,* employee newsletter of Weyerhaeuser Packaging Division)

Like almost everything else, the image of the chemist is changing. Once thought of by many as a world of burbling test tubes and vials of questionable looking liquids, chemistry is changing to meet the technical and environmental needs of the microchip age. (*Current News,* employee newsletter of Delmarva Power)

Setting the scene:

It's 5:30 on a Monday afternoon and you've just finished one of *those* days. Not only did the never-ending pile of work on your desk cease to go away, but you just received two additional "A" priority assignments. On top of that, the phones wouldn't stop ringing and the air conditioning wouldn't start working, even though the temperature hit 95. (*Spectra,* employee newsletter of the SAIF Corporation)

It's pretty quiet at Merwin Dam in southwest Washington. Two generators are running. The water level is down a little so folks along the reservoir can repair some docks while the weather stays nice.

    For the 21 people working at the dam, it's business as usual. But, there is a subtle change. There's no longer a threat hanging over their heads that Pacific might not own or operate the dam. The court case that could have forced Pacific to give it up was finally resolved at the end of February. (*Pacific Power Bulletin,* employee newsletter of Pacific Power)

Cramming Mom, Dad, the kids and perhaps a pet together in a car, camper, cabin or hotel for a two-week vacation will either bring day-to-day tensions to a boil—or draw everyone wonderfully closer.

    The key to a successful vacation is preparation. With adequate planning, you can return home a stronger family—not a carload of bitter enemies. (*Bottom Line/Personal,* a digest-type newsletter for subscribers published by Boardroom Reports, Inc.)

Leading with a metaphor/simile:

Recession fears faded like Presidential Candidates this spring. Markets were jolted by the February employment release which showed an increase in employment of over 500,000.... The mood has gone full circle as there is renewed focus on the strength of the economy with its 5.4 percent unemployment rate, and the whiff of higher inflation in the air. (*Northwest Business Barometer,* a quarterly economic review for customers from U.S. Bank)

Writing the Story

Once the lead is conceived and written, the story must elaborate on it. If possible, make points one by one, explaining each as you go. Get the who, what, when, where, and how down in the most interesting way possible—but get to the point early.

The body of the article must support your main point, hopefully already made in the lead, and elaborate on it. Anticipate questions your reader might have, and answer them satisfactorily. Remember to utilize logical transitional devices when moving from one point to another. Subheads, while technically sound, don't alleviate the need for thoughtful transitions.

Back up your statements with facts and support your generalizations with specifics. Although newsletter articles seldom use footnotes, they are not completely inappropriate. Usually, however, citation can be taken care of in the body of the text. If, however, you are quoting someone, be sure to use attribution. Don't just give the person's name. A person's title or job may lend your quote authority if that person is considered knowledgeable or an expert on your subject.

In a feature, cover the news angle in a more people-oriented way. Use color, paint word pictures to help readers hear, smell, and feel the story. If your story has a possible human-interest angle, use it. It helps your readers relate to the message through other human beings. Above all, don't be afraid to experiment with different approaches to the same topic. Try a straight news approach, then a human-interest angle or maybe a dramatic dialogue. In every case, try to make your story specific to your audience. Remember, they are major players in your scripts, in reality or vicariously (see **Figure 11.5**).

Formatting Your Content

Depending on the nature of your publication, contents can vary widely. Here are some of the most common editorial inclusions.

- **Articles**
- **Table of contents**: Usually run on the first page.
- **Masthead**: Gives publication information (editor, publisher, etc.) and usually run on the second or back page.
- **Announcements**: Usually as boxed information, but sometimes run as regular columns for job placement, promotions, etc.
- **Letters:** If the publication is designed for two-way communication, a letters column is a common addition.
- **Editorial**: Can be in the form of a "President's Column," a signed editorial from management or the publication's editor.
- **News Notes**: A quick (and brief) look at what's happening—often a boxed item or sometimes run in very narrow columns as *marginalia*.
- **Mailer**: This is the spot reserved for mailing labels, postage-paid information and return address; however, it is often used as a place to put masthead information.
- **Calendar**: Upcoming events of interest to readers.

Although there are variations on these elements, most newsletters include at least some of these items.

Fully Loaded

Playing Tag with the Competition

Can the lowly load tag become a competitive advantage? Several plants are learning the answer is yes, if it's a load tag produced on BOXIS. BOXIS, the Packaging Division's Box Information System, has been around a while, and most plants are currently using computer generated load tags. But Portland folks, among others are getting a feel for just how useful BOXIS load tags can be – for themselves and their customers.

"Most load tags are handwritten, often difficult to read," notes Don McLaurin, BOXIS manager in Tacoma. "BOXIS produces a computer generated tag that's easy to read, even in dark warehouses."

But the beauty of the BOXIS load tag is more than skin deep. It also carries bar code information, the foundation of automated operations that improve productivity and customer service.

For instance, while an order is still being produced, load tags help the finishing department run more smoothly. According to Portland's Chuck Goodrich, production supervisor, the load tag's bar coding has helped Portland increase strapper throughput 15 to 20%.

"As a unit comes down the line, a laser scanner reads the bar code information on the load tag. The information is used by a computer to set the strapping pattern, automatically strap the unit, and send it down the correct spur line," Chuck explains.

Automated strapping is an easy way to make sure the load is strapped to the customer's specs. It also can improve finishing department productivity, decrease bottlenecks at the strapper, and free employees to dress the load and correct problems before they happen.

"It has really made a big difference," adds Chuck. "Before, the line would get so backed up, we'd have to put three people on the strapper. Now, we're able to run it smoothly most of the time with just one person."

Another advantage of the bar code system is that it provides instant access to order status.

"By simply scanning the bar code on a completed unit, we can tell a customer exactly how many units of the order have been completed that moment," explains Don. But load tag customer service doesn't stop there. Packaging Division customers are learning how our load tags can help them with computerized inventory and other needs.

Tom Booth, production planner at Salinas, says the flexibility of the load tag and help from information systems expert Del Green allowed them to quickly and easily modify the load tag when a key agricultural customer, Bud of California, asked them to add a special numeric inventory code.

"Hey, this is a competitive business," Tom says, "and anytime you can provide an additional service – particularly when it doesn't cost much – that's a real advantage. The customer was very, very pleased."

Brendan Doherty, Charlotte sales rep, says a customized load tag was one factor solidifying Charlotte's position in a trial with Kimberly Clark. "We developed a special corner tag that included a calendar. They were impressed. We're still on a trial basis, but it looks very good. The load tag is an advantage that sets us apart just that much more.

That's not the end of the story; BOXIS users are still learning just what the system can do. But one thing's certain: once they see Weyerhaeuser load tags, customers are beginning to request similar load tags from all their packaging suppliers.

A major Rochester customer, Central New York Bottle, liked the tag so much they asked competitors to produce a similar one. "This customer buys $5 million of corrugated a year," says senior sales rep John McCormick. "We are currently a minority supplier. But this could easily gain us $200,000 in new business because our competitors are scratching their heads wondering how they will do it."

"They don't have the system.'

(continued on next page)

Figure 11.5

Newsletter Articles. (following pages) Both of the following articles appeared in corporate newsletters and deal with innovation—one with a new product development and the other with a management technique. Notice the strong similarities between the two articles in style, use of quotes, presentation of information and level of language.

Focused teamwork is key to 'Just in Time'

What moves at a consistent pace with 40 arms and legs, operates 20 brains simultaneously and changes speed and direction at will? You may thin we're talking about ghastly creatures from Hollywood or complex robots from futuristic sci-fi films, but we're not.

It's all part of a new set of manufacturing techniques PCD currently is experimenting with called Just In Time (JIT). The entity mentioned above is a JIT Team, 20 PCD assemblers, technicians and inspectors working as a team under a new production philosophy aimed at conserving resources and increasing the quality and consistency of units rolling off the floor each day.

JIT, derived from successful Japanese manufacturing practices, is based on the notion that "small is better." In this case, "small" refers to reducing nearly every phase of the production process, including parts inventories, lot sizes and labor time. This will theoretically lead to significant dollar savings in areas such as engineering, work-in-process and rework time.

The experiment is being conducted in PCD manufacturing and involves restructuring the operating methods of two programs, the 4-055 and 4-411 power supplies. In a JIT production configuration, assembly personnel build units in small lot sizes at a consistent rate, two per day in PCD's case, instead of larger batches every so often. According to JIT theory, the team in this scenario is more likely to solve problems as they arise because they deal with a smaller quantity of the same units over a longer period of time.

"We don't want to build or buy anything we don't need," says Don Neff, Manager of Electronics Production. "If we are only going to ship two units per day, then we'll only build two per day. The idea is to avoid tying up our resources, human or otherwise, in idle inventories of parts or products."

Two committees have bee formed to oversee the implementation of the changes JIT has brought: an operating committee headed by Production Control Supervisor Tara Mattie and a management support group led by Neff.

The operating committee, making the actual changes on the production floor has concentrated on reducing set-up times by limiting parts handling.

"The assemblers have designed their own parts kits containing every part necessary for constructing one unit," says Mattie. "Each morning the people in stores will fill two kits for each assembler and have them waiting for work to begin."

Each kit is made of pieces of foam in a parts tub die-cut to fit specific parts. If anything is missing, assemblers will know right away because an empty part space will be readily visible.

In contrast to the traditional way of operation, the parts-sorting process is moved off the floor and into stores. Ths eliminates double-handling and repackaging of parts, and removes large inventories of parts from the workplace.

With shorter set-up times, similar parts kits for a variety of ELDEC products and a smaller number of units tied up in the working process, JIT could conceivably provide the production line with greater flexibility: assembly lines turning out one unit have the ability to change to a different one within a matter of minutes.

Another visible change has been to move JIT team members close to each other. Circuit board assembly, high voltage module assembly, inspection, end item assembly and final test areas are all positioned next to each other for easy access and close communication.

In a perfectly balanced JIT line, when a technician places a finished product on the cart, she should receive a unit ready for test from the final assembler, who in turn should receive another circuit board and voltage module from those areas, and so on.

"We have communication and closer proximity between team members," says Mattie. "This way, people can put their heads together on problems as they arise, rather than putting things off till a later date."

Should a problem pop up, production stops and all team-members are informed about it at once. Not only do they cooper-

(continued on next page)

ated in finding a solution, they eliminate the problem early, assuring it will not repeat itself during future production. This should decrease rework and engineering time spent debugging before shipping.

To help the program establish itself, engineering has committed itself to respond to specific JIT problems within one hour, so the team's ability to produce consistently shouldn't be hampered.

"Because of the way things are being built (in a JIT situation), any possible problems become ore visible," says Ted Meinhardt, Manufacturing Engineer. "If there is a problem that requires our help, we can respond and get it solved earlier, so problems don't repeat and the volume of bad pieces decreases."

It all adds up to a big quality boost according to Mattie.

"We think quality will improve immensely because the people involved will be cross-trained in a number of jobs. This way, the team can check and critique its own work collectively," she says.

People involved with the experiment have expressed enthusiasm about the prospects of working within a JIT framework.

"We have more freedom to get our jobs done, so we have a more relaxed production cycle," says Assembler Betty Daniels. "We're responding very accurately to the customer's needs and expanding our own knowledge at the same time."

Laura Blystone, another assembler, agrees. "We think it's great. The smoothness of how it works, even this early, is impressive."

Test Technician Nadia Jorgensen particularly enjoys the teamwork atmosphere surrounding the project. "The close proximity is the best. All th solutions are right here. If problems arise, they don't repeat because people get immediate feedback. Corrective steps are taken right away."

Jorgensen offered an example: A solder ring on a circuit board wasn't melting around a wire, leaving a loose connection. She detected it while testing, informed the inspector and assem-

bler next to her, and they began paying special attention to the particular connection. The problem hasn't resurfaced.

Planning for JIT's trial run began in late March this year, when Neff, Mattie and their committee members began touring various companies in the Northwest that already use JIT, such as Tektronics, Hewlett Packard and Opcon. After attending a series fo seminars and compiling extensive data on the topic, Mattie, Neff and Manufacturing Engineer Larry Wever made a presentation to PCD's executive group in May, which was accepted.

"At this point we want to see if JIT will work, if it is adaptable to our special characteristics," comments PCD Manufacturing Director Ken Jenkins, who helped procure approval for the project. "From what we've seen in other companies, we know it's a proven management tool."

How Much Is Enough?

How many articles to run depends on the focus and length of your publication, but fortunately, newsletters are extremely flexible. If you run a four-page newsletter but you always have more information than room, you can expand to six or eight pages. A one-page insert (loose, or run on a larger sheet with a folder-type fold) will give you enough room for two or three more stories—more if your articles are short (see **Figure 11.4**).

There is truly no set figure for how much is enough; however, here are some contents from a variety of newsletters.

- *Oregon Columbia IABC Ampersand*: A regional monthly association newsletter of the International Association of Business Communicators.
  Number of Pages: 4
  Number of Articles: 4

Average Length: 500 words
Other Editorial Matter: table of contents, announcements, masthead, help wanted.

- *Action Connection*: A monthly institutional newsletter for employees of the Weyerhaeuser Paper Company Packaging Division.
  Number of Pages: 8
  Number of Articles: 7
  Average Length: 447 words
  Other Editorial Matter: recognition by plant site, employee recognition, masthead.

- *Resource:* A monthly institutional newsletter for employees of the Western Wood Products manufacturing Division of Georgia Pacific.
  Number of Pages: 4
  Number of Articles: 5
  Average Length: 65 words
  Other Editorial Matter: table of contents, a news notes column, employee recognition, masthead information on mailer.

- *The Sampler from Response Analysis*: A digest newsletter for clients and prospective clients featuring articles on research findings from Response Analysis Corporation of Princeton, New Jersey.
  Number of Pages: 4
  Number of Articles: 10
  Average Length: 252 words
  Other Editorial Matter: table of contents, editorial, masthead.

- *Northwest Business Barometer*: A quarterly economic review for customers from the Department of Economics, U.S. Bancorp.
  Number of Pages: 8
  Number of Articles: 6 (Divided geographically and topically)
  Average Length: 850 words
  Other Editorial Matter: a news notes called "Random Thoughts." Masthead information is included as part of the nameplate or banner.

- *N.E.T.M.A. (Nobody Ever Tells Me Anything)*: An employee/public news briefs newsletter from Eugene, Oregon, Development Department/ Business Development Division.
  Number of Pages: 4
  Number of Articles: 14 (not articles in the true sense, but digested news)
  Average Length: 90 words
  Other Editorial Matter: a list of publications of interest to the business community, business community recognition column, calendar of events, trivia column.

Making Your Articles Fit

Most newsletters lead off with the most topical or interesting story on the front page—much like a newspaper. Your choice of lead article will be based on management dictates or your assessment of reader interest.

Before you begin to lay out your newsletter, you should list all your potential articles, their lengths, and approximate placement by importance/interest in the newsletter. This way, if space gets tight, you can edit from the bottom up. A secondary choice is to carry over articles that aren't "time bound"—that is, articles that could just as well wait for the next issue. And, finally, you can edit each story until *all* of them fit in the space you have. This assumes that some information in each article is superfluous which, under ideal editorial circumstances, shouldn't happen. But, as any experienced editor can tell you, there is always something you can cut.

Standing columns—articles such as editorials or employee recognition that recur from issue to issue—should already have a reserved space in your layout. It is in your best interest to allot a certain amount of space to these recurring articles and stick to it. That way, your other articles will have the space they need and deserve.

If you run out of space and can afford it, consider adding two pages (a single page run on both sides) either as an insert or an extra fold. If you only have enough copy to add literally one page (a single sheet printed only on one side) don't do it. Nothing is as unattractive as a publication page printed only on one side.

Editorial Considerations for Display Copy

Display copy, from an editorial viewpoint, includes headlines, subheads, captions, and pull quotes. Each of these elements has to be written for best effect. Ideally,

Figure 11.6 _____

Newsletter inserts. A one-page addition (printed both sides) can be inserted as a loose page into a standard four-page newsletter; however, many of these loose pages fall out or become lost during distribution or reading. If you opt for an attached page as part of a two-fold format, the last page should fold inward.

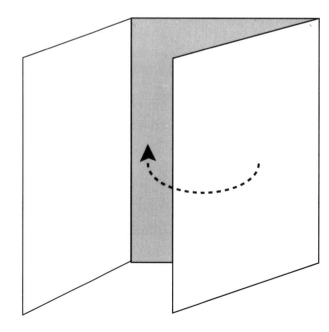

Illustration by Thomas H. Bivins © 1990

each should contribute to the article to which it refers by adding to, elaborating or amplifying on, or drawing attention to information already presented in the article.

Writing Headlines

Headlines are important to any publication, but especially so for newsletters. Headlines should grab the readers' attention and make them want to read the article. They should be informative and brief. Here are some guidelines that should help you in constructing good headlines.

- Keep them short. Space is always a problem in newsletters. Be aware of column widths and how much space that sentence-long headline you are proposing will take up. Every column inch you devote to your headline will have to be subtracted somewhere else. Headlines don't have to be complete sentences, nor do they have to be punctuated unless they are.

- Avoid vague words or phrases. Your headline should contribute to the article, not detract from it. Cute or vague headlines that play on words should be left for entertainment publications like *Variety* (famous for its convoluted headlines). Don't use standing heads for recurring articles such as "President's Message" or "Employee Recognition." It is better to mention something of the article's content in the headline, such as "Packaging Division wins company-wide contest."

- Use short words. Nothing is worse than a long word in a headline that has to be hyphenated or left on a line by itself. You can always come up with an alternative that is shorter.

Writing Subheads and Crossheads

Subheads are explanatory heads, usually set in a smaller type (or italics), that appear under the headline. For example:

> **ACME buyout impending**
> *Statewide Telecom makes takeover bid*

In most cases, a headline is sufficient; however, there are times when a rather lengthy subhead is necessary, especially if the headline is brief or cryptic.

> **'A drama of national failure'**
> *A best-selling author talks about reporting on AIDS*

Subheads should be used sparingly, if at all, and only for clarity's sake.

Crossheads are the smaller, transitional heads within an article. You shouldn't need them in a typical newsletter article. About the only time they might be useful is in a longer article—perhaps a newsletter devoted to a single subject. Crossheads should be very short and should simply indicate a change in subject or direction. Most writers use crossheads in place of elaborate transitional devices. Since space is always a consideration, using a crosshead instead of a longer transitional device will save you several column inches.

However, if you do use crossheads, make sure that more than one is warranted. Like subpoints in an outline, crossheads don't come solo. Either delete a single crosshead, or expand your points to include another one.

Writing Captions

Captions, or cutlines, are the informational blurbs that appear below or next to photographs or other illustrations. They are usually set in a smaller point size. Like headlines, they should contribute to the overall information of an article, not detract from it.

Keep captions brief. Make sure they relate directly to the photograph. (The best captions also add information that may not be included in the article itself.)

If your caption is necessarily long, make sure it is clear. If you are naming a number of people in a photo, for example, establish a recognizable order (*clockwise from the top, right to left, from the top, from the left*, etc.)

Captions, like headlines, should not be vague or cute. You simply don't have enough space to waste developing that groaner of a pun you've been dying to try out.

Writing Pull Quotes

Pull quotes are relatively new to newsletters. Traditionally a magazine device, they draw a reader's attention to a point within an article. They almost always appear close to the place in the article from which the quote is taken.

Pull quotes don't have to be actual quotes, but they should at least be an edited version of the article copy. Pull quotes usually suggest themselves. If you have a number of good quotes from an interviewee, you can always find a good one to use as a pull quote. Or, if you simply want to stress an important point in an article, use it as a pull quote.

Pull quotes can also create white space or fill up unused space left over from a short article. A good pull quote can be as long or as short as you want and still make sense. They can span several columns, be constrained to a single column, head the page, appear in the center of a copy-heavy page, or help balance some other graphic element on the page.

Remember, good pull quotes reflect the best your article has to offer. A mundane pull quote is wasted space.

"A pull quote can can be used at the top of a page as a kind of headline introducing the key idea on that page."

"A pull quote can be used in a one-column format with extended white space following."

"A pull quote can extend across two columns breaking up a copy-heavy page and creating more white space."

"Pull quotes can be used to balance other pull quotes or other graphic elements on the page."

Figure 11.7

Pull quote placement. *(Clockwise from top left) Used as an introduction to the page; to add white space; a one-column pull quote used to balance a picture in the far right column; across two columns.*

Newsletters aren't what they used to be. As their name implies, newsletters originally provided news to their readers through a letter format. For the most part, they were informal, unpretentious and direct. And they looked like letters—set single column with long, ragged right lines and unit-spaced type.

Their publishers and audience weren't particularly concerned with journalistic style, slick production methods and photography. Instead, they focused on timely information. Consequently, most newsletters appeared irregularly, whenever a hot tip, recent change or other significant information mandated that the audience be brought up to date.

Technically, the original newsletter format was equally simplistic. Ordinary typewriters produced the headlines, copy and most of whatever other typography existed—with the possible exclusion of the nameplate and fixed design features that didn't vary from issue to issue. Moreover, the unaffected format—the letter—lent itself to the no-frills look of the early newsletter, and it was familiar to the audience.

More recently, though, thanks to the revolution in printing caused by the microcomputer and desktop publishing, this medium has shed its modest appearance and taken on a more sophisticated look. In fact, today's average newsletter more closely resembles the magazine and newspaper than its original form. Because the great majority of newsletters share an 8-1/2" x 11" page size, it shouldn't seem surprising that so many of them resemble magazines. But newsletters aren't limited to this format; in fact, many adopt the larger tabloid format. Desktop publishing and its ever-improving software allow newsletters to finesse the most complicated layout problems into submission.

Newsletters have their respective parts: cover or front page, back page and interior pages. And although structuring the newsletter means employing the design principles learned earlier, this publication has its own idiosyncrasies and inherent peculiarities.

The Newsletter Cover

Due to obvious space constraints, the newsletter cover tends to be a self-cover, literally and figuratively. In fact, it really isn't really a cover in the conventional sense. Because it is a combination cover and interior page, it looks more like a miniature newspaper front page than anything else.

Despite other obvious linkages, the newsletter cover bears little resemblance to its magazine counterpart. Because of its very limited number of pages, the newsletter can't afford to use the entire cover to flaunt fully bled artwork.

Figure 11.8 _____

Today's newsletters tend to be sophisticated and often don newspaper and magazine styles. The Services Quarterly, for example, is an elegant mix of flashy graphics and modern design, much of which is computer-generated. It is designed by Jack Anderson and Cheri Huber of Hornall Anderson, Seattle. Anderson is also responsible for the art direction and Dean Williams worked as the illustrator. Reprinted with permission from Stevedoring Services of America and Hornall Anderson Design Works.

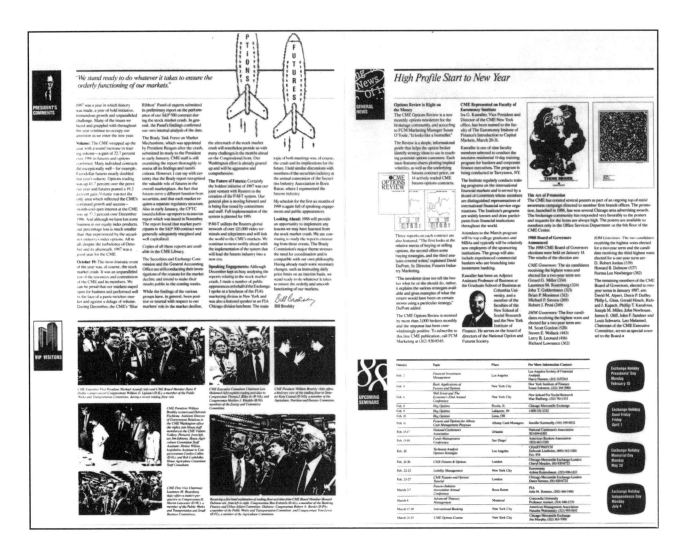

Figure 11.9 _____

Open Outcry *is a monthly newsletter designed and produced by Liska and Associates for the members and staff of the Chicago Mercantile Exchange. Its tabloid format gives it the look of a newspaper, and its illustrations and use of two color in captions, rules and graphs dress it out smartly. Designed by Liska and Associates; illustrator Mary Flock. Reprinted with permission from the Chicago Mercantile Exchange and Liska and Associates.*

There are exceptions of course, but they more closely resemble magazine or tabloid formats. Nonetheless, visuals are common to contemporary newsletter covers; they might be anything from a strong photograph to an appropriate information graphic or chart. A single visual is unlikely to take up much more than a quarter of the cover's area. More common are visuals approximately the size of a playing card. Whatever the visual, it ought to reflect the character and image of the publication and serve a function beyond simple illustration.

If you intend to use a strong photograph, the cover is probably the best place to display it. Unless it is a remarkably self-standing image—a unique or powerful photograph that does not connect to any of the stories on that page—it ought to relate to your lead story or issue theme. Be especially selective with the photography you choose to use.

Basically, newsletters carry three types of photography, any of which may end up on this publication's cover. The most common variety of the three are posed images. These are the ribbon-cutting, hand-shaking, award-holding photographs we all know and detest. Also included in this category are the group shots—one to three rows of people lined up for the firing squad—and office action pictures. You know, the secretary-at-work shot, complete with its subject holding a telephone. They are predictable and common to the point of being photographic clichés. The second type, common to all publications, is the mug shot—a simple head and shoulders image. However mundane, head shots are

expected by your readers and may be used for anything from illustrating a standing column to providing simple visual identification. Last of all and least common are well-composed images; these may be news, action, environmental or set-up photographs. They are compositionally and technically superior to the other imagery.

If newsletters have a single glaring weakness, it is photography, dominated by snapshots and posed imagery that is predictable and unprofessional. If the publication is only to be shared with your employees, this may be forgivable. However, if your audience is more varied and sophisticated, consider your photography strategies carefully. Review composition and structuring photographs in **Chapter 4**.

Remember, too, *captions should accompany every photograph in the newsletter*, with the exception of column illustrations and the like—that means that all mugshots deserve a simple identification line. See **Chapter 4** for particulars on writing captions.

The nameplate or flag is an expected component of the newsletter cover. As a rule of thumb, it should not take up more than one-fourth of the page's area. Also, the fewer pages you have, the smaller this area should be. All of this presumes that you have important information to share in a very limited amount of space. A typical newsletter nameplate bears its logotype, a date, issue number and slogan—if that is deemed important.

Figure 11.10

Steve Liska uses a very large nameplate and illustrations to dominate the cover and back page of Open Outcry. *The artwork is neatly wrapped in type and generous white space. Compare this figure with the previous one for continuity purposes. Design by Liska and Associates. Reprinted with permission from the Chicago Mercantile Exchange and Liska and Associates.*

Because of the peculiar nature of newsletter covers and because space is so limited, coverlines are seldom used. The same is generally true of blurbs, teaseboxes and other items often found on magazine and other covers.

Structuring the Newsletter Page

Figure 11.11

This two-page spread from Leo Burnett's theBurnettwork is an explosion of full-color art: illustration, stripped out photography, advertising video stills and packaging. It features modular design in a tabloid format. What's more, its full-color production is impeccable, rivaling the production standards of any magazine. Designed by Robert Feie, Boller/Coates/Spadaro, Ltd. Reprinted with permission from Leo Burnett Co., Inc., Chicago.

Although the newsletter borrows a great deal from magazine design, it takes at least as much from newspaper design—most notably the grid or modular approach to design. Grids help organize your materials, producing layouts that are not only logical, but well ordered and easy to read.

Grids break your stories, visuals and charts neatly into modules that are arranged within the layout in much the same way as hand-hewn stones are placed into a wall. They fit cleanly and squarely through the grid's precise geometry. What's more, each module individually echoes the grid's overall shape, which not only helps order the page's parts but reinforces the layout's motif. In addition, they bring still another kind of order to the design—a sequential order that is accomplished through optical weight. Optical weight prioritizes our vision; that is, we tend to look first at larger, darker or colored modules. In effect, grid parts provide a natural sequencing to your designs. Large modules and those you screen, tint or box will command more attention. Newsletters often saddle you

with very important information that may take up considerably less space than other articles on the page. By screening or tinting a module, you can make it stand out from the rest of the material on the page without affecting the design at large.

Technically, this tactic may involve counterchange, which alternates units and their alignments within a grid. For example, a large module may be counterweighted optically by a smaller, darker one. This asymmetric patchwork plays an important part in arranging gridded layouts and in establishing sequence. Newsletters usually run very short articles; grids allow you to assemble these without turning the page into a checkerboard.

Grids can accommodate vertical layouts as easily as horizontal ones, and often handle both concurrently. And there are no limitations as to how modules within the grid may be shaped and sized. In fact, a good many newsletters use modular layout for that reason alone; some even build gridded newsletter templates that change only to vary the size of a module or two.

What's more, the orderly subdivision of space makes designing easier, something very important to newsletters, because grids work out balance, proportion, sequence and emphasis from within themselves, and the margin or surrounding border unifies from the outside. Your copy may be quickly edited and fitted into the modules, and the photographs or illustrations stretched or cropped to fit the holes left for them. Or the grid can be reapportioned to better accommodate some or all of the above elements.

Figure 11.12 _____

Here, the Burnettwork *shows more of a horizontal layout. The very heavy rules are bifunctional: they carry reversed headlines and demarcate space. In this instance, the grid is more conservative; modules are indicated through the rules, screens and tint blocks. Artwork further breaks larger modules. Compare and contrast the two Burnett layouts. Designed by Robert Feie, Boller/Coates/ Spadaro, Ltd. Reprinted with permission from Leo Burnett Co., Inc., Chicago.*

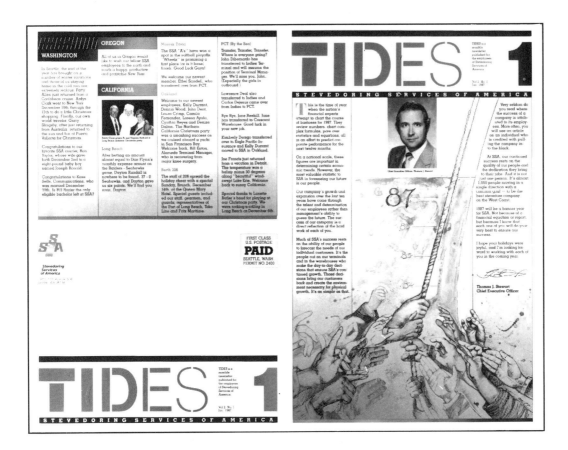

Figure 11.13 _____

Although the rules in the nameplate of TIDES *are considerably lighter than those in the* Burnettwork, *they are still bi-functional. The lower rule on the cover bears the organization's name and encloses the nameplate. Elsewhere, wider, one-column rules carry article heads. Do you find similarities between this design and that of* **Figure 11.8**? *You should. Although the publications are distinct from one another, both were designed for the same organization, the Stevedoring Services of America, by Hornall Anderson. Jack Anderson, art director; Jack Anderson and Cheri Huber, designers. Illustration by Dean Williams. Reprinted with permission from the Stevedoring Services of America and Hornall Anderson Design Works.*

The perpendicular, straight-lined geometry inherent to the grid system is also clean and pleasing to the eye. And although its architecture is direct and minimal, grids bring an incredible amount of versatility and flexibility to any design. When they are used correctly, grids consistently provide orderly design solutions.

Plotting Your Course—Plotting the Design

Establishing a basic grid design for the page itself takes imagination and experimentation. Decide if you're going to work with a three- or four-column design, or a grid which varies column widths within a page. Next, plug in a series of modules to examine how it will fracture out. Implant sample visuals as well, using the media and sizes you'd be inserting for your real newsletter. Experiment with typefaces, point sizes, styles, leading and other type specifications in order to gain a real sense of the combinations, textures and contrasts that are available to you. Of course this includes settling on rule sizes and other graphic particulars. If color is going to be part of your publication, test it as well. After you've come to terms with these and other questions, note which combinations and arrangements are most favorable to you. Refine them until you're content.

Then plot the front and back pages of your newsletter, using what you feel are your strongest preliminary designs. Of all your newsletter pages, these two should be the most distinctive. (See **Figure 11.12**.) One serves as the cover, your opening design statement which must adroitly balance your image, nameplate,

text, visuals and, of course, present the design itself. It sets the stage, order and look of your publication. The other page puts the finishing touches on all of these. It might turn out to be your mailer page as well, or it might function as a calendar, photography or planning page. In any case, although it is different from all the other pages, it must maintain the publication's continuity.

Inside pages should be similarly tailored and carry the same basic look and design but make provisions for individual wrinkles. Their grids should look like the others, accommodating columns, editorial sections and other elements common to inside pages. Columns and regularly appearing departments should be fixed to the page design, appearing in the same spot each issue. Regular placement anchors the design and is reassuring to readers. Pages subsequent to the front page carry **folio lines**. Sometimes they carry page number only; more often, however, they'll include the name of the publication and/or the date or number of the issue. In addition to the type and style sheet particulars, all the newsletter pages should share grid and basic design linkages.

Figure 11.14 _____

These are the two inside pages of TIDES' four-page newsletter. If you look closely, you'll see that by themselves each of these pages is asymmetrical; together, however, they are nearly symmetrical. Notice how the second column from the left is used for pullouts, and how they are integrated into the page. What you cannot see is how Hornall Anderson graduated colors within the illustrations and color bars. See previous caption for credit particulars. Reprinted with permission from the Stevedoring Services of America and Hornall Anderson.

Typography and Newsletters

Some designers feel strongly that because newsletters are a separate publication form, they should have their own look and typographical nuances. In other words, the type choices and specifications in newsletters should not look analogous to those of newspapers and magazines.

Because the newsletter is a comparatively modern medium, think modern. Selecting a sans serif as your text and display type might follow this logic.

Taking this still another step, you might choose a recently designed sans serif to add even more contemporary flavor to your publication. In most instances, though, either Helvetica (still today's most popular and best selling computer typeface) or Futura would serve you well for text and/or display purposes.

A handful of typefaces have been specifically designed for computer use and today's laser printer technology. One of these, Stone—designed by Sumner Stone at Adobe—is available as a serif, sans serif and an informal or contemporary serif. If you're considering mixing races for your newsletter and are looking to invest in a couple new typefaces, you might wish to give these a close look. The congruity and integrity of design in Stone carries beautifully from one race to the other. To date, each version also comes with italic, semibold, semibold italic, bold and bold italic weights and styles.

There are other interesting sans serif choices available to you, some fitted for newsletter text and display purposes.

◀ **Figure 11.15** _____

Designer Michael Gunselman uses the original newsletter format—one-sheet/two page (front and back) 8-1/2" x 11"—for this Du Pont marketing publication, but that is about the only thing traditional about it. Diagonal elemental form, graduated three color (black, yellow and turquoise) and circularly cropped photography make for a lively design. Notice how the circular form from the photo crop is repeated in spot color as an enclosed dropped initial letter at the top of the page. Designer: Michael Gunselman. Reprinted with permission from The Du Pont Company and Michael Gunselman.

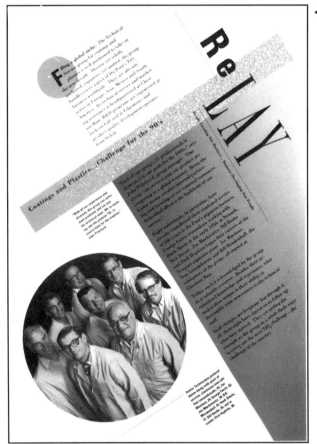

Figure 11.16 _____

Gunselman's unusual design is carried over to the back: more three color, diagonal form and rounded photo crops. Note how the larger image (top right) is counterbalanced by the six mugshots in the opposite lower corner. Finally, the Du Pont logotype is placed in the lower right corner. Striking design work. See credits above. Reprinted with permission from The Du Pont Company and Michael Gunselman.

- Avant Garde may work as text face if space isn't a concern, or if you run it small enough—no larger than 9 point, say. This 1970 Lubalin/Carnase design reflects the functional and geometric concerns of the Bauhaus and is probably the most modern-looking sans serif. It is widely used for display purposes and renowned for very large x-height and letter width. Avant Garde is clean, crisp and more legible than it is readable.

- Franklin Gothic doesn't have the same aesthetic styling as the others included in this list, but it is a very economical and practical typeface that it uses very little space. Today, bolded versions of Franklin Gothic are quite popular as a display face, in newspapers and magazines alike. It has a decent x-height and legibility, but it looks monotonal in large doses. Nonetheless, it is widely used in newsletters.

- Lucida Sans, like Stone, is another double-barreled creation. One of the newest typefaces available, it was developed with both sans serif and roman variations, and specifically designed with desktop technology in mind. Like Optima, it has some variations in its letter strokes; this provides text blocks more color or texture. Lucida Sans has good x-height and tends to run a little large. Should you select this typeface for text, you might wish to run it a point or two smaller than normal.

- News Gothic, considered a classic sans serif type, has a news or journalistic look to it. More importantly, it is a very readable sans serif with a good x-height and a fairly narrow letter, which means that you can pack more information into small areas. It is also considered stylish by today's design standards, probably because of its sleek, leggy look. All of these are good reasons to consider it for your text.

- Optima might be the ideal solution, depending upon how adamant you are in having the type look sans serif. It sometimes passes as a serif because, unlike most all sans serifs, it has both thick and thin strokes. That brings texture, high readability, variety and elegance to your pages—something few sans serifs can boast. Optima is a Hermann Zapf-designed typeface that mixes well with serifs or sans serifs. Because of its high-quality look, it is as well suited for newsletters as it is annual reports.

- Univers, sometimes confused with Helvetica, is also especially well suited as a text face for newsletters. Created in 1956 by Adrian Frutiger, it is not quite as popular as Helvetica, although it provides some interesting benefits Helvetica does not. Adobe points out that "its more pronounced stress to the stroke weights makes it very readable in lengthy body type." Despite good letter width, it doesn't take up much space or look as monotonal as other sans serifs.

If you prefer the trendy newsletter look of sleek, stripped-down sans serifs and modular design, there are two other sans serifs you might wish to consider: Helvetica and Futura.

It's no accident that most computers come with Helvetica. Max Miedinger's near flawless typeface, most popular worldwide, is a clean, highly readable type whose design fits most any printing situation. Because of the incredible demand for it, Helvetica probably has more style and weight variations than any other typeface.

Among the sans serifs, Futura is probably second only to Avant Garde in geometric precision. Although it has been around considerably longer—it was

Avant Garde

Franklin Gothic

Lucida Sans

News Gothic

Optima

Univers

Figure 11.17 _____
Type samples.

created in 1927 by Paul Renner—it has proven to be the classic sans serif. And like Avant Garde, it is connected to the Bauhaus philosophy of design that form follows function. Futura's applications know no bounds; it is functional as text and display. It is today's display darling, run in everything from BMW advertising to annual reports and in a many of today's magazines. It is highly fashionable of late to run its display versions extra bold in all uppercase, tightly kerned and leaded—and in reverse. It does make a dramatic statement with those parameters.

But utilizing sans serifs for a modern, newsletter look isn't your only choice. And while defensible, it is not necessarily the last word on the subject. There is absolutely nothing wrong with using roman typefaces for this publication form. Many designers would argue that serif type is more readable anyway, and that if you prefer a more contemporary look, there are a good many modern romans to choose from. What's more, there are many other stylish serifs that—despite their age—read and look quite contemporary, including Baskerville, Caslon, Century Schoolbook, Cheltenham, Garamond, Goudy, Palatino and Times Roman. Stone and Lucida are two more recently designed typefaces that are especially well suited for desktop-produced newsletters. There are many others, but this grouping—however brief—is not only fashionable, it's functional. Here is a short overview of their particulars.

Baskerville

- Baskerville is a transitional roman celebrated for its elegance, grace and function. It was originally designed in 1772 by John Baskerville, an Englishman, who said that he was looking for perfection in the letter structure, according to what he perceived to be their true proportion, when designing it. This is a classic typeface sure to bring elegance and precision to a newsletter—or any publication, for that matter. Its average x-height is very readable, and it uses space economically. Audience and image considerations are crucial; this face says "class" all the way.

Caslon

- Caslon, another English face, was first cut by William Caslon about the same time as Baskerville's creation. An old-style roman face, its pinched, bracketed serifs and letters reveal a certain amount of irregularity, which gives Caslon its own informal elegance. Because Caslon copied imperfections from original Roman letters to maintain their structural integrity, this face brings honesty, informality and warmth to the page. Caslon is a fairly compact face with good x-height. A typographical adage that still stands says "when in doubt, use Caslon."

New Century Schoolbook

- New Century Schoolbook was specifically designed for readability and legibility; that is, its design is based on reading and letter recognition research. It is characterized by good x-height, long ascenders and disproportionately shorter descenders. Its lack of stylistic affectation makes it a good text and display face that mixes well with serif and sans serif faces alike. Century Schoolbook is a rather large face, but is quickly made suitable for newsletters through smaller than normal point sizes. Many designers like to use its uppercase letters as dropped initial letters.

Cheltenham

- Cheltenham is an old-style roman that was created around the turn of the century. Because it has a very lean look, it's not uncommon to find it used when the image or idea being promoted centers around being slim or sleek. Its original versions tend to be on the spindly side because it has a smaller than average x-height, narrow letters and long ascenders. Despite those limitations, its decent readability and compact structure make it especially

Figure 11.18 _____
More type samples.

appropriate as a newsletter face. If you're considering this type, take a good look at the more recent book versions of Cheltenham.

- Garamond is an old-style roman whose French designer, Claude Garamond (or Garamont), is thought to have cut the face in the mid-1500s. Many herald it as *the* classic roman typeface. Most designers, regardless of backgrounds, will include this typeface among their five or ten best. Its original versions had longer ascenders, but ITC has modified Garamond by giving it a larger x-height and proportionally shorter ascenders, without damaging the face's beauty. As elegant and useful as ever, its outstanding readability and compact structure make it an especially appealing face for newsletters. It's another very classy type that can be used for just about any purpose.

Garamond

- Goudy is one of the most distinctively stylized serif faces. It was designed by American Frederic Goudy in 1915. Unlike many of the other old-style romans, Goudy is somewhat easy to identify by its diamond-shaped punctuation marks. An amazingly versatile face, Goudy provides a highly readable and beautiful type without sacrificing space.

Goudy

- Palatino is a marvel. It is another of Hermann Zapf's typographic creations. (Zapf is also responsible for Zapf Chancery, Zapf Dingbats, Optima and Melior, among others.) Created in 1950, it is a curious combination of old and new design. Although it is a transitional roman, Zapf designed this face to meet the needs and peculiarities of today's audience and technology. Palatino is highly valued as a text face—not so valued for display purposes by some—because of its good x-height, strong readability and texture. It is truly a contemporary classic.

Palatino

- Times Roman, designed in 1931 by Stanley Morison for *The Times* (London), has had many immitations—most notably what is available in most computer font libraries as Times, a good desktop adaptation of the original. Somewhat smaller in stature, it has less contrast between thick and thin strokes and was developed specifically for computer and electronic technology. Its readability and efficiency make it a very common newsletter face. More than anything else, its strong newspaper look and familiarity may make it a less tantalizing choice. Nonetheless, it is a hard-working typeface.

Times Roman

These faces are all strong candidates for newsletters. They are employed regularly and fashionably throughout the realm of publications—but that isn't any reason to ignore them. Romans have as much a place in newsletters as they do any publication. Note the particulars of all the faces discussed through their descriptions, and look through samples furnished.

A Checklist of Other Typographical Tactics for Newsletters

Typography is probably the most critical part of newsletter design. The final list of type tactics listed below, although not carved in stone, is especially appropriate and suitable for newsletters.

- Choose a fairly compact but readable face that has good x-height and matches your publication image and audience. Sometimes it's a good idea

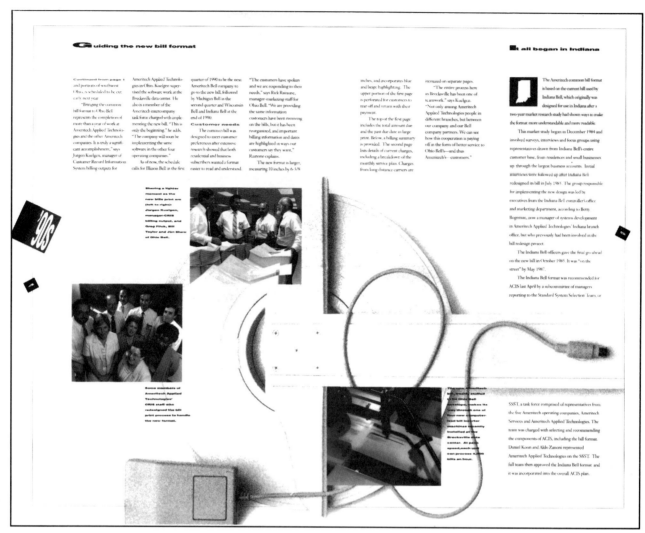

Figure 11.19 _____

Artwork dominates this exciting layout. Let's dissect it. Three equally sized photographs share the upper and lower horizontal axes of the far left image. The T-square runs the lower axis out to the right. Vision is directed into the photos (far left) through the folio and the (black and red) two-color DESIGN FOR THE 90s graphic, and across the page. Jim Hardy's design also uses red for the captions and the for both the head and text of the right article. Note how your vision is pulled to the graphic (the outline of Indiana in black box) in the righthand story, "It all began in Indiana." Link *is a publication for the employees of American Applied Technologies. Photography by Jack Van Antwerp. Reprinted with permission from American Applied Technologies and Samata Associates.*

to write a two- or three-sentence statement that outlines your space situation, typographic needs, image, audience and expectations.

- Because your design space is considerably less than other publications, you cannot afford to waste space with your display type. A good rule of thumb to consider for your stylebook is this: for average heads, add two points to the text point size and bold. In especially tight quarters, you might try to simply bold your text for heads.

- Use the smallest possible number of typefaces, sizes and weights. With type, less is more, especially in newsletters, where space, too, is less.

- Using the same family for display and text will help the continuity and general design of your pages—and perhaps save you the price of an additional face, if you're shopping for type. Typically, using this scenario, the text would be set normal, captions in italic and the headlines bold and larger.

- On the other hand, don't be afraid to mix races, but if you do, make sure they're compatible and restrict what each does functionally. For example, use one for display and crossheads, and the other, say, for text, by-line, credits and the like. A healthy and fashionable mix might be Garamond for your copy and Futura for the display.

- It's crucial to show sequence or to alert the reader to the hierarchial structure of your content. Help your reader determine at a glance which stories are more important by using optical weight through size, borders, tints, screens and boxes. Remember, too, the more important the story or article, the higher on the page it should be.

- Use bullets, dropped initial letters, crossheads and screens to help direct visual traffic and to add emphasis and texture to your pages.

- Give your pages added contrast through sidebars, boxes, screens and tints.

- Serif faces bring more texture to your pages. Of the sans serif faces, Optima and Lucida Sans provide decent texture; most other sans serifs are monotonal.

- If you are using a sans serif face for your text type, be sure to inject texture through bullets, dropped initial letters, tint blocks, screens, boxes, photos and other graphic devices to offset the lack of color on the page.

Figures 11.20 and **11.21** _____

This photograph dominates this Link *page through its exaggerated format and location in the layout; it splits both the article and the page, and the reverse block/caption makes it even stronger. Also, the reverse color, a brown, was achieved by mixing screens of black and red. Subtle overprinting can extend two-color possibilities. Both of these pages are unique; they don't resemble typical newspaper or magazine layouts. And like most good designs, they are simple and carefully ordered. This lower* Link *page was also shaped by the very capable hands of Samata Associates. The sunburst screen on the layout below was also created by overprinting screens of red and black. Jim Hardy, designer. Photography by Peter Yates, Jack Van Antwerp and Bob Tolchin. Reprinted with permission from American Applied Technologies and Samata Associates.*

Figure 11.22

NT Enterprise is designed and produced for Northern Telecom by the Thomas Ryan Design. It is both specialized and internal, directing timely information on networking to employees. This design features a single article on the large, tabloid-sized front page. Although the layout is based on five-columns, only three are used for the story area. The fourth column supports part of the art and a ragged edged tab (top right), which provides an overview of the issue. The fifth column is used for a vertical nameplate. The publication is printed in three color (black, violet and green), and the headline, blurb and most of the nameplate is run in violet. Design by Thomas Ryan; photography by Mark Avery. Reprinted with permission from Northern Telecom and the Thomas Ryan Design.

Some Final Thoughts

Today's newsletter differs dramatically from other publication formats. This, despite the fact that, often, differentiating between newsletters and other publications is often impossible. The point is that company magazines, tabloids and a number of undefinable formats sometimes refer to themselves as newsletters.

Recently, when I judged the National Food Institute publication designs and writing to make annual awards to their editors and designers across the country, I encountered several magazines that referred to themselves as newsletters and vice versa. I also discovered some very high-quality, well-designed and thoughtfully written newsletters, tabloids and magazines. There was also the opposite end of the spectrum—publications that looked like exemplary models of how not to design a newsletter. Many of the Food Institute's state directors and editors confirmed what I have preached, and their comments are startling.

They told me that most of their newsletter editors had little experience or education in journalistic writing, computers and desktop publishing, design or photography—despite the fact that most are graduated from communications and public relations programs. What's more, on average they are expected to perform or coordinate all of these skills. The typical editor probably writes, edits, designs, photographs for and is involved in the production of each publication. Usually, they have a limited background in one of the four areas cited. Most often, they possess some writing skills and training. And although they may have worked with computers, it's seldom with desktop publishing and even less frequently with any kind of designing. Few have any formal experience in photography. Although the majority of those hired graduated from public relations and communications programs, very few expected that publication and

Figure 11.23

Lyphomed Report's *nameplate is broken; that is, it runs* Lyphomed *along with its logotype in black atop brown, and* Report *vertically down the outside margin—a very uncommon tactic. This design uses a four-column layout with very generous alleys and outside margins. White space also airs out the Question/Answer department on the back page (left). Despite ample room, the designers have chosen to run photography small, while featuring large graphic areas— nameplate and department graphic. Hill and Knowlton produces* Lyphomed Report *for Lyphomed of Chicago. Kathy Keen directed the design. Reprinted with permission from Lyphomed and Hill and Knowlton.*

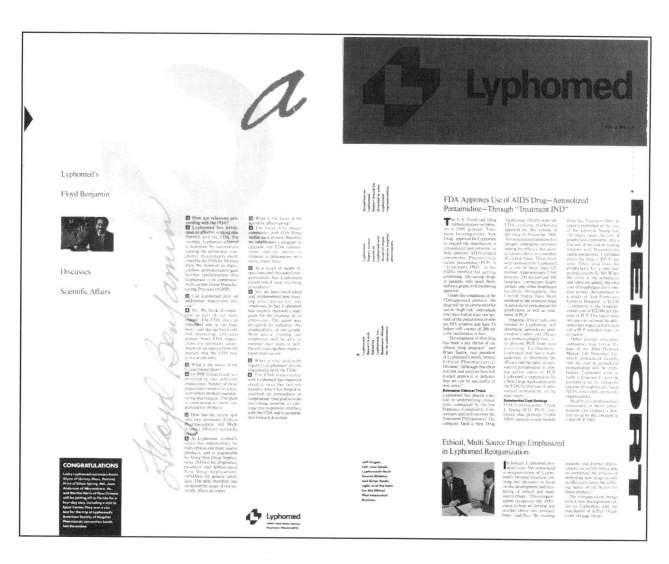

Figure 11.24

Although taken from a different issue, this is the inside spread of the four-page newsletter, Lyphomed Report. *Here, the photography is much larger and has a stronger bearing on the design. Notice the very fashionable ragged bottoms on all four articles—and the strong use of a second color (a dark blue-green in this issue) in the sidebar. The circular LYPOMED SERVICE, with its half-reversed/half-straight treatment, is eye-catching and a nice touch. Notice, too, how the abundant white space makes the stories more inviting. Design by Hill and Knowlton, Kathy Keen, designer. Reprinted with permission from Lyphomed and Hill and Knowlton.*

production skills would be an important part of their jobs! In most instances, in fact, it is their primary function; that is, the public relations person wears most of the publications hats as well, particularly in the case of smaller organizations.

Today's colleges and universities need to scrutinize their curricula and modernize courses. Along with current requirements, colleges should offer reporting and editing classes, at least one desktop publishing and productions course, a basic photography class and some sort of visual communications, visual literacy or graphic design class.

Newsletters are currently the most popular business communication publication, and their number and importance continue to grow. Newsletters generally take one of two basic forms; they are either specialized or internal and external business communications publications.

The specialized publication is characterized as being the less slick of the two forms and its audience is fiercely loyal. The *Kiplinger Newsletter* is a marvelous example. This group has stayed with the original concept, design and intent of the newsletter: it is simple, direct, unaffected and focused on content. Although desktop publishing figures largely into their design and production now, the general look of these publications has changed little. Specialized publications are not only alive and well, but are growing at an astonishing rate.

Internal and external business communications newsletters are the slicker and more professional-looking of the two types of newsletters. Desktop publishing is central to their viability and vitality. Indeed, a substantial part of today's software and hardware is targeted specifically at their editors. The sophistication of this newsletter depends upon the size of the company or organization, its main audience, design, preparation and production budgets, the method of production, and the skills of editors, writers, designers and photographers.

Obviously, the larger corporations have the money, size, talent and production capabilities to generate larger and more professional-looking pieces. However, a single editor with good design, writing, graphics and photography skills can produce work on a par with the spendier newsletters, if provided the time and situation.

When designing your newsletter, give some thought to its intent and audience. If your newsletter is intended to be nothing more than an informal employee morale booster, there is no reason to invest additional time and money in professional photography, and high-end, full-color production. They will only take away from the personal and unpretentious mission of the publication. On the other hand, however, if your audience is composed of professionals or shareholders who expect a highly stylized, slick newsletter, you'd better be sure that your design, type, color, writing and photography is up to the task.

If the best-designed piece misses its audience, it has failed and so have you. The point is clear. Review your publication goals regularly to make sure that your newsletter is correctly aligned and designed to your mission and audience.

Newsletters are read carefully and religiously because your audience either has tremendous confidence in your information and publication, or because it keeps them informed of friends, colleagues and company activities or policy. These are good reasons to maintain a logic and simplicity in your design. To guarantee an easy read for your audience, eliminate design bottlenecks and mixed messages wherever they exist, and strive to grease the flow of your information to your readers.

Appendix

Setting Up a Desktop Publishing System

So, you're ready to set yourself up with a desktop publishing system, but you don't have any idea where to start. It wasn't all that long ago that the choices were amazingly simple—you just bought a Macintosh and a copy of *PageMaker* and you were set. Today, the choices for hardware and software are far more complex, and depend on at least two factors: what you intend to publish and how much you have to spend. Even the most basic publications require some fairly sophisticated hardware and software, and it behooves you to make the right choices now so that you can expand later with the least amount of trouble and cost.

Your hardware choices are especially dictated by your needs and your pocketbook, although personal preference is undoubtedly a factor. For example, if you have already been working on a PC (IBM or compatible) don't assume that you'll have to switch to Apple Macintosh just to get involved in desktop publishing. Software layout programs such as *Ventura Publisher* and *Quark Xpress* can turn your PC into a superb desktop publishing system. And, with the advances in special add-ons to non-*PostScript* laser printers, you can now rival the output of a standard *PostScript* printer with your PC system.

Hardware

Whether you're starting from scratch or adding to an existing system, at the very minimum you'll need the following hardware.

- A computer with enough RAM to handle the larger layout and art programs. For example, *PageMaker* 4.0 requires 4 MGBs to run efficiently.

423

- At least a 20 MGB hard drive. The fact is, most layout programs now require a hard drive to work, and you're going to need the storage space and room to work.

- At least one floppy disk drive for backup file storage.

- A monochrome monitor.

- A printer. For the beginner who will be sending, or taking, final output to a Linotronic, a dot-matrix will do for rough drafts.

If you aspire to a more advanced system, you'll probably be considering the following as either basics or add-ons:

- A high resolution monitor. Although you can certainly get by with less, if you're going to be working with photographs, you'll want a monitor that will show you a complete range of grays.

And, if you're going to be working on publications with large page sizes, double-page spreads, or just want to see an entire page at once and still be able to read the body type, look into a large-screen monitor. These vary in price (none are cheap) and configuration. The most typical large-screen monitors come in either landscape (wide) or portrait (tall) configurations. If you work on magazines and newsletters, a landscape orientation would be best.

If you are working in color (either for printing color comps or for creating separations for Linotronic printouts) you'll eventually want a color monitor. Again, be prepared to pay the price.

Exhibit A.1 _____

Basic configuration*. A single-person operation can get by with a computer and a printer—preferably, a laser printer.*

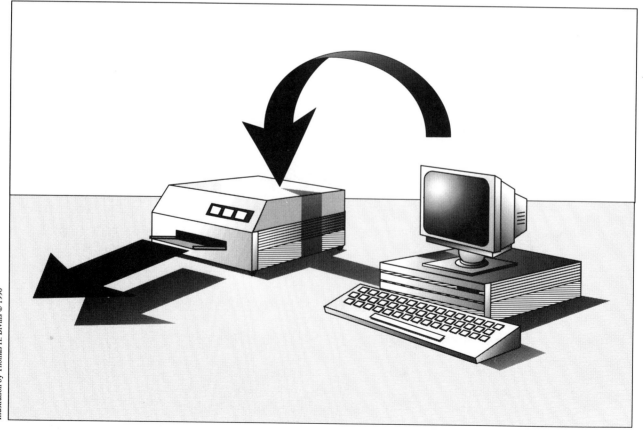

Illustration by Thomas H. Bivins © 1990

- A laser printer. Although you can get by with a dot-matrix printer for drafts, you'll want the kind of precision a laser printer can deliver. Many of your less prestigious layouts can often be run right from laser-printed masters.

- A scanner, especially if you want to use photographs or if you're tired of trying to calculate just where your artwork will fit in your computer layout by holding it against your screen.

- A color printer, especially if you want to run color comps or proofs. For most art directors, a color printer isn't necessary; however, if you're trying to impress your clients, nothing works like a color comp.

There is always something you can add—a more expensive computer, expanded memory, a better laser printer, a graphics tablet, and so on. Just make sure that you will get your money's worth out of that fancy, new piece of hardware before you buy into it.

Exhibit A.2

Advanced hardware configuration. One of the most common desktop publishing setups includes some sort of input device (keyboard, mouse, stylus) as well as peripheral devices such as a scanner which feed into the computer itself. From there, the infomation is sent to an output device such as a laser printer or, for finished work, a phototypesetter such as a Linotronic.

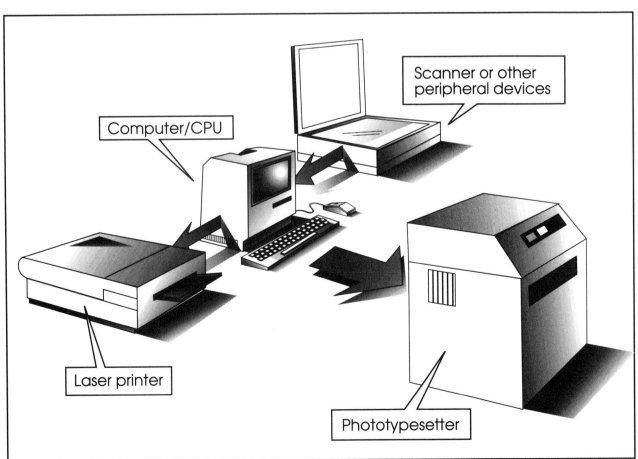

Scanner or other peripheral devices

Computer/CPU

Laser printer

Phototypesetter

Illustration by Thomas H. Bivins © 1990

Software

These days, you can purchase a word-processing program that will do a bit of page layout (simple blocks, columns, lines, etc.), or a layout program that will do a bit of word processing. But, what you really want is the best of each, since no one program can yet deliver in all areas.

As with hardware purchases, buy what you need to do the job, but be aware of your future needs as well. Software, unlike hardware, isn't easily extended by adding a peripheral device. If you buy into a word-processing program that will only do short documents because that's all you do right now, you'll just have to buy a whole new program later if you decide you need greater capabilities. Plan ahead and purchase software that you can use both now and in the predictable future.

Again, there are basic needs and more elaborate needs. For the beginning desktop publisher, the following types of programs are recommended at a minimum:

- A good word-processing program—one that will serve your current *and* future needs. The industry standards are relatively expensive, but programs such as *WordPerfect* for the PC and Microsoft *Word* for the Mac have become leaders in word processing for good reason. These, and others like them, have limited layout capabilities and can sometimes even use imported graphics. The key to their success, however, is the fact that they can adjust to longer and more complex documents easily. For example, both *WordPerfect* and Microsoft *Word* can perform various indexing, sorting and text calculation functions as well as execute excellent spell checks.

  Remember, word-processing programs are also a matter of taste; however, don't assume that your favorite PC-based program will be as good in its Macintosh version. It's been our experience that there are good PC word-processing programs and good Macintosh word-processing programs, and *they are different programs entirely*. Read some reviews, try out sample programs, and, above all, project your needs as far ahead as you can.

- A page-layout program. As with the word-processing programs, what's good for the goose isn't necessarily good for the gander. What works well on a Macintosh doesn't necessarily work well for a PC desktop publishing system. Industry standards such as *PageMaker* (for the Macintosh) and *Ventura Publisher* and Quark *XPress* (for the PC) are your best bet. Don't skimp on quality. A low-end page layout program will give you low-end results—if you survive the frustration factor.

Aside from these basic requirements, the serious art director will want access to various add-on programs that will enhance the job and reduce the number of intermediaries involved in the publication process. Take a look at these software extras.

- A graphics program (or programs). This is an area in which your talent is the deciding factor. For those with little or no artistic or design talent, some basic (but fairly inflexible) programs are best. Object-oriented programs such as *MacDraw* and *Cricket Draw* provide you with clean, *PostScript-*

printable lines, but are limited to basic and somewhat static forms. Of course, bit-mapped images can be created on a number of paint programs including *MacPaint* and *FullPaint*, but they aren't for polished ads.

Judging by the multiplicity of newspaper graphics being generated using *MacDraw*, you might think it is a superb artist's tool; however, programs such as Adobe *Illustrator* and Aldus *FreeHand* are actually the software of choice for experienced designers and artists. Be warned, these programs are not for the inexperienced designer. They are complex to learn and use, but the results can be astonishing.

- A color graphics program. If you work in color, this can be useful. However, the two most popular programs mentioned above, *Illustrator* and *FreeHand*, can also be used in color and can produce color separations. Although a color graphics program such as *PixelPaint* or *Modern Artist* can be fun to use, especially if you have a color monitor, they are truly luxuries if you already own an illustration program. And, since they produce bit-mapped images, they are of limited use in ads.

- A photo manipulation program such as *Image Studio* or *Digital Darkroom*. If you have a scanner and work with photos on a regular basis (either as finished art or simple placeholders for the screened art) you'll want one of these programs. They allow for the kind of fine tuning many scanners don't provide including brightness and contrast adjustments, gray-scale manipulation, photo retouching, and myriad other tasks. These programs are not toys; they are serious graphics tools that, as they become more sophisticated, may actually replace the traditional methods of working with photographs.

- A font editing/creation program such as *Fontographer* or *Letra Studio* allows you to create your own type fonts. These are terrific fun for novice and experienced type designers alike, but they can be difficult to learn if you know absolutely nothing about type. They are especially good for developing logotypes and creating special letters for illustrations.

The Proof Is In the Pudding

There's a lot to be said for that old saw. Ultimately, your final, printed publication is going to determine how successful your desktop publishing system is—and a lot of that success depends not on your hardware and software, but on you.

You are the final ingredient in this system. Your energy, talent, interest and organizational abilities will determine the success or failure of your ads. Truthfully, you can get by on a lot less than you think you can if you possess the right attitude and the requisite abilities. Fancy hardware and expensive software only enhance and streamline a process you should already have down to a fine art.

The fact is that many excellent publications are still laid out the "old-fashioned" way. There is no substitute for being able to accomplish the task this way. (For instance, what happens when the power goes out or your only computer breaks down?) Don't get the wrong idea—computers have made and are continuing to make a huge difference in publishing. Just remember: that multi-thousand dollar system you sit down in front of every day is only a tool.

Simply holding a brush in your hand doesn't make you an artist, the same as sitting in front of a typewriter doesn't make you a writer. Dedication, hard work and talent will.

Take a hard look at your publications and ask yourself a few questions:

- Are they already the best they can be without the addition of desktop publishing? If they are, you probably already know the basics and are ready for desktop publishing. If they're not, why not? Will the technology help the look or simply add to the clutter? Be honest. Don't expect desktop publishing to give you something you don't already possess.

- What, exactly, do you expect desktop publishing to add to your layouts or the process of developing them? Again, if you're looking for an answer to your design problems, check out your own abilities first. On the other hand, if you're expecting the technology to streamline the process and save you some money—you're probably right.

- Will the savings you accrue be offset by the cost of the system? It takes a lot of savings in typesetting to counter balance a $25,000 investment. On the other hand, a basic setup might pay for itself in the person-hours normally used up to do the same thing by hand.

- Are you willing to take the time needed to make yourself an expert on your system. If you aren't willing to become an expert, you're wasting your money. Anyone can learn the basics (or just enough to cause trouble). If you're serious about desktop publishing, you'd best dedicate yourself to the long haul. The authors of this text aren't exactly beginners, yet they both learn something new almost every day. Be prepared to immerse yourself in the process, the programs and the machinery. The more you know, the more streamlined the publications' process becomes.

Above all, don't set yourself up for frustration. Realize the limitations of your system and of desktop publishing in general. Understand how it works and why it does what it does. You don't have to become a "computer nerd" to gain a fairly complete understanding of your hardware and software. The more you know, the less frustrated you'll be when something does go wrong. Most of the frustration of working with computers comes from not knowing what's happening in software or hardware problem situations. Keep those technical support hotline numbers close at hand and use them. Don't be afraid to ask questions, but read your manuals first so you'll know what to ask.

Finally, take it all with a grain of salt. Don't talk to your computer. You probably don't talk to your typewriter. They're both just tools of the trade. Misuse them, and your shortcomings will become apparent to everyone who reads your ads. Use them wisely and they'll show off for you.

Colophon

How This Book Was Put Together

T his entire book was written, designed, and laid out using desktop publishing. We have learned a great deal during the experience that will serve us in the future. We have explored new avenues and developed techniques that are invaluable to any desktop publisher. Many of these techniques are shared within the chapters of this book. Some, we will introduce or reinforce here.

The Tools

A number of software and hardware considerations are important to any desktop publishing endeavor. These are usually dictated by the complexity of the job as mentioned in the preceding appendix on setting up a system of your own.

Hardware

For our purposes, we needed the most powerful hardware available to accomplish such a large publication effectively. For starters, we used a Mac II (the earliest model) with an 80-MGB hard drive and 4 MGBs of RAM. Storage space for such a large publication is always a problem. Fortunately, we also have access to a 275-MGB file server on which we kept backup copies of all our chapters and stored the scanned images for **Chapter 4** on photography. The 4 MGBs of RAM were needed to run such memory-eating programs as *Image Studio* and the latest version of *PageMaker* (4.0).

We couldn't have begun to do justice to our layouts without a large-screen monitor. We have a high-resolution Radius two-page monochrome monitor capable of displaying 256 shades of grey. Many of the images seen in **Chapters 4, 5**, and **6** were scanned in using a Hewlett Packard ScanJet Plus.

Drafts were printed on an Apple LaserWriter II NTX, a powerful and speedy machine. Final, camera-ready copy was produced on a Linotronic 300 at 1270 dpi. Scanned photographs in **Chapters 4**, **5**, and **6** were run with 90 lpi screens to increase contrast. As pointed out in **Chapter 4**, scanned photographs increase in clarity with lower resolution. Efforts to run photos at the standard 133 line screen produced high resolution but extremely dense proofs which muddied when printed. The rest of the examples, not produced originally on the computer, were halftoned the traditional way using a 133-line screen.

Software

PageMaker has always been our layout software of choice. Version 4.0 came out just in time to accomplish our final layouts and includes a number of time-saving functions designed specifically for book production. Chief among them is an automatic indexing function that keys to page layouts instead of word-processing files (eliminating the very tedious step of matching indexed word-processed files to page layouts). The index can be viewed at any time and includes all documents linked under the *book* designator. The table of contents was also generated in *PageMaker* 4.0 simply by designating all chapter heads and all subheads as entries. This can be done from the *define styles* menu for each chapter/file. Both indexing and compiling a table of contents are generated across documents stored in separate files but linked as a single publication under *PageMaker's* new *book* function.

In addition, the new version comes with a built-in word processor. All final spell checks and those tedious global search and replace jobs can now be done in the page-layout program. This was especially handy when we decided to raise the point size of the bullets that appear so often throughout this book. We simply called up the word processing editor in each chapter, searched for bullets and replaced them with a larger point size.

Style sheets, a fixture in *PageMaker* 3.0 and now in version 4.0, are still the mainstay of any long publication. Without them, we couldn't have laid out this book. Our style sheet became quite lengthy. Here is what we eventually settled on.

Body Text—11-point Times, leaded 13, justified, first indents .25 inches.

Chapter Number—18-point Avant Garde, normal face, flush left.

Chapter Title—24-point Avant Garde, normal face, flush right.

Chapter Section—14-point Avant Garde, bold, flush right.

Captions—9-point Times, italic, leaded 11, flush left.

Drop Caps (for chapter title pages)—48-point Avant Garde, bold, pasted to the scrapbook and placed in *PageMaker* as a graphic element which then permitted textwrap.

Sub Points (bulleted and numbered items)—11-point Times, leaded 13, justified, indented .25 inches. Space between bulleted items was leaded 6 points to tighten up the lists. This leading was also saved as a style called "bullet leading" so that the leading could be clicked and set quickly.

A-level Subheads—13-point Avant Garde, bold, flush left with 1.5 spaces following between it and text.

B-level Subheads—11-point Avant Garde, bold, flush left with .5 space following.

C-level Subheads—11-point Avant Garde, bold, indented .25 inches, body text leading.

Figure Numbers—9-point Avant Garde, bold, flush left with a .5-point rule following to the right edge of the copy block. (This new function in *PageMaker* 4.0 allows you to set ruler lines anywhere above or below a beginning paragraph. We simply designated a baseline placement for a .5-point line and indented it .65 inches so as to follow the figure number. Several had to be created due to the varying lengths of the figure numbers.)

A number of other software programs were used for specialized work. For photo manipulation, we used *Image Studio*. For illustration, we used Aldus *Freehand*. Several illustrations were traced using Adobe *Streamline* and then further enhanced in *Freehand*. We also used Adobe *Type Manager* to spec our type for alignment in critical places.

And, finally, all our word processing was accomplished in Microsoft *Word* 4.0—for our money, the most efficient program on the market for the Macintosh.

The Layout

We worked from a template we developed early on using a 30 pica text column thrown to the inside leaving a 12 pica margin on the outside for captions, small illustrations, and overflow illustrations from the text column. Running feet were 9-point Helvetica with 10-point Avant Garde page numbers. These were set on the master pages along with the column guides.

During the later stages of the layout process, we purchased a brand new book called *Real World PageMaker 4.0: Industrial Strength Techniques* by Olav Kvern and Stephen Roth. This book proved to be invaluable in speeding up the final layout. It contains hundreds of shortcuts, many not mentioned in the *PageMaker* 4.0 documentation. Probably the most helpful hints were directions for setting up several *Quickeys* that take the place of tedious and repetitious mouse movements or multiple key strokes. *Quickeys* is a program developed by CE Software that allows you to assign key strokes to commonly used functions so that you don't have to go to the menus. For example, since we used the text wrap function of *PageMaker* constantly, we simply set up a single key stroke that would automatically outline selected items, saving us having to go through several menu manipulations. And, even though PageMaker has key strokes designed to change *toolbox* icons, they are double strokes involving the shift and function keys and requiring the finger spread of a concert pianist. We consigned the most frequently used icons—the pointer and text icons—to single keys which we could reach with ease.

On the whole, this entire project has been an incredible learning experience. As desktop publishers, we have at least doubled our own proficiency. The moral, of course, is practice, practice, practice.

Chapter number—*18 point Avant Garde, normal face, flush left.*

Chapter title—*24 point Avant Garde, normal face, flush right.*

Drop caps *(for chapter title pages)—48 point Avant Garde, bold, pasted to the scrapbook and placed in PageMaker as a graphic element which then permitted textwrap.*

Photography is not only the most commonly used means of visual communication in publications, it has become, in one form or another, central to our experience. We use it to document both important and mundane events in our own lives. Photography has a marvelous power to fix our image and the images around us almost instantaneously. Its imagery links us to the world, and beyond.

Its highly graphic or representational nature is what makes it such a potent medium. Photography has such tremendous credibility that we often confuse it with truth, forgetting that photographs are *images* of reality and not the real thing. We believe something when we see it with our eyes, and so we believe photographs. Today, however, that credibility is strained, because photography is easily manipulated. Through computerized or digitized photography, images can be altered and overlaid with such precision that we cannot differentiate between the original and doctored imagery.

A second characteristic of photography is as fascinating as it can be troublesome. Photographic images are captured on film in split seconds. In a sense, they stop time, freezing it on a single frame of film. One of the charming things about photographs is that our images remain static over time even though we change. However, images recorded in fractions of a second can be quite deceiving. All of us have seen outrageous pictures of ourselves. Frames of film that caught us mid-word or while we blinked. Aside from not being flattering, these images are deceiving. Still another problem is that viewers tend to bring their own interpretations to the photographic image. That is why captions are so important. For these and other reasons, photography must be used with great care. Indeed, questions of ethics and photography arise often in journalism.

It is important to know up front the strengths and weaknesses of the medium, and, in at least two instances, to realize that photography's strengths and weaknesses are one and the same.

129

Sub points *(bulleted and numbered items)— 11 point Times, leaded 13, justified, indented .25 inches. Space between bulleted items was leaded 6 points to tighten up the lists.*

Body text—*11 point Times, leaded 13, justified, first indents .25 inches.*

- What do they know about your topic already? Never assume they know anything; however, don't talk down to them. How do you reach a compromise? Find out what they do know. Remember, people like to learn something from communication. It is best, however, to limit the amount of new information somewhat so as not to overwhelm your readers.

- What is their attitude toward you? Remember the three basic audiences for any persuasive piece? You'll need to determine whether your audience is on your side, against you, or unconvinced. This is a primary concern. To the extent possible, it is also a good idea to try to determine what their image of you or your organization is. Determining audience attitude is often an expensive proposition because it usually requires formal research; however, if the best you can do is make an educated guess based on a small focus group or even intuition—it's better than nothing at all. It is much easier to persuade when you know that you have credibility with your reader.

- Is your publication to be used in a larger context? In other words, is your publication part of a press kit, for instance, or a direct-mail package, or one of many handouts at a trade show? This knowledge will determine your readers' level of attention and their receptiveness. Always consider the surroundings in which your piece will be used if you want it to have the maximum impact.

Choosing the Appropriate Medium

It's strange to note that most nonwriters who are seeking some sort of publicity automatically assume that a brochure is the route to take, or, if the message is meant for employees, a newsletter. Of course, these may both turn out to be sound suggestions. The problem is that any *assumptions* you make concerning the most appropriate medium for your message could be disastrous. As in all stages of the planning process, selecting the right medium or media is a decision that should be based on sound knowledge of a number of factors. Doug Newsom and Alan Scott have designed a series of important considerations to be used in choosing the right medium for your message.[1]

- **What audience are you trying to reach and what do you know about its media usage patterns and the credibility ratings for each medium?** Many target audiences, for instance, simply do not watch television or listen to the radio. Others don't read newspapers regularly or subscribe to magazines. You need to know, first off, whether your intended audience will even see your message if it is presented in a medium they don't regularly use. Research tells us, for example, that businesspeople read the newspaper more than do some other groups, and rely on it for basic news and information. Other groups may rely on television almost exclusively for their news and information. For each of these groups, the credibility of the medium in question is vital. Again, businesspeople cite newspapers as a more credible source for news and information than television; however, for many people, television is far more credible.

- **When do you need to reach this audience in order for your message to be effective?** If time is of the essence, you'd best not leave your message for the next issue of the corporate magazine.

A-level subheads—13 point Avant Garde, bold, flush left with 1.5 spaces following between it and text.

B-level subheads—11 point Avant Garde, bold, flush left with .5 space following.

C-level subheads—11 point Avant Garde, bold, indented .25 inches, body text leading.

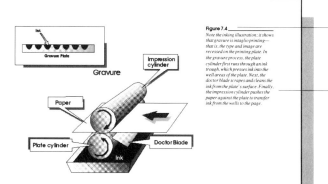
Figure numbers—9 point Avant Garde, bold, flush left with a .5 point rule following to the right edge of the copy block.

Captions—9 point Times, italic, leaded 11, flush left.